D0606031

EVERYMAN, I will go with thee,

and be thy guide,

In thy most need to go by thy side

JOSEPH ADDISON

Born at Milston in Wiltshire, 1672; educated at Lichfield Grammar School, the Charterhouse and Magdalen College, Oxford, where he was a Demy and Fellow. M.P. for Malmesbury, Under-Secretary of State, Secretary of the Irish Government and Secretary of State in England, he died in 1719 at Holland House, his wife's London residence.

SIR RICHARD STEELE

Born at Dublin in 1672; educated at the Charterhouse and Merton College, Oxford. He was elected M.P. for Stockbridge in 1713, for Boroughbridge in 1715 (in which year he was knighted) and for Wendover in 1722. He died at Llangunnor in 1729.

ADDISON & STEELE
AND OTHERS

The Spectator

IN FOUR VOLUMES · VOLUME TWO

EDITED BY
GREGORY SMITH

INTRODUCTION BY
PETER SMITHERS, D.PHIL.(OXON.)

DENT: LONDON
EVERYMAN'S LIBRARY
DUTTON: NEW YORK

All rights reserved
Made in Great Britain
at the
Aldine Press · Letchworth · Herts
for
J. M. DENT & SONS LTD
Aldine House · Bedford Street · London
First included in Everyman's Library 1907
Reset, with minor revisions, 1945
Last reprinted 1970

NO. *165*

ISBN: 0 460 00165 5

CONTENTS

HENRY BOYLE, Esq.

SIR,

As the profest Design of this Work is to Entertain its Readers in general, without giving Offence to any particular Person, it would be difficult to find out so proper a Patron for it as Your self, there being none whose Merit is more universally acknowledged by all Parties, and who has made himself more Friends, and fewer Enemies. Your great Abilities, and unquestioned Integrity, in those High Employments which You have passed through, would not have been able to have raised You this general Approbation, had they not been accompanied with that Moderation in an high Fortune, and that Affability of Manners, which are so conspicuous through all parts of Your Life. Your Aversion to any Ostentatious Arts of Setting to show those Great Services which You have done the Publick, has not likewise a little contributed to that Universal Acknowledgment which is paid You by Your Country.

The Consideration of this Part of Your Character is that which hinders me from enlarging on those Extraordinary Talents, which have given You so great a Figure in the *British* Senate, as well as on that Elegance and Politeness, which appear in your more retired Conversation. I should be unpardonable, if, after what I have said, I should longer detain You with an Address of this Nature; I cannot, however, conclude it without owning those great Obligations which You have laid upon,

SIR,

Your most Obedient,

Humble Servant,

THE SPECTATOR.

THE SPECTATOR.

VOL. III.

No. 170.

[ADDISON.]   Friday, September 14, 1711.

> *In amore haec omnia insunt vitia: injuriae,*
> *Suspiciones, inimicitiae, induciae,*
> *Bellum, pax rursum. . . .*—Ter. *Eun.*

UPON looking over the Letters of my female Correspondents, I find several from Women complaining of jealous Husbands, and at the same time protesting their own Innocence; and desiring my Advice on this Occasion. I shall therefore take this Subject into my Consideration, and the more willingly, because I find that the Marquis of *Hallifax*, who in his Advice to a Daughter has instructed a Wife how to behave her self towards a false, an intemperate, a cholerick, a sullen, a covetous, or a silly Husband, has not spoken one Word of a jealous Husband.

Jealousie is that Pain which a Man feels from the Apprehension that he is not equally beloved by the Person whom he entirely loves. Now, because our inward Passions and Inclinations can never make themselves visible, it is impossible for a jealous Man to be throughly cured of his Suspicions. His Thoughts hang at best in a State of Doubtfulness and Uncertainty; and are never capable of receiving any Satisfaction on the advantageous Side; so that his Enquiries are most successful when they discover nothing: His Pleasure arises from his Disappointments, and his Life is spent in Pursuit of a Secret that destroys his Happiness if he chance to find it.

An ardent Love is always a strong Ingredient in this Passion; for the same Affection which stirs up the jealous Man's Desires, and gives the Party beloved so beautiful a Figure in his Imagination, makes him believe she kindles the same Passion in others, and appears as amiable to all Beholders. And as Jealousie thus arises from an extraordinary Love, it is of so delicate a Nature that it scorns to take up with any thing less than an equal Return of Love. Not the warmest Expressions of Affection, the softest and most tender Hypocrisie, are able to give any Satisfaction, where we are not perswaded that the Affection is real and the Satisfaction mutual. For the jealous Man wishes himself a kind of Deity to the Person he loves: He would be the only Pleasure of her Senses, the Employment of her Thoughts; and is angry at every thing she admires, or takes Delight in, besides himself.

Phaedria's Request to his Mistress, upon his leaving her for three Days, is inimitably beautiful and natural.

> *Cum milite isto praesens, absens ut sies:*
> *Dies noctesque me ames: me desideres:*
> *Me somnies: me exspectes: de me cogites:*
> *Me speres: me te oblectes: mecum tota sis:*
> *Meus fac sis postremo animus, quando ego sum tuus.*
>
> —Ter. *Eun.*

The jealous Man's Disease is of so malignant a nature, that it converts all he takes into its own Nourishment. A cool Behaviour sets him on the Rack, and is interpreted as an Instance of Aversion or Indifference; a fond one raises his Suspicions, and looks too much like Dissimulation and Artifice. If the Person he loves be cheerful, her Thoughts must be employed on another; and if sad, she is certainly thinking on himself. In short, there is no Word or Gesture so insignificant but it gives him new Hints, feeds his Suspicions, and furnishes him with fresh Matters of Discovery: So that if we consider the Effects of this Passion, one would rather think it proceeded from an inveterate Hatred than an excessive Love; for certainly none can meet with more Disquietude and Uneasiness than a suspected Wife, if we except the jealous Husband.

But the great Unhappiness of this Passion is, that it naturally tends to alienate the Affection which it is so sollicitous to engross; and that for these two Reasons, because it lays too great a Constraint on the Words and Actions of the suspected Person, and at the same time shews you have no honourable Opinion of her; both of which are strong Motives to Aversion.

Nor is this the worst Effect of Jealousie; for it often draws after it a more fatal Train of Consequences, and makes the Person you suspect guilty of the very Crimes you are so much afraid of. It is very natural for such who are treated ill and upbraided falsely, to find out an intimate Friend that will hear their Complaints, condole their Sufferings, and endeavour to sooth and asswage their secret Resentments. Besides, Jealousie puts a Woman often in Mind of an ill thing that she would not otherwise perhaps have thought of, and fills her Imagination with such an unlucky Idea, as in Time grows familiar, excites Desire, and loses all the Shame and Horrour which might at first attend it. Nor is it a Wonder, if she who suffers wrongfully in a Man's Opinion of her, and has therefore nothing to forfeit in his Esteem, resolves to give him Reason for his Suspicions, and to enjoy the Pleasure of the Crime since she must undergo the Ignominy. Such probably were the Considerations that directed the wise Man in his Advice to Husbands; *Be not jealous over the Wife of thy Bosom, and teach her not an evil Lesson against thyself.* Ecclus.

And here, among the other Torments which this Passion produces, we may usually observe that none are greater Mourners than jealous Men, when the Person who provoked their Jealousie is taken from them. Then it is that their Love breaks out furiously, and throws off all the Mixtures of Suspicion which choaked and smothered it before. The beautiful Parts of the Character rise uppermost in the jealous Husband's Memory, and upbraid him with the ill Usage of so divine a Creature as was once in his Possession; whilst all the little Imperfections that were before so uneasie to him wear off from his Remembrance, and shew themselves no more.

We may see, by what has been said, that Jealousie takes the deepest Root in Men of amorous Dispositions; and of these we may find three Kinds who are most over-run with it.

The First are those who are conscious to themselves of any Infirmity, whether it be Weakness, old Age, Deformity, Ignorance, or the like. These Men are so well acquainted with the unamiable Part of themselves, that they have not the Confidence to think they are really beloved; and are so distrustful of their own Merits, that all Fondness towards them puts them out of Countenance, and looks like a Jest upon their Persons. They grow suspicious on their first looking in a Glass, and are stung with Jealousie at the Sight of a Wrinkle. A handsome Fellow immediately allarms them, and every thing that looks young or gay turns their Thoughts upon their Wives.

A Second sort of Men, who are most liable to this Passion, are those of cunning, wary and distrustful Tempers. It is a Fault very justly found in Histories composed by Politicians, that they leave nothing to Chance or Humour, but are still for deriving every Action from some Plot and Contrivance, for drawing up a perpetual Scheme of Causes and Events, and preserving a constant Correspondence between the Camp and the Council-Table. And thus it happens in the Affairs of Love with Men of too refined a Thought. They put a Construction on a Look, and find out a Design in a Smile; they give new Senses and Significations to Words and Actions; and are ever tormenting themselves with Fancies of their own raising: They generally act in a Disguise themselves, and therefore mistake all outward Shows and Appearances for Hipocrisie in others; so that I believe no Men see less of the Truth and Reality of things, than these great Refiners upon Incidents, who are so wonderfully subtile and over-wise in their Conceptions.

Now what these Men fancy they know of Women by Reflection, your lewd and vicious Men believe they have learn'd by Experience. They have seen the poor Husband so mis-led by Tricks and Artifices, and in the Midst of his Enquiries so lost and bewildered in a crooked Intreague, that they will suspect an Under-plot in every female Action; and especially where they see any Resemblance in the Behaviour of two Persons, are apt to fancy it proceeds from the same Design in both. These Men therefore bear hard upon the suspected Party, pursue her close through all her Turns and Windings, and are too well acquainted with the Chace to be flung off by any false Steps or Doubles: Besides, their Acquaintance and Conversation has lain wholly among the vicious Part of Womankind, and therefore it is no Wonder they censure all alike, and look upon the whole Sex as a Species of Impostors. But if, notwithstanding their private Experience, they can get over these Prejudices, and entertain a favourable Opinion of some *Women*; yet their own loose Desires will stir up new Suspicions from another Side, and make them believe all *Men* subject to the same Inclinations with themselves.

Whether these or other Motives are most predominant, we learn from the modern Histories of *America*, as well as from our own Experience in this Part of the World, that Jealousie is no Northern Passion, but rages most in those Nations that lie nearest the Influence of the Sun. It is a Misfortune for a Woman to be born between the Tropicks, for there lie the hottest Regions of Jealousie; which as you come Northward cools all along with the Climate, till you scarce meet with any thing like it in the Polar Circle. Our own Nation is very temperately situated in this Respect, and if we meet with some few disordered with the Violence of this Passion, they are not the proper Growth of our Country, but are many Degrees nearer the Sun in their Constitutions than in their Climate.

After this frightful Account of Jealousie, and the Persons who are most subject to it, it will be but fair to shew by what Means the Passion may be best allay'd, and those who are possessed with it set at Ease. Other Faults indeed are not under the Wife's Jurisdiction, and should, if possible, escape her Observation; but Jealousie calls upon her particularly for its Cure, and deserves all her Art and Application in the Attempt: Besides, she has this for her Encouragement, that her Endeavours will be always pleasing, and that she will still find the Affection of her Husband rising towards her in proportion as his Doubts and Suspicions vanish; for, as we have seen all along, there is so great a Mixture of Love in Jealousie as is well worth the separating. But this shall be the Subject of another Paper.   L

No. 171.

[ADDISON.]   Saturday, September 15.

Credula res amor est . . .—Ovid. *Met.*

HAVING in my Yesterday's Paper discovered the Nature of Jealousie, and pointed out the Persons who are most subject to it, I must here apply my self to my Fair Correspondents, who desire to live well with a jealous Husband, and to ease his Mind of its unjust Suspicions.

The first Rule I shall propose to be observed is, that you never seem to dislike in another what the Jealous Man is himself guilty of, or to admire any thing in which he himself does not excell. A Jealous Man is very quick in his Applications; he knows how to find a double Edge in an Invective, and to draw a Satyr on himself out of a Panegyrick on another. He does not trouble himself to consider the Person, but to direct the Character; and is secretly pleased or confounded as he finds more or less of himself in it. The Commendation of any thing in another, stirs up his Jealousie, as it shews you have a Value for others, besides himself; but the Commendation of that which he himself wants, inflames him more, as it shews that in some Respects you prefer others before him. Jealousie is admirably described in this view by *Horace* in his Ode to *Lydia*;

> *Quum tu, Lydia, Telephi*
> *Cervicem roseam, cerea Telephi*
> *Laudas brachia, vae meum*
> *Fervens difficili bile tumet jecur:*
> *Tunc nec mens mihi, nec color*
> *Certa sede manet; humor & in genas*
> *Furtim labitur arguens*
> *Quam lentis penitus macerer ignibus.*

> *When* Telephus *his youthful Charms,*
> *His rosie Neck and winding Arms,*
> *With endless Rapture you recite,*
> *And in the pleasing Name delight,*
> *My Heart, inflam'd by jealous Heats,*
> *With numberless Resentments beats;*
> *From my pale Cheek the Colour flies,*
> *And all the Man within me Dies:*
> *By turns my hidden Grief appears*
> *In rising Sighs and falling Tears,*
> *That shew too well the warm Desires,*
> *The silent, slow, consuming Fires,*
> *Which on my inmost Vitals prey,*
> *And melt my very Soul away.*

The Jealous Man is not indeed angry, if you dislike another;

but if you find those Faults which are to be found in his own Character, you discover not only your Dislike of another but of himself.   In short, he is so desirous of engrossing all your Love, that he is grieved at the want of any Charm, which, he believes, has power to raise it; and if he finds, by your Censures on others, that he is not so agreeable in your Opinion as he might be, he naturally concludes you could love him better, if he had other Qualifications, and that by Consequence your Affection does not arise so high as he thinks it ought.   If therefore his Temper be Grave or Sullen, you must not be too much pleased with a jest, or transported with any thing that is gay and diverting.   If his Beauty be none of the best, you must be a profest Admirer of Prudence, or any other Quality he is Master of, or at least vain enough to think he is.

In the next place, you must be sure to be free and open in your Conversation with him, and to let in Light upon your Actions, to unravel all your Designs, and discover every Secret however trifling or indifferent.   A jealous Husband has a particular Aversion to Winks and Whispers, and if he does not see to the Bottom of every thing, will be sure to go beyond it in his Fears and Suspicions.   He will always expect to be your chief Confident, and where he finds himself kept out of a Secret, will believe there is more in it than there should be.   And here it is of great concern, that you preserve the Character of your Sincerity uniform and of a piece: for if he once finds a false gloss put upon any single Action, he quickly suspects all the rest; his working Imagination immediately takes a false hint, and runs off with it into several remote Consequences, till he has proved very ingenious in working out his own Misery.

If both these Methods fail, the best way will be to let him see, you are much cast down and afflicted for the ill Opinion he entertains of you, and the Disquietudes he himself suffers for your sake.   There are many, who take a kind of barbarous Pleasure in the Jealousie of those who love them, that insult over an aking Heart, and triumph in their Charms which are able to excite so much Uneasiness.

Ardeat ipsa licet, tormentis gaudet amantis.—Juv.

But these often carry the Humour so far, till their affected Coldness and Indifference quite kills all the Fondness of a Lover, and are then sure to meet in their turn with all the Contempt and Scorn that is due to so insolent a Behaviour, On the contrary, it is very probable, a melancholy, dejected Carriage, the usual effects of injured Innocence, may soften the Jealous Husband into Pity, make him sensible of the Wrong he does you, and work out of his Mind all those Fears and Suspicions that make you both unhappy. At least it will have this good Effect, that he will keep his Jealousie to himself, and repine in private, either because he is sensible it is a Weakness, and will therefore hide it from your Knowledge, or because he will be apt to fear some ill Effect it may produce, in cooling your Love towards him, or diverting it to another.

There is still another Secret that can never fail, if you can once get it believ'd, and which is often practis'd by Women of greater Cunning than Virtue: This is to change Sides for a while with the Jealous Man, and to turn his own Passion upon himself; to take some Occasion of growing Jealous of him, and to follow the Example he himself hath set you. This Counterfeited Jealousie will bring him a great deal of Pleasure, if he thinks it real; for he knows experimentally how much Love goes along with this Passion, and will besides feel something like the Satisfaction of a Revenge, in seeing you undergo all his own Tortures. But this, indeed, is an Artifice so difficult, and at the same time so dis-ingenuous, that it ought never to be put in Practice, but by such as have Skill enough to cover the Deceit, and Innocence to render it excusable.

I shall conclude this Essay with the Story of *Herod* and *Mariamne*, as I have collected it out of *Josephus*, which may serve almost as an Example to whatever can be said on this Subject.

Mariamne had all the Charms that Beauty, Birth, Wit and Youth could give a Woman, and *Herod* all the Love that such Charms are able to raise in a warm and amorous Disposition. In the midst of this his Fondness for *Mariamne*, he put her Brother to Death, as he did her Father not many Years after. The Barbarity of the Action was represented to *Mark Antony*, who immediately summoned *Herod* into *Egypt*, to answer for the Crime that was there laid to his Charge. *Herod* attributed the Summons to *Antony's* Desire of *Mariamne*, whom therefore before his Departure he gave into the Custody of his Uncle *Joseph*, with private Orders to put her to Death, if any such Violence was offer'd to himself. This *Joseph* was much delighted with *Mariamne's* Conversation, and endeavour'd with all his Art and Rhetorick to set out the Excess of *Herod's* Passion for her; but when he still found her Cold and Incredulous, he inconsiderately told her, as a certain Instance of her Lord's Affection, the private Orders he had left behind him, which plainly shew'd, according to *Joseph's* Interpretation, that he could neither Live nor Die without her. This Barbarous Instance of a wild unreasonable Passion quite put out, for a time, those little Remains of Affection she still had for her Lord: Her Thoughts were so wholly taken up with the

Cruelty of his Orders, that she could not consider the Kindness
that produced them, and therefore represented him in her
Imagination, rather under the frightful Idea of a Murderer than
a Lover. *Herod* was at length acquitted and dismissed by
Mark Antony, when his Soul was all in Flames for his *Mariamne*;
but before their Meeting he was not a little alarm'd at the
Report he had heard of his Uncle's Conversation and Familiarity with her in his Absence.   This therefore was the first
Discourse he entertain'd her with, in which she found it no
easie Matter to quiet his Suspicions.   But at last he appear'd
so well satisfied of her Innocence, that from Reproaches and
Wranglings he fell to Tears and Embraces.   Both of them wept
very tenderly at their Reconciliation, and *Herod* poured out
his whole Soul to her in the warmest Protestations of Love and
Constancy; when amidst all his Sighs and Languishings she
ask'd him, whether the private Orders he left with his Uncle
Joseph were an instance of such an inflamed Affection.   The
jealous King was immediately roused at so unexpected a
Question, and concluded his Uncle must have been too Familiar
with her, before he would have discovered such a Secret.   In
short, he put his Uncle to Death, and very difficultly prevailed
upon himself to spare *Mariamne*.

After this he was forced on a second Journey into *Egypt*,
when he committed his Lady to the Care of *Sohemus*, with the
same private Orders he had before given his Uncle, if any Mischief befel himself.   In the mean while *Mariamne* so won upon
Sohemus by her Presents and obliging Conversation, that she
drew all the Secret from him, with which *Herod* had entrusted
him; so that after his Return, when he flew to her with all the
Transports of Joy and Love, she received him coldly with Sighs
and Tears, and all the Marks of Indifference and Aversion.
This Reception so stirred up his Indignation, that he had certainly slain her with his own Hands, had not he feared he himself should have become the greater Sufferer by it.   It was not
long after this when he had another violent Return of Love
upon him; *Mariamne* was therefore sent for to him, whom he
endeavoured to soften and reconcile with all possible Conjugal
Caresses and Endearments; but she declin'd his Embraces, and
answer'd all his Fondness with bitter Invectives for the Death
of her Father and her Brother.   This Behaviour so incensed
Herod, that he very hardly refrain'd from striking her; when in
the heat of their Quarrel there came in a Witness, suborn'd by
some of *Mariamne*'s Enemies, who accused her to the King of a
Design to poison him.   *Herod* was now prepared to hear any
thing in her Prejudice, and immediately ordered her Servant to
be stretch'd upon the Rack; who in the Extremity of his

Tortures confest, that his Mistress's Aversion to the King arose from something *Sohemus* had told her; but as for any Design of poisoning, he utterly disowned the least Knowledge of it. This Confession quickly proved fatal to *Sohemus*, who now lay under the same Suspicions and Sentence that *Joseph* had before him on the like Occasion. Nor would *Herod* rest here; but accused her with great Vehemence of a Design upon his Life, and by his Authority with the Judges had her publickly Condemned and Executed. *Herod* soon after her Death grew melancholy and dejected, retiring from the Publick Administration of Affairs into a solitary Forest, and there abandoning himself to all the black Considerations which naturally arise from a Passion made up of Love, Remorse, Pity and Despair. He used to rave for his *Mariamne*, and to call upon her in his distracted Fits; and in all Probability would soon have followed her, had not his Thoughts been seasonably called off from so sad an Object by Publick Storms, which at that time very nearly threatned him.

L

No. 172.

[STEELE.] Monday, September 17.

Non solum scientia, quae est remota a justitia, calliditas potius quam sapientia est appellanda; verum etiam animus paratus ad periculum, si sua cupiditate, non utilitate communi impellitur, audaciae potius nomen habeat, quam fortitudinis.—Plato apud Tull.

THERE can be no greater Injury to humane Society, than that good Talents among Men should be held honourable to those who are endowed with them, without any Regard how they are applied. The Gifts of Nature and Accomplishments of Art are valuable, but as they are exerted in the Interests of Virtue, or governed by the Rules of Honour. We ought to abstract our Minds from the Observation of any Excellence in those we converse with, 'till we have taken some Notice, or received some good Information of the Disposition of their Minds; otherwise the Beauty of their Persons, or the Charms of their Wit, may make us fond of those whom our Reason and Judgment will tell us we ought to abhor.

When we suffer our selves to be thus carried away by meer Beauty or meer Wit, *Omnamante* with all her Vice will bear away as much of our Good-will as the most innocent Virgin or discreetest Matron; and there cannot be a more abject Slavery in this World, than to doat upon what we think we ought to condemn: Yet this must be our Condition in all the Parts of Life, if we suffer our selves to approve any thing but what tends to the Promotion of what is good and honourable. If we would take true Pains with our selves to consider all things by the Light of Reason and Justice, tho' a Man were in the Height of Youth and amorous Inclinations, he would look upon a Coquet with the same Contempt or Indifference as he would upon a Coxcomb: The wanton Carriage in a Woman, would disappoint her of the Admiration which she aims at; and the vain Dress or Discourse of a Man, would destroy the Comliness of his Shape, or Goodness of his Understanding. I say the Goodness of his Understanding, for it is no less common to see Men of Sense commence Coxcombs, than beautiful Women become immodest. When this happens in either, the Favour we are naturally inclined to give to the good Qualities they have from Nature, should abate in Proportion. But however just it is to measure the Value of Men by the Application of their Talents, and not by the Eminence of those Qualities abstracted from their Use; I say, however just such a way of judging is, in all Ages as well as this, the Contrary has prevailed upon the Generality of Mankind. How many lewd Devices have been preserved from one Age to another, which had perished as soon as they were made, if Painters and Sculptors had been esteemed as much for the Purpose as the Execution of their Designs? Modest and well-governed Imaginations, have by this Means lost the Representations of Ten thousand charming Portraitures, filled with Images of innate Truth, generous Zeal, couragious Faith, and tender Humanity; instead of which Satyrs, Furies, and Monsters, are recommended by those Arts to a shameful Eternity.

The unjust Application of laudable Talents, is tolerated in the general Opinion of Men, not only in such Cases as are here mentioned, but also in Matters which concern ordinary Life. If a Lawyer were to be esteemed only as he uses his Parts in contending for Justice, and were immediately despicable when he appeared in a Cause which he could not but know was an unjust one, how honourable would his Character be? And how honourable is it in such among us, who follow the Profession no otherwise than as labouring to protect the Injured, to subdue the Oppressor, to imprison the careless Debtor, and do Right to the painful Artificer? But many of this excellent Character are overlooked by the greater Number; who affect covering a weak Place in a Client's Title, diverting the Course of an Enquiry, or finding a skilful Refuge to palliate a Falshood: Yet it is still called Eloquence in the latter, though thus unjustly employed; but Resolution in an Assassin is according to Reason quite as laudable, as Knowledge and Wisdom exercised in the Defence of an ill Cause.

Were the Intention stedfastly considered, as the Measure of Approbation, all Falshood would soon be out of Countenance; and an Address in imposing upon Mankind, would be as contemptible in one State of Life as another. A couple of Courtiers making Professions of Esteem, would make the same Figure after Breach of Promise, as two Knights of the Post convicted of Perjury. But Conversation is fallen so low in point of Morality, that as they say in a Bargain, 'Let the Buyer look to it': so in Friendship he is the Man in Danger who is most apt to believe: He is the more likely to suffer in the Commerce, who begins with the Obligation of being the more ready to enter into it.

But those Men only are truly great, who place their Ambition rather in acquiring to themselves the Conscience of worthy Enterprizes, than in the Prospect of Glory which attends them. These exalted Spirits would rather be secretly the Authors of Events which are serviceable to Mankind, than without being such, to have the publick Fame of it. Where therefore an eminent Merit is robbed by Artifice or Detraction, it does but encrease by such Endeavours of its Enemies: The impotent Pains which are taken to sully it, or diffuse it among a Crowd to the Injury of a single Person, will naturally produce the contrary Effect; the Fire will blaze out, and burn up all that attempt to smother what they cannot extinguish.

There is but one thing necessary to keep the Possession of true Glory, which is to hear the Opposers of it with Patience, and preserve the Virtue by which it was acquired. When a Man is thoroughly perswaded that he ought neither to admire, wish for, or pursue any thing but what is exactly his Duty, it is not in the Power of Seasons, Persons or Accidents to diminish his Value: He only is a great Man who can neglect the Applause of the Multitude, and enjoy himself independent of its Favour. This is indeed an arduous Task; but it should comfort a glorious Spirit that it is the highest Step to which humane Nature can arrive. Triumph, Applause, Acclamation, are dear to the Mind of Man; but it is still a more exquisite Delight to say to your self, you have done well, than to hear the whole humane Race pronounce you glorious, except you your self can join with them in your own Reflexions. A Mind thus equal and uniform may be deserted by little fashionable Admirers and Followers, but will ever be had in Reverence by Souls like it self. The Branches of the Oak endure all the Seasons of the Year, though its Leaves fall off in Autumn; and these too will be restored with the returning Spring.   T

No. 173.

[ADDISON.]   Tuesday, September 18.

> . . . *Remove fera monstra, tuaeque*
> *Saxificos vultus, quaecunque ea, tolle Medusae.*
>   —Ovid. *Met.*

In a late Paper I mentioned the Project of an ingenious Author for the erecting of several Handicraft Prizes to be contended for by our *British* Artizans, and the Influence they might have towards the Improvement of our several Manufactures.   I have since that been very much surpriz'd by the following Advertisement which I find in the *Post-Boy* of the 11th Instant, and again repeated in the *Post-Boy* of the 15th.

On the 9th of October next will be run for upon Coleshill-Heath in Warwickshire, a Plate of 6 Guineas value, 3 Heats, by any Horse, Mare or Gelding that hath not won above the Value of 5 *l.*, the winning Horse to be Sold for 10 *l.*, to carry 10 Stone weight, if 14 Hands high, if above or under, to carry or be allowed weight for Inches, and to be entred Friday the 5th at the Swan in Coleshill, before 6 in the Evening.   Also a Plate of less Value to be run for by Asses.   The same Day a Gold Ring to be Grinn'd for by Men.

The first of these Diversions, that is to be exhibited by the 10*l.* Race-Horses, may probably have its use; but the two last, in which the Asses and Men are concerned, seem to me altogether extraordinary and unaccountable.   Why they should keep running Asses at *Coleshill*, or how making Mouths turns to account in *Warwickshire*, more than in any other Parts of *England*, I cannot comprehend.   I have looked over all the Olympick Games, and do not find any thing in them like an Ass Race, or a Match at Grinning.   However it be, I am informed that several Asses are now kept in Body-Cloaths, and sweated every Morning upon the Heath, and that all the Country Fellows within ten Miles of the *Swan*, grinn an Hour or two in their Glasses every Morning, in order to qualifie themselves for the 9th of *October*.   The Prize which is proposed to be grinn'd for, has raised such an Ambition among the Common People of Out-grinning one another, that many very discerning Persons are afraid it should spoil most of the Faces in the County; and that a *Warwickshire* Man will be known by his Grinn, as Roman Catholicks imagine a *Kentish* Man is by his Tail.   The Gold Ring which is made the Prize of Deformity, is just the Reverse of the Golden Apple that was formerly made the Prize of Beauty, and should carry for its Posie the old Motto inverted.

Detur tetriori.

Or to accommodate it to the Capacity of the Combatants,

> *The frightfull'st Grinner*
> *Be the Winner.*

In the mean while I would advise a *Dutch* Painter to be present at this great Controversie of Faces, in order to make a Collection of the most remarkable Grinns that shall be there exhibited.

I must not here omit an Account which I lately received of one of these Grinning Matches from a Gentleman, who upon reading the above-mentioned Advertisement, entertained a Coffee-house with the following Narrative.   Upon the taking of *Namur,* amidst other Publick Rejoicings made on that Occasion, there was a Gold Ring given by a Whig Justice of Peace to be grinn'd for.   The first Competitor that entred the Lists, was a black swarthy *French* Man, who accidentally passed that way, and being a Man naturally of a wither'd Look, and hard Features, promised himself good Success.   He was placed upon a Table in the Great Point of View, and looking upon the Company like *Milton*'s Death,

> *Grinn'd horribly a Ghastly Smile—*

His Muscles were so drawn together on each side of his Face, that he shewed twenty Teeth at a Grinn, and put the Country in some pain, least a Foreigner should carry away the Honour of the Day; but upon a further Tryal they found he was Master only of the Merry Grinn.

The next that mounted the Table was a Male-content in those Days, and a great Master in the whole Art of Grinning, but particularly excelled in the angry Grinn.   He did his Part so well that he is said to have made half a Dozen Women miscarry; but the Justice being apprised by one who stood near him, that the Fellow who Grinned in his Face was a *Jacobite,* and being unwilling that a Disaffected Person should win the Gold Ring, and be looked upon as the best Grinner in the Country, he ordered the Oaths to be tendered him upon his quitting the Table, which the Grinner refusing, he was set aside as an unqualified Person.   There were several other Grotesque Figures that presented themselves, which it would be too tedious to describe.   I must not however omit a Plow-man who lived in the further Part of the Country, and being very lucky in a Pair of long Lanthorn-Jaws, wrung his Face into such an hideous Grimace that every Feature of it appeared under a different Distortion.   The whole Company stood astonished at such a complicated Grinn, and were ready to assign the Prize to him, had it not been proved by one of his Antagonists that he had practised with Verjuice for some Days before, and had a Crab found upon him at the very time of Grinning; upon which the best Judges of Grinning declared it, as their Opinion, that he was not to be looked upon as a fair Grinner, and therefore ordered him to be set aside as a Cheat.

The Prize, it seems, fell at length upon a Cobler, *Giles Gorgon* by Name, who produced several new Grinns of his own Invention, having been used to cut Faces for many Years together over his Last. At the very first Grinn he cast every Human Feature out of his Countenance; at the second he became the Face of a Spout; at the third a Baboon, at the fourth the Head of a Base-Viol, and at the fifth a Pair of Nut-crackers. The whole Assembly wondered at his Accomplishments, and bestowed the Ring on him unanimously; but, what he esteemed more than all the rest, a Country Wench whom he had wooed in vain for above five Years before, was so charmed with his Grinns and the Applauses which he received on all sides, that she Married him the Week following, and to this Day wears the Prize upon her Finger, the Cobler having made use of it as his Wedding Ring.

This Paper might perhaps seem very impertinent if it grew serious in the Conclusion. I would nevertheless leave it to the Consideration of those who are the Patrons of this monstrous Tryal of Skill, whether or no they are not guilty, in some measure, of an Affront to their Species, in treating after this manner the *Human Face Divine*, and turning that part of us, which has so great an Image impressed upon it, into the Image of a Monkey; whether the raising such silly Competitions among the Ignorant, proposing Prizes for such useless Accomplishments, filling the common People's Heads with such Senseless Ambitions, and inspiring them with such absurd Ideas of Superiority and Preheminence, has not in it something Immoral as well as Ridiculous.   L

No. 174.

[STEELE.]   Wednesday, September 19.

Haec memini & victum frustra contendere Thyrsin.—Virg.

THERE is scarce any thing more common than Animosities between Parties that cannot subsist but by their Agreement: This was well represented in the Sedition of the Members of the human Body in the old *Roman* Fable. It is often the Case of lesser confederate States against a superior Power, which are hardly held together though their Unanimity is necessary tor their common Safety: And this is always the Case of the landed and trading Interest of *Great Britain*; the Trader is fed by the Product of the Land, and the landed Man cannot be cloathed but by the Skill of the Trader; and yet those Interests are ever jarring.

We had last Winter an Instance of this at our Club, in Sir ROGER DE COVERLY and Sir ANDREW FREEPORT, between whom there is generally a constant, though friendly, Opposition of Opinions. It happened that one of the Company, in an historical Discourse, was observing, that *Carthaginian* Faith was a proverbial Phrase to intimate Breach of Leagues. Sir ROGER said it could hardly be otherwise: That the *Carthaginians* were the greatest Traders in the World; and as Gain is the chief End of such a People, they never pursue any other: The Means to it are never regarded; they will, if it comes easily, get Money honestly; but if not, they will not scruple to attain it by Fraud or Cosenage: And indeed what is the whole Business of the Trader's Accompt, but to over-reach him who trusts to his Memory? But were that not so, what can there great and noble be expected from him whose Attention is for ever fixed upon ballancing his Books, and watching over his Expences? And at best, let Frugality and Parsimony be the Virtues of the Merchant, how much is his punctual Dealing below a Gentleman's Charity to the Poor, or Hospitality among his Neighbours?

CAPTAIN SENTRY observed Sir ANDREW very diligent in hearing Sir ROGER, and had a Mind to turn the Discourse, by taking Notice in general from the highest to the lowest Parts of humane Society, there was a secret, tho' unjust Way among Men, of indulging the Seeds of Ill-nature and Envy, by comparing their own State of Life to that of another, and grudging the Approach of their Neighbour to their own Happiness; and on the other Side, he who is the less at his Ease repines at the other who, he thinks, has unjustly the Advantage over him. Thus the civil and military List look upon each other with much Ill-nature; the Soldier repines at the Courtier's Power, and the Courtier rallies the Soldier's Honour; or, to come to lower Instances, the private Men in the Horse and Foot of an Army, the Carmen and Coachmen in the City-streets, mutually look upon each other with Ill-will, when they are in Competition for Quarters or the Way in their respective Motions.

It is very well, good Captain, interrupted Sir ANDREW: You may attempt to turn the Discourse, if you think fit, but I must however have a Word or two with Sir ROGER; who, I see, thinks he has paid off, and been very severe upon the Merchant. I shall not, continued he, at this Time remind Sir ROGER of the

great and noble Monuments of Charity and publick Spirit which
have been erected by Merchants since the Reformation, but at
present content my self with what he allows us, Parsimony and
Frugality. If it were consistent with the Quality of so antient
a Baronet as Sir ROGER, to keep an Accompt or measure things
by the most infallible Way, that of Numbers, he would prefer
our Parsimony to his Hospitality. If to drink so many Hogsheads is to be hospitable, we do not contend for the Fame of
that Virtue; but it would be worth while to consider, whether
so many Artificers at work ten Days together by my Appointment, or so many Peasants made merry on Sir ROGER's
Charge, are the Men more obliged: I believe the Families of
the Artificers will thank me, more than the Housholds of the
Peasants shall Sir ROGER. Sir ROGER gives to his Men, but I
place mine above the Necessity or Obligation of my Bounty.
I am in very little Pain for the *Roman* Proverb upon the *Carthaginian* Traders; the *Romans* were their professed Enemies:
I am only sorry no *Carthaginian* Histories have come to our
Hands; we might have been taught perhaps by them some
Proverbs against the *Roman* Generosity, in fighting for and
bestowing other People's Goods. But since Sir ROGER has
taken Occasion from an old Proverb to be out of Humour with
Merchants, it should be no Offence to offer one not quite so old
in their Defence. When a Man happens to break in *Holland,*
they say of him that *he has not kept true Accompts.* This
Phrase, perhaps, among us would appear a soft or humorous
way of speaking, but with that exact Nation it bears the
highest Reproach; for a Man to be mistaken in the Calculation
of his Expence, in his Ability to answer future Demands, or to
be impertinently sanguine in putting his Credit to too great
Adventure, are all Instances of as much Infamy, as with gayer
Nations to be failing in Courage or common Honesty.

Numbers are so much the Measure of every thing that is
valuable, that it is not possible to demonstrate the Success of
any Action, or the Prudence of any Undertaking, without them.
I say this in Answer to what Sir ROGER is pleased to say, That
little that is truly noble can be expected from one who is ever
poring on his Cash-book or ballancing his Accompts. When I
have my Returns from Abroad, I can tell to a Shilling by the
Help of Numbers the Profit or Loss by my Adventure; but I
ought also to be able to shew that I had Reason for making it,
either from my own Experience or that of other People, or
from a reasonable Presumption that my Returns will be sufficient to answer my Expence and Hazard; and this is never to
be done without the Skill of Numbers. For Instance, if I am
to trade to *Turkey,* I ought beforehand to know the Demand of

our Manufactures there as well as of their Silks in *England*, and
the customary Prices that are given for both in each Country.
I ought to have a clear Knowledge of these Matters before-
hand, that I may presume upon sufficient Returns to answer
the Charge of the Cargo I have fitted out, the Freight and
Assurance out and home, the Customs to the Queen, and the
Interest of my own Money, and besides all these Expences a
reasonable Profit to my self.   Now what is there of Scandal in
this Skill?   What has the Merchant done that he should be so
little in the good Graces of Sir ROGER? he throws down no
Man's Enclosures, and tramples upon no Man's Corn; he takes
nothing from the industrious Labourer; he pays the poor Man
for his Work; he communicates his Profit with Mankind; by the
Preparation of his Cargo and the Manufacture of his Returns,
he furnishes Employment and Subsistance to greater Numbers
than the richest Nobleman; and even the Nobleman is obliged
to him for finding out foreign Markets for the Produce of his
Estate, and for making a great Addition to his Rents; and yet
'tis certain that none of all these Things could be done by him
without the Exercise of his Skill in Numbers.

This is the Oeconomy of the Merchant, and the Conduct of
the Gentleman must be the same, unless by scorning to be the
Steward, he resolves the Steward shall be the Gentleman.   The
Gentleman no more than the Merchant is able without the Help
of Numbers to account for the Success of any Action, or the
Prudence of any Adventure.   If, for Instance, the Chace is his
whole Adventure, his only Returns must be the Stag's Horns
in the great Hall, and the Fox's Nose upon the Stable Door.
Without Doubt Sir ROGER knows the full Value of these Returns; and if before-hand he had computed the Charges of the
Chace, a Gentleman of his Discretion would certainly have
hang'd up all his Dogs, he would never have brought back so
many fine Horses to the Kennel, he would never have gone so
often like a Blast over Fields of Corn.   If such too had been the
Conduct of all his Ancestors, he might truly have boasted at this
Day that the Antiquity of his Family had never been sullied
by a Trade; a Merchant had never been permitted with his
whole Estate to purchase a Room for his Picture in the Gallery
of the COVERLYS, or to claim his Descent from the Maid of
Honour.   But 'tis very happy for Sir ROGER that the Merchant
paid so dear for his Ambition.   'Tis the Misfortune of many
other Gentlemen to turn out of the Seats of their Ancestors, to
make Way for such new Masters as have been more exact in
their Accompts than themselves; and certainly he deserves the
Estate a great deal better who has got it by his Industry, than
he who has lost it by his Negligence.   **T**

No. 175.

[BUDGELL.]   Thursday, September 20.

Proximus a tectis ignis defenditur aegre.—Ovid. *Rem. Am.*

I SHALL this Day entertain my Readers with two or three
Letters I have received from my Correspondents: The first discovers to me a Species of Females which have hitherto escaped
my Notice, and is as follows.

'*Mr.* SPECTATOR,

I am a young Gentleman of a competent Fortune, and a
sufficient Taste of Learning, to spend five or six Hours every
Day very agreeably among my Books. That I might have
nothing to divert me from my Studies, and to avoid the Noises
of Coaches and Chair-men, I have taken Lodgings in a very
narrow Street, not far from *White-hall*; but it is my Misfortune
to be so posted, that my Lodgings are directly opposite to those
of a *Jezebel*. You are to know, Sir, that a *Jezebel* (so called by
the Neighbourhood from displaying her pernicious Charms at
her Window) appears constantly dress'd at her Sash, and has a
thousand little Tricks and Fooleries to attract the Eyes of all
the idle young Fellows in the Neighbourhood. I have seen
more than six Persons at once from their several Windows
observing the *Jezebel* I am now complaining of. I at first
looked on her my self with the highest Contempt, could divert
my self with her Airs for half an Hour, and afterwards take up
my *Plutarch* with great Tranquility of Mind; but was a little
vexed to find that in less than a Month she had considerably
stoln upon my Time, so that I resolved to look at her no more.
But the *Jezebel*, who, as I suppose, might think it a diminution
to her Honour, to have the Number of her Gazers lessen'd, resolved not to part with me so, and begun to play so many new
Tricks at her Window, that it was impossible for me to forbear
observing her. I verily believe she put her self to the Expence
of a new Wax Baby on purpose to plague me; she used to
dandle and play with this Figure as impertinently as if it had
been a real Child: Sometimes she would let fall a Glove or a
Pin-Cushion in the Street, and shut or open her Casement three
or four times in a Minute. When I had almost weaned my self
from this, she came in her Shift Sleeves, and dress'd at the
Window. I had no way left but to let down my Curtains, which
I submitted to, though it considerably darknd my Room, and
was pleased to think that I had at last got the better of her;
but was surprized the next Morning to hear her talking out of
her Window quite cross the Street, with another Woman that

lodges over me: I am since informed, that she made her a Visit, and got acquainted with her, within three Hours after the Fall of my Window-Curtains.

Sir, I am plagued every Moment in the Day one way or other in my own Chambers; and the *Jezebel* has the Satisfaction to know, that, though I am not looking at her, I am list'ning to her impertinent Dialogues that pass over my Head. I would immediately change my Lodgings, but that I think it might look like a plain Confession that I am conquered; and besides this, I am told that most Quarters of the Town are infested with these Creatures. If they are so, I am sure 'tis such an Abuse, as a Lover of Learning and Silence ought to take Notice of.

I am, Sir, Yours, &c.'

I am afraid, by some Lines in this Letter, that my young Student is touched with a Distemper which he hardly seems to dream of, and is too far gone in it to receive Advice. However, I shall Animadvert in due time on the Abuse which he mentions, having my self observed a Nest of *Jezebels* near the *Temple*, who make it their Diversion to draw up the Eyes of young Templars, that at the same time they may see them stumble in an unlucky Gutter which runs under the Window.

'*Mr.* Spectator,

I have lately read the Conclusion of your forty-seventh Speculation upon *Butts* with great Pleasure, and have ever since been throughly perswaded that one of those Gentlemen is extreamly necessary to enliven Conversation. I had an Entertainment last Week upon the Water for a Lady to whom I make my Addresses, with several of our Friends of both Sexes. To divert the Company in general, and to shew my Mistress in particular my Genius for Raillery, I took one of the most celebrated *Butts* in Town along with me. It is with the utmost Shame and Confusion that I must acquaint you with the Sequel of my Adventure: As soon as we were got into the Boat I played a Sentence or two at my *Butt* which I thought very smart, when my ill Genius, who I verily believe inspired him purely for my Destruction, suggested to him such a Reply, as got all the Laughter on his side. I was dashed at so unexpected a Turn, which the *Butt* perceiving, resolved not to let me recover my self, and pursuing his Victory, rallied and tossed me in a most unmerciful and barbarous manner 'till we came to *Chelsea*. I had some small Success while we were eating Cheese-Cakes; but coming Home he renewed his Attacks with his former good Fortune, and equal Diversion to the whole Company.

In short, Sir, I must ingenuously own that I was never so handled in all my Life; and to compleat my Misfortune, I am since told that the *Butt*, flushed with his late Victory, has made a Visit or two to the dear Object of my Wishes, so that I am at once in danger of losing all my Pretensions to Wit, and my Mistress into the Bargain.   This, Sir, is a true Account of my present Troubles, which you are the more obliged to assist me in, as you were your self in a great measure the Cause of them, by recommending to us an Instrument, and not instructing us at the same time how to play upon it.

I have been thinking whether it might not be highly convenient, that all *Butts* should wear an Inscription affixed to some Part of their Bodies, shewing on which side they are to be come at, and that if any of them are Persons of unequal Tempers, there should be some Method taken to inform the World at what Time it is safe to attack them, and when you had best let them alone.   But submitting these Matters to your more serious Consideration,

I am, Sir, Yours, &c.'

I have, indeed, seen and heard of several young Gentlemen under the same Misfortune with my present Correspondent. The best Rule I can lay down for them to avoid the like Calamities for the future, is, throughly to consider not only *Whether their Companions are weak*, but *Whether themselves are Wits*.

The following Letter comes to me from *Exeter*, and being credibly informed that what it contains is Matter of Fact, I shall give it my Reader as it was sent me.

'*Mr.* Spectator,   *Exeter, Sept.* 7.

You were pleased in a late Speculation to take Notice of the Inconvenience we lie under in the Country, in not being able to keep Pace with the Fashion; but there is another Misfortune which we are subject to, and is no less grievous than the former, which has hitherto escaped your Observation.   I mean, the having things palmed upon us for *London* Fashions, which were never once heard of there.

A Lady of this Place had some time since a Box of the newest Ribbons sent down by the Coach: Whether it was her own malicious Invention, or the Wantonness of a *London* Milliner, I am not able to inform you; but, among the rest, there was one Cherry-coloured Ribbon, consisting of about half a dozen Yards, made up in the Figure of a Small Head-dress.   The foresaid Lady had the Assurance to affirm, amidst a Circle of Female Inquisitors, who were present at the opening of the Box, that this was the newest Fashion worn at Court.   Accordingly the next *Sunday* we had several Females, who came to Church with their Heads dress'd wholly in Ribbons, and looked like so many Victims ready to be Sacrificed. This is still a reigning Mode among us. At the same time we have a Sett of Gentlemen, who take the Liberty to appear in all publick Places without any Buttons to their Coats, which they supply with several little silver Hasps; tho' our freshest Advices from *London* make no mention of any such Fashion; and we are something shy of affording Matter to the Button-makers for a second Petition.

What I would humbly propose to the Publick is, that there may be a Society erected in *London*, to consist of the most skilful Persons of both Sexes for the *Inspection of Modes and Fashions*; and that hereafter no Person or Persons shall presume to appear singularly habited in any Part of the Country, without a Testimonial from the foresaid Society that their Dress is answerable to the Mode at *London*. By this means, Sir, we shall know a little whereabout we are.

If you could bring this Matter to bear, you would very much oblige great Numbers of your Country Friends, and among the rest,

Your very Humble Servant,

X   Jack Modish.'

No. 176.

[STEELE.]   Friday, September 21.

Parvula, pumilio, χαρίτων μία, tota merum sal.—Luc.

THERE are in the following Letter Matters which I, a Batchelor, cannot be supposed to be acquainted with; therefore shall not pretend to explain upon it till further Consideration, but leave the Author of the Epistle to express his Condition his own Way.

   '*Mr.* SPECTATOR,

I do not deny but you appear in many of your Papers to understand humane Life pretty well; but there are very many things which you cannot possibly have a true Notion of, in a single Life; these are such as respect the married State; otherwise I cannot account for your having over-looked a very good sort of People, which are commonly called in Scorn the *Henpeckt*. You are to understand that I am one of those innocent Mortals, who suffer Derision under that Word, for being governed by the best of Wives. It would be worth your Consideration to enter into the Nature of Affection it self, and tell us, according to your Philosophy, why it is that our Dears should do what they will with us, shall be froward, ill-natured, assuming, sometimes whine, at others rail, then swoon away, then come to Life, have the Use of Speech to the greatest Fluency imaginable, and then sink away again, and all because they fear we do not love them enough; that is, the poor things love us so heartily, that they cannot think it possible we should be able to love them in so great a Degree, which makes them take on so.   I say, Sir, a true good-natur'd Man, whom Rakes and Libertines call *Hen-peckt*, shall fall into all these different Moods with his dear Life, and at the same time see they are wholly put on; and yet not be hard-hearted enough to tell the dear good Creature that she is an Hypocrite.   This sort of good Man is very frequent in the populous and wealthy City of *London*, and is the true *hen-peckt* Man; the kind Creature cannot break through his Kindnesses so far as to come to an Explanation with the tender Soul, and therefore goes on to comfort her when nothing ails her, to appease her when she is not angry, and to give her his Cash when he knows she does not want it; rather than be uneasie for a whole Month, which is computed by hard-hearted Men the Space of Time which a froward Woman takes to come to her self if you have Courage to stand out.

There are indeed several other Species of the *Hen-peckt*, and in my Opinion they are certainly the best Subjects the Queen has; and for that Reason I take it to be your Duty to keep us above Contempt.

I do not know whether I make my self understood in the Representation of an hen-peckt Life, but I shall take Leave to give you an Account of my self, and my own Spouse.   You are to know that I am reckoned no Fool, have on several Occasions been tried whether I will take ill Usage, and yet the Event has been to my Advantage; and yet there is not such a Slave in *Turkey* as I am to my Dear.   She has a good Share of Wit, and is what you call a very pretty agreeable Woman.   I perfectly doat on her, and my Affection to her gives me all the Anxieties imaginable but that of Jealousie.   My being thus confident of her, I take, as much as I can judge of my Heart, to be the Reason, that whatever she does, tho' it be never so much against my Inclination, there is still left something in her Manner that is amiable.   She will sometimes look at me with an assumed Grandeur, and pretend to resent that I have not had Respect enough for her Opinion in such an Instance in Company.   I cannot but smile at the pretty Anger she is in, and then she pretends she is used like a Child.   In a Word, our great Debate is which has the Superiority in Point of Understanding.   She is eternally forming an Argument of

Debate; to which I very indolently answer, Thou art mighty pretty. To this she answers, All the World but you think I have as much Sense as your self. I repeat to her, Indeed you are pretty. Upon this there is no Patience; she will throw down any thing about her, stamp, and pull off her Head-Cloaths. Fie, my Dear, say I; how can a Woman of your Sense fall into such an intemperate Rage? This is an Argument which never fails. Indeed, my Dear, says she, you make me mad sometimes, so you do, with the silly Way you have of treating me like a pretty Idiot. Well, what have I got by putting her into good Humour? Nothing, but that I must convince her of my good Opinion by my Practice; and then I am to give her Possession of my little ready Money, and for a Day and a half following dislike all she dislikes, and extol every thing she approves. I am so exquisitely fond of this Darling, that I seldom see any of my Friends, am uneasie in all Companies till I see her again; and when I come home she is in the Dumps, because she says she's sure I came so soon only because I think her handsome. I dare not upon this Occasion laugh; but tho' I am one of the warmest Churchmen in the Kingdom I am forced to rail at the Times, because she is a violent Whig. Upon this we talk Politicks so long, that she is convinc'd I kiss her for her Wisdom. It is a common Practice with me to ask her some Question concerning the Constitution, which she answers me in general out of *Harington's Oceana*: Then I commend her strange Memory, and her Arm is immediately locked in mine. While I keep her in this Temper she plays before me, sometimes dancing in the Midst of the Room, sometimes striking an Air at her Spinet, varying her Posture and her Charms in such a Manner that I am in continual Pleasure: She will play the Fool if I allow her to be wise, but if she suspects I like her for her trifling she immediately grows grave.

These are the Toils in which I am taken, and I carry off my Servitude as well as most Men; but my Application to you is in Behalf of the *Hen-peckt* in general, and I desire a Dissertation from you in Defence of us. You have, as I am informed, very good Authorities in our Favour, and hope you will not omit the Mention of the renowned *Socrates*, and his philosophick Resignation to his Wife *Xantippe*. This would be a very good Office to the World in general, for the *Hen-peckt* are powerful; in their Quality and Numbers, not only in Cities but in Courts; in the latter they are ever the most obsequious, in the former the most wealthy of all Men. When you have considered Wedlock throughly, you ought to enter into the Suburbs of Matrimony, and give us an Account of the Thraldom of kind Keepers and irresolute Lovers; the Keepers who cannot quit their fair ones tho' they see their approaching Ruin; the Lovers who dare not marry, tho' they know they shall never be happy without the Mistresses whom they cannot purchase on other Terms.

What will be a great Embellishment to your Discourse, will be, that you may find Instances of the Haughty, the Proud, the Frolick, the Stubborn, who are each of them in secret down-right Slaves to their Wives or Mistresses. I must beg of you in the last Place to dwell upon this, That the Wise and Valiant in all Ages have been *hen-peckt*; and that the sturdy Tempers who are not Slaves to Affection, owe that Exemption to their being enthraled by Ambition, Avarice, or some meaner Passion. I have ten thousand thousand things more to say, but my Wife sees me Writing, and will, according to Custom, be consulted, if I do not seal this immediately.

Yours,

Nathaniel Henroost.'

T

No. 177.

[ADDISON.]   Saturday, September 22.

> . . . *Quis enim bonus, aut face dignus*
> *Arcana, qualem Cereris vult esse sacerdos,*
> *Ulla aliena sibi credat mala?* . . .—Juv.

In one of my last Week's Papers I treated of Good-nature, as it is the effect of Constitution, I shall now speak of it as it is a Moral Virtue. The first may make a Man easie in himself, and agreeable to others, but implies no Merit in him that is possessed of it. A Man is no more to be praised upon this Account, than because he has a regular Pulse or a good Digestion. This Good-nature however in the Constitution, which Mr. *Dryden* somewhere calls a *Milkiness of Blood*, is an admirable Groundwork for the other. In order therefore to try our Good-nature, whether it arises from the Body or the Mind, whether it be founded in the Animal or Rational Part of our Nature, in a word, whether it be such as is entituled to any other Reward, besides that secret Satisfaction and Contentment of Mind which is essential to it, and the kind Reception it procures us in the World, we must examine it by the following Rules.

First, Whether it acts with Steadiness and Uniformity in Sickness and in Health, in Prosperity and in Adversity; if otherwise, it is to be looked upon as nothing else but an Irradiation of the Mind from some new Supply of Spirits, or a more kindly Circulation of the Blood. Sir *Francis Bacon* mentions a cunning Sollicitor, who would never ask a Favour of a great Man before Dinner; but took care to prefer his

Petition at a time when the Party petitioned had his Mind free from Care, and his Appetites in good Humour. Such a transient Temporary Good-nature as this, is not that *Philanthrophie*, the Love of Mankind, which deserves the Title of a Moral Virtue.

The next way of a Man's bringing his Good-nature to the Test is, to consider whether it operates according to the Rules of Reason and Duty: For if, notwithstanding its general Benevolence to Mankind, it makes no distinction between its Objects, if it exerts it self promiscuously towards the Deserving and the Undeserving, if it relieves alike the Idle and the Indigent, if it gives it self up to the first Petitioner, and lights upon any one rather by Accident than Choice, it may pass for an amiable Instinct, but must not assume the Name of a Moral Virtue.

The third Tryal of Good-nature will be the examining our selves, whether or no we are able to exert it to our own Disadvantage, and employ it on proper Objects, notwithstanding any little Pain, Want or Inconvenience which may arise to our selves from it: In a word, whether we are willing to risque any part of our Fortune, our Reputation, our Health or Ease, for the Benefit of Mankind. Among all these Expressions of Good-nature, I shall single out that which goes under the general Name of Charity, as it consists in relieving the Indigent; that being a Tryal of this kind which offers it self to us almost at all Times and in every Place.

I should propose it as a Rule to every one, who is provided with any Competency of Fortune more than sufficient for the Necessaries of Life, to lay aside a certain Proportion of his Income for the use of the Poor. This I would look upon as an Offering to him who has a Right to the whole, for the Use of those, whom, in the Passage hereafter mentioned, he has described as his own Representatives upon Earth. At the same time we should manage our Charity with such Prudence and Caution, that we may not hurt our own Friends or Relations, whilst we are doing good to those who are Strangers to us.

This may possibly be explained better by an Example than by a Rule.

Eugenius is a Man of an Universal Good-nature, and Generous beyond the Extent of his Fortune, but withal so prudent in the Oeconomy of his Affairs, that what goes out in Charity is made up by Good Management. *Eugenius* has what the World calls Two hundred Pounds a Year; but never values himself above Nine-score, as not thinking he has a right to the Tenth Part, which he always appropriates to charitable Uses. To this Sum he frequently makes other voluntary Additions, insomuch that in a good Year, for such he accounts those in which he has been able to make greater Bounties than ordinary, he has given above twice that Sum to the Sickly and Indigent. *Eugenius* prescribes to himself many particular Days of Fasting and Abstinence, in order to encrease his private Bank of Charity, and sets aside what would be the current Expences of those Times for the use of the Poor. He often goes a-foot where his Business calls him, and at the End of his Walk has given a Shilling, which in his ordinary Methods of Expence would have gone for Coach-hire, to the first necessitous Person that has fallen in his way. I have known him, when he has been going to a Play, or an Opera, divert the Mony which was designed for that Purpose, upon an Object of Charity whom he has met with in the Street, and afterwards pass his Evening in a Coffee-house, or at a Friend's Fireside, with much greater Satisfaction to himself than he could have received from the most exquisite Entertainments of the Theatre. By these means he is generous without impoverishing himself, and enjoys his Estate by making it the Property of others.

There are few Men so cramped in their private Affairs, who may not be charitable after this maner, without any Disadvantage to themselves, or Prejudice to their Families. It is but sometimes sacrificing a Diversion or Convenience to the Poor, and turning the usual Course of our Expences into a better Channel. This is, I think, not only the most prudent and convenient, but the most meritorious Piece of Charity, which we can put in Practice. By this Method we in some measure share the Necessities of the Poor at the same time that we relieve them, and make our selves not only their Patrons, but their Fellow-Sufferers.

Sir *Thomas Brown* in the last Part of his *Religio Medici,* in which he describes his Charity in several Heroic Instances, and with a noble Heat of Sentiments mentions that Verse in the Proverbs of *Solomon, He that giveth to the Poor lendeth to the Lord*: 'There is more Rhetorick in that one Sentence,' says he, 'than in a Library of Sermons; and indeed if those Sentences were understood by the Reader, with the same Emphasis as they are delivered by the Author, we needed not those Volumes of Instructions, but might be honest by an Epitome.'

This Passage in Scripture is indeed wonderfully persuasive, but I think the same Thought is carried much further in the New Testament, where our Saviour tells us in a most pathetick manner that he shall hereafter regard the cloathing of the Naked, the feeding of the Hungry, and the visiting of the Imprisoned, as Offices done to himself, and reward them accordingly. Pursuant to those Passages in Holy Scripture,

I have some where met with the Epitaph of a charitable Man which has very much pleased me. I cannot recollect the Words, but the Sense of it is to this Purpose. What I spent I lost. What I possessed is left to others. What I gave away remains with me.

Since I am thus insensibly engaged in Sacred Writ, I cannot forbear making an Extract of several Passages which I have always read with great Delight in the Book of *Job*. It is the Account which that Holy Man gives of his Behaviour in the Days of his Prosperity, and if considered only as a human Composition, is a finer Picture of a charitable and good-natured Man than is to be met with in any other Author.

Oh that I were as in months past, as in the days when God pre-served me: When his candle shined upon my head, and when by his light I walked through darkness: When the Almighty was yet with me; when my Children were about me: When I washed my steps with butter, and the rock poured out rivers of oyl.

When the ear heard me, then it blessed me; and when the Eye saw me it gave witness to me. Because I delivered the poor that cried, and the fatherless, and him that had none to help him. The blessing of him that was ready to perish came upon me, and I caused the Widow's heart to sing for joy. I was eyes to the blind, and feet was I to the lame; I was a father to the poor, and the cause which I knew not I searched out. Did not I weep for him that was in trouble, was not my soul grieved for the poor? Let me be weighed in an even ballance, that God may know mine integrity. If I did despise the cause of my man-servant or of my maid-servant when they contended with me: What then shall I do when God riseth up? and when he visiteth what shall I answer him? Did not he that made me in the womb, make him? and did not one fashion us in the womb? If I have with-held the poor from their desire, or have caused the eyes of the widow to fail; or have eaten my morsel my self alone, and the fatherless hath not eaten thereof: If I have seen any perish for want of cloathing, or any poor without covering: If his loyns have not blessed me, and if he were not warmed with the fleece of my sheep: If I have lift up my hand against the fatherless when I saw my help in the gate: Then let mine arm fall from my shoulder-blade, and mine arm be broken from the bone. If I have rejoiced at the Destruction of him that hated me, or lift up my self when evil found him: Neither have I suffered my mouth to sin, by wishing a curse to his soul. The stranger did not lodge in the street; but I opened my doors to the traveller. If my land cry against me, or that the furrows likewise thereof com-plain: If I have eaten the fruits thereof without mony, or have caused the owners thereof to lose their life; Let thistles grow instead of wheat, and cockle instead of barley. **L**

No. 178.

[STEELE.]   Monday, September 24.

Comis in uxorem . . .—Hor.

I CANNOT defer taking Notice of this Letter.

'Mr SPECTATOR,

I am but too good a Judge of your Paper of the 15th Instant,
which is a Master-Piece; I mean that of Jealousie: But I think
it unworthy of you to speak of that Torture in the Breast of a
Man, and not to mention also the Pangs of it in the Heart of a
Woman. You have very judiciously, and with the greatest
Penetration imaginable, considered it as Woman is the Creature
of whom the Diffidence is raised; but not a Word of a Man who
is so unmerciful as to move Jealousie in his Wife, and not care
whether she is so or not. It is possible you may not believe
there are such Tyrants in the World; but alas I can tell you of a
Man who is ever out of Humour in his Wife's Company, and the
pleasantest Man in the World every where else; the greatest
Sloven at Home when he appears to none but his Family, and
most exactly well-dressed in all other Places. Alas, Sir, is it
of Course, that to deliver one's self wholly into a Man's Power
without Possibility of Appeal to any other Jurisdiction but to
his own Reflexions, is so little an Obligation to a Gentleman
that he can be offended and fall into a Rage, because my
Heart swells Tears into my Eyes when I see him in a cloudy
Mood? I pretend to no Succour, and hope for no Relief but
from himself; and yet he that has Sense and Justice in every
thing else, never reflects, that to come home only to sleep off an
Intemperance, and spend all the Time he is there as if it were a
Punishment, cannot but give the Anguish of a jealous Mind.
He always leaves his Home as if he were going to Court, and
returns as if he were entring a Gaol. I could add to this, that
from his Company and his usual Discourse, he does not scruple
being thought an abandoned Man as to his Morals. Your own
Imagination will say enough to you concerning the Condition
of me his Wife; and I wish you would be so good as to represent
to him, for he is not ill-natured and reads you much, that the
Moment I hear the Door shut after him, I throw my self upon
my Bed, and drown the Child he is so fond of with my Tears,
and often frighten it with my Cries; that I curse my Being;
that I run to my Glass all over-bathed in Sorrows, and help the
Utterance of my inward Anguish by beholding the Gush of my
own Calamiti.s as my Tears fall from my Eyes. This looks
like an imagined Picture to tell you, but indeed this is one of
my Pastimes. Hitherto I have only told you the general

Temper of my Mind, but how shall I give you an Account of the Distraction of it? Could you but conceive how cruel I am one Moment in my Resentment, and, at the ensuing Minute, when I place him in the Condition my Anger would bring him to, how compassionate; it would give you some Notion how miserable I am, and how little I deserve it. When I remonstrate with the greatest Gentleness that is possible against unhandsome Appearances, and that married Persons are under particular Rules; when he is in the best Humour to receive this, I am answered only, That I expose my own Reputation and Sense if I appear jealous. I wish, good Sir, you would take this into serious Consideration, and admonish Husbands and Wives what Terms they ought to keep towards each other. Your Thoughts on this important Subject will have the greatest Reward, that which descends on such as feel the Sorrows of the Afflicted. Give me Leave to subscribe my self,

Your unfortunate,

humble Servant,

CELINDA.'

I had it in my Thoughts, before I received the Letter of this Lady, to consider this dreadful Passion in the Mind of a Woman; and the Smart she seems to feel, does not abate the Inclination I had to recommend to Husbands a more regular Behaviour, than to give the most exquisite of Torments to those who love them, nay whose Torment would be abated if they did not love them.

It is wonderful to observe how little is made of this inexpressible Injury, and how easily Men get into an Habit of being least agreeable where they are most obliged to be so. But this Subject deserves a distinct Speculation, and I shall observe for a Day or two the Behaviour of two or three happy Pair I am acquainted with, before I pretend to make a System of Conjugal Morality. I design in the first Place to go a few Miles out of Town, and there I know where to meet one who practises all the Parts of a fine Gentleman in the Duty of an Husband. When he was a Batchelor much Business made him particularly negligent in his Habit; but now there is no young Lover living so exact in the Care of his Person. One who asked why he was so long washing his Mouth, and so delicate in the Choice and Wearing of his Linnen? was answered, Because there is a Woman of Merit obliged to receive me kindly, and I think it incumbent upon me to make her Inclination go along with her Duty.

If a Man would give himself leave to think, he would not be so unreasonable as to expect Debauchery and Innocence could live in Commerce together; or hope that Flesh and Blood is capable of so strict an Allegiance, as that a fine Woman must go on to improve her self 'till she is as good and impassive as an Angel, only to preserve a Fidelity to a Brute and a Satyr.   The Lady who desires me for her Sake to end one of my Papers with the following Letter, I am perswaded thinks such a Perseverance very impracticable.

'*Husband*,

Stay more at Home. I know where you visited at Seven of Clock on *Thursday* Evening. The Colonel whom you charged me to see no more, is in Town.

T   *Martha Housewife.*'

No. 179.

[ADDISON.]   Tuesday, September 25.

Centuriae seniorum agitant expertia frugis:
Celsi praetereunt austera poemata Rhamnes.
Omne tulit punctum qui miscuit utile dulci,
Lectorem delectando pariterque monendo.—Hor.

I MAY cast my Readers under two general Divisions, the *Mercurial* and the *Saturnine*.   The first are the gay part of my Disciples, who require Speculations of Wit and Humour; the others are those of a more solemn and sober Turn, who find no Pleasure but in Papers of Morality and sound Sense; the former call everything that is Serious Stupid.   The latter look upon every thing as Impertinent that is Ludicrous.   Were I always Grave one half of my Readers would fall off from me: Were I always Merry I should lose the other.   I make it therefore my endeavour to find out Entertainments of both kinds, and by that means perhaps consult the good of both more than I should do, did I always write to the particular Taste of either.   As they neither of them know what I proceed upon, the sprightly Reader, who takes up my Paper in order to be diverted, very often finds himself engaged unawares in a serious and profitable Course of thinking; as on the contrary the Thoughtful Man, who perhaps may hope to find something Solid, and full of deep Reflection, is very often insensibly betrayed into a Fit of Mirth.   In a word, the Reader sits down to my Entertainment without knowing his Bill of Fare, and has therefore at least the Pleasure of hoping there may be a Dish to his Palate.

I must confess, were I left to my self, I should rather aim at Instruction than Diverting; but if we will be useful to the World, we must take it as we find it.   Authors of professed

Severity discourage the looser part of Mankind from having any thing to do with their Writings.   A Man must have Virtue in him, before he will enter upon the Reading of a *Seneca* or an *Epictetus.*   The very Title of a Moral Treatise has something in it Austere and Shocking to the Careless and Inconsiderate.

For this reason several unthinking Persons fall in my way, who would give no attention to Lectures delivered with a Religious Seriousness or a Philosophic Gravity.   They are insnared into Sentiments of Wisdom and Virtue when they do not think of it; and if by that means they arrive only at such a degree of Consideration as may dispose them to listen to more studied and elaborate Discourses, I shall not think my Speculations useless.   I might likewise observe, that the Gloominess in which sometimes the Minds of the best Men are involved, very often stands in need of such little incitements to Mirth and Laughter, as are apt to disperse Melancholy, and put our Faculties in good Humour.   To which some will add, that the *British* Climate, more than any other, makes Entertainments of this nature in a manner necessary.

If what I have here said does not recommend, it will at least excuse, the Variety of my Speculations.   I would not willingly Laugh but in order to Instruct, or if I sometimes fail in this Point, when my Mirth ceases to be Instructive, it shall never cease to be Innocent.   A Scrupulous Conduct in this Particular has, perhaps, more Merit in it than the generality of Readers imagine; did they know how many Thoughts occur in a point of Humour, which a discreet Author in Modesty suppresses; how many Stroaks of Railery present themselves, which could not fail to please the ordinary Taste of Mankind, but are stifled in their Birth by reason of some remote Tendency which they carry in them to corrupt the Minds of those who read them; did they know how many glances of Ill-nature are industriously avoided for fear of doing Injury to the Reputation of another, they would be apt to think kindly of those Writers who endeavour to make themselves diverting without being Immoral. One may apply to these Authors that Passage in *Waller,*

> *Poets lose half the Praise they would have got,*
> *Were it known what they discreetly blot.*

As nothing is more easie than to be a Wit with all the above-mentioned Liberties, it requires some Genius and Invention to appear such without them.

What I have here said is not only in regard to the Publick, but with an Eye to my particular Correspondent who has sent me the following Letter, which I have castrated in some places upon these Considerations.

'Sir,

Having lately seen your Discourse upon a Match of Grinning,
I cannot forbear giving you an account of a Whistling Match,
which, with many others, I was entertained with about three
Years since at the *Bath*. The Prize was a Guinea, to be conferred upon the ablest Whistler, that is, on him who could
Whistle clearest, and go through his Tune without Laughing, to
which at the same time he was provoked by the Antick Postures
of a *Merry-Andrew*, who was to stand upon the Stage and play
his Tricks in the Eye of the Performer. There were three
Competitors for the Ring. The first was a Plow-man of a very
promising Aspect; his Features were steady, and his Muscles
composed in so inflexible a stupidity, that upon his first appearance every one gave the Guinea for lost. The Pickled-Herring
however found the way to shake him, for upon his Whistling a
Country Jigg this unlucky Wagg danced to it with such a
variety of Distortions and Grimaces, that the Country Man
could not forbear smiling upon him, and by that means spoiled
his Whistle and lost the Prize.

The next that mounted the Stage was an Under-Citizen of
the *Bath*, a Person remarkable among the inferior People of
that Place for his great Wisdom and his broad Band. He contracted his Mouth with much Gravity, and, that he might dispose his Mind to be more serious than ordinary, begun the
Tune of *the Children in the Wood*, and went through part of it
with good Success, when on a sudden the Wit at his Elbow, who
had appeared wonderfully grave and attentive for some time,
gave him a touch upon the left Shoulder, and stared him in the
Face with so bewitching a Grinn, that the Whistler relaxed his
Fibres into a kind of Simper, and at length burst out into an
open Laugh. The third who entered the Lists was a Footman,
who in defiance of the *Merry-Andrew*, and all his Arts, whistled
a *Scotch* Tune and an *Italian* Sonata, with so setled a Countenance, that he bore away the Prize, to the great Admiration of
some Hundreds of Persons, who, as well as my self, were present
at this Tryal of Skill. Now, Sir, I humbly conceive, whatever
you have determined of the Grinners, the Whistlers ought to be
encouraged, not only as their Art is practised without Distortion, but as it improves Country Musick, promotes Gravity, and
teaches ordinary People to keep their Countenances, if they see
any thing ridiculous in their Betters; besides that it seems an
Entertainment very particularly adapted to the *Bath*, as it
is usual for a Rider to Whistle to his Horse when he would
make his Waters pass.

                                              I am, Sir, &c.

Postcript.

After having dispatched these two important Points of Grinning and Whistling, I hope you will oblige the World with some Reflections upon Yawning, as I have seen it practised on a Twelfth-Night, among other *Christmas* Gambols, at the House of a very worthy Gentleman, who always entertains his Tenants at that time of the Year. They Yawn for a *Cheshire* Cheese, and begin about Mid-night, when the whole Company is disposed to be drowsie. He that Yawns widest, and at the same time so naturally as to produce the most Yawns among his Spectators, carries home the Cheese. If you handle this Subject as you ought, I question not but your Paper will set half the Kingdom a Yawning, tho' I dare promise you it will never make any Body fall asleep.'   L

No. 180.

[STEELE.]   Wednesday, September 26.

. . . *Delirant reges, plectuntur Achivi.*—Hor.

THE following Letter has so much Weight and good Sense, that I cannot forbear inserting it, tho' it relates to an hardened Sinner, whom I have very little Hopes of reforming, *viz.* Lewis XIV. of *France.*

'*Mr.* SPECTATOR,

Amidst the Variety of Subjects of which you have treated, I could wish it had fallen in your Way to expose the Vanity of Conquests. This Thought would naturally lead one to the *French* King, who has been generally esteemed the greatest Conquerour of our Age, till her Majesty's Armies had torn from him so many of his Countries, and deprived him of the Fruit of all his former Victories. For my own Part, if I were to draw his Picture, I should be for taking him no lower than to the Peace of *Reswick,* just at the End of his Triumphs, and before his Reverse of Fortune; and even then I should not forbear thinking his Ambition had been vain and unprofitable to himself and his People.

As for himself, it is certain he can have gained nothing by his Conquests, if they have not rendered him Master of more Subjects, more Riches, or greater Power. What I shall be able to offer upon these Heads, I resolve to submit to your Consideration.

To begin then with his Increase of Subjects. From the

Time he came of Age, and has been a Manager for himself, all the People he had acquired were such only as he had reduced by his Wars, and were left in his Possession by the Peace; he had conquered not above one Third Part of *Flanders*, and consequently no more than one Third Part of the Inhabitants of that Province.

About 100 Years ago the Houses in that Country were all numbered, and by a just Computation the Inhabitants of all sorts could not then exceed 750000 Souls. And if any Man will consider the Desolation by almost perpetual Wars, the numerous Armies that have lived almost ever since at Discretion upon the People, and how much of their Commerce has removed for more Security to other Places, he will have little Reason to imagine that their Numbers have since increased; and therefore with one Third Part of that Province that Prince can have gained no more than one Third Part of the Inhabitants, or 250000 new Subjects, even though it should be supposed they were all contented to live still in their native Country, and transfer their Allegiance to a new Master.

The Fertility of this Province, its convenient Situation for Trade and Commerce, its Capacity for furnishing Employment and Subsistence to great Numbers, and the vast Armies that have been maintained here, make it credible that the remaining two Thirds of *Flanders* are equal to all his other Conquests; and consequently by all he cannot have gained more than 750000 new Subjects, Men, Women, and Children, especially if a Deduction shall be made of such as have retired from the Conqueror to live under their old Masters.

It is Time now to set his Loss against his Profit, and to shew for the new Subjects he had acquired how many old ones he had lost in the Acquisition: I think that in his Wars he has seldom brought less into the Field in all Places than 200000 fighting Men, besides what have been left in Garrisons; and I think the common Computation is, that of an Army, at the latter End of a Campaign, without Sieges or Battle, scarce four Fifths can be mustered of those that came into the Field at the Beginning of the Year. His Wars at several Times till the last Peace have held about 20 Years; and if 40000 yearly lost, or a fifth Part of his Armies, are to be multiply'd by 20, he cannot have lost less than 800000 of his old Subjects, all able-body'd Men, a greater Number than the new Subjects he had acquired.

But this Loss is not all: Providence seems to have equally divided the whole Mass of Mankind into different Sexes, that every Woman may have her Husband, and that both may equally contribute to the Continuance of the Species. It follows then that for all the Men that have been lost as many

Women must have lived single, and it were but Charity to believe they have not done all the Service they were capable of doing in their Generation. In so long a Course of Years great Part of them must have dyed, and all the rest must go off at last without leaving any Representatives behind. By this Account he must have lost not only 800000 Subjects, but double that Number, and all the Increase that was reasonably to be expected from it.

It is said in the last War there was a Famine in his Kingdom which swept away two Millions of his People. This is hardly credible; if the Loss was only of one Fifth Part of that Sum it was very great. But 'tis no Wonder there should be Famine where so much of the People's Substance is taken away for the King's use that they have not sufficient left to provide against Accidents, where so many of the Men are taken from the Plough to serve the King in his Wars, and a great Part of the Tillage is left to the weaker Hands of so many Women and Children. Whatever was the Loss, it must undoubtedly be placed to the Account of his Ambition.

And so must also the Destruction or Banishment of 3 or 400000 of his reformed Subjects; he could have no other Reasons for valuing those Lives so very cheap, but only to recommend himself to the Bigotry of the *Spanish* Nation.

How should there be Industry in a Country where all Property is precarious? What Subject will sow his Land that his Prince may reap the whole Harvest? Parsimony and Frugality must be Strangers to such a People; for will any Man save to Day what he has Reason to fear will be taken from him To-morrow? And where is the Encouragement for marrying? Will any Man think of raising Children without any Assurance of Cloathing for their Backs, or so much as Food for their Bellies? And thus by his fatal Ambition he must have lessened the Number of his Subjects, not only by Slaughter and Destruction, but by preventing their very Births, he has done as much as was possible towards destroying Posterity it self.

Is this then the great, the invincible *Lewis*? This the immortal Man, the *tout puissant*, or the Almighty, as his Flatterers have called him? Is this the Man that is so celebrated for his Conquests? For every Subject he has acquired, has he not lost three that were his Inheritance? Are not his Troops fewer, and those neither so well fed, or cloathed, or paid, as they were formerly, tho' he has now so much greater Cause to exert himself? And what can be the Reason of all this, but that his Revenue is a great deal less, his Subjects are either poorer, or not so many to be plundered by constant Taxes for his Use?

It is well for him he had found out a Way to steal a King-
dom; if he had gone on conquering as he did before, his
Ruin had been long since finished.   This brings to my Mind a
Saying of King *Pyrrhus*, after he had a second Time beat the
Romans in a pitched Battel, and was complimented by his
Generals, *Yes*, says he, *such another Victory and I am quite undone*.   And since I have mentioned *Pyrrhus*, I will end with a
very good though known Story of this ambitious Mad-man:
When he had shewn the utmost Fondness for his Expedition
against the *Romans*, *Cyneas* his chief Minister asked him what
he proposed to himself by this War?   Why, says *Pyrrhus*, to
conquer the *Romans*, and reduce all *Italy* to my Obedience.
What then? says *Cyneas*.   To pass over into *Sicily*, says
Pyrrhus, and then all the *Sicilians* must be our Subjects.   And
what does your Majesty intend next?   Why truly, says the
King, to conquer *Carthage*, and make my self Master of all
Africa.   And what, Sir, says the Minister, is to be the End of
all your Expeditions?   Why then, says the King, for the rest
of our Lives we 'll sit down to good Wine.   How, Sir, replyed
Cyneas, to better than we have now before us?   Have we not
already as much as we can drink?

Riot and Excess are not the becoming Characters of Princes;
but if *Pyrrhus* and *Lewis* had debauched like *Vitellius* they had
been less hurtful to their People.

Your humble Servant,

T   PHILARITHMUS.'

No. 181.
[ADDISON.]   Thursday, September 27.

His lacrimis vitam damus, & miserescimus ultro.—Virg.

I AM more pleased with a Letter that is filled with Touches of
Nature than of Wit.   The following one is of this kind.

'*Sir*,

Among all the Distresses which happen in Families, I do not
remember that you have touched upon the Marriage of Children
without the Consent of their Parents.   I am one of these unfortunate Persons.   I was about Fifteen when I took the
Liberty to chuse for my self, and have ever since languished
under the Displeasure of an inexorable Father, who, though he
sees me happy in the best of Husbands, and blessed with very
fine children, can never be prevailed upon to forgive me.   He
was so kind to me before this unhappy Accident, that indeed it
makes my Breach of Duty, in some measure, inexcusable; and

at the same time creates in me such a Tenderness towards him, that I love him above all things, and would die to be reconciled to him. I have thrown my self at his Feet, and besought him with Tears to pardon me, but he always pushes me away, and spurns me from him; I have written several Letters to him, but he will neither open nor receive them. About two Years ago I sent my little Boy to him, dressed in a new Apparel, but the Child returned to me crying, because he said his Grand-father would not see him, and had ordered him to be put out of his House. My Mother is won over to my side, but dares not mention me to my Father for fear of provoking him. About a Month ago he lay sick upon his Bed, and in great Danger of his Life; I was pierced to the Heart at the News, and could not forbear going to enquire after his Health. My Mother took this Opportunity of speaking in my behalf: She told him with abundance of Tears that I was come to see him, that I could not speak to her for weeping, and that I should certainly break my Heart if he refused at that time to give me his Blessing, and be reconciled to me. He was so far from relenting towards me, that he bid her speak no more of me, unless she had a Mind to disturb him in his last Moments: for, Sir, you must know that he has the Reputation of an honest and religious Man, which makes my Misfortune so much the greater. God be thanked he is since recovered, but his severe Usage has given me such a Blow that I shall soon sink under it, unless I may be relieved by any Impressions which the reading of this in your Paper may make upon him.

> *I am, &c.'*

Of all Hardnesses of Heart, there is none so inexcusable as that of Parents towards their Children. An obstinate, inflexible, unforgiving Temper, is odious upon all Occasions, but here it is unnatural. The Love, Tenderness and Compassion, which are apt to arise in us towards those who depend upon us, is that by which the whole World of Life is upheld. The Supreme Being, by the transcendent Excellency and Goodness of his Nature, extends his Mercy towards all his Works; and because his Creatures have not such a spontaneous Benevolence and Compassion towards those who are under their Care and Protection, he has implanted in them an Instinct, that supplies the Place of this inherent Goodness. I have illustrated this kind of Instinct in former Papers, and have shewn how it runs thro' all the Species of Brute Creatures, as indeed the whole Animal Creation subsists by it.

This Instinct in Man is more general and uncircumscribed than in Brutes, as being enlarged by the Dictates of Reason and Duty. For if we consider our selves attentively, we shall find that we are not only enclined to Love those who descend from us, but that we bear a kind of στοργή or natural Affection to every thing which relies upon us for its Good and Preservation. Dependance is a perpetual Call upon Humanity, and a greater Incitement to Tenderness and Pity than any other Motive whatsoever.

The Man therefore who, notwithstanding any Passion or Resentment, can overcome this powerful Instinct, and extinguish natural Affection, debases his Mind even below Brutality, frustrates, as much as in him lies, the great Design of Providence, and strikes out of his Nature one of the most Divine Principles that is planted in it.

Among innumerable Arguments which might be brought against such an unreasonable Proceeding, I shall only insist on one. We make it the Condition of our Forgiveness that we forgive others. In our very Prayers we desire no more than to be treated by this kind of Retaliation. The Case therefore before us seems to be what they call a *Case in point*; the relation between the Child and Father, being what comes nearest to that between a Creature and its Creator. If the Father is inexorable to the Child who has offended, let the Offence be of never so high a Nature, how will he address him self to the Supreme Being, under the tender Appellation of a Father, and desire of him such a Forgiveness as he him self refuses to grant?

To this I might add many other Religious, as well as many Prudential Considerations; but if the last mentioned Motive does not prevail, I despair of succeeding by any other, and shall therefore conclude my Paper with a very remarkable Story, which is recorded in an old Chronicle published by *Freher* among the Writers of the *German* History.

Eginhart, who was Secretary to *Charles* the Great, became exceeding Popular by his Behaviour in that Post. His great Abilities gained him the Favour of his Master, and the Esteem of the whole Court. *Imma*, the Daughter of the Emperor, was so pleased with his Person and Conversation, that she fell in Love with him. As she was one of the greatest Beauties of the Age, *Eginhart* answered her with a more than equal Return of Passion. They stifled their Flames for some time, under Apprehension of the fatal Consequences that might ensue. *Eginhart* at length resolving to hazard all, rather than live deprived of one whom his Heart was so much set upon, conveyed himself one Night into the Princess's Apartment, and knocking gently at the Door, was admitted as a Person who had something to communicate to her from the Emperor. He was with her in private most part of the Night; but upon his preparing to go away about

Break of Day, he observed that there had fallen a great Snow during his Stay with the Princess: This very much perplexed him, lest the Prints of his Feet in the Snow might make Discoveries to the King, who often used to visit his Daughter in the Morning. He acquainted the Princess *Imma* with his Fears, who after some Consultations upon the Matter, prevailed upon him to let her carry him through the Snow upon her own Shoulders. It happened, that the Emperor not being able to sleep, was at that time up and walking in his Chamber, when upon looking through the Window he perceived his Daughter tottering under her Burden, and carrying his first Minister across the Snow; which she had no sooner done, but she returned again with the utmost speed to her own Apartment. The Emperor was extremely troubled and astonished at this Accident; but resolved to speak nothing of it 'till a proper Opportunity. In the mean time *Eginhart* knowing that what he had done could not be long a Secret; determined to retire from Court, and in order to it begged the Emperor that he would be pleased to dismiss him, pretending a kind of Discontent at his not having been rewarded for his long Services. The Emperor would not give a direct Answer to his Petition, but told him he would think of it, and appointed a certain Day when he would let him know his Pleasure. He then called together the most faithful of his Counsellors, and acquainting them with his Secretary's Crime, asked them their Advice in so delicate an Affair. They most of them gave their Opinion, that the Person could not be too severely punished, who had thus dishonoured his Master. Upon the whole Debate, the Emperor declared it was his Opinion, that *Eginhart*'s Punishment would rather encrease than diminish the Shame of his Family; and that therefore he thought it the most adviseable to wear out the Memory of the Fact, by Marrying him to his Daughter. Accordingly *Eginhart* was called in, and acquainted by the Emperor, that he should no longer have any Pretence of complaining his Services were not rewarded, for that the Princess *Imma* should be given him in Marriage, with a Dower suitable to her Quality; which was soon after performed accordingly.   L

No. 182.

[STEELE.]   Friday, September 28.

Plus aloes quam mellis habet . . .—Juv.

As all Parts of humane Life come under my Observation, my Reader must not make uncharitable Inferences from my

speaking knowingly of that sort of Crime which is at present
treated of.   He will, I hope, suppose I know it only from the
Letters of Correspondents, two of which you shall have as
follow.

· *Mr.* SPECTATOR,

It is wonderful to me, that among the many Enormities
which you have treated of you have not mentioned that of
Wenching, and particularly the insnaring Part; I mean, that it
is a thing very fit for your Pen to expose the Villany of the
Practice of deluding Women.   You are to know, Sir, that I my
self am a Woman who have been one of the Unhappy that have
fallen into this Misfortune, and that by the Insinuation of a very
worthless Fellow who served others in the same Manner both
before my Ruin and since that Time.   I had, as soon as the
Rascal left me, so much Indignation and Resolution, as not
to go upon the Town, as the Phrase is, but took to work for my
Living in an obscure Place, out of the Knowledge of all with
whom I was before acquainted.

It is the ordinary Practice and Business of Life with a Sett
of idle Fellows about this Town, to write Letters, send Messages, and form Appointments with little raw unthinking Girls,
and leave them after Possession of them without any Mercy to
Shame, Infamy, Poverty, and Disease.   Were you to read the
nauseous Impertinencies which are written on these Occasions,
and to see the silly Creatures sighing over them, it could not but
be Matter of Mirth as well as Pity.   A little Prentice Girl of
mine has been for some time applied to by an *Irish* Fellow, who
dresses very fine, and struts in a lac'd Coat, and is the Admiration of Semstresses who are under Age in Town.   Ever since
I have had some Knowledge of the Matter, I have debarred my
Prentice from Pen, Ink, and Paper.   But the other Day he bespoke some Cravats of me: I went out of the Shop, and left his
Mistress to put them up into a Band-Box in order to be sent
to him when his Man called.   When I came into the Shop
again I took Occasion to send her away, and found in the
Bottom of the Box written these Words, *Why would you ruin a
harmless Creature that loves you ?* then in the Lid, *There is no re-
sisting* Strephon: I searched a little further, and found in the
Rim of the Box, *At Eleven of Clock at Night come in an Hackney-
Coach at the End of our Street.*   This was enough to alarm me;
I sent away the things, and took my Measures accordingly.   An
Hour or two before the appointed Time I examined my young
Lady, and found her Trunk stuffed with impertinent Letters,
and an old Scrole of Parchment in Latin, which her Lover had
sent her as a Settlement of fifty Pounds a Year; among other

things there was also the best Lace I had in my Shop to make
him a Present for Cravats. I was very glad of this last Circumstance, because I could very conscienciously swear against him
that he had enticed my Servant away, and was her Accomplice
in robbing me. I procured a Warrant against him accordingly.
Every thing was now prepared, and the tender Hour of Love
approaching, I who had acted for my self in my Youth the same
senseless Part, knew how to manage accordingly. Therefore
after having locked up my Maid, and not being so much unlike
her in Height and Shape, as in a huddled way not to pass for
her, I delivered the Bundle designed to be carried off to her
Lover's Man, who came with the Signal to receive them. Thus
I followed after to the Coach, where when I saw his Master
take them in, I cryed out Thieves! Thieves! and the Constable
with his Attendants seized my expecting Lover. I kept my
self unobserved 'till I saw the Crowd sufficiently encreased, and
then appeared to declare the Goods to be mine; and had the
Satisfaction to see my Man of Mode put into the Round-house
with the stolen Wares by him, to be produced in Evidence
against the next Morning. This Matter is notoriously known
to be Fact, and I have been contented to save my Prentice, and
take a Year's Rent of this mortified Lover not to appear further
in the Matter. This was some Penance; but, Sir, is this enough
for a Villany of much more pernicious Consequence than the
Trifles of which he was to have been indicted? Should not you,
and all Men of any Parts or Honour, put things upon so right a
Foot, as that such a Rascal should not laugh at the Imputation
of what he was really guilty, and dread being accused of that
for which he was arrested?

In a Word, Sir, it is in the Power of you, and such as I hope
you are, to make it as infamous to rob a poor Creature of her
Honour as her Cloaths. I leave this to your Consideration,
only take Leave (which I cannot do without sighing) to remark
to you, that if this had been the Sense of Mankind thirty Years
ago, I should have avoided a Life spent in Poverty and Shame.

> *I am, Sir,*
>> *Your most humble Servant,*
>>> Alice Threadneedle.'

'*Mr.* SPECTATOR, *Round-house, Sept.* 9.

I am a Man of Pleasure about Town, but by the Stupidity
of a dull Rogue of a Justice of Peace and an insolent Constable,
upon the Oath of an old Harridan, am imprisoned here for
Theft when I designed only Fornication. The Midnight Magistrate as he conveyed me along had you in his Mouth, and said

this would make a pure Story for the SPECTATOR.   I hope, Sir,
you won't pretend to Wit, and take the Part of dull Rogues of
Business.   The World is so altered of late Years, that there was
not a Man who would knock down a Watchman in my Behalf,
but I was carried off with as much Triumph as if I had been a
Pick-pocket.   At this Rate there is an End of all the Wit and
Humour in the World.   The Time was when all the honest
Whoremasters in the Neighbourhood, would have rose against
the Cuckolds to my Rescue.   If Fornication is to be scandalous,
half the fine Things that have been writ by most of the Wits of
the last Age may be burnt by the common Hangman.   Harkee,
SPEC. do not be queer; after having done some things pretty
well, don't begin to write at that Rate that no Gentleman can
read thee.   Be true to Love, and burn your *Seneca.*   You do
not expect me to write my Name from hence, but I am

Your unknown humble, &c.'

No. 183.
[ADDISON.]   Saturday, September 29.

"Ἴδμεν ψεύδεα πολλὰ λέγειν ἐτύμοισιν ὁμοῖα,
"Ἴδμεν δ', εὖτ' ἐθέλωμεν, ἀληθέα μυθήσασθαι.

FABLES were the first Pieces of Wit that made their Appearance
in the World, and have been still highly valued, not only in
times of the greatest Simplicity, but among the most polite
Ages of Mankind.   *Jothram's* Fable of the Trees is the oldest
that is extant, and as beautiful as any which have been made
since that time.   *Nathan's* Fable of the poor Man and his Lamb
is likewise more Ancient than any that is extant, besides the
above-mentioned, and had so good an effect as to convey Instruction to the Ear of a King without offending it, and to bring
the Man after God's own Heart to a right Sense of his Guilt and
his Duty.   We find *Aesop* in the most distant Ages of *Greece;*
and if we look into the very Beginnings of the Commonwealth
of *Rome,* we see a Mutiny among the Common People appeased
by a Fable of the Belly and the Limbs, which was indeed very
proper to gain the Attention of an incensed Rabble, at a time
when perhaps they would have torn to Pieces any Man who had
preached the same Doctrine to them in an open and direct
manner.   As Fables took their Birth in the very Infancy of
Learning, they never flourished more than when Learning was
at its greatest Height.   To justifie this Assertion, I shall put my
Reader in mind of *Horace,* the greatest Wit and Critick in the
Augustan Age; and of *Boileau,* the most correct Poet among the

Moderns: Not to mention *la Fontaine*, who by this way of Writing is come more into Vogue than any other Author of our times.

The Fables I have here mentioned are raised altogether upon Brutes and Vegetables, with some of our own Species mixt among them, when the Moral hath so required. But besides this kind of Fable there is another in which the Actors are Passions, Virtues, Vices, and other imaginary Persons of the like Nature. Some of the Ancient Criticks will have it that the Iliad and Odissey of *Homer* are Fables of this nature; and that the several Names of Gods and Heroes are nothing else but the Affections of the Mind in a visible Shape and Character. Thus they tell us, that *Achilles*, in the first Iliad, represents Anger, or the Irascible part of Human Nature. That upon drawing his Sword against his Superior in a full Assembly, *Pallas* is only another Name for Reason, which checks and advises him upon that occasion; and at her first Appearance touches him upon the Head, that part of the Man being looked upon as the Seat of Reason. And thus of the rest of the Poem. As for the Odissey, I think it is plain that *Horace* considered it as one of these Allegorical Fables, by the Moral which he has given us of several Parts of it. The greatest *Italian* Wits have applied themselves to the Writing of this latter kind of Fables; As *Spencer's Fairy-Queen* is one continued Series of them from the Beginning to the end of that admirable Work. If we look into the finest Prose-Authors of Antiquity, such as *Cicero, Plato, Xenophon*, and many others, we shall find that this was likewise their favourite kind of Fable. I shall only further observe upon it, that the first of this sort that made any considerable Figure in the World was that of *Hercules* meeting with Pleasure and Virtue, which was invented by *Prodicus*, who lived before *Socrates*, and in the first Dawnings of Philosophy. He used to Travel through *Greece* by vertue of this Fable, which procured him a kind Reception in all the Market Towns, where he never failed telling it as soon as he had gathered an Audience about him.

After this short Preface, which I have made up of such Materials as my Memory does at present suggest to me, before I present my Reader with a Fable of this kind, which I design as the Entertainment of the present Paper, I must in a few Words open the occasion of it.

In the Account which *Plato* gives us of the Conversation and Behaviour of *Socrates* the Morning he was to Die, he tells the following Circumstance.

When *Socrates* his Fetters were knocked off (as was usual to be done on the Day that the Condemn'd Person was to be executed) being seated in the midst of his Disciples, and laying one of his Legs over the other, in a very unconcerned Posture, he began to rub it where it had been galled by the Iron; and whether it was to shew the Indifference with which he entertained the Thoughts of his approaching Death, or after his usual manner, to take every occasion of Philosophizing upon some useful Subject, he observed the Pleasure of that Sensation which now arose in those very Parts of his Leg, that just before had been so much pained by the Fetter. Upon this he reflected on the Nature of Pleasure and Pain in general, and how constantly they succeed one another. To this he added, that if a Man of a good Genius for a Fable were to represent the Nature of Pleasure and Pain in that way of Writing, he would probably join them together after such a manner, that it would be impossible for the one to come into any Place, without being followed by the other.

It is possible, that if *Plato* had thought it proper at such a time to describe *Socrates* launching out into a Discourse which was not of a Piece with the Business of the Day, he would have enlarged upon this Hint, and have drawn it out into some beautiful Allegory or Fable. But since he has not done it, I shall attempt to write one my self in the Spirit of that Divine Author.

There were two Families which from the beginning of the World were as opposite to each other as Light and Darkness. The one of them lived in Heaven and the other in Hell. The youngest Descendant of the first Family was Pleasure, who was the Daughter of Happiness, who was the Child of Virtue, who was the Offspring of the Gods. These, as I said before, had their Habitation in Heaven. The youngest of the opposite Family was Pain, who was the Son of Misery, who was the Child of Vice, who was the Offspring of the Furies. The Habitation of this Race of Beings was in Hell.

The middle Station of Nature between these two opposite Extreams was the Earth, which was inhabited by Creatures of a middle Kind, neither so Virtuous as the one, nor so Vicious as the other, but partaking of the good and bad Qualities of these two opposite Families. Jupiter *considering that this Species, commonly called Man, was too virtuous to be miserable, and too vicious to be happy; that he might make a Distinction between the Good and the Bad, ordered the two youngest of the above-mentioned Families, Pleasure who was the Daughter of Happiness, and Pain who was the Son of Misery, to meet one another upon this part of Nature which lay in the half way between them, having promised to settle it upon them both, provided they could agree upon the Division of it, so as to share Mankind between them.*

Pleasure and Pain were no sooner met in their new Habitation, but they immediately agreed upon this point, that Pleasure should take Possession of the Virtuous, and Pain of the Vicious part of that Species which was given up to them. But upon examining to which of them any Individual they met with belonged, they found each of them had a Right to him; for that, contrary to what they had seen in their old places of Residence, there was no Person so Vicious who had not some Good in him, nor any Person so Virtuous who had not in him some Evil. The Truth of it is, they generally found upon Search that in the most vicious Man Pleasure might lay a claim to an hundredth part, and that in the most virtuous Man Pain might come in for at least two thirds. This they saw would occasion endless Disputes between them, unless they could come to some Accommodation. To this End there was a Marriage proposed between them, and at length concluded: By this means it is that we find Pleasure and Pain are such constant Yoke-fellows, and that they either make their Visits together, or are never far asunder. If Pain comes into an Heart he is quickly followed by Pleasure; and if Pleasure enters, you may be sure Pain is not far off.

But notwithstanding this Marriage was very convenient for the two Parties, it did not seem to answer the Intention of Jupiter *in sending them among Mankind. To remedy therefore this Inconvenience, it was stipulated between them by Article, and confirmed by the consent of each Family, that notwithstanding they here possessed the Species indifferently; upon the Death of every single Person, if he was found to have in him a certain Proportion of Evil, he should be dispatched into the infernal Regions by a Passport from Pain, there to dwell with Misery, Vice, and the Furies. Or on the contrary, if he had in him a certain Proportion of Good, he should be dispatched into Heaven by a Passport from Pleasure, there to dwell with Happiness, Virtue and the Gods.*

L

No. 184.
[ADDISON.] Monday, October 1.

. . . *Opere in longo fas est obrepere somnum.*—Hor.

WHEN a Man has discovered a new Vein of Humour, it often carries him much further than he expected from it. My Correspondents take the Hint I give them, and pursue it into Speculations which I never thought of at my first starting it. This has been the Fate of my Paper on the Match of Grinning, which has already produced a second Paper on parallel Subjects, and brought me the following Letter by the last Post.

I shall not premise any thing to it further than that it is built
on Matter of Fact, and is as follows.

'*Sir,*

You have already obliged the World with a Discourse upon
Grinning, and have since proceeded to Whistling, from whence
you are at length come to Yawning; from this I think you may
make a very natural Transition to Sleeping.   I therefore recommend to you for the Subject of a Paper the following Advertisement, which about two Months ago was given into every Body's
Hands, and may be seen with some Additions in the *Daily
Courant* of *August* the Ninth.

Nicholas Hart, *who slept last Year in St.* Bartholomew's
Hospital, intends to sleep this Year at the Cock *and* Bottle *in*
Little Britain.

Having since enquired into the Matter of Fact, I find that
the above-mentioned *Nicholas Hart* is every Year seized with
a periodical Fit of Sleeping, which begins upon the Fifth of
August, and ends on the Eleventh of the same Month: That

On the First of that Month he grew dull;
On the Second appeared drowsy;
On the Third fell a yawning;
On the Fourth began to nod;
On the Fifth dropped asleep;
On the Sixth was heard to snore;
On the Seventh turned himself in his Bed;
On the Eighth recovered his former Posture;
On the Ninth fell a stretching;
On the Tenth about Midnight awaked;
On the Eleventh in the Morning called for a little Small-Beer.

This Account I have extracted out of the Journal of this
sleeping Worthy, as it has been faithfully kept by a Gentleman
of *Lincoln's-Inn* who has undertaken to be his Historiographer.
I have sent it to you, not only as it represents the Actions of
Nicholas Hart, but as it seems a very natural Picture of the
Life of many an honest *English* Gentleman, whose whole
History very often consists of Yawning, Nodding, Stretching,
Turning, Sleeping, Drinking, and the like extraordinary Par-
ticulars.   I do not question, Sir, that if you pleased you could
put out an Advertisement not unlike the above-mentioned of
several Men of Figure, that Mr. *John* such a one, Gentleman, or
Thomas such a one, Esquire, who slept in the Country last
Summer, intends to sleep in Town this Winter.   The worst of

it is, that the drowsie Part of our Species is chiefly made up of very honest Gentlemen, who live quietly among their Neighbours without ever disturbing the publick Peace: They are Drones without Stings. I could heartily wish that several turbulent, restless, ambitious Spirits would for a while change Places with these good Men, and enter themselves into *Nicholas Hart's* Fraternity. Could one but lay asleep a few busie Heads which I could name, from the first of *November* next to the first of *May* ensuing, I question not but it would very much redound to the Quiet of particular Persons as well as to the Benefit of the Publick.

But to return to *Nicholas Hart*: I believe, Sir, you will think it a very extraordinary Circumstance for a Man to gain his Livelihood by Sleeping, and that Rest should procure a Man Sustenance as well as Industry; yet so it is that *Nicholas* got last Year enough to support himself for a Twelvemonth. I am likewise informed that he has this Year had a very comfortable Nap. The Poets value themselves very much for sleeping on *Parnassus*, but I never heard they got a Groat by it: On the contrary, our Friend *Nicholas* gets more by sleeping than he could by working, and may be more properly said, than ever *Homer* was, to have had Golden Dreams. *Juvenal* indeed mentions a drowsie Husband who raised an Estate by Snoring, but then he is represented to have slept what the Common People call a Dog's Sleep; or if his Sleep was real, his Wife was awake and about her Business. Your Pen, which loves to moralize upon all Subjects, may raise something methinks on this Circumstance also, and point out to us those Sets of Men, who instead of growing rich by an honest Industry, recommend themselves to the Favours of the Great, by making themselves agreeable Companions in the Participations of Luxury and Pleasure.

I must further acquaint you, Sir, that one of the most eminent Pens in *Grub-street* is now employed in Writing the Dream of this miraculous Sleeper, which I hear will be of a more than ordinary Length, as it must contain all the Particulars that are supposed to have passed in his Imagination during so long a Sleep. He is said to have gone already through three Days and three Nights of it, and to have comprised in them the most remarkable Passages of the four first Empires of the World. If he can keep free from Party-Strokes his Work may be of use; but this I much doubt, having been informed by one of his Friends and Confidents that he has spoken some things of *Nimrod* with too great Freedom.

L   *I am ever, Sir, &c.'*

No. 185.

[ADDISON]   Tuesday, October 2.

> . . . *Tantaene animis coelestibus irae?*—Virg.

THERE is nothing in which Men more deceive themselves than in what the World calls Zeal. There are so many Passions which hide themselves under it, and so many Mischiefs arising from it, that some have gone so far as to say it would have been for the Benefit of Mankind if it had never been reckoned in the Catalogue of Virtues. It is certain where it is once Laudable and Prudential it is an hundred times Criminal and Erroneous, nor can it be otherwise if we consider that it operates with equal Violence in all Religions, however opposite they may be to one another, and in all the Subdivisions of each Religion in particular.

We are told by some of the *Jewish Rabbins*, that the first Murder was occasioned by a Religious Controversie; and if we had the whole History of Zeal from the Days of *Cain* to our own Times, we should see it filled with so many Scenes of Slaughter and Bloodshed, as would make a wise Man very careful how he suffers himself to be actuated by such a Principle, when it only regards Matters of Opinion and Speculation.

I would have every Zealous Man examine his Heart throughly, and, I believe, he will often find that what he calls a Zeal for his Religion is either Pride, Interest, or Ill-nature. A Man who differs from another in Opinion sets himself above him in his own Judgment, and in several Particulars pretends to be the wiser Person. This is a great Provocation to the Proud Man, and gives a very keen Edge to what he calls his Zeal. And that this is the Case very often, we may observe from the Behaviour of some of the most Zealous for Orthodoxy, who have often great Friendships and Intimacies with vitious Immoral Men, provided they do but agree with them in the same Scheme of Belief. The Reason is, Because the vitious Believer gives the Precedency to the virtuous Man, and allows the good Christian to be the worthier Person, at the same time that he cannot come up to his Perfections. This we find exemplified in that trite Passage which we see quoted in almost every System of Ethics, tho' upon another Occasion.

> . . . *Video meliora proboque,*
> *Deteriora sequor . . .*—Ov.

On the contrary, it is certain if our Zeal were true and genuine, we should be much more angry with a Sinner than a Heretick, since there are several Cases which may excuse the latter before his great Judge, but none which can excuse the former.

Interest is likewise a great Inflamer, and sets a Man on
Persecution under the Colour of Zeal. For this Reason we find
none are so forward to promote the true Worship by Fire and
Sword, as those who find their present account in it. But I
shall extend the Word Interest to a larger Meaning than what
is generally given it, as it relates to our Spiritual Safety and
Welfare, as well as to our Temporal. A Man is glad to gain
Numbers on his side, as they serve to strengthen him in his
private Opinions. Every Proselyte is like a new Argument for
the Establishment of his Faith. It makes him believe that his
Principles carry Conviction with them, and are the more likely
to be true, when he finds they are conformable to the Reason of
others, as well as to his own. And that this Temper of Mind
deludes a Man very often into an Opinion of his Zeal, may
appear from the common Behaviour of the Atheist, who maintains and spreads his Opinions with as much heat as those who
believe they do it only out of a Passion for God's Glory.

Ill-nature is another dreadful Imitator of Zeal. Many a
good Man may have a Natural Rancour and Malice in his Heart,
which has been in some measure quelled and subdued by
Religion; but if it finds any Pretence of breaking out, which
does not seem to him inconsistent with the Duties of a Christian,
it throws off all Restraint, and rages in its full Fury. Zeal is
therefore a great Ease to a malicious Man, by making him believe he does God Service, whilst he is gratifying the bent of a
perverse revengeful Temper. For this Reason we find that
most of the Massacres and Devastations which have been in the
World, have taken their Rise from a furious pretended Zeal.

I love to see a Man zealous in a good Matter, and especially
when his Zeal shews it self for advancing Morality, and promoting the Happiness of Mankind: But when I find the Instruments he works with are Racks and Gibbets, Gallies and
Dungeons; when he Imprisons Men's Persons, Confiscates their
Estates, Ruins their Families, and Burns the Body to save the
Soul, I cannot stick to pronounce of such a one, that (whatever
he may think of his Faith and Religion) his Faith is vain, and
his Religion unprofitable.

After having treated of these false Zealots in Religion, I
cannot forbear mentioning a monstrous Species of Men, who
one would not think had any Existence in Nature, were they
not to be met with in ordinary Conversation, I mean the
Zealots in Atheism. One would fancy that these Men, tho'
they fall short, in every other respect, of those who make a
Profession of Religion, would at least out-shine them in this
Particular, and be exempt from that single Fault which seems
to grow out of the Imprudent Fervours of Religion; but so it is,

that Infidelity is propagated with as much Fierceness and Contention, Wrath and Indignation, as if the Safety of Mankind depended upon it. There is something so ridiculous and perverse in this kind of Zealots, that one does not know how to set them out in their proper Colours. They are a sort of Gamesters who are eternally upon the Fret, though they play for nothing. They are perpetually teizing their Friends to come over to them, though at the same time they allow that neither of them shall get any thing by the Bargain. In short, the Zeal of spreading Atheism is, if possible, more absurd than Atheism it self.

Since I have mentioned this unaccountable Zeal which appears in Atheists and Infidels, I must further observe that they are likewise in a most particular manner possessed with the Spirit of Bigottry. They are wedded to Opinions full of Contradiction and Impossibility, and at the same time look upon the smallest Difficulty in an Article of Faith as a sufficient Reason for rejecting it. Notions that fall in with the common Reasons of Mankind, that are conformable to the Sense of all Ages, and all Nations, not to mention their tendency for promoting the happiness of Societies, or of particular Persons, are exploded as Errors and Prejudices; and Schemes erected in their stead that are altogether Monstrous and Irrational, and require the most extravagant Credulity to embrace them. I would fain ask one of these bigotted Infidels, supposing all the great Points of Atheism, as the casual or eternal Formation of the World, the Materiality of a thinking Substance, the Mortality of the Soul, the fortuitous Organization of the Body, the Motions and Gravitation of Matter, with the like Particulars, were laid together and formed in a kind of Creed, according to the Opinions of the most celebrated Atheists, I say, supposing such a Creed as this were formed and imposed upon any one People in the World, whether it would not require an infinitely greater measure of Faith than any Sett of Articles which they so violently oppose. Let me therefore advise this Generation of Wranglers, for their own and for the Publick good, to act at least so consistently with themselves, as not to burn with Zeal for Irreligion and with Bigottry for Nonsense.   C

No. 186.

[ADDISON.]   Wednesday, October 3.

Coelum ipsum petimus stultitia.—Hor.

UPON my Return to my Lodgings last Night, I found a Letter from my worthy Friend the Clergyman, whom I have given some Account of in my former Papers. He tells me in it that he was particularly pleased with the latter Part of my Yesterday's Speculation; and at the same Time enclosed the following Essay, which he desires me to publish as the Sequel of that Discourse. It consists partly of uncommon Reflections, and partly of such as have been already used, but now set in a stronger Light.

'A Believer may be excused by the most hardened Atheist for endeavouring to make him a Convert, because he does it with an Eye to both their Interests. The Atheist is inexcusable who tries to gain over a Believer, because he does not propose the doing himself or Believer any Good by such a Conversion.

The Prospect of a future State is the secret Comfort and Refreshment of my Soul; it is that which makes Nature look gay about me: it doubles all my Pleasures, and supports me under all my Afflictions. I can look at Disappointments and Misfortunes, Pain and Sickness, Death it self, and, what is worse than Death, the Loss of those who are dearest to me, with Indifference, so long as I keep in view the Pleasures of Eternity, and the State of Being in which there will be no Fears nor Apprehensions, Pains nor Sorrows, Sickness nor Separation. Why will any Man be so impertinently officious, as to tell me all this is only Fancy and Delusion? Is there any Merit in being the Messenger of ill News? If it is a Dream let me enjoy it, since it makes me both the happier and better Man.

I must confess I do not know how to trust a Man who believes neither Heaven nor Hell, or in other Words, a future State of Rewards and Punishments. Not only natural Self-love, but Reason directs us, to promote our own Interest above all things. It can never be for the Interest of a Believer to do me a Mischief, because he is sure upon the Ballance of Accompts, to find himself a Loser by it. On the contrary, if he considers his own Welfare in his Behaviour towards me, it will lead him to do me all the Good he can, and at the same Time restrain him from doing me an Injury. An Unbeliever does not act like a reasonable Creature, if he favours me contrary to his present Interest, or does not distress me when it turns to his present Advantage. Honour and Good-nature may indeed tie up his Hands; but as these would be very much strengthened by Reason and Principle, so without them they are only Instincts, or wavering unsettled Notions which rest on no Foundation.

Infidelity has been attacked with so good Success of late Years, that it is driven out of all its Outworks. The Atheist has not found his Post tenable, and is therefore retired into

Deism, and a Disbelief of revealed Religion only. But the Truth of it is, the greatest Number of this Sett of Men, are those who for want of a virtuous Education, or examining the Grounds of Religion, know so very little of the Matter in question that their Infidelity is but another Term for their Ignorance.

As Folly and Inconsiderateness are the Foundations of Infidelity, the great Pillars and Supports of it are either a Vanity of appearing wiser than the rest of Mankind, or an Ostentation of Courage in despising the Terrors of another World, which have so great an Influence on what they call weaker Minds; or an Aversion to a Belief that must cut them off from many of those Pleasures they propose to themselves, and fill them with Remorse for many of those they have already tasted.

The great received Articles of the Christian Religion, have been so clearly proved from the Authority of that Divine Revelation in which they are delivered, that it is impossible for those who have Ears to hear and Eyes to see, not to be convinced of them. But were it possible for any thing in the Christian Faith to be erroneous, I can find no ill Consequences in adhering to it. The great Points of the Incarnation and Sufferings of our Saviour, produce naturally such Habits of Virtue in the Mind of Man, that, I say, supposing it were possible for us to be mistaken in them, the Infidel himself must at least allow that no other System of Religion could so effectually contribute to the heightening of Morality. They give us great Ideas of the Dignity of humane Nature, and of the Love which the supreme Being bears to his Creatures, and consequently engage us in the highest Acts of Duty towards our Creator, our Neighbour, and our selves. How many noble Arguments has Saint *Paul* raised from the chief Articles of our Religion, for the advancing of Morality in its three great Branches? To give a single Example in each Kind: What can be a stronger Motive to a firm Trust and Reliance on the Mercies of our Maker, than the giving us his Son to suffer for us? What can make us love and esteem even the most inconsiderable of Mankind, more than the Thought that Christ died for him? Or what dispose us to set a stricter Guard upon the Purity of our own Hearts, than our being Members of Christ, and a Part of the Society of which that immaculate Person is the Head? But these are only a Specimen of those admirable Enforcements of Morality which the Apostle has drawn from the History of our blessed Saviour.

If our Modern Infidels considered these Matters with that Candour and Seriousness which they deserve, we should not see them act with such a Spirit of Bitterness, Arrogance, and

Malice; They would not be raising such insignificant Cavils, Doubts, and Scruples, as may be started against every thing that is not capable of mathematical Demonstration; in order to unsettle the Minds of the Ignorant, disturb the publick Peace, subvert Morality, and throw all things into Confusion and Disorder. If none of these Reflections can have any Influence on them, there is one that perhaps may; because it is adapted to their Vanity, by which they seem to be guided much more than their Reason. I would therefore have them consider that the wisest and best of Men in all Ages of the World, have been those who lived up to the Religion of their Country, when they saw nothing in it opposite to Morality, and to the best Lights they had of the divine Nature. *Pythagoras's* first Rule directs us to worship the Gods *as it is ordained by Law,* for that is the most natural Interpretation of the Precept. *Socrates,* who was the most renowned among the Heathens both for Wisdom and Virtue, in his last Moments desires his Friends to offer a Cock to *Aesculapius;* doubtless out of a submissive Deference to the established Worship of his Country. *Xenophon* tells us, that his Prince (whom he sets forth as a Pattern of Perfection) when he found his Death approaching, offered Sacrifices on the Mountains to the *Persian Jupiter* and the Sun, *according to the Custom of the Persians;* for those are the Words of the Historian. Nay, the *Epicureans* and Atomical Philosophers shewed a very remarkable Modesty in this Particular; for though the Being of a God was entirely repugnant to their Schemes of natural Philosophy, they contented themselves with the Denial of a Providence, asserting at the same Time the Existence of Gods in general; because they would not shock the common Belief of Mankind, and the Religion of their Country.' L

No. 187.
[STEELE.]   Thursday, October 4.

. . . *Miseri quibus*
Intentata nites . . .—Hor.

THE Intelligence given by this Correspondent is so important and useful, in order to avoid the Persons he speaks of, that I shall insert his Letter at length.

'Mr. SPECTATOR,

I do not know that you have ever touched upon a certain Species of Women, whom we ordinarily call Jilts. You cannot possibly go upon a more useful Work, than the Consideration

of these dangerous Animals. The Coquet is indeed one degree
towards the Jilt; but the Heart of the former is bent upon
admiring her self, and giving false Hopes to her Lovers; but the
latter is not contented to be extreamly Amiable, but she must
add to that Advantage a certain Delight in being a Torment to
others. Thus when her Lover is in the full Expectation of
Success, the Jilt shall meet him with a sudden Indifference, an
Admiration in her Face at his being surprized that he is received like a Stranger, and a Cast of her Head another way
with a pleasant Scorn of the Fellow's Insolence. It is very
probable the Lover goes Home utterly astonished and dejected, sits down to his Scrutore, sends her Word, in the most
abject Terms, That he knows not what he has done, that all
which was desirable in this Life is so suddenly vanished from
him, that the Charmer of his Soul should withdraw the vital
Heat from the Heart which pants for her. He continues a
Mournful Absence for some time pining in Secret, and out of
Humour with all things which he meets with. At length he
takes a Resolution to try his Fate, and explain with her resolutely upon her unaccountable Carriage. He walks up to her
Apartment with a thousand Inquietudes and Doubts in what
manner he shall meet the first Cast of her Eye; when upon his
first Appearance she flies towards him, wonders where he has
been, accuses him of his Absence, and treats him with a
Familiarity as surprizing as her former Coldness. This good
Correspondence continues 'till the Lady observes the Lover
grows happy in it, and then she interrupts it with some new
Inconsistency of Behaviour. For (as I just now said) the
Happiness of a Jilt consists only in the Power of making others
uneasie. But such is the Folly of this Sect of Women, that
they carry on this pretty skittish Behaviour, 'till they have no
Charms left to render it supportable. *Corinna*, that used to
torment all who conversed with her with false Glances, and little
heedless unguarded Motions, that were to betray some Inclination towards the Man she would insnare, finds at present all
she attempts that way unregarded; and is obliged to indulge
the Jilt in her Constitution, by laying Artificial Plots, writing
perplexing Letters from unknown Hands, and making all the
young Fellows in Love with her, 'till they find out who she is.
Thus, as before she gave Torment by disguising her Inclination,
she now is obliged to do it by hiding her Person.

As for my own part, *Mr.* SPECTATOR, it has been my Unhappy
Fate to be Jilted from my Youth upward, and as my Taste has
been very much towards Intreague, and having Intelligence
with Women of Wit, my whole Life has passed away in a Series
of Impositions. I shall, for the Benefit of the present Race of

young Men, give some account of my Loves. I know not whether you have ever heard of the famous Girl about Town called *Kitty*; this Creature (for I must take Shame upon my self) was my Mistress in the Days when Keeping was in Fashion. *Kitty*, under the Appearance of being Wild, Thoughtless and Irregular in all her Words and Actions, concealed the most accomplished Jilt of her Time. Her Negligence had to me a Charm in it like that of Chastity, and want of Desires seemed as great a Merit as the Conquest of them. The Air she gave her self was that of a Romping Girl, and whenever I talked to her with any Turn of Fondness, she would immediately snatch off my Perriwig, try it upon her self in the Glass, clap her Arms a Kimbow, draw my Sword, and make Passes on the Wall, take off my Cravat, and seize it to make some other use of the Lace, or run into some other unaccountable Rompishness, 'till the time I had appointed to pass away with her was over: I went from her full of Pleasure at the Reflection that I had the keeping of so much Beauty in a Woman, who as she was too heedless to please me, was also too unattentive to form a Design to wrong me. Long did I divert every Hour that hung heavy upon me in the Company of this Creature, whom I looked upon as neither Guilty or Innocent, but could laugh at my self for my unaccountable Pleasure in an Expence upon her, 'till in the end it appeared my pretty Insensible was with Child by my Footman.

This Accident roused me into a Disdain against all Libertine Women, under what Appearance soever they hid their Insincerity, and I resolved after that Time to converse with none but those who lived within the Rules of Decency and Honour. To this End, I formed my self into a more regular Turn of Behaviour, and began to make Visits, frequent Assemblies, and lead out Ladies from the Theatres, with all the other insignificant Duties which the professed Servants of the Fair place themselves in constant readiness to perform. In a very little time, (having a plentiful Fortune) Fathers and Mothers began to regard me as a good Match, and I found easie Admittance into the best Families in Town to observe their Daughters; but I, who was born to follow the Fair to no purpose, have by the force of my ill Stars made my Application to three Jilts successively.

Hyaena is one of those who form themselves into a melancholy and indolent Air, and endeavour to gain Admirers from their Inattention to all around them. *Hyaena* can loll in her Coach, with something so fixed in her Countenance, that it is impossible to conceive her Meditation is employed only on her Dress and her Charms in that posture. If it were not too coarse a Simile, I should say *Hyaena,* in the Figure she affects to appear in, is a Spider in the midst of a Cobweb, that is sure to destroy every Fly that approaches it.   The Net *Hyaena* throws is so fine, that you are taken in it before you can observe any Part of her Work.   I attempted her for a long and weary Season; but I found her Passion went no further than to be admired, and she is of that unreasonable Temper as not to value the Inconstancy of her Lovers, provided she can boast she once had their Addresses.

Biblis was the second I aimed at, and her Vanity lay in purchasing the Adorers of others, and not in rejoicing in their Love it self.   *Biblis* is no Man's Mistress, but every Woman's Rival. As soon as I found this, I fell in Love with *Chloe,* who is my present Pleasure and Torment.   I have writ to her, danced with her, and fought for her, and have been her Man in the sight and expectation of the whole Town this three Years, and thought my self near the end of my Wishes, when the other Day she called me into her Closet, and told me, with a very grave Face, that she was a Woman of Honour, and scorned to deceive a Man who loved her with so much Sincerity as she saw I did, and therefore she must inform me that she was by Nature the most inconstant Creature breathing, and begg'd of me not to marry her: If I insisted upon it, I should; but that she was lately fallen in Love with another.   What to do or say I know not, but desire you to inform me, and you will infinitely oblige,

Sir,

Your most humble Servant,

Charles Yellow.'

ADVERTISEMENT.

Mr. Sly, Haberdasher of Hats at the Corner of Devereux Court in the Strand, gives Notice, that he has prepared very neat Hats, Rubbers and Brushes, for the Use of young Tradesmen in their last Year of Apprenticeship, at reasonable Rates.   T

No. 188.

[STEELE.]   Friday, October 5.

Laetus sum laudari a te laudato viro.—Tull.

HE is a very unhappy Man who sets his Heart upon being admired by the Multitude, or affects a general and undistinguishing Applause among Men.   What pious Men call the Testimony of a good Conscience, should be the Measure of our

Ambition in this Kind; that is to say, a Man of Spirit should contemn the Praise of the Ignorant, and like being applauded for nothing but what he knows in his own Heart he deserves. Besides which, the Character of the Person who commends you is to be considered, before you set a Value upon his Esteem. The Praise of an ignorant Man is only Good-will, and you should receive his Kindness as he is a good Neighbour in Society, and not as a good Judge of your Actions in Point of Fame and Reputation. The Satyrist said very well of popular Praise and Acclamations, *Give the Tinkers and Coblers their Presents again, and learn to live of your self.* It is an Argument of a loose and ungoverned Mind, to be affected with the promiscuous Approbation of the Generality of Mankind; and a Man of Virtue should be too delicate for so coarse an Appetite of Fame. Men of Honour should endeavour only to please the Worthy, and the Man of Merit should desire to be tried only by his Peers. I thought it a noble Sentiment which I heard Yesterday uttered in Conversation; *I know,* said a Gentleman, *a Way to be greater than any Man: If he has Worth in him I can rejoyce in his Superiority to me; and that Satisfaction is a greater Act of the Soul in me, than any in him which can possibly appear to me.* This Thought could not proceed but from a candid and generous Spirit, and the Approbation of such Minds is what may be esteemed true Praise. For with the common Rate of Men there is nothing commendable but what they themselves may hope to be Partakers of or arrive at; but the Motive truly glorious is, when the Mind is set rather to do things laudable than to purchase Reputation. Where there is that Sincerity as the Foundation of a good Name, the kind Opinion of virtuous Men will be an unsought but a necessary Consequence. The *Lacedemonians,* tho' a plain People, and no Pretenders to Politeness, had a certain Delicacy in their Sense of Glory, and sacrificed to the Muses when they entered upon any great Enterprize. They would have the Commemoration of their Actions be transmitted by the purest and most untainted Memorialists. The Din which attends Victories and publick Triumphs, is by far less eligible, than the Recital of the Actions of great Men by honest and wise Historians. It is a frivolous Pleasure to be the Admiration of gaping Crowds; but to have the Approbation of a good Man in the cool Reflections of his Closet, is a Gratification worthy an heroick Spirit. The Applause of the Crowd makes the Head giddy, but the Attestation of a reasonable Man makes the Heart glad.

What makes the Love of popular or general Praise still more ridiculous, is, that it is usually given for Circumstances which are foreign to the Persons admired. Thus they are the ordinary Attendants on Power and Riches, which may be taken out of one Man's Hands and put into another's. The Application only, and not the Possession, makes those outward things honourable. The Vulgar and Men of Sense agree in admiring Men for having what they themselves would rather be possessed of; the wise Man applauds him whom he thinks most virtuous; the rest of the World, him who is most wealthy.

When a Man is in this Way of Thinking, I do not know what can occur to one more monstrous than to see Persons of Ingenuity address their Services and Performances to Men no Way addicted to liberal Arts: In these Cases, the Praise on one Hand and the Patronage on the other, are equally the Objects of Ridicule. Dedications to ignorant Men, are as absurd as any of the Speeches of *Bulfinch* in the Drol: Such an Address one is apt to translate into other Words; and when the different Parties are thoroughly considered, the Panegyric generally implies no more than if the Author should say to the Patron, My very good Lord, You and I can never understand one another, therefore I humbly desire we may be intimate Friends for the future.

The Rich may as well ask to borrow of the Poor, as the Man of Virtue or Merit hope for Addition to his Character from any but such as himself. He that commends another, engages so much of his own Reputation as he gives to that Person commended; and he that has nothing laudable in himself, is not of Ability to be such a Surety. The wise *Phocion* was so sensible how dangerous it was to be touched with what the Multitude approved, that upon a general Acclamation made when he was making an Oration, he turned to an intelligent Friend who stood near him, and asked, in a surprized Manner, What Slip have I made?

I shall conclude this Paper with a Billet which has fallen into my Hands, and was written to a Lady from a Gentleman whom she had highly commended. The Author of it had formerly been her Lover. When all Possibility of Commerce between them on the Subject of Love was cut off, she spoke so handsomly of him, as to give Occasion for this Letter.

'*Madam,*

I should be insensible to a Stupidity, if I could forbear making you my Acknowledgments for your late Mention of me with so much Applause. It is, I think, your Fate to give me new Sentiments; as you formerly inspired me with the true Sense of Love, so do you now with the true Sense of Glory. As Desire had the least Part in the Passion I heretofore professed towards you, so has Vanity no Share in the Glory to which you have now raised me.   Innocence, Knowledge, Beauty, Virtue, Sincerity and Discretion, are the constant Ornaments of her who has said this of me.   Fame is a Babler, but I have arrived at the highest Glory in this World, the Commendation of the most deserving Person in it.'   T

No. 189.

[ADDISON.]   Saturday, October 6.

Patriae pietatis imago.—Virg.

THE following Letter being written to my Bookseller, upon a Subject of which I treated some time since, I shall publish it in this Paper, together with the Letter that was inclosed in it.

'*Mr. Buckley,*

Mr. SPECTATOR having of late descanted upon the Cruelty of Parents to their Children, I have been induced (at the Request of several of Mr. SPECTATOR's Admirers) to enclose this Letter, which I assure you is the Original from a Father to his own Son, notwithstanding the latter gave but little or no Provocation.   It would be wonderfully obliging to the World, if Mr. SPECTATOR would give his Opinion of it, in some of his Speculations, and particularly to

(Mr. *Buckley*)

Your humble Servant.

'*Sirrah,*

You are a sawcy audacious Rascal, and both Fool and Mad, and I care not a Farthing whether you comply or no; that does not raze out my Impressions of your Insolence, going about Railing at me, and the next Day to sollicit my Favour: These are Inconsistencies, such as discover thy Reason depraved. To be brief, I never desire to see your Face; and, Sirrah, if you go to the Work-house, it's no Disgrace to me for you to be supported there; and if you Starve in the Streets, I'll never give any thing underhand in your behalf.   If I have any more of your scribling Nonsense, I'll break your Head, the first time I set Sight on you: You are a stubborn Beast; is this your Gratitude for my giving you Mony?   You Rogue I'll better your Judgment, and give you a greater Sense of your Duty to (I regret to say) your Father, *&c.*

P. S. It's Prudence for you to keep out of my Sight; for to reproach me, that Might overcomes Right, on the outside of your Letter, I shall give you a great Knock on the Skull for it.'

Was there ever such an Image of Paternal Tenderness!   It

was usual among some of the *Greeks* to make their Slaves drink to excess, and then expose them to their Children, who by that means conceived an early Aversion to a Vice which makes Men appear so monstrous and irrational. I have exposed this Picture of an unnatural Father with the same Intention, that its Deformity may deter others from its Resemblance. If the Reader has a mind to see a Father of the same Stamp represented in the most exquisite Stroaks of Humour, he may meet with it in one of the finest Comedies that ever appeared upon the *English* Stage: I mean the part of Sir *Sampson* in *Love for Love*.

I must not however engage my self blindly on the side of the Son, to whom the fond Letter above-written was directed. His Father calls him a *sawcy and audacious Rascal* in the first Line, and I am afraid upon Examination he will prove but an ungracious Youth. *To go about Railing* at his Father, and to find no other place but the *outside of his Letter* to tell him *that Might overcomes Right*, if it does not discover *his Reason to be depraved*, and *that he is either Fool or Mad*, as the Cholerick old Gentleman tells him, we may at least allow that the Father will do very well in endeavouring to *better his Judgment, and give him a greater Sense of his Duty.* But whether this may be brought about *by breaking his Head,* or *giving him a great Knock on the Skull,* ought I think to be well considered. Upon the whole, I wish the Father has not met with his Match, and that he may not be as equally paired with a Son, as the Mother in *Virgil.*

> . . . *Crudelis tu quoque mater:*
> *Crudelis mater magis an puer improbus ille?*
> *Improbus ille puer, crudelis tu quoque mater.*

Or like the Crow and her Egg in the *Greek* Proverb.

> *Κακοῦ κόρακος κακὸν ᾠόν.*

I must here take Notice of a Letter which I have received from an unknown Correspondent, upon the Subject of my Paper, upon which the foregoing Letter is likewise founded. The Writer of it seems very much concerned lest that Paper should seem to give Encouragement to the Disobedience of Children towards their Parents; but if the Writer of it will take the Pains to read it over again attentively, I dare say his Apprehensions will vanish. Pardon and Reconciliation are all the Penitent Daughter requests, and all that I contend for in her behalf; and in this Case I may use the Saying of an eminent Wit, who upon some great Men's pressing him to forgive his Daughter who had married against his Consent, told them he could refuse nothing to their Instances, but that he would have them remember there was Difference between *Giving* and *Forgiving*.

I must confess, in all Controversies between Parents and their Children, I am naturally prejudiced in favour of the former. The Obligations on that side can never be acquitted, and I think it is one of the greatest Reflections upon Humane Nature that Paternal Instinct should be a stronger Motive to Love than Filial Gratitude; that the receiving of Favours should be a less Inducement to Good-will, Tenderness and Commiseration, than the conferring of them; and that the taking Care of any Person should endear the Child or Dependant more to the Parent or Benefactor, than the Parent or Benefactor to the Child or Dependant; yet so it happens, that for one cruel Parent we meet with a thousand undutiful Children. This is indeed wonderfully contrived (as I have formerly observed) for the Support of every living Species; but at the same time that it shews the Wisdom of the Creator, it discovers the Imperfection and Degeneracy of the Creature.

The Obedience of Children to their Parents is the Basis of all Government, and set forth as the measure of that Obedience which we owe to those whom Providence hath placed over us.

It is Father *le Conte*, if I am not mistaken, who tells us how want of Duty in this Particular is punished among the *Chinese*, insomuch that if a Son should be known to kill or so much as to strike his Father, not only the Criminal but his whole Family would be rooted out, nay the Inhabitants of the Place where he lived would be put to the Sword, nay the Place it self would be razed to the Ground, and its Foundations sown with Salt: For, say they, there must have been an utter Depravation of Manners in that Clan or Society of People, who could have bred up among them so horrid an Offender. To this I shall add a Passage out of the first Book of *Herodotus*. That Historian in his Account of the *Persian* Customs and Religion tells us, it is their Opinion that no Man ever killed his Father, or that it is possible such a Crime should be in Nature; but that if any thing like it should ever happen, they conclude that the reputed Son must have been Illegitimate, Supposititious, or begotten in Adultery. Their Opinion in this Particular shews sufficiently what a Notion they must have had of Undutifulness in general.   L

No. 190.

[STEELE.]

Monday, October 8.

Servitus crescit nova . . .—Hor.

SINCE I made some Reflections upon the general Negligence used in the Case of Regard towards Women, or, in other Words, since I talked of Wenching, I have had Epistles upon that Subject, which I shall, for the present Entertainment, insert as they lye before me.

'*Mr.* SPECTATOR,

As your Speculations are not confined to any Part of Human Life, but concern the Wicked as well as the Good, I must desire your favourable Acceptance of what I, a poor stroling Girl about Town, have to say to you. I was told by a Roman-Catholick Gentleman who picked me up last Week, and who, I hope, is absolved for what passed between us; I say, I was told by such a Person, who endeavoured to convert me to his own Religion, that in Countries where Popery prevails, besides the Advantage of licensed Stews, there are large Endowments given for the *Incurabili*, I think he called them, such as are past all Remedy, and are allowed such Maintenance and Support as to keep them without further Care 'till they expire. This Manner of treating poor Sinners, has, methinks, great Humanity in it; and as you are a Person who pretend to carry your Reflections upon all Subjects, whatever occur to you, with Candour, and act above the Sense of what Misinterpretation you may meet with, I beg the Favour of you to lay before all the World the unhappy Condition of us poor Vagrants, who are really in a Way of Labour instead of Idleness. There are Crowds of us whose Manner of Livelihood has long ceased to be pleasing to us; and who would willingly lead a new Life, if the Rigour of the Virtuous did not for ever expel us from coming into the World again. As it now happens, to the eternal Infamy of the Male Sex, Falshood among you is not reproachful, but Credulity in Women is infamous.

Give me Leave, Sir, to give you my History. You are to know that I am Daughter of a Man of good Reputation, Tenant to a Man of Quality. The Heir of this great House took it in his Head to cast a favourable Eye upon me, and succeeded. I do not pretend to say he promised me Marriage: I was not a Creature silly enough to be taken by so foolish a Story: But he ran away with me up to this Town; and introduced me to a grave Matron, with whom I boarded for a Day or two with great Gravity, and was not a little pleased with the Change of my Condition, from that of a Country Life to the finest Company, as I believed, in the whole World. My humble Servant made me to understand that I should be always kept in the plentiful Condition I then enjoyed; when after a very great Fondness towards me, he one Day took his Leave of me for four or five Days. In the Evening of the same Day my good Landlady came to me, and observing me very pensive began to comfort me, and with a Smile told me I must see the World. When I was deaf to all she could say to divert me, she began to tell me with a very frank Air that I must be treated as I ought, and not take these squeamish Humours upon me, for my Friend had left me to the Town; and, as their Phrase is, she expected I would see Company, or I must be treated like what I had brought my self to. This put me into a Fit of Crying: And I immediately, in a true Sense of my Condition, threw my self on the Floor, deploring my Fate, calling upon all that was good and sacred to succour me. While I was in all this Agony, I observed a decrepid old Fellow come into the Room, and, looking with a Sense of Pleasure in his Face at all my Vehemence and Transport. In a Pause of my Distress I heard him say to the shameless old Woman who stood by me, She is certainly a new Face, or else she acts it rarely. With that the Gentlewoman, who was making her Market of me, in all the Turn of my Person, the Heaves of my Passion, and the suitable Changes of my Posture, took Occasion to commend my Neck, my Shape, my Eyes, my Limbs. All this was accompanied with such Speeches as you may have heard Horse-coursers make in the Sale of Nags when they are warranted for their Soundness. You understand by this time that I was left in a Brothel, and exposed to the next Bidder that could purchase me of my Patroness. This is so much the Work of Hell; the Pleasure in the Possession of us Wenches, abates in Proportion to the Degrees we go beyond the Bounds of Innocence; and no Man is gratified, if there is nothing left for him to debauch. Well, Sir, my first Man, when I came upon the Town, was Sir *Jeoffrey Foible,* who was extremely lavish to me of his Money, and took such a Fancy to me that he would have carried me off, if my Patroness would have taken any reasonable Terms for me: But as he was old, his Covetousness was his strongest Passion, and poor I was soon left exposed to be the common Refuse of all the Rakes and Debauchees in Town. I cannot tell whether you will do me Justice or no, 'till I see whether you print this or not; otherwise, as I now live with *Sal,* I could give you a very just Account of who and who is together in this Town. You perhaps won't believe it; but I know of one who pretends to be a very good Protestant who lies with a Roman-

Catholick: But more of this hereafter, as you please me.   There do come to our House the greatest Politicians of the Age; and *Sal* is more shrewd than any Body thinks: No Body can believe that such wise Men could go to Baudy-houses out of idle Purposes; I have heard them often talk of *Augustus Caesar*, who had Intrigues with the Wives of Senators, not out of Wantonness but Stratagem.

It is a thousand Pities you should be so severely virtuous as I fear you are; otherwise, after one Visit or two, you would soon understand that we Women of the Town are not such useless Correspondents as you may imagine: You have undoubtedly heard that it was a Courtesan who discovered *Cataline*'s Conspiracy.   If you print this I'll tell you more; and am in the mean time,

> Sir,
>> *Your most humble Servant,*
>>> REBECCA NETTLETOP.'

'*Mr.* SPECTATOR,

I am an idle young Woman that would work for my Livelihood, but that I am kept in such a Manner as I cannot stir out. My Tyrant is an old jealous Fellow, who allows me nothing to appear in.   I have but one Shooe and one Slipper; no Headdress, and no upper Petticoat.   As you set up for a Reformer, I desire you would take me out of this wicked Way, and keep me your self.

>> EVE AFTERDAY.'

'*Mr.* SPECTATOR,

I am to complain to you of a Set of impertinent Coxcombs, who visit the Apartments of us Women of the Town, only, as they call it, to see the World.   I must confess to you, this to Men of Delicacy might have an Effect to cure them; but as they are stupid, noisy, and drunken Fellows, it tends only to make Vice in themselves, as they think, pleasant and humorous, and at the same Time nauseous in us.   I shall, Sir, hereafter from Time to Time give you the Names of these Wretches who pretend to enter our Houses meerly as Spectators.   These Men think it Wit to use us ill: Pray tell them however worthy we are of such Treatment, it is unworthy them to be guilty of it towards us.   Pray, Sir, take Notice of this, and pity the Oppressed: I wish we could add to it, the Innocent.'

>>> T

No. 191.

[ADDISON.]   Tuesday, October 9.

. . . οὖλον ὄνειρον.

SOME ludicrous Schoolmen have put the case, that if an Ass were placed between two bundles of Hay, which affected his Senses equally on each side, and tempted him in the very same degree, whether it would be possible for him to Eat of either. They generally determine this Question to the Disadvantage of the Ass, who they say would Starve in the midst of Plenty, as not having a single Grain of Free-will to determine him more to the one than to the other. The bundle of Hay on either side striking his Sight and Smell in the same proportion, would keep him in a perpetual Suspence, like the two Magnets which Travellers have told us, are placed one of them in the Roof, and the other in the Floor of *Mahomet*'s Burying Place at *Mecca*, and by that means, say they, pull the Impostor's Iron Coffin with such an equal Attraction, that it hangs in the Air between both of them. As for the Ass's Behaviour in such nice Circumstances, whether he would Starve sooner than violate his Neutrality to the two bundles of Hay, I shall not presume to determine; but only take Notice of the Conduct of our own Species in the same Perplexity. When a Man has a mind to venture his Mony in a Lottery, every Figure of it appears equally alluring, and as likely to succeed as any of its fellows. They all of them have the same Pretensions to good Luck, stand upon the same foot of Competition, and no manner of Reason can be given why a Man should prefer one to the other before the Lottery is drawn. In this Case therefore Caprice very often acts in the Place of Reason, and forms to it self some Groundless Imaginary Motive, where real and substantial ones are wanting. I know a well-meaning Man that is very well pleased to risque his good Fortune upon the Number 1711, because it is the Year of our Lord. I am acquainted with a Tacker that would give a good deal for the Number 134. On the contrary I have been told of a certain Zealous Dissenter who being a great Enemy to Popery, and believing that bad Men are the most fortunate in this World, will lay two to one on the Number 666 against any other Number, because, says he, it is the Number of the Beast. Several would prefer the Number 12000 before any other, as it is the Number of the Pounds in the great Prize. In short, some are pleased to find their own Age in their Number; some that they have got a Number which makes a pretty Appearance in the Cyphers, and others because it is the same Number that succeeded in the last Lottery. Each of these, upon no other Grounds, thinks he stands fairest for the great Lot, and that he is possessed of what may not be improperly called the *Golden Number*.

These Principles of Election are the Pastimes and Extravagances of Human Reason, which is of so busie a Nature, that it will be exerting it self in the meanest Trifles, and working even when it wants Materials. The wisest of Men are sometimes acted by such unaccountable Motives, as the Life of the Fool and the Superstitious is guided by nothing else.

I am surprised that none of the Fortune-tellers, or as the *French* call them, the *Diseurs de bonne aventure*, who publish their Bills in every Quarter of the Town, have not turned our Lotteries to their Advantage: did any of them set up for a Caster of Fortunate Figures, what might he not get by his pretended Discoveries and Predictions?

I remember among the Advertisements in the *Post-Boy* of *September* the 27th, I was surprized to see the following one.

This is to give Notice, That Ten Shillings over and above the Market Price, will be given for the Ticket in the 1500000*l. Lottery, No.* 132, *by Nath. Cliff at the Bible and Three Crowns in Cheapside.*

This Advertisement has given great Matter of Speculation to Coffee-house Theorists. Mr. *Cliff*'s Principles and Conversation have been canvassed upon this Occasion, and various Conjectures made why he should thus set his Heart upon No. 132. I have examined all the Powers in those Numbers, broken them into Fractions, extracted the Square and Cube Root, divided and multiplied them all ways, but could not arrive at the Secret till about three Days ago, when I received the following Letter from an unknown Hand; by which I find that Mr. *Nathaniel Cliff* is only the Agent, and not the Principal, in this Advertisement.

'*Mr.* SPECTATOR,

I am the Person that lately advertised I would give ten Shillings more than the Current Price for the Ticket No. 132 in the Lottery now Drawing, which is a Secret I have communicated to some Friends, who rally me incessantly upon that account. You must know I have but one Ticket, for which Reason, and a certain Dream I have lately had more than once, I was resolved it should be the Number I most approved. I am so positive I have pitched upon the great Lot, that I could almost lay all I am worth of it. My visions are so frequent and strong upon this Occasion, that I have not only possessed the Lot, but disposed of the Money which in all probability it will sell for. This Morning, in particular, I set up an Equipage which I look upon to be the gayest in the Town. The Liveries are very Rich, but not Gaudy. I should be very glad to see a

Speculation or two upon Lottery Subjects, in which you would oblige all People concerned, and in particular

Your most humble Servant,

George Gossling.

P. S. Dear Spec, If I get the 12000 Pound I 'll make thee a handsome Present.'

After having wished my Correspondent good Luck, and thanked him for his intended Kindness, I shall for this time dismiss the Subject of the Lottery, and only observe that the greatest part of Mankind are in some degree guilty of my Friend *Gossling's* Extravagance. We are apt to rely upon future Prospects, and become really expensive while we are only rich in Possibility. We live up to our Expectations, not to our Possessions, and make a Figure proportionable to what we may be, not what we are. We out-run our present Income, as not doubting to disburse our selves out of the Profits of some future Place, Project or Reversion that we have in view. It is through this Temper of Mind, which is so common among us, that we see Tradesmen break, who have met with no Misfortunes in their Business, and Men of Estates reduced to Poverty, who have never suffered from Losses or Repairs, Tenants, Taxes or Law-suits. In short, it is this foolish sanguine Temper, this depending upon Contingent Futurities that occasions Romantick Generosity, Chymerical Grandeur, Senseless Ostentation, and generally ends in Beggary and Ruin. The Man, who will live above his present Circumstances, is in great Danger of living in a little time much beneath them, or, as the *Italian* Proverb runs, The Man who lives by Hope will die by Hunger.

It should be an indispensable Rule in Life, to contract our Desires to our present Condition, and, whatever may be our Expectations, to live within the compass of what we actually possess. It will be time enough to enjoy an Estate when it comes into our Hands; but if we anticipate our good Fortune we shall lose the Pleasure of it when it arrives, and may possibly never possess what we have so foolishly counted upon. L

No. 192.

[STEELE.] Wednesday, October 10.

> . . . *Uno ore omnes omnia*
> *Bona dicere, & laudare fortunas meas,*
> *Qui gnatum haberem tali ingenio praeditum.*—Ter.

I stood the other Day and beheld a Father sitting in the Middle of a Room with a large Family of Children about him; and

methought I could observe in his Countenance different Motions
of Delight, as he turned his Eye towards the one and the other of
them. The Man is a Person moderate in his Designs for their
Preferment and Welfare; and as he has an easie Fortune, he is
not sollicitous to make a great one. His eldest Son is a Child
of a very towardly Disposition, and as much as the Father loves
him I dare say he will never be a Knave to improve his Fortune.
I do not know any Man who has a juster Relish of Life than the
Person I am speaking of, or keeps a better Guard against the
Terrours of Want or the Hopes of Gain. It is usual, in a
Crowd of Children, for the Parent to name out of his own
Flock all the great Officers of the Kingdom. There is something so very surprizing in the Parts of a Child of a Man's own,
that there is nothing too great to be expected from his Endowments. I know a good Woman who has but three Sons, and
there is, she says, nothing she expects with more Certainty than
that she shall see one a Bishop, the other a Judge, and the third
a Court Physician. The Humour is, that any thing which can
happen to any Man's Child, is expected by every Man for his
own: But my Friend whom I was going to speak of, does not
flatter himself with such vain Expectations, but has his Eye
more upon the Virtue and Disposition of his Children, than
their Advancement or Wealth. Good Habits are what will
certainly improve a Man's Fortune and Reputation; but on the
other Side, Affluence of Fortune will not as probably produce
good Affections of the Mind.

It is very natural for a Man of a kind Disposition to amuse
himself with the Promises his Imagination makes to him of the
future Condition of his Children, and to represent to himself the
Figure they shall bear in the World after he has left it. When
his Prospects of this Kind are agreeable, his Fondness gives as
it were a longer Date to his own Life; and the Survivorship of a
worthy Man to his Son, is a Pleasure scarce inferior to the
Hopes of the Continuance of his own Life. That Man is happy
who can believe of his Son, that he will escape the Follies and
Indiscretions of which he himself was guilty, and pursue and
improve every thing that was valuable in him. The Continuance of his Virtue is much more to be regarded than that
of his Life; but it is the most lamentable of all Reflections, to
think that the Heir of a Man's Fortune is such a one as wiil be
a Stranger to his Friends, alienated from the same Interests,
and a Promoter of every thing which he himself disapproved
An Estate in Possession of such a Successor to a good Man, is
worse than laid waste; and the Family of which he is the Head,
is in a more deplorable Condition than that of being extinct.

When I visit the agreeable Seat of my honoured Friend

Ruricola, and walk from Room to Room revolving many
pleasing Occurrences, and the Expressions of many just Sentiments I have heard him utter, and see the Booby his Heir in
Pain while he is doing the Honours of his House to the Friend
of his Father, the Heaviness it gives one is not to be expressed.
Want of Genius is not to be imputed to any Man; but want of
Humanity is a Man's own Fault.   The Son of *Ruricola* (whose
Life was one continued Series of worthy Actions and Gentle-
man-like Inclinations) is the Companion of drunken Clowns,
and knows no Sense of Praise but in the Flattery he receives
from his own Servants; his Pleasures are mean and inordinate,
his Language base and filthy, his Behaviour rough and absurd.
Is this Creature to be accounted the Successor of a Man of
Virtue, Wit, and Breeding?   At the same time that I have
this melancholy Prospect at the House where I miss my old
Friend, I can go to a Gentleman's not far off it, where he has a
Daughter who is the Picture both of his Body and Mind; but
both improved with the Beauty and Modesty peculiar to her
Sex.   It is she who supplies the Loss of her Father to the
World: She without his Name or Fortune is a truer Memorial
of him, than her Brother who succeeds him in both.   Such an
Offspring as the eldest Son of my Friend, perpetuates his
Father in the same manner as the Appearance of his Ghost
would: It is indeed *Ruricola*, but it is *Ruricola* grown frightful.

I know not to what to attribute the brutal Turn which this
young Man has taken, except it may be to a certain Severity
and Distance which his Father used towards him; and might,
perhaps, have occasioned a Dislike to those Modes of Life which
were not made amiable to him by Freedom and Affability.

We may promise our selves that no such Excrescence will
appear in the Family of the *Cornelii*, where the Father lives
with his Sons like their eldest Brother, and the Sons converse
with him as if they did it for no other Reason but that he is the
wisest Man of their Acquaintance.   As the *Cornelii* are eminent
Traders, their good Correspondence with each other is useful
to all that know them as well as to themselves: And their
Friendship, Good-will, and kind Offices, are disposed of jointly
as well as their Fortune; so that no one ever obliged one of
them, who had not the Obligation multiplied in Returns from
them all.

It is the most beautiful Object the Eyes of Man can behold,
to see a Man of Worth and his Son live in an entire unreserved
Correspondence.   The mutual Kindness and Affection between
them give an inexpressible Satisfaction to all who know them.
It is a sublime Pleasure which encreases by the Participation.
It is as sacred as Friendship, as pleasurable as Love, and as

joyful as Religion.   This State of Mind does not only dissipate
Sorrow, which would be extream without it, but enlarges
Pleasures which would otherwise be contemptible.   The most
indifferent thing has its Force and Beauty when it is spoke by
a kind Father, and an insignificant Trifle has its Weight when
offered by a dutiful Child.   I know not how to express it, but
I think I may call it a transplanted Self-love.   All the Enjoyments and Sufferings which a Man meets with, are regarded
only as they concern him in the Relation he has to another.
A Man's very Honour receives a new Value to him, when he
thinks that when he is in his Grave it will be had in Remembrance that such an Action was done by such a one's Father.
Such Considerations sweeten the old Man's Evening, and his
Soliloquy delights him when he can say to himself, No Man
can tell my Child his Father was either unmerciful or unjust.
My Son shall meet many a Man who shall say to him, I was
obliged to thy Father, and be my Child a Friend to his Child
for ever.

It is not in the Power of all Men to leave illustrious Names or
great Fortunes to their Posterity, but they can very much
conduce to their having Industry, Probity, Valour, and Justice.
It is in every Man's Power to leave his Son the Honour of
descending from a virtuous Man, and add the Blessings of
Heaven to whatever he leaves him.   I shall end this Rhapsody
with a Letter to an excellent young Man of my Acquaintance
who has lately lost a worthy Father.

'*Dear Sir,*

I know no Part of Life more impertinent than the Office of
administring Consolation: I will not enter into it, for I cannot
but applaud your Grief.   The virtuous Principles you had
from that excellent Man whom you have lost, have wrought in
you as they ought, to make a Youth of Three and Twenty
incapable of Comfort upon coming into Possession of a great
Fortune.   I doubt not but you will honour his Memory by a
modest Enjoyment of his Estate; and scorn to triumph over his
Grave by employing in Riot, Excess, and Debauchery, what he
purchased with so much Industry, Prudence, and Wisdom.
This is the true Way to shew the Sense you have of your Loss,
and to take away the Distress of others upon the Occasion.
You cannot recall your Father by your Grief, but you may
revive him to his Friends by your Conduct.'   T

No. 193.
[STEELE.]   Thursday, October 11.

> . . . *Ingentem foribus domus alta superbis*
> *Mane salutantum totis vomit aedibus undam.*—Virg.

WHEN we look round us, and behold the strange Variety of
Faces and Persons which fill the Streets with Business and
Hurry, it is no unpleasant Amusement to make Guesses at their
different Pursuits, and judge by their Countenances what it is
that so anxiously engages their present Attention.   Of all this
busie Crowd, there are none who would give a Man inclined to
such Inquiries better Diversion for his Thoughts, than those
whom we call good Courtiers, and such as are assiduous at the
Levées of Great Men.   These Worthies are got into an Habit
of being Servile with an Air, and enjoy a certain Vanity in
being known for understanding how the World passes.   In the
pleasure of this they can rise early, go abroad sleek and well-
dressed, with no other Hope or Purpose but to make a Bow to
a Man in Court Favour, and be thought, by some insignificant
Smile of his, not a little engaged in his Interests and Fortunes.
It is wondrous that a Man can get over the Natural Existence
and Possession of his own Mind so far, as to take delight either
in paying or receiving such cold and repeated Civilities.   But
what maintains the Humour is, that outward Show is what
most Men pursue, rather than real Happiness.   Thus both the
Idol and Idolater equally impose upon themselves in pleasing
their Imaginations this way.   But as there are very many of
her Majesty's good Subjects who are extremely uneasie at their
own Seats in the Country, where all from the Skies to the
Center of the Earth is their own, and have a mighty longing
to shine in Courts, or be Partners in the Power of the World; I
say, for the Benefit of these, and others who hanker after being
in the Whisper with great Men, and vexing their Neighbours
with the Changes they would be capable of making in the
Appearance at a Country Sessions, it would not methinks be
amiss to give an Account of that Market for Preferment, a
great Man's Levée.

For ought I know, this Commerce between the Mighty and
their Slaves, very justly represented, might do so much good,
as to incline the Great to regard Business rather than Ostentation; and make the Little know the Use of their Time too well,
to spend it in vain Applications and Addresses.

The Famous Doctor in *Moorfields*, who gained so much
Reputation for his Horary Predictions, is said to have had in
his Parlour different Ropes to little Bells, which hung in the
Room above Stairs, where the Doctor thought fit to be oraculous.

If a Girl had been deceived by her Lover, one Bell was pulled; and if a Peasant had lost a Cow, the Servant rung another. This Method was kept in respect to all other Passions and Concerns, and the skilful Waiter below sifted the Enquirer, and gave the Doctor Notice accordingly.   The Levée of a great Man is laid after the same manner, and twenty Whispers, false Alarms, and private Intimations pass backward and forward, from the Porter, the Valet, and the Patron himself, before the gaping Crew who are to pay their Court are gathered together: when the Scene is ready, the Doors fly open and discover his Lordship.

There are several Ways of making this first Appearance: You may be either half dressed, and washing your self, which is, indeed, the most stately; but this way of opening is peculiar to Military Men, in whom there is something graceful in exposing themselves naked; but the Politicians, or Civil Officers, have usually affected to be more reserved, and preserve a certain Chastity of Deportment.   Whether it be Hieroglyphical, or not, this Difference in the Military and Civil List, I will not say, but have ever understood the Fact to be, that the close Minister is buttoned up, and the brave Officer open-breasted on these Occasions.

However that is, I humbly conceive the Business of a Levée is to receive the Acknowledgments of a Multitude, that a Man is Wise, Bounteous, Valiant, and Powerful.   When the first Shot of Eyes are made, it is wonderful to observe how much Submission the Patron's Modesty can bear, and how much Servitude the Client's Spirit can descend to.   In the vast multiplicity of Business, and the Crowd about him, my Lord's Parts are usually so great, that, to the Astonishment of the whole Assembly, he has something to say to every Man there, and that so suitable to his Capacity, as any Man may judge that it is not without Talents that Men can arrive at great Employments.   I have known a great Man ask a Flag-Officer, which way was the Wind, a Commander of Horse the present Price of Oats, and a Stock-Jobber at what Discount such a Fund was, with as much ease as if he had been bred to each of those several ways of Life.   Now this is extremely obliging; for at the same time that the Patron informs himself of Matters, he gives the Person of whom he enquires an Opportunity to exert himself.   What adds to the Pomp of those Interviews is, that it is performed with the greatest Silence and Order imaginable.   The Patron is usually in the midst of the Room, and some humble Person gives him a Whisper, which his Lordship answers aloud, *It is well.   Yes, I am of your Opinion. Pray inform your self further, you may be sure of my Part in it.*

This happy Man is dismissed, and my Lord can turn himself to a Business of a quite different Nature, and off-hand give as good an Answer as any great Man is obliged to. For the chief Point is to keep in Generals, and if there be any thing offered that's Particular, to be in haste.

But we are now in the Height of the Affair, and my Lord's Creatures have all had their Whispers round to keep up the Farce of the thing, and the Dumb Show is become more general. He casts his Eye to that Corner, and there to Mr. such a one; to the other, *and when did you come to Town?* and perhaps just before he nods to another, and enters with him, *but, Sir, I am glad to see you, now I think of it.* Each of those are happy for the next four and twenty Hours; and those who bow in Ranks undistinguished, and by Dozens at a Time, think they have very good Prospects if they may hope to arrive at such Notices half a Year hence.

The Satyrist says there is seldom common Sense in high Fortune; and one would think, to behold a Levée, that the Great were not only infatuated with their Station, but also that they believed all below were seized too, else how is it possible they could think of imposing upon themselves and others in such a degree, as to set up a Levée for any thing but a direct Farce? But such is the Weakness of our Nature, that when Men are a little exalted in their Condition, they immediately conceive they have additional Senses, and their Capacities enlarged not only above other Men, but above human Comprehension it self. Thus it is ordinary to see a great Man attend one listning, bow to one at a distance, and call to a third at the same instant. A Girl in new Ribbands is not more taken with her self, nor does she betray more apparent Coquetries, than even a Wise Man in such a Circumstance of Courtship. I do not know any thing that I ever thought so very distasteful as the Affectation which is recorded of *Caesar*, to wit, that he would dictate to three several Writers at the same time. This was an Ambition below the Greatness and Candour of his Mind. He indeed (if any Man had Pretensions to greater Faculties than any other Mortal) was the Person; but such a way of acting is Childish, and Inconsistent with the manner of our Being. And it appears from the very Nature of things that there cannot be any thing effectually dispatched in the Distraction of a Publick Levée, but the whole seems to be a Conspiracy of a Sett of Servile Slaves, to give up their own Liberty to take away their Patron's Understanding. T

No. 194.

[STEELE.]   Friday, October 12.

        . . . *Difficili bile tumet jecur.*—Hor.

THE present Paper shall consist of two Letters, which observe
upon Faults that are easily cured both in Love and Friendship.
In the latter, as far as it meerly regards Conversation, the Person who neglects visiting an agreeable Friend is punished in
the very Transgression; for a good Companion is not found in
every Room we go into.   But the Case of Love is of a more
delicate Nature, and the Anxiety is inexpressible if every little
Instance of Kindness is not reciprocal.   There are things in
this sort of Commerce which there are not Words to express,
and a Man may not possibly know how to represent, which yet
may tear his Heart into ten Thousand Tortures.   To be grave
to a Man's Mirth, unattentive to his Discourse, or to interrupt
either with something that argues a Disinclination to be entertained by him, has in it something so disagreeable, that the
utmost Steps which may be made in further Enmity cannot give
greater Torment.   The gay *Corinna*, who sets up for an Indifference and becoming Heedlessness, gives her Husband all
the Torment imaginable out of mere Indolence, with this
peculiar Vanity, That she is to look as gay as a Maid in the
Character of a Wife.   It is no Matter what is the Reason of a
Man's Grief, if it be heavy as it is.   Her unhappy Man is convinced that she means him no Dishonour, but pines to Death
because she will not have so much Deference to him as to avoid
the Appearances of it.   The Author of the following Letter is
perplexed with an Injury that is in a Degree yet less criminal,
and yet the Source of the utmost Unhappiness.

   '*Mr.* SPECTATOR,

   I have read your Papers which relate to Jealousie, and desire
your Advice in my Case, which you will say is not common.
I have a Wife of whose Virtue I am not in the least doubtful;
yet I cannot be satisfied she loves me, which gives me as great
Uneasiness as being faulty the other way would do.   I know
not whether I am not yet more miserable than in that Case,
for she keeps Possession of my Heart without the Return of
her's.   I would desire your Observations upon that Temper in
some Women, who will not condescend to convince their Husbands of their Innocence or their Love, but are wholly negligent of what Reflections the poor Men make upon their Conduct (so they cannot call it criminal), when at the same time
a little Tenderness of Behaviour, or Regard to shew an Inclina-

tion to please them, would make them entirely at ease. Do not such Women deserve all the Misinterpretation which they neglect to avoid? or are they not in the actual Practice of Guilt, who care not whether they are thought guilty or not? If my Wife does the most ordinary thing, as visiting her Sister, or taking the Air with her Mother, it is always carried with the Air of a Secret: Then she will sometimes tell a thing of no Consequence, as if it was only want of Memory made her conceal it before; and this only to dally with my Anxiety. I have complained to her of this Behaviour in the gentlest Terms imaginable, and beseeched her not to use him who desired only to live with her like an indulgent Friend, as the most morose and unsociable Husband in the World. It is no easie Matter to describe our Circumstance, but it is miserable with this Aggravation, That it might be easily mended, and yet no Remedy endeavoured. She reads you, and there is a Phrase or two in this Letter which she will know came from me. If we enter into an Explanation which may tend to our future Quiet by your Means, you shall have our joint Thanks: In the mean time I am (as much as I can in this ambiguous Condition be any thing),

Sir,

Your Humble Servant.'

'*Mr.* SPECTATOR,

Give me Leave to make you a Present of a Character not yet described in your Papers; which is that of a Man who treats his Friend with the same odd Variety which a Fantastical Female Tyrant practises towards her Lover. I have for some Time had a Friendship with one of these mercurial Persons: The Rogue I know loves me, yet takes Advantage of my Fondness for him to use me as he pleases: We are by Turns the best Friends, and the greatest Strangers imaginable: Sometimes you would think us inseparable; at other Times he avoids me for a long Time, yet neither he nor I know why. When we meet next by Chance, he is amazed he has not seen me, is impatient for an Appointment the same Evening; and when I expect he should have kept it, I have known him slip away to another Place; where he has sate reading the News, when there is no Post; smoaking his Pipe, which he seldom cares for; and staring about him in Company with whom he has had nothing to do, as if he wonder'd how he came there.

That I may state my Case to you the more fully, I shall transcribe some short Minutes I have taken of him in my Almanack since last Spring; for you must know there are certain Seasons of the Year, according to which, I will not say our

Friendship, but the Enjoyment of it rises or falls: In *March* and *April* he was as various as the Weather; In *May* and Part of *June*, I found him the sprightliest best-humoured Fellow in the World; In the Dog-days, he was much upon the Indolent; In *September* very agreeable, but very busie; and since the Glass fell last to changeable, he has made three Appointments with me, and broke them every one.   However I have good Hopes of him this Winter, especially if you will lend me your Assistance to reform him, which will be a great Ease and Pleasure to,

October 9,

1711.
T

Sir,

Your most humble Servant.'

No. 195.
[ADDISON.]   Saturday, October 13.

Νήπιοι, οὐδ' ἴσασιν, ὅσῳ πλέον ἥμισυ παντός,
Οὐδ' ὅσον ἐν μαλάχῃ τε καὶ ἀσφοδέλῳ μέγ' ὄνειαρ.—Hes.

THERE is a Story in the *Arabian Nights Tales*, of a King who had long languished under an ill Habit of Body, and had taken abundance of Remedies to no purpose.   At length, says the Fable, a Physician cured him by the following Method.   He took an Hollow Ball of Wood, and filled it with several Drugs, after which he clos'd it up so artificially that nothing appeared. He likewise took a Mall, and after having hollowed the Handle, and that Part which strikes the Ball, he enclosed in them several Drugs after the same manner as in the Ball it self. He then ordered the Sultan, who was his Patient, to exercise himself early in the Morning with these *rightly prepared* Instruments, 'till such time as he should Sweat: When, as the Story goes, the Virtue of the Medicaments perspiring through the Wood, had so good an Influence on the Sultan's Constitution, that they cured him of an Indisposition which all the Compositions he had taken inwardly had not been able to remove.   This Eastern Allegory is finely contrived to shew us how beneficial Bodily Labour is to Health, and that Exercise is the most effectual Physick.   I have described, in my Hundred and Fifteenth Paper, from the general Structure and Mechanism of an Human Body, how absolutely necessary Exercise is for its Preservation.   I shall in this Place recommend another great Preservative of Health, which in many Cases produces the same Effects as Exercise, and may, in some measure, supply its Place, where Opportunities of Exercise are wanting. The Preservative I am speaking of is Temperance, which has those particular Advantages above all other Means of Health, that it may be practised by all Ranks and Conditions, at any Season, or in any Place. It is a kind of Regimen, into which every Man may put himself, without Interruption to Business, Expence of Mony, or Loss of Time. If Exercise throws off all Superfluities, Temperance prevents them. If Exercise clears the Vessels, Temperance neither satiates nor overstrains them. If Exercise raises proper Ferments in the Humours, and promotes the Circulation of the Blood, Temperance gives Nature her full Play, and enables her to exert her self in all her Force and Vigour. If Exercise dissipates a growing Distemper, Temperance starves it.

Physick, for the most part, is nothing else but the Substitute of Exercise or Temperance. Medicines are indeed absolutely necessary in acute Distempers, that cannot wait the slow Operations of these two great Instruments of Health; but did Men live in an habitual Course of Exercise and Temperance, there would be but little Occasion for them. Accordingly we find that those Parts of the World are the most healthy, where they subsist by the Chace; and that Men lived longest when their Lives were employed in hunting, and when they had little Food besides what they caught. Blistering, Cupping, Bleeding are seldom of use but to the Idle and Intemperate; as all those inward Applications which are so much in practice among us, are for the most part nothing else but Expedients to make Luxury consistent with Health. The Apothecary is perpetually employed in countermining the Cook and the Vintner. It is said of *Diogenes*, that meeting a young Man who was going to a Feast, he took him up in the Street and carried him Home to his Friends, as one who was running into imminent Danger, had not he prevented him. What would that Philosopher have said, had he been present at the Gluttony of a modern Meal? Would not he have thought the Master of a Family mad, and have begged his Servants to tie down his Hands, had he seen him devour Fowl, Fish and Flesh; swallow Oyl and Vinegar, Wines and Spices; throw down Sallads of twenty different Herbs, Sauces of an hundred Ingredients, Confections and Fruits of numberless Sweets and Flavours? What unnatural Motions and Counterferments must such a Medley of Intemperance produce in the Body? For my Part, when I behold a Fashionable Table set out in all its Magnificence, I fancy that I see Gouts and Dropsies, Feavers and Lethargies, with other innumerable Distempers lying in Ambuscade among the Dishes.

Nature delights in the most plain and simple Diet. Every

Animal, but Man, keeps to one Dish. Herbs are the Food of this Species, Fish of that, and Flesh of a Third. Man falls upon every thing that comes in his way, not the smallest Fruit or Excrescence of the Earth, scarce a Berry or a Mushroom, can escape him.

It is impossible to lay down any determinate Rule for Temperance, because what is Luxury in one may be Temperance in another; but there are few that have lived any time in the World who are not Judges of their own Constitutions, so far as to know what Kinds and what Proportions of Food do best agree with them. Were I to consider my Readers as my Patients, and to prescribe such a kind of Temperance as is accommodated to all Persons, and such as is particularly suitable to our Climate and way of Living, I would copy the following Rules of a very eminent Physician. Make your whole Repast out of one Dish. If you indulge in a second, avoid drinking any thing Strong 'till you have finished your Meal; at the same time abstain from all Sauces, or at least such as are not the most plain and simple. A Man could not be well guilty of Gluttony, if he stuck to these few obvious and easie Rules. In the first case there would be no Variety of Tastes to sollicit his Palate, and occasion Excess; nor in the second any artificial Provocatives to relieve Satiety, and create a false Appetite. Were I to prescribe a Rule for drinking, it should be form'd upon a Saying quoted by Sir *William Temple; the first Glass for my self, the second for my Friends, the third for good Humour, and the fourth for mine Enemies.* But because it is impossible for one who lives in the World to Diet himself always in so Philosophical a manner, I think every Man should have his Days of Abstinence, according as his Constitution will permit. These are great Reliefs to Nature, as they qualifie her for strugling with Hunger and Thirst, whenever any Distemper or Duty of Life may put her upon such Difficulties; and at the same time give her an Opportunity of extricating her self from her Oppressions, and recovering the several Tones and Springs of her distended Vessels. Besides, that Abstinence well timed often kills a Sickness in Embrio, and destroys the first Seeds of an Indisposition. It is observed by two or three ancient Authors, that *Socrates,* notwithstanding he lived in *Athens* during that great Plague, which has made so much Noise through all Ages, and has been celebrated at different times by such eminent Hands, I say, notwithstanding that he lived in the time of this devouring Pestilence, he never caught the least Infection, which those Writers unanimously ascribe to that uninterrupted Temperance which he always observed.

And here I cannot but mention an Observation which I have

often made, upon Reading the Lives of the Philosophers, and comparing it with any Series of Kings or great Men of the same number.   If we consider these ancient Sages, a great part of whose Philosophy consisted in a temperate and abstemious Course of Life, one would think the Life of a Philosopher, and the Life of a Man, were of two different Dates.   For we find that the generality of these wise Men were nearer an hundred than sixty Years of Age at the time of their respective Deaths. But the most remarkable Instance of the Efficacy of Temperance towards the procuring of long Life, is what we meet with in a little Book published by *Lewis Cornaro* the *Venetian*, which I the rather mention, because it is of undoubted Credit, as the late *Venetian* Ambassador, who was of the same Family, attested more than once in Conversation, when he resided in *England.*   *Cornaro*, who was the Author of the little Treatise I am mentioning, was of an infirm Constitution 'till about forty, when by obstinately persisting in an exact Course of Temperance, he recovered a perfect State of Health; insomuch that at fourscore he published his Book, which has been translated into *English* under the title of *The sure Way of attaining a long and healthful Life.*   He lived to give a third or fourth Edition of it, and after having passed his hundredth Year, died without Pain or Agony, and like one who falls asleep.   The Treatise I mention has been taken Notice of by several Eminent Authors, and is written with such a Spirit of Chearfulness, Religion, and good Sense, as are the natural Concomitants of Temperance and Sobriety.   The mixture of the old Man in it is rather a Recommendation than a Discredit to it.

   Having designed this Paper as the Sequel to that upon Exercise, I have not here considered Temperance as it is a Moral Virtue, which I shall make the Subject of a future Speculation, but only as it is the Means of Health.   L

No. 196.
[STEELE.]   Monday, October 15.

Est Ulubris, animus si te non deficit aequus.—Hor.

   '*Mr.* SPECTATOR,

THERE is a particular Fault which I have observed in most of the Moralists in all Ages, and that is, that they are always professing themselves and teaching others to be happy.   This State is not to be arrived at in this Life, therefore I would recommend to you to talk in an humbler Strain than your Predecessors have done, and instead of presuming to be happy, instruct us only to be easy. The Thoughts of him who would be discreet, and aim at practicable Things, should turn upon allaying our Pain rather than promoting our Joy. Great Inquietude is to be avoided, but great Felicity is not to be attained. The great Lesson is Aequanimity, a Regularity of Spirit, which is a little above Chearfulness and below Mirth. Chearfulness is always to be supported if a Man is out of Pain, but Mirth to a prudent Man should always be accidental: It should naturally arise out of the Occasion, and the Occasion seldom be laid for it: for those Tempers who want Mirth to be pleased, are like the Constitutions which flag without the use of Brandy. Therefore, I say, let your Precept be, *Be easy*. That Mind is dissolute and ungoverned, which must be hurried out of it self by loud Laughter or sensual Pleasure, or else be wholly unactive.

There are a Couple of old Fellows of my Acquaintance, who meet every Day and smoak a Pipe, and by their mutual Love to each other, tho' they have been Men of Business and Bustle in the World, enjoy a greater Tranquility than either could have worked himself into by any Chapter of *Seneca*. Indolence of Body and Mind, when we aim at no more, is very frequently enjoyed; but the very Enquiry after Happiness has something restless in it, which a Man who lives in a Series of temperate Meals, friendly Conversations, and easy Slumbers, gives himself no Trouble about. While Men of Refinement are talking of Tranquility, he possesses it.

What I would by these broken Expressions recommend to you, *Mr.* SPECTATOR, is, that you would speak of the Way of Life which plain Men may pursue, to fill up the Spaces of Time with Satisfaction. It is a lamentable Circumstance, that Wisdom, or, as you call it, Philosophy, should furnish Ideas only for the Learned; and that a Man must be a Philosopher to know how to pass away his Time agreeably. It would therefore be worth your Pains to place in an handsome Light the Relations and Affinities among Men, which render their Conversation with each other so grateful, that the highest Talents give but an impotent Pleasure in Comparison with them. You may find Descriptions and Discourses which will render the Fire-Side of an honest Artificer as entertaining as your own Club is to you. Good-nature has an endless Source of Pleasures in it; and the Representation of domestick Life, filled with its natural Gratifications (instead of the necessary Vexations which are generally insisted upon in the Writings of the Witty) will be a good Office to Society.

The Vicissitudes of Labour and Rest in the lower Part of Mankind, make their Being pass away with that Sort of Relish

which we express by the Word Comfort; and should be treated
of by you, who are a SPECTATOR, as well as such Subjects which
appear indeed more speculative, but are less instructive. In
a word, Sir, I would have your turn your Thoughts to the
Advantage of such as want you most; and shew that Simplicity, Innocence, Industry and Temperance, are Arts which
lead to Tranquility, as much as Learning, Wisdom, Knowledge,
and Contemplation.

I am, Sir,
Your most humble Servant,

T. B.'

' *Mr.* SPECTATOR,

Hackney, October 12.

I am the young Woman whom you did so much Justice to
some time ago, in acknowledging that I am perfect Mistress of
the Fan, and use it with the utmost Knowledge and Dexterity.
Indeed the World, as malicious as it is, will allow, that from an
Hurry of Laughter I recollect my self the most suddenly, make
a Curtsie, and let fall my Hands before me, closing my Fan at
the same Instant, the best of any Woman in *England.* I am
not a little delighted that I have had your Notice and Approbation; and however other young Women may rally me out of
Envy, I triumph in it, and demand a Place in your Friendship.
You must therefore permit me to lay before you the present
state of my Mind. I was reading your *Spectator* of the 9th
Instant, and thought the Circumstance of the Ass divided
between two Bundles of Hay which equally affected his Senses,
was a lively Representation of my present Condition: For you
are to know that I am extremely enamoured with two young
Gentlemen who at this Time pretend to me. One must hide
nothing when one is asking Advice, therefore I will own to you,
that I am very amorous and very covetous. My Lover *Will* is
very rich, and my Lover *Tom* very handsome. I can have
either of them when I please; but when I debate the Question
in my own Mind, I cannot take *Tom* for fear of losing *Will's*
Estate, nor enter upon *Will's* Estate and bid adieu to *Tom's*
Person. I am very young, and yet no one in the World, dear
Sir, has the main Chance more in her Head than my self.
Tom is the gayest, the blithest Creature! He dances well, is
very civil, and diverting at all Hours and Seasons: Oh he is the
Joy of my Eyes! But then again *Will* is so very rich and
careful of the Main. How many pretty Dresses does *Tom*
appear in to charm me: But then it immediately occurs to me
that a Man of his Circumstances is so much the poorer. Upon
the whole, I have at last examined both these Desires of Love

and Avarice, and upon strictly weighing the Matter I begin to think I shall be covetous longer than fond: therefore if you have nothing to say to the contrary, I shall take *Will*.   Alas poor *Tom*!

Your Humble Servant,

T   BIDDY LOVELESS.'

No. 197.
[BUDGELL.]   Tuesday, October 16.

> *Alter rixatur de lana saepe caprina,*
> *Propugnat nugis armatus: scilicet, ut non*
> *Sit mihi prima fides, &, vere quod placet, ut non*
> *Acriter elatrem, pretium aetas altera sordet.*
> *Ambigitur quid enim?   Castor sciat, an Dolichos plus;*
> *Brundusium Minuci melius via ducat an Appi.*—Hor.

EVERY Age a Man passes through, and Way of Life he engages in, has some particular Vice or Imperfection naturally cleaving to it, which it will require his nicest Care to avoid.   The several Weaknesses, to which Youth, old Age, and Manhood are exposed, have long since been set down by many both of the Poets and Philosophers; but I do not remember to have met with any Author who has treated of those ill Habits Men are subject to, not so much by reason of their different Ages and Tempers, as the particular Profession or Business in which they were educated and brought up.

I am the more surprised to find this Subject so little touched on, since what I am here speaking of is so apparent as not to escape the most vulgar Observation.   The Business Men are chiefly conversant in, does not only give a certain Cast or Turn to their Minds, but is very often apparent in their outward Behaviour, and some of the most indifferent Actions of their Lives.   It is this Air diffusing it self over the whole Man, which helps us to find out a Person at his first Appearance: So that the most careless Observer fancies he can scarce be mistaken in the Carriage of a Seaman, or the Gaite of a Tailor.

The liberal Arts, though they may possibly have less Effect on our External Mien and Behaviour, make so deep an Impression on the Mind, as is very apt to bend it wholly one way.

The Mathematician will take little less than Demonstration in the most common Discourse, and the Schoolman is as great a Friend to Definitions and Syllogisms.   The Physician and Divine are often heard to dictate in private Companies with the same Authority which they exercise over their Patients and

Disciples; while the Lawyer is putting Cases, and raising Matter for Disputation out of every thing that occurs.

I may possibly some time or other animadvert more at large on the particular Fault each Profession is most infected with; but shall at present wholly apply my self to the Cure of what I have mentioned, namely, That Spirit of Strife and Contention in the Conversations of Gentlemen of the Long Robe.

This is the more ordinary, because these Gentlemen regarding Argument as their own proper Province, and very often making ready Money of it, think it unsafe to yield before Company. They are shewing in common Talk how zealously they could defend a Cause in Court, and therefore frequently forget to keep that Temper which is absolutely requisite to render Conversation pleasant and instructive.

Captain SENTRY pushes this Matter so far, that I have heard him say, *He has known but few Pleaders that were tolerable Company.*

The Captain, who is a Man of good Sense, but dry Conversation, was last Night giving me an Account of a Discourse, in which he had lately been engaged with a young Wrangler in the Law. I was giving my Opinion, says the Captain, without apprehending any Debate that might arise from it, of a General's Behaviour in a Battel that was fought some Years before either the Templer or my self were born. The young Lawyer immediately took me up, and by reasoning above a Quarter of an Hour upon a Subject which I saw he understood nothing of, endeavoured to shew me that my Opinions were ill grounded. Upon which, says the Captain, to avoid any farther Contests, I told him, that truly I had not consider'd those several Arguments which he had brought against me; and that there might be a great deal in them. Ay, but says my Antagonist, who would not let me escape so, there are several things to be urged in favour of your Opinion which you have omitted, and thereupon begun to shine on the other side of the Question; upon this, says the Captain, I came over to my first Sentiments, and entirely acquiesced in his Reasons for my so doing. Upon which the Templer again recovered his former Posture, and confuted both himself and me a third Time. In short, says my Friend, I found he was resolved to keep me at Sword's length, and never let me close with him, so that I had nothing left but to hold my Tongue, and give my Antagonist free leave to smile at his Victories, who I found, like *Hudibras, could still change sides, and still confute.*

For my own part I have ever regarded our Inns of Court as Nurseries of Statesmen and Law-givers, which makes me often frequent that part of the Town with great Pleasure.

Upon my Calling in lately at one of the most noted *Temple* Coffee-houses, I found the whole Room, which was full of young Students, divided into several Parties, each of which was deeply engaged in some Controversie. The Management of the late Ministry was attacked, and defended, with great Vigour; and several Preliminaries to the Peace were proposed by some, and rejected by others; the Demolishing of *Dunkirk* was so eagerly insisted on, and so warmly controverted, as had like to have produced a Challenge. In short, I observed that the Desire of Victory, whetted with the little Prejudices of Party and Interest, generally carried the Argument to such an height, as made the Disputants insensibly conceive an Aversion towards each other, and part with the highest Dissatisfaction on both sides.

The managing an Argument handsomly being so nice a Point, and what I have seen so very few excell in, I shall here set down a few Rules on that Head, which, among other things, I gave in Writing to a young Kinsman of mine who had made so great a Proficiency in the Law, that he began to plead in Company upon every Subject that was started.

Having the entire Manuscript by me, I may, perhaps, from time to time publish such Parts of it as I shall think requisite for the Instruction of the *British* Youth. What regards my present Purpose is as follows:

Avoid Disputes as much as possible. In order to appear easie and well-bred in Conversation, you may assure your self that it requires more Wit, as well as more good Humour, to improve than to contradict the Notions of another: But if you are at any time obliged to enter on an Argument, give your Reasons with the utmost Coolness and Modesty, two things which scarce ever fail of making an Impression on the Hearers. Besides, if you are neither Dogmatical, nor shew either by your Actions or Words, that you are full of your self, all will the more heartily rejoice at your Victory. Nay, should you be pinched in your Argument, you may make your Retreat with a very good Grace: You were never positive, and are now glad to be better informed. This has made some approve the Socratical way of Reasoning, where while you scarce affirm any thing, you can hardly be caught in an Absurdity, and though possibly you are endeavouring to bring over another to your Opinion, which is firmly fix'd, you seem only to desire Information from him.

In order to keep that Temper, which it is so difficult, and yet so necessary to preserve, you may please to consider that nothing can be more unjust or ridiculous than to be angry with another, because he is not of your Opinion. The Interests,

Education, and Means by which Men attain their Knowledge are so very different, that it is impossible they should all think alike; and he has at least as much Reason to be angry with you, as you with him. Sometimes to keep your self cool, it may be of Service to ask your self fairly, What might have been your Opinion, had you all the Biasses of Education and Interest, your Adversary may possibly have? But if you contend for the Honour of Victory alone, you may lay down this as an infallible Maxim, That you cannot make a more false Step, or give your Antagonists a greater Advantage over you, than by falling into a Passion.

When an Argument is over, how many weighty Reasons does a Man recollect, which his Heat and Violence made him utterly forget?

It is yet more absurd to be angry with a Man because he does not apprehend the force of your Reasons, or give weak ones of his own. If you argue for Reputation, this makes your Victory the easier; he is certainly in all Respects an Object of your Pity, rather than Anger; and if he cannot comprehend what you do, you ought to thank Nature for her Favours, who has given you so much the clearer Understanding.

You may please to add this Consideration, That among your Equals no one values your Anger, which only preys upon its Master; and perhaps you may find it not very consistent either with Prudence or your Ease, to punish your self, whenever you meet with a Fool or a Knave.

Lastly, If you propose to your self the true End of Argument, which is Information, it may be a seasonable Check to your Passion; for if you search purely after Truth, 'twill be almost indifferent to you where you find it. I cannot in this Place omit an Observation which I have often made, namely, That nothing procures a Man more Esteem and less Envy from the whole Company, than if he chuses the Part of Moderator, without engaging directly on either side in a Dispute. This gives him the Character of Impartial, furnishes him with an Opportunity of Sifting things to the Bottom, shewing his Judgment, and of sometimes making handsome Compliments to each of the contending Parties.

I shall close this Subject with giving you one Caution. When you have gained a Victory do not push it too far; 'tis sufficient to let the Company and your Adversary see 'tis in your Power, but that you are too generous to make use of it.

X

No. 198.

[ADDISON.]   Wednesday, October 17.

> *Cervae, luporum praeda rapacium,*
> *Sectamur ultro, quos opimus*
> *Fallere & effugere est triumphus.*—Hor.

THERE is a Species of Women, whom I shall distinguish by
the Name of Salamanders. Now a Salamander is a kind of
Heroine in Chastity, that treads upon Fire, and lives in the
midst of Flames without being hurt.   A Salamander knows no
Distinction of Sex in those she converses with, grows familiar
with a Stranger at first Sight, and is not so narrow-spirited as to
observe whether the Person she talks to be in Breeches or in
Petticoats.   She admits a Male Visitant to her Bed-side, plays
with him a whole Afternoon at Pickette, walks with him two
or three Hours by Moon-light; and is extremely Scandalized
at the unreasonableness of an Husband, or the Severity of a
Parent, that would debar the Sex from such innocent Liberties.
Your Salamander is therefore a perpetual Declaimer against
Jealousie, and Admirer of the *French* Good-breeding, and a
great Stickler for Freedom in Conversation.   In short, the
Salamander lives in an invincible State of Simplicity and
Innocence: Her Constitution is *preserv'd* in a kind of natural
Frost; She wonders what People mean by Temptations; and
defies Mankind to do their worst.   Her Chastity is engaged in
a constant *Ordeal*, or fiery Trial: (like good Queen *Emma*) the
pretty Innocent walks blindfold among burning Plough-shares,
without being scorched or singed by them.

It is not therefore for the use of the Salamander, whether
in a married or single State of Life, that I design the
following Paper; but for such Females only as are made of
Flesh and Blood, and find themselves subject to Human
Frailties.

As for this Part of the Fair Sex who are not of the Salamander Kind, I would most earnestly advise them to observe
a quite different Conduct in their Behaviour; and to avoid as
much as possible what Religion calls *Temptations*, and the
World *Opportunities*.   Did they but know how many Thousands of their Sex have been gradually betrayed from innocent
Freedoms to Ruin and Infamy; and how many Millions of ours
have begun with Flatteries, Protestations and Endearments,
but ended with Reproaches, Perjury and Perfidiousness; they
would shun like Death the very first Approaches of one that
might lead them into inextricable Labyrinths of Guilt and
Misery.   I must so far give up the Cause of the Male World,

as to exhort the Female Sex in the Language of *Chamont* in the *Orphan*.

> *Trust not a Man, we are by Nature false,*
> *Dissembling, Subtle, Cruel, and Unconstant:*
> *When a Man talks of Love, with caution trust him;*
> *But if he Swears, he'll certainly deceive thee.*

I might very much enlarge upon this Subject, but shall conclude it with a Story which I lately heard from one of our *Spanish* Officers, and which may shew the Danger a Woman incurs by too great Familiarities with a Male Companion.

An Inhabitant of the Kingdom of *Castile*, being a Man of more than ordinary Prudence, and of a grave composed Behaviour, determined about the fiftieth Year of his Age to enter upon Wedlock. In order to make himself easie in it, he cast his Eye upon a young Woman who had nothing to recommend her but her Beauty and her Education, her Parents having been reduced to great Poverty by the Wars which for some Years have laid that whole Country waste. The *Castilian* having made his Addresses to her and married her, they lived together in perfect Happiness for some time; when at length the Husband's Affairs made it necessary for him to take a Voyage to the Kingdom of *Naples*, where a great Part of his Estate lay. The wife loved him too tenderly to be left behind him. They had not been a Ship-board above a Day, when they unluckily fell into the hands of an *Algerine* Pyrate, who carried the whole company on Shore, and made them Slaves. The *Castilian* and his Wife had the Comfort to be under the same Master; who seeing how dearly they loved one another, and gasped after their Liberty, demanded a most exorbitant Price for their Ransom. The *Castilian*, though he would rather have died in Slavery himself, than have paid such a Sum as he found would go near to ruin him, was so moved with Compassion towards his wife, that he sent repeated Orders to his Friend in *Spain* (who happened to be his next Relation) to sell his Estate, and transmit the Mony to him. His Friend, hoping that the Terms of his Ransome might be made more reasonable, and unwilling to sell an Estate which he himself had some Prospect of inheriting, formed so many Delays, that three whole Years passed away without any thing being done for the setting them at Liberty.

There happened to live a *French* Renegado in the same Place where the *Castilian* and his Wife were kept Prisoners. As this Fellow had in him all the Vivacity of his Nation, he often entertained the Captives with Accounts of his own Adventures; to which he sometimes added a Song, or a Dance, or some other

Piece of Mirth, to divert them during their Confinement.   His
Acquaintance with the Manners of the *Algerines*, enabled him
likewise to do them several good Offices.   The *Castilian*, as he
was one Day in Conversation with this Renegado, discovered to
him the Negligence and Treachery of his Correspondent in
Castile, and at the same Time asked his Advice how he should
behave himself in that Exigency: He further told the Renegado,
that he found it would be impossible for him to raise the Mony,
unless he himself might go over to dispose of his Estate.   The
Renegado, after having represented to him that his *Algerine*
Master would never consent to his Release upon such a Pretence, at length contrived a Method for the *Castilian* to make
his Escape in the Habit of a Seaman.   The *Castilian* succeeded
in his Attempt; and having sold his Estate, being afraid lest
the Mony should miscarry by the Way, and determining to
perish with it rather than lose one who was much dearer to him
than his Life, he returned himself in a little Vessel that was
going to *Algiers*.   It is impossible to describe the Joy he felt
upon this Occasion, when he considered that he should soon
see the Wife whom he so much loved, and endear himself more
to her by his uncommon Piece of Generosity.

The Renegado, during the Husband's Absence, so insinuated
himself into the good Graces of his young Wife, and so turned
her Head with Stories of Gallantry, that she quickly thought
him the finest Gentleman she had ever conversed with.   To be
brief, her Mind was quite alienated from the honest *Castilian*,
whom she was taught to look upon as a formal old Fellow unworthy the Possession of so charming a Creature.   She had
been instructed by the Renegado how to manage her self upon
his Arrival; so that she received him with an Appearance of the
utmost Love and Gratitude, and at length perswaded him to
trust their common Friend the Renegado with the Mony he had
brought over for their Ransome; as not questioning but he
would beat down the Terms of it, and negociate the Affair more
to their Advantage than they themselves could do.   The good
Man admired her Prudence, and followed her Advice.   I wish
I could conceal the Sequel of this Story, but since I cannot I
shall dispatch it in as few Words as possible.   The *Castilian*
having slept longer than ordinary the next Morning, upon his
awaking found his wife had left him: He immediately rose and
enquired after her, but was told that she was seen with the
Renegado about Break of Day.   In a Word, her Lover having
got all Things ready for their Departure, they soon made their
Escape out of the Territories of *Algiers*, carried away the Mony,
and left the *Castilian* in Captivity; who partly through the
cruel Treatment of the incensed *Algerine* his Master, and partly

through the unkind Usage of his unfaithful Wife, died some few months after.   I.

No. 199.
[STEELE.]   Thursday, October 18.

     . . . *Scribere jussit amor.*—Ovid.

THE following Letters are written with such an Air of Sincerity, that I cannot deny the inserting of them.

   '*Mr.* SPECTATOR,

Tho' you are every where in your Writings a Friend to Women, I do not remember that you have directly considered the mercenary Practice of Men in the Choice of Wives. If you would please to employ your Thoughts upon that Subject, you would easily conceive the miserable Condition many of us are in, who not only from the Laws of Custom and Modesty are restrained from making any Advances towards our Wishes, but are also from the Circumstance of Fortune out of all Hope of being addressed to by those whom we love. Under all these Disadvantages I am obliged to apply my self to you, and hope I shall prevail with you to print in your very next Paper the following Letter, which is a Declaration of Passion to one who has made some feint Addresses to me for some Time. I believe he ardently loves me, but the Inequality of my Fortune makes him think he cannot answer it to the World, if he pursues his Designs by way of Marriage; and I believe, as he does not want Discerning, he discovered me looking at him the other Day unawares, in such a manner as has raised his Hopes of gaining me on Terms the Men call easier. But my Heart is very full on this Occasion, and if you know what Love and Honour are, you will pardon me that I use no farther Arguments with you, but hasten to my Letter to him, whom I call *Oroondates*, because if I do not succeed it shall look like Romance; and if I am regarded you shall receive a Pair of Gloves at my Wedding, sent you under the name of *Statira.*'

                        '*To* OROONDATES.
    Sir,

After very much Perplexity in my self, and revolving how to acquaint you with my own Sentiments, and expostulate with you concerning yours, I have chosen this Way, by which means I can be at once revealed to you, or, if you please, lye concealed. If I do not within few Days find the Effect which I hope from this, the whole Affair shall be buried in Oblivion.

But alas! what am I going to do, when I am about to tell you that I love you? But after I have done so, I am to assure you, that with all the Passion which ever entered a tender Heart, I know I can banish you from my Sight for ever, when I am convinced that you have no Inclinations towards me but to my Dishonour. But, alas, Sir, why should you sacrifice the real and essential Happiness of Life to the Opinion of a World, that moves upon no other Foundation but profess'd Error and Prejudice? You all can observe that Riches do not alone make you happy, and yet give up every thing else when it stands in Competition with Riches. Since the World is so bad that Religion is left to us silly Women, and you Men act generally upon Principles of Profit and Pleasure, I will talk to you without arguing from any thing but what may be most to your Advantage, as a Man of the World. And I will lay before you the State of the Case, supposing that you had it in your Power to make me your Mistress, or your Wife, and hope to convince you that the latter is more for your Interest, and will contribute more to your Pleasure.

We will suppose then the Scene was laid, and you were now in Expectation of the approaching Evening wherein I was to meet you, and be carried to what Corner of the Town you thought fit, to consummate all which your wanton Imagination has promised you in the Possession of one who is in the Bloom of Youth, and in the Reputation of Innocence: You would soon have enough of me, as I am Sprightly, Young, Gay and Airy. When Fancy is sated, and finds all the Promises it made it self false, where is now the Innocence which charmed you? The first Hour you are alone you will find that the Pleasure of a Debauchee is only that of a Destroyer: He blasts all the Fruit he tastes, and where the Brute has been devouring there is nothing left worthy the Relish of the Man. Reason resumes her Place after Imagination is cloyed; and I am, with the utmost Distress and Confusion, to behold my self the Cause of uneasie Reflections to you, to be visited by Stealth, and dwell for the future with the two Companions (the most unfit for each other in the World) Solitude and Guilt. I will not insist upon the shameful Obscurity we should pass our Time in, nor run over the little short snatches of fresh Air and free Commerce which all People must be satisfied with, whose Actions will not bear Examination, but leave them to your Reflections, who have seen of that Life of which I have but a meer Idea.

On the other hand, If you can be so good and generous as to make me your Wife, you may promise your self all the Obedience and Tenderness with which Gratitude can inspire a virtuous Woman. Whatever Gratifications you may promise your self from an agreeable Person, whatever Compliances from an easie Temper, whatever Consolations from a Sincere Friendship, you may expect as the Due of your Generosity.   What at present in your ill View you promise your self from me, will be followed by Distaste and Satiety; but the Transports of a virtuous Love are the least Part of its Happiness.   The Raptures of Innocent Passion are but like Lightning to the Day, they rather interrupt than advance the Pleasure of it: How happy then is that life to be where the highest Pleasures of Sense are but the lowest parts of its Felicity!

Now am I to repeat to you the unnatural Request of taking me in direct Terms.   I know there stands between me and that Happiness the haughty Daughter of a Man who can give you suitably to your Fortune.   But if you weigh the Attendance and Behaviour of her who comes to you in Partnership of your Fortune, and expects an Equivalent, with that of her who enters your House as honoured and obliged by that Permission, whom of the two will you chuse?   You, perhaps, will think fit to spend a Day abroad in the common Entertainments of Men of Sense and Fortune, she will think her self ill used in that Absence, and contrive at home an Expence proportioned to the Appearance which you make in the World. She is in all Things to have a regard to the Fortune which she brought you, I to the Fortune to which you introduced me. The Commerce between you two will eternally have the Air of a Bargain, between us of a Friendship: Joy will ever enter into the Room with you, and kind Wishes attend my Benefactor when he leaves it.   Ask your self, how would you be pleased to enjoy for ever the Pleasure of having laid an immediate Obligation on a grateful Mind: such will be your case with Me.   In the other Marriage you will live in a constant Comparison of Benefits and never know the Happiness of conferring or receiving any.

It may be you will, after all, act rather in the prudential way, according to the Sense of the ordinary World.   I know not what I think or say, when that Melancholy Reflection comes upon me; but shall only add more, that it is in your Power to make me your Grateful Wife, but never your Abandoned Mistress.'   T

No. 200.

Friday, October 19.

Vincit amor patriae . . .—Virg.

THE Ambition of Princes is many times as hurtful to themselves as their People.   This cannot be doubted of such as prove unfortunate in their Wars, but it is often true too of those who are celebrated for their Successes.   If a severe View were to be taken of their Conduct, if the Profit and Loss by their Wars could be justly ballanc'd, it would be rarely found that the Conquest is sufficient to repay the Cost.

As I was the other Day looking over the Letters of my Correspondents, I took this Hint from that of *Philarithmus*; which has turn'd my present Thoughts upon Political Arithmetick, an Art of greater Use than Entertainment.   My Friend has offer'd an Essay towards proving, that *Lewis* XIV., with all his Acquisitions, is not Master of more People than at the Beginning of his Wars; nay, that for every Subject he had acquir'd, he had lost three that were his Inheritance: If *Phil arithmus* is not mistaken in his Calculations, *Lewis* must have been impoverish'd by his Ambition.

The Prince for the publick Good has a Sovereign Property in every private Person's Estate; and consequently his Riches must encrease or decrease in Proportion to the Number and Riches of his Subjects.   For Example: If Sword or Pestilence should destroy all the People of this Metropolis (God forbid there should be Room for such a Supposition! but if this should be the Case), the Queen must needs lose a great Part of her Revenue, or, at least, what is charg'd upon the City must encrease the Burthen upon the rest of her Subjects.   Perhaps the Inhabitants here are not above a tenth Part of the Whole; yet as they are better fed, and cloath'd, and lodg'd than her other Subjects, the Customs and Excises upon their Consumption, the Imposts upon their Houses, and other Taxes, do very probably make a fifth Part of the whole Revenue of the Crown.   But this is not all; the Consumption of the City takes off a great Part of the Fruits of the whole Island; and as it pays such a Proportion of the Rent or yearly Value of the Lands in the Country, so it is the Cause of paying such a Proportion of Taxes upon those Lands.   The Loss then of such a People must needs be sensible to the Prince, and visible to the whole Kingdom.

On the other Hand, if it should please God to drop from Heaven a new People equal in Number and Riches to the City, I should be ready to think their Excises, Customs, and House-Rent would raise as great a Revenue as to the Crown as would be lost in the former Case.   And as the Consumption of this new Body would be a new Market for the Fruits of the Country, all the Lands, especially those most adjacent, would rise in their yearly Value, and pay greater yearly Taxes to the Publick.   The Gain in this Case would be as sensible as the former Loss.

Whatsoever is assess'd upon the General is levied upon Individuals. It were worth the while then to consider what is paid by, or by Means of, the meanest Subjects, in order to compute the Value of every Subject to the Prince.

For my own Part, I should believe that seven Eighths of the People are without Property in themselves or the Heads of their Families, and forc'd to work for their daily Bread; and that of this Sort there are seven Millions in the whole Island of *Great Britain*: And yet one would imagine that seven Eighths of the whole People should consume at least three Fourths of the whole Fruits of the Country. If this is the Case, the Subjects without Property pay three Fourths of the Rents, and consequently enable the landed Men to pay three Fourths of their Taxes. Now if so great a Part of the Land-Tax were to be divided by seven Millions, it would amount to more than three Shillings to every Head. And thus as the Poor are the Cause, without which the Rich could not pay this Tax, even the poorest Subject is upon this Account worth three Shillings yearly to the Prince.

Again: One would imagine the Consumption of seven Eighths of the whole People should pay two Thirds of all the Customs and Excises. And if this Sum too should be divided by seven Millions, *viz.* the Number of poor People, it will amount to more than seven Shillings to every Head: And therefore with this and the former Sum, every poor Subject, without Property, except of his Limbs or Labour, is worth at least ten Shillings yearly to the Sovereign. So much then the Queen loses with every one of her old, and gains with every one of her new Subjects.

When I was got into this way of thinking, I presently grew conceited of the Argument, and was just preparing to write a letter of Advice to a Member of Parliament, for opening the Freedom of our Towns and Trades, for taking away all manner of Distinctions between the Natives and Foreigners, for repealing our Laws of Parish Settlements, and removing every other Obstacle to the Increase of the People. But as soon as I had recollected with what inimitable Eloquence my Fellow Labourers had exaggerated the Mischiefs of selling the Birthright of *Britons* for a Shilling, of spoiling the pure *British* Blood with foreign Mixtures, of introducing a Confusion of Languages and Religions, and of letting in Strangers to eat the Bread out of the Mouths of our own People, I became so humble as to let my Project fall to the Ground, and leave my Country to encrease by the ordinary way of Generation.

As I have always at Heart the Publick Good, so I am ever contriving Schemes to promote it; and I think I may without

Vanity pretend to have contriv'd some as wise as any of the Castle-builders. I had no sooner given up my former Project, but my Head was presently full of draining Fens and Marshes, banking out the Sea, and joining new Lands to my Country; for since it is thought impracticable to increase the People to the Land, I fell immediately to consider how much would be gained to the Prince by increasing the Land to the People.

If the same Omnipotent Power which made the World, should at this Time raise out of the Ocean and join to *Great Britain* an equal Extent of Land, with equal Buildings, Corn, Cattle, and other Conveniences and Necessaries of Life, but no Men, Women, nor Children, I should hardly believe this would add either to the Riches of the People or Revenue of the Prince; for since the present Buildings are sufficient for all the Inhabitants, if any of them should forsake the old to inhabit the new Part of the Island, the Increase of House-Rent in this would be attended with at least an equal Decrease of it in the other: Besides, we have such a Sufficiency of Corn and Cattle, that we give Bounties to our Neighbours to take what exceeds of the former off our Hands, and we will not suffer any of the latter to be imported upon us by our Fellow Subjects; and for the remaining Product of the Country, 'tis already equal to all our Markets: But if all these things should be doubled to the same Buyers, the Owners must be glad with half their present Prices, the Landlords with half their present Rents; and thus by so great an Enlargement of the Country, the Rents in the whole would not increase, nor the Taxes to the Publick.

On the contrary, I should believe they would be very much diminished; for as the Land is only valuable for its Fruits, and these are all perishable, and for the most Part must either be used within the Year, or perish without Use, the Owners will get rid of them at any Rate, rather than they should waste in their Possession: So that 'tis probable the annual Production of those perishable things, even of one Tenth Part of them, beyond all Possibility of Use, will reduce one half of their Value. It seems to be for this Reason that our Neighbour Merchants who engross all the Spices, and know how great a Quantity is equal to the Demand, destroy all that exceeds it. It were natural then to think that the Annual Production of twice as much as can be used, must reduce all to an Eighth Part of their present Prices; and thus this extended Island would not exceed one Fourth Part of its present Value, or pay more than one Fourth Part of the present Tax.

It is generally observed, That in Countries of the greatest Plenty there is the poorest Living; like the Schoolmen's Ass, in one of my Speculations, the People almost starve between two Meals. The Truth is, the Poor, which are the Bulk of a Nation, work only that they may live; and if with two Days Labour they can get a wretched Subsistence for a Week, they will hardly be brought to work the other four: But then with the Wages of two Days they can neither pay such Prices for their Provisions, nor such Excises to the Government.

That Paradox therefore in old *Hesiod* πλέον ἥμισυ παντός, or Half is more than the Whole, is very applicable to the present Case; since nothing is more true in political Arithmetick, than that the same People with half a Country is more valuable than with the whole. I begin to think there was nothing absurd in Sir *W. Petty*, when he fancied if all the Highlands of *Scotland*, and the whole Kingdom of *Ireland* were sunk in the Ocean, so that the People were all saved and brought into the Lowlands of *Great Britain*; nay tho' they were to be reimburst the Value of their Estates by the Body of the People, yet both the Sovereign and the Subjects in general would be enriched by the very Loss.

If the People only make the Riches, the Father of ten Children is a greater Benefactor to his Country than he who has added to it 10000 Acres of Land and no People. It is certain *Lewis* has join'd vast Tracts of Land to his Dominions: But if *Philarithmus* says true, that he is not now Master of so many Subjects as before; we may then account for his not being able to bring such mighty Armies into the Field, and for their being neither so well fed, nor cloathed, nor paid as formerly. The Reason is plain, *Lewis* must needs have been impoverished not only by his Loss of Subjects, but by his Acquisition of Lands.   T

No. 201.

[ADDISON.]   Saturday, October 20.

Religentem esse oportet, religiosum nefas.
                    —Incerti Autoris apud Aul. Gell.

It is of the last Importance to season the Passions of a Child with Devotion, which seldom dies in a Mind that has received an early Tincture of it. Though it may seem extinguished for a while by the Cares of the World, the Heats of Youth, or the Allurements of Vice, it generally breaks out and discovers it self again as soon as Discretion, Consideration, Age or Misfortunes have brought the Man to himself. The Fire may be covered and overlaid, but cannot be entirely quenched and smothered.

A State of Temperance, Sobriety and Justice without Devotion, is a cold, lifeless, insipid Condition of Virtue; and is rather to be stiled Philosophy than Religion. Devotion opens the Mind to great Conceptions, and fills it with more sublime Ideas than any that are to be met with in the most exalted Science; and at the same time warms and agitates the Soul more than with sensual Pleasure.

It has been observed by some Writers, that Man is more distinguished from the Animal World by Devotion than by Reason, as several Brute Creatures discover in their Actions something like a faint glimmering of Reason, though they betray in no single Circumstance of their Behaviour any thing that bears the least Affinity to Devotion. It is certain, the Propensity of the Mind to Religious Worship; the Natural Tendency of the Soul to fly to some Superior Being for Succour in Dangers and Distresses; the Gratitude to an invisible Superintendent which rises in us upon receiving any extraordinary and unexpected good Fortune; the Acts of Love and Admiration with which the Thoughts of Men are so wonderfully transported in meditating upon the Divine Perfections; and the universal Concurrence of all the Nations under Heaven in the great Article of Adoration, plainly shew that Devotion or Religious Worship must be the effect of a Tradition from some first Founder of Mankind, or that it is conformable to the Natural Light of Reason, or that it proceeds from an Instinct implanted in the Soul it self. For my part I look upon all these to be the concurrent Causes, but which-ever of them shall be assigned as the Principle of Divine Worship, it manifestly points to a Supreme Being as the first Author of it.

I may take some other Opportunity of considering those particular Forms and Methods of Devotion which are taught us by Christianity, but shall here observe into what Errors even this Divine Principle may sometimes lead us, when it is not moderated by that right Reason which was given us as the Guide of all our Actions.

The two great Errors into which a mistaken Devotion may betray us, are Enthusiasm and Superstition.

There is not a more melancholy Object than a Man who has his Head turned with Religious Enthusiasm. A Person that is crazed, though with Pride or Malice, is a Sight very mortifying to Human Nature; but when the Distemper arises from any indiscreet Fervours of Devotion, or too intense an Application of the Mind to its mistaken Duties, it deserves our Compassion in a more particular manner. We may however learn this Lesson from it, that since Devotion it self (which one would be apt to think could not be too warm) may disorder the Mind, unless its Heats are tempered with Caution and Prudence, we should be particularly careful to keep our Reason as cool as possible, and to guard our selves in all Parts of Life against the Influence of Passion, Imagination, and Constitution.

Devotion, when it does not lie under the check of Reason, is very apt to degenerate into Enthusiasm. When the Mind finds her self very much inflamed with her Devotions, she is too much inclined to think they are not of her own kindling, but blown up by something Divine within her. If she indulges this Thought too far, and humours the growing Passion, she at last flings her self into imaginary Raptures and Extasies; and when once she fancies her self under the Influence of a Divine Impulse, it is no wonder if she slights Human Ordinances, and refuses to comply with any established Form of Religion, as thinking her self directed by a much superior Guide.

As Enthusiasm is a kind of Excess in Devotion, Superstition is the Excess not only of Devotion, but of Religion in general, according to an old Heathen Saying, quoted by *Aulus Gellius, Religentem esse oportet, Religiosum nefas :* A Man should be Religious, not Superstitious: For as the Author tells us, *Nigidius* observed upon this Passage, that the *Latin* Words which terminate in *osus* generally imply vitious Characters, and the having of any Quality to an Excess.

An Enthusiast in Religion is like an obstinate Clown, a Superstitious Man like an insipid Courtier. Enthusiasm has something in it of Madness, Superstition of Folly. Most of the Sects that fall short of the Church of *England*, have in them strong Tinctures of Enthusiasm, as the *Roman* Catholick Religion is one huge overgrown Body of childish and idle Superstitions.

The *Roman* Catholick Church seems indeed irrecoverably lost in this Particular. If an absurd Dress or Behaviour be introduced in the World, it will soon be found out and discarded: On the contrary, a Habit or Ceremony, though never so ridiculous, which has taken Sanctuary in the Church, sticks in it for ever. A *Gothic* Bishop, perhaps, thought it proper to repeat such a Form in such particular Shoes or Slippers. Another fancied it would be very decent if such a Part of publick Devotions were performed with a Mitre on his Head, and a Crosier in his Hand. To this a Brother *Vandal*, as wise as the others, adds an antick Dress, which he conceived would allude very aptly to such and such Mysteries, till by Degrees the whole Office has degenerated into an empty Show.

Their Successors see the Vanity and Inconvenience of these Ceremonies, but instead of reforming, perhaps add others, which they think more significant, and which take Possession in the same manner, and are never to be driven out after they have been once admitted. I have seen the Pope officiate at Saint *Peter's*, where, for two Hours together, he was busied in putting on or off his different Accoutrements, according to the different Parts he was to act in them.

Nothing is so glorious in the Eyes of Mankind, and ornamental to Human Nature, setting aside the infinite Advantages which arise from it, as a strong steady masculine Piety; but Enthusiasm and Superstition are the Weaknesses of Human Reason, that expose us to the Scorn and Derision of Infidels, and sink us even below the Beasts that perish.

Idolatry may be looked upon as another Error arising from mistaken Devotion; but because Reflections on that Subject would be of no use to an *English* Reader, I shall not enlarge upon it.   L

No. 202.

[STEELE.]   Monday, October 22.

Saepe decem vitiis instructior odit & horret.—Hor.

THE other Day as I passed along the Street, I saw a sturdy Prentice-Boy Disputing with an Hackney-Coachman; and in an Instant, upon some word of Provocation, throw off his Hat and Perriwig, clench his Fist, and strike the Fellow a Cut on the Face; at the same time calling him Rascal, and telling him he was a Gentleman's Son. The young Gentleman was, it seems, bound to a Blacksmith; and the Debate arose about Payment for some Work done about a Coach, near which they fought. His Master, during the Combat, was full of his Boy's Praises; and as he called to him to play with Hand and Foot, and throw in his Head, he made all us who stood round him of his Party, by declaring the Boy had very good Friends, and he could trust him with untold Gold. As I am generally in the Theory of Mankind, I could not but make my Reflections upon the sudden Popularity which was raised about the Lad; and perhaps, with my Friend *Tacitus*, fell into Observations upon it which were too great for the Occasion; or ascribed this general Favour to Causes which had nothing to do towards it. But the young Blacksmith's being a Gentleman, was, methought, what created him good Will from his present equality with the Mob about him: Add to this, that he was not so much a Gentleman, as not, at the same time that he called himself such, to use as rough Methods for his Defence as his Antagonist. The Advantage of his having good Friends, as his Master expressed it, was not lazily urged; but he shewed himself Superior to the Coachman in his Personal Qualities of Courage and Activity, to confirm that of his being well Allyed, before his Birth was of any Service to him.

If one might Moralize from this silly Story, a Man wou'd say, that whatever advantages of Fortune, Birth, or any other Good, People possess above the rest of the World, they should shew collateral Eminence besides those Distinctions; or those Distinctions will avail only to keep up common Decencies and Ceremonies, and not to preserve a real place of Favour or Esteem in the Opinion and common Sense of their Fellow Creatures.

The Folly of People's procedure, in imagining that nothing more is necessary than Property and superior Circumstances to support them in Distinction, appears in no way so much as in the Domestick part of Life. It is ordinary to feed their Humours into unnatural Excrescences, if I may so speak, and make their whole Being a wayward and uneasie Condition, for want of the obvious Reflection that all parts of Human Life is a Commerce. It is not only paying Wages, and giving Commands, that Constitutes a Master of a Family; but Prudence, equal Behaviour, with readiness to Protect and Cherish them, is what entitles a Man to that Character in their very Hearts and Sentiments. It is pleasant enough to observe, that Men expect from their Dependants, from their sole Motive of Fear, all the good Effects which a liberal Education, and affluent Fortune, and every other Advantage cannot produce in themselves. A Man will have his Servant just, diligent, sober, and chaste, for no other Reasons but the Terrour of losing his Master's Favour; when all the Laws Divine and Human cannot keep him whom he serves within Bounds with Relation to any one of those Virtues. But both in great and ordinary Affairs, all Superiority which is not founded on Merit and Virtue, is supported only by Artifice and Stratagem. Thus you see Flatterers are the Agents in Families of Humourists, and those who govern themselves by any thing but Reason. Make-Bates, distant Relations, poor Kinsmen, and indigent Followers, are the Fry which support the Oeconomy of an humoursome rich Man. He is eternally whispered with Intelligence of who are true or false to him in Matters of no Consequence; and he maintains twenty Friends to defend him against the Insinuations of one who would perhaps cheat him of an old Coat.

I shall not enter into further Speculation upon this Subject at present, but think the following Letters and Petition are made up of proper Sentiments on this Occasion.

' *Mr.* Spectator,

I am Servant to an old Lady who is governed by one she calls her Friend; who is so familiar an one, that she takes upon her to advise her without being called to it, and makes her uneasie with all about her. Pray, Sir, be pleased to give us some Remarks upon voluntary Counsellors; and let these People know, that to give any Body Advice, is to say to that Person I am your Betters. Pray, Sir, as near as you can, describe that eternal Flirt and Disturber of Families Mrs. *Taperty*, who is always visiting, and putting People in a Way, as they call it. If you can make her stay at home one Evening, you will be a general Benefactor to all the Ladies' Women in Town, and particularly to

> *Your loving Friend,*
> Susan Civil.'

' *Mr.* Spectator,

I am a Footman, and live with one of those Men, each of whom is said to be one of the best humoured Men in the World, but that he is passionate. Pray be pleased to inform them, that he who is passionate, and takes no Care to command his Hastiness, does more Injury to his Friends and Servants in one half Hour than whole Years can attone for. This Master of mine, who is the best Man alive in common Fame, disobliges Somebody every Day he lives; and strikes me for the next thing I do because he is out of Humour at it. If these Gentlemen know that they do all the Mischief that is ever done in Conversation, they would reform; and I who have been a Spectator of Gentlemen at Dinner for many Years, have seen that Indiscretion does ten times more Mischief than Ill-nature. But you will represent this better than

> *Your abused*
> *Humble Servant,*
> Thomas Smoaky.'

' *To the* Spectator,

The humble Petition of *John Steward, Robert Butler, Harry Cook*, and *Abigail Chambers*, in Behalf of themselves and their Relations, belonging to and dispersed in the several Services of most of the great Families within the Cities of *London* and *Westminster*;

Sheweth,

That in many of the Families in which your Petitioners live and are employeâ, the several Heads of them are wholly unacquainted with what is Business, and are very little Judges when they are well or ill used by us your said Petitioners.

That for want of such Skill in their own Affairs, and by Indulgence of their own Laziness and Pride, they continually keep about them certain mischievous Animals called Spies.

That whenever a Spy is entertained, the Peace of that House is from that Moment banished.

That Spies never give an Account of good Services, but represent our Mirth and Freedom by the Words Wantonness and Disorder.

That in all Families where there are Spies, there is a general Jealousie and Misunderstanding.

That the Masters and Mistresses of such Houses live in continual Suspicion of their ingenuous and true Servants, and are given up to the Management of those who are false and perfidious.

That such Masters and Mistresses who entertain Spies, are no longer more than Cyphers in their own Families; and that we your Petitioners are with great Disdain obliged to pay all our Respect, and expect all our Maintenance from such Spies.

> Your Petitioners therefore most humbly pray, that you would represent the Premises to all Persons of Condition; and your Petitioners, as in Duty bound, shall for ever Pray, *&c.*'

T

No. 203.
[ADDISON.]   Tuesday, October 23.

Phoebe pater, si das hujus mihi nominis usum,
Nec falsa Clymene culpam sub imagine celat;
Pignora da, genitor. . . .—Ov. Met.

THERE is a loose Tribe of Men whom I have not yet taken Notice of, that ramble into all the Corners of this great City, in order to seduce such unfortunate Females as fall into their Walks. These abandoned Profligates raise up Issue in every Quarter of the Town, and very often for a valuable Consideration father it upon the Church-warden. By this means there are several Married Men who have a little Family in most of the Parishes of *London* and *Westminster*, and several Batchelors who are undone by a Charge of Children.

When a Man once gives himself this Liberty of preying at large, and living upon the Common, he finds so much Game in a populous City, that it is surprising to consider the Numbers which he sometimes Propagates. We see many a young

Fellow, who is scarce of Age, that could lay his Claim to the *Jus trium Liberorum*, or the Privileges which were granted by the *Roman* Laws to all such as were Fathers of three Children: Nay, I have heard a Rake who was not quite Five and Twenty declare himself the Father of a Seventh Son, and very prudently determine to breed him up a Physician. In short, the Town is full of these young Patriarchs, not to mention several battered Beaus, who, like heedless Spend-thrifts that squander away their Estates before they are Masters of them, have raised up their whole stock of Children before Marriage.

I must not here omit the particular Whim of an Impudent Libertine that had a little smattering of Heraldry, and observing how the Genealogies of great Families were often drawn up in the shape of Trees, had taken a Fancy to dispose of his own Illegitimate Issue in a Figure of the same kind.

> . . . *Nec longum tempus et ingens*
> *Exiit ad coelum ramis felicibus arbos,*
> *Miraturque novas frondes, et non sua poma.*—Virg.

The Trunk of the Tree was marked with his own Name, *Will Maple*. Out of the Side of it grew a large Barren Branch, Inscribed *Mary Maple*, the Name of his unhappy Wife. The Head was adorned with five high Boughs. On the bottom of the first was Written in Capital Characters *Kate Cole*, who branched out into three Sprigs, *viz. William, Richard* and *Rebecca*. *Sal Twiford* gave birth to another Bough that shot up into *Sarah, Tom. Will.* and *Frank*. The third Arm of the Tree had only a single Infant in it, with a space left for a second, the Parent from whom it sprung being near her time, when the Author took this Ingenious Device into his Head. The two other great Boughs were very plentifully loaden with Fruit of the same kind; besides which there were many Ornamental Branches that did not bear. In short, a more flourishing Tree never came out of the Herald's Office.

What makes this Generation of Vermin so very Prolifick, is the indefatigable Diligence with which they apply themselves to their Business. A Man does not undergo more watchings and fatigues in a Campaign, than in the Course of a vicious Amour. As it is said of some Men, that they make their Business their Pleasure, these Sons of Darkness may be said to make their Pleasure their Business. They might conquer their corrupt Inclinations with half the Pains they are at in gratifying them.

Nor is the Invention of these Men less to be admired than their Industry and Vigilance. There is a Fragment of *Apollodorus* the Comick Poet (who was Contemporary with *Menander*) which is full of Humour, as follows. *Thou may'st shut up thy Doors,* says he, *with Bars and Bolts: It will be impossible for the Blacksmith to make them so fast, but a Cat and a Whore-master will find a way through them.* In a Word, there is no Head so full of Stratagems as that of a Libidinous Man.

Were I to propose a Punishment for this infamous Race of Propagators, it should be to send them, after the second or third Offence, into our *American* Colonies, in order to People those Parts of her Majesty's Dominions where there is a want of Inhabitants, and in the Phrase of *Diogenes* to *Plant Men.* Some Countries punish this Crime with Death; but I think such a Banishment would be sufficient, and might turn this generative Faculty to the Advantage of the Publick.

In the mean time, till these Gentlemen may be thus disposed of, I would earnestly exhort them to take Care of those unfortunate Creatures whom they have brought into the World by these indirect Methods, and to give their spurious Children such an Education as may render them more virtuous than their Parents. This is the best Attonement they can make for their own Crimes, and indeed the only Method that is left them to repair their past Miscarriages.

I would likewise desire them to consider, whether they are not bound in common Humanity, as well as by all the Obligations of Religion and Nature, to make some Provision for those whom they have not only given Life to, but entailed upon them, though very unreasonably, a degree of Shame and Disgrace. And here I cannot but take notice of those depraved Notions which prevail among us, and which must have taken Rise from our natural Inclination to favour a Vice to which we are so very prone, namely, that *Bastardy* and *Cuckoldom* should be looked upon as Reproaches, and that the Ignominy which is only due to Lewdness and Falshood, should fall in so unreasonable a manner upon the Persons who are Innocent.

I have been insensibly drawn into this Discourse by the following Letter, which is drawn up with such a Spirit of Sincerity, that I question not but the Writer of it has represented his Case in a true and genuine Light.

'*Sir,*

I am one of those People who by the general Opinion of the World are counted both Infamous and Unhappy.

My Father is a very eminent Man in this Kingdom, and one who bears considerable Offices in it. I am his Son, but my Misfortune is, that I dare not call him Father, nor he without shame own me as his Issue, I being Illegitimate, and therefore deprived of that endearing Tenderness and unparallel'd

Satisfaction which a good Man finds in the Love and Conversation of a Parent; Neither have I the Opportunities to render him the Duties of a Son, he having always carried himself at so vast a Distance, and with such Superiority towards me, that by long use I have contracted a Timorousness when before him, which hinders me from declaring my own Necessities, and giving him to understand the Inconveniences I undergo.

It is my Misfortune to have been neither bred a Scholar, a Soldier, nor to any kind of Business, which renders me entirely uncapable of making Provision for my self without his Assistance; and this creates a continual Uneasiness in my Mind, fearing I shall in time want Bread; my Father, if I may so call him, giving me but very faint Assurances of doing any thing for me.

I have hitherto lived somewhat like a Gentleman, and it would be very hard for me to labour for my Living. I am in continual Anxiety for my future Fortune, and under a great Unhappiness in losing the sweet Conversation and Friendly Advice of my Parents; so that I cannot look upon my self otherwise than as a Monster, strangely sprung up in Nature, which every one is ashamed to own.

I am thought to be a Man of some natural Parts, and by the continual reading what you have offered the World, become an Admirer thereof, which has drawn me to make this Confession; at the same time hoping, if any thing herein shall touch you with a Sense of Pity, you would then allow me the favour of your Opinion thereupon, as also what part, I, being unlawfully born, may claim of the Man's Affection who begot me, and how far in your Opinion I am to be thought his Son, or he acknowledged as my Father. Your Sentiments and Advice herein will be a great Consolation and Satisfaction to,

Sir,

Your Admirer and
Humble Servant,

C   W. B.'

No. 204.
[STEELE.]   Wednesday, October 24.

> *Urit grata protervitas,*
> *Et vultus nimium lubricus aspici.*—Hor.

I am not at all displeased that I am become the Courier of Love, and that the Distressed in that Passion convey their Complaints to each other by my Means. The following Letters have lately come to my Hands, and shall have their Place with great Willingness. As to the Reader's Entertainment, he will, I hope, forgive the inserting such Particulars as to him may perhaps seem frivolous, but are to the Persons who wrote them of the highest Consequence. I shall not trouble you with the Prefaces, Compliments, and Apologies made to me before each Epistle when it was desired to be inserted; but in general they tell me, that the Persons to whom they are addressed have Intimations, by Phrases and Allusions in them, from whence they came.

'To the Sothades.

The Word by which I address you, gives you who understand *Portuguese* a lively Image of the tender Regard I have for you. The SPECTATOR'S late Letter from *Statira* gave me the Hint to use the same Method of explaining my self to you. I am not affronted at the Design your late Behaviour discovered you had in your Addresses to me; but I impute it to the Degeneracy of the Age rather than your particular Fault. As I aim at nothing more than being yours, I am willing to be a Stranger to your Name, your Fortune, or any Figure which your Wife might expect to make in the World, provided my Commerce with you is not to be a guilty one. I resign gay Dress, the Pleasures of Visits, Equipage, Plays, Balls, and Operas, for that one Satisfaction of having you for ever mine. I am willing you shall industriously conceal the only Cause of Triumph which I can know in this Life. I wish only to have it my Duty, as well as my Inclination, to study your Happiness. If this has not the Effect this Letter seems to aim at, you are to understand that I had a Mind to be rid of you, and took the readiest Way to pall you with an Offer of what you would never desist pursuing while you received ill Usage. Be a true Man; be my Slave while you doubt me, and neglect me when you think I love you. I defy you to find out what is your present Circumstance with me; but I know while I can keep this Suspence,

I am your admired
Bellinda.'

'Madam,

It is a strange State of Mind a Man is in, when the very Imperfections of a Woman he loves turn into Excellencies and Advantages. I do assure you I am very much afraid of venturing upon you. I now like you in spite of my Reason, and think it an ill Circumstance to owe one's Happiness to nothing but Infatuation. I can see you ogle all the young Fellows who look at you, and observe your Eye wander after new Conquests every Moment you are in a publick place; and yet there is such a Beauty in all your Looks and Gestures, that I cannot but admire you in the very Act of endeavouring to gain the Hearts of others. My Condition is the same with that of the Lover in the Way of the World. I have studied your Faults so long, that they are become as familiar to me, and I like them as well as I do my own. Look to it, Madam, and consider whether you think this gay Behaviour will appear to me as amiable when an Husband, as it does now to me a Lover. Things are so far advanced, that we must proceed; and I hope you will lay it to Heart, that it will be becoming in me to appear still your Lover, but not in you to be still my Mistress. Gaiety in the Matrimonial Life is graceful in one Sex, but exceptionable in the other. As you improve these little Hints, you will ascertain the Happiness or Uneasiness of,

> *Madam,*
> *Your most obedient,*
> *Most humble Servant,*
>
> T. D.'

'*Sir,*

When I sat at the Window, and you at the other End of the Room by my Cousin, I saw you catch me looking at you. Since you have the Secret at last, which I am sure you should never have known but by Inadvertency, what my Eyes said was true. But it is too soon to confirm it with my Hand, therefore shall not subscribe my Name.'

'*Sir,*

There were other Gentlemen nearer, and I know no Necessity you were under to take up that flippant Creature's Fan last Night; but you shall never touch a Stick of mine more, that's pos.

> *Phillis.'*

'*To Collonel* R———s *in* Spain.

Before this can reach the best of Husbands and the fondest Lover, those tender Names will be on more of Concern to me. The Indisposition in which you, to obey the Dictates of your Honour and Duty, left me, has encreased upon me; and I am acquainted by my Physicians I cannot live a Week longer. At this time my Spirits fail me; and it is the ardent Love I have for you that carries me beyond my Strength, and enables me to tell you the most painful thing in the Prospect of Death, is, that I must part with you. But let it be a Comfort to you, that I have no Guilt hangs upon me, no unrepented Folly that retards me; but I pass away my last Hours in Reflexion upon the Happiness we have lived in together, and in Sorrow that it is so soon to have an End. This is a Frailty which I hope is so far from criminal, that, methinks, there is a kind of Piety in being so unwilling to be separated from a State which is the Institution of Heaven, and in which we have lived according to its Laws. As we know no more of the next Life, but that it will be an happy one to the Good, and miserable to the Wicked, why may we not please our selves at least to alleviate the Difficulty of resigning this Being, in imagining that we shall have a Sense of what passes below, and may possibly be imployed in guiding the Steps of those with whom we walked with Innocence when mortal? Why may not I hope to go on in my usual Work, and, though unknown to you, be assistant in all the Conflicts of your Mind? Give me leave to say to you, Oh best of Men, that I cannot figure to my self a greater Happiness than in such an Employment: To be present at all the Adventures to which humane Life is exposed, to administer Slumber to thy Eyelids in the Agonies of a Fever, to cover thy beloved Face in the Day of Battel, to go with thee a Guardian Angel incapable of Wound or Pain, where I have longed to attend thee when a weak, a fearful Woman. These, my Dear, are the Thoughts with which I warm my poor languid Heart; but indeed I am not capable under my present Weakness of bearing the strong Agonies of Mind I fall into, when I form to my self the Grief you will be in upon your first hearing of my Departure. I will not dwell upon this, because your kind and generous Heart will be but the more afflicted, the more the Person for whom you lament offers you Consolation. My last Breath will, if I am my self, expire in a Prayer for you. I shall never see thy Face again. Farewell for ever.'   **T**

No. 205.

[ADDISON.]   Thursday, October 25.

Decipimur specie recti.—Hor.

WHEN I meet with any vicious Character, that is not generally known, in order to prevent its doing Mischief, I draw it at length, and set it up as a Scarecrow: By which means I do not only make an Example of the Person to whom it belongs, but give Warning to all her Majesty's Subjects, that they may not suffer by it. Thus, to change the Allusion, I have marked out several of the Shoals and Quicksands of Life, and am continually employed in discovering those which are still concealed, in order to keep the Ignorant and Unwary from running upon

them.   It is with this Intention that I publish the following
Letter, which brings to light some Secrets of this Nature.

'Mr. SPECTATOR,

There are none of your Speculations which I read over with
greater Delight, than those which are designed for the Improvement of our Sex.   You have endeavoured to correct our unreasonable Fears and Superstitions, in your Seventh and
Twelfth Papers; our Fancy for Equipage, in your Fifteenth;
our Love of Puppet-Shows, in your Thirty First; our Notions
of Beauty, in your Thirty Third; our Inclination for Romances,
in your Thirty Seventh; our Passion for *French* Fopperies, in
your Forty Fifth; our Manhood and Party-Zeal, in your Fifty
Seventh; our Abuse of Dancing, in your Sixty Sixth and Sixty
Seventh; our Levity, in your Hundred and Twenty Eighth;
our Love of Coxcombs, in your Hundred and Fifty Fourth and
Hundred and Fifty Seventh; our Tyranny over the Henpeckt,
in your Hundred and Seventy Sixth.   You have described the
Pict in your Forty First; the Idol, in your Seventy Third; the
Demurrer, in your Eighty Ninth; the Salamander, in your
Hundred and Ninety Eighth.   You have likewise taken to
pieces our Dress, and represented to us the Extravagancies
we are often guilty of in that Particular.   You have fallen
upon our Patches, in your Fiftieth and Eighty First; Our
Commodes, in your Ninety Eighth; our Fans, in your Hundred
and Second; our Riding-habits in your Hundred and Fourth;
our Hoop-petticoats, in your Hundred and Twenty-Seventh;
besides a great many little Blemishes, which you have touched
upon in your several other Papers, and in those many Letters
that are scattered up and down your Works.   At the same time
we must own, that the Complements you pay our Sex are innumerable, and that those very Faults, which you represent
in us, are neither black in themselves, nor, as you own, universal
among us.   But, Sir, it is plain that these your Discourses are
calculated for none but the fashionable Part of Womankind,
and for the Use of those who are rather indiscreet than vicious.
But, Sir, there is a sort of Prostitutes in the lower part of our
Sex, who are a Scandal to us, and very well deserve to fall under
your Censure.   I know it would debase your Paper too much
to enter into the Behaviour of these female Libertines; but as
your Remarks on some part of it would be a doing of Justice to
several Women of Virtue and Honour, whose Reputations
suffer by it, I hope you will not think it improper to give the
Publick some Accounts of this nature.   You must know, Sir, I
am provoked to write you this Letter by the Behaviour of
an infamous Woman, who having passed her Youth in a most

shameless State of Prostitution, is now one of those who gain their Livelihood by seducing others, that are younger than themselves, and by establishing a Criminal Commerce between the two Sexes. Among several of her Artifices to get Mony, she frequently perswades a vain young Fellow, that such a Woman of Quality, or such a celebrated Toast, entertains a secret Passion for him, and wants nothing but an Opportunity of revealing it. Nay, she has gone so far as to write Letters in the Name of a Woman of Figure, to borrow Mony of one of these foolish *Roderigos*, which she has afterwards appropriated to her own use: In the mean time, the Person, who has lent the Mony, has thought a Lady under Obligations to him, who scarce knew his Name; and wondered at her Ingratitude when he has been with her, that she has not owned the Favour, though at the same time he was too much a Man of Honour to put her in mind of it.

When this abandoned Baggage meets with a Man who has Vanity enough to give Credit to Relations of this nature, she turns him to very good Account, by repeating Praises that were never uttered and delivering Messages that were never sent. As the House of this shameless Creature is frequented by several Foreigners, I have heard of another Artifice, out of which she often raises Mony. The Foreigner sighs after some *British* Beauty, whom he only knows by Fame: Upon which she promises, if he can be secret, to procure him a Meeting. The Stranger, ravish'd at his good Fortune, gives her a Present, and in a little time is introduced to some Imaginary Title. For you must know that this cunning Purveyor has her Representatives, upon this Occasion, of some of the finest Ladies in the Kingdom. By this Means, as I am informed, it is usual enough to meet with a *German* Count in Foreign Countries, that shall make his Boasts of Favours he has received from Women of the highest Ranks, and the most unblemished Characters. Now Sir, what Safety is there for a Woman's Reputation, when a Lady may be thus prostituted as it were by Proxy, and be reputed an unchaste Woman; as the Hero in the Ninth Book of *Dryden's Virgil* is looked upon as a Coward, because the Phantom which appeared in his Likeness, ran away from *Turnus.* You may depend upon what I relate to you to be matter of Fact, and the Practice of more than one of these Female Panders. If you Print this Letter, I may give you some further Accounts of this vicious Race of Women.

Your humble Servant,

BELVIDERA.'

I shall add two other Letters on different Subjects, to fill up my Paper.

'*Mr.* SPECTATOR,

I am a Country Clergyman, and hope you will lend me your
Assistance, in ridiculing some little Indecencies which cannot
so properly be exposed from the Pulpit.

A Widow Lady, who straggled this Summer from *London*
into my Parish for the Benefit of the Air, as she says, appears
every *Sunday* at Church with many fashionable Extravagances,
to the great Astonishment of my Congregation.

But what gives us the most Offence is her Theatrical manner
of Singing the Psalms. She introduces above fifty *Italian* Airs
into the Hundredth Psalm, and whilst we begin *All People* in
the old Solemn Tune of our Fore-fathers, she in a quite different
Key runs Divisions on the Vowels, and adorns them with the
Graces of *Nicolini*; if she meets with Eke or Aye, which are
frequent in the Metre of *Hopkins* and *Sternhold*, we are certain
to hear her quavering them half a Minute after us to some
sprightly Airs of the Opera.

I am very far from being an Enemy to Church Musick; but
fear this Abuse of it may make my Parish ridiculous, who
already look on the Singing Psalms as an Entertainment, and
not part of their Devotion: besides, I am apprehensive that the
Infection may spread, for Squire *Squeekum*, who by his Voice
seems (if I may use the Expression) to be cut out for an
Italian Singer, was last *Sunday* practising the same Airs.

I know the Lady's Principles, and that she will plead the
Toleration, which (as she fancies) allows her Non-Conformity
in this Particular; but I beg you to acquaint her, that Singing
the Psalms in a different Tune from the rest of the Congregation, is a sort of Schism not tolerated by that Act.

I am, Sir, your very humble Servant,

R. S.'

'*Mr.* SPECTATOR,

In your Paper upon Temperance you prescribe to us a Rule
for Drinking, out of Sir *William Temple*, in the following
Words, *The first Glass for my self, the second for my Friends, the
third for good Humour, and the fourth for mine Enemies.* Now,
Sir, you must know that I have read this your SPECTATOR in a
Club whereof I am a Member, when our President told us
there was certainly an Error in the Print, and that the Word
Glass should be *Bottle*, and therefore has ordered me to inform
you of this Mistake, and to desire you to publish the following
Errata. In the Paper of *Saturday, October* 13, Col. 3. Line 11.
for *Glass* read *Bottle*.

L

Yours, Robin Good-Fellow.'

No. 206
[STEELE.]
                                          Friday, October 26.

Quanto quisque sibi plura negaverit,
A Diis plura feret. . . .—Hor.

THERE is a Call upon Mankind to value and esteem those who set a moderate Price upon their own Merit; and Self-denial is frequently attended with unexpected Blessings, which in the End abundantly recompence such Losses as the Modest seem to suffer in the ordinary Occurrences of Life.   The Curious tell us, a Determination in our Favour or to our Disadvantage is made upon our first Appearance, even before they know any thing of our Characters, but from the Intimations Men gather from our Aspect.   A Man, they say, wears the Picture of his Mind in his Countenance; and one Man's Eyes are Spectacles to his who looks at him to read his Heart.   But tho' that Way of raising an Opinion of those we behold in Publick is very fallacious, certain it is, that those who by their Words and Actions take as much upon themselves as they can but barely demand in the strict Scrutiny of their Deserts, will find their Accompt lessen every Day.   A modest Man preserves his Character, as a frugal Man does his Fortune; if either of them live to the Height of either, one will find Losses, the other Errours which he has not Stock by him to make up.   It were therefore a just Rule to keep your Desires, your Words and Actions, within the Regard you observe your Friends have for you; and never, if it were in a Man's Power, to take as much as he possibly might either in Preferment of Reputation.   My Walks have lately been among the mercantile Part of the World; and one gets Phrases naturally from those with whom one converses: I say then, he that in his Air, his Treatment of others, or an habitual Arrogance to himself, gives himself Credit for the least Article of more Wit, Wisdom, Goodness, or Valour than he can possibly produce if he is called upon, will find the World break in upon him, and consider him as one who has cheated them of all the Esteem they had before allowed him.   This brings a Commission of Bankruptcy upon him, and he that might have gone on to his Life's End in a prosperous Way, by aiming at more than he should, is no longer Proprietor of what he really had before, but his Pretensions fare as all things do which are torn instead of being divided.

There is no one living would deny *Cinna* the Applause of an agreeable and facetious Wit; or could possibly pretend that there is not something inimitably unforced and diverting in his Manner of delivering all his Sentiments in his Conversation, if he were able to conceal the strong Desire of Applause which he betrays in every Syllable he utters.   But they who converse with him, see that all the Civilities they could do to him, or the kind things they could say to him, would fall short of what he expects; and therefore instead of shewing him the Esteem they have for his Merit, their Reflexions turn only upon that they observe he has of it himself.

If you go among the Women, and behold *Gloriana* trip into a Room with that theatrical Ostentation of her Charms, *Mirtilla* with that soft Regularity in her Motion, *Cloe* with such an indifferent Familiarity, *Corinna* with such a fond Approach, and *Roxana* with such a Demand of Respect in the great Gravity of her Entrance; you find all the Sex who understand themselves, and act naturally, wait only for their Absence to tell you that all these Ladies would impose themselves upon you; and each of them carry in their Behaviour a Consciousness of so much more than they should pretend to, that they lose what would otherwise be given them.

I remember the last time I saw *Mackbeth*, I was wonderfully taken with the Skill of the Poet, in making the Murderer form Fears to himself from the Moderation of the Prince whose Life he was going to take away.   He says of the King, *He bore his Faculties so meekly*; and justly inferred from thence, that all divine and humane Power would join to avenge his Death, who had made such an abstinent Use of Dominion.   All that is in a Man's Power to do to advance his own Pomp and Glory, and forbears, is so much laid up against the Day of Distress; and Pity will always be his Portion in Adversity, who acted with Gentleness in Prosperity.

The great Officer who foregoes the Advantages he might take to himself, and renounces all prudential Regards to his own Person in Danger, has so far the Merit of a Volunteer; and all his Honours and Glories are unenvied, for sharing the common Fate with the same Frankness as they do who have no such endearing Circumstances to part with.   But if there were no such Considerations as the good Effect which Self-Denial has upon the Sense of other Men towards us, it is of all Qualities the most desirable for the agreeable Disposition in which it places our own Minds.   I cannot tell what better to say of it, than that it is the very Contrary of Ambition; and that Modesty allays all those Passions and Inquietudes to which that Vice exposes us.   He that is moderate in his Wishes from Reason and Choice, and not resign'd from Sowerness, Distaste, or Disappointment, doubles all the Pleasures of his Life.   The Air, the Season, a Sun-shine Day, or a Fair Prospect, are Instances of Happiness, and that which he enjoys in common with all the World (by his Exemption from the Enchantments

with which all the World are bewitched) are to him uncommon
Benefits and new Acquisitions. Health is not eaten up with
Care, nor Pleasure interrupted by Envy. It is not to him of
any Consequence what this Man is famed for, or for what the
other is preferred. He knows there is in such a Place an uninterrupted Walk; he can meet in such a Company an agreeable Conversation. He has no Emulation; he is no Man's
Rival, but every Man's Well-wisher; can look at a prosperous
Man, with a Pleasure in reflecting that he hopes he is as happy
as himself; and has his Mind and his Fortune (as far as Prudence
will allow) open to the Unhappy and to the Stranger.

Lucceius has Learning, Wit, Humour, Eloquence, but no
ambitious Prospects to pursue with these Advantages; therefore to the ordinary World he is perhaps thought to want
Spirit, but known among his Friends to have a Mind of the
most consummate Greatness. He wants no Man's Admiration,
is in no Need of Pomp. His Cloaths please him if they are
fashionable and warm, his Companions are agreeable if they
are civil and well-natured. There is with him no Occasion
for Superfluity at Meals, for Jollity in Company, in a Word, for
any thing extraordinary to administer Delight to him. Want
of Prejudice and Command of Appetite, are the Companions
which make his Journey of Life so easy, that he in all Places
meets with more Wit, more good Chear, and more Good-
Humour, than is necessary to make him enjoy himself with
Pleasure and Satisfaction.   T

No. 207.
[ADDISON.]   Saturday, October 27.

> *Omnibus in terris quae sunt a Gadibus usque*
> *Auroram & Gangem, pauci dignoscere possunt*
> *Vera bona, atque illis multum diversa, remota*
> *Erroris nebula. . . .* —Juv.

IN my last *Saturday's* Paper I laid down some Thoughts upon
Devotion in general, and shall here shew what were the Notions
of the most refined Heathens on this Subject, as they are
represented in *Plato's* Dialogue upon Prayer, Entituled Alcibiades *the Second*, which doubtless gave Occasion to *Juvenal's*
Tenth Satyr, and to the Second Satyr of *Persius*; as the last of
these Authors has almost transcribed the preceding Dialogue,
Entitled Alcibiades *the First*, in his Fourth Satyr.

The Speakers in this Dialogue upon Prayer, are *Socrates* and

Alcibiades, and the Substance of it (when drawn together out of the Intricacies and Digressions) as follows.

Socrates meeting his Pupil *Alcibiades*, as he was going to his Devotions, and observing his Eyes to be fixed upon the Earth with great Seriousness and Attention, tells him, That he had Reason to be thoughtful on that Occasion, since it was possible for a Man to bring down Evils upon himself by his own Prayers, and that those things, which the Gods send him in Answer to his Petitions, might turn to his Destruction. This, says he, may not only happen when a Man prays for what he knows is mischievous in its own Nature, as *Oedipus* implored the Gods to sow Dissention between his Sons, but when he prays for what he believes would be for his Good, and against what he believes would be to his Detriment. This the Philosopher shews must necessarily happen among us, since most Men are blinded with Ignorance, Prejudice or Passion, which hinder them from seeing such things as are really beneficial to them. For an Instance, he asks *Alcibiades* whether he would not be thoroughly pleased and satisfied if that God, to whom he was going to address himself should promise to make him the Soveraign of the whole Earth. *Alcibiades* answers, That he should doubtless look upon such a Promise as the greatest Favour that could be bestowed upon him. *Socrates* then asks him, If after having received this great Favour he would be contented to lose his Life, or if he would receive it tho' he was sure he should make an ill use of it? To both which Questions *Alcibiades* answers in the Negative. *Socrates* then shews him, from the Examples of others, how these might very probably be the Effects of such a Blessing. He then adds, that other reputed Pieces of good Fortune, as that of having a Son, or procuring the highest Post in a Government, are subject to the like fatal Consequences; which nevertheless, says he, Men ardently desire, and would not fail to pray for, if they thought their Prayers might be effectual for the obtaining of them.

Having established this great Point, That all the most apparent Blessings in this Life are obnoxious to such dreadful Consequences, and that no Man knows what in its Events would prove to him a Blessing or a Curse, he teaches *Alcibiades* after what manner he ought to pray.

In the first Place he recommends to him, as the Model of his Devotions, a short Prayer, which a *Greek* Poet composed for the use of his Friends, in the following Words. *O* Jupiter, *give us those things which are good for us, whether they are such things as we pray for, or such things as we do not pray for; and remove from us those things which are hurtful, though they are such things as we pray for.*

In the second Place, that his Disciple may ask such things as are expedient for him, he shews him that it is absolutely necessary to apply himself to the Study of true Wisdom, and to the Knowledge of that which is his chief Good, and the most suitable to the Excellency of his Nature.

In the third and last Place, he informs him that the best Methods he could make use of to draw down Blessings upon himself, and to render his Prayers acceptable, would be to live in a Constant Practice of his Duty towards the Gods, and towards Men. Under this Head he very much recommends a Form of Prayer the *Lacedemonians* made use of, in which they petition the Gods *to give them all good things, so long as they were virtuous.* Under this Head likewise he gives a very remarkable Account of an Oracle to the following Purpose.

When the *Athenians* in the War with the *Lacedemonians* received many Defeats both by Sea and Land, they sent a Message to the Oracle of *Jupiter Ammon*, to ask the Reason why they who erected so many Temples to the Gods, and adorned them with such costly Offerings; why they who had instituted so many Festivals, and accompanied them with such Pomps and Ceremonies; in short, why they who had slain so many Hecatombs at their Altars, should be less successful than the *Lacedemonians*, who fell so short of them in all these Particulars. To this, says he, the Oracle made the following Reply, *I am better pleased with the Prayer of the* Lacedemonians, *than with all the Oblations of the* Greeks. As this Prayer implied and encouraged Virtue in those who made it; the Philosopher proceeds to shew how the most vicious Man might be devout, so far as Victims could make him, but that his Offerings were regarded by the Gods as Bribes, and his Petitions as Blasphemies. He likewise quotes on this Occasion two Verses out of *Homer*, in which the Poet says, that the Scent of the *Trojan* Sacrifices was carried up to Heaven by the Winds; but that it was not acceptable to the Gods, who were displeased with *Priam* and all his People.

The Conclusion of this Dialogue is very remarkable. *Socrates* having deterred *Alcibiades* from the Prayers and Sacrifice which he was going to offer, by setting forth the above-mentioned Difficulties of performing that Duty as he ought, adds these Words, *We must therefore wait 'till such time as we may learn how we ought to behave our selves towards the Gods, and towards Men.* But when will that time come, says *Alcibiades*, and who is it that will instruct us? For I would fain see this Man, whoever he is. It is one, says *Socrates*, who takes Care of you; but as *Homer* tells us, that *Minerva* removed the Mist from *Diomedes* his Eyes, that he might plainly discover both Gods and Men, so that Darkness that hangs upon your Mind must be removed before you are able to discern what is Good and what is Evil. Let him remove from my Mind, says *Alcibiades*, the Darkness and what else he pleases, I am determined to refuse nothing he shall order me, whoever he is, so that I may become the better Man by it.   The remaining part of this Dialogue is very obscure: There is something in it that would make us think *Socrates* hinted at himself, when he spoke of this Divine Teacher who was to come into the World, did not he own that he himself was in this Respect as much at a Loss, and in as great Distress as the rest of Mankind.

Some learned Men look upon this Conclusion as a Prediction of our Saviour, or at least that *Socrates*, like the High Priest, prophesied unknowingly, and pointed at that Divine Teacher who was to come into the World some Ages after him.   However that may be, we find that this great Philosopher saw, by the Light of Reason, that it was suitable to the Goodness of the Divine Nature to send a Person into the World, who should instruct Mankind in the Duties of Religion, and in particular, teach them how to Pray.

Whoever reads this Abstract of *Plato*'s Discourse on Prayer, will, I believe, naturally make this Reflection.   That the great Founder of our Religion, as well by his own Example, as in the Form of Prayer which he taught his Disciples, did not only keep up to those Rules which the Light of Nature had suggested to this great Philosopher, but instructed his Disciples in the whole Extent of this Duty, as well as of all others.   He directed them to the proper Object of Adoration, and taught them, according to the third Rule above-mentioned, to apply themselves to him in their Closets, without Show or Ostentation, and to worship him in Spirit and in Truth.   As the *Lacedemonians* in their Form of Prayer implored the Gods in general to give them all good Things so long as they were Virtuous, we ask in particular *that our Offences may be forgiven, as we forgive those of others.*   If we look into the second Rule which *Socrates* has prescribed, namely, That we should apply our selves to the Knowledge of such Things as are best for us, this too is explained at large in the Doctrines of the Gospel, where we are taught in several Instances to regard those things as Curses, which appear as Blessings in the Eye of the World; and on the contrary to esteem those things as Blessings, which to the Generality of Mankind appear as Curses.   Thus in the Form which is prescribed to us, we only pray for that Happiness which is our chief Good, and the great End of our Existence, when we Petition the Supreme Being for the *coming of his Kingdom,* being sollicitous for no other Temporal Blessings but our *daily Sustenance*. On the other side, we pray against nothing but Sin, and against *Evil* in general, leaving it with Omniscience to determine what is really such. If we look into the first of *Socrates* his Rules of Prayer, in which he recommends the above-mentioned Form of the Ancient Poet, we find that Form not only comprehended, but very much improved in the Petition, wherein we Pray to the Supreme Being that *his Will may be done*: Which is of the same force with that Form which our Saviour used, when he prayed against the most painful and most ignominious of Deaths, *Nevertheless not my Will, but thine be done.* This comprehensive Petition is the most humble, as well as the most prudent that can be offered up from the Creature to his Creator, as it supposes the Supreme Being wills nothing but what is for our Good, and that he knows better than our selves what is so.

No. 208.
[STEELE.]   Monday, October 29.

. . . *Veniunt spectentur ut ipsae.*—Ov.

I HAVE several Letters from People of good Sense, who lament the Depravity or Poverty of Taste the Town is fallen into with relation to Plays and publick Spectacles. A Lady in particular observes, that there is such a Levity in the Minds of her own Sex, that they seldom attend any thing but Impertinences. It is indeed prodigious to observe how little Notice is taken of the most exalted Parts of the best Tragedies in *Shakespear*; nay it is not only visible that Sensuality has devoured all Greatness of Soul, but the under Passion (as I may so call it) of a noble Spirit, Pity, seems to be a Stranger to the Generality of an Audience. The Minds of Men are indeed very differently disposed; and the Reliefs from Care and Attention are of one Sort in a great Spirit, and of another in an ordinary one. The Man of a great Heart and a serious Complexion, is more pleased with Instances of Generosity and Pity, than the light and ludicrous Spirit can possibly be with the highest Strains of Mirth and Laughter: It is therefore a melancholy Prospect, when we see a numerous Assembly lost to all serious Entertainments, and such Incidents as should move one sort of Concern, excite in them a quite contrary one. In the Tragedy of *Mackbeth* the other Night, when the Lady who is conscious of the Crime of murdering the King seems utterly astonished at the News, and makes an Exclamation at it; instead of the Indignation which is natural to the Occasion, that Expression is received with a loud Laugh: They were as merry when a Criminal was stabbed. It is certainly an Occasion of Rejoycing when the Wicked are seized in their Designs; but, I think, it is not such a Triumph as is exerted by Laughter.

You may generally observe, that the Appetites are sooner moved than the Passions: A sly Expression which alludes to Bawdry, puts a whole Row into a pleasing Smirk; when a good Sentence that describes an inward Sentiment of the Soul, is received with the greatest Coldness and Indifference. A Correspondent of mine, upon this Subject, has divided the Female Part of the Audience, and accounts for their Prepossession against this reasonable Delight in the following Manner. The Prude, says he, as she acts always in Contradiction, so she is gravely sullen at a Comedy, and extravagantly gay at a Tragedy. The Coquet is so much taken up with throwing her Eyes around the Audience, and considering the Effect of them, that she cannot be expected to observe the Actors but as they are her Rivals, and take off the Observation of the Men from herself. Besides these Species of Women, there are the *Examples*, or the first of the Mode: These are to be supposed too well acquainted with what the Actor is going to say to be moved at it. After these one might mention a certain flippant Set of Females, who are Mimicks, and are wonderfully diverted with the Conduct of all the People around them, and are Spectators only of the Audience. But what is of all the most to be lamented, is, the Loss of a Party whom it would be worth preserving in their right Senses upon all Occasions, and these are those whom we may indifferently call the Innocent or the Unaffected. You may sometimes see one of these sensibly touched with a well wrought Incident; but then she is immediately so impertinently observed by the Men, and frowned at by some insensible Superiour of her own Sex, that she is ashamed, and loses the Enjoyment of the most laudable Concern, Pity. Thus the whole Audience is afraid of letting fall a Tear, and shun as a Weakness the best and worthiest Part of our Sense.

'*Sir*,

As you are one that doth not only pretend to reform, but effects it amongst People of any Sense; makes me (who am one of the greatest of your Admirers) give you this Trouble, to desire you will settle the Method of us Females knowing when one another is in Town: For they have now got a Trick of never sending to their Acquaintance when they first come; and if one does not visit them within the Week which they stay at home, it is a mortal Quarrel. Now, dear Mr. SPEC. either command them to put it in the Advertisement of your Paper, which is generally read by our Sex, or else order them to breathe their saucy Footmen, (who are good for nothing else) by sending them to tell all their Acquaintance.   If you think to print this, pray put it into a better Stile as to the spelling Part.   The Town is now filling every Day, and it cannot be deferred, because People take Advantage of one another by this Means, and break off Acquaintance, and are rude: Therefore pray put this in your Paper as soon as you can possibly, to prevent any future Miscarriages of this Nature.   I am, as I ever shall be,

Dear SPEC.

Pray settle what is to be a proper Notification of a Person's being in Town, and how that differs according to People's Quality.

Your most obedient,
Humble Servant,
Mary Meanwell.'

'*Mr.* SPECTATOR,   October *the* 20*th*.

I have been out of Town, so did not meet with your Paper dated *September* the 28th, wherein you to my Heart's Desire expose that cursed Vice of insnaring poor young Girls, and drawing them from their Friends.   I assure you without Flattery it has saved a Prentice of mine from Ruin; and in Token of Gratitude, as well as for the Benefit of my Family, I have put it in a Frame and Glass, and hung it behind my Counter.   I shall take Care to make my young ones read it every Morning, to fortify them against such pernicious Rascals. I know not whether what you writ was Matter of Fact, or your own Invention; but this I will take my Oath on, the first Part is so exactly like what happened to my Prentice, that had I read your Paper then, I should have taken your method to have secured a Villain.   Go on and Prosper.

Your most obliged humble Servant.'

'*Mr.* SPECTATOR,

Without Raillery I desire you to insert this Word for Word in your next, as you value a Lover's Prayers.   You see it is an Hue and Cry after a stray Heart (with the Marks and Blemishes underwritten) which whoever shall bring to you shall receive Satisfaction.   Let me beg of you not to fail, as you remember the Passion you had for her to whom you lately ended a Paper.

Noble, Generous, Great, and Good,
But never to be understood;
Fickle as the Wind, still changing,
After every Female ranging;

> *Panting, trembling, sighing, dying,*
> *But addicted much to lying:*
> *When the Siren Songs repeats,*
> *Equal Measures still it beats;*
> *Whoe'er shall wear it, it will smart her,*
> *And whoe'er takes it, takes a Tartar.*

T

No. 209.
[ADDISON.]   Tuesday, October 30.

Γυναικὸς οὐδὲ χρῆμ' ἀνὴρ ληίζεται
Ἐσθλῆς ἄμεινον, οὐδὲ ῥίγιον κακῆς.—Simonides.

THERE are no Authors I am more pleased with than those who shew Human Nature in a variety of Views, and describe the several Ages of the World in their different Manners. A Reader cannot be more rationally entertained, than by comparing the Virtues and Vices of his own Times, with those which prevailed in the times of his Forefathers; and drawing a Parallel in his Mind between his own private Character, and that of other Persons, whether of his own Age, or of the Ages that went before him. The Contemplation of Mankind under these changeable Colours is apt to shame us out of any particular Vice, or animate us to any particular Virtue, to make us pleased or displeased with our selves in the most proper Points, to clear our Minds of Prejudice and Prepossession, and rectifie that Narrowness of Temper which inclines us to think amiss of those who differ from our selves.

If we look into the Manners of the most remote Ages of the World, we discover Human Nature in her Simplicity; and the more we come downward towards our own Times, may observe her hiding herself in Artifices and Refinements, Polished insensibly out of her Original Plainness, and at length entirely lost under Form and Ceremony, and (what we call) Good-breeding. Read the Accounts of Men and Women as they are given us by the most Ancient Writers, both Sacred and Prophane, and you would think you were reading the History of another Species.

Among the Writers of Antiquity, there are none who instruct us more openly in the Manners of their respective Times in which they lived, than those who have employed themselves in Satyr, under what Dress soever it may appear; as there are no other Authors, whose Province it is to enter so directly into the ways of Men, and set their Miscarriages in so strong a Light.

Simonides, a Poet famous in his Generation, is I think Author of the oldest Satyr that is now extant; and, as some say, of the first that was ever written. This Poet flourished about four hundred Years after the Siege of *Troy*, and shews by his way of Writing, the Simplicity or rather Coarseness of the Age in which he lived. I have taken notice, in my Hundred and sixty first Speculation, that the Rule of observing what the *French* call the *bienséance*, in an Allusion, has been found out of latter Years; and that the Ancients, provided there was a Likeness in their Similitudes, did not much trouble themselves about the Decency of the Comparison. The Satyr or Iambicks of *Simonides*, with which I shall entertain my Readers in the present Paper, are a remarkable Instance of what I formerly advanced. The Subject of this Satyr is Woman. He describes the Sex in their several Characters, which he derives to them from a fanciful Supposition raised upon the Doctrine of Prae-existence. He tells us, that the Gods formed the Souls of Women out of those Seeds and Principles which compose several kinds of Animals and Elements, and that their Good or Bad Dispositions arise in them according as such and such Seeds and Principles predominate in their Constitutions. I have translated the Author very faithfully, and if not Word for Word (which our Language would not bear), at least so as to comprehend every one of his Sentiments, without adding any thing of my own. I have already apologized for this Author's want of Delicacy, and must further premise, that the following Satyr affects only some of the lower part of the Sex, and not those who have been refined by a Polite Education, which was not so common in the Age of this Poet.

In the Beginning God made the Souls of Womankind out of different Materials, and in separate State from their Bodies.

The Souls of one kind of Women were formed out of those Ingredients which compose a Swine. A Woman of this Make is a Slut in her House, and a Glutton at her Table. She is uncleanly in her Person, a Slattern in her Dress; and her Family is no better than a Dunghill.

A Second sort of Female Soul was formed out of the same Materials that enter into the Composition of a Fox. Such an one is what we call a notable discerning Woman, who has an Insight into every thing, whether it be good or bad. In this Species of Females there are some Virtuous and some Vicious.

A Third Kind of Women were made up of Canine Particles. These are what we commonly call Scolds, *who imitate the Animals out of which they were taken, that are always busy and barking, that snarl at every one who comes in their way, and live in perpetual Clamour.*

The Fourth Kind of Women were made out of the Earth. These are your Sluggards, who pass away their Time in Indolence and Ignorance, hover over the Fire a whole Winter, and apply themselves with Alacrity to no kind of Business but Eating.

The Fifth Species of Females were made out of the Sea. These are Women of variable uneven Tempers, sometimes all Storm and Tempests, sometimes all Calm and Sunshine. The Stranger who sees one of these in her Smiles and Smoothness would cry her up for a Miracle of good Humour; but on a sudden her Looks and her Words are changed, she is nothing but Fury and Outrage, Noise and Hurricane.

The Sixth Species were made up of the Ingredients which compose an Ass, or a Beast of Burden. These are naturally exceeding Slothful, but upon the Husband's exerting his Authority will live upon hard Fare, and do every thing to please him. They are however far from being averse to Venereal Pleasure, and seldom refuse a Male Companion.

The Cat furnished Materials for a seventh Species of Women, who are of a melancholy, froward, unamiable Nature, and so repugnant to the Offers of Love, that they fly in the Face of their Husband when he approaches them with Conjugal Endearments. This Species of Women are likewise subject to little Thefts, Cheats and Pilferings.

The Mare with a flowing Mane, which was never broke to any Servile Toil and Labour, composed an Eighth Species of Women. These are they who have little regard for their Husbands, who pass away their Time in Dressing, Bathing and Perfuming; who throw their Hair into the nicest Curls, and trick it up with the fairest Flowers and Garlands. A Woman of this Species is a very pretty thing for a Stranger to look upon, but very detrimental to the Owner, unless it be a King or Prince, who takes a Fancy to such a Toy.

The Ninth Species of Females were taken out of the Ape. These are such as are both ugly and ill-natured, who have nothing beautiful in themselves, and endeavour to detract from or ridicule every thing which appears so in others.

The Tenth and Last Species of Women were made out of the Bee, and happy is the Man who gets such an one for his Wife. She is altogether faultless and unblameable. Her family flourishes and improves by her good Management. She loves her Husband, and is beloved by him. She brings him a Race of beautiful and virtuous Children. She distinguishes her self among her Sex. She is surrounded with Graces. She never sits among the loose Tribe of Women, nor passes away her Time with them in wanton Discourses. She is full of Virtue and Prudence, and is the best Wife Jupiter *can bestow on Man.*

I shall conclude these Iambicks with the Motto of this Paper, which is a Fragment of the same Author. *A Man cannot possess any thing that is better than a good Woman, nor any thing that is worse than a bad one.*

As the Poet has shewn a great Penetration in this Diversity of Female Characters, he has avoided the Fault which *Juvenal* and Monsieur *Boileau* are guilty of, the former in his Sixth, and the other in his last Satyr, where they have endeavoured to expose the Sex in general, without doing Justice to the valuable Part of it.   Such levelling Satyrs are of no use to the World, and for this reason I have often wondered how the *French* Author above mentioned, who was a Man of exquisite Judgment, and a Lover of Virtue, could think Human Nature a proper Subject for Satyr in another of his celebrated Pieces, which is called *The Satyr upon Man*.   What Vice or Frailty can a Discourse correct, which censures the whole Species alike, and endeavours to shew by some Superficial Strokes of Wit, that Brutes are the most excellent Creatures of the two?   A Satyr should expose nothing but what is corrigible, and make a due Discrimination between those who are, and those who are not the proper Objects of it.   L

No. 210.

[HUGHES.]   Wednesday, October 31.

Nescio quomodo inhaeret in mentibus quasi seculorum quoddam augurium futurorum; idque in maximis ingeniis altissimisque animis & existit maxime & apparet facillime.

                                            Cic. *Tusc. Quaest.*

'To the SPECTATOR.

   Sir,

I AM fully perswaded that one of the best Springs of generous and worthy Actions, is the having generous and worthy Thoughts of our selves.   Whoever has a mean Opinion of the Dignity of his Nature, will act in no higher a Rank than he has allotted himself in his own Estimation: If he considers his Being as circumscribed by the uncertain Term of a few Years, his Designs will be contracted into the same narrow Span he imagines is to bound to his Existence.   How can he exalt his Thoughts to any thing great and noble, who only believes that, after a short Turn to the Stage of this World, he is to sink into Oblivion, and to lose his Consciousness for ever?

   For this Reason I am of Opinion, that so useful and elevated a Contemplation as that of the *Soul's Immortality* cannot be resum'd too often.   There is not a more improving Exercise to the human Mind, than to be frequently reviewing its own great Privileges and Endowments; nor a more effectual Means to awaken in us an Ambition rais'd above low Objects and little Pursuits, than to value our selves as Heirs of Eternity.

It is a very great Satisfaction to consider the best and wisest of Mankind in all Nations and Ages asserting, as with one Voice, this their Birthright, and to find it ratify'd by an express Revelation. At the same time, if we turn our Thoughts inward upon our selves, we may meet with a kind of secret Sense concurring with the Proofs of our own Immortality.

You have in my Opinion rais'd a good presumptive Argument from the encreasing Appetite the Mind has to Knowledge, and to the extending its own Faculties, which cannot be accomplish'd, as the more restrain'd Perfection of lower Creatures may, in the Limits of a short Life. I think another probable Conjecture may be rais'd from our Appetite to Duration it self, and from a Reflection on our Progress through the several Stages of it: *We are complaining,* as you observe in a former Speculation, *of the Shortness of Life, and yet are perpetually hurrying over the Parts of it, to arrive at certain little Settlements or imaginary Points of Rest which are dispersed up and down in it.*

Now let us consider what happens to us when we arrive at these *imaginary Points of Rest.* Do we stop our Motion, and sit down satisfy'd in the Settlement we have gain'd? or are we not removing the Boundary, and marking out new Points of Rest, to which we press forward with the like Eagerness, and which cease to be such as fast as we attain them? Our Case is like that of a Traveller upon the *Alps,* who should fancy that the Top of the next Hill must end his Journey because it terminates his Prospect; but he no sooner arrives at it than he sees new Ground and other Hills beyond it, and continues to travel on as before.

This is so plainly every Man's Condition in Life, that there is no one who has observ'd any thing but may observe, that as fast as his Time wears away, his Appetite to something future remains. The Use therefore I would make of it is this, that since Nature (as some love to express it) does nothing in vain, or, to speak properly, since the Author of our Being has planted no wandering Passion in it, no Desire which has not its Object, Futurity is the proper Object of the Passion so constantly exercis'd about it; and this Restlessness in the present, this assigning our selves over to farther Stages of Duration, this successive grasping at somewhat still to come, appears to me (whatever it may to others) as a kind of Instinct or natural Symptom which the Mind of Man has of its own Immortality.

I take it at the same time for granted, that the Immortality of the Soul is sufficiently established by other Arguments; and if so, this Appetite, which otherwise would be very unaccountable and absurd, seems very reasonable, and adds Strength to the Conclusion. But I am amazed when I consider there are Creatures capable of Thought, who, in spight of every Argument, can form to themselves a sullen Satisfaction in thinking otherwise. There is something so pitifully mean in the inverted Ambition of that Man who can hope for Annihilation, and please himself to think that his whole Fabrick shall one Day crumble into Dust, and mix with the Mass of inanimate Beings, that it equally deserves our Admiration and Pity. The Mystery of such Men's Unbelief is not hard to be penetrated; and indeed amounts to nothing more than a sordid Hope, that they shall not be immortal because they dare not be so.

This brings me back to my first Observation, and gives me Occasion to say further, that as worthy Actions spring from worthy Thoughts, so worthy Thoughts are likewise the Consequence of worthy Actions: But the Wretch who has degraded himself below the Character of Immortality, is very willing to resign his Pretensions to it, and to substitute in its Room a dark negative Happiness in the Extinction of his Being.

The admirable *Shakespear* has given us a strong Image of the unsupported Condition of such a Person in his last Minutes, in the second Part of King *Henry* the Sixth, where Cardinal *Beaufort*, who had been concern'd in the Murder of the good Duke *Humphrey*, is represented on his Death-Bed. After some short confus'd Speeches which shew an Imagination disturbed with Guilt, just as he is expiring, King *Henry* standing by him full of Compassion, says,

> *Lord Cardinal! if thou think'st on Heaven's Bliss*
> *Hold up thy Hand, make Signal of that Hope!*
> *He dies, and makes no Sign!* . . .

The Despair which is here shewn, without a Word or Action on the Part of the dying Person, is beyond what cou'd be painted by the most forcible Expressions whatever.

I shall not pursue this Thought further, but only add, that as Annihilation is not to be had with a Wish, so it is the most abject thing in the World to wish it. What are Honour, Fame, Wealth, or Power, when compared with the generous Expectation of a Being without End, and a Happiness adequate to that Being?

I shall trouble you no further; but, with a certain Gravity which these Thoughts have given me, I reflect upon some things People say of you (as they will of Men who distinguish

themselves), which I hope are not true; and wish you as good a
Man as you are an Author.

I am, Sir,
Your most obedient humble Servant,

Z   T. D.'

No. 211.

[ADDISON.]   Thursday, November 1.

Fictis jocari nos meminerit fabulis.—Phaed.

HAVING lately translated the Fragment of an old Poet, which
describes Womankind under several Characters, and supposes
them to have drawn their different Manners and Dispositions
from those Animals and Elements out of which he tells us they
were compounded; I had some Thoughts of giving the Sex their
Revenge, by laying together in another Paper the many vicious
Characters which prevail in the Male World, and shewing the
different Ingredients that go to the making up of such different
Humours and Constitutions. *Horace* has a Thought which is
something a-kin to this, when, in order to excuse himself to his
Mistress, for an Invective which he had written against her, and
to account for that unreasonable Fury with which the Heart of
Man is often transported, he tells us, that when *Prometheus*
made his Man of Clay, in the kneading up of the Heart he
seasoned it with some furious Particles of the Lion. But upon
turning this Plan to and fro in my Thoughts, I observed so
many unaccountable Humours in Man, that I did not know out
of what Animals to fetch them. Male Souls are diversifyed
with so many Characters that the World has not Variety
of Materials sufficient to furnish out their different Tempers
and Inclinations. The Creation, with all its Animals and
Elements, would not be large enough to supply their several
Extravagances.

Instead therefore of pursuing the Thought of *Simonides*, I
shall observe that as he has exposed the vicious Part of Women
from the Doctrine of Prae-existence, some of the ancient
Philosophers have, in a manner, satyrized the vicious Part of
the Human Species in general, from a Notion of the Soul's
Post-existence, if I may so call it; and that as *Simonides*
describes Brutes entering into the Composition of Women,
others have represented human Souls as entering into Brutes.
This is commonly termed the Doctrine of Transmigration,
which supposes that human Souls, upon their leaving the Body,
become the Souls of such Kinds of Brutes as they most resemble

in their Manners; or to give an Account of it, as Mr. *Dryden* has described it in his Translation of *Pythagoras* his Speech in the Fifteenth Book of *Ovid*, where that Philosopher dissuades his Hearers from eating Flesh:

> *Thus all things are but alter'd, nothing dies,*
> *And here and there th' unbody'd Spirit flies:*
> *By Time, or Force, or Sickness dispossess'd,*
> *And lodges where it lights in Bird or Beast,*
> *Or hunts without till ready Limbs it find,*
> *And actuates those according to their Kind:*
> *From Tenement to Tenement is toss'd,*
> *The Soul is still the same; the Figure only lost.*

> *Then let not Piety be put to flight,*
> *To please the Taste of Glutton-Appetite;*
> *But suffer Inmate Souls secure to dwell,*
> *Lest from their Seats your Parents you expel;*
> *With rabid Hunger feed upon your Kind,*
> *Or from a Beast dislodge a Brother's Mind.*

Plato in the Vision of *Erus* the *Armenian*, which I may possibly make the Subject of a future Speculation, records some beautiful Transmigrations; as that the Soul of *Orpheus* who was musical, melancholy, and a Woman-hater, entered into a Swan; the Soul of *Ajax*, which was all Wrath and Fierceness, into a Lion; the Soul of *Agamemnon*, that was Rapacious and Imperial, into an Eagle; and the Soul of *Thersites*, who was a Mimick and a Buffoon, into a Monkey.

Mr. *Congreve*, in a Prologue to one of his Comedies, has touched upon this Doctrine with great Humour.

> *Thus* Aristotle's *Soul, of old that was,*
> *May now be damn'd to animate an Ass;*
> *Or in this very House, for ought we know,*
> *Is doing painful Penance in some Beau.*

I shall fill up this Paper with some Letters, which my last *Tuesday*'s Speculation has produced. My following Correspondents will shew, what I there observed, that the Speculation of that Day affects only the lower part of the Sex.

'*From my House in the* Strand, *Octob.* 30, 1711.

Mr. SPECTATOR,

Upon Reading your *Tuesday*'s Paper, I find by several Symptoms in my Constitution, that I am a Bee. My Shop, or if you please to call it so, my Cell, is in that great Hive of Females which goes by the Name of the *New-Exchange*, where I am daily employed in gathering together a little Stock of

Gain from the finest Flowers about the Town, I mean the Ladies and the Beaus. I have a numerous Swarm of Children, to whom I give the best Education I am able: But, Sir, it is my Misfortune to be married to a Drone who lives upon what I get, without bringing any thing into the Common Stock. Now, Sir, as on the one Hand I take care not to behave my self towards him like a Wasp, so likewise I would not have him look upon me as an Humble-Bee; for which Reason I do all I can to put him upon laying up Provisions for a Bad Day, and frequently represent to him the fatal Effects his Sloth and Negligence may bring upon us in our old Age. I must beg that you will join with me in your good Advice upon this Occasion, and you will for ever oblige

Your humble Servant,

MELISSA.'

'*Sir,*   *Picadilly, October* 31, 1711.

I am joined in Wedlock for my Sins to one of those Fillies who are described in the old Poet with that hard Name you gave us the other Day. She has a flowing Mane, and a Skin as soft as Silk: But, Sir, she passes half her Life at her Glass, and almost ruins me in Ribbons. For my own part I am a plain Handicraft Man, and in danger of Breaking by her Laziness and Expensiveness. Pray Master, tell me in your next Paper, whether I may not expect of her so much Drudgery as to take care of her Family, and Curry her Hide in case of Refusal.

Your loving Friend,

Barnaby Brittle.'

'*Mr.* Spectator,   *Cheapside, October* 30.

I am mightily pleased with the Humour of the Cat, be so kind as to enlarge upon that Subject.

Yours till Death,

Josiah Henpeck.

P. S. You must know I am Married to a *Grimalkin.*'

'*Sir,*   *Wapping, October* 31, 1711.

Ever since your *Spectator* of *Tuesday* last came into our Family, my Husband is pleased to call me his *Oceana,* because the foolish old Poet that you have Translated says, That the Souls of some Women are made of Sea Water. This, it seems, has encouraged my Sauce-Box to be Witty upon me. When I am Angry, he cries Prithee my Dear *be Calm*; when I chide one of my Servants, Prithee Child *do not bluster.* He had the Impudence about an Hour ago to tell me, That he was a Seafaring Man, and must expect to divide his Life between *Storm* and *Sunshine*. When I bestir my self with any Spirit in my Family, it is *high Sea* in his House; and when I sit still without doing any thing, his Affairs forsooth are *Wind-bound*. When I ask him whether it Rains, he makes Answer, It is no matter, so that it be *fair Weather* within Doors. In short, Sir, I cannot speak my Mind freely to him, but I either *swell* or *rage*, or do something that is not fit for a Civil Woman to hear. Pray, Mr. SPECTATOR, since you are so sharp upon other Women, let us know what Materials your Wife is made of, if you have one. I suppose you would make us a Parcel of poor-spirited tame insipid Creatures. But, Sir, I would have you to know, we have as good Passions in us as your self, and that a Woman was never designed to be a Milk-Sop.

L *Martha Tempest.*'

No. 212.

[STEELE.] Friday, November 2.

. . . *Eripe turpi*
Colla jugo, liber, liber sum, dic age. . . .—Hor.

'*Mr.* SPECTATOR,

I NEVER look upon my dear Wife, but I think of the Happiness Sir ROGER DE COVERLEY enjoys, in having such a Friend as you to expose in proper Colours the Cruelty and Perverseness of his Mistress. I have very often wished you visited in our Family, and were acquainted with my Spouse; she would afford you for some Months at least Matter enough for one *Spectator* a Week. Since we are not so happy as to be of your Acquaintance, give me Leave to represent to you our present Circumstances as well as I can in Writing, You are to know then that I am not of a very different Constitution from *Nathaniel Henroost*, whom you have lately recorded in your Speculations; and have a Wife who makes a more tyrannical Use of the Knowledge of my easie Temper, than that Lady ever pretended to. We had not been a Month married when she found in me a certain Pain to give Offence, and an Indolence that made me bear little Inconveniences rather than dispute about them. From this Observation it soon came to that Pass, that if I offered to go abroad, she would get between me and the Door, kiss me, and say she could not part with me; then down again I sat. In a Day or two after this first pleasant Step towards confining me, she declared to me, that I was all the World to her, and she thought she ought to be all the World to me. If,

*E 165

said she, my Dear loves me as much as I love him, he will never be tired of my Company. This Declaration was followed by my being denied to all my Acquaintance; and it very soon came to that Pass, that to give an Answer at the Door before my Face, the Servants would ask her whether I was within or not; and she would answer No with great Fondness, and tell me I was a good Dear. I will not enumerate more little Circumstances to give you a livelier Sense of my Condition, but tell you in general, that from such Steps as these at first, I now live the Life of a Prisoner of State; my Letters are opened, and I have not the Use of Pen, Ink, and Paper but in her Presence. I never go abroad except she sometimes takes me with her in her Coach to take the Air, if it may be called so, when we drive, as we generally do, with the Glasses up. I have overheard my Servants lament my Condition; but they dare not bring me Messages without her Knowledge, because they doubt my Resolution to stand by 'em. In the Midst of this insipid Way of Life, an old Acquaintance of mine, *Tom Meggot*, who is a Favourite with her, and allowed to visit me in her Company because he sings prettily, has roused me to rebell, and conveyed his Intelligence to me in the following Manner. My Wife is a great Pretender to Musick, and very ignorant of it; but far gone in the *Italian* Taste. *Tom* goes to *Armstrong*, the famous fine Writer of Musick, and desires him to put this Sentence of *Tully* in the *Scale* of an *Italian* Air, and write it out for my Spouse from him. *An ille mihi liber cui mulier imperat? Cui leges imponit, praescribit, jubet, vetat quod videtur? Qui nihil imperanti negare potest, nihil recusare audet? Poscit? dandum est. Vocat? veniendum. Ejicit? abeundum. Minitatur? extimescendum. Does he live like a Gentleman who is commanded by a Woman? He to whom she gives Law, grants and denies what she pleases? who can neither deny her any thing she asks, or refuse to do any thing she commands?*

To be short, my Wife was extremely pleased with it; said the *Italian* was the only Language for Musick; and admired how wonderfully tender the Sentiment was, and how pretty the Accent is of that Language; with the rest that is said by Rote on that Occasion. Mr. *Meggot* is sent for to sing this Air, which he performs with mighty Applause; and my Wife is in Exstasy on the Occasion, and glad to find, by my being so much pleased, that I was at last come into the Notion of the *Italian*; for, said she, it grows upon one when one once comes to know a little of the Language; and pray, Mr. *Meggot*, sing again those Notes, *Nihil imperanti negare, nihil recusare.* You may believe I was not a little delighted with my Friend *Tom's* Expedient to alarm me, and in Obedience to his Summons I give all this Story thus at large; and I am resolved, when this appears in the *Spectator*, to declare for my self. The Manner of the Insurrection I contrive by your Means, which shall be no other than that *Tom Meggot*, who is at our Tea-Table every Morning, shall read it to us; and if my Dear can take the Hint, and say not one Word, but let this be the Beginning of a new Life without further Explanation, it is very well; for as soon as the *Spectator* is read out, I shall, without more ado, call for the Coach, name the Hour when I shall be at home, if I come at all, if I do not they may go to Dinner. If my Spouse only swells and says nothing, *Tom* and I go out together, and all is well, as I said before; but if she begins to command or expostulate, you shall in my next to you receive a full Account of her Resistance and Submission; for submit the dear thing must to,

> *Sir,*
>
> *Your most obedient humble Servant,*
>
> Anthony Freeman.

P. S. I hope I need not tell you that I desire this may be in your very next.'   T

No. 213.

[ADDISON.]   Saturday, November 3.

. . . *Mens sibi conscia recti.*—Virg.

It is the great Art and Secret of Christianity, if I may use that Phrase, to manage our Actions to the best Advantage, and direct them in such a manner, that every thing we do may turn to Account at that great Day, when every thing we have done will be set before us.

In order to give this Consideration its full weight, we may cast all our Actions under the Division of such as are in themselves either Good, Evil or Indifferent. If we divide our Intentions after the same manner, and consider them with regard to our Actions, we may discover that great Art and Secret of Religion which I have here mentioned.

A Good Intention joined to a Good Action, gives it its proper Force and Efficacy; joined to an Evil Action, extenuates its Malignity, and in some cases may take it wholly away; and joined to an Indifferent Action, turns it to a Virtue, and makes it meritorious, as far as Human Actions can be so.

In the next Place, to consider in the same manner the Influence of an Evil Intention upon our Actions. An Evil Intention perverts the best of Actions, and makes them in reality what the Fathers with a witty kind of Zeal have termed the Virtues of the Heathen World, so many *shining Sins*. It destroys the Innocence of an Indifferent Action, and gives an Evil Action all possible Blackness and Horror, or in the emphatical Language of Sacred Writ makes Sin *exceeding Sinful*.

If, in the last Place, we consider the Nature of an Indifferent Intention, we shall find that it destroys the Merit of a Good Action; abates, but never takes away, the Malignity of an Evil Action; and leaves an Indifferent Action in its natural state of Indifference.

It is therefore of unspeakable Advantage to possess our Minds with an habitual Good Intention, and to aim all our Thoughts, Words and Actions at some laudable End, whether it be the Glory of our Maker, the Good of Mankind, or the Benefit of our own Souls.

This is a sort of Thrift or Good Husbandry in Moral Life, which does not throw away any single Action, but makes every one go as far as it can. It multiplies the Means of Salvation, encreases the number of our Virtues, and diminishes that of our Vices.

There is something very Devout, tho' not so solid, in *Acosta*'s Answer to *Limborck*, who Objects to him the Multiplicity of Ceremonies in the Jewish Religion, as Washings, Dresses, Meats, Purgations, and the like. The reply which the Jew makes upon this Occasion, is, to the best of my Remembrance, as follows: 'There are not Duties enough (says he) in the essential Parts of the Law for a zealous and active Obedience. Time, Place and Person are requisite, before you have an Opportunity of putting a Moral Virtue into Practice. We have therefore, says he, enlarged the Sphere of our Duty, and made many things which are in themselves Indifferent a Part of our Religion, that we may have more Occasions of shewing our Love to God, and in all the Circumstances of Life be doing something to please him.'

Monsieur *St. Evremont* has endeavoured to palliate the Superstitions of the Roman Catholick Religion with the same kind of Apology, where he pretends to consider the different Spirit of the Papists and the Calvinists, as to the great Points wherein they disagree. He tells us, that the former are actuated by Love, and the other by Fear; and that in their Expressions of Duty and Devotion towards the Supreme Being, the former seem particularly careful to do every thing which may possibly please him, and the other to abstain from every thing which may possibly displease him.

But notwithstanding this plausible Reason with which both the Jew and the Roman Catholick would excuse their respective Superstitions, it is certain there is something in them very pernicious to Mankind, and destructive to Religion. Because, the Injunction of superfluous Ceremonies make such Actions Duties, as were before Indifferent, and by that means renders Religion more burdensome and difficult than it is in its own Nature, betrays many into Sins of Omission which they could not otherwise be guilty of, and fixes the Minds of the Vulgar to the shadowy unessential Points, instead of the more weighty and more important Matters of the Law.

This zealous and active Obedience however takes Place in the great Point we are recommending: for if, instead of prescribing to our selves indifferent Actions as Duties, we apply a good Intention to all our most indifferent Actions, we make our very Existence one continued Act of Obedience, we turn our Diversions and Amusements to our Eternal Advantage, and are pleasing him (whom we are made to please) in all the Circumstances and Occurrences of Life.

It is this Excellent Frame of Mind, this *holy Officiousness* (if I may be allowed to call it such) which is recommended to us by the Apostle in that uncommon Precept, wherein he directs us to propose to our selves the Glory of our Creator in all our most indifferent Actions, *whether we eat or drink, or whatsoever we do.*

A Person therefore, who is possessed with such an habitual good Intention as that which I have been here speaking of, enters upon no single Circumstance of Life, without considering it as well-pleasing to the great Author of his Being, conformable to the Dictates of Reason, suitable to human Nature in general, or to that particular Station in which Providence has placed him. He lives in a perpetual Sense of the Divine Presence, regards himself as acting, in the whole Course of his Existence, under the Observation and Inspection of that Being, who is privy to all his Motions and all his Thoughts, who knows his *down-sitting and his up-rising, who is about his Path, and about his Bed, and spieth out all his Ways.* In a Word, he remembers that the Eye of his Judge is always upon him, and in every Action he reflects that he is doing what is commanded or allowed by Him who will hereafter either reward or punish it. This was the Character of those Holy Men of old, who in that beautiful Phrase of Scripture are said to have *walked with God.*

When I employ my self upon a Paper of Morality, I generally consider how I may recommend the particular Virtue, which I treat of, by the Precepts or Examples of the ancient Heathens; by that means, if possible, to shame those who have greater Advantages of knowing their Duty, and therefore greater Obligations to perform it, into a better Course of Life: Besides, that many among us are unreasonably disposed to give a fairer hearing to a Pagan Philosopher, than to a Christian Writer.

I shall therefore produce an Instance of this excellent Frame of Mind in a Speech of *Socrates*, which is quoted by *Erasmus*. This great Philosopher on the Day of his Execution, a little before the Draught of Poison was brought to him, entertaining his Friends with a Discourse on the Immortality of the Soul, has these Words. *Whether or no God will approve of my Actions I know not, but this I am sure of, that I have at all times made it my Endeavour to please him; and I have a good Hope that this my Endeavour will be accepted by him.* We find in these Words of that great Man the habitual good Intention which I would here inculcate, and with which that Divine Philosopher always acted. I shall only add that *Erasmus*, who was an unbigotted Roman Catholick, was so much transported with this Passage of *Socrates*, that he could scarce forbear looking upon him as a Saint, and desiring him to pray for him; or as that ingenious and learned Writer has expressed himself in a much more lively manner, *When I reflect on such a Speech pronounced by such a Person, I can scarce forbear crying out,* Sancte Socrates, ora pro nobis: *O holy* Socrates, *pray for us.*　　　　　　L

No. 214.

[STEELE.]　　　　　　　　　　　　　　Monday, November 5.

> . . . *Perierunt tempora longi*
> *Servitii . . .*—Juv.

I DID some Time ago lay before the World the unhappy Condition of the trading Part of Mankind, who suffer by want of Punctuality in the Dealings of Persons above them; but there is a Set of Men who are much more the Objects of Compassion than even those, and these are the Dependants on great Men, whom they are pleased to take under their Protection as such as are to share in their Friendship and Favour. These indeed, as well from the Homage that is accepted from them, as the Hopes which are given to them, are become a sort of Creditors; and these Debts, being Debts of Honour, ought, according to the accustomed Maxime, to be first discharged.

When I speak of Dependants, I would not be understood to mean those who are worthless in themselves, or who, without any Call, will press into the Company of their Betters. Nor, when I speak of Patrons, do I mean those who either have it not in their Power, or have no Obligation to assist their Friends; but I speak of such Leagues where there is Power and Obligation on the one Part, and Merit and Expectation on the other.

The Division of Patron and Client, may, I believe, include a Third of our Nation; the Want of Merit and real Worth in the Client, will strike out about Ninety nine in a Hundred of these; and the Want of Ability in Patrons, as many of that Kind. But however, I must beg leave to say, that he who will take up another's Time and Fortune in his Service tho' he has no Prospect of rewarding his Merit towards him, is as unjust in his Dealings as he who takes up Goods of a Tradesman without Intention or Ability to pay him. Of the few of the Class which I think fit to consider, there are not two in ten who succeed; insomuch, that I know a Man of good Sense who put his Son to a Black-smith, tho' an Offer was made him of his being received as a Page to a Man of Quality. There are not more Cripples come out of the Wars, than there are from those great Services; some through Discontent lose their Speech, some their Memories, others their Senses or their Lives; and I seldom see a Man thorowly discontented, but I conclude he has had the Favour of some great Man. I have known of such as have been for twenty Years together within a Month of a good Employment, but never arrived at the Happiness of being possessed of any thing.

There is nothing more ordinary, than that a Man who is got into a considerable Station, shall immediately alter his manner of treating all his Friends, and from that moment he is to deal with you as if he were your Fate. You are no longer to be consulted, even in Matters which concern your self, but your Patron is of a Species above you, and a free Communication with you is not to be expected. This perhaps may be your Condition all the while he bears Office, and when that is at an End you are as intimate as ever you were, and he will take it very ill if you keep the Distance he prescribed you towards him in his Grandeur. One would think this should be a Behaviour a Man could fall into with the worst Grace imaginable; but they who know the World have seen it more than once. I have often, with secret Pity, heard the same Man who has professed his abhorrence against all kind of passive Behaviour, lose Minutes, Hours, Days, and Years, in a fruitless Attendance on one who had no Inclination to befriend him. It is very much to be regarded, that the Great have one particular Privilege above the rest of the World, of being slow in receiving Impressions of Kindness, and quick in taking Offence. The Elevation above the rest of Mankind, except in very great Minds, makes Men so giddy that they do not see after the same Manner they did before: Thus they despise their old Friends, and strive to extend their Interest to new Pretenders. By this Means it often happens, that when you come to know how you lost such an Employment, you will find the Man who got it never dreamed of it; but, forsooth, he was to be surprized into it, or perhaps sollicited to receive it. Upon such Occasions as these a Man may perhaps grow out of Humour; if you are so, all Mankind will fall in with the Patron, and you are an Humourist and untractable if you are capable of being sower at a Disappointment: But it is the same thing, whether you do or do not resent ill Usage, you will be used after the same Manner; as some good Mothers will be sure to whip their Children till they cry, and then whip them for crying.

There are but two Ways of doing any thing with great People, and those are by making your self either considerable or agreeable: The former is not to be attained but by finding a Way to live without them, or concealing that you want them; the latter, is only by falling into their Taste and Pleasures: This is of all the Employments in the World the most servile, except it happens to be of your own natural Humour. For to be agreeable to another, especially if he be above you, is not to be possessed of such Qualities and Accomplishments as should render you agreeable in your self, but such as make you agreeable in respect to him. An Imitation of his Faults, or a Compliance, if not Subservience, to his Vices, must be the Measures of your Conduct.

When it comes to that, the unnatural State a Man lives in, when his Patron pleases, is ended; and his Guilt and Complaisance are objected to him, though the Man who rejects him for his Vices was not only his Partner but Seducer. Thus the Client (like a young Woman who has given up the Innocence which made her charming) has not only lost his Time, but also the Virtue which could render him capable of resenting the Injury which is done him.

It would be endless to recount the Tricks of turning you off from themselves to Persons who have less Power to serve you, the Art of being sorry for such an unaccountable Accident in your Behaviour, that such a one (who, perhaps, has never heard of you) opposes your Advancement; and if you have any thing more than ordinary in you, you are flattered with a Whisper, that 'tis no Wonder People are so slow in doing for a Man of your Talents, and the like.

After all this Treatment, I must still add the pleasantest Insolence of all, which I have once or twice seen; to wit, That when a silly Rogue has thrown away one Part in three of his Life in unprofitable Attendance, it is taken wonderfully ill that he withdraws, and is resolved to employ the rest for himself.

When we consider these things, and reflect upon so many honest Natures (which one, who makes Observation of what

passes may have seen) that have miscarried by such sort of
Applications, it is too melancholy a Scene to dwell upon;
therefore I shall take another Opportunity to discourse of
good Patrons, and distinguish such as have done their Duty to
those who have depended upon them, and were not able to
act without their Favour.   Worthy Patrons are like *Plato*'s
Guardian Angels, who are always doing good to their Wards;
but negligent Patrons are like *Epicurus*'s Gods, that lye lolling
on the Clouds, and instead of Blessings pour down Storms and
Tempests on the Heads of those that are offering Incense to
them.   T

No. 215.

[ADDISON.]   Tuesday, November 6.

> . . . *Ingenuas didicisse fideliter artes*
> *Emollit mores, nec sinit esse feros.*—Ov.

I CONSIDER an Human Soul without Education like Marble
in the Quarry, which shews none of its inherent Beauties, till
the Skill of the Polisher fetches out the Colours, makes the
Surface shine, and discovers every ornamental Cloud, Spot and
Vein that runs thro' the Body of it.   Education, after the same
manner, when it works upon a noble Mind, draws out to View
every latent Virtue and Perfection, which without such Helps
are never able to make their Appearance.

If my Reader will give me leave to change the Allusion so
soon upon him, I shall make use of the same Instance to
illustrate the Force of Education, which *Aristotle* has brought
to explain his Doctrine of Substantial Forms, when he tells us,
that a Statue lies hid in a Block of Marble; and that the Art of
the Statuary only clears away the superfluous Matter, and
removes the Rubbish.   The Figure is in the Stone, the Sculptor
only finds it.   What Sculpture is to a Block of Marble, Education is to an Human Soul.   The Philosopher, the Saint, or the
Hero, the Wise, the Good, or the Great Man, very often lie
hid and concealed in a Plebean, which a proper Education
might have disenterred, and have brought to Light.   I am
therefore much delighted with Reading the Accounts of Savage
Nations, and with contemplating those Virtues which are wild
and uncultivated; to see Courage exerting it self in Fierceness,
Resolution in Obstinacy, Wisdom in Cunning, Patience in
Sullenness and Despair.

Men's Passions operate variously, and appear in different
kinds of Actions, according as they are more or less rectified

and swayed by Reason. When one hears of Negroes, who upon the Death of their Masters, or upon changing their Service, hang themselves upon the next Tree, as it frequently happens in our *American* Plantations, who can forbear admiring their Fidelity, though it expresses it self in so dreadful a manner? What might not that Savage Greatness of Soul, which appears in these poor Wretches on many Occasions, be raised to, were it rightly cultivated? And what Colour of Excuse can there be for the Contempt with which we treat this Part of our Species; That we should not put them upon the common foot of Humanity, that we should only set an insignificant Fine upon the Man who murders them; nay, that we should, as much as in us lies, cut them off from the Prospects of Happiness in another World as well as in this, and deny them that which we look upon as the proper Means for attaining it?

Since I am engaged on this Subject, I cannot forbear mentioning a Story which I have lately heard, and which is so well attested, that I have no manner of reason to suspect the Truth of it. I may call it a kind of wild Tragedy that passed about twelve Years ago at St. *Christopher*'s, one of our *British* Leeward Islands. The Negroes who were the Persons concerned in it, were all of them the Slaves of a Gentleman who is now in *England*.

This Gentleman among his Negroes had a young Woman, who was looked upon as a most extraordinary Beauty by those of her own Complexion. He had at the same time two young Fellows who were likewise Negroes and Slaves, remarkable for the Comeliness of their Persons, and for the Friendship which they bore to one another. It unfortunately happened that both of them fell in Love with the Female Negro abovementioned, who would have been very glad to have taken either of them for her Husband, provided they could agree between themselves which should be the Man. But they were both so passionately in Love with her, that neither of them could think of giving her up to his Rival; and at the same time were so true to one another, that neither of them would think of gaining her without his Friend's Consent. The Torments of these two Lovers were the Discourse of the Family to which they belonged, who could not forbear observing the strange Complication of Passions which perplexed the Hearts of the poor Negroes, that often dropped Expressions of the Uneasiness they underwent, and how impossible it was for either of them ever to be happy.

After a long Struggle between Love and Friendship, Truth and Jealousie, they one Day took a Walk together into a Wood, carrying their Mistress along with them: Where, after abundance of Lamentations, they stabbed her to the Heart, of which she immediately died. A Slave who was at his Work not far from the Place where this astonishing piece of Cruelty was committed, hearing the Shrieks of the dying Person, ran to see what was the Occasion of them. He there discovered the Woman lying dead upon the Ground, with the two Negroes on each side of her, kissing the dead Corps, weeping over it, and beating their Breasts in the utmost Agonies of Grief and Despair. He immediately ran to the *English* Family with the News of what he had seen; who upon coming to the Place saw the Woman dead, and the two Negroes expiring by her with Wounds they had given themselves.

We see, in this amazing instance of Barbarity, what strange Disorders are bred in the Minds of those Men whose Passions are not regulated by Virtue, and disciplined by Reason. Though the Action which I have recited is in it self full of Guilt and Horror, it proceeded from a Temper of Mind which might have produced very noble Fruits, had it been informed and guided by a suitable Education.

It is therefore an unspeakable Blessing to be born in those Parts of the World where Wisdom and Knowledge flourish; though it must be confest, there are, even in these Parts, several poor uninstructed Persons, who are but little above the Inhabitants of those Nations of which I have been here speaking; as those who have had the Advantages of a more liberal Education rise above one another, by several different degrees of Perfection. For to return to our Statue in the Block of Marble, we see it sometimes only begun to be chipped, sometimes rough-hewn and but just sketched into an human Figure, sometimes we see the Man appearing distinctly in all his Limbs and Features, sometimes we find the Figure wrought up to a great Elegancy, but seldom meet with any to which the Hand of a *Phidias* or *Praxiteles* could not give several nice Touches and Finishings.

Discourses of Morality, and Reflections upon human Nature, are the best Means we can make use of to improve our Minds, and gain a true Knowledge of our selves, and consequently to recover our Souls out of the Vice, Ignorance and Prejudice which naturally cleave to them. I have all along profest my self in this Paper a Promoter of these great Ends, and I flatter my self that I do from Day to Day contribute something to the polishing of Men's Minds; at least my Design is laudable, whatever the Execution may be. I must confess I am not a little encouraged in it by many Letters, which I receive from unknown Hands, in Approbation of my Endeavours, and must take this Opportunity of returning my Thanks to those who write them, and excusing my self for not inserting several of them in my Papers, which I am sensible would be a very great Ornament to them.   Should I publish the Praises which are so well penned, they would do Honour to the Persons who write them; but my publishing of them would I fear be a sufficient Instance to the World that I did not deserve them.   **C**

No. 216.

[STEELE.]   Wednesday, November **7**.

> *Siquidem hercle possis, nil prius neque fortius;*
> *Verum si incipies neque pertendes naviter,*
> *Atque ubi pati non poteris, cum nemo expetet,*
> *Infecta pace, ultro ad eam venies, indicans*
> *Te amare, & ferre non posse: actum est, ilicet,*
> *Peristi: eludet, ubi te victum senserit.*—Ter.

'To Mr. SPECTATOR.

Sir,

THIS is to inform you, that Mr. *Freeman* had no sooner taken Coach, but his Lady was taken with a terrible Fit of the Vapours, which, 'tis feared, will make her miscarry, if not endanger her Life; therefore, dear Sir, if you know of any Receipt that is good against this fashionable reigning Distemper, be pleased to communicate it for the Good of the Publick, and you will oblige

                    Yours,

                              A. NOEWILL.'

'Mr. SPECTATOR,

The Uproar was so great as soon as I had read the *Spectator* concerning Mrs. *Freeman,* that after many Revolutions in her Temper of raging, swooning, railing, fainting, pitying her self, and reviling her Husband, upon an accidental coming in of a neighbouring Lady (who says she has writ to you also) she had nothing left for it but to fall in a Fit.   I had the Honour to read the Paper to her, and have a pretty good Command of my Countenance and Temper on such Occasions; and soon found my historical Name to be *Tom Meggot* in your Writings, but concealed my self till I saw how it affected Mrs. *Freeman.* She looked frequently at her Husband, as often at me; and she did not tremble as she filled Tea, till she came to the Circumstance of *Armstrong's* writing out a Piece of *Tully* for an Opera Tune: Then she burst out she was exposed, she was deceived, she was wronged and abused. The Tea-Cup was thrown in the Fire; and without taking Vengeance on her Spouse, she said of me, that I was a pretending Coxcomb, a Medler that knew not what it was to interpose in so nice an Affair as between a Man and his Wife. To which Mr. *Freeman*; Madam, Were I less fond of you than I am I should not have taken this Way of writing to the SPECTATOR, to inform a Woman whom God and Nature has placed under my Direction with what I request of her; but since you are so indiscreet as not to take the Hint which I gave you in that Paper, I must tell you, Madam, in so many Words, that you have for a long and tedious Space of Time acted a Part unsuitable to the Sense you ought to have of the Subordination in which you are placed. And I must acquaint you once for all, that the Fellow without, ha *Tom !* (here the Footman entered and answered Madam) Sirrah don't you know my Voice; look upon me when I speak to you; I say, Madam, this Fellow here is to know of me my self, whether I am at Leisure to see Company or not. I am from this Hour Master of this House; and my Business in it, and every where else, is to behave my self in such a Manner as it shall be hereafter an Honour to you to bear my Name; and your Pride that you are the Delight, the Darling, and Ornament of a Man of Honour, useful and esteemed by his Friends; and I no longer one that has buried some Merit in the World, in Compliance to a froward Humour which has grown upon an agreeable Woman by his Indulgence. Mr. *Freeman* ended this with a Tenderness in his Aspect and a downcast Eye, which shew'd he was extremely moved at the Anguish he saw her in; for she sat swelling with Passion, and her Eyes firmly fixed on the Fire; when I fearing he would lose all again, took upon me to provoke her out of that amiable Sorrow she was in to fall upon me; upon which I said very seasonably for my Friend, that indeed Mr. *Freeman* was become the common Talk of the Town; and that nothing was so much a Jest as when it was said in Company Mr. *Freeman* had promised to come to such a Place. Upon which the good Lady turned her Softness into downright Rage, and threw the scalding Tea-Kettle upon your humble Servant; flew into the Middle of the Room, and cried out she was the unfortunatest of all Women: Others kept Family Dissatisfactions for Hours of Privacy and Retirement: No Apology was to be made to her, no Expedient to be found, no previous Manner of breaking what was amiss in her; but all the World was to be acquainted with her Errours without the least Admonition. Mr. *Freeman* was going to make a softening Speech, but I interposed. Look you, Madam, I have nothing to say to this Matter, but you ought to consider you are now past a Chicken; this Humour, which was well enough in a Girl, is unsufferable in one of your Motherly Character. With that she lost all Patience, and flew directly at her Husband's Periwig. I got her in my Arms, and defended my Friend: He making Signs at the same time that it was too much; I beckening, nodding, and frowning over her Shoulder that he was lost if he did not persist. In this Manner she flew round and round the Room in a Moment, till the Lady I spoke of above and Servants entered, upon which she fell on a Couch as breathless. I still kept up my Friend; but he, with a very silly Air, bid them bring the Coach to the Door, and we went off, I being forced to bid the Coachman drive on. We were no sooner come to my Lodgings but all his Wife's Relations came to inquire after him; and Mrs. *Freeman*'s Mother Writ a Note, wherein she thought never to have seen this Day, and so forth.

In a Word, Sir, I am afraid we are upon a thing we have not Talents for; and I can observe already my Friend looks upon me rather as a Man that knows a Weakness of him that he is ashamed of, than one who has rescued him from Slavery. Mr. SPECTATOR, I am but a young Fellow, and if Mr. *Freeman* submits, I shall be looked upon as an Incendiary, and never get a Wife as long as I breathe. He has indeed sent Word home he shall lie at *Hampstead* to Night; but I believe Fear of the first Onset after this Rupture has too great a Place in this Resolution. Mrs. *Freeman* has a very pretty Sister; suppose I delivered him up, and articled with the Mother for her for bringing him home. If he has not Courage to stand it, (you are a great Casuist) is it such an ill thing to bring my self off as well as I can? What makes me doubt my Man, is, that I find he thinks it reasonable to expostulate at least with her; and Captain SENTREY will tell you, if you let your Orders be disputed you are no longer a Commander. I wish you could advise me how to get clear of this Business handsomely,

Yours,

T   Tom Meggot.'

No. 217.

[BUDGELL.]   Thursday, November 8.

> . . . *Tunc foemina simplex,*
> *Et pariter toto repetitus clamor ab antro.*—Juv. *Sat.* 6.

I SHALL entertain my Reader to day with some Letters from my Correspondents. The first of them is the Description of a

Club, whether real or imaginary I cannot determine; but am apt to fancy, that the Writer of it, whoever she is, has formed a kind of Nocturnal Orgie out of her own Fancy; whether this be so, or not, her Letter may conduce to the Amendment of that kind of Persons who are represented in it, and whose Characters are frequent enough in the World.

' *Mr.* SPECTATOR,

In some of your first Papers you were pleased to give the Publick a very diverting Account of several Clubs and nocturnal Assemblies; but I am a Member of a Society which has wholly escaped your Notice: I mean a Club of She-Romps. We take each a Hackney-Coach, and meet once a Week in a large upper Chamber, which we hire by the Year for that Purpose; our Landlord and his Family, who are quiet People, constantly contriving to be abroad on our Club-night. We are no sooner come together than we throw off all that Modesty and Reservedness with which our Sex are obliged to disguise themselves in publick Places. I am not able to express the Pleasure we enjoy from ten at Night till four in the Morning, in being as rude as you Men can be, for your Lives. As our Play runs high the Room is immediately filled with broken Fans, torn Petticoats, Lappets of Head-dresses, Flounces, Furbelows, Garters, and Working-Aprons. I had forgot to tell you at first, that besides the Coaches we come in our selves, there is one which stands always empty to carry off our *dead Men,* for so we call all those Fragments and Tatters with which the Room is strewed, and which we pack up together in Bundles, and put into the aforesaid Coach. It is no small Diversion for us to meet the next Night at some Member's Chamber, where every one is to pick out what belonged to her, from this confused Bundle of Silks, Stuffs, Laces, and Ribbands. I have hitherto given you an Account of our Diversion on Ordinary Club-Nights; but must acquaint you farther, that once a Month we *Demolish a Prude,* that is, we get some queer formal Creature in among us, and unrig her in an instant. Our last Month's Prude was so armed and fortified in Whale-bone and Buckram that we had much ado to come at her, but you would have died with laughing to have seen how the sober aukward Thing looked, when she was forced out of her Intrenchments. In short, Sir, 'tis impossible to give you a true Notion of our Sport, unless you would come one Night amongst us; and tho' it be directly against the Rules of our Society to admit a Male Visitant, we repose so much Confidence in your Silence and Taciturnity, that 'twas agreed by the whole Club, at our last Meeting, to give you Entrance for one Night as a Spectator.

I am

Your Humble Servant,

Kitty Termagant.

P.S. *We shall Demolish a Prude next Thursday.*'

Tho' I thank *Kitty* for her kind Offer, I do not at present find in my self any Inclination to venture my Person with her and her romping Companions. I should regard my self as a second *Clodius* intruding on the Mysterious Rites of the *Bona Dea,* and should apprehend being *Demolished* as much as the *Prude.*

The following Letter comes from a Gentleman, whose Taste I find is much too delicate to endure the least Advance towards Romping. I may perhaps hereafter improve upon the Hint he has given me, and make it the Subject of a whole *Spectator*; in the mean time take it as it follows in his own Words.'

'*Mr.* Spectator,

It is my Misfortune to be in Love with a young Creature who is daily committing Faults, which though they give me the utmost Uneasiness, I know not how to reprove her, or even acquaint her with. She is pretty, dresses well, is rich, and good-humoured; but either wholly neglects, or has no Notion of that which Polite People have agreed to distinguish by the Name of *Delicacy.* After our Return from a Walk the other Day, she threw her self into an Elbow Chair, and professed before a large Company, that *she was all over in a Sweat.* She told me this Afternoon that her *Stomach aked;* and was complaining yesterday at Dinner of something that *stuck in her Teeth.* I treated her with a Basket of Fruit last Summer, which she eat so very greedily, as almost made me resolve never to see her more. In short, Sir, I begin to tremble whenever I see her about to speak or move. As she does not want Sense, if she takes these Hints, I am happy. If not, I am more than afraid, that these things which shock me even in the Behaviour of a Mistress, will appear insupportable in that of a Wife.

I am,

Sir,

Yours, &c.'

My next Letter comes from a Correspondent whom I cannot but very much value, upon the Account which she gives of herself.

'*Mr.* Spectator,

I am happily arrived at a State of Tranquility which few

People envy, I mean that of an old Maid; therefore being wholly unconcerned in all that Medley of Follies which our Sex is apt to contract from their silly Fondness of yours, I read your Railleries on us without Provocation. I can say with *Hamlet,*

> . . . *Man delights not me,*
> *Nor Woman neither . . .*

Therefore, dear Sir, as you never spare your own Sex, do not be afraid of reproving what is ridiculous in ours, and you will oblige at least one Woman, who is,

Your humble Servant,

Susanna Frost.'

'*Mr.* SPECTATOR,

I am Wife to a Clergyman, and cannot help thinking that in your Tenth or Tithe-Character of Womankind you meant my self, therefore I have no Quarrel against you for the other Nine Characters.

Your humble Servant,

X   A. B.'

No. 218.

[STEELE.]   Friday, November 9.

Quid de quoque viro & cui dicas saepe videto.—Hor.

I HAPPENED the other Day, as my Way is, to strole into a little Coffee-house beyond *Aldgate*; and as I sat there, two or three very plain sensible Men were talking of the SPECTATOR. One said, he had that Morning drawn the great Benefit Ticket; another wished he had; but a third shaked his Head and said, it was pity that the Writer of that Paper was such a sort of Man, that it was no great Matter whether he had it or no. He is, it seems, said the good Man, the most extravagant Creature in the World; has run through vast Sums, and yet been in continual Want; a Man, for all he talks so well of Oeconomy, unfit for any of the Offices of Life, by reason of his Profuseness. It would be an unhappy thing to be his Wife, his Child, or his Friend; and yet he talks as well of those Duties of Life as any one. Much Reflection has brought me to so easie a Contempt for every thing which is false, that this heavy Accusation gave me no Manner of Uneasiness; but at the same time it threw me into deep Thought upon the Subject of Fame in general; and I could not but pity such as were so weak, as to value what the common People say, out of their own talkative Temper, to

the Advantage and Diminution of those whom they mention,
without being moved either by Malice or Goodwill. It would
be too long to expatiate upon the Sense all Mankind have of
Fame, and the inexpressible Pleasure which there is in the
Approbation of worthy Men, to all who are capable of worthy
Actions; but methinks one may divide the general Word Fame
into three different Species, as it regards the different Orders
of Mankind who have any thing to do with it. Fame therefore
may be divided into Glory, which respects the Hero; Reputation, which is preserved by every Gentleman; and Credit, which
must be supported by every Tradesman. These Possessions in
Fame are dearer than Life to these Characters of Men, or
rather are the Life of those Characters. Glory, while the Hero
pursues great and noble Enterprizes, is impregnable; and all
the Assailants of his Renown do but shew their Pain and
Impatience of its Brightness, without throwing the least Shade
upon it. If the Foundation of an high Name be Virtue and
Service, all that is offered against it is but Rumour, which is
too short-lived to stand up in Competition with Glory, which is
everlasting.

Reputation, which is the Portion of every Man who would
live with the elegant and knowing Part of Mankind, is as stable
as Glory if it be as well founded; and the common Cause of
human Society is thought concerned when we hear a Man of
good Behaviour calumniated: Besides which, according to a
prevailing Custom amongst us, every Man has his Defence in
his own Arm; and Reproach is soon checked, put out of
Countenance, and overtaken by Disgrace.

The most unhappy of all Men, and the most exposed to the
Malignity or Wantonness of the common Voice, is the Trader.
Credit is undone in Whispers: The Tradesman's Wound is
received from one who is more private and more cruel than the
Ruffian with the Lanthorn and Dagger. The Manner of repeating a Man's Name, As *Mr.* Cash, *Oh! do you leave your
Money at his Shop? Why do you know Mr.* Searoom? *He is
indeed a general Merchant.* I say, I have seen, from the
Iteration of a Man's Name, hiding one Thought of him, and
explaining what you hide by saying something to his Advantage when you speak, a Merchant hurt in his Credit; and him
who every Day he lived litterally added to the Value of his
native Country, undone by one who was only a Burthen and a
Blemish to it. Since every Body who knows the World is
sensible of this great Evil, how careful ought a Man to be in his
Language of a Merchant. It may possibly be in the Power of a
very shallow Creature to lay the Ruin of the best Family in the
most opulent City; and the more so, the more highly he deserves

of his Country; that is to say, the farther he places his Wealth out of his Hands, to draw home that of another Climate.

In this Case an ill Word may change Plenty into Want, and by a rash Sentence a free and generous Fortune may in a few Days be reduced to Beggary.   How little does a giddy Prater imagine, that an idle Phrase to the Disfavour of a Merchant may be as pernicious in the Consequence, as the Forgery of a Deed to bar an Inheritance would be to a Gentleman?   Land stands where it did before a Gentleman was calumniated, and the State of a great Action is just as it was before Calumny was offered to diminish it, and there is Time, Place, and Occasion expected to unravel all that is contrived against those Characters; but the Trader who is ready only for probable Demands upon him, can have no Armour against the Inquisitive, the Malicious, and the Envious, who are prepared to fill the Cry to his Dishonour.   Fire and Sword are slow Engines of Destruction, in Comparison of the Babbler in the case of the Merchant.

For this Reason I thought it an imitable Piece of Humanity of a Gentleman of my Acquaintance, who had great Variety of Affairs, and used to talk with Warmth enough against Gentlemen by whom he thought himself ill dealt with; but he would never let any thing be urged against a Merchant (with whom he had any Difference) except in a Court of Justice.   He used to say, that to speak ill of a Merchant was to begin his Suit with Judgment and Execution.   One cannot, I think, say more on this Occasion, than to repeat, That the Merit of the Merchant is above that of all other Subjects; for while he is untouched in his Credit, his Hand-writing is a more portable Coin for the Service of his Fellow-Citizens, and his Word the Gold of *Ophir* to the Country wherein he resides.   T

No. 219.
[ADDISON.]   Saturday, November 10.

Vix ea nostra voco.—Ov.

THERE are but few Men who are not Ambitious of distinguishing themselves in the Nation or Country where they live, and of growing Considerable among those with whom they converse. There is a kind of Grandeur and Respect, which the meanest and most insignificant part of Mankind endeavour to procure in the little Circle of their Friends and Acquaintance.   The poorest Mechanick, nay, the Man who lives upon common Alms, gets him his Sett of Admirers, and delights in that Superiority which he enjoys over those who are in some

Respects beneath him. This Ambition, which is natural to the Soul of Man, might methinks receive a very happy turn; and, if it were rightly directed, contribute as much to a Person's Advantage, as it generally does to his Uneasiness and Disquiet.

I shall therefore put together some Thoughts on this Subject, which I have not met with in other Writers; and shall set them down as they have occurred to me, without being at the Pains to Connect or Methodise them.

All Superiority and Prae-eminence that one Man can have over another, may be reduced to the Notion of *Quality*, which considered at large, is either that of Fortune, Body, or Mind. The first is that which consists in Birth, Title or Riches; and is the most foreign to our Natures, and what we can the least call our own of any of the three kinds of Quality. In relation to the Body, Quality arises from Health, Strength or Beauty, which are nearer to us, and more a Part of our selves than the former. Quality as it regards the Mind, has its rise from Knowledge or Virtue; and is that which is more essential to us, and more intimately united with us than either of the other two.

The Quality of Fortune, tho' a Man has less reason to value himself upon it than on that of the Body or Mind, is however the kind of Quality which makes the most shining Figure in the Eye of the World.

As Virtue is the most reasonable and genuine Source of Honour, we generally find in Titles an Intimation of some particular Merit that should recommend Men to the high Stations which they possess. Holiness is ascribed to the Pope; Majesty to Kings; Serenity or Mildness of Temper to Princes; Excellence or Perfection to Ambassadors; Grace to Arch-Bishops; Honour to Peers; Worship or Venerable Behaviour to Magistrates; and Reverence, which is of the same Import as the former, to the inferior Clergy.

In the Founders of great Families such Attributes of Honour are generally correspondent with the Virtues of the Person to whom they are applied; but in the Descendants they are too often the Marks rather of Grandeur than of Merit. The Stamp and Denomination still continues, but the Intrinsick Value is frequently lost.

The Death-Bed shews the Emptiness of Titles in a true Light. A poor dispirited Sinner lies trembling under the Apprehensions of the State he is entering on; and is asked by a grave Attendant how his Holiness does? Another hears himself addressed to under the Title of Highness or Excellency, who lies under such mean Circumstances of Mortality as are the Disgrace of Human Nature. Titles at such a time look rather like Insults and Mockery than Respect.

The truth of it is, Honours are in this World under no Regulation; true Quality is neglected, Virtue is oppressed, and Vice triumphant. The last Day will rectifie this Disorder, and assign to every one a Station suitable to the Dignity of his Character; Ranks will be then adjusted, and Precedency set right.

Methinks we should have an Ambition, if not to advance our selves in another World, at least to preserve our Post in it, and outshine our Inferiors in Virtue here, that they may not be put above us in a State which is to settle the Distinction for Eternity.

Men in Scripture are called *Strangers* and *Sojourners upon Earth*, and Life a *Pilgrimage*. Several Heathen as well as Christian Authors, under the same kind of Metaphor, have represented the World as an Inn, which was only designed to furnish us with Accommodations in this our Passage. It is therefore very absurd to think of setting up our Rest before we come to our Journey's End, and not rather to take care of the Reception we shall there meet, than to fix our Thoughts on the little Conveniences and Advantages which we enjoy one above another in the Way to it.

Epictetus makes use of another kind of Allusion, which is very beautiful, and wonderfully proper to incline us to be satisfyed with the Post in which Providence has placed us. We are here, says he, as in a Theatre, where every one has a Part allotted to him. The great Duty which lies upon a Man is to act his Part in Perfection. We may, indeed, say that our Part does not suit us, and that we could act another better. But this (says the Philosopher) is not our Business. All that we are concerned in is to excel in the Part which is given us. If it be an improper one the Fault is not in us, but in him who has *cast* our several Parts, and is the great Disposer of the Drama.

The Part that was acted by this Philosopher himself was but a very indifferent one, for he lived and died a Slave. His Motive to Contentment in this particular receives a very great Inforcement from the above-mentioned Consideration, if we remember that our Parts in the other World will be *new cast*, and that Mankind will be there ranged in different Stations of Superiority and Prae-eminence, in Proportion as they have here excelled one another in Virtue, and performed in their several Posts of Life the Duties which belong to them.

There are many beautiful Passages in the little Apocryphal Book, entituled *The Wisdom of Solomon*, to set forth the Vanity of Honour, and the like Temporal Blessings, which are in so great Repute among Men, and to comfort those who have not the Possession of them. It represents in very warm and

noble Terms this Advancement of a good Man in the other
World, and the great Surprize which it will produce among
those who are his Superiors in this. 'Then shall the Righteous
Man stand in great Boldness before the Face of such as have
afflicted him, and made no Account of his Labours. When they
see it they shall be troubled with terrible Fear, and shall be
amazed at the strangeness of his Salvation, so far beyond all
that they looked for. And they repenting, and groaning for
Anguish of Spirit, shall say within themselves, This was he
whom we had sometime in Derision, and a Proverb of Reproach.
We Fools accounted his Life Madness, and his End to be without Honour. How is he numbered among the Children of
God, and his Lot is among the Saints!'

If the Reader would see the Description of a Life that is
passed away in Vanity, and among the Shadows of Pomp and
Greatness, he may see it very finely drawn in the same Place.
In the mean time, since it is necessary, in the present Constitution of things, that Order and Distinction should be kept
up in the World, we should be happy if those who enjoy the
upper Stations in it would endeavour to surpass others in
Virtue, as much as in Rank, and by their Humanity and Con-
descension make their Superiority easie and acceptable to those
who are beneath them; and if, on the contrary, those who are in
meaner Posts of Life, would consider how they may better their
Condition hereafter, and by a just Deference and Submission to
their Superiors, make them happy in those Blessings with which
Providence has thought fit to distinguish them.   C

No. 220.
[STEELE.]   Monday, November 12.

Rumoresque serit varios . . .—Virg.

'*Sir,*

WHY will you apply to my Father for my Love? I cannot
help it if he will give you my Person; but I assure you it is not
in his Power, nor even in my own, to give you my Heart. Dear
Sir, do but consider the ill Consequence of such a Match; you
are fifty five, I twenty one. You are a Man of Business, and
mightily conversant in Arithmetick and making Calculations;
be pleased therefore to consider what Proportion your Spirits
bear to mine; and when you have made a just Estimate of the
necessary Decay on one Side, and the Redundance on the other,
you will act accordingly. This, perhaps, is such Language as
you may not expect from a young Lady; but my Happiness is

at Stake, and I must talk plainly. I mortally hate you; and so, as you and my Father agree, you may take me or leave me: But if you will be so good as never to see me more, you will for ever oblige,

Sir,

Your most humble Servant,

HENRIETTA.'

'Mr. SPECTATOR,

There are so many Artifices and Modes of false Wit, and such a Variety of Humour discovers it self among its Votaries, that it would be impossible to exhaust so fertile a Subject if you would think fit to resume it. The following Instances may, if you think fit, be added by Way of Appendix to your Discourses on that Subject.

That Feat of poetical Activity, mentioned by *Horace*, of an Author who could compose two hundred Verses while he stood upon one Leg, has been imitated (as I have heard) by a modern Writer; who priding himself on the Hurry of his Invention, thought it no small Addition to his Fame to have each Piece minuted with the exact Number of Hours or Days it cost him in the Composition. He could taste no Praise till he had acquainted you in how short Space of Time he had deserved it; and was not so much led to an Ostentation of his Art, as of his Dispatch.

. . . Accipe si vis,
Accipe jam tabulas; detur nobis locus, hora,
Custodes: videamus uter plus scribere possit.—Hor.

This was the whole of his Ambition; and therefore I cannot but think the Flights of this rapid Author very proper to be opposed to those long laborious Nothings which you have observed were the Delight of the *German* Wits, and in which they so happily got rid of such a tedious Quantity of their Time.

I have known a Gentleman of another Turn of Humour, who, despising the Name of an Author, never printed his Works, but contracted his Talent, and by the Help of a very fine Diamond which he wore on his little Finger, was a considerable Poet upon Glass. He had a very good Epigrammatick Wit; and there was not a Parlour or Tavern Window where he visited or dined for some Years, which did not receive some Sketches or Memorials of it. It was his Misfortune at last to lose his Genius and his Ring to a Sharper at play; and he has not attempted to make a Verse since.

But of all Contractions or Expedients for Wit, I admire that of an ingenious Projector whose Book I have seen: This

Virtuoso being a Mathematician, has, according to his Taste, thrown the Art of Poetry into a short Problem, and contriv'd Tables by which any one, without knowing a Word of Grammar or Sense, may, to his great Comfort, be able to compose or rather to erect Latin Verses. His Tables are a kind of poetical Logarithms, which being divided into several Squares, and all inscribed with so many incoherent Words, appear to the Eye somewhat like a Fortune-telling Screen. What a Joy must it be to the unlearned Operator, to find that these Words, being carefully collected and writ down in order according to the Problem, start of themselves into Hexameter and Pentameter Verses? A Friend of mine, who is a Student in Astrology, meeting with this Book, perform'd the Operation by the Rules there set down; he shew'd his Verses to the next of his Acquaintance, who happened to understand Latin; and being informed they described a Tempest of Wind, very luckily prefix'd them, together with a Translation, to an Almanack he was just then printing, and was supposed to have foretold the last great Storm.

I think the only Improvement beyond this, would be that which the late Duke of *Buckingham* mention'd to a stupid Pretender to Poetry, as the Project of a *Dutch* Mechanick, *viz.* a Mill to make Verses. This being the most compendious Method of all which have yet been propos'd, may deserve the Thoughts of our modern Virtuosi who are employ'd in new Discoveries for the publick Good; and it may be worth the while to consider, whether, in an Island where few are content without being thought Wits, it will not be a common Benefit that Wit as well as Labour should be made cheap.

> *I am,*
> > *Sir,*
> > > *Your humble Servant, &c.'*

'*Mr.* SPECTATOR,

I often dine at a Gentleman's House, where there are two young Ladies, in themselves very agreeable, but very cold in their Behaviour, because they understand me for a Person that is to break my Mind, as the Phrase is, very suddenly to one of them. But I take this Way to acquaint them, that I am not in Love with either of them, in hopes they will use me with that agreeable Freedom and Indifference which they do all the rest of the World, and not to drink to one another only, but sometimes cast a kind Look, with their Service to,

> > *Sir,*
> > > *Your humble Servant.'*

'Mr. Spectator,

I am a young Gentleman, and take it for a Piece of Good-breeding to pull off my Hat when I see any thing peculiarly charming in any Woman, whether I know her or not. I take Care that there is nothing ludicrous or arch in my Manner, as if I were to betray a Woman into a Salutation by Way of Jest or Humour; and yet except I am acquainted with her, I find she ever takes it for a Rule, that she is to look upon this Civility and Homage I pay to her supposed Merit, as an Impertinence or Forwardness which she is to observe and neglect. I wish, Sir, you would settle the Business of Salutation; and please to inform me how I shall resist the sudden Impulse I have to be civil to what gives an Idea of Merit; or tell these Creatures how to behave themselves in Return to the Esteem I have for them. My Affairs are such, that your Decision will be a Favour to me, if it be only to save the unnecessary Expence of wearing out my Hat so fast as I do at present.

I am, Sir,

Yours,

T. D.

P.S. *There are some that do know me and won't bow to me.*'

T

No. 221.
[ADDISON.]

Tuesday, November 13.

. . *Ab ovo*
Usque ad mala . . .—Hor.

WHEN I have finished any of my Speculations, it is my Method to consider which of the Ancient Authors have touched upon the Subject that I treat of. By this means I meet with some celebrated Thought upon it, or a Thought of my own expressed in better Words, or some Similitude for the Illustration of my Subject. This is what gives Birth to the Motto of a Speculation, which I rather chuse to take out of the Poets than the Prose Writers, as the former generally give a finer Turn to a Thought than the latter, and by couching it in few Words, and in harmonious Numbers, make it more portable to the Memory.

My Reader is therefore sure to meet with at least one good Line in every Paper, and very often finds his Imagination entertained by a Hint that awakens in his Memory some beautiful Passage of a Classick Author.

It was a Saying of an Ancient Philosopher, which I find some of our Writers have ascribed to Queen *Elizabeth*, who perhaps might have taken occasion to repeat it, That a good Face is a Letter of Recommendation. It naturally makes the Beholders inquisitive into the Person who is the Owner of it, and generally prepossesses them in his Favour. A handsom Motto has the same Effect. Besides that, it always gives a Supernumerary Beauty to a Paper, and is sometimes in a manner necessary when the Writer is engaged in what may appear a Paradox to vulgar Minds, as it shews that he is supported by good Authorities, and is not singular in his Opinion.

I must confess the Motto is of little use to an unlearned Reader. For which Reason I consider it only as a *Word to the Wise*. But as for my unlearned Friends, if they cannot relish the Motto, I take care to make Provision for them in the Body of my Paper. If they do not understand the Sign that is hung out, they know very well by it, that they may meet with Entertainment in the House; and I think I was never better pleased than with a plain Man's Compliment, who upon his Friend's telling him that he would like the *Spectator* much better if he understood the Motto, replied, *That good Wine needs no Bush.*

I have heard of a couple of Preachers in a Country Town, who endeavoured which should outshine one another, and draw together the greatest Congregation. One of them being well versed in the Fathers, used to quote every now and then a *Latin* Sentence to his Illiterate Hearers, who it seems found themselves so edified by it, that they flocked in greater Numbers to this Learned Man, than to his Rival. The other finding his Congregation mouldering every *Sunday*, and hearing at length what was the Occasion of it, resolved to give his Parish a little *Latin* in his turn; but being unacquainted with any of the Fathers, he digested into his Sermons the whole Book of *Quae Genus*, adding however such Explications to it as he thought might be for the Benefit of his People. He afterwards entered upon *As in praesenti*, which he converted in the same manner to the Use of his Parishioners. This in a very little time thickned his Audience, filled his Church, and routed his Antagonist.

The natural Love to *Latin* which is so prevalent in our common People, makes me think that my Speculations fare never the worse among them for that little Scrap which appears at the Head of them; and what the more encourages me in the use of Quotations in an unknown Tongue, is, that I hear the Ladies, whose Approbation I value more than that of the whole Learned World, declare themselves in a more particular manner pleas'd with my *Greek* Mottos.

Designing this Day's Work for a Dissertation upon the two

Extremities of my Paper, and having already dispatched my Motto, I shall, in the next place, discourse upon those single Capital Letters which are placed at the End of it, and which have afforded great Matter of Speculation to the Curious. I have heard various Conjectures upon this Subject. Some tell us, that C is the Mark of those Papers that are written by the Clergyman, though others ascribe them to the Club in general. That the Papers marked with R were written by my Friend Sir ROGER. That L signifies the Lawyer, whom I have described in my Second Speculation; and that T stands for the Trader or Merchant: But the Letter X, which is placed at the End of some few of my Papers, is that which has puzled the whole Town, as they cannot think of any Name which begins with that Letter, except *Xenophon* and *Xerxes*, who can neither of them be supposed to have had any Hand in these Speculations.

In Answer to these inquisitive Gentlemen, who have many of them made Enquiries of me by Letter, I must tell them the Reply of an ancient Philosopher, who carried something hidden under his Cloak. A certain Acquaintance desiring him to let him know what it was he covered so carefully; *I cover it*, says he, *on purpose that you should not know.* I have made use of these obscure Marks for the same purpose. They are, perhaps, little Amulets or Charms to preserve the Paper against the Fascination and Malice of Evil Eyes; for which Reason I would not have my Reader surprized, if hereafter he sees any of my Papers marked with a Q, a Z, a Y, an &c. or with the Word *Abracadabra.*

I shall however so far explain my self to the Reader, as to let him know that the Letters C, L and X are Cabalistical, and carry more in them than it is proper for the World to be acquainted with. Those who are versed in the Philosophy of *Pythagoras*, and swear by the *Tetrachtys*, that is, the number Four, will know very well that the Number *Ten*, which is signified by the Letter X, (and which has so much perplexed the Town) has in it many particular Powers; that it is called by *Platonick* Writers the Compleat Number; that One, Two, Three and Four put together make up the Number Ten; and that Ten is all. But these are not the Mysteries for ordinary Readers to be let into. A Man must have spent many Years in hard Study before he can arrive at the Knowledge of them.

We had a Rabbinnical Divine in *England*, who was Chaplain to the Earl of *Essex* in Queen *Elizabeth*'s Time, that had an admirable Head for Secrets of this Nature. Upon his taking the Doctor of Divinity's Degree he preached before the University of *Cambridge*, upon the *First* Verse of the *First* Chapter of

the *First* Book of *Chronicles*, in which, says he, you will see the
three following Words,

> *Adam, Sheth, Enosh.*

He divided this short Text into many Parts, and by discovering several Mysteries in each Word, made a most Learned and
Elaborate Discourse. The Name of this profound Preacher
was Doctor *Alabaster*, of whom the Reader may find a more
particular Account in Doctor *Fuller*'s Book of *English* Worthies.
This Instance will, I hope, convince my Readers that there may
be a great deal of fine Writing in the Capital Letters which bring
up the Rear of my Paper, and give them some Satisfaction in
that Particular. But as for the full Explication of these
Matters, I must refer them to Time, which discovers all Things.

C

No. 222.

[STEELE.]   Wednesday, November 14.

> *Cur alter fratrum cessare, & ludere, & ungi,*
> *Praeferat Herodis palmetis pinguibus . . .*—Hor.

'Mr. SPECTATOR,

THERE is one thing I have often looked for in your Papers,
and have as often wonder'd to find my self disappointed; the
rather, because I think it a Subject every way agreeable to your
Design, and by being left unattempted by others seems reserved as a proper Employment for you: I mean a Disquisition,
from whence it proceeds, that Men of the brightest Parts
and most comprehensive Genius, compleatly furnished with
Talents for any Province in humane Affairs; such as by their
wise Lessons of Oeconomy to others have made it evident, that
they have the justest Notions of Life and of true Sense in the
Conduct of it ——; from what unhappy contradictious Cause it
proceeds, that Persons thus finished by Nature and by Art
should so often fail in the Management of that which they so
well understand, and want the Address to make a right Application of their own Rules. This is certainly a prodigious Inconsistency in Behaviour, and makes much such a Figure in
Morals as a monstrous Birth in Naturals, with this Difference
only, which greatly aggravates the Wonder, that it happens
much more frequently; and what a Blemish does it cast upon
Wit and Learning in the general Account of the World? and in
how disadvantageous a Light does it expose them to the busie
Class of Mankind, that there should be so many Instances of
Persons who have so conducted their Lives in spite of these
transcendent Advantages. as neither to be happy in themselves

nor useful to their Friends; when every Body sees it was entirely in their own Power to be eminent in both these Characters? For my Part, I think there is no Reflexion more astonishing, than to consider one of these Gentleman spending a fair Fortune, running in every Body's Debt without the least Apprehension of a future Reckoning, and at last leaving not only his own Children, but possibly those of other People, by his Means in starving Circumstances; while a Fellow whom one would scarce suspect to have a humane Soul, shall perhaps raise a vast Estate out of nothing, and be the Founder of a Family capable of being very considerable in their Country, and doing many illustrious Services to it. That this observation is just, Experience has put beyond all Dispute. But though the Fact be so evident and glaring, yet the Causes of it are still in the dark; which makes me perswade my self that it would be no unacceptable Piece of Entertainment to the Town, to inquire into the hidden Sources of so unaccountable an Evil.

> *I am, Sir,*
> *Your most humble Servant.'*

What this Correspondent wonders at, has been Matter of Admiration ever since there was any such thing as humane Life. *Horace* reflects upon this Inconsistency very agreeably in the Character of *Tigellius*, whom he makes a mighty Pretender to Oeconomy, and tells you, you might one Day hear him speak the most philosophick things imaginable concerning being contented with a Little, and his Contempt of every thing but mere Necessaries, and in Half a Week after spend a thousand Pound. When he says this of him with Relation to Expence, he describes him as unequal to himself in every other Circumstance of Life. And indeed if we consider lavish Men carefully, we shall find it always proceeds from a certain Incapacity of possessing themselves, and finding Enjoyment in their own Minds. Mr. *Dryden* has expressed this very excellently in the Character of *Zimri*.

> *A Man so various, that he seem'd to be*
> *Not one, but all Mankind's Epitome.*
> *Stiff in Opinion, always in the Wrong,*
> *Was every thing by Starts, and nothing long;*
> *But in the Course of one revolving Moon,*
> *Was Chymist, Fidler, Statesman, and Buffoon.*
> *Then all for Women, Painting, Rhiming, Drinking,*
> *Besides ten thousand Freaks that dy'd in thinking;*
> *Blest Mad-man, who could every Hour employ,*
> *In something new to wish or to enjoy!*
> *In squandring Wealth was his peculiar Art,*
> *Nothing went unrewarded but Desert.*

This loose State of the Soul hurries the Extravagant from one Pursuit to another; and the Reason that his Expences are greater than another's, is, that his Wants are also more numerous. But what makes so many go on in this Way to their Lives' End, is, that they certainly do not know how contemptible they are in the Eyes of the rest of Mankind, or rather, that indeed they are not so contemptible as they deserve. *Tully* says it is the greatest of Wickedness to lessen your paternal Estate: And if a Man would thoroughly consider how much worse than Banishment it must be to his Child to ride by the Estate which should have been his had it not been for his Father's injustice to him, he would be smitten with the Reflection more deeply than can be understood by any but one who is a Father. Sure there can be nothing more afflicting, than to think it had been happier for his Son to have been born of any other Man living than himself.

It is not perhaps much thought of, but it is certainly a very important Lesson to learn how to enjoy ordinary Life, and to be able to relish your Being without the Transport of some Passion, or Gratification of some Appetite. For want of this Capacity the World is filled with Whetters, Tipplers, Cutters, Sippers, and all the numerous Train of those who for want of Thinking are forced to be ever exercising their Feeling or Tasting. It would be hard on this Occasion to mention the harmless Smoakers of Tobacco and Takers of Snuff.

The slower Part of Mankind, whom my Correspondent wonders should get Estates, are the more immediately formed for that Pursuit: They can expect distant things without Impatience, because they are not carried out of their Way either by violent Passion, or keen Appetite to any thing. To Men addicted to Delight, Business is an Interruption; to such as are cold to Delights, Business is an Entertainment. For which Reason it was said by one who commended a dull Man for his Application, *No Thanks to him; if he had no Business, he would have nothing to do.* T

No. 223.

[ADDISON.]   Thursday, November 15.

> *O suavis anima! quale in te dicam bonum*
> *Antehac fuisse, tales cum sint reliquiae!*—Phaed.

WHEN I reflect upon the various Fate of those multitudes of Ancient Writers who flourished in *Greece* and *Italy*, I consider Time as an Immense Ocean, in which many noble Authors are entirely swallowed up, many very much shattered and damaged, some quite dis-jointed and broken into pieces, while some have wholly escaped the Common Wreck; but the Number of the last is very small:

> *Apparent rari nantes in gurgite vasto.*

Among the mutilated Poets of Antiquity, there is none whose Fragments are so beautiful as those of *Sappho*. They give us a Taste of her way of Writing, which is perfectly conformable with that extraordinary Character we find of her, in the Remarks of those great Criticks who were conversant with her Works when they were entire. One may see, by what is left of them, that she followed Nature in all her Thoughts, without descending to those little Points, Conceits and Turns of Wit with which many of our Modern Lyricks are so miserably infected. Her Soul seems to have been made up of Love and Poetry: She felt the Passion in all its Warmth, and described it in all its Symptoms. She is called by Ancient Authors the Tenth Muse; and by *Plutarch* is compared to *Cacus* the Son of *Vulcan*, who breathed out nothing but Flame. I do not know, by the Character that is given of her Works, whether it is not for the Benefit of Mankind that they are lost. They were filled with such bewitching Tenderness and Rapture, that it might have been dangerous to have given them a Reading.

An Inconstant Lover, called *Phaon*, occasioned great Calamities to this Poetical Lady. She fell desperately in Love with him, and took a Voyage into *Sicily*, in Pursuit of him, he having withdrawn himself thither on purpose to avoid her. It was in that Island, and on this Occasion, she is supposed to have made the Hymn to *Venus*, with a Translation of which I shall present my Reader. Her Hymn was ineffectual for the procuring that Happiness which she prayed for in it. *Phaon* was still obdurate, and *Sappho* so transported with the Violence of her Passion, that she was resolved to get rid of it at any Price.

There was a Promontory in *Acarnania* called *Leucate*, on the Top of which was a little Temple dedicated to *Apollo*. In this Temple it was usual for despairing Lovers to make their Vows in secret, and afterwards to fling themselves from the Top of the Precipice into the Sea, where they were sometimes taken up alive. This Place was therefore called, the Lovers-Leap; and whether or no the Fright they had been in, or the Resolution that could push them to so dreadful a Remedy, or the Bruises which they often received in their Fall, banished all the Tender Sentiments of Love, and gave their Spirits another Turn; those who had taken this Leap were observed never to Relapse into that Passion. *Sappho* tried the Cure, but perished in the Experiment.

After having given this short Account of *Sappho* so far as it regards the following Ode, I shall subjoin the Translation of it as it was sent me by a Friend, whose admirable Pastorals and *Winter-Piece* have been already so well received. The Reader will find in it that Pathetick Simplicity which is so peculiar to him, and so suitable to the Ode he has here Translated. This Ode in the *Greek* (besides those Beauties observed by Madam *Dacier*) has several harmonious Turns in the Words, which are not lost in the *English*. I must further add, that the Translation has preserved every Image and Sentiment of *Sappho*, notwithstanding it has all the Ease and Spirit of an Original. In a Word, if the Ladies have a mind to know the manner of Writing practised by the so much celebrated *Sappho*, they may here see it in its genuine and natural Beauty, without any foreign or affected Ornaments.

An HYMN to *VENUS.*

I.

O Venus, *Beauty of the Skies,*
To whom a thousand Temples rise,
Gayly false in gentle Smiles,
Full of Love-perplexing Wiles;
O Goddess! from my Heart remove
The wasting Cares and Pains of Love.

II.

If ever thou hast kindly heard
A Song in soft Distress preferr'd,
Propitious to my tuneful Vow,
O gentle Goddess! hear me now,
Descend, thou bright, immortal Guest,
In all thy radiant Charms confest.

III.

Thou once didst leave Almighty Jove,
And all the Golden Roofs above:
The Carr thy wanton Sparrows drew;
Hov'ring in Air they lightly flew,
As to my Bow'r they wing'd their Way:
I saw their quiv'ring Pinions play.

VI.

The Birds dismist (while you remain)
Bore back their empty Carr again;

Then you, with Looks divinely mild,
In ev'ry heav'nly Feature smil'd,
And ask'd, what new Complaints I made,
And why I call'd you to my Aid?

V.

What Phrenzy in my Bosom raged,
And by what Cure to be asswaged?
What gentle Youth I would allure,
Whom in my artful Toiles secure?
Who does thy tender Heart subdue,
Tell me, my Sappho, *tell me Who?*

VI.

Tho' now he Shuns thy longing Arms,
He soon shall court thy slighted Charms;
Tho' now thy Off'rings he despise,
He soon to Thee shall Sacrifice;
Tho' now he freeze, he soon shall burn,
And be thy Victim in his turn.

VII.

Celestial Visitant, once more
Thy needful Presence I implore!
In Pity come and ease my Grief,
Bring my distemper'd Soul Relief;
Favour thy Suppliant's hidden Fires,
And give me All my Heart desires.

Madam *Dacier* observes there is something very pretty in that Circumstance of this Ode, wherein *Venus* is described as sending away her Chariot upon her Arrival at *Sappho's* Lodgings, to denote that it was not a short transient Visit which she intended to make her. This Ode was preserved by an Eminent *Greek* Critick, who inserted it intire in his Works, as a Pattern of Perfection in the Structure of it.

Longinus has quoted another Ode of this great Poetess, which is likewise admirable in its kind, and has been translated by the same Hand with the foregoing one. I shall oblige my Reader with it in another Paper. In the mean while, I cannot but wonder, that these two finished Pieces have never been attempted before by any of our own Countrymen. But the Truth of it is, the Compositions of the Ancients, which have not in them any of those unnatural Witicisms, that are the Delight of ordinary Readers, are extreamly difficult to render into another Tongue, so as the Beauties of the Original may not appear weak and faded in the Translation.   C

No. 224.
[HUGHES.]   Friday, November 16.

> . . . *Fulgente trahit constrictos Gloria curru*
> *Non minus ignotos generosis* . . .—Hor. *Sat.* 6.

IF we look abroad upon the great Multitude of Mankind, and
endeavour to trace out the Principles of Action in every
Individual, it will, I think, seem highly probable that Ambition runs through the whole Species, and that every Man in
Proportion to the Vigour of his Complection is more or less
actuated by it.   It is indeed no uncommon thing to meet with
Men, who, by the natural Bent of their Inclinations, and without the Discipline of Philosophy, aspire not to the Heights of
Power and Grandeur; who never set their Hearts upon a
numerous Train of Clients and Dependancies, nor other gay
Appendages of Greatness; who are contented with a Competency, and will not molest their Tranquility to gain an
Abundance: But it is not therefore to be concluded that such
a Man is not ambitious: his Desires may have cut out another
Channel, and determin'd him to other Pursuits; the Motive
however may be still the same; and in these Cases likewise the
Man may be equally pushed on with the Desire of Distinction.

Though the pure Consciousness of worthy Actions, abstracted
from the Views of popular Applause, be to a generous Mind
an ample Reward, yet the Desire of Distinction was doubtless
implanted in our Natures as an additional Incentive to exert
our selves in virtuous Excellence.

This Passion indeed, like all others, is frequently perverted
to evil and ignoble Purposes; so that we may account for many
of the Excellencies and Follies of Life upon the same innate
Principle, to wit, the Desire of being remarkable: For this as
it has been differently cultivated by Education, Study, and
Converse, will bring forth suitable Effects as it falls in with an
ingenuous Disposition or a corrupt Mind; it does accordingly
express it self in Acts of Magnanimity or selfish Cunning, as it
meets with a good or a weak Understanding.   As it has been
employed in embellishing the Mind or adorning the Outside;
it renders the Man eminently Praise-worthy or ridiculous.
Ambition therefore is not to be confined only to one Passion
or Pursuit; for as the same Humours in Constitutions otherwise
different affect the Body after different Manners, so the same
aspiring Principle within us sometimes breaks forth upon one
Object, sometimes upon another.

It cannot be doubted but that there is as great a Desire of
Glory in a Ring of Wrestlers, or Cudgel-Players, as in any other
more refined Competition for Superiority.   No Man that could

avoid it, would ever suffer his Head to be broken but out of a Principle of Honour; this is the secret Spring that pushes them forward, and the Superiority which they gain above the undistinguished Many, does more than repair those Wounds they have received in the Combat. 'Tis Mr. *Waller*'s Opinion, that *Julius Caesar*, had he not been Master of the *Roman* Empire, would in all Probability have made an excellent Wrestler.

> *Great* Julius *on the Mountains bred,*
> *A Flock perhaps or Herd had led:*
> *He that the World subdued, had been*
> *But the best Wrestler on the Green.*

That he subdued the World, was owing to the Accidents of Art and Knowledge; had he not met with those Advantages, the same Sparks of Emulation would have kindled within him, and prompted him to distinguish himself in some Enterprize of a lower Nature. Since therefore no Man's Lot is so unalterably fixed in this Life, but that a thousand Accidents may either forward or disappoint his Advancement, it is, methinks, a pleasant and inoffensive Speculation, to consider a great Man as divested of all the adventitious Circumstances of Fortune, and to bring him down in one's Imagination to that low Station of Life, the Nature of which bears some distant Resemblance to that high one he is at present possessed of. Thus one may view him exercising in Miniature those Talents of Nature, which being drawn out by Education to their full Length, enable him for the Discharge of some important Employment. On the other Hand, one may raise uneducated Merit to such a Pitch of Greatness, as may seem equal to the possible Extent of his improved Capacity.

Thus Nature furnishes a Man with a general Appetite of Glory, Education determines it to this or that particular Object. The Desire of Distinction is not, I think, in any Instance more observable than in the variety of Out-sides and new Appearances, which the Modish part of the World are oblig'd to provide, in order to make themselves remarkable; for any thing glaring and particular, either in Behaviour or Apparel, is known to have this good Effect, that it catches the Eye, and will not suffer you to pass over the Person so adorned without due Notice and Observation. It has likewise, upon this Account, been frequently resented as a very great Slight, to leave any Gentleman out of a Lampoon or Satyr, who has as much right to be there as his Neighbour, because it supposes the Person not eminent enough to be taken notice of. To this passionate fondness for Distinction are owing various frolick-some and irregular Practises, as sallying out into Nocturnal

Exploits, breaking of Windows, singing of Catches, beating the Watch, getting Drunk twice a Day, killing a great Number of Horses; with many other Enterprizes of the like fiery Nature; For certainly many a Man is more Rakish and Extravagant than he would willingly be, were there not others to look on and give their Approbation.

One very common, and at the same time the most absurd Ambition that ever shew'd it self in Humane Nature, is that which comes upon a Man with Experience and old Age, the Season when it might be expected he should be wisest; and therefore it cannot receive any of those lessening Circumstances which do, in some measure, excuse the disorderly Ferments of youthful Blood: I mean the passion for getting Money, exclusive of the Character of the Provident Father, the Affectionate Husband, or the Generous Friend. It may be remarked for the Comfort of honest Poverty, that this Desire reigns most in those who have but few good Qualities to recommend 'em. This is a Weed that will grow in a barren Soil. Humanity, Good Nature, and the Advantages of a Liberal Education, are incompatible with Avarice. 'Tis strange to see how suddenly this abject Passion kills all the noble Sentiments and generous Ambitions that adorn Humane Nature; it renders the Man who is over-run with it a peevish and cruel Master, a severe Parent, an unsociable Husband, a distant and mistrustful Friend. But it is more to the present Purpose to consider it as an absurd Passion of the Heart, rather than as a vicious Affection of the Mind. As there are frequent Instances to be met with of a Proud Humility, so this Passion, contrary to most others, affects Applause, by avoiding all Shew and Appearance; for this reason it will not sometimes endure even the common Decencies of Apparel. *A Covetous Man will call himself poor, that you may sooth his Vanity by contradicting him.* Love, and the Desire of Glory, as they are the most natural, so they are capable of being refined into the most delicate and rational Passions. 'Tis true, the wise Man who strikes out of the secret Paths of a private Life for Honour and Dignity, allured by the Splendor of a Court, and the unfelt Weight of publick Employment, whether he succeeds in his Attempts or no, usually comes near enough to this painted Greatness to discern the Dawbing; he is then desirous of extricating himself out of the Hurry of Life, that he may pass away the Remainder of his Days in Tranquility and Retirement.

It may be thought then but common Prudence in a Man not to change a better State for a worse, nor ever to quit that which he knows he shall take up again with Pleasure; and yet if human Life be not a little moved with the gentle Gales of

Hopes and Fears, there may be some Danger of its stagnating in an unmanly Indolence and Security. It is a known Story of *Domitian*, that after he had possessed himself of the *Roman* Empire his Desires turn'd upon catching Flies. Active and Masculine Spirits in the Vigour of Youth neither can nor ought to remain at Rest: If they debar themselves from aiming at a noble Object, their Desires will move downwards, and they will feel themselves actuated by some low and abject Passion. Thus if you cut off the top Branches of a Tree, and will not suffer it to grow any higher, it will not therefore cease to grow, but will quickly shoot out at the Bottom. The Man indeed who goes into the World only with the narrow Views of Self-Interest, who catches at the Applause of an idle Multitude, as he can find no solid Contentment at the End of his Journey, so he deserves to meet with Disappointments in his Way: But he who is actuated by a nobler Principle, whose Mind is so far enlarged as to take in the Prospect of his Country's Good, who is enamour'd with that Praise which is one of the fair Attendants of Virtue, and values not those Acclamations which are not seconded by the impartial Testimony of his own Mind; who repines not at the low Station which Providence has at present allotted him, but yet would willingly advance himself by justifiable Means to a more rising and advantageous Ground; such a Man is warmed with a generous Emulation; it is a virtuous Movement in him to wish and to endeavour that his Power of doing Good may be equal to his Will.

The Man who is fitted out by Nature, and sent into the World with great Abilities, is capable of doing great Good or Mischief in it. It ought therefore to be the Care of Education to infuse into the untainted Youth early Notices of Justice and Honour, that so the possible Advantages of good Parts may not take an evil Turn, nor be perverted to base and unworthy Purposes. It is the Business of Religion and Philosophy not so much to extinguish our Passions, as to regulate and direct them to valuable well-chosen Objects: When these have pointed out to us which Course we may lawfully steer, 'tis no Harm to set out all our Sail; if the Storms and Tempests of Adversity should rise upon us, and not suffer us to make the Haven where we would be, it will however prove no small Consolation to us in these Circumstances, that we have neither mistaken our Course, nor fallen into Calamities of our own procuring.

Religion therefore (were we to consider it no further than as it interposes in the Affairs of this Life) is highly valuable, and worthy of great Veneration; as it settles the various Pretensions, and otherwise interfering Interests of mortal Men, and thereby consults the Harmony and Order of the great

Community; as it gives a Man room to play his Part, and exert his Abilities; as it animates to Actions truly laudable in themselves, in their Effects beneficial to Society; as it inspires rational Ambition, correct Love, and elegant Desire.

No. 225.

[ADDISON.] Saturday, November 17.

Nullum numen abest si sit prudentia.—Juv.

I HAVE often thought if the Minds of Men were laid open, we should see but little Difference between that of the Wise Man and that of the Fool. There are infinite *Reveries*, numberless Extravagancies, and a perpetual Train of Vanities which pass through both. The great Difference is, that the first knows how to pick and cull his Thoughts for Conversation, by suppressing some, and communicating others; whereas the other lets them all indifferently fly out in Words. This sort of Discretion, however, has no Place in private Conversation between intimate Friends. On such Occasions the wisest Men very often Talk like the weakest; for indeed the Talking with a Friend is nothing else but *thinking aloud*.

Tully has therefore very justly exposed a Precept delivered by some Ancient Writers, That a Man should live with his Enemy in such a manner, as might leave him room to become his Friend; and with his Friend in such a manner, that if he became his Enemy it should not be in his Power to hurt him. The first part of this Rule, which regards our Behaviour towards an Enemy, is indeed very reasonable, as well as very prudential; but the latter part of it, which regards our Behaviour towards a Friend, savours more of Cunning than of Discretion, and would cut a Man off from the greatest Pleasures of Life, which are the Freedoms of Conversation with a bosom Friend. Besides, that when a Friend is turned into an Enemy, and (as the Son of *Sirach* calls himself) a Bewrayer of Secrets, the World is just enough to accuse the Perfidiousness of the Friend, rather than the Indiscretion of the Person who confided in him.

Discretion does not only shew it self in Words, but in all the Circumstances of Action, and is like an Under-Agent of Providence to guide and direct us in the ordinary Concerns of Life.

There are many more shining Qualities in the Mind of Man, but there is none so useful as Discretion; it is this indeed which gives a Value to all the rest, which sets them at work in their proper Times and Places, and turns them to the Advantage of the Person who is possessed of them. Without it Learning is Pedantry, and Wit Impertinence; Virtue it self looks like Weakness; the best Parts only qualifie a Man to be more sprightly in Errors, and active to his own Prejudice.

Nor does Discretion only make a Man the Master of his own Parts, but of other Men's. The discreet Man finds out the Talents of those he Converses with, and knows how to apply them to proper Uses. Accordingly if we look into particular Communities and Divisions of Men, we may observe that it is the Discreet Man, not the Witty, nor the Learned, nor the Brave who guides the Conversation, and gives Measures to the Society. A Man with great Talents, but void of Discretion, is like *Polyphemus* in the Fable, Strong and Blind, endued with an Irresistible Force which for want of Sight is of no use to him.

Though a Man has all other Perfections, and wants Discretion, he will be of no great Consequence in the World; but if he has this single Talent in Perfection, and but a common share of others, he may do what he pleases in his particular Station of Life.

At the same time that I think Discretion the most useful Talent a Man can be Master of, I look upon Cunning to be the Accomplishment of little, mean, ungenerous Minds. Discretion points out the noblest Ends to us, and pursues the most proper and laudable Methods of attaining them: Cunning has only private selfish Aims, and sticks at nothing which may make them succeed. Discretion has large and extended Views, and, like a well-formed Eye, commands a whole Horizon: Cunning is a kind of Short-sightedness, that discovers the minutest Objects which are near at hand, but is not able to discern things at a distance. Discretion the more it is discovered, gives a greater Authority to the Person who possesses it: Cunning, when it is once detected, loses its force, and makes a Man incapable of bringing about even those Events which he might have done, had he passed only for a plain Man. Discretion is the Perfection of Reason, and a Guide to us in all the Duties of Life: Cunning is a kind of Instinct, that only looks out after our immediate Interest and Welfare. Discretion is only found in Men of strong Sense and good Understandings: Cunning is often to be met with in Brutes themselves, and in Persons who are but the fewest Removes from them. In short, Cunning is only the Mimick of Discretion, and may pass upon weak Men, in the same manner as Vivacity is often mistaken for Wit, and Gravity for Wisdom.

The Cast of Mind which is natural to a discreet Man makes him look forward into Futurity, and consider what will be his Condition millions of Ages hence, as well as what it is at present. He knows that the Misery or Happiness which are reserved for him in another World, lose nothing of their Reality by being placed at so great a distance from him. The Objects do not appear little to him because they are remote. He considers that those Pleasures and Pains which lie hid in Eternity approach nearer to him every Moment, and will be present with him in their full Weight and Measure, as much as those Pains and Pleasures which he feels at this very Instant. For this Reason he is careful to secure to himself that which is the proper Happiness of his Nature, and the ultimate Design of his Being. He carries his Thoughts to the End of every Action, and considers the most distant as well as the most immediate Effects of it. He supersedes every little Prospect of Gain and Advantage which offers it self here, if he does not find it consistent with his Views of an Hereafter. In a Word, his Hopes are full of Immortality, his Schemes are large and glorious, and his Conduct suitable to one who knows his true Interest, and how to pursue it by proper Methods.

I have, in this Essay upon Discretion, considered it both as an Accomplishment and as a Virtue, and have therefore described it in its full Extent; not only as it is conversant about worldly Affairs, but as it regards our whole Existence; not only as it is the Guide of a mortal Creature, but as it is in general the Director of a reasonable Being. It is in this Light that Discretion is represented by the Wise Man, who sometimes mentions it under the name of Discretion, and sometimes under that of Wisdom. It is indeed (as described in the latter part of this Paper) the greatest Wisdom, but at the same time in the Power of every one to attain. Its Advantages are infinite, but its Acquisition easie; or, to speak of her in the Words of the Apocryphal Writer whom I quoted in my last *Saturday*'s Paper, *Wisdom is glorious, and never fadeth away, yet she is easily seen of them that love her, and found of such as seek her. She preventeth them that desire her, in making herself first known unto them. He that seeketh her early shall have no great Travel: for he shall find her sitting at his Doors. To think therefore upon her is perfection of Wisdom, and whoso watcheth for her shall quickly be without Care. For she goeth about seeking such as are worthy of her, sheweth herself favourably unto them in the Ways, and meeteth them in every Thought.* C

No. 226.
[STEELE.]   Monday, November 19.

Mutum est pictura poema.

I have very often lamented and hinted my Sorrow in several Speculations, that the Art of Painting is made so little Use of to the Improvement of our Manners. When we consider that it places the Action of the Person represented in the most agreeable Aspect imaginable, that it does not only express the Passion or Concern as it sits upon him who is drawn, but has under those Features the Height of the Painter's Imagination, What strong Images of Virtue and Humanity might we not expect would be instilled into the Mind from the Labours of the Pencil? This is a Poetry which would be understood with much less Capacity, and less Expence of Time, than what is taught by Writings; but the Use of it is generally perverted, and that admirable Skill prostituted to the basest and most unworthy Ends. Who is the better Man for beholding the most beautiful *Venus*, the best wrought *Bacchanal*, the Images of sleeping *Cupids*, languishing Nymphs, or any of the Representations of Gods, Goddesses, Demygods, Satyrs, *Polyphemes*, Sphinxes or Fauns? But if the Virtues and Vices which are sometimes pretended to be represented under such Draughts, were given us by the Painter in the Characters of real Life, and the Persons of Men and Women whose Actions have rendered them laudable or infamous; we should not see a good History-Piece without receiving an instructive Lecture. There needs no other Proof of this Truth, than the Testimony of every reasonable Creature who has seen the Cartons in her Majesty's Gallery at *Hampton-Court*: These are Representations of no less Actions than those of our Blessed Saviour and his Apostles. As I now sit and recollect the warm Images which the admirable *Raphael* has raised, it is impossible, even from the faint Traces in one's Memory of what one has not seen these two Years, to be unmoved at the Horrour and Reverence which appears in the whole Assembly when the mercenary Man fell down dead; at the Amazement of the Man born blind, when he first receives Sight; or at the graceless Indignation of the Sorcerer, when he is struck blind. The Lame, when they first find Strength in their Feet, stand Doubtful of their new Vigour. The heavenly Apostles appear acting these great things, with a deep Sense of the Infirmities which they relieve, but no Value of themselves who administer to their Weakness. They know themselves to be but Instruments; and the generous Distress they are painted in when divine Honours are offered to them, is a Representation in the most exquisite Degree of the Beauty of Holiness. When St. *Paul* is preaching to the *Athenians*, with what wonderful Art are almost all the different Tempers of Mankind represented in that elegant Audience? You see one credulous of all that is said, another wrapt up in deep Suspence, another saying there is some Reason in what he says, another angry that the Apostle destroys a favourite Opinion which he is unwilling to give up, another wholly convinced and holding out his Hands in Rapture; while the Generality attend, and wait for the Opinion of those who are of leading Characters in the Assembly. I will not pretend so much as to mention that Chart on which is drawn the Appearance of our Blessed Lord after his Resurrection. Present Authority, late Suffering, Humility and Majesty, Despotick Command and Divine Love, are at once seated in his Celestial Aspect. The Figures of the Eleven Apostles are all in the same Passion of Admiration, but discover it differently according to their Characters. *Peter* receives his Master's Orders on his Knees with an Admiration mixed with a more particular Attention: The two next with a more open Extasie, though still constrained by the Awe of the Divine Presence: The beloved Disciple, whom I take to be the Right of the two first Figures, has in his Countenance Wonder drowned in Love; and the last Personage, whose Back is towards the Spectator and his Side towards the Presence, one would fancy to be St. *Thomas*, as abashed by the Conscience of his former Diffidence; which perplexed Concern it is possible *Raphael* thought too hard a Task to draw but by this Acknowledgment of the Difficulty to describe it.

The whole Work is an Exercise of the highest Piety in the Painter; and all the Touches of a Religious Mind are expressed in a manner much more forcible than can possibly be performed by the most moving Eloquence. These invaluable Pieces are very justly in the Hands of the greatest and most pious Soveraign in the World; and cannot be the frequent Object of every one at their own Leisure: But as an Engraver is to the Painter, what a Printer is to an Author, it is worthy Her Majesty's Name, that she has encouraged that noble Artist, Monsieur *Dorigny*, to publish these Works of *Raphael*. We have of this Gentleman a Piece of the Transfiguration, which is held a Work second to none in the World.

Methinks it would be ridiculous in our People of Condition, after their large Bounties to Foreigners of no Name or Merit, should they overlook this Occasion of having, for a trifling Subscription, a Work which it is impossible for a Man of Sense to behold, without being warmed with the noblest Sentiments that can be inspired by Love, Admiration, Compassion, Contempt of this World, and Expectation of a Better.

It is certainly the greatest Honour we can do our Country, to distinguish Strangers of Merit who apply to us with Modesty and Diffidence, which generally accompanies Merit. No Opportunity of this Kind ought to be neglected; and a modest Behaviour should alarm us to examine whether we do not lose something excellent under that Disadvantage in the Possessor of that Quality. My Skill in Paintings, where one is not directed by the Passion of the Pictures, is so inconsiderable, that I am in very great Perplexity when I offer to speak of any Performance of Painters of Landskips, Buildings, or single Figures. This makes me at a Loss how to mention the Pieces which Mr. *Boul* exposes to Sale by Auction on *Wednesday* next in *Shandois-street*: But having heard him commended by those who have bought of him heretofore for great Integrity in his Dealing, and overheard him himself (tho' a laudable Painter) say nothing of his own was fit to come into the Room with those he had to sell, I feared I should lose an Occasion of serving a Man of Worth in omitting to speak of his Auction.

ADVERTISEMENT

There is arrived from Italy *a Painter who acknowledges himself the greatest Person of the Age in that Art, and is willing to be as renowned in this Island as he declares he is in foreign Parts.*

The Doctor paints the Poor for nothing.

T

No. 227.
[ADDISON.]   Tuesday, November 20.

'Ὦ μοι ἐγὼ τί πάθω; τί ὁ δύσσοος; οὐχ ὑπακούεις;
Τὰν βαίταν ἀποδὺς εἰς κύματα τῆνα ἁλεῦμαι,
Ὧπερ τὼς θύννως σκοπιάζεται "Ολπις ὁ γριπεύς·
Κἤκα μὴ 'ποθάνω, τό γε μὰν τεὸν ἁδὺ τέτυκται.—Theoc.

In my last *Thursday*'s Paper I made mention of a Place called *The Lover's Leap*, which I find has raised a great Curiosity among several of my Correspondents. I there told them that this Leap was used to be taken from a Promontory of *Leucas*. This *Leucas* was formerly a Part of *Acarnania*, being joined to it by a narrow Neck of Land, which the Sea has by length of time overflowed and washed away; so that at present *Leucas* is divided from the Continent, and is a little Island in the *Ionian* Sea. The Promontory of this Island, from whence the Lover took his Leap, was formerly called *Leucate*. If the Reader has a mind to know both the Island and the Promontory by their Modern Titles, he will find in his Map the Ancient Island of *Leucas* under the Name of St. *Mauro*, and the Ancient Promontory of *Leucate* under the Name of the Cape of St. *Mauro*.

Since I am engaged thus far in Antiquity, I must observe that *Theocritus* in the Motto prefixed to my Paper, describes one of his despairing Shepherds addressing himself to his Mistress after the following manner. *Alas! What will become of me? Wretch that I am! Will you not hear me? I'll throw off my Cloaths, and take a Leap into that part of the Sea which is so much frequented by* Olphis *the Fisherman. And tho' I should escape with my Life, I know you will be pleased with it.* I shall leave it with the Criticks to determine whether the Place which the Shepherd so particularly points out, was not the above-mentioned *Leucate*, or at least some other Lover's Leap, which was supposed to have had the same Effect. I cannot believe, as all the Interpreters do, that the Shepherd means nothing further here, than that he would drown himself, since he represents the Issue of his Leap as doubtful, by adding that if he should escape with Life, he knows his Mistress would be pleased with it; which is, according to our Interpretation, that she would rejoice any way to get rid of a Lover, who was so troublesome to her.

After this short Preface I shall present my Reader with some Letters which I have received upon this Subject. The first is sent me by a Physician.

'*Mr.* Spectator,

The Lover's Leap which you mention in your Two hundred and twenty third Paper, was generally, I believe, a very effectual Cure for Love, and not only for Love, but for all other Evils. In short, Sir, I am afraid it was such a Leap as that which *Hero* took to get rid of her Passion for *Leander*. A Man is in no danger of breaking his Heart, who breaks his Neck to prevent it. I know very well the Wonders which Ancient Authors relate concerning this Leap; and in particular, that very many Persons who tried it escaped not only with their Lives, but their Limbs. If by this means they got rid of their Love, tho' it may in part be ascribed to the Reasons you give for it; why may not we suppose, that the Cold Bath into which they plunged themselves, had also some share in their Cure? A Leap into the Sea, or into any Creek of Salt Waters, very often gives a new Motion to the Spirits, and a new Turn to the Blood, for which reason we prescribe it in Distempers which no other Medicine will reach. I could produce a Quotation out of a very venerable Author, in which the Phrenzy produced by Love is compared to that which is produced by the biting of a mad Dog. But as this Comparison is a little too coarse for your Paper, and might look as if it were cited to ridicule the Author who has made use of it, I shall only hint at it, and desire you to consider whether if the Phrenzy produced by these two different Causes be of the same Nature, it may not very properly be cured by the same Means.

I am, Sir,

Your most humble Servant,
and Well-wisher,

ESCULAPIUS.'

'*Mr.* Spectator,

I am a young Woman crossed in Love. My Story is very long and melancholy. To give you the Heads of it, a young Gentleman, after having made his Applications to me for three Years together, and filled my Head with a thousand Dreams of Happiness, some few Days since married another. Pray tell me in what Part of the World your Promontory lies, which you call the Lover's Leap, and whether one may go to it by Land. But alas I am afraid it has lost its Virtue, and that a Woman of our Times would find no more Relief in taking such a Leap, than in singing an Hymn to *Venus*. So that I must cry out with *Dido* in *Dryden's Virgil,*

Ah! cruel Heav'n, that made no Cure for Love!

Your disconsolate Servant,

ATHENAIS.'

'Mister Spictatur,

My Heart is so full of Loves and Passions for Mrs. *Gwinifrid,* and she is so pettish, and over-run with Cholers against me, that if I had the good Happiness to have my Dwelling (which is placed by my great Cran-Father upon the Pottom of an Hill) no farther distance but twenty Mile from the Lofers Leap, I would indeed indeafour to preak my Neck upon it on purpose. Now, good Mister Spictatur of *Crete Prittain,* you must know it, there iss in *Caernarvanshire* a fery pig Mountain, the Clory of all *Wales,* which iss named *Penmainmaure,* and you must also know, it iss no great Journey on Foot from me; but the Road is stony and bad for Shoes. Now there is upon the Forehead of this Mountain a very high Rock, (like a Parish Steeple) that cometh a huge deal over the Sea; so when I am in my Melancholies, and I do throw my self from it, I do desire my fery good Friend to tell me in his Spictatur, if I shall be cure of my griefous Lofes; for there is the Sea clear as the Glass, and ass creen as the Leek: Then likewise, if I be drown, and preak my Neck, if Mrs. *Gwinifrid* will not lofe me afterwards. Pray be speedy in your Answers, for I am in crete haste, and it is my

Tesires to do my Pusiness without loss of Time. I remain, with cordial Affections, your ever loving Friend,

Davyth ap Shenkyn.

P. S. My Law Suits have brought me to *London*, but I have lost my Causes; and so have made my Resolutions to go down and Leap before the Frosts begin; for I am apt to take Colds.'

Ridicule, perhaps, is a better Expedient against Love than sober Advice, and I am of opinion that *Hudibras* and Don Quixote may be as effectual to cure the Extravagancies of this Passion, as any of the old Philosophers. I shall therefore publish, very speedily, the Translation of a little *Greek* Manuscript, which is sent me by a Learned Friend. It appears to have been a Piece of those Records which were kept in the Temple of *Apollo*, that stood upon the Promontory of *Leucate*. The Reader will find it to be a Summary Account of several Persons who tried the Lover's Leap, and of the Success they found in it. As there seem to be in it some Anachronisms and Deviations from the Ancient Orthography, I am not wholly satisfied my self that it is authentick, and not rather the Production of one of those *Graecian* Sophisters, who have imposed upon the World several spurious Works of this Nature. I speak this by way of Precaution, because I know there are several Writers of uncommon Erudition, who would not fail to expose my Ignorance, if they caught me tripping in a matter of so great Moment.   C

No. 228.

[STEELE.]   Wednesday, November 21.

Percunctatorem fugito, nam garrulus idem est.—Hor.

THERE is a Creature who has all the Organs of Speech, a tolerable good Capacity for conceiving what is said to it, together with a pretty proper Behaviour in all the Occurrences of common Life; but naturally very vacant of Thought in its self, and therefore forced to apply it self to foreign Assistances. Of this Make is that Man who is very inquisitive: You may often observe, that though he speaks as good Sense as any Man upon any thing with which he is well acquainted, he cannot trust to the Range of his own Fancy to entertain himself upon that Foundation, but goes on to still new Enquiries. Thus, though you know he is fit for the most polite Conversation, you shall see him very well contented to sit by a Jockey giving an Account of the many Revolutions in his Horse's Health, what

Potion he made him take, how that agreed with him, how afterwards he came to his Stomach and his Exercise, or any the like Impertinence; and be as well pleased as if you talked to him on the most important Truths. This Humour is far from making a Man unhappy, though it may subject him to Raillery; for he generally falls in with a Person who seems to be born for him, which is your talkative Fellow. It is so ordered that there is a secret Bent, as natural as the Meeting of different Sexes, in these two Characters, to supply each others Wants. I had the Honour the other Day to sit in a publick Room, and saw an inquisitive Man look with an Air of Satisfaction upon the Approach of one of these Talkers. The Man of ready Utterance sat down by him; and rubbing his Head, leaning on his Arm, and making an uneasie Countenance, he began; 'There is no Manner of News to Day. I cannot tell what is the Matter with me, but I slept very ill last Night; whether I caught Cold or no I know not, but I fancy I do not wear Shoes thick enough for the Weather, and I have coughed all this Week: It must be so, for the Custom of washing my Head Winter and Summer with cold Water, prevents any Injury from the Season entering that Way; so it must come in at my Feet: But I take no Notice of it, as it comes so it goes. Most of our Evils proceed from too much Tenderness; and our Faces are naturally as little able to resist the Cold as other Parts. The *Indian* answered very well to an *European*, who asked him how he could go naked; I am all Face.'

I observed this Discourse was as welcome to my general Inquirer as any other of more Consequence could have been; but some Body calling our Talker to another Part of the Room, the Inquirer told the next Man who sat by him, that Mr. such a one, who was just gone from him, used to wash his Head in cold Water every Morning; and so repeated almost *Verbatim* all that had been said to him. The Truth is, the Inquisitive are the Funnels of Conversation; they do not take in any thing for their own Use, but merely to pass it to another: They are the Channels thro' which all the Good and Evil that is spoken in Town are conveyed. Such as are offended at them, or think they suffer by their Behaviour, may themselves mend that Inconvenience; for they are not a malicious People, and if you will supply them, you may contradict any thing they have said before by their own Mouths. A further Account of a thing is one of the gratefullest Goods that can arrive to them; and it is seldom that they are more particular than to say, The Town will have it, or, I have it from a good Hand: So that there is Room for the Town to know the Matter more particularly, and for a better Hand to contradict what was said by a good one.

I have not known this Humour more ridiculous than in a Father, who has been earnestly sollicitous to have an Account how his Son has passed his leisure Hours; if it be in a Way thoroughly insignificant, there cannot be a greater Joy than an Inquirer discovers in seeing him follow so hopefully his own Steps: But this Humour among Men is most pleasant when they are saying something which is not wholly proper for a third Person to hear, and yet is in it self indifferent. The other Day there came in a well-dressed young Fellow, and two Gentlemen of this Species immediately fell a whispering his Pedigree. I could over-hear, by Breaks, She was his Aunt; then an Answer, Ay, she was of the Mother's Side: Then again in a little lower Voice, His Father wore generally a darker Wig; Answer, Not much. But this Gentleman wears higher Heels to his Shooes.

As the Inquisitive, in my Opinion, are such merely from a Vacancy in their own Imaginations, there is nothing, methinks, so dangerous as to communicate Secrets to them; for the same Temper of Inquiry makes them as impertinently communicative: But no Man though he converses with them need put himself in their Power, for they will be contented with Matters of less Moment as well. When there is Fewel enough, no Matter what it is———Thus the Ends of Sentences in the News Papers, as *This wants Confirmation, This occasions many Speculations, And Time will discover the Event*, are read by them, and considered not as meer Expletives.

One may see now and then this Humour accompanied with an insatiable Desire of knowing what passes, without turning it to any Use in the World but meerly their own Entertainment. A Mind which is gratified this Way is adapted to Humour and Pleasantry, and formed for an unconcerned Character in the World; and like my self to be a meer Spectator. This Curiosity, without Malice or Self-Interest, lays up in the Imagination a Magazine of Circumstances which cannot but entertain when they are produced in Conversation. If one were to know from the Man of the first Quality to the meanest Servant, the different Intrigues, Sentiments, Pleasures and Interests of Mankind, would it not be the most pleasing Entertainment imaginable to enjoy so constant a Farce, as the observing Mankind much more different from themselves in their secret Thoughts and publick Actions, than in their Night-Caps and long Periwiggs?

'*Mr.* SPECTATOR,

Plutarch tells us, that *Caius Gracchus*, the *Roman*, was frequently hurried by his Passion into so loud and tumultuous a Way of speaking, and so strained his Voice as not to be able to proceed. To remedy this Excess, he had an ingenious Servant, by Name *Licinius*, always attending him with a Pitch Pipe, or Instrument, to regulate the Voice; who, whenever he heard his Master begin to be high, immediately touched a soft Note; at which, 'tis said, *Caius* would presently abate and grow calm.

Upon recollecting this Story, I have frequently wondered that this useful Instrument should have been so long discontinued; especially since we find that this good Office of *Licinius* has preserved his Memory for many hundred Years, which, methinks, should have encouraged some one to have revived it, if not for the publick Good, yet for his own Credit. It may be objected, that our loud Talkers are so fond of their own Noise, that they would not take it well to be checked by their Servants: But granting this to be true, surely any of their Hearers have a very good Title to play a soft Note in their own Defence. To be short, no *Licinius* appearing, and the Noise encreasing, I was resolved to give this late long Vacation to the Good of my Country; and I have at length, by the Assistance of an ingenious Artist, (who works for the Royal Society) almost compleated my Design, and shall be ready in a short Time to furnish the Publick with what Number of these Instruments they please, either to lodge at Coffee-houses, or carry for their own private Use. In the mean Time I shall pay that Respect to several Gentlemen who I know will be in Danger of offending against this Instrument, to give them Notice of it by private Letters, in which I shall only write, *Get a* Licinius.

I should now trouble you no longer, but that I must not conclude without desiring you to accept one of these Pipes, which shall be left for you with *Buckley*; and which I hope will be serviceable to you, since as you are silent your self, you are most open to the Insults of the Noisy.

I am, Sir, &c. W. B.

I had almost forgot to inform you, that as an Improvement in this Instrument there will be a particular Note which I call a Hush-note; and this is to be made use of against a long Story, Swearing, Obsceneness, and the like.'　　　　　　　　T

No. 229.

[ADDISON.]   Thursday, November 22.

> . . . *Spirat adhuc amor,*
> *Vivuntque commissi calores*
> *Aeoliae fidibus puellae.*—Hor.

AMONG the many famous Pieces of Antiquity which are still
to be seen at *Rome*, there is the Trunc of a Statue which has lost
the Arms, Legs and Head, but discovers such an exquisite
Workmanship in what remains of it, that *Michael Angelo*
declared he had learned his whole Art from it. Indeed he
studied it so attentively, that he made most of his Statues, and
even his Pictures in that *gusto*, to make use of the *Italian*
Phrase; for which reason this maimed Statue is still called
Michael Angelo's School.

A Fragment of *Sappho*, which I design for the Subject of
this Paper, is in as great Reputation among the Poets and
Criticks, as the mutilated Figure Above-mentioned is among
the Statuaries and Painters. Several of our Country-men, and
Mr. *Dryden* in particular, seem very often to have copied after
it in their Dramatick Writings, and in their Poems upon Love.

Whatever might have been the Occasion of this Ode, the
English Reader will enter into the Beauties of it, if he supposes
it to have been written in the Person of a Lover sitting by his
Mistress. I shall set to view three different Copies of this
beautiful Original. The first is a Translation by *Catullus*, the
second by Monsieur *Boileau*, and the last by a Gentleman,
whose Translation of the *Hymn to Venus* has been so deservedly admired.

Ad LESBIAM.

> *Ille mi par esse Deo videtur,*
> *Ille, si fas est, superare divos,*
> *Qui sedens adversus identidem te,*
>   *Spectat, & audit*
>
> *Dulce ridentem, misero quod omnis*
> *Eripit sensus mihi: nam simul te*
> *Lesbia adspexi, nihil est super mi*
>   Quod loquar amens.
>
> *Lingua sed torpet, tenuis sub artus*
> *Flamma dimanat, sonitu suopte*
> *Tinniunt aures, gemina teguntur*
>   *Lumina nocte.*

My Learned Reader will know very well the Reason why one
of these Verses is Printed in *Roman* Letter; and if he compares
this Translation with the Original, will find that the three first

Stanzas are rendered almost Word for Word, and not only with the same Elegance, but with the same short Turn of Expression which is so remarkable in the *Greek*, and so peculiar to the *Sapphick* Ode. I cannot imagine for what reason Madam *Dacier* has told us that this Ode of *Sappho* is preserved entire in *Longinus*, since it is manifest to any one who looks into that Author's Quotation of it, that there must at least have been another Stanza, which is not transmitted to us.

The second Translation of this Fragment which I shall here cite, is that of Monsieur *Boileau*'s.

> *Heureux! qui près de toi, pour toi seule soûpire :*
> *Qui joûit du plaisir de t'entendre parler :*
> *Qui te voit quelquefois doucement lui soûrire,*
> *Les Dieux, dans son bonheur, peuvent-ils l'égaler ?*
>
> *Je sens de veine en veine une subtile flamme*
> *Courir par tout mon corps, si-tost que je te vois :*
> *Et dans les doux transports, où s'égare mon ame,*
> *Je ne sçaurois trouver de langue, ni de voix.*
>
> *Un nuage confus se répand sur ma vuë,*
> *Je n'entens plus, je tombe en de douces langueurs ;*
> *Et pasle, sans haleine, interdite, esperduë,*
> *Un frisson me saisit, je tremble, je me meurs.*

The Reader will see that this is rather an Imitation than a Translation. The Circumstances do not lie so thick together, and follow one another witn that Vehemence and Emotion as in the Original. In short, Monsieur *Boileau* has given us all the Poetry, but not all the Passion of this famous Fragment.

I shall in the last Place present my Reader with the *English* Translation.

I.

> *Blest as th' Immortal Gods is he,*
> *The Youth who fondly sits by thee,*
> *And hears and sees thee all the while*
> *Softly speak and sweetly smile.*

II.

> *'Twas this depriv'd my Soul of Rest,*
> *And rais'd such Tumults in my Breast;*
> *For while I gaz'd, in Transport tost,*
> *My Breath was gone, my Voice was lost:*

III.

> *My Bosom glow'd: the subtle Flame*
> *Ran quick thro' all my vital Frame;*
> *O'er my dim Eyes a Darkness hung;*
> *My Ears with hollow Murmurs rung:*

IV.

In dewy Damps my Limbs were chill'd;
My Blood with gentle Horrours thrill'd;
My feeble Pulse forgot to play;
I fainted, sunk, and dy'd away.

Instead of giving any Character of this last Translation, I shall desire my Learned Reader to look into the Criticisms which *Longinus* has made upon the Original. By that means he will know to which of the Translations he ought to give the Preference. I shall only add, that this Translation is written in the very Spirit of *Sappho*, and as near the *Greek* as the Genius of our Language will possibly suffer.

Longinus has observed, that this Description of Love in *Sappho* is an exact Copy of Nature, and that all the Circumstances, which follow one another in such an hurry of Sentiments, notwithstanding they appear repugnant to each other, are really such as happen in the Phrenzies of Love.

I wonder that not one of the Criticks or Editors, through whose Hands this Ode has passed, has taken occasion from it to mention a Circumstance related by *Plutarch.* That Author in the Famous Story of *Antiochus*, who fell in Love with *Stratonice*, his Mother-in-law, and (not daring to discover his Passion) pretended to be confined to his Bed by Sickness, tells us, that *Erasistratus*, the Physician, found out the Nature of his Distemper by those Symptoms of Love which he had learnt from *Sappho*'s Writings. *Stratonice* was in the Room of the Love-sick Prince, when these Symptoms discovered themselves to his Physician; and it is probable that they were not very different from those which *Sappho* here describes in a Lover sitting by his Mistress. This Story of *Antiochus* is so well known, that I need not add the Sequel of it, which has no Relation to my present Subject. C

No. 230.

[STEELE.]   Friday, November 23.

Homines ad Deos nulla re propius accedunt, quam salutem hominibus
dando.—Tull.

HUMAN Nature appears a very deformed, or a very beautiful Object, according to the different Lights in which it is view'd. When we see Men of inflamed Passions, or of wicked Designs, tearing one another to Pieces by open Violence, or undermining each other by secret Treachery; when we observe base and narrow Ends pursued by ignominious and dishonest Means; when we behold Men mix'd in Society as if it were for the Destruction of it; we are even ashamed of our Species, and out of Humour with our own Being: But in another Light, when we behold them mild, good, and benevolent, full of a generous Regard for the publick Prosperity, compassionating each other's Distresses and relieving each other's Wants, we can hardly believe they are Creatures of the same Kind. In this View they appear Gods to each other, in the Exercise of the noblest Power, that of doing Good; and the greatest Compliment we have ever been able to make to our own Being, has been by calling this Disposition of Mind Humanity. We cannot but observe a Pleasure arising in our own Breast upon the seeing or hearing of a generous Action, even when we are wholly disinterested in it. I cannot give a more proper Instance of this, than by a Letter from *Pliny*, in which he recommends a Friend in the most handsome Manner; and, methinks, it would be a great Pleasure to know the Success of this Epistle, though each Party concerned in it has been so many hundred Years in his Grave.

'To MAXIMUS.

What I should gladly do for any Friend of yours, I think I may now with Confidence request for a Friend of mine. *Arrianus Maturius* is the most considerable Man of his Country; when I call him so, I do not speak with Relation to his Fortune, though that is very plentiful, but to his Integrity, Justice, Gravity and Prudence; his Advice is useful to me in Business, and his Judgment in Matters of Learning: His Fidelity, Truth, and good Understanding, are very great; besides this, he loves me as you do, than which I cannot say any thing that signifies a warmer Affection. He has nothing that 's aspiring; and tho' he may rise to the highest Order of Nobility, he keeps himself in an inferiour Rank; yet I think my self bound to use my Endeavours to serve and promote him; and would therefore find the Means of adding something to his Honours while he neither expects nor knows it, nay though he should refuse it. Something, in short, I would have for him that may be honourable, but not troublesome; and I entreat that you will procure him the first thing of this Kind that offers, by which you will not only oblige me, but him also; for though he does not covet it, I know he will be as grateful in acknowledging your Favour as if he had asked it.'

'*Mr*. SPECTATOR,

The Reflections in some of your Papers on the servile Manner of Education now in use, have given Birth to an Ambition, which unless you discountenance it, will, I doubt, engage me in a very difficult, tho' not ungrateful Adventure. I am about to undertake for the sake of the *British* Youth, to instruct them in such a Manner, that the most dangerous Page in *Virgil* or *Homer* may be read by them with much Pleasure, and with perfect Safety to their Persons.

Could I prevail so far as to be honoured with the Protection of some few of them (for I am not Heroe enough to rescue many), my Design is to retire with them to an agreeable Solitude; tho' within the Neighbourhood of a City, for the Convenience of their being instructed in Musick, Dancing, Drawing, Designing, or any other such Accomplishments, which it is conceived may make as proper Diversions for them, and almost as pleasant, as the little sordid Games which dirty School-boys are so much delighted with. It may easily be imagined how such a pretty Society, conversing with none beneath themselves, and sometimes admitted as perhaps not unentertaining Parties amongst better Company, commended and caressed for their little Performances, and turned by such Conversations to a certain Gallantry of Soul, might be brought early acquainted with some of the most polite *English* Writers. This having given them some tolerable Taste of Books, they would make themselves Masters of the *Latin* Tongue by Methods far easier than those in *Lilly*, with as little Difficulty or Reluctance as young Ladies learn to speak *French* or to sing *Italian* Operas. When they had advanced thus far, it would be Time to form their Taste something more exactly: One that had any true Relish of fine Writing, might with great Pleasure, both to himself and them, run over together with them the best *Roman* Historians, Poets, and Orators, and point out their more remarkable Beauties; give them a short Scheme of Chronology, a little View of Geography, Medals, Astronomy, or what else might best feed the busie inquisitive Humour so natural to that Age. Such of them as had the least Spark of Genius, when it was once awakened by the shining Thoughts and great Sentiments of those admired Writers, could not, I believe, be easily with-held from attempting that more difficult Sister Language, whose exalted Beauties they would have heard so often celebrated as the Pride and Wonder of the whole learned World. In the mean while it would be requisite to exercise their Stile in writing any light Pieces that ask more of Fancy than of Judgment; and that frequently in their native Language, which every one methinks should be most concerned to cultivate, especially Letters in which a Gentleman must have so frequent Occasions to distinguish himself. A Set of genteel good-natur'd Youths fallen into such a Manner of Life, would form almost a little Academy, and doubtless prove no such contemptible Companions, as might not often tempt a wiser Man to mingle himself in their Diversions, and draw them into such serious Sports as might prove nothing less instructing than the gravest Lessons: I doubt not but it might be made some of their favourite Plays, to contend which of them should recite a beautiful Part of a Poem or Oration most gracefully, or sometimes to join in acting a Scene of *Terence*, *Sophocles*, or our own *Shakespear*. The Cause of *Milo* might again be pleaded before more favourable Judges, *Caesar* a second Time be taught to tremble, and another race of *Athenians* be afresh enraged at the Ambition of another *Philip*. Amidst these noble Amusements we could hope to see the early Dawnings of their Imagination daily brighten into Sense, their Innocence improve into Virtue, and their unexperienc'd Good-nature directed to a generous Love of their Country.

T   *I am, &c.'*

No. 231.
[ADDISON.]   Saturday, November 24.

O pudor! O pietas! . . .—Mart.

LOOKING over the Letters, which I have lately received from my Correspondents, I met with the following one, which is written with such a Spirit of Politeness, that I could not but be very much pleased with it my self, and question not but it will be as acceptable to the Reader.

'*Mr.* SPECTATOR,

You, who are no Stranger to Publick Assemblies, cannot but have observed the Awe they often strike on such as are obliged to exert any Talent before them. This is a sort of Elegant Distress, to which ingenuous Minds are the most liable, and may therefore deserve some Remarks in your Paper. Many a brave Fellow, who has put his Enemy to Flight in the Field, has been in the utmost Disorder upon making a Speech before a Body of his Friends at home: One would think there was some kind of Fascination in the Eyes of a large Circle of People, when darting all together upon one Person. I have seen a new Actor in a Tragedy so bound up by it as to be scarce able to speak or move, and have expected he would have died above three Acts before the Dagger or Cup of Poison were brought in. It would not be amiss, if such an one were at first introduced as a Ghost, or a Statue, till he recovered his Spirits, and grew fit for some living Part.

As this sudden Desertion of ones-self shews a Diffidence, which is not displeasing, it implies at the same time the greatest Respect to an Audience that can be. It is a sort of Mute Eloquence, which pleads for their Favour much better than Words could do; and we find their Generosity naturally moved to support those who are in so much Perplexity to entertain them. I was extreamly pleased with a late Instance of this kind at the Opera of *Almahide*, in the Encouragement given to a young Singer, whose more than ordinary Concern on her First Appearance, recommended her no less than her agreeable Voice, and just Performance. Meer Bashfulness, without Merit, is awkward; and Merit. without Modesty, in-solent: But Modest Merit has a double Claim to Acceptance, and generally meets with as many Patrons as Beholders.

I am, &c.'

It is impossible that a Person should exert himself to Advan-tage in an Assembly, whether it be his part either to sing or speak, who lies under too great Oppressions of Modesty. I remember, upon talking with a Friend of mine concerning the force of Pronunciation, our Discourse led us into the Enumera-tion of the several Organs of Speech, which an Orator ought to have in Perfection, as the Tongue, the Teeth, the Lips, the Nose, the Palate, and the Wind-pipe. Upon which, says my Friend, you have omitted the most material Organ of them all, and that is the Forehead.

But notwithstanding an Excess of Modesty obstructs the Tongue, and renders it unfit for its Offices, a due Proportion of it is thought so requisite to an Orator, that Rhetoricians have recommended it to their Disciples as a Particular in their Art. *Cicero* tells us, that he never liked an Orator, who did not appear in some little Confusion at the beginning of his Speech, and confesses that he himself never entered upon an Oration without trembling and concern. It is indeed a kind of Deference which is due to a great Assembly, and seldom fails to raise a Benevolence in the Audience towards the Per-son who speaks. My Correspondent has taken notice, that the bravest Men often appear timorous on these Occasions; as indeed we may observe that there is generally no Creature more impudent than a Coward.

> . . . *Lingua melior sed frigida bello*
> *Dextera . . .*

A bold Tongue, and a feeble Arm, are the Qualifications of *Drances* in *Virgil*; as *Homer*, to express a Man both timorous and sawcy, makes use of a kind of Point, which is very rarely to be met with in his Writings; namely, that he had the Eyes of a Dog, but the Heart of a Deer.

A just and reasonable Modesty does not only recommend Eloquence, but sets off every great Talent which a Man can be possessed of. It heightens all the Virtues which it accompanies; like the Shades in Paintings, it raises and rounds every Figure, and makes the Colours more beautiful, tho' not so glaring as they would be without it.

Modesty is not only an Ornament, but also a Guard to Virtue. It is a kind of quick and delicate *feeling* in the Soul, which makes her shrink and withdraw her self from every thing that has Danger in it. It is such an exquisite Sensibility as warns her to shun the first appearance of every thing which is hurtful.

I cannot at present recollect either the Place or Time of what I am going to mention; but I have read somewhere in the History of Ancient *Greece*, that the Women of the Country were seiz'd with an unaccountable Melancholy, which disposed several of them to make away with themselves. The Senate, after having tryed many Expedients to prevent this Self-Murder, which was so frequent among them, Published an Edict, that if any Woman whatever should lay violent Hands upon her self, her Corps should be exposed Naked in the Street, and dragged about the City in the most publick manner. This Edict immediately put a stop to the Practice which was before so common. We may see in this Instance the Strength of Female Modesty, which was able to overcome the Violence even of Madness and Despair. The Fear of Shame in the Fair Sex, was in those Days more prevalent than that of Death.

If Modesty has so great an Influence over our Actions, and is in many cases so impregnable a Fence to Virtue; what can more undermine Morality than that Politeness which reigns among the unthinking part of Mankind, and treats as unfashionable the most ingenuous part of our Behaviour; which recommends Impudence as Good-Breeding, and keeps a Man always in Countenance, not because he is Innocent, but because he is Shameless?

Seneca thought Modesty so great a Check to Vice, that he prescribes to us the Practice of it in Secret, and advises us to raise it in our selves upon imaginary Occasions, when such as are real do not offer themselves; for this is the Meaning of his Precept, that when we are by our selves, and in our greatest Solitudes, we should fancy that *Cato* stands before us, and sees every thing we do. In short, if you banish Modesty out of the World, she carries away with her half the Virtue that is in it.

After these Reflections on Modesty, as it is a Virtue, I must observe, that there is a vicious Modesty, which justly deserves to be ridiculed, and which those Persons very often discover, who value themselves most upon a well-bred Confidence. This happens when a Man is ashamed to act up to his Reason, and would not upon any Consideration be surprized in the Practice of those Duties, for the Performance of which he was sent into the World. Many an Impudent Libertine would blush to be caught in a serious Discourse, and would scarce be able to shew his Head, after having disclosed a Religious Thought. Decency of Behaviour, all outward Show of Virtue, and Abhorrence of Vice, are carefully avoided by this Sett of shamefaced People, as what would disparage their gayety of Temper, and infallibly bring them to Dishonour. This is such a Poorness of Spirit, such a despicable Cowardice, such a degenerate abject State of Mind, as one would think Human Nature incapable of, did we not meet with frequent Instances of it in ordinary Conversation.

There is another kind of Vicious Modesty which makes a Man ashamed of his Person, his Birth, his Profession, his Poverty, or the like Misfortunes, which it was not in his Choice to prevent, and is not in his Power to rectifie. If a Man appears ridiculous by any of the aforementioned Circumstances, he becomes much more so by being out of Countenance for them. They should rather give him occasion to exert a noble Spirit, and to palliate those Imperfections which are not in his Power, by those Perfections which are; or to use a very witty Allusion of an eminent Author, he should imitate *Caesar*, who because his Head was bald, covered that Defect with Laurels.   C

No. 232.

Monday, November 26.

Nihil largiundo gloriam adeptus est.—Sallust.

MY wise and good Friend Sir ANDREW FREEPORT divides himself almost equally between the Town and the Country: His Time in Town is given up to the Publick and the Management of his private Fortune; and after every three or four Days spent in this Manner, he retires for as many to his Seat within a few Miles of the Town, to the Enjoyment of himself, his Family, and his Friends. Thus Business and Pleasure, or rather, in Sir ANDREW, Labour and Rest, recommend each other: They take their Turns with so quick a Vicissitude, that neither becomes a Habit, or takes Possession of the whole Man; nor is it possible he should be surfeited with either. I often see him at our Club in good Humour, and yet sometimes too with an Air of Care in his Looks: But in his Country Retreat he is always unbent, and such a Companion as I could desire; and therefore I seldom fail to make one with him when he is pleased to invite me.

The other Day, as soon as we were got into his Chariot, two or three Beggars on each side hung upon the Doors, and sollicited our Charity with the usual Rhetoric of a sick Wife or Husband at Home, three or four helpless little Children all starving with Cold and Hunger. We were forc'd to part with some Money to get rid of their Importunity; and then we proceeded on our Journey with the Blessings and Acclamations of these People.

'Well then,' says Sir ANDREW, 'we go off with the Prayers and good Wishes of the Beggars, and perhaps too our Healths will be drank at the next Ale-House: So all we shall be able to value our selves upon, is, that we have promoted the Trade of the Victualler, and the Excises of the Government. But how few Ounces of Wooll do we see upon the Backs of those poor Creatures? And when they shall next fall in our Way, they will hardly be better drest; they must always live in Rags to look like Objects of Compassion. If their Families too are such as they are represented, 'tis certain they cannot be better cloathed, and must be a great deal worse fed: One would think Potatoes should be all their Bread, and their Drink the pure Element; and then what goodly Customers are the Farmers like to have for their Wooll, Corn and Cattel? Such Customers and such a Consumption cannot chuse but advance the landed Interest, and hold up the Rents of the Gentlemen.

But of all Men living, we Merchants, who live by Buying and Selling, ought never to encourage Beggars. The Goods which we export are indeed the Product of the Lands, but much the greatest Part of their Value is the Labour of the People: But how much of these People's Labour shall we export, whilst we hire them to sit still? The very Alms they receive from us, are the Wages of Idleness. I have often thought that no Man should be permitted to take Relief from the Parish, or to ask it in the Street, till he has first purchas'd as much as possible of his own Livelihood by the Labour of his own Hands; and then the Publick ought only to be tax'd to make good the Deficiency. If this Rule was strictly observed, we should see every where such a Multitude of new Labourers, as would in all Probability reduce the Prices of all our Manufactures. It is the very Life of Merchandise to buy cheap and sell dear. The Merchant ought to make his Out-set as cheap as possible, that he may find the greater Profit upon his Returns; and nothing will enable him to do this like the Reduction of the Price of Labour upon all our Manufactures. This too would be the ready Way to increase the Number of our foreign Markets: The Abatement of the Price of the Manufacture would pay for the Carriage of it to more distant Countries; and this Consequence would be equally beneficial both to the landed and trading Interests. As so great an Addition of labouring Hands would produce this happy Consequence both to the Merchant and the Gentleman; our Liberality to common Beggars, and every other Obstruction to the Increase of Labourers, must be equally pernicious to both.'

Sir ANDREW then went on to affirm, That the Reduction of the Prices of our Manufactures by the Addition of so many new Hands, would be no Inconvenience to any Man: But observing I was something startled at the Assertion, he made a short Pause, and then resumed the Discourse. 'It may seem,' says he, 'a Paradox, that the Price of Labour should be reduced without an Abatement of Wages, or that Wages can be abated without any Inconvenience to the Labourer; and yet nothing is more certain than that both these things may happen. The Wages of the Labourers make the greatest Part of the Price of every thing that is useful; and if in Proportion with the Wages the Prices of all other things shall be abated, every Labourer with less Wages would be still able to purchase as many Necessaries of Life; where then would be the Inconvenience? But the Price of Labour may be reduced by the Addition of more Hands to a Manufacture, and yet the Wages of Persons remain as high as ever. The admirable Sir *William Petty* has given Examples of this in some of his Writings: One of them, as I remember, is that of a Watch, which I shall endeavour to explain so as shall suit my present Purpose. It is certain that a single Watch could not be made so cheap in Proportion by one only Man, as a hundred Watches by a hundred; for as there is vast Variety in the Work, no one Person could equally suit himself to all the Parts of it; the Manufacture would be tedious, and at last but clumsily performed: But if an hundred Watches were to be made by a hundred Men, the Cases may be assigned to one, the Dials to another, the Wheels to another, the Springs to another, and every other Part to a proper Artist; as there would be no need of perplexing any one Person with too much Variety, every one would be able to perform his single Part with greater Skill and Expedition; and the hundred Watches would be finished in one fourth Part of the Time of the first one, and every one of them at one fourth Part of the Cost, though the Wages of every Man were equal. The Reduction of the Price of the Manufacture would increase the Demand of it, all the same Hands would be still employed and as well paid. The same Rule will hold in the Cloathing, the Shipping, and all the other Trades whatsoever. And thus an Addition of Hands to our Manufactures will only reduce the Price of them; the Labourer will still have as much Wages, and will consequently be enabled to purchase more Conveniences of Life; so that every Interest in the Nation would receive a Benefit from the Increase of our working People.

Besides, I see no Occasion for this Charity to common Beggars, since every Beggar is an Inhabitant of a Parish, and every Parish is taxed to the Maintenance of their own Poor. For my own Part, I cannot be mightily pleas'd with the Laws which have done this, which have provided better to feed than employ the Poor. We have a Tradition from our Forefathers, that after the first of those Laws was made, they were insulted with that famous Song;

> *Hang Sorrow, and cast away Care,*
> *The Parish is bound to find us, &c.*

And if we will be so good-natured as to maintain them without Work, they can do no less in Return than sing us *The merry Beggars.*

What then? am I against all Acts of Charity? God forbid! I know of no Virtue in the Gospel that is in more pathetical Expressions recommended to our Practice. *I was hungry and you gave me no Meat, thirsty and you gave me no Drink; naked and you cloathed me not, a Stranger and you took me not in; sick and in Prison and you visited me not.* Our Blessed Saviour treats the Exercise or Neglect of Charity towards a poor Man, as the Performance or Breach of this Duty towards himself. I shall endeavour to obey the Will of my Lord and Master. And therefore if an industrious Man shall submit to the hardest Labour and coarsest Fare, rather than endure the Shame of taking Relief from the Parish or asking it in the Street, this is the Hungry, the Thirsty, the Naked; and I ought to believe if any Man is come hither for Shelter against Persecution or Oppression, this is the Stranger and I ought to take him in. If any Countryman of our own is fallen into the Hands of Infidels, and lives in a State of miserable Captivity, this is the Man in Prison, and I should contribute to his Ransom. I ought to give to an Hospital of Invalids, to recover as many useful Subjects as I can; but I shall bestow none of my Bounties upon an Alms-house of idle People; and for the same Reason I shall not think it a Reproach to me if I had with-held my Charity from those common Beggars. But we prescribe better Rules than we are able to practise; we are ashamed not to give into the mistaken Customs of our Country: But at the same Time I cannot but think it a Reproach worse than that of common Swearing, that the Idle and the Abandoned are suffered in the Name of Heaven and all that is sacred, to extort from christian and tender Minds a Supply to a profligate Way of Life, that is always to be supported but never relieved.'   Z

No. 233.

[ADDISON.]   Tuesday, November 27.

> *. . . Tanquam haec sint nostri medicina furoris,*
> *Aut Deus ille malis hominum mitescere discat.*—Virg.

I SHALL, in this Paper, discharge my self of the Promise I have made to the Publick, by obliging them with a Translation of the little *Greek* Manuscript, which is said to have been a Piece of those Records that were preserved in the Temple of *Apollo*, upon the Promontory of *Leucate*: It is a short History of the Lover's Leap and is inscribed, *An Account of Persons Male and Female, who offered up their Vows in the Temple of the* Pythian Apollo, *in the Forty sixth Olympiad, and leaped from the Promontory of* Leucate *into the* Ionian Sea, *in order to cure themselves of the Passion of Love.*

This Account is very dry in many Parts, as only mentioning the Name of the Lover who leaped, the Person he leaped for, and relating in short, that he was either cured, or killed, or maimed, by the Fall. It indeed gives the Names of so many who died by it, that it would have looked like a Bill of Mortality, had I translated it at full length: I have therefore made an Abridgment of it, and only extracted such particular Passages as have something extraordinary, either in the Case, or in the Cure, or in the Fate of the Person who is mentioned in it. After this short Preface, take the Account as follows.

Battus, the Son of *Menalcas* the *Sicilian*, leaped for *Bombyca* the Musician: Got rid of his Passion with the Loss of his Right Leg and Arm, which were broken in the Fall.

Melissa, in Love with *Daphnis*, very much bruised, but escaped with Life.

Cynisca, the Wife of *Eschines*, being in Love with *Lycus*; and *Eschines* her Husband being in Love with *Eurilla*; (which had made this Married Couple very uneasie to one another for several Years) both the Husband and the Wife took the Leap by consent; they both of them escaped, and have lived very happily together ever since.

Larissa, a Virgin of *Thessaly*, deserted by *Plexippus*, after a Courtship of Three Years; She stood upon the Brow of the

Promontory for some time, and after having thrown down a Ring, a Bracelet, and a little Picture, with other Presents which she had received from *Plexippus*, she threw her self into the Sea, and was taken up alive.

N.B. Larissa, before she leaped, made an Offering of a Silver *Cupid* in the Temple of *Apollo*.

Simaetha, in Love with *Daphnis* the *Myndian*, perished in the Fall.

Charixus, the Brother of *Sappho*, in Love with *Rhodope* the Courtezan, having spent his whole Estate upon her, was advised by his Sister to Leap in the beginning of his Amour, but would not hearken to her 'till he was reduced to his last Talent; being forsaken by *Rhodope*, at length resolved to take the Leap. Perished in it.

Aridaeus, a beautiful Youth of *Epirus*, in Love with *Praxinoe*, the Wife of *Thespis*, escaped without Damage, saving only that two of his fore Teeth were struck out, and his Nose a little flatted.

Cleora, a Widow of *Ephesus*, being inconsolable for the Death of her Husband, was resolved to take this Leap, in order to get rid of her Passion for his Memory; but being arrived at the Promontory, she there met with *Dimmachus* the *Miletian*, and after a short Conversation with him, laid aside the Thoughts of her Leap, and Married him in the Temple of *Apollo*.

N.B. Her Widow's Weeds are still to be seen hanging up in the Western Corner of the Temple.

Olphis, the Fisherman, having received a Box on the Ear from *Thestylis* the Day before, and being determined to have no more to do with her, leaped, and escaped with Life.

Atalanta, an old Maid, whose Cruelty had several Years before driven two or three despairing Lovers to this Leap; being now in the Fifty fifth Year of her Age, and in Love with an Officer of *Sparta*. Broke her Neck in the Fall.

Hipparchus being passionately fond of his own Wife, who was Enamour'd of *Bathyllus*, leaped and died of his Fall; upon which his Wife married her Gallant.

Tettyx, the Dancing-Master, in Love with *Olympia*, an *Athenian* Matron, threw himself from the Rock with great Agility, but was crippled in the Fall.

Diagoras, the Usurer, in Love with his Cook-Maid; he peeped several times over the Precipice, but his Heart misgiving him, he went back, and Married her that Evening.

Cinaedus, after having entred his own Name in the *Pythian* Records, being asked the Name of the Person whom he leaped for, and being ashamed to discover it, he was set aside, and not suffered to Leap.

Eunica, a Maid of *Paphos*, aged Nineteen, in Love with *Eurybates*. Hurt in the Fall, but recovered.

N.B. This was her second Time of Leaping.

Hesperus, a young Man of *Tarentum*, in Love with his Master's Daughter. Drowned, the Boats not coming in soon enough to his Relief.

Sappho, the *Lesbian*, in Love with *Phaon*, arrived at the Temple of *Apollo*, habited like a Bride in Garments as white as Snow. She wore a Garland of Mirtle on her Head, and carried in her Hand the little Musical Instrument of her own Invention. After having Sung an Hymn to *Apollo*, she hung up her Garland on one side of his Altar, and her Harp on the other. She then tucked up her Vestments like a *Spartan* Virgin, and amidst thousands of Spectators, who were anxious for her Safety, and offered up Vows for her Deliverance, marched directly forwards to the utmost Summit of the Promontory, where after having repeated a Stanza of her own Verses, which we could not hear, she threw her self off the Rock with such an Intrepidity, as was never before observed in any who had attempted that dangerous Leap. Many, who were present, related, that they saw her fall into the Sea, from whence she never rose again; though there were others who affirmed, that she never came to the bottom of her Leap; but that she was changed into a Swan as she fell, and that they saw her hovering in the Air under that Shape. But whether or no the whiteness and fluttering of her Garments might not deceive those who looked upon her, or whether she might not really be Metamorphosed into that Musical and Melancholy Bird, is still a Doubt among the *Lesbians*.

Alcaeus, the famous *Lyrick* Poet, who had for some time been passionately in Love with *Sappho*, arrived at the Promontory of *Leucate* that very Evening, in order to take the Leap upon her Account; but hearing that *Sappho* had been there before him, and that her Body could be no where found, he very generously lamented her Fall, and is said to have written his Hundred and twenty fifth Ode upon that Occasion.

Leaped in this Olympiad 350.

Males	124
Females	126

Cured   120

Males	51
Females	69

No. 234.

[STEELE.]   Wednesday, November 28.

Vellem in amicitia sic erraremus . . .—Hor.

You very often hear People, after a Story has been told with some entertaining Circumstances, tell it over again with Particulars that destroy the Jest, but give Light into the Truth of the Narration. This sort of Veracity, though it is impertinent, has something amiable in it, because it proceeds from the Love of Truth even in frivolous Occasions. If such honest Amendments do not promise an agreeable Companion, they do a sincere Friend; for which Reason one should allow them so much of our Time, if we fall into their Company, as to set us right in Matters that can do us no manner of Harm, whether the Facts be one Way or the other. Lies which are told out of Arrogance and Ostentation a Man should detect in his own Defence, because he should not be triumph'd over; Lies which are told out of Malice he should expose, both for his own Sake and that of the rest of Mankind, because every Man should rise against a common Enemy: but the officious Liar many have argued is to be excused, because it does some Man Good and no Man Hurt. The Man who made more than ordinary Speed from a Fight in which the *Athenians* were beaten, and told them they had obtained a compleat Victory, and put the whole City into the utmost Joy and Exultation, was checked by the Magistrates for his Falshood; but excused himself by saying, Oh *Athenians !* am I your Enemy because I gave ye two happy Days? This Fellow did to a whole People what an Acquaintance of mine does every Day he lives in some eminent Degree to particular Persons. He is ever lying People into good Humour, and as *Plato* said it was allowable in Physicians to lie to their Patients to keep up their Spirits, I am half doubtful whether my Friend's Behaviour is not as excusable. His Manner is to express himself surprised at the chearful Countenance of a Man whom he observes diffident of himself; and generally by that Means makes his Lie a Truth. He will, as if he did not know any thing of the Circumstance, ask one whom he knows at Variance with another, what is the Meaning that Mr. such a one, naming his Adversary, does not applaud him with that Heartiness which formerly he has heard him? He said indeed (continues he) I would rather have that Man for my Friend than any Man in *England*; but for an Enemy—— This melts the Person he talks to, who expected nothing but downright Raillery from that Side. According as he sees his Practice succeed, he goes to the opposite Party and tells him, he cannot imagine how it happens that some People know one another so little; you spoke with so much Coldness of a Gentleman who said more Good of you, than, let me tell you, any Man living deserves. The Success of one of these Incidents was, that the next Time that one of the Adversaries spy'd the other, he hems after him in the publick Street; and they must crack a Bottle at the next Tavern, that used to turn out of the other's Way to avoid one another's Eyeshot. He will tell one Beauty she was commended by another, nay, he will say she gave the Woman he speaks to the Preference in a Particular for which she her self is admired. The pleasantest Confusion imaginable is made through the whole Town by my Friend's indirect Offices; you shall have a Visit returned after half a Year's Absence, and mutual Railing at each other every Day of that Time. They meet with a thousand Lamentations for so long a Separation, each Party naming her self for the greater Delinquent, if the other can possibly be so good as to forgive her, which she has no Reason in the World but from the Knowledge of her Goodness to hope for. Very often a whole Train of Railers of each Side tire their Horses in setting Matters right which they have said during the War between the Parties, and a whole Circle of Acquaintance are put into a thousand pleasing Passions and Sentiments, instead of the Pangs of Anger, Envy, Detraction and Malice.

The worst Evil I ever observed this Man's Falshood occasion, has been that he turned Detraction into Flattery. He is well skilled in the Manners of the World, and by over-looking what Men really are, he grounds his Artifices upon what they have a Mind to be: Upon this Foundation, if two distant Friends are brought together, and the Cement seems to be weak, he never rests till he finds new Appearances to take off all Remains of Ill-will; and that by new Misunderstandings they are thoroughly reconciled.

'*To the* SPECTATOR,

'*Sir,*   *Devonshire, Nov.* 14, 1711.

There arrived in this Neighbourhood two Days ago one of your gay Gentlemen of the Town, who being attended at his Entry with a Servant of his own, besides a Countryman he had taken up for a Guide, excited the Curiosity of the Village to learn whence and what he might be. The Countryman (to whom they applied as most easie of Access) knew little more than that the Gentleman came from *London* to travel and see Fashions, and was, as he heard say, a Free-thinker: What Religion that might be, he could not tell, and for his own part, if they had not told him the Man was a Free-thinker, he should have guessed, by his way of talking, he was little better than a Heathen; excepting only that he had been a good Gentleman to him, and made him drunk twice in one Day, over and above what they had bargain'd for.

I do not look upon the Simplicity of this, and several odd Enquiries with which I shall trouble you, to be wondered at, much less can I think that our Youths of fine Wit and enlarged Understandings have any Reason to laugh. There is no necessity that every Squire in *Great-Britain* should know what the Word Free-thinker stands for; but it were much to be wish'd, that they who value themselves upon that conceited Title were a little better instructed what it ought to stand for; and that they would not perswade themselves a Man is really and truly a Free-thinker in any tolerable Sense, merely by vertue of his being an Atheist, or an Infidel of any other Distinction. It may be doubted, with good Reason, whether there ever was in Nature a more abject, slavish, and bigotted Generation than the Tribe of *Beaux Esprits*, at present so prevailing in this Island. Their Pretension to be Free-Thinkers, is no other than Rakes have to be Free-livers, and Savages to be Free-men; that is, they can think whatever they have a mind to, and give themselves up to whatever Conceit the Extravagancy of their Inclination, or their Fancy, shall suggest; they can think as wildly as they talk and act, and will not endure that their Wit should be controuled by such Formal Things as Decency and common Sense: Deduction, Coherence, Consistency, and all the Rules of Reason they accordingly disdain, as too precise and Mechanical for Men of a Liberal Education.

This, as far as I could ever learn from their Writings, or my own Observation, is a true Account of the *British* Free-thinker. Our Visitant here, who gave Occasion to this Paper, has brought with him a New System of common Sense, the Particulars of which I am not yet acquainted with, but will lose no Opportunity of informing my self whether it contain any thing worth Mr. SPECTATOR's Notice. In the mean time, Sir, I cannot but think it would be for the good of Mankind, if you would take this Subject into your own Consideration, and convince the hopeful Youth of our Nation, that Licentiousness is not Freedom; or, if such a Paradox will not be understood, that a Prejudice towards Atheism is not Impartiality.

I am, Sir,

Your most humble Servant,

T   PHILONOUS.'

No. 235.
[ADDISON.]   Thursday, November 29

. . . *Populares*
Vincentum strepitus . . .—Hor.

THERE is nothing which lies more within the Province of a
Spectator than Publick Shows and Diversions; and as among
these there are none which can pretend to vie with those
Elegant Entertainments that are exhibited in our Theatres,
I think it particularly Incumbent on me to take Notice of
every thing that is remarkable in such numerous and refined
Assemblies.

It is observed, that of late Years, there has been a certain
Person in the Upper Gallery of the Play-house, who when he is
pleased with any thing that is acted upon the Stage, expresses
his Approbation by a loud Knock upon the Benches or the
Wainscot, which may be heard over the whole Theatre.   This
Person is commonly known by the Name of the *Trunk-maker in
the Upper Gallery*.   Whether it be, that the Blow he gives on
these Occasions resembles that which is often heard in the
Shops of such Artizans, or that he was supposed to have been a
real Trunk-maker, who after the finishing of his Day's Work,
used to unbend his Mind at these Publick Diversions with his
Hammer in his Hand, I cannot certainly tell.   There are some,
I know, who have been foolish enough to imagine it is a Spirit
which haunts the Upper-Gallery, and from time to time, makes
those strange Noises; and the rather, because he is observed to
be louder than ordinary every time the Ghost of *Hamlet*
appears.   Others have reported, that it is a Dumb Man, who
has chosen this way of uttering himself, when he is transported
with any thing he sees or hears.   Others will have it to be the
Play-house Thunderer, that exerts himself after this manner in
the Upper-Gallery, when he has nothing to do upon the Roof.

But having made it my business to get the best Information
I cou'd in a matter of this Moment, I find that the Trunk-
maker, as he is commonly called, is a large black Man, whom no
body knows.   He generally leans forward on a huge Oaken
Plant with great Attention to every thing that passes upon the
Stage.   He is never seen to Smile; but upon hearing any thing
that pleases him, he takes up his Staff with both Hands, and
lays it upon the next piece of Timber that stands in his way
with exceeding Vehemence: After which he composes himself
in his former Posture, 'till such time as something new sets
him again at work.

It has been observed his Blow is so well timed, that the most
judicious Critick could never except against it.   As soon as any

shining Thought is expressed in the Poet, or any uncommon Grace appears in the Actor, he smites the Bench or Wainscot. If the Audience does not concur with him, he smites a second time; and if the Audience is not yet awaked, looks round him with great Wrath, and repeats the Blow a third time, which never fails to produce the Clap. He sometimes lets the Audience begin the Clap of themselves, and at the Conclusion of their Applause ratifies it with a single Thwack.

He is of so great Use to the Play-house, that it is said a former Director of it, upon his not being able to pay his Attendance by reason of Sickness, kept one in Pay to officiate for him 'till such time as he recovered; but the Person so employed, tho' he laid about him with incredible Violence, did it in such wrong Places, that the Audience soon found out it was not their old Friend the Trunk-maker.

It has been remarked, that he has not yet exerted himself with Vigour this Season. He sometimes plies at the Opera; and upon *Nicolini*'s first Appearance, was said to have demolished three Benches in the Fury of his Applause. He has broken half a dozen Oaken Plants upon *Dogget*, and seldom goes away from a Tragedy of *Shakespear*, without leaving the Wainscot extreamly shattered.

The Players do not only connive at this his obstreperous Approbation, but very chearfully repair at their own Cost whatever Damages he makes. They had once a Thought of erecting a kind of Wooden Anvil for his use, that should be made of a very sounding Plank, in order to render his Stroaks more deep and mellow; but as this might not have been distinguished from the Musick of a Kettle Drum, the Project was laid aside.

In the mean while I cannot but take notice of the great use it is to an Audience, that a Person should thus preside over their Heads, like the Director of a Consort, in order to awaken their Attention, and beat Time to their Applauses. Or to raise my Simile, I have sometimes fancied the Trunk-maker in the Upper Gallery to be like *Virgil*'s Ruler of the Winds, seated upon the Top of a Mountain, who, when he struck his Sceptre upon the side of it, roused an Hurricane, and set the whole Cavern in an Uproar.

It is certain the Trunk-maker has saved many a good Play, and brought many a graceful Actor into Reputation, who would not otherwise have been taken notice of. It is very visible, as the Audience is not a little abashed, if they find themselves betrayed into a Clap, when their Friend in the Upper-Gallery does not come into it; so the Actors do not value themselves upon the Clap, but regard it as a meer *Brutum fulmen*, or empty

Noise, when it has not the Sound of the Oaken Plant in it.
I know it has been given out by those who are Enemies to the
Trunk-maker, that he has sometimes been bribed to be in the
Interest of a bad Poet, or a vicious Player; but this is a Surmise,
which has no Foundation; his Stroaks are always just, and his
Admonitions seasonable; he does not deal about his Blows at
Random, but always hits the right Nail upon the Head.   The
inexpressible Force wherewith he lays them on, sufficiently
shews the Evidence and Strength of his Conviction.   His Zeal
for a good Author is indeed outragious, and breaks down every
Force and Partition, every Board and Plank, that stands within
the Expression of his Applause.

As I do not care for terminating my Thoughts in Barren
Speculations, or in Reports of pure Matter of Fact, without
drawing something from them for the Advantage of my
Countrymen, I shall take the Liberty to make an humble
Proposal, that whenever the Trunk-maker shall depart this
Life, or whenever he shall have lost the Spring of his Arm by
Sickness, Old Age, Infirmity, or the like, some able-bodied
Critick should be advanced to this Post, and have a competent
Salary settled on him for Life, to be furnished with Bamboos
for Operas, Crabtree-Cudgels for Comedies, and Oaken Plants
for Tragedy, at the publick Expence.   And to the End that this
Place should always be disposed of, according to Merit, I would
have none preferred to it, who has not given convincing Proofs,
both of a sound Judgment and a strong Arm, and who could
not, upon Occasion, either knock down an Ox or write a Comment upon *Horace*'s Art of Poetry.   In short, I would have
him a due Composition of *Hercules* and *Apollo*, and so rightly
qualify'd for this important Office, that the *Trunk-maker* may
not be missed by our Posterity.   C

No. 236.
[STEELE.]   Friday, November 30.

. . . *Dare jura maritis.*—Hor.

  '*Mr.* SPECTATOR,
YOU have not spoken in so direct a Manner upon the Subject
of Marriage as that important Case deserves.   It would not be
improper to observe, upon the Peculiarity in the Youth of
Great Britain, of Railling and Laughing at that Institution;
and when they fall into it, from a profligate Habit of Mind,
being insensible to the Satisfactions in that Way of Life, and
treating their Wives with the most barbarous Disrespect.

Particular Circumstances and Cast of Temper must teach a
Man the Probability of mighty Uneasinesses in that State (for

unquestionably some there are whose very Dispositions are strangely averse to conjugal Friendship); but no one, I believe, is by his own natural Complexion prompted to teaze and torment another for no Reason but being nearly allied to him: And can there be any thing more base, or serve to sink a Man so much below his own distinguishing Characteristick (I mean Reason), than returning Evil for Good in so open a Manner, as that of treating an helpless Creature with Unkindness, who has had so good an Opinion of him as to believe what he said relating to one of the greatest Concerns of Life, by delivering her Happiness in this World to his Care and Protection? Must not that Man be abandoned even to all manner of Humanity, who can deceive a Woman with Appearances of Affection and Kindness, for no other End but to torment her with more Ease and Authority? Is any thing more unlike a Gentleman, than when his Honour is engaged for the performing his Promises, because nothing but that can oblige him to it, to become afterwards false to his Word, and be alone the Occasion of Misery to one whose Happiness he but lately pretended was dearer to him than his own? Ought such a one to be trusted in his common Affairs? or treated but as one whose Honesty consisted only in his Incapacity of being otherwise?

There is one Cause of this Usage no less absurd than common, which takes Place among the more unthinking Men; and that is the Desire to appear to their Friends free and at Liberty, and without those Trammells they have so much ridiculed: To avoid this they fly into the other Extream, and grow Tyrants that they may seem Masters. Because an uncontroulable Command of their own Actions is a certain Sign of entire Dominion, they won't so much as recede from the Government even in one Muscle of their Faces. A kind Look they believe would be fawning, and a civil Answer yielding the Superiority. To this must we attribute an Austerity they betray in every Action: What but this can put a Man out of Humour in his Wife's Company, tho' he is so distinguishingly pleasant every where else? The Bitterness of his Replies and the Severity of his Frowns to the tenderest of Wives, clearly demonstrate, that an ill-grounded Fear of being thought too submissive is at the Bottom of this, as I am willing to call it, affected Moroseness; but if it be such only, put on to convince his Acquaintance of his entire Dominion, let him take care of the Consequence, which will be certain, and worse than the present Evil; his seeming Indifference will by degrees grow into real Contempt, and if it doth not wholly alienate the Affections of his Wife for ever from him, make both him and her more miserable than if it really did so.

However inconsistent it may appear, to be thought a well-bred Person has no small Share in this clownish Behaviour: A Discourse therefore relating to Good-breeding towards a loving and a tender Wife would be of great use to this sort of Gentlemen. Could you but once convince them, that to be civil at least is not beneath the Character of a Gentleman, nor even tender Affection, towards one who would make it reciprocal, betray any Softness of Effeminacy that the most masculine Disposition need be ashamed of; Could you satisfie them of the Generosity of voluntary Civility, and the Greatness of Soul that is conspicuous in Benevolence without immediate Obligations; Could you recommend to People's Practice the Saying of the Gentleman quoted in one of your Speculations, *That he thought it incumbent upon him to make the Inclinations of a Woman of Merit go along with her Duty:* Could you, I say, perswade these Men of the Beauty and Reasonableness of this sort of Behaviour, I have so much Charity for some of them at least, to believe you would convince them of a thing they are only ashamed to allow: Besides, you would recommend that State in its truest, and consequently its most agreeable Colours; and the Gentlemen who have for any Time been such professed Enemies to it, when Occasion should serve would return you their Thanks for assisting their Interest in prevailing over their Prejudices. Marriage in general would by this Means be a more easie and comfortable Condition; the Husband would be no where so well satisfied as in his own Parlour, nor the Wife so pleasant as in the Company of her Husband; a Desire of being agreeable in the Lover would be increased in the Husband, and the Mistress be more amiable by becoming the Wife. Besides all which, I am apt to believe we should find the Race of Men grow wiser as their Progenitors grew kinder, and the Affection of the Parents would be conspicuous in the Wisdom of their Children; in short, Men would in general be much better humoured than they are, did not they so frequently exercise the worst Turns of their Temper where they ought to exert the best.'

'*Mr.* SPECTATOR,

I am a Woman who left the Admiration of this whole Town, to throw my self (by Love of Wealth) into the Arms of a Fool. When I married him I could have had any one of several Men of Sense who languished for me; but my Case is just, I believed my Superior Understanding would form him into a tractable Creature. But alas my Spouse has Cunning and Suspicion, the inseparable Companions of little Minds; and every Attempt I make to divert, by putting on an agreeable Air, a sudden

Chearfulness, or kind Behaviour, he looks upon as the first Acts towards an Insurrection against his undeserved Dominion over me. Let every one who is still to chuse, and hopes to govern a Fool, remember

TRISTISSA.'

'*Mr.* SPECTATOR,   *St. Martins, Nov.* 25.

This is to complain of an evil Practice which I think very well deserves a Redress, tho' you have not as yet taken any Notice of it: If you mention it in your Paper, it may perhaps have a very good Effect. What I mean is the Disturbance some People give to others at Church, by their Repetition of the Prayers after the Minister, and that not only in the Prayers, but also the Absolution and the Commandments fare no better, which are in a particular Manner the Priest's Office: This I have known done in so audible a Manner, that sometimes their Voices have been as loud as his. As little as you would think it, this is frequently done by People seemingly devout. This irreligious Inadvertency is a Thing extreamly offensive: but I do not recommend it as a thing I give you Liberty to ridicule, but hope it may be amended by the bare Mention.

Sir,

Your very humble Servant,

T   T. S.'

No. 237.
[ADDISON.]   Saturday, December 1.

Visu carentem magna pars veri latet.—Senec. in Oedip.

IT is very reasonable to believe, that part of the Pleasure which happy Minds shall enjoy in a future State, will arise from an enlarged Contemplation of the Divine Wisdom in the Government of the World, and a Discovery of the secret and amazing Steps of Providence, from the Beginning to the End of Time. Nothing seems to be an Entertainment more adapted to the Nature of Man, if we consider that curiosity is one of the strongest and most lasting Appetites implanted in us, and that Admiration is one of our most pleasing Passions; and what a perpetual Succession of Enjoyments will be afforded to both these, in a Scene so large and various as shall then be laid open to our View in the Society of superior Spirits, who will perhaps joyn with us in so delightful a Prospect.

It is not impossible, on the contrary, that part of the Punishment of such as are excluded from Bliss may consist not only in their being denied this Privilege, but in having their Appetites at the same time vastly encreased, without any Satisfaction afforded to them. In these, the vain Pursuit of Knowledge shall, perhaps, add to their Infelicity, and bewilder them in Labyrinths of Error, Darkness, Distraction, and Uncertainty of every thing but their own Evil State. *Milton* has thus represented the fallen Angels reasoning together in a kind of Respite from their Torments, and creating to themselves a new Disquiet amidst their very Amusements; he could not properly have described the Sports of condemned Spirits, without that Cast of Horror and Melancholy he has so judiciously mingled with them.

> *Others apart sate on a Hill retir'd,*
> *In Thoughts more elevate, and reason'd high*
> *Of Providence, Fore-knowledge, Will, and Fate,*
> *Fixt Fate, Free-will, Fore-knowledge absolute,*
> *And found no End, in wandering Mazes lost.*

In our present Condition, which is a middle State, our Minds are, as it were, chequered with Truth and Falshood; and as our Faculties are narrow and our Views imperfect, it is impossible but our Curiosity must meet with many Repulses. The Business of Mankind in this Life being rather to act than to know, their Portion of Knowledge is dealt to them accordingly.

From hence it is, that the Reason of the Inquisitive has so long been exercised with Difficulties, in accounting for the promiscuous Distribution of Good and Evil to the Virtuous and the Wicked in this World. From hence come all those Pathetical Complaints of so many Tragical Events, which happen to the Wise and the Good; and of such surprizing Prosperity, which is often the Reward of the Guilty and the Foolish; that Reason is sometimes puzzled, and at a loss what to pronounce upon so mysterious a Dispensation.

Plato expresses his Abhorrence of some Fables of the Poets, which seem to reflect on the Gods as the Authors of Injustice; and lays it down as a Principle, that whatever is permitted to befal a Just Man, whether Poverty, Sickness, or any of those things which seem to be Evils, shall either in Life or Death conduce to his Good. My Reader will observe how agreeable this Maxim is to what we find delivered by a greater Authority. *Seneca* has written a Discourse purposely on this Subject, in which he takes Pains, after the Doctrine of the *Stoicks*, to shew, that Adversity is not in it self an Evil; and mentions a noble Saying of *Demetrius*, That *nothing wou'd be more Unhappy than a Man who had never known Affliction.* He compares Prosperity to the Indulgence of a fond Mother to a Child, which often proves his Ruin; but the Affection of the Divine Being to that of a Wise Father, who would have his Sons exercised with Labour, Disappointment and Pain, that they may gather

Strength, and improve their Fortitude. On this Occasion the Philosopher rises into that celebrated Sentiment, that there is not on Earth a Spectacle more worthy for a Creator intent on his Works, than a brave Man superior to his Sufferings; to which he adds, that it must be a Pleasure to *Jupiter* himself to look down from Heaven, and see *Cato* amidst the Ruins of his Country preserving his Integrity.

This Thought will appear yet more reasonable, if we consider Human Life as a State of Probation, and Adversity as the Post of Honour in it, assigned often to the best and most select Spirits.

But what I would chiefly insist on here, is, that we are not at present in a proper Situation to judge of the Counsels by which Providence acts, since but little arrives at our Knowledge, and even that little we discern imperfectly; or, according to the elegant Figure in Holy Writ, *we see but in part, and as in a Glass darkly.* Since Providence therefore in its Oeconomy regards the whole System of Time and Things together, we cannot discover the beautiful Connexions between Incidents which lye widely separated in Time, and by losing so many Links of the Chain, our Reasonings become broken and imperfect. Thus those Parts of the Moral World which have not an absolute, may yet have a relative Beauty, in respect of some other Parts concealed from us, but open to his Eye before whom *Past, Present* and *To come*, are set together in one Point of View: and those Events, the Permission of which seems now to accuse his Goodness, may in the Consummation of Things, both magnifie his Goodness, and exalt his Wisdom. And this is enough to check our Presumption, since it is in vain to apply our Measures of Regularity to Matters of which we know neither the Antecedents nor the Consequents, the Beginning nor the End.

I shall relieve my Readers from this abstracted Thought, by relating here a *Jewish* Tradition concerning *Moses*, which seems to be a kind of Parable, illustrating what I have last mentioned. That great Prophet, it is said, was called up by a Voice from Heaven to the Top of a Mountain; where, in a Conference with the Supreme Being, he was permitted to propose to him some Questions concerning his Administration of the Universe. In the midst of this Divine Conference he was commanded to look down on the Plain below. At the Foot of the Mountain there issued out a clear Spring of Water, at which a Soldier alighted from his Horse to Drink. He was no sooner gone than a little Boy came to the same Place, and finding a Purse of Gold which the Soldier had dropped, took it up and went away with it. Immediately after this came an Infirm old Man, weary with

Age and Travelling, and having quenched his Thirst, sat down to rest himself by the side of the Spring. The Soldier missing his Purse returns to search for it, and demands it of the old Man, who affirms he had not seen it, and appeals to Heaven in witness of his Innocence. The Soldier not believing his Protestations, kills him. *Moses* fell on his Face with Horror and Amazement, when the Divine Voice thus prevented his Expostulation, 'Be not surprised, *Moses*, nor ask why the Judge of the whole Earth hath suffered this thing to come to pass; the Child is the Occasion that the Blood of the old Man is spilt; but know, that the old Man whom thou sawest was the Murderer of that Child's Father.'

No. 238.
[STEELE.]   Monday, December 3.

> *Nequicquam populo bibulas donaveris aures,*
> *Respue quod non es. . . .* —Persius, *Sat.* 4.

AMONG all the Diseases of the Mind there is not one more epidemical or more pernicious than the Love of Flattery. For as where the Juices of the Body are prepared to receive a malignant Influence, there the Disease rages with most Violence; so, in this Distemper of the Mind, where there is ever a Propensity and Inclination to suck in the Poison, it cannot be but that the whole Order of reasonable Action must be overturned; for, like Musick, it

> *. . . So softens and disarms the Mind,*
> *That not one Arrow can Resistance find.*

First we flatter our selves, and then the Flattery of others is sure of Success. It awakens our Self-Love within, a Party which is ever ready to revolt from our better Judgment, and joyn the Enemy without. Hence it is, that the Profusion of Favours we so often see poured upon the Parasite, are represented to us by our Self-Love; as Justice done to the Man so agreeably, reconciles us to our selves. When we are overcome by such soft Insinuations and ensnaring Compliances, we gladly recompence the Artifices which are made Use of to blind our Reason, and which triumph over the Weaknesses of our Temper and Inclinations.

But were every Man perswaded from how mean and low a Principle this Passion is derived, there can be no Doubt but the Person who should attempt to gratifie it, would then be as contemptible as he is now successful. 'Tis the Desire of some

Quality we are not possessed of, or Inclination to be something
we are not, which are the Causes of our giving our selves up to
that Man; who bestows upon us the Characters and Qualities
of others, which perhaps suit us as ill, and were as little designed for our wearing as their Cloaths.   Instead of going out
of our own complectional Nature into that of others, 'twere a
better and more laudable Industry to improve our own, and
instead of a miserable Copy become a good Original; for there
is no Temper, no Disposition so rude and untractable, but may
in its own peculiar Cast and Turn be brought to some agreeable Use in Conversation, or in the Affairs of Life.   A Person of
a rougher Deportment, and less tied up to the usual Ceremonies
of Behaviour, will, like *Manly* in the Play, please by the Grace
which Nature gives to every Action wherein she is complied
with; the Brisk and Lively will not want their Admirers, and
even a more Reserved and Melancholy Temper may at some
Times be agreeable.

When there is not Vanity enough awake in a Man to undo
him, the Flatterer stirs up that dormant Weakness, and inspires him with Merit enough to be a Coxcomb.   But if Flattery
be the most sordid Act that can be complied with, the Art of
Praising justly is as commendable: For 'tis laudable to praise
well; as Poets at one and the same Time give Immortality, and
receive it themselves for a Reward: Both are pleased, the one
whilst he receives the Recompence of Merit, the other, whilst
he shews he knows how to discern it; but above all that Man
is happy in this Art, who, like a skilful Painter, retains the
Features and Complection, but still softens the Picture into the
most agreeable Likeness.

There can hardly, I believe, be imagined a more desirable
Pleasure, than that of Praise unmixed with any Possibility of
Flattery.   Such was that which *Germanicus* enjoyed, when,
the Night before a Battle, desirous of some sincere Mark of the
Esteem of his Legions for him, he is described by *Tacitus*
list'ning in a Disguise to the Discourse of a Soldier, and wrapt
up in the Fruition of his Glory, whilst with an undesigned Sincerity they praised his noble and majestick Mein, his Affability,
his Valour, Conduct, and Success in War.   How must a Man
have his Heart full-blown with Joy in such an Article of Glory
as this?   What a Spur and Encouragement still to proceed
in those Steps which had already brought him to so pure a
Taste of the greatest of mortal Enjoyments?

It sometimes happens that even Enemies and envious Persons bestow the sincerest Marks of Esteem when they least
design it.   Such afford a greater Pleasure, as extorted by Merit,
and freed from all Suspicion of Favour or Flattery.   Thus it is

with *Malvolio*, he has Wit, Learning, and Discernment, but temper'd with an Allay of Envy, Self-Love, and Detraction: *Malvolio* turns pale at the Mirth and good Humour of the Company, if it centre not in his Person; he grows jealous and displeased when he ceases to be the only Person admired, and looks upon the Commendations paid to another as a Detraction from his Merit, and an Attempt to lessen the Superiority he affects; but by this very Method he bestows such Praise as can never be suspected of Flattery.   His Uneasiness and Distastes are so many sure and certain Signs of another's Title to that Glory he desires, and has the Mortification to find himself not possessed of.

A good Name is fitly compared to a precious Ointment, and when we are praised with Skill and Decency, 'tis indeed the most agreeable Perfume; but if too strongly admitted into a Brain of a less vigorous and happy Texture, 'twill like too strong an Odour overcome the Senses, and prove pernicious to those Nerves 'twas intended to refresh.   A generous Mind is of all others the most sensible of Praise and Dispraise; and a noble Spirit is as much invigorated with its due Proportion of Honour and Applause, as 'tis depressed by Neglect and Contempt: But 'tis only Persons far above the common Level who are thus affected with either of these Extreams; as in a Thermometer 'tis only the purest and most sublimated Spirit, that is either contracted or delated by the Benignity or Inclemency of the Season.

'*Mr.* SPECTATOR,

The Translations which you have lately given us from the *Greek* in some of your last Papers, have been the Occasion of my looking into some of those Authors; among whom I chanced on a Collection of Letters which pass under the Name of *Aristaenetus*.   Of all the Remains of Antiquity I believe there can be nothing produced of an Air so gallant and polite; each Letter contains a little Novel or Adventure, which is told with all the Beauties of Language, and heightened with a Luxuriance of Wit.   There are several of them translated, but with such wide Deviations from the Original, and in a Stile so far differing from the Author's, that the Translator seems rather to have taken Hints for the expressing his own Sense and Thoughts, than to have endeavoured to render those of *Aristaenetus*.   In the following Translation I have kept as near the Meaning of the *Greek* as I could, and have only added a few Words to make the Sentences in *English* fit together a little better than they would otherwise have done.   The Story seems to be taken from that of *Pigmalion* and the Statue in *Ovid*:

Some of the Thoughts are of the same Turn, and the Whole is written in a kind of Poetical Prose.

" *Philopinax* to *Chromation.*

Never was Man more overcome with so fantastical a Passion as mine. I have painted a beautiful Woman, and am despairing, dying for the Picture. My own Skill has undone me; 'tis not the Dart of *Venus*, but my own Pencil has thus wounded me. Ah me! with what Anxiety am I necessitated to adore my own Idol? How miserable am I, whilst every one must as much pity the Painter as he praises the Picture, and own my Torment more than equal to my Art. But why do I thus complain? have there not been more unhappy and unnatural Passions than mine? Yes, I have seen the Representations of *Phaedra, Narcissus,* and *Pasiphae. Phaedra* was unhappy in her Love; that of *Pasiphae* was monstrous; and whilst the other caught at his beloved Likeness, he destroyed the watry Image, which ever eluded his Embraces: The Fountain represented *Narcissus* to himself, and the Picture both that and him, thirsting after his adored Image. But I am yet less unhappy, I enjoy her Presence continually, and if I touch her I destroy not the beauteous Form, but she looks pleas'd, and a sweet Smile sits in the charming Space which divides her lips. One would swear that Voice and Speech were issuing out, and that one's Ears felt the melodious Sound. How often have I, deceived by a Lover's Credulity, hearkened if she had not something to whisper me? and when frustrated of my Hopes, how often have I taken my Revenge in Kisses from her Cheeks and Eyes, and softly wooed her to my Embrace? whilst she (as to me it seemed) only with-held her Tongue, the more to enflame me. But, Madman that I am, shall I be thus taken with the Representation only of a beauteous Face and flowing Hair, and thus waste my self and melt to Tears for a Shadow? Ah sure 'tis something more, 'tis a Reality! for see her Beauties shine out with new Lustre, and she seems to upbraid me with such unkind Reproaches. O may I have a living Mistress of this Form, that when I shall compare the Work of Nature and that of Art, I may be still at a Loss which to chuse, and be long perplex'd with the pleasing Uncertainty."' T

No. 239.
[ADDISON.] Tuesday, December 4.
. . . *Bella, horrida bella!*—Virg.

I HAVE sometimes amused my self with considering the several

Methods of managing a Debate, which have obtained in the World.

The first Races of Mankind used to dispute, as our ordinary People do now-a-days, in a kind of wild Logick, uncultivated by Rules of Art.

Socrates introduced a Catechetical Method of Arguing. He would ask his Adversary Question upon Question, till he had convinced him out of his own Mouth that his Opinions were wrong. This way of debating drives an Enemy up into a Corner, seizes all the Passes through which he can make an Escape, and forces him to surrender at Discretion.

Aristotle changed this Method of Attack, and invented a great variety of little Weapons, called Syllogisms. As in the *Socratic* way of Dispute you agree to every thing which your Opponent advances, in the *Aristotelic* you are still denying and contradicting some part or other of what he says. *Socrates* conquers you by Stratagem, *Aristotle* by Force: The one takes the Town by Sapp, the other Sword in Hand.

The Universities of *Europe*, for many Years, carried on their Debates by Syllogism, insomuch that we see the Knowledge of several Centuries laid out into Objections and Answers, and all the good Sense of the Age cut and minced into almost an Infinitude of Distinctions.

When our Universities found that there was no End of wrangling this way, they invented a kind of Argument, which is not reducible to any Mood or Figure in *Aristotle*. It was called the *Argumentum Basilinum* (others write it *Bacilinum* or *Baculinum*) which is pretty well expressed in our *English* Word Club-Law. When they were not able to confute their Antagonist, they knock'd him down. It was their Method in these Polemical Debates first to discharge their Syllogisms, and afterwards to betake themselves to their Clubs, till such time as they had one way or other confounded their Gainsayers. There is in *Oxford* a narrow Defilé, (to make use of a Military Term) where the Partisans used to Encounter, for which Reason it still retains the Name of *Logic Lane*. I have heard an old Gentleman, a Physician, make his Boasts, that when he was a young Fellow he marched several times at the Head of a Troop of *Scotists*, and Cudgell'd a Body of *Smiglesians* half the length of *High-street*; till they had dispersed themselves for Shelter into their respective Garrisons.

This Humour, I find, went very far in *Erasmus*'s Time. For that Author tells us, That upon the Revival of *Greek* Letters, most of the Universities in *Europe* were divided into *Greeks* and *Trojans*. The latter were those who bore a mortal Enmity to the Language of the *Grecians*, insomuch that if they met with any who understood it, they did not fail to treat him as a Foe. *Erasmus* himself had, it seems, the Misfortune to fall into the Hands of a Party of *Trojans*, who laid him on with so many Blows and Buffets, that he never forgot their Hostilities to his dying Day.

There is a way of managing an Argument not much unlike the former, which is made use of by States and Communities, when they draw up a hundred thousand Disputants on each side, and convince one another by dint of Sword. A certain grand Monarch was so sensible of his Strength in this way of Reasoning, that he writ upon his great Guns—*Ratio ultima Regum*, The Logick of Kings. But God be thanked he is now pretty well baffled at his own Weapons. When one has to do with a Philosopher of this kind, one should remember the old Gentleman's Saying who had been engaged in an Argument with one of the *Roman* Emperors. Upon his Friend's telling him, That he wonder'd he would give up the Question, when he had visibly the better of the Dispute, *I am never ashamed*, says he, *to be Confuted by one who is Master of Fifty Legions.*

I shall but just mention another kind of Reasoning, which may be called Arguing by Poll; and another which is of equal force, in which Wagers are made use of as Arguments, according to the celebrated Line in *Hudibras*.

But the most notable way of managing a Controversie is that which we may call *Arguing by Torture*. This is a Method of Reasoning which has been made use of with the poor Refugees, and which was so fashionable in our Country during the Reign of Queen *Mary*, that in a Passage of an Author quoted by Monsieur *Bayle*, it is said, the Price of Wood was raised in *England*, by reason of the Executions that were made in *Smithfield*. These Disputants convince their Adversaries with a *Sorites* commonly called a Pile of Faggots. The Rack is also a kind of Syllogism which has been used with good Effect, and has made multitudes of Converts. Men were formerly disputed out of their Doubts, reconciled to Truth by Force of Reason, and won over to Opinions by the Candour, Sense and Ingenuity of those who had the Right on their Side; but this method of Conviction operated too slowly. Pain was found to be much more Enlightning than Reason. Every Scruple was looked upon as Obstinacy, and not to be removed but by several Engines invented for that purpose. In a Word, the Application of Whips, Racks, Gibbets, Gallies, Dungeons, Fire and Faggot, in a Dispute, may be looked upon as Popish Refinements upon the old Heathen Logick.

There is another way of Reasoning which seldom fails, tho' it be of a quite different Nature to that I have last mentioned.

I mean convincing a Man by ready Mony, or, as it is ordinarily called, Bribing a Man to an Opinion. This Method has often proved successful, when all the others have been made use of to no purpose. A Man who is furnished with Arguments from the Mint, will convince his Antagonist much sooner than one who draws them from Reason and Philosophy. Gold is a wonderful Clearer of the Understanding: It dissipates every Doubt and Scruple in an Instant: Accommodates it self to the meanest Capacities, Silences the Loud and Clamorous, and brings over the most Obstinate and Inflexible. *Philip* of *Macedon* was a Man of most Invincible Reason this way. He refuted by it all the Wisdom of *Athens*, confounded their Statesmen, struck their Orators Dumb, and at length argued them out of all their Liberties.

Having here touched upon the several Methods of Disputing, as they have prevailed in different Ages of the World, I shall very suddenly give my Reader an Account of the whole Art of Cavilling; which shall be a full and satisfactory Answer to all such Papers and Pamphlets as have yet appeared against the *Spectator.*   C

No. 240.
[STEELE.]   Wednesday, December 5.
. . . *Aliter not fit, Avite, liber.*—Mart.

'*Mr.* SPECTATOR,

I AM of one of the most gentile Trades in the City, and understand this much of liberal Education, as to have an ardent Ambition of being useful to Mankind, and to think That the chief End of Being as to this Life. I had these good Impressions given me from the handsome Behaviour of a learned, generous, and wealthy Man towards me when I first began the World. Some Dissatisfactions between me and my Parents made me enter into it with less Relish of Business than I ought, and to turn off this Uneasiness I gave my self to criminal Pleasures, some Excesses, and a general loose Conduct. I know not what the excellent Man above-mentioned saw in me, but he descended from the Superiority of his Wisdom and Merit, to throw himself frequently into my Company: This made me soon hope that I had something in me worth cultivating; and his Conversation made me sensible of Satisfactions in a regular Way, which I had never before imagined. When he was grown familiar with me, he opened himself like a good Angel, and told me, he had long laboured to ripen me into a Preparation to receive his Friendship and Advice, both which I should daily command, and the Use of any Part of his Fortune, to apply the Measures he should propose to me, for the Improvement of my own. I assure you I cannot recollect the Goodness and Confusion of the good Man when he spoke to this Purpose to me without melting into Tears; but in a Word, Sir, I must hasten to tell you, that my Heart burns with Gratitude towards him, and he is so happy a Man that it can never be in my Power to return him his Favours in Kind, but I am sure I have made him the most agreeable Satisfaction I could possibly, in being ready to serve others to my utmost Ability, as far as is consistent with the Prudence he prescribes to me. Dear Mr. SPECTATOR, I do not owe to him only the Goodwill and Esteem of my own Relations (who are People of Distinction) the present Ease and Plenty of my Circumstances, but also the Government of my Passions, and Regulation of my Desires. I doubt not, Sir, but in your Imagination such Virtues as these of my worthy Friend, bear as great a Figure, as Actions which are more glittering in the common Estimation. What I would ask of you is, to give us a whole *Spectator* upon Heroick Virtue in common Life, which may incite Men to the same generous Inclinations, as have by this admirable Person been shewn to, and rais'd in,

Sir,
Your most humble Servant.'

'Mr. SPECTATOR,

I am a Country Gentleman, of a good plentiful Estate, and live as the rest of my Neighbours with great Hospitality. I have been ever reckoned among the Ladies the best Company in the World, and have Access as a sort of Favourite. I never came in publick, but I saluted them tho' in great Assemblies all around, where it was seen how genteely I avoided hampering my Spurs in their Petticoats, while I moved amongst them; and on the other Side, how prettily how they curtsied and received me, standing in proper Rows, and advancing as fast as they saw their Elders or their Betters dispatched by me. But so it is, Mr. SPECTATOR, that all our good Breeding is of late lost by the unhappy Arrival of a Courtier, or Town-Gentleman, who came lately among us: This Person where-ever he came into a Room, made a profound Bow and fell back, then recovered with a soft Air and made a Bow to the next, and so to one or two more, and then took the Gross of the Room, by passing by them in a continued Bow till he arrived at the Person he thought proper particularly to entertain. This he did with so good a Grace and Assurance, that it is taken for the present Fashion; and there is no young Gentlewoman within several Miles of this

Place has been kissed ever since his first Appearance among us. We Country Gentlemen cannot begin again and learn these fine and reserved Airs; and our Conversation is at a Stand, till we have your Judgment for or against Kissing, by Way of Civility or Salutation, which is impatiently expected by your Friends of both Sexes, but by none so much as

Your humble Servant,

RUSTICK SPRIGHTLY.'

'*Mr.* SPECTATOR,   *Decemb.* 3, 1711.

I was the other Night at *Philaster*, where I expected to hear your famous Trunk-maker, but was unhappily disappointed of his Company; and saw another Person who had the like Ambition to distinguish himself in a noisie Manner, partly by Vociferation or talking loud, and partly by his bodily Agility. This was a very lusty Fellow but withal a sort of Beau, who getting into one of the Side-Boxes on the Stage before the Curtain drew, was disposed to shew the whole Audience his Activity by leaping over the Spikes; he passed from thence to one of the ent'ring Doors, where he took Snuff with a tolerable good Grace, display'd his fine Cloaths, made two or three feint Passes at the Curtain with his Cane, then faced about and appear'd at the other Door: Here he affected to survey the whole House, bow'd and smil'd at Random, and then shew'd his Teeth (which were some of them indeed very white): After this he retir'd behind the Curtain, and obliged us with several Views of his Person from every Opening.

During the Time of Acting he appear'd frequently in the Prince's Apartment, made one at the Hunting-Match, and was very forward in the Rebellion.   If there were no Injunctions to the contrary, yet this Practice must be confess'd to diminish the Pleasure of the Audience, and for that Reason presumptuous and unwarrantable: But since her Majesty's late Command has made it criminal, you have Authority to take notice of it.

Sir,

Your humble Servant,

T

Charles Easy.'

No. 241.
[ADDISON.]   Thursday, December 6.

> . . . *Semperque relinqui*
> *Sola sibi, semper longam incomitata videtur*
> *Ire viam* . . .—Virg.

'*Mr.* SPECTATOR,

THOUGH you have considered virtuous Love in most of its Distresses, I do not remember that you have given us any Dissertation upon the Absence of Lovers, or laid down any Methods how they should support themselves under those long Separations which they are sometimes forced to undergo. I am at present in this unhappy Circumstance, having parted with the best of Husbands, who is abroad in the Service of his Country, and may not possibly return for some Years. His warm and generous Affection while we were together, with the Tenderness which he expressed to me at parting, made his Absence almost insupportable. I think of him every Moment of the Day, and meet him every Night in my Dreams. Every thing I see puts me in mind of him, I apply my self with more than ordinary Diligence to the Care of his Family and his Estate; but this, instead of relieving me, gives me but so many Occasions of wishing for his Return. I frequent the Rooms where I used to converse with him, and not meeting him there, sit down in his Chair and fall a weeping. I love to read the Books he delighted in, and to converse with the Persons whom he esteem'd. I visit his Picture an hundred times a Day, and place my self against it whole Hours together. I pass a great Part of my Time in the Walks where I used to lean upon his Arm, and recollect in my Mind the Discourses which have there passed between us: I look over the several Prospects and Points of View which we used to survey together, fix my Eye upon the Objects which he has made me take Notice of, and call to mind a thousand agreeable Remarks which he has made on those Occasions. I write to him by every Conveyance, and, contrary to other People, am always in good Humour when an East Wind blows, because it seldom fails of bringing me a Letter from him. Let me intreat you, Sir, to give me your Advice upon this Occasion, and to let me know how I may relieve my self in this my Widowhood.

> *I am, Sir,*
> *Your most humble Servant,*
> ASTERIA.'

Absence is what the Poets call Death in Love, and has given Occasion to abundance of beautiful Complaints in those Authors, who have treated of this Passion in Verse. *Ovid's* Epistles are full of them. *Otway's Monimia* talks very tenderly upon this Subject.

> *. . . It was not kind*
> *To leave me, like a Turtle, here alone,*
> *To droop and mourn the Absence of my Mate.*
> *When thou art from me every Place is desart:*
> *And I methinks am savage and forlorn.*
> *Thy Presence only 'tis can make me blessed,*
> *Heal my unquiet Mind, and tune my Soul.*

The Consolations of Lovers on these Occasions are very extraordinary. Besides those mentioned by *Asteria*, there are many other Motives of Comfort, which are made use of by absent Lovers.

I remember in one of *Scudery*'s Romances, a couple of honourable Lovers agreed at their Parting to set aside one half Hour in the Day to think of each other during a tedious Absence. The Romance tells us, that they both of them punctually observed the time thus agreed upon; and that whatever Company or Business they were engaged in, they left it abruptly as soon as the Clock warned them to retire. The Romance further adds, That the Lovers expected the Return of this stated Hour with as much Impatience, as if it had been a real Assignation, and enjoy'd an imaginary Happiness, almost as pleasing to them as what they would have found from a real Meeting. It was an inexpressible Satisfaction to these divided Lovers to be assured that each was at the same time employed in the same kind of Contemplation, and making equal Returns of Tenderness and Affection.

If I may be allowed to mention a more Serious Expedient for the alleviating of Absence, I shall take Notice of one which I have known two Persons practise, who joined Religion to that Elegance of Sentiments with which the Passion of Love generally inspires its Votaries. This was, at the Return of such an Hour to offer up a certain Prayer for each other, which they had agreed upon before their Parting. The Husband, who is a Man that makes a Figure in the polite World, as well as in his own Family, has often told me that he could not have supported an Absence of three Years without this Expedient.

Strada in one of his Prolusions gives an Account of a chimerical Correspondence between two Friends, by the Help of a certain Loadstone, which had such Vertue in it, that if it touched two several Needles, when one of the Needles so touched begun to move, the other, tho' at never so great a Distance, moved at the same Time, and in the same Manner. He tells us, That the two Friends, being each of them possessed of one of these Needles, made a kind of a Dial-plate, inscribing it with the four and twenty Letters, in the same manner as the Hours of the Day are marked upon the ordinary Dial-plate. They then fix'd one of the Needles on each of these Plates in such a manner that it could move round without Impediment, so as to touch any of the four and twenty Letters. Upon their separating from one another into distant Countries, they agreed to withdraw themselves punctually into their Closets at a certain Hour of the Day, and to converse with one another by Means of this their Invention. Accordingly when they were some hundred Miles asunder, each of them shut himself up in his Closet at the Time appointed, and immediately cast his Eye upon his Dial-plate. If he had a mind to write any thing to his Friend, he directed his Needle to every Letter that formed the Words which he had Occasion for, making a little Pause at the End of every Word or Sentence to avoid Confusion. The Friend, in the mean while, saw his own Sympathetick Needle moving of it self to every Letter which that of his Correspondent pointed at. By this Means they talked together across a whole Continent, and conveyed their Thoughts to one another in an Instant over Cities or Mountains, Seas or Desarts.

If Monsieur *Scudery*, or any other Writer of Romance, had introduced a Necromancer, who is generally in the Train of a Knight-Errant, making a Present to two Lovers of a Couple of these above-mentioned Needles, the Reader would not have been a little pleased to have seen them corresponding with one another, when they were guarded by Spies and Watches, or separated by Castles and Adventures.

In the mean while, if ever this Invention should be revived or put in Practice, I would propose that upon the Lover's Dial-plate there should be written not only the four and twenty Letters, but several entire Words which have always a Place in passionate Epistles, as *Flames, Darts, Die, Languish, Absence, Cupid, Heart, Eyes, Hang, Drown,* and the like. This would very much abridge the Lover's Pains in this way of writing a Letter, as it would enable him to express the most useful and significant Words with a single Touch of the Needle.

C

No. 242.
[STEELE.]   Friday, December 7.

Creditur, ex medio quia res arcessit, habere
Sudoris minimum . . .—Hor.

'*Mr.* SPECTATOR,

YOUR Speculations do not so generally prevail over Men's Manners as I could wish. A former Paper of yours, concerning the Misbehaviour of People, who are necessarily in each other's Company in travelling, ought to have been a lasting Admonition against Transgressions of that kind: But I had the Fate of your Quaker, in meeting with a rude Fellow in a Stage-Coach, who entertain'd two or three Women of us (for there was no Man besides himself) with Language as indecent as ever was heard upon the Water. The impertinent Observations which the Coxcomb made upon our Shame and Confusion, were such, that it is an unspeakable Grief to reflect upon them.   As much as you have declaimed against Duelling, I hope you will do us the Justice to declare, that if the Brute has Courage enough to send to the Place where he saw us all alight together to get rid of him, there is not one of us but has a Lover who shall avenge the Insult.   It would certainly be worth your Consideration, to look into the frequent Misfortunes of this kind, to which the Modest and Innocent are expos'd, by the licentious Behaviour of such, as are as much Strangers to good Breeding as to Virtue.   Could we avoid hearing what we do not approve, as easily as we can seeing what is disagreeable, there were some Consolation; but since, in a Box at a Play, in an Assembly of Ladies, or even in a Pew at Church, it is in the Power of a gross Coxcomb to utter what a Woman cannot avoid hearing, how miserable is her Condition who comes within the Power of such Impertinents? and how necessary is it to repeat Invectives against such a Behaviour?   If the Licentious had not utterly forgot what it is to be modest, they would know, that offended Modesty labours under one of the greatest Sufferings to which human Life can be exposed.   If one of these Brutes could reflect thus much, though they want Shame, they would be moved, by their Pity, to abhor an impudent Behaviour in the Presence of the Chaste and Innocent.   If you will oblige us with a *Spectator* on this Subject, and procure it to be pasted against every Stage-Coach in *Great-Britain* as the Law of the Journey, you will highly oblige the whole Sex, for which you have professed so great an Esteem; and, in particular, the two Ladies, my late Fellow-Sufferers, and,

Sir,

Your most Humble Servant,

Rebecca Ridinghood.'

'*Mr.* Spectator,

The Matter which I am now going to send you is an unhappy Story in low Life, and will recommend it self, so that you must excuse the Manner of expressing it.   A poor idle drunken Weaver in *Spittle-Fields* has a faithful laborious Wife, who by her Frugality and Industry had laid by her as much Money as purchased her a Ticket in the present Lottery.   She had hid this very privately in the Bottom of a Trunk, and had given her Number to a Friend and Confident, who had promis'd to keep the Secret, and bring her News of the Success.   The poor Adventurer was one Day gone abroad, when her careless Husband, suspecting she had saved some Money, searches every Corner, till at length he finds this same Ticket; which he immediately carries abroad, sells, and squanders away the

Money, without the Wife's suspecting any thing of the Matter. A Day or two after this, this Friend, who was a Woman, comes, and brings the Wife Word that she had a Benefit of five hundred Pounds. The poor Creature overjoy'd, flies up Stairs to her Husband, who was then at work, and desires him to leave his Loom for that Evening, and come and drink with a Friend of his and hers below. The Man received this chearful Invitation, as bad Husbands sometimes do; and after a cross Word or two told her he wou'dn't come. His Wife with Tenderness renewed her Importunity, and at length said to him, My Love! I have within these few Months, unknown to you, scrap'd together as much Money as has bought us a Ticket in the Lottery, and now here is Mrs. *Quick* come to tell me, that 'tis come up this Morning a five hundred Pound Prize. The Husband replies immediately, You lie you Slut, you have no Ticket, for I have sold it. The poor Woman upon this faints away in a Fit, recovers, and is now run distracted. As she had no Design to defraud her Husband, but was willing only to participate in his good Fortune, every one pities her, but thinks her Husband's Punishment but just. This, Sir, is Matter of Fact, and would, if the Persons and Circumstances were greater, in a well wrought Play be call'd Beautiful Distress. I have only sketch'd it out with Chalk, and know a good Hand can make a Moving-Picture with worse Materials.

Sir, &c.'

'*Mr.* SPECTATOR,

I am what the World calls a warm Fellow, and by good Success in Trade I have raised my self to a Capacity of making some Figure in the World; but no Matter for that: I have now under my Guardianship a Couple of Neices, who will certainly make me run mad; which you will not wonder at when I tell you they are female Virtuosos, and during the three Years and a half that I have had them under my Care, they never in the least inclined their Thoughts towards any one single Part of the Character of a notable Woman. Whilst they should have been considering the proper Ingredients for a Sack-Posset, you should hear a Dispute concerning the Magnetical Virtue of the Loadstone, or perhaps the Pressure of the Atmosphere: Their Language is peculiar to themselves, and they scorn to express themselves on the meanest Trifle, with Words that are not of a *Latin* Derivation. But this were supportable still, would they suffer me to enjoy an uninterrupted Ignorance; but, unless I fall in with their abstracted Ideas of Things (as they call them) I must not expect to smoak one Pipe in quiet. In a late Fit of the Gout I complained of the Pain of that Distemper, when my Neice *Kitty* begged leave to assure me, that whatever I might think, several great Philosophers, both Ancient and Modern, were of Opinion, that both Pleasure and Pain were imaginary Distinctions; and that there was no such thing as either *in rerum Naturâ*.   I have often heard them affirm that the Fire was not hot; and one Day when I, with the Authority of an old Fellow, desired one of them to put my Blue Cloak on my Knees, she answered, Sir, I will reach the Cloak; but, take notice, I do not do it as allowing your Description, for it might as well be called Yellow as Blue; for Colour is nothing but the various Infractions of the Rays of the Sun.   Miss *Molly* told me one Day, That to say Snow is white, is allowing a vulgar Error; for as it contains a great Quantity of Nitrous Particles, it may more reasonably be supposed to be Black.   In short, the young Husseys would perswade me, that to believe one's Eyes, is a sure way to be deceived; and have often advised me, by no means, to trust any Thing so fallible as my Senses. What I have to beg of you now, is, to turn one Speculation to the due Regulation of Female Literature, so far at least, as to make it consistent with the Quiet of such, whose Fate it is to be liable to its Insults; and to tell us the difference between a Gentleman that should make Cheescakes, and raise Paste, and a Lady that reads *Lock*, and understands the Mathematicks. In which you will extremely oblige

Your hearty Friend and Humble Servant,

T   Abraham Thrifty.'

No. 243.

[ADDISON.]   Saturday, December 8.

*Formam quidem ipsam, Marce fili, & tanquam faciem honesti vides:
    quae si oculis cerneretur, mirabiles amores (ut ait Plato) excitaret
    sapientiae.*—Tull. *Offic.*

I DO not remember to have read any Discourse written expressly upon the Beauty and Loveliness of Virtue, without considering it as a Duty, and as the Means of making us happy both now and hereafter.   I design therefore this Speculation as an Essay upon that Subject, in which I shall consider Virtue no further than as it is in it self of an amiable Nature, after having premised that I understand by the word Virtue such a general Notion as is affixed to it by the Writers of Morality, and which by Devout Men generally goes under the Name of Religion, and by Men of the World under the Name of Honour.

Hypocrisie it self does great Honour, or rather Justice, to Religion, and tacitly acknowledges it to be an Ornament to Human Nature. The Hypocrite would not be at so much Pains to put on the Appearance of Virtue, if he did not know it was the most proper and effectual Means to gain the Love and Esteem of Mankind.

We learn from *Hierocles* it was a common Saying among the Heathens, that the Wise Man hates no Body, but only loves the Virtuous.

Tully has a very beautiful Gradation of Thoughts, to shew how amiable Virtue is. We love a Virtuous Man, says he, who lives in the remotest Parts of the Earth, tho' we are altogether out of the reach of his Virtue, and can receive from it no manner of Benefit; nay, one who died several Ages ago, raises a secret Fondness and Benevolence for him in our Minds, when we read his Story: Nay, what is still more, one who has been the Enemy of our Country, provided his Wars were regulated by Justice and Humanity, as in the Instance of *Pyrrhus*, whom *Tully* mentions on this Occasion in opposition to *Hannibal.* Such is the natural Beauty and Loveliness of Virtue.

Stoicism, which was the Pedantry of Virtue, ascribes all good Qualifications of what kind soever to the Virtuous Man. Accordingly *Cato*, in the Character *Tully* has left of him, carried Matters so far, that he would not allow any one but a Virtuous Man to be handsom. This indeed looks more like a Philosophical Rant, than the real Opinion of a Wise Man: Yet this was what *Cato* very seriously maintained. In short, the Stoicks thought they cou'd not sufficiently represent the Excellence of Virtue, if they did not comprehend in the Notion of it all possible Perfection; and therefore did not only suppose, that it was transcendently Beautiful in it self, but that it made the very Body amiable, and banished every kind of Deformity from the Person in whom it resided.

It is a common Observation, that the most abandoned to all Sense of Goodness are apt to wish those who are related to them of a different Character; and it is very observable, that none are more struck with the Charms of Virtue in the fair Sex, than those who by their very Admiration of it are carried to a Desire of ruining it.

A virtuous Mind in a fair Body is indeed a fine Picture in a good Light, and therefore it is no wonder that it makes the beautiful Sex all over Charms.

As Virtue in general is of an amiable and lovely Nature, there are some particular kinds of it which are more so than others, and these are such as dispose us to do Good to Mankind. Temperance and Abstinence, Faith and Devotion, are in themselves perhaps as laudable as any other Virtues; but those which make a Man popular and beloved are Justice, Charity, Munificence, and in short all the good Qualities that render us beneficial to each other. For which Reason even an extravagant Man, who has nothing else to recommend him but a false Generosity, is often more beloved and esteemed than a Person of a much more finished Character, who is defective in this Particular.

The two great Ornaments of Virtue, which shew her in the most advantageous Views, and make her altogether lovely, are Chearfulness and Good-nature. These generally go together, as a Man cannot be agreeable to others who is not easie within himself. They are both very requisite in a Virtuous Mind, to keep out Melancholy from the many serious Thoughts it is engaged in, and to hinder its natural Hatred of Vice from sowering into Severity and Censoriousness.

If Virtue is of this amiable nature, what can we think of those who can look upon it with an Eye of Hatred and Ill-Will, or can suffer their Aversion for a Party to blot out all the Merit of the Person who is engaged in it. A Man must be excessively stupid, as well as uncharitable, who believes that there is no Virtue but on his own Side, and that there are not Men as honest as himself who may differ from him in political Principles. Men may oppose one another in some Particulars, but ought not to carry their Hatred to those Qualities which are of so amiable a Nature in themselves, and have nothing to do with the Points in dispute. Men of Virtue, though of different Interests, ought to consider themselves as more nearly united with one another, than with the vicious Part of Mankind, who embark with them in the same civil Concerns. We should bear the same Love towards a Man of Honour, who is a living Antagonist, which *Tully* tells us in the forementioned Passage every one naturally does to an Enemy that is dead. In short, we should esteem Virtue though in a Foe, and abhor Vice though in a Friend.

I speak this with an Eye to those cruel Treatments which Men of all sides are apt to give the Characters of those who do not agree with them. How many Persons of undoubted Probity and exemplary Virtue, on either Side, are blackned and defamed: How many Men of Honour exposed to publick Obloquy and Reproach? Those therefore who are either the Instruments or Abettors in such infernal Dealings, ought to be looked upon as Persons who make use of Religion to promote their Cause, not of their Cause to promote Religion.

C

No. 244.
[STEELE.]   Monday, December 10.

. . . *Judex & callidus audis.*—Hor.

'*Mr.* SPECTATOR,   *Covent-Garden, Nov.* 7.

I CANNOT without a double Injustice forbear expressing to you the Satisfaction which a whole Clan of Virtuosos have received from those Hints which you have lately given the Town on the Cartons of the inimitable *Raphael*. It should be methinks the Business of a SPECTATOR to improve the Pleasures of Sight, and there cannot be a more immediate Way to it than recommending the Study and Observation of excellent Drawings and Pictures. When I first went to view those of *Raphael* which you have celebrated, I must confess I was but barely pleas'd; the next Time I liked them better, but at last as I grew better acquainted with them I fell deeply in love with them, like wise Speeches they sunk deep into my Heart; for you know, *Mr.* SPECTATOR, that a Man of Wit may extreamly affect one for the present, but if he has not Discretion his Merit soon vanishes away, while a wise Man that has not so great a Stock of Wit shall nevertheless give you a far greater and more lasting Satisfaction: Just so it is in a Picture that is smartly touch'd but not well study'd, one may call it a witty Picture, tho' the Painter in the mean time may be in Danger of being called a Fool. On the other Hand a Picture that is thoroughly understood in the Whole, and well performed in the Particulars, that is begun on a Foundation of Geometry, carry'd on by the Rules of Perspective, Architecture, and Anatomy, and perfected by a good Harmony, a just and natural Colouring, and such Passions and Expressions of the Mind as are almost peculiar to *Raphael*, this is what you may justly stile a wise Picture, and which seldom fails to strike us dumb, till we can assemble all our Faculties to make but a tolerable Judgment upon it. Other Pictures are made for the Eyes only, as Rattles are made for Children's Ears; and certainly that Picture that only pleases the Eye, without representing some well-chosen Part of Nature or other, does but shew what fine Colours are to be sold at the Colour-shop, and mocks the Works of the Creator. If the best Imitator of Nature is not to be esteemed the best Painter, but he that makes the greatest Show and Glare of Colours; it will necessarily follow, that he who can array himself in the most gaudy Draperies is best Drest, and he that can speak loudest the best Orator. Every Man when he looks on a Picture should examine it according to that Share of Reason he is Master of, or he will be in Danger of making a wrong Judgment

If Men as they walk abroad would make more frequent Observations on those Beauties of Nature which every Moment present themselves to their View, they would be better Judges when they saw her well imitated at home: This would help to correct those Errors which most Pretenders fall into, who are over hasty in their Judgments, and will not stay to let Reason come in for a Share in the Decision: 'Tis for want of this that Men mistake in this Case, and in common Life, a wild extravagant Pencil for one that is truly bold and great, an impudent Fellow for a Man of true Courage and Bravery, hasty and unreasonable Actions for Enterprizes of Spirit and Resolution, gaudy Colouring for that which is truly beautiful, a false and insinuating Discourse for simple Truth elegantly recommended. The Parallel will hold through all the Parts of Life and Painting too; and the Virtuosos abovementioned will be glad to see you draw it with your Terms of Art. As the Shadows in Picture represent the serious or melancholy, so the Lights do the bright and lively Thoughts; As there should be but one forcible Light in a Picture which should catch the Eye and fall on the Heroe, so there should be but one Object of our Love, even the Author of Nature. These and the like Reflections well improved, might very much contribute to open the Beauty of that Art, and prevent young People from being poisoned by the ill Gusto of any extravagant Workman that should be impos'd upon us.

> *I am, Sir,*
>
> *Your most humble Servant.'*

'*Mr.* SPECTATOR,

Though I am a Woman, yet I am one of those who confess themselves highly pleased with a Speculation you obliged the World with some time ago, from an old *Greek* Poet you called *Simonides*, in relation to the several Natures and Distinctions of our own Sex. I could not but admire how justly the Characters of Women in this Age fall in with the Times of *Simonides*, there being no one of those sorts I have not at some time or other of my Life met with a Sample of: But, Sir, the Subject of this present Address, are a Set of Women comprehended, I think, in the Ninth Specie of that Speculation, call'd the Apes; the Description of whom I find to be, "That they are such as are both ugly and ill-natured, who have nothing beautiful themselves, and endeavour to detract from or ridicule every thing that appears so in others.' Now, Sir, this Sect, as I have been told, is very frequent in the great Town where you live; but as my Circumstance of Life obliges me to reside altogether in the Country, though not many Miles from *London*, I can't have met with a great number of 'em, nor indeed is it a desirable Acquaintance, as I have lately found by Experience. You must know, Sir, that at the Beginning of this Summer a Family of these Apes came and settled for the Season not far from the Place where I live: As they were Strangers in the Country they were visited by the Ladies about 'em, of whom I was, with an Humanity usual in those who pass most of their Time in Solitude. The Apes lived with us very agreeably our own Way till towards the End of the Summer, when they began to bethink themselves of returning to Town; then it was, Mr. SPECTATOR, that they began to set themselves about the proper and distinguishing Business of their Character; and, as 'tis said of evil Spirits, that they are apt to carry away a Piece of the House they are about to leave, the Apes, without regard to common Mercy, Civility, or Gratitude, thought fit to mimick and fall foul on the Faces, Dress and Behaviour of their innocent Neighbours, bestowing abominable Censures and disgraceful Appellations, commonly call'd Nick-names, on all of 'em; and in short, like true fine Ladies, made their honest Plainness and Sincerity Matter of Ridicule. I could not but acquaint you with these Grievances, as well at the Desire of all the Parties injured, as from mine own Inclination. I hope, Sir, if you can't propose intirely to reform this Evil, you will take such Notice of it in some of your future Speculations, as may put the deserving Part of our Sex on their Guard against these Creatures; and at the same Time the Apes may be sensible, that this sort of Mirth is so far from an innocent Diversion, that it is in the highest Degree that Vice which is said to comprehend all others.

> *I am, Sir,*
> *Your humble Servant,*

T   Constantia Feild.'

No. 245.
[ADDISON.]   Tuesday, December 11.

Ficta voluptatis causa sint proxima veris.—Hor.

THERE is nothing which one regards so much with an Eye of Mirth and Pity as Innocence, when it has in it a Dash of Folly. At the same time that one esteems the Virtue, one is tempted to laugh at the Simplicity which accompanies it. When a Man is made up wholly of the Dove, without the least Grain of the Serpent in his Composition, he becomes ridiculous in many Circumstances of Life, and very often discredits his best

Actions. The *Cordeliers* tell a Story of their Founder St. *Francis*, that as he passed the Streets in the Dusk of the Evening, he discovered a young Fellow with a Maid in a Corner; upon which the good Man, say they, lifted up his Hands to Heaven with a Secret Thanksgiving, that there was still so much Christian Charity in the World. The Innocence of the Saint made him mistake the Kiss of a Lover for a Salute of Charity. I am heartily concerned when I see a Virtuous Man without a competent Knowledge of the World; and if there be any use in these my Papers, it is this, that without representing Vice under any false alluring Notions, they give my Reader an Insight into the Ways of Men, and represent Human Nature in all its changeable Colours. The Man who has not been engaged in any of the Follies of the World, or as *Shakespear* expresses, *Hackney'd in the Ways of Men*, may here find a Picture of its Follies and Extravagancies. The Virtuous and the Innocent may know in Speculation what they could never arrive at by Practice, and by this means avoid the Snares of the Crafty, the Corruptions of the Vicious, and the Reasonings of the Prejudiced. Their Minds may be opened without being vitiated.

It is with an Eye to my following Correspondent, Mr. *Timothy Doodle*, who seems a very well meaning Man, that I have written this short Preface, to which I shall subjoin a Letter from the said Mr. *Doodle*.

'*Sir*,

I could heartily wish that you would let us know your Opinion upon several Innocent Diversions which are in use among us, and which are very proper to pass away a Winter Night for those who do not care to throw away their Time at an Opera, or at the Play-house. I would gladly know in particular what Notion you have of Hot-Cockles; as also whether you think that Questions and Commands, Mottoes, Similies and Cross-Purposes have not more Mirth and Wit in them, than those publick Diversions which are grown so very fashionable among us. If you would recommend to our Wives and Daughters, who read your Papers with a great deal of Pleasure, some of those Sports and Pastimes that may be practised within Doors, and by the Fire side, we who are Masters of Families should be hugely obliged to you. I need not tell you that I would have these Sports and Pastimes not only Merry, but Innocent, for which Reason I have not mentioned either Whisk or Lanterloo, nor indeed so much as One and Thirty. After having communicated to you my Request upon this Subject, I will be so free as to tell you how my Wife and I pass away these tedious Winter Evenings with a great deal of

Pleasure. Tho' she be young and handsome, and good-humoured to a Miracle, she does not care for gadding abroad like others of her Sex. There is a very friendly Man, a Colonel in the Army, whom I am mightily obliged to for his Civilities, that comes to see me almost every Night; for he is not one of those giddy young Fellows that cannot live out of a Play-house. When we are together we very often make a Party at blind Man's Buff, which is a Sport that I like the better, because there is a good deal of Exercise in it. The Colonel and I are blinded by Turns, and you would laugh your Heart out to see what Pains my Dear takes to Hoodwink us, so that it is impossible for us to see the least glimpse of Light. The poor Colonel sometimes hits his Nose against a Post, and makes us die with Laughing. I have generally the good Luck not to hurt my self, but am very often above half an Hour before I can catch either of them; for you must know we hide our selves up and down in Corners, that we may have the more Sport. I only give you this Hint as a Sample of such Innocent Diversions as I would have you recommend; and am,

> *Most Esteemed Sir,*
>> *Your ever Loving Friend,*
>>> Timothy Doodle.'

The following Letter was occasioned by my last *Thursday*'s Paper upon the Absence of Lovers, and the Methods therein mentioned, of making such Absence supportable.

'*Sir,*
Among the several Ways of Consolation, which absent Lovers make use of while their Souls are in that State of Departure, which, you say, is Death in Love, there are some very material ones, that have escaped your Notice. Among these, the First and most received is a crooked Shilling, which has administered great Comfort to our Fore-fathers, and is still made use of on this Occasion with very good Effect in most Parts of Her Majesty's Dominions. There are some, I know, who think a Crown Piece cut into two equal Parts, and preserved by the distant Lovers, is of more Sovereign Vertue than the former. But since Opinions are divided in this Particular, why may not the same Persons make use of both? The Figure of a Heart, whether cut in Stone or cast in Metal, whether bleeding upon an Altar, stuck with Darts, or held in the Hand of a *Cupid*, has always been looked upon as Talismanick in Distresses of this nature. I am acquainted with many a brave Fellow, who carries his Mistress in the Lid of his Snuff box, and by that Expedient has supported himself under the Absence of a whole Campaign. For my own part, I have tried all these

Remedies, but never found so much Benefit from any as from a Ring, in which my Mistress's Hair is platted together very artificialy in a kind of True-Lover's Knot.   As I have received great Benefit from this Secret, I think my self obliged to communicate it to the Publick, for the good of my Fellow Subjects. I desire you will add this Letter as an Appendix to your Consolations upon Absence, and am,

Your very Humble Servant,

T. B.'

I shall conclude this Paper with a Letter from an University Gentleman, occasioned by my last *Tuesday*'s Paper, wherein I gave some Account of the great Feuds which happened formerly in those learned Bodies, between the modern *Greeks* and *Trojans.*

' *Sir,*

This will give you to understand, that there is at present in this Society whereof I am a Member a very considerable Body of *Trojans,* who, upon a proper Occasion, would not fail to declare our selves.   In the mean while we do all we can to annoy our Enemies by Stratagem, and are resolved, by the first Opportunity, to attack Mr. *Joshua Barnes,* whom we look upon as the *Achilles* of the opposite Party.   As for my self, I have had the Reputation, ever since I came from School, of being a trusty *Trojan,* and am resolved never to give Quarter to the smallest Particle of *Greek,* where-ever I chance to meet it.   It is for this reason I take it very ill of you, that you sometimes hang out *Greek* Colours at the Head of your Paper, and sometimes give a Word of the Enemy even in the Body of it. When I meet with any thing of this Nature I throw down your Speculations upon the Table; with that Form of Words which we make use of when we declare War upon an Author,

Graecum est, non potest legi.

I give you this Hint, that you may for the future abstain from any such Hostilities at your Peril.

C   *Troilus.*'

No. 246.

[STEELE.]   Wednesday, December 12.

. . . Οὐκ ἄρα σοί γε πατὴρ ἦν ἱππότα Πηλεύς,
Οὐδὲ Θέτις μήτηρ· γλαυκὴ δέ σε τίκτε θάλασσα
Πέτραι τ' ἠλίβατοι, ὅτι τοι νόος ἐστὶν ἀπηνής.

' *Mr.* Spectator,

As your Paper is Part of the Equipage of the Tea-Table, I

conjure you to print what I now write to you; for I have no other Way to communicate what I have to say to the fair Sex on the most important Circumstance of Life, even the Care of Children. I do not understand that you profess your Paper is always to consist of Matters which are only to entertain the Learned and Polite, but that it may agree with your Design to Publish some which may tend to the Information of Mankind in general; and when it does so, you do more than writing Wit and Humour. Give me Leave then to tell you, that of all the Abuses that ever you have as yet endeavoured to reform, certainly not one wanted so much your Assistance as the Abuse in nursing of Children. It is unmerciful to see, that a Woman endowed with all the Perfections and Blessings of Nature, can, as soon as she is delivered, turn off her innocent, tender, and helpless Infant, and give it up to a Woman that is (ten thousand to one) neither in Health nor good Condition, neither sound in Mind nor Body, that has neither Honour nor Reputation, neither Love nor Pity for the poor Babe, but more Regard for the Money than for the whole Child, and never will take further Care of it than what by all the Encouragement of Money and Presents she is forced to; like *Aesop's* Earth, which would not nurse the Plant of another Ground, altho' never so much improved, by Reason that Plant was not of its own Production. And since another's Child is no more natural to a Nurse than a Plant to a strange and different Ground, how can it be supposed that the Child should thrive? and if it thrives, must it not imbibe the gross Humours and Qualities of the Nurse, like a Plant in a different Ground, or like a Graft upon a different Stock? Do we not observe, that a Lamb sucking a Goat changes very much its Nature, nay even its Skin and Wooll into the Goat kind? The Power of a Nurse over a Child, by infusing into it with her Milk her Qualities and Disposition, is sufficiently and daily observed. Hence came that old Saying concerning an Ill-natured and malicious Fellow, that he had imbibed his Malice with his Nurse's Milk, or that some Brute or other had been his Nurse. Hence *Romulus* and *Remus* were said to have been nursed by a Wolf, *Telephus* the Son of *Hercules* by a Hind, *Pelias* the Son of *Neptune* by a Mare, and *Aegistus* by a Goat; not that they had actually sucked such Creatures, as some Simpletons have imagined, but that their Nurses had been of such a Nature and Temper, and infused such into them.

Many Instances may be produced from good Authorities and daily Experience, that Children actually suck in the several Passions and depraved Inclinations of their Nurses, as Anger, Malice, Fear, Melancholy, Sadness, Desire, and Aversion.

This *Diodorus, Lib.* 2. witnesses, when he speaks saying, That *Nero* the Emperor's Nurse had been very much addicted to Drinking, which Habit *Nero* received from his Nurse, and was so very particular in this, that the People took so much Notice of it, as instead of *Tiberius Nero*, they call'd him *Biberius Mero*. The same *Diodorus* also relates of *Caligula*, predecessor to *Nero*, that his Nurse used to moisten the Nipples of her Breast frequently with Blood, to make *Caligula* take the better Hold of them; which, says *Diodorus*, was the Cause that made him so blood-thirsty and cruel all his Life-time after, that he not only committed frequent Murder by his own Hand, but likewise wish'd that all human Kind were but one Neck, that he might have the Pleasure to cut it off. Such like Degeneracies astonish the Parents, not knowing after whom the Child can take, seeing the one to incline to Stealing, another Drinking, Cruelty, Stupidity; yet all these are not minded: Nay, it is easie to demonstrate, that a Child, although it be born from the best of Parents, may be corrupted by an ill-tempered Nurse. How many Children do we see daily brought into Fits, Consumptions, Rickets, *&c.* meerly by sucking their Nurses when in a Passion or Fury. But indeed almost any Disorder of the Nurse is a Disorder to the Child, and few Nurses can be found in this Town but what labour under some Distemper or other. The first Question that is generally asked a young Woman that wants to be a Nurse, why she should be a Nurse to other People's Children; is answered by her having an ill Husband, and that she must make Shift to live. I think now this very Answer is enough to give any Body a Shock if duly considered; for an ill Husband may, or ten to one if he does not, bring home to his Wife an ill Distemper, or at least Vexation and Disturbance. Besides, as she takes the Child out of meer Necessity, her Food will be accordingly, or else very coarse at best; whence proceeds an ill concocted and coarse Food for the Child, for as the Blood so is the Milk; and hence I am very well assured proceeds the Scurvy, the Evil, and many other Distempers. I beg of you, for the Sake of the many poor Infants that may and will be saved, by weighing this Case seriously, to exhort the People with the utmost Vehemence to let the Children suck their own Mother, both for the Benefit of Mother and Child. For the general Argument, that a Mother is weakned by giving Suck to her Children, is vain and simple; I will maintain, that the Mother grows stronger by it, and will have her Health better than she would have otherwise: She will find it the greatest Cure and Preservative for the Vapours and future Miscarriages, much beyond any other Remedy whatsoever: Her Children will be like Giants, whereas otherwise they are but living Shadows and like unripe Fruit; and certainly, if a Woman is strong enough to bring forth a Child, she is beyond all Doubt strong enough to nurse it afterwards. It grieves me to observe and consider how many poor Children are daily ruined by careless Nurses; and yet how tender they ought to be of a poor Infant, since the least Hurt or Blow, especially upon the Head, may make it senseless, stupid, or otherwise miserable for ever?

But I cannot well leave this Subject as yet; for it seems to me very unnatural that a Woman that has fed a Child as Part of her self for nine Months, should have no Desire to nurse it farther, when brought to Light and before her Eyes, and when by its Cry it implores her Assistance and the Office of a Mother. Do not the very cruellest of Brutes tend their young Ones with all the Care and Delight imaginable? For how can she be called a Mother that will not nurse its young Ones? The Earth is called the Mother of all things, not because she produces, but because she maintains and nurses what she produces. The Generation of the Infant is the Effect of Desire, but the Care of it argues Virtue and Choice. I am not ignorant but that there are some Cases of Necessity where a Mother cannot give suck, and then out of two Evils the least must be chosen; but there are so very few, that I am sure in a thousand there is hardly one real Instance; for if a Woman does but know that her Husband can spare about three or six Shillings a Week extraordinary (although this is but seldom considered), she certainly, with the Assistance of her Gossips, will soon persuade the good Man to send the Child to Nurse, and easily impose upon him by pretending Indisposition. This Cruelty is supported by Fashion, and Nature gives Place to Custom.

Sir,

T   *Your humble Servant.'*

No. 247.
[ADDISON.]   Thursday, December 13.

$$\ldots \; \Tau\hat{\omega}\nu \; \delta' \; \dot{\alpha}\kappa\dot{\alpha}\mu\alpha\tau\sigma\varsigma \; \dot{\rho}\acute{\epsilon}\epsilon\iota \; \alpha\dot{\upsilon}\delta\dot{\eta}$$
$$\text{'}E\kappa \; \sigma\tau\sigma\mu\acute{\alpha}\tau\omega\nu \; \dot{\eta}\delta\epsilon\hat{\iota}\alpha. \; \ldots$$ —Hes.

WE are told by some ancient Authors, that *Socrates* was instructed in Eloquence by a Woman, whose Name, if I am not mistaken, was *Aspasia*. I have indeed very often looked upon that Art as the most proper for the Female Sex, and I think the Universities would do well to consider whether they should not fill the Rhetorick Chairs with She-Professors.

It has been said in the Praise of some Men, that they could talk whole Hours together upon any thing; but it must be owned to the Honour of the other Sex, that there are many among them who can talk whole Hours together upon nothing. I have known a Woman branch out into a long extempore Dissertation upon the Edging of a Petticoat, and chide her Servant for breaking a China Cup in all the Figures of Rhetorick.

Were Women admitted to plead in Courts of Judicature, I am persuaded they would carry the Eloquence of the Bar to greater Heights than it has yet arrived at. If any one doubts this, let him but be present at those Debates which frequently arise among the Ladies of the *British* Fishery.

The first kind therefore of Female Orators which I shall take notice of, are those who are employed in stirring up the Passions, a part of Rhetorick in which *Socrates* his Wife had perhaps made a greater Proficiency than his above-mentioned Teacher.

The second kind of Female Orators are those who deal in Invectives, and who are commonly known by the Name of the Censorious. The Imagination and Elocution of this Sett of Rhetoricians is wonderful. With what a Fluency of Invention, and Copiousness of Expression, will they enlarge upon every little Slip in the Behaviour of another? With how many different Circumstances, and with what variety of Phrases, will they tell over the same Story? I have known an old Lady make an unhappy Marriage the Subject of a Month's Conversation. She blamed the Bride in one place; pitied her in another; laught at her in a third; wondered at her in a fourth; was angry with her in a fifth; and in short, wore out a pair of Coachhorses in expressing her Concern for her. At length, after having quite exhausted the Subject on this side, she made a Visit to the new-married Pair, praised the Wife for the prudent Choice she had made, told her the unreasonable Reflections which some malicious People had cast upon her, and desired that they might be better acquainted. The Censure and Approbation of this kind of Women are therefore only to be considered as Helps to Discourse.

A third kind of Female Orators may be comprehended under the Word Gossips. Mrs. *Fiddle Faddle* is perfectly accomplished in this sort of Eloquence; she launches out into Descriptions of Christenings, runs Divisions upon an Head-dress, knows every Dish of Meat that is served up in her Neighbourhood, and entertains her Company a whole Afternoon together with the Wit of her little Boy, before he is able to speak.

The Coquet may be looked upon as a fourth kind of Female Orator. To give her self the larger Field for Discourse, she

Hates and Loves in the same Breath, talks to her Lap-Dog or Parrot, is uneasie in all kinds of Weather, and in every part of the Room: She has false Quarrels, and feigned Obligations, to all the Men of her Acquaintance; Sighs when she is not Sad, and Laughs when she is not Merry. The Coquet is in particular a great Mistress of that part of Oratory which is called Action, and indeed seems to speak for no other Purpose, but as it gives her an Opportunity of stirring a Limb, or varying a Feature, of glancing her Eyes, or playing with her Fan.

As for News-mongers, Politicians, Mimicks, Story-Tellers, with other Characters of that nature, which give Birth to Loquacity, they are as commonly found among the Men as the Women; for which Reason I shall pass them over in Silence.

I have often been puzzled to assign a Cause, why Women should have this Talent of a ready Utterance in so much greater Perfection than Men. I have sometimes fancied that they have not a Retentive Power, or the Faculty of suppressing their Thoughts, as Men have, but that they are necessitated to speak every thing they think; and if so, it would perhaps furnish a very strong Argument to the *Cartesians*, for the supporting of their Doctrine, that the Soul always thinks. But as several are of Opinion that the Fair Sex are not altogether Strangers to the Arts of Dissembling, and concealing their Thoughts, I have been forced to relinquish that Opinion, and have therefore endeavoured to seek after some better Reason. In order to it, a Friend of mine, who is an excellent Anatomist, has promised me by the first Opportunity to dissect a Woman's Tongue, and to examine whether there may not be in it certain Juices which render it so wonderfully voluble and flippant, or whether the Fibres of it may not be made up of a finer or more pliant Thread, or whether there are not in it some particular Muscles, which dart it up and down by such sudden Glances and Vibrations; or whether, in the last place, there may not be certain undiscovered Channels running from the Head and the Heart, to this little Instrument of Loquacity, and conveying into it a perpetual Affluence of animal Spirits. Nor must I omit the Reason which *Hudibras* has given, why those who can talk on Trifles, speak with the greatest Fluency; namely, that the Tongue is like a Race-Horse, which runs the faster the lesser Weight it carries.

Which of these Reasons so ever may be looked upon as the most probable, I think the *Irishman*'s Thought was very natural, who after some Hours Conversation with a Female Orator told her, that he believed her Tongue was very glad when she was asleep, for that it had not a Moment's Rest all the while she was awake.

That excellent old Ballad of the *Wanton Wife of Bath* has the following remarkable lines.

> *I think, quoth* Thomas, *Women's Tongues*
> *Of Aspen Leaves are made.*

And *Ovid*, though in the description of a very Barbarous Circumstance, tells us, that when the Tongue of a beautiful Female was cut out, and thrown upon the Ground, it could not forbear muttering even in that posture.

> *. . . Comprensam forcipe linguam*
> *Abstulit ense fero.   Radix micat ultima linguae.*
> *Ipsa jacet, terraeque tremens immurmurat atrae;*
> *Utque salire solet mutilatae cauda colubrae*
> *Palpitat . . .*

If a Tongue would be talking without a Mouth, what could it have done when it had all its Organs of Speech, and Accomplices of Sound about it! I might here mention the Story of the Pippin Woman, had not I some reason to look upon it as Fabulous.

I must confess, I am so wonderfully charmed with the Musick of this little Instrument, that I would by no Means discourage it. All that I aim at, by this Dissertation, is, to cure it of several disagreeable Notes, and in particular of those little Jarrings and Dissonances which arise from Anger, Censoriousness, Gossiping and Coquetry. In short, I would have it always tuned by Good-nature, Truth, Discretion and Sincerity.   C

No. 248.

[STEELE.]   Friday, December 14.

Hoc maxime officii est, ut quisque maxime opis indigeat, ita ei potissimum opitulari.—Tull.

THERE are none who deserve Superiority over others in the Esteem of Mankind, who do not make it their Endeavour to be beneficial to Society; and who, upon all Occasions which their Circumstances of Life can administer, do not take a certain unfeigned Pleasure in confessing Benefits of one Kind or other. Those whose great Talents and high Birth have placed them in conspicuous Stations of Life, are indispensibly obliged to exert some noble Inclinations for the Service of the World, or else such Advantages become Misfortunes, and Shade and Privacy are a more eligible Portion. Where Opportunities and Inclinations are given to the same Person,

we sometimes see sublime Instances of Virtue, which so dazzle
our Imaginations, that we look with Scorn on all which in lower
Scenes of Life we may our selves be able to practise.   But this
is a vicious Way of Thinking; and it bears some Spice of romantick Madness for a Man to imagine that he must grow ambitious,
or seek Adventures, to be able to do great Actions.   It is in
every Man's Power in the World, who is above meer Poverty,
not only to do things worthy but heroick.   The great Foundation of civil Virtue is Self-Denial; and there is no one above the
Necessities of Life, but has Opportunities of exercising that
noble Quality, and doing as much as his Circumstances wil'
bear for the Ease and Convenience of other Men; and he who
does more than ordinarily Men practise upon such Occasions as
occur in his Life, deserves the Value of his Friends as if he had
done Enterprizes which are usually attended with the highest
Glory.   Men of publick Spirit differ rather in their Circumstances than their Virtue; and the Man who does all he can in a
low Station, is more an Hero than he who omits any worthy
Action he is able to accomplish in a great one.   It is not many
Years ago since *Lapirius*, in Wrong of his elder Brother, came
to a great Estate by Gift of his Father, by reason of the dissolute Behaviour of the First-Born.   Shame and Contrition reformed the Life of the disinherited Youth, and he became as
remarkable for his good Qualities, as formerly for his Errors.
Lapirius, who observed his Brother's Amendment, sent him on
a New-Year's Day in the Morning the following Letter:

   '*Honoured Brother,*

   I enclose to you the Deeds whereby my Father gave me this
House and Land: Had he lived till now he would not have
bestowed it in that manner; he took it from the Man you were,
and I restore it to the Man you are.   I am,
               Sir,
                     Your affectionate Brother
                        and humble Servant,
                                          P. T.'

   As great and exalted Spirits undertake the Pursuit of hazar-
dous Actions for the Good of others, at the same Time gratifying their Passion for Glory; so do worthy Minds in the domestick
Way of Life deny themselves many Advantages, to satisfie a
generous Benevolence which they bear to their Friends oppressed with Distresses and Calamities.   Such Natures one
may call Stores of Providence, which are actuated by a secret
celestial Influence to undervalue the ordinary Gratifications of
Wealth, to give Comfort to an Heart loaded with Affliction, to

save a falling Family, to preserve a Branch of Trade in their Neighbourhood, and give Work to the Industrious, preserve the Portion of the helpless Infant, and raise the Head of the mourning Father. People whose Hearts are wholly bent towards Pleasure, or intent upon Gain, never hear of the noble Occurrences among Men of Industry and Humanity. It would look like a City Romance, to tell them of the generous Merchant who the other Day sent this Billet to an eminent Trader under Difficulties to support himself, in whose Fall many hundreds besides himself had perished; but because I think there is more Spirit and true Gallantry in it than in any Letter I have ever read from *Strephon* to *Phillis*, I shall insert it even in the mercantile honest Stile in which it was sent.

'*Sir*,

I have heard of the Casualties which have involved you in extreme Distress at this Time; and knowing you to be a Man of great Good-nature, Industry, and Probity, have resolved to stand by you. Be of good Chear, the Bearer brings with him five thousand Pounds, and has my Order to answer your drawing as much more on my Account. I did this in Haste, for Fear I should come too late for your Relief; but you may value your self with me to the Sum of fifty thousand Pounds; for I can very chearfully run the Hazard of being so much less rich than I am now, to save an honest Man whom I love.

Your Friend and Servant,

W. S.'

I think there is somewhere in *Montaigne* Mention made of a Family-Book, wherein all the Occurrences that happened from one Generation of that House to another were recorded. Were there such a Method in the Families which are concerned in this Generosity, it would be an hard Task for the greatest in *Europe* to give in their own, an Instance of a Benefit better placed, or conferred with a more graceful Air. It has been heretofore urged, how barbarous and inhuman is any unjust Step made to the Disadvantage of a Trader; and by how much such an Act towards him is detestable, by so much an Act of Kindness to him is laudable. I remember to have heard a Bencher of the *Temple* tell a Story of a Tradition in their House, where they had formerly a Custom of chusing Kings for such a Season, and allowing him his Expences at the Charge of the Society: One of our Kings, said my Friend, carried his royal Inclination a little too far, and there was a Committee ordered to look into the Management of his Treasury. Among other things it appeared, that his Majesty walking *incog.* in the Cloyster, had overheard a poor Man say to another, Such a

small Sum would make me the happiest Man in the World.
The King out of his royal Compassion privately enquired into
his Character, and finding him a proper Object of Charity sent
him the Money.   When the Committee read their Report the
House passed his Accompts with a Plaudite without farther
Examination, upon Recital of this Article in them.

	l.	s.	d.
For making a Man happy	10	00	00

T

No. 249.
[ADDISON.]   Saturday, December 15.

Γέλως ἄκαιρος ἐν βροτοῖς δεινὸν κακόν.—Frag. Vet. Poet.

WHEN I make Choice of a Subject that has not been treated of
by others, I throw together my Reflections on it without any
Order or Method, so that they may appear rather in the Loose-
ness and Freedom of an Essay, than in the Regularity of a Set
Discourse.   It is after this manner that I shall consider
Laughter and Ridicule in my present Paper.

Man is the merriest Species of the Creation, all above and
below him are serious.   He sees things in a different Light from
other Beings, and finds his Mirth rising from Objects which
perhaps cause something like Pity or Displeasure in higher
Natures.   Laughter is indeed a very good Counterpoise to the
Spleen; and it seems but reasonable that we should be capable
of receiving Joy from what is no real Good to us, since we can
receive Grief from what is no real Evil.

I have in my Forty seventh Paper raised a Speculation on the
Notion of a modern Philosopher, who describes the first
Motive of Laughter to be a secret Comparison which we make
between our selves and the Persons we laugh at; or, in other
Words, that Satisfaction which we receive from the Opinion of
some Pre-eminence in our selves, when we see the Absurdities of
another, or when we reflect on any past Absurdities of our own.
This seems to hold in most Cases, and we may observe that the
vainest Part of Mankind are the most addicted to this Passion.

I have read a Sermon of a Conventual in the Church of
Rome, on those Words of the Wise Man, *I said of Laughter it is
mad, and of Mirth what does it?*   Upon which he laid it down as
a Point of Doctrine, that Laughter was the Effect of Original
Sin, and that *Adam* could not laugh before the Fall.

Laughter, while it lasts, slackens and unbraces the Mind,
weakens the Faculties, and causes a Kind of Remisness, and

Dissolution in all the Powers of the Soul: And thus far it may be looked upon as a Weakness in the Composition of human Nature. But if we consider the frequent Reliefs we receive from it, and how often it breaks the Gloom which is apt to depress the Mind and damp our Spirits with transient unexpected Gleams of Joy, one would take Care not to grow too wise for so great a Pleasure of Life.

The Talent of turning Men into Ridicule, and exposing to Laughter those one converses with, is the Qualification of little ungenerous Tempers. A young Man with this Cast of Mind cuts himself off from all manner of Improvement. Every one has his Flaws and Weaknesses; nay, the greatest Blemishes are often found in the most shining Characters; but what an absurd thing is it to pass over all the valuable Parts of a Man, and fix our Attention on his Infirmities; to observe his Imperfections more than his Virtues; and to make use of him for the Sport of others, rather than for our own Improvement.

We therefore very often find that Persons the most accomplished in Ridicule, are those who are very shrewd at hitting a Blot, without exerting any thing Masterly in themselves. As there are many eminent Criticks who never writ a good Line, there are many admirable Buffoons that animadvert upon every single Defect in another, without ever discovering the least Beauty of their own. By this Means these unlucky little Wits often gain Reputation in the Esteem of vulgar Minds, and raise themselves above Persons of much more laudable Characters.

If the Talent of Ridicule were employed to laugh Men out of Vice and Folly, it might be of some Use to the World; but instead of this, we find that it is generally made Use of to laugh Men out of Virtue and good Sense, by attacking every thing that is Solemn and Serious, Decent and Praise-worthy in human Life.

We may observe, that in the First Ages of the World, when the great Souls and Master-pieces of human Nature were produced, Men shined by a noble Simplicity of Behaviour, and were Strangers to those little Embellishments which are so fashionable in our present Conversation. And it is very remarkable, that notwithstanding we fall short at present of the Ancients in Poetry, Painting, Oratory, History, Architecture, and all the noble Arts and Sciences which depend more upon Genius than Experience, we exceed them as much in Doggerel, Humour, Burlesque, and all the trivial Arts of Ridicule. We meet with more Raillery among the Moderns, but more good Sense among the Ancients.

The two great Branches of Ridicule in Writing are Comedy

and Burlesque. The first ridicules Persons by drawing them in their proper Characters, the other by drawing them quite unlike themselves. Burlesque is therefore of two kinds, the first represents mean Persons in the Accoutrements of Heroes; the other describes great Persons acting and speaking, like the basest among the People. *Don Quixote* is an Instance of the first, and *Lucian's* Gods of the second. It is a Dispute among the Criticks, whether Burlesque Poetry runs best in Heroic Verse, like that of *The Dispensary*, or in Doggerel, like that of *Hudibras*. I think where the low Character is to be raised the Heroic is the proper Measure, but when an Hero is to be pulled down and degraded, it is done best in Doggerel.

If *Hudibras* had been set out with as much Wit and Humour in Heroic Verse as he is in Doggerel, he would have made a much more agreeable Figure than he does; tho' the generality of his Readers are so wonderfully pleased with the double Rhimes, that I do not expect many will be of my Opinion in this Particular.

I shall conclude this Essay upon Laughter with observing that the Metaphor of Laughing, applied to Fields and Meadows when they are in Flower, or to Trees when they are in Blossom, runs through all Languages; which I have not observed of any other Metaphor, excepting that of Fire, and Burning, when they are applied to Love. This shews that we naturally regard Laughter, as what is both in it self amiable and beautiful. For this Reason likewise *Venus* has gained the Title of Φιλομμειδής, the Laughter-loving Dame, as *Waller* has translated it, and is represented by *Horace* as the Goddess who delights in Laughter. *Milton*, in a joyous Assembly of imaginary Persons, has given us a very poetical Figure of Laughter. His whole Band of Mirth is so finely described that I shall set down the Passage at length.

> *But come thou Goddess fair and free,*
> *In Heav'n ycleap'd Euphrosyne,*
> *And by Men, heart-easing Mirth,*
> *Whom lovely Venus at a Birth*
> *With two Sister Graces more*
> *To Ivy-crowned Bacchus bore:*
> *Haste thee Nymph, and bring with thee*
> *Jest and youthful Jollity,*
> *Quips and Cranks, and Wanton Wiles,*
> *Nods, and Becks, and wreathed Smiles,*
> *Such as hang on Hebe's Cheek,*
> *And love to live in dimple sleek;*
> *Sport that wrinkled Care derides,*
> *And Laughter holding both his Sides.*

Come, and trip it as you go
On the light fantastick Toe,
And in thy right Hand lead with thee,
The Mountain Nymph, sweet Liberty;
And if I give thee Honour due,
Mirth, admit me of thy Crue
To live with her, and live with thee,
In unreproved Pleasures free.

No. 250.

Monday, December 17.

Disce, docendus adhuc quae censet amiculus, ut si
Caecus iter monstrare velit; tamen aspice si quid
Et nos, quod cures proprium fecisse, loquamur.—Hor.

'*Mr.* SPECTATOR,

YOU see the Nature of my Request by the *Latin* Motto which I address to you: I am very sensible I ought not to use many Words to you, who are one of but few; but the following Piece, as it relates to Speculation in Propriety of Speech, being a Curiosity in its Kind, begs your Patience: It was found in a Poetical Virtuoso's Closet among his Rarities; and since the several Treaties of Thumbs, Ears and Noses have obliged the World, this of Eyes is at your Service.

The first Eye of Consequence (under the invisible Author of all) is the visible Luminary of the Universe: This glorious Spectator is said never to open his Eyes at his Rising in a Morning, without having a whole Kingdom of Adorers in *Persian* Silk waiting at his Levée. Millions of Creatures derive their Sight from this Original, who, besides his being the great Director of Opticks, is the surest Test whether Eyes be of the same Species with that of an Eagle or that of an Owl: The one he emboldens with a manly Assurance to look, speak, act or plead before the Faces of a numerous Assembly; the other he dazzles out of Countenance into a sheepish Dejectedness. The Sun-Proof Eye dares lead up a Dance in a full Court; and without blinking at the Lustre of Beauty, can distribute an Eye of proper Complaisance to a Room crowded with Company, each of which deserves particular Regard; while the other sneaks from Conversation, like a fearful Debtor, who never dares to look out, but when he can see no Body, and no Body him.

The next Instance of Opticks is the famous *Argus*, who (to speak the Language of *Cambridge*) was one of an hundred; and being us'd as a Spy in the Affairs of Jealousie, was obliged to have all his Eyes about him. We have no Account of the particular Colours, Casts, and Turns of this Body of Eyes; but as he was Pimp for his Mistress *Juno*, 'tis probable he us'd all the modern Leers, sly Glances, and other ocular Activities to serve his Purpose. Some look upon him as the then King at Arms to the Heathenish Deities, and make no more of his Eyes than as so many Spangles of his Herald's Coat.

The next upon the Optick List is old *Janus*, who stood in a double-sighted Capacity like a Person placed betwixt two opposite Looking-Glasses, and so took a sort of Retrospective Cast at one View. Copies of this double-faced Way are not yet out of Fashion with many Professions, and the ingenious Artists pretend to keep up this Species by double-headed Canes and Spoons; but there is no Mark of this Faculty except in the emblematical Way of a wise General having an Eye to both Front and Rear, or a pious Man taking a Review and Prospect of his Past and Future State at the same Time.

I must own that the Names, Colours, Qualities, and Turns of Eyes vary almost in every Head; for, not to mention the common Appellations of the Black, the Blue, the White, the Grey, and the like, the most remarkable are those that borrow their Title from Animals, by Vertue of some particular Quality or Resemblance they bear to the Eyes of the respective Creature; as that of a greedy rapacious Aspect takes its Name from the Cat, that of a sharp piercing Nature from the Hawk, those of an amorous roguish Look derive their Title even from the Sheep, and we say such a one has a Sheep's Eye, not so much to denote the Innocence as the simple Slyness of the Cast; Nor is this metaphorical Inoculation a modern Invention, for we find *Homer* taking the Freedom to place the Eye of an Ox, Bull, or Cow in one of his principal Goddesses, by that frequent Expression of

$$Βοῶπις\ πότνια\ ″Ηρη\ .\ .\ .$$

Now as to the peculiar Qualities of the Eye, that fine Part of our Constitution seems as much the Receptacle and Seat of our Passions, Appetites, and Inclinations, as the Mind it self; at least 'tis as the outward Portal to introduce them to the House within, or rather the common Thorough-fare to let our Affections pass in and out; Love, Anger, Pride, and Avarice all visibly move in those little Orbs. I know a young Lady that can't see a certain Gentleman pass by, without shewing a secret Desire of seeing him again by a Dance in her Eye-balls; nay, she can't for the Heart of her help looking half a Street's Length after any Man in a gay Dress. You cannot behold a covetous Spirit walk by a Goldsmith's Shop, without casting a wishful Eye at the Heaps upon the Counter. Does not a haughty Person shew the Temper of his Soul in the super-cilious Rowl of his Eye? and how frequently in the Height of Passion does that moving Picture in our Head start and stare, gather a Redness and quick Flashes of Lightning, and makes all its Humours sparkle with Fire, as *Virgil* finely describes it,

> . . . *Ardentis ab ore*
> *Scintillae absistunt: oculis micat acribus ignis.*

As for the various Turns of the Eye-sight, such as the voluntary or involuntary, the half or the whole Leer, I shall not enter into a very particular Account of them; but let me ob-serve, that oblique Vision, when natural, was anciently the Mark of Bewitchery and magical Fascination, and to this Day 'tis a malignant ill Look; but when 'tis forc'd and affected it carries a wanton Design, and in Play-houses, and other publick Places, this ocular Intimation is often an Assignation for bad Practices: But this Irregularity in Vision, together with such Enormities as tipping the Wink, the circumspective Rowl, the Side-Peep thro' a thin Hood or Fan, must be put in the Class of Heter-opticks, as all wrong Notions of Religion are rank'd under the general Name of Heterodox. All the pernicious Applications of Sight are more immediately under the Direction of a SPECTATOR; and I hope you will arm your Readers against the Mischiefs which are daily done by killing Eyes, in which you will highly oblige your wounded unknown Friend,

T. B.'

'*Mr.* SPECTATOR,

You professed in several Papers your particular Endeavours, in the Province of SPECTATOR, to correct the Offences com-mitted by Starers, who disturbed whole Assemblies, without any Regard to Time, Place or Modesty. You complained also, that a Starer is not usually a Person to be convinced by the Reason of the Thing; nor so easily rebuked, as to amend by Admonitions. I thought therefore fit to acquaint you with a convenient Mechanical way, which may easily prevent or correct Staring, by an Optical Contrivance of new Perspective-Glasses, short and commodious like Opera-Glasses, fit for short-sighted People as well as others; these Glasses making the Objects appear, either as they are seen by the naked Eye, or more distinct, though somewhat less than Life, or bigger and nearer. A Person may by the Help of this Invention take a View of another, without the Impertinence of Staring; at the same time it shall not be possible to know whom or what he is looking at. One may look towards his right or left Hand, when he is sup-posed to look forwards: This is set forth at large in the printed Proposals for the Sale of these Glasses, to be had at Mr. *Dillon*'s in *Long-Acre*, next door to the *White Hart*: Now, Sir, as your *Spectator* has occasion'd the publishing of this Invention, for the Benefit of modest Spectators, the Inventor desires your Admonitions, concerning the decent Use of it, and hopes by your Recommendation that for the future Beauty may be beheld, without the Torture and Confusion which it suffers from the Insolence of Starers. By this Means you will relieve the Innocent from an Insult which there is no Law to punish, though it is a greater Offence than many which are within Cognizance of Justice. I am,

Sir,

Your most Humble Servant,

Q   Abraham Spy.'

No. 251.

[ADDISON.]   Tuesday, December 18.

> . . . *Linguae centum sunt, oraque centum.*
> *Ferrea vox* . . .—Virg.

THERE is nothing which more astonishes a Foreigner, and frights a Country Squire, than the *Cries of London*. My good Friend Sir ROGER often declares, that he cannot get them out of his Head, or go to sleep for them the first Week that he is in Town. On the contrary, WILL HONEYCOMB calls them the *Ramage de la Ville*, and prefers them to the Sounds of Larks and Nightingales, with all the Musick of the Fields and Woods. I have lately received a Letter from some very odd Fellow upon this Subject, which I shall leave with my Reader, without saying any thing further of it.

'*Sir,*

I am a Man out of all Business, and would willingly turn my Head to any thing for an honest Livelihood. I have invented several Projects for raising many Millions of Money without burdening the Subject, but I cannot get the Parliament to listen to me, who look upon me, forsooth, as a Projector; so that despairing to enrich either my self or my Country by this Publick-spiritedness, I would make some Proposals to you relating to a Design which I have very much at Heart, and which may procure me an handsome Subsistance, if you will be pleased to recommend it to the Cities of *London* and *Westminster*.

The Post I would aim at is to be Comptroller general of the *London* Cries, which are at present under no manner of Rules or Discipline. I think I am pretty well qualified for this Place, as being a Man of very strong Lungs, of great Insight into all the Branches of our *British* Trades and Manufactures, and of a competent Skill in Musick.

The Cries of *London* may be divided into Vocal and Instrumental. As for the latter, they are at present under a very great Disorder. A Freeman of *London* has the Privilege of disturbing a whole Street for an Hour together, with the Twancking of a brass Kettle or a Frying-pan. The Watchman's Thump at Midnight startles us in our Beds, as much as the breaking in of a Thief. The Sow-gelder's Horn has indeed something musical in it, but this is seldom heard within the Liberties. I would therefore propose, that no Instrument of this Nature should be made use of, which I have not tuned and licensed, after having carefully examined in what manner it may affect the Ears of her Majesty's liege Subjects.

Vocal Cries are of a much larger Extent, and indeed so full of Incongruities and Barbarisms, that we appear a distracted City to Foreigners, who do not comprehend the Meaning of such enormous Outcries. Milk is generally sold in a Note above *Elah*, and in Sounds so exceeding Shrill, that it often sets our Teeth an edge. The Chimney-sweeper is confined to no certain Pitch; he sometimes utters himself in the deepest Base, and sometimes in the sharpest Treble; sometimes in the highest, and sometimes in the lowest Note of the Gamut. The same Observation might be made on the Retailers of Smallcoal, not to mention broken Glasses or Brick-dust. In these, therefore, and the like Cases, it should be my Care to sweeten and mellow the Voices of these itinerant Tradesmen, before they make their Appearance in our Streets; as also to accommodate their Cries to their respective Wares; and to take Care in particular that those may not make the most Noise, who have the least to sell, which is very observable in the Venders of Card-matches, to whom I cannot but apply that old Proverb of *Much Cry but little Wool.*

Some of these last-mentioned Musicians are so very loud in the Sale of these trifling Manufactures, that an honest splenetick Gentleman of my Acquaintance bargained with one of them never to come into the Street where he lived: But what was the Effect of this Contract? why, the whole Tribe of Cardmatch-makers which frequent that Quarter, passed by his Door the very next Day, in hopes of being bought off after the same manner.

It is another great Imperfection in our *London* Cries, that there is no just Time nor Measure observed in them. Our News should indeed be published in a very quick Time, because it is a Commodity that will not keep cold. It should not however be cried with the same Precipitation as *Fire*: Yet this is generally the Case: A bloody battel alarms the Town from one End to another in an Instant. Every Motion of the *French* is published in so great an Hurry, that one would think the Enemy were at our Gates. This likewise I would take upon me to regulate in such a manner, that there should be some Distinction made between the spreading of a Victory, a March, or an Incampment, a *Dutch,* a *Portugal,* or a *Spanish* Mail. Nor must I omit under this Head, those excessive Alarms with which several boisterous Rusticks infest our Streets in Turnip Season; and which are more inexcusable, because these are Wares which are in no Danger of Cooling upon their Hands.

There are others who affect a very slow Time, and are in my Opinion much more tuneable than the former; the Cooper in particular swells his last Note in an hollow Voice, that is not without its Harmony; nor can I forbear being inspired with a most agreeable Melancholy, when I hear that sad and solemn Air with which the Publick is very often asked, if they have any Chairs to mend. Your own Memory may suggest to you many other lamentable Ditties of the same Nature, in which the Musick is wonderfully languishing and melodious.

I am always pleased with that particular Time of the Year which is proper for the pickling of Dill and Cucumbers; but alas this Cry, like the Song of the Nightingales, is not heard above two Months. It would therefore be worth while to consider whether the same Air might not in some Cases be adapted to other Words.

It might likewise deserve our most serious Consideration, how far, in a well-regulated City, those Humourists are to be tolerated, who not contented with the traditional Cries of their Fore-fathers, have invented particular Songs and Tunes of their own: Such as was, not many Years since, the Pastry-man commonly known by the Name of the Colly-Molly-Puff; and such as is at this Day the Vender of Powder and Washballs, who, if I am rightly informed, goes under the Name of *Powder-Watt.*

I must not here omit one particular Absurdity which runs thro' this whole vociferous Generation, and which renders their Cries very often not only incommodious, but altogether useless to the Publick. I mean that idle Accomplishment which they all of them aim at, of Crying so as not to be understood. Whether or no they have learned this from several of our affected Singers, I will not take upon me to say; but most certain it is, that People know the Wares they deal in rather by their Tunes than by their Words; insomuch that I have sometimes seen a Country Boy run out to buy Apples of a Bellows-mender, and Ginger-bread from a Grinder of Knives and Scissars. Nay, so strangely infatuated are some very eminent Artists of this particular Grace in a Cry, that none but their Acquaintance are able to guess at their Profession; for who else can know, that *Work if I had it*, should be the Signification of a Corn-Cutter?

Forasmuch therefore as Persons of this Rank are seldom Men of Genius or Capacity, I think it would be very proper that some Man of good Sense and sound Judgment should preside over these publick Cries, who should permit none to lift up their Voices in our Streets, that have not tuneable Throats, and are not only able to overcome the Noise of the Croud, and the rattling of Coaches, but also to vend their respective Merchandizes in apt Phrases, and in the most distinct and agreeable Sounds. I do therefore humbly recommend my self as a Person rightly qualified for this Post, and if I meet with fitting Encouragement, shall communicate some other Projects which I have by me, that may no less conduce to the Emolument of the Publick.

> *I am,*
>
> > *Sir, &c.*

C   Ralph Crotchett.'

The End of the Third Volume.

TO THE

DUKE OF MARLBOROUGH.

MY LORD,

As it is natural to have a Fondness for what has cost us much Time and Attention to produce, I hope Your Grace will forgive an Endeavour to preserve this Work from Oblivion, by affixing it to Your memorable Name.

I shall not here presume to mention the illustrious Passages of Your Life, which are celebrated by the whole Age, and have been the Subject of the most sublime Pens; but if I could convey You to Posterity in Your private Character, and describe the Stature, the Behaviour and Aspect of the Duke of *Marlborough*, I question not but it would fill the Reader with more agreeable Images, and give him a more delightful Entertainment than what can be found in the following, or any other Book.

One cannot indeed without Offence, to Yourself, observe, that You excel the rest of Mankind in the least, as well as the greatest Endowments. Nor were it a Circumstance to be mentioned, if the Graces and Attractions of Your Person were not the only Preheminence You have above others, which is left, almost, unobserved by greater Writers.

Yet how pleasing would it be to those who shall read the surprising Revolutions in Your Story, to be made acquainted with Your ordinary Life and Deportment? How pleasing would it be to hear that the same Man who had carried Fire and Sword into the Countries of all that had opposed the Cause of Liberty, and struck a Terrour into the Armies of *France*, had in the midst of His high Station a Behaviour as gentle as is usual in the first Steps towards Greatness? And if it were possible to express that easy Grandeur, which did at once persuade and command; it would appear as clearly to those to come, as it does to His Contemporaries, that all the great Events which were brought to pass under the Conduct of so well-govern'd a Spirit, were the Blessings of Heaven upon Wisdom and Valour; and all which seem adverse fell out by divine Permission, which we are not to search into.

You have pass'd that Year of Life wherein the most able and fortunate Captain, before Your Time, declared he had lived enough both to Nature and to Glory; and Your Grace may make that Reflection with much more Justice. He spoke it after he had arrived at Empire, by an Usurpation upon those whom he had enslaved; but the Prince of *Mindelheim* may rejoyce in a Soveraignty which was the Gift of Him whose Dominions He had preserved.

Glory established upon the uninterrupted Success of honourable Designs and Actions is not subject to Diminution; nor can any Attempts prevail against it, but in the Proportion which the narrow Circuit of Rumour bears to the unlimited Extent of Fame.

We may congratulate Your Grace not only upon Your high Atcheivements, but likewise upon the happy Expiration of Your Command, by which Your Glory is put out of the Power of Fortune: And when Your Person shall be so too, that the Author and Disposer of all Things may place You in that higher Mansion of Bliss and Immortality which is prepared for good Princes, Lawgivers, and Heroes, when HE in HIS due Time removes them from the Envy of Mankind, is the hearty Prayer of,

    My LORD,
        Your Grace's
            Most Obedient,
                Most Devoted
                    Humble Servant,
                        THE SPECTATOR.

THE SPECTATOR.

VOL. IV.

No. 252.

[STEELE.]   Wednesday, December 19, 1711.

Erranti, passimque oculos per cuncta ferenti.—Virg.

'*Mr.* Spectator,

I am very sorry to find by your Discourse upon the Eye, that
you have not thoroughly studied the Nature and Force of that
Part of a beauteous Face. Had you ever been in Love, you
would have said ten thousand Things, which it seems did not
occur to you: Do but reflect upon the Nonsense it makes Men
talk, the Flames which it is said to kindle, the Transport it
raises, the Dejection it causes in the bravest Men; and if you
do believe those Things are expressed to an Extravagance, yet
you will own, that the Influence of it is very great which moves
Men to that Extravagance. Certain it is, that the whole
Strength of the Mind is sometimes seated there; that a kind
Look imparts all, that a Year's Discourse could give you, in
one Moment. What matters it what she says to you, see how
she looks is the Language of all who know what Love is. When
the Mind is thus summed up and expressed in a Glance, did
you never observe a sudden Joy arise in the Countenance of a
Lover? Did you never see the Attendance of Years paid, over-
paid, in an Instant? You a Spectator, and not know that
the Intelligence of Affection is carried on by the Eye only;
that Good-breeding has made the Tongue falsify the Heart,
and act a Part of continual Constraint, while Nature has preserved the Eyes to her self, that she may not be disguised or
misrepresented. The poor Bride can give her Hand, and say,
I do, with a languishing Air to the Man she is obliged by cruel
Parents to take for mercenary Reasons, but at the same Time
she cannot look as if she loved; her Eye is full of Sorrow, and
Reluctance sits in a Tear, while the Offering of the Sacrifice is
performed in what we call the Marriage Ceremony. Do you
never go to Plays? Cannot you distinguish between the Eyes
of those who go to see, from those who come to be seen? I am
a Woman turned of Thirty, and am on the Observation a little;
therefore if you or your Correspondent had consulted me in
your Discourse on the Eye, I could have told you that the Eye
of *Leonora* is slyly watchful while it looks negligent; she looks
round her without the Help of the Glasses you speak of, and yet

seems to be employed on Objects directly before her. This Eye is what affects Chance-medley, and on a sudden, as if it attended to another Thing, turns all its Charms against an Ogler. The Eye of *Lusitania* is an Instrument of premeditated Murder, but the Design being visible, destroys the Execution of it; and with much more Beauty than that of *Leonora*, it is not half so mischievous. There is a brave Soldier's Daughter in Town, that by her Eye has been the Death of more than ever her Father made fly before him. A beautiful Eye makes Silence eloquent, a kind Eye makes Contradiction an Assent, an enraged Eye makes Beauty deformed. This little Member gives Life to every other Part about us, and I believe the Story of *Argus* implies no more than that the Eye is in every Part, that is to say, every other Part would be mutilated, were not its Force represented more by the Eye than even by it self. But this is Heathen *Greek* to those who have not conversed by Glances. This, Sir, is a Language in which there can be no Deceit, nor can a skilful Observer be imposed upon by Looks even among Politicians and Courtiers. If you do me the Honour to print this among your Speculations, I shall in my next, make you a Present of secret History, by translating all the Looks of the next Assembly of Ladies and Gentlemen into Words, to adorn some future Paper.

> *I am,*
> > *Sir,*
> > > *Your faithful Friend,*
> > > > Mary Heartfree.'

'*Dear Mr.* SPECTATOR,

I have a Sot of a Husband that lives a very scandalous Life, and wastes away his Body and Fortune in Debauches; and is immoveable to all the Arguments I can urge to him. I would gladly know whether in some Cases a Cudgel may not be allowed as a good Figure of Speech, and whether it may not be lawfully used by a female Orator.

> *Your humble Servant,*
> > Barbara Crabtree.'

'*Mr.* SPECTATOR,

Though I am a Practitioner in the Law of some standing, and have heard many eminent Pleaders in my Time, as well as other eloquent Speakers of both Universities, yet I agree with you that Women are better qualified to succeed in Oratory than the Men, and believe this is to be resolved into natural Causes. You have mentioned only the Volubility of their Tongue; but what do you think of the silent Flattery of their pretty Faces, and the Perswasion which even an insipid Discourse carries with it when flowing from beautiful Lips, to which it would be cruel to deny any Thing? It is certain too that they are possessed of some Springs of Rhetorick which Men want, such as Tears, fainting Fits, and the like, which I have seen employed upon Occasion with good Success. You must know I am a plain Man and love my Money; yet I have a Spouse who is so great an Orator in this Way, that she draws from me what Sums she pleases. Every Room in my House is furnished with Trophies of her Eloquence, rich Cabinets, Piles of China, Japan Screens, and costly Jarrs; and if you were to come into my great Parlour, you would fancy your self in an *India* Warehouse: Besides this, she keeps a Squirrel, and I am doubly taxed to pay for the China he breaks. She is seized with periodical Fits about the Time of the Subscriptions to a new Opera, and is drowned in Tears after having seen any Woman there in finer Cloaths than her self: These are Arts of Perswasion purely Feminine, and which a tender Heart cannot resist. What I would therefore desire of you, is, to prevail with your Friend who has promised to dissect a Female Tongue, that he would at the same Time give us the Anatomy of a female Eye, and explain the Springs and Sluices which feed it with such ready Supplies of Moisture; and likewise shew by what Means, if possible, they may be stopped at a reasonable Expence: Or indeed, since there is something so moving in the very Image of weeping Beauty, it would be worthy his Art to provide, that these eloquent Drops may no more be lavished on Trifles, or employed as Servants to their wayward Wills; but reserved for serious Occasions in Life, to adorn generous Pity, true Penitence, or real Sorrow.

T   *I am, &c.*'

No. 253.

[ADDISON.]   Thursday, December 20.

*Indignor quicquam reprehendi, non quia crasse
Compositum illepideve putetur, sed quia nuper.*—Hor.

THERE is nothing which more denotes a great Mind, than the Abhorrence of Envy and Detraction. This Passion reigns more among bad Poets, than among any other Set of Men.

As there are none more ambitious of Fame, than those who are conversant in Poetry, it is very natural for such as have not succeeded in it to depreciate the Works of those who have. For since they cannot raise themselves to the Reputation of their Fellow-Writers, they must endeavour to sink it to their own Pitch, if they would still keep themselves upon a Level with them.

The greatest Wits that ever were produced in one Age, lived together in so good an Understanding, and celebrated one another with so much Generosity, that each of them receives an additional Lustre from his Contemporaries, and is more famous for having lived with Men of so extraordinary a Genius, than if he had himself been the sole Wonder of the Age. I need not tell my Reader, that I here point at the Reign of *Augustus,* and I believe he will be of my Opinion, that neither *Virgil* nor *Horace* would have gained so great a Reputation in the World, had they not been the Friends and Admirers of each other. Indeed all the great Writers of that Age, for whom singly we have so great an Esteem, stand up together as Vouchers for one another's Reputation. But at the same time that *Virgil* was celebrated by *Gallus, Propertius, Horace, Varius, Tucca* and *Ovid,* we know that *Bavius* and *Maevius* were his declared Foes and Calumniators.

In our own Country a Man seldom sets up for a Poet, without attacking the Reputation of all his Brothers in the Art. The Ignorance of the Moderns, the Scribblers of the Age, the Decay of Poetry, are the Topicks of Detraction, with which he makes his Entrance into the World: But how much more noble is the Fame that is built on Candour and Ingenuity, according to those beautiful Lines of Sir *John Denham,* in his Poem on *Fletcher's* Works!

> *But whither am I straid? I need not raise*
> *Trophies to thee from other Men's Dispraise;*
> *Nor is thy Fame on lesser Ruins built,*
> *Nor needs thy juster Title the foul Guilt*
> *Of Eastern Kings, who to secure their Reign*
> *Must have their Brothers, Sons, and Kindred slain.*

I am sorry to find that an Author, who is very justly esteemed among the best Judges, has admitted some Stroaks of this Nature into a very fine Poem, I mean *The Art of Criticism,* which was published some Months since, and is a Master-piece in its Kind. The Observations follow one another like those in *Horace's Art of Poetry,* without that methodical Regularity which would have been requisite in a Prose Author. They are some of them uncommon, but such as the Reader must assent to, when he sees them explained with that Elegance and Perspicuity in which they are delivered. As for those which are the most known, and the most received, they are placed in so beautiful a Light, and illustrated with such apt Allusions, that they have in them all the Graces of Novelty, and make the Reader, who was before acquainted with them, still more convinced of their Truth and Solidity. And here give me Leave to mention what Monsieur *Boileau* has so very well enlarged upon in the Preface to his Works, that Wit and fine Writing doth not consist so much in advancing Things that are new, as in giving things that are known an agreeable Turn. It is impossible, for us who live in the later Ages of the World, to make Observations in Criticism, Morality, or in any Art or Science, which have not been touched upon by others. We have little else left us, but to represent the common Sense of Mankind in more strong, more beautiful, or more uncommon Lights. If a Reader examines *Horace's* Art of Poetry, he will find but very few precepts in it, which he may not meet with in *Aristotle,* and which were not commonly known by all the Poets of the *Augustan* Age. His Way of Expressing and Applying them, not his Invention of them, is what we are chiefly to admire.

For this Reason I think there is nothing in the World so tiresome as the Works of those Criticks, who write in a positive dogmatick Way, without either Language, Genius or Imagination. If the Reader would see how the best of the *Latin* Criticks writ, he may find their Manner very beautifully described in the Characters of *Horace, Petronius, Quintilian* and *Longinus,* as they are drawn in the Essay of which I am now speaking.

Since I have mentioned *Longinus,* who in his Reflections has given us the same Kind of Sublime, which he observes in the several Passages that occasioned them; I cannot but take notice that our *English* Author has after the same manner exemplified several of his Precepts in the very Precepts themselves. I shall produce two or three Instances of this Kind. Speaking of the insipid Smoothness which some Readers are so much in Love with, he has the following Verses.

> *These* Equal Syllables *alone require,*
> *Tho' oft the Ear the* open Vowels *tire,*
> *While* Expletives *their feeble Aid* do *join,*
> *And ten low Words oft creep in one dull Line.*

The gaping of the Vowels in the second Line, the Expletive *do* in the third, and the ten Monosyllables in the fourth, give such a Beauty to this Passage, as would have been very much admired in an Ancient Poet. The Reader may observe the following Lines in the same View.

> *A* needless Alexandrine *ends the Song,*
> *That like a wounded Snake, drags its slow Length along.*

And afterwards,

> *'Tis not enough no Harshness gives Offence,*
> *The* Sound *must seem an* Eccho *to the Sense.*

Soft *is the Strain when* Zephir *gently blows,*
And the smooth Stream *in* smoother Numbers *flows;*
But when loud Surges lash the sounding Shore,
The hoarse, rough Verse *shou'd like the* Torrent *roar.*
When Ajax *strives, some Rock's vast Weight to throw,*
The Line too labours, *and the Words move* slow;
Not so, when swift Camilla *scours the Plain,*
Flies o'er th' unbending Corn, and skims along the Main.

The beautiful Distich upon *Ajax* in the foregoing Lines, puts
me in mind of a Description in *Homer's* Odyssey, which none
of the Criticks have taken notice of. It is where *Sisyphus* is
represented lifting his Stone up the Hill, which is no sooner
carried to the Top of it, but it immediately tumbles to the
Bottom. This double Motion of the Stone is admirably described in the Numbers of these Verses. As in the four first it
is heaved up by several *Spondees*, intermixed with proper
Breathing-places, and at last trundles down in a continued
Line of *Dactyls*.

Καὶ μὴν Σίσυφον εἰσεῖδον, κρατέρ' ἄλγε' ἔχοντα,
Λᾶαν βαστάζοντα πελώριον ἀμφοτέρῃσιν.
Ἤτοι ὁ μὲν σκηριπτόμενος χερσίν τε ποσίν τε
Λᾶαν ἄνω ὤθεσκε ποτὶ λόφον· ἀλλ' ὅτε μέλλοι
Ἄκρον ὑπερβαλέειν, τότ' ἀποστρέψασκε Κραταιΐς,
Αὖτις ἔπειτα πέδονδε κυλίνδετο λᾶας ἀναιδής.

It would be endless to quote Verses out of *Virgil* which have
this particular Kind of Beauty in the Numbers; but I may
take an Occasion in a future Paper to shew several of them
which have escaped the Observation of others.

I cannot conclude this Paper without taking notice that we
have three Poems in our Tongue, which are of the same Nature,
and each of them a Master-piece in its Kind; the Essay on
Translated Verse, the Essay on the Art of Poetry, and the
Essay upon Criticism.   C

No. 254.
[STEELE.]   Friday, December 21.

Σεμνὸς ἔρως ἀρετῆς, ὁ δὲ κύπριδος ἄχος ὀφέλλει.

WHEN I consider the false Impressions which are received by
the Generality of the World, I am troubled at none more than
a certain Levity of Thought which many young Women of
Quality have entertained, to the Hazard of their Characters
and the certain Misfortune of their Lives. The first of the

following Letters may best represent the Faults I would now point at, and the Answer to it the Temper of Mind in a contrary Character.

'*My dear* Harriot,

If thou art she, but oh how fall'n, how chang'd, what an Apostate! How lost to all that's gay and agreeable! To be marry'd I find is to be bury'd alive; I can't conceive it more dismal to be shut up in a Vault to converse with the Shades of my Ancestors, than to be carried down to an old Mannor House in the Country, and confin'd to the Conversation of a sober Husband and an aukward Chambermaid. For Variety I suppose you may entertain your self with Madam in her Grogram Gown, the Spouse of your Parish Vicar, who has by this Time I am sure well furnish'd you with Receipts for making Salves and Possets, distilling Cordial Waters, making Syrups, and applying Poultices.

Blest Solitude! I wish thee Joy, my Dear, of thy lov'd Retirement, which indeed you would perswade me is very agreeable, and different enough from what I have here describ'd: But, Child, I am afraid thy Brains are a little disordered with Romances and Novels: After six Month's Marriage to hear thee talk of Love and paint the Country Scenes so softly, is a little extravagant; one would think you lived the Lives of *Sylvan* Deities, or roved among the Walks of *Paradise* like the first happy Pair. But prithee leave these Whimsies, and come to Town in order to live and talk like other Mortals. However, as I am extremely interested in your Reputation, I would willingly give you a little good Advice at your first Appearance under the Character of a married Woman: 'Tis a little Insolence in me, perhaps, to advise a Matron; but I am so afraid you'll make so silly a Figure as a fond Wife, that I cannot help warning you not to appear in any publick Places with your Husband, and never to saunter about St. *James's Park* together: If you presume to enter the Ring at *Hide-Park* together, you are ruin'd for ever; nor must you take the least Notice of one another at the Play-House or Opera, unless you would be laugh'd at for a very loving Couple most happily pair'd in the Yoke of Wedlock. I would recommend the Example of an Acquaintance of ours to your Imitation; she is the most negligent and fashionable Wife in the World; she is hardly ever seen in the same Place with her Husband, and if they happen to meet you would think them perfect Strangers: She never was heard to name him in his Absence, and takes Care he shall never be the Subject of any Discourse that she has a Share in. I hope you'll propose this Lady as a Pattern, tho' I am very much afraid you 'll be so silly to think *Porcia, &c. Sabine* and *Roman* Wives, much brighter Examples. I wish it may never come into your Head to imitate those antiquated Creatures so far, as to come into Publick in the Habit as well as Air of a *Roman* Matron. You make already the Entertainment at Mrs. *Modish's* Tea-Table; she says she always thought you a discreet Person, and qualified to manage a Family with admirable Prudence; she dies to see what demure and serious Airs Wedlock has given you, but she says she shall never forgive your Choice of so gallant a Man as *Bellamour* to transform him in to a meer sober Husband; 'twas unpardonable: You see, my Dear, we all envy your Happiness, and no Person more than,

> *Your humble Servant,*
>
> Lydia.'

'Be not in Pain, good Madam, for my Appearance in Town; I shall frequent no publick places, or make any Visits where the Character of a modest Wife is ridiculous: As for your wild Raillery on Matrimony, 'tis all Hypocrisy; you and all the handsome young Women of your Acquaintance shew your selves to no other Purpose than to gain a Conquest over some Man of Worth, in order to bestow your Charms and Fortune on him. There 's no Indecency in the Confession, the Design is modest and honourable, and all your Affectation can't disguise it.

I am marry'd, and have no other Concern but to please the Man I love: he 's the End of every Care I have; if I dress 'tis for him, if I read a Poem or a Play 'tis to qualify my self for a Conversation agreeable to his Taste: He 's almost the End of my Devotions, half my Prayers are for his Happiness—I love to talk of him, and never hear him named but with Pleasure and Emotion. I am your Friend and wish you Happiness, but am sorry to see by the Air of your Letter that there are a Set of Women who are got into the common-Place Raillery of every Thing that is sober, decent, and proper: Matrimony and the Clergy are the Topicks of People of little Wit and no Understanding. I own to you I have learned of the Vicar's Wife all you tax me with: She is a discreet, ingenious, pleasant, pious Woman; I wish she had the handling of you and Mrs. *Modish*; you would find, if you were too free with her, she would soon make you as charming as ever you were, she would make you blush as much as if you never had been fine Ladies. The Vicar, Madam, is so kind as to visit my Husband, and his agreeable Conversation has brought him to enjoy many sober happy Hours when even I am shut out, and my dear Master is entertained only with his own Thoughts. These Things, dear

Madam, will be lasting Satisfactions, when the fine Ladies and the Coxcombs by whom they form themselves are irreparably ridiculous, ridiculous in old Age.

> *I am, Madam,*
>> *Your most humble Servant,*
>>> Mary Home.'

'*Dear Mr.* SPECTATOR,

You have no Goodness in the World, and are not in Earnest in any Thing you say that is serious, if you do not send me a plain Answer to this: I happened some Days past to be at the Play, where, during the Time of Performance, I could not keep my Eyes off from a beautiful young Creature who sat just before me, and who I have been since informed has no Fortune. It would utterly ruin my Reputation for Discretion to marry such a one, and by what I can learn she has a Character of great Modesty, so that there is nothing to be thought on any other Way. My Mind has ever since been so wholly bent on her, that I am much in Danger of doing Something very extravagant without your speedy Advice to,

> *Sir,*
>> *Your most humble Servant.*'

I am sorry I cannot answer this impatient Gentleman but by another Question.

> *Dear Correspondent,*

Would you marry to please other People, or your self?   T

No. 255.

[ADDISON.]   Saturday, December 22.

> *Laudis amore tumes? sunt certa piacula quae te*
> *Ter pure lecto poterunt recreare libello.*—Hor.

THE Soul, considered abstractedly from its Passions, is of a remiss and sedentary Nature, slow in its Resolves, and languishing in its Executions.   The Use therefore of the Passions, is to stir it up and put it upon Action, to awaken the Understanding, to enforce the Will, and to make the whole Man more vigorous and attentive in the Prosecution of his Designs.   As this is the End of the Passions in general, so it is particularly of Ambition, which pushes the Soul to such Actions as are apt to procure Honour and Reputation to the Actor.   But if we carry our Reflections higher, we may discover further Ends of Providence in implanting this Passion in Mankind.

It was necessary for the World, that Arts should be invented and improved, Books written and transmitted to Posterity, Nations conquered and civilized: Now since the proper and genuine Motives to these and the like great Actions, would only influence vertuous Minds; there would be but small Improvements in the World, were there not some common Principle of Action working equally with all Men. And such a Principle is Ambition or a desire of Fame, by which great Endowments are not suffer'd to lie idle and useless to the Publick, and many vicious Men over-reached, as it were, and engaged contrary to their natural Inclinations in a glorious and laudable Course of Action. For we may further observe, that Men of the greatest Abilities are most fired with Ambition: and that, on the contrary, mean and narrow Minds are the least actuated by it; whether it be that a Man's Sense of his own Incapacities makes him despair of coming at Fame, or that he has not enough Range of Thought to look out for any Good which does not more immediately relate to his interest or Convenience, or that Providence, in the very Frame of his Soul, would not subject him to such a Passion as would be useless to the World, and a Torment to himself.

Were not this Desire of Fame very strong, the Difficulty of obtaining it, and the Danger of losing it when obtained, would be sufficient to deter a Man from so vain a Pursuit.

How few are there who are furnished with Abilities sufficient to recommend their Actions to the Admiration of the World, and to distinguish themselves from the rest of Mankind? Providence for the most part sets us upon a Level, and observes a Kind of Proportion in its Dispensations towards us. If it renders us perfect in one Accomplishment, it generally leaves us defective in another, and seems careful rather of preserving every Person from being mean and deficient in his Qualifications, than of making any single one eminent or extraordinary.

And among those, who are the most richly endow'd by Nature, and accomplished by their own Industry, how few are there whose Vertues are not obscured by the Ignorance, Prejudice or Envy of their Beholders? Some Men cannot discern between a noble and a mean Action. Others are apt to attribute them to some false End or Intention; and others purposely misrepresent, or put a wrong Interpretation on them.

But the more to enforce this Consideration, we may observe that those are generally most unsuccessful in their Pursuit after Fame, who are most desirous of obtaining it. It is *Sallust*'s Remark upon *Cato*, that the less he coveted Glory the more he acquired it.

Men take an ill-natured Pleasure in crossing our Inclinations, and disappointing us in what our Hearts are most set upon. When therefore they have discovered the passionate Desire of Fame in the ambitious Man, (as no Temper of Mind is more apt to shew it self) they become sparing and reserved in their Commendations, they envy him the Satisfaction of an Applause, and look on their Praises rather as a Kindness done to his Person, than as a Tribute paid to his Merit. Others who are free from this natural Perverseness of Temper, grow wary in their Praises of one, who sets too great a Value on them, lest they should raise him too high in his own Imagination, and by Consequence remove him to a greater Distance from themselves.

But further, this Desire of Fame naturally betrays the ambitious Man into such Indecencies as are a lessening to his Reputation. He is still afraid lest any of his Actions should be thrown away in private, lest his Deserts should be concealed from the Notice of the World, or receive any Disadvantage from the Reports which others make of them. This often sets him on empty Boasts and Ostentations of himself, and betrays him into vain fantastick Recitals of his own Performances: His Discourse generally leans one Way, and whatever is the Subject of it, tends obliquely either to the detracting from others, or the extolling of himself. Vanity is the natural Weakness of an ambitious Man, which exposes him to the secret Scorn and Derision of those he converses with, and ruins the Character he is so industrious to advance by it. For tho' his Actions are never so glorious, they lose their Luster when they are drawn at large, and set to show by his own Hand; and as the World is more apt to find Fault than to commend, the Boast will probably be censured when the great Action that occasioned it is forgotten.

Besides, this very Desire of Fame is looked on as a Meanness and Imperfection in the greatest Character. A solid and substantial Greatness of Soul looks down with a generous Neglect on the Censures and Applauses of the Multitude, and places a Man beyond the little Noise and Strife of Tongues. Accordingly we find in our selves a secret Awe and Veneration for the Character of one who moves above us in a regular and illustrious Course of Vertue, without any Regard to our good or ill Opinions of him, to our Reproaches or Commendations. As on the contrary it is usual for us, when we would take off from the Fame and Reputation of an Action, to ascribe it to Vain-Glory, and a Desire of Fame in the Actor. Nor is this common Judgment and Opinion of Mankind ill-founded; for certainly it denotes no great Bravery of Mind to be worked up to any noble Action by so selfish a Motive, and to do that out of a Desire of Fame, which we could not be prompted to by a disinterested Love to Mankind, or by a generous Passion for the Glory of him that made us.

Thus is Fame a Thing difficult to be obtained by all, but particularly by those who thirst after it, since most Men have so much either of Ill-nature or of Wariness, as not to gratifie and sooth the Vanity of the ambitious Man and since this very Thirst after Fame naturally betrays him into such Indecencies as are a lessening to his Reputation, and is it self looked upon as a Weakness in the greatest Characters.

In the next Place, Fame is easily lost, and as difficult to be preserved as it was at first to be acquired. But this I shall make the Subject of a following Paper.   C

No. 256.

[ADDISON.]   Monday, December 24.

Φήμη γάρ τε κακὴ πέλεται· κούφη μὲν ἀεῖραι
'Ρεῖα μάλ', ἀργαλέη δὲ φέρειν . . .—Hes.

THERE are many Passions and Tempers of Mind which naturally dispose us to depress and vilify the Merit of one rising in the Esteem of Mankind. All those who made their Entrance into the World with the same Advantages, and were once looked on as his Equals, are apt to think the Fame of his Merits a Reflection on their own Indeserts; and will therefore take Care to reproach him with the Scandal of some past Action, or derogate from the Worth of the present, that they may still keep him on the same Level with themselves. The like Kind of Consideration often stirs up the Envy of such as were once his Superiours, who think it a Detraction from their Merit to see another get Ground upon them and overtake them in the Pursuits of Glory; and will therefore endeavour to sink his Reputation, that they may the better preserve their own. Those who were once his Equals envy and defame him, because they now see him their Superiour; and those who were once his Superiours, because they look upon him as their Equal.

But further, a Man whose extraordinary Reputation thus lifts him up to the Notice and Observation of Mankind, draws a Multitude of Eyes upon him that will narrowly inspect every Part of him, consider him nicely in all Views, and not be a little pleased when they have taken him in the worst and most disadvantagious Light: There are many who find a Pleasure in contradicting the common Reports of Fame, and in spreading abroad the Weaknesses of an exalted Character. They publish their ill-natured Discoveries with a secret Pride, and applaud themselves for the Singularity of their Judgment which has searched deeper than others, detected what the rest of the World have over-looked, and found a Flaw in what the Generality of Mankind admires. Others there are who proclaim the Errours and Infirmities of a great Man with an inward Satisfaction and Complacency, if they discover none of the like Errours and Infirmities in themselves; for while they are exposing another's Weaknesses, they are tacitly aiming at their own Commendations who are not subject to the like Infirmities, and are apt to be transported with a secret Kind of Vanity, to see themselves superiour in some Respects to one of a sublime and celebrated Reputation. Nay it very often happens, that none are more industrious in publishing the Blemishes of an extraordinary Reputation, than such as lie open to the same Censures in their own Characters; as either hoping to excuse their own Defects by the Authority of so high an Example, or raising an imaginary Applause to themselves for resembling a Person of an exalted Reputation, though in the blameable Parts of his Character. If all these secret Springs of Detraction fail, yet very often a vain Ostentation of Wit sets a Man on attacking an established Name, and sacrificing it to the Mirth and Laughter of those about him. A Satyr or a Libel on one of the common Stamp, never meets with that Reception and Approbation among its Readers, as what is aimed at a Person whose Merit places him upon an Eminence, and gives him a more conspicuous Figure among Men. Whether it be that we think it shews greater Art to expose and turn to Ridicule a Man whose Character seems so improper a Subject for it, or that we are pleased by some implicit Kind of Revenge to see him taken down and humbled in his Reputation, and in some Measure reduced to our own Rank, who had so far raised himself above us in the Reports and Opinions of Mankind.

Thus we see how many dark and intricate Motives there are to Detraction and Defamation, and how many malicious Spies are searching into the Actions of a great Man, who is not always the best prepared for so narrow an Inspection. For we may generally observe, that our Admiration of a famous Man lessens upon our nearer Acquaintance with him; and that we seldom hear the Description of a celebrated Person, without a Catalogue of some notorious Weaknesses and Infirmities. The Reason may be, because any little Slip is more conspicuous and observable in his Conduct than in another's, as it is not of a Piece with the rest of his Character, or because it is impossible for a Man at the same Time to be attentive to the more important Part of his Life, and to keep a watchful Eye over all the inconsiderable Circumstances of his Behaviour and

Conversation; or because, as we have before observed, the same Temper of Mind which enclines us to a Desire of Fame, naturally betrays us into such Slips and Unwarinesses as are not incident to Men of a contrary Disposition.

After all it must be confess'd, that a noble and triumphant Merit often breaks through and dissipates these little Spots and Sullies in its Reputation; but if by a mistaken Pursuit after Fame, or through humane Infirmity, any false Step be made in the more momentous Concerns of Life, the whole Scheme of ambitious Designs is broken and disappointed.   The smaller Stains and Blemishes may die away and disappear amidst the Brightness that surrounds them; but a Blot of a deeper Nature casts a Shade on all the other Beauties, and darkens the whole Character.   How difficult therefore is it to preserve a great Name, when he that has acquired it is so obnoxious to such little Weaknesses and Infirmities as are no small Diminution to it when discovered, especially when they are so industriously proclaimed, and aggravated by such as were once his Superiours or Equals; by such as would set to show their Judgment or their Wit, and by such as are guilty or innocent of the same Slips or Misconducts in their own Behaviour.

But were there none of these Dispositions in others to censure a famous Man, nor any such Miscarriages in himself, yet would he meet with no small Trouble in keeping up his Reputation in all its Height and Splendour.   There must be always a noble Train of Actions to preserve his Fame in Life and Motion.   For when it is once at a Stand, it naturally flags and languishes. Admiration is a very short-lived Passion, that immediately decays upon growing familiar with its Object, unless it be still fed with fresh Discoveries, and kept alive by a new perpetual Succession of Miracles rising up to its View.   And even the greatest Actions of a celebrated Person labour under this Disadvantage, that however surprizing and extraordinary they may be, they are no more than what are expected from him; but on the contrary, if they fall any thing below the Opinion that is conceived of him, tho' they might raise the Reputation of another, they are a Diminution to *his*.

One would think there should be something wonderfully pleasing in the Possession of Fame, that, notwithstanding all these mortifying Considerations, can engage a Man in so desperate a Pursuit; and yet if we consider the little Happiness that attends a great Character, and the Multitude of Disquietudes to which the Desire of it subjects an ambitious Mind, one would be still the more surprised to see so many restless Candidates for Glory.

Ambition raises a secret Tumult in the Soul, it inflames the

Mind, and puts it into a violent Hurry of Thought: It is still reaching after an empty imaginary Good; that has not in it the Power to abate or satisfy it. Most other Things we long for can allay the Cravings of their proper Sense, and for a while set the Appetite at Rest: But Fame is a Good so wholly foreign to our Natures, that we have no Faculty in the Soul adapted to it, nor any Organ in the Body to relish it; an Object of Desire placed out of the Possibility of Fruition. It may indeed fill the Mind for a while with a giddy Kind of Pleasure, but it is such a Pleasure as makes a Man restless and uneasy under it; and which does not so much satisfy the present Thirst, as it excites fresh Desires, and sets the Soul on new Enterprises. For how few ambitious Men are there, who have got as much Fame as they desired, and whose Thirst after it has not been as eager in the very Height of their Reputation, as it was before they became known and eminent among Men? There is not any Circumstance in *Caesar's* Character which gives me a greater Idea of him, than a Saying which *Cicero* tells us he frequently made use of in private Conversation, *That he was satisfied with his Share of Life and Fame. Se satis vel ad Naturam, vel ad Gloriam vixisse.* Many indeed have given over their Pursuits after Fame, but that has proceeded either from the Disappointments they have met in it, or from their Experience of the little Pleasure which attends it, or from the better Informations or natural Coldness of Old-Age; but seldom from a full Satisfaction and Acquiescence in their present Enjoyments of it.

Nor is Fame only unsatisfying in it self, but the Desire of it lays us open to many accidental Troubles, which those are free from who have no such a tender Regard for it. How often is the ambitious Man cast down and disappointed, if he receives no Praise where he expected it? Nay how often is he mortifyed with the very Praises he receives, if they do not rise so high as he thinks they ought, which they seldom do unless increased by Flattery, since few Men have so good an Opinion of us as we have of our selves? But if the ambitious Man can be so much grieved even with Praise itself, how will he be able to bear up under Scandal and Defamation? For the same Temper of Mind which makes him desire Fame, makes him hate Reproach. If he can be transported with the extraordinary Praises of Men, he will be as much dejected by their Censures. How little therefore is the Happiness of an ambitious Man, who gives every one a Dominion over it, who thus subjects himself to the good or ill Speeches of others, and puts it in the Power of every malicious Tongue to throw him into a Fit of Melancholy, and destroy his natural Rest and Repose of Mind?

Especially when we consider that the World is more apt to censure than applaud, and himself fuller of Imperfections than Virtues.

We may further observe, that such a Man will be more grieved for the Loss of Fame, than he could have been pleased with the Enjoyment of it. For tho' the Presence of this imaginary Good cannot make us happy, the Absence of it may make us miserable: Because in the Enjoyment of an Object we only find that Share of Pleasure which it is capable of giving us, but in the Loss of it we do not proportion our Grief to the real Value it bears, but to the Value our Fancies and Imaginations set upon it.

So inconsiderable is the Satisfaction that Fame brings along with it, and so great the Disquietudes to which it makes us liable. The Desire of it stirs up very uneasy Motions in the Mind, and is rather enflamed than satisfied by the Presence of the Thing desired. The Enjoyment of it brings but very little Pleasure, tho' the Loss or Want of it be very sensible and afflicting; and even this little Happiness is so very precarious, that it wholly depends on the Will of others. We are not only tortured by the Reproaches which are offered us, but are disappointed by the Silence of Men when it is unexpected; and humbled even by their Praises.   C

No. 257.
[ADDISON.]   Tuesday, December 25.

. . . Οὐχ' εὕδει Διὸς
'Οφθαλμός· ἐγγὺς δ' ἔστι καὶ παρὼν πόνῳ.—Incert. ex Stob.

THAT I might not lose my self upon a Subject of so great Extent as that of Fame, I have treated it in a particular Order and Method. I have first of all considered the Reasons why Providence may have implanted in our Minds such a Principle of Action. I have in the next Place shewn, from many Considerations, first, that Fame is a Thing difficult to be obtained, and easily lost; Secondly, that it brings the ambitious Man very little Happiness, but subjects him to much Uneasiness and Dissatisfaction. I shall in the last Place shew that it hinders us from obtaining an End which we have Abilities to acquire, and which is accompanied with Fulness of Satisfaction. I need not tell my Reader, that I mean by this End, that Happiness which is reserved for us in another World, which every one has Abilities to procure, and which will bring along with it Fulness of Joy and Pleasures for evermore.

How the Pursuit after Fame may hinder us in the Attainment of this great End, I shall leave the Reader to collect from the three following Considerations.

First, Because the strong Desire of Fame breeds several vicious Habits in the Mind.

Secondly, Because many of those Actions, which are apt to procure Fame, are not in their Nature conducive to this our ultimate Happiness.

Thirdly, Because if we should allow the same Actions to be the proper Instruments, both of acquiring Fame, and of procuring this Happiness, they would nevertheless fail in the Attainment of this last End, if they proceeded from a Desire of the first.

These three Propositions are self-evident to those who are versed in Speculations of Morality. For which Reason I shall not enlarge upon them, but proceed to a Point of the same Nature, which may open to us a more uncommon Field of Speculation.

From what has been already observed, I think we may make a natural Conclusion, that it is the greatest Folly to seek the Praise or Approbation of any Being, besides the Supream, and that for these two Reasons, because no other Being can make a right Judgment of us, and esteem us according to our Merits; and because we can procure no considerable Benefit or Advantage from the Esteem and Approbation of any other Being.

In the first Place no other Being can make a right Judgment of us, and esteem us according to our Merits. Created Beings see nothing but our Outside, and can therefore only frame a Judgment of us from our exteriour Actions and Behaviour; but how unfit these are to give us a right Notion of each other's Perfections, may appear from several Considerations. There are many Vertues, which in their own Nature are incapable of any outward Representation: Many silent Perfections in the Soul of a good Man, which are great Ornaments to Humane Nature, but not able to discover themselves to the Knowledge of others; they are transacted in private, without Noise or Show, and are only visible to the great Searcher of Hearts. What Actions can express the entire Purity of Thought which refines and sanctifies a virtuous Man? That secret Rest and Contentedness of Mind, which gives him a perfect Enjoyment of his present Condition? That inward Pleasure and Complacency, which he feels in doing Good? That Delight and Satisfaction which he takes in the Prosperity and Happiness of another? These and the like Vertues are the hidden Beauties of a Soul, the secret Graces which cannot be discovered by a mortal Eye, but make the Soul lovely and precious in his

Sight, from whom no Secrets are concealed. Again, there are many Virtues which want an Opportunity of exerting and shewing themselves in Actions. Every Virtue requires Time and Place, a proper Object and a fit Conjuncture of Circumstances, for the due Exercise of it. A State of Poverty obscures all the Virtues of Liberality and Munificence. The Patience and Fortitude of a Martyr or Confessor lye concealed in the flourishing Times of Christianity. Some Virtues are only seen in Affliction, and some in Prosperity; some in a private, and others in a publick Capacity. But the great Sovereign of the World beholds every Perfection in its Obscurity, and not only sees what we do, but what we would do. He views our Behaviour in every Concurrence of Affairs, and sees us engaged in all the Possibilities of Action. He discovers the Martyr and Confessor without the Tryal of Flames and Tortures, and will hereafter entitle many to the Reward of Actions, which they had never the Opportunity of performing. Another Reason why Men cannot form a right Judgment of us is, because the same Actions may be aimed at different Ends, and arise from quite contrary Principles. Actions are of so mixt a Nature, and so full of Circumstances, that as Men pry into them more or less, or observe some Parts more than others, they take different Hints, and put contrary Interpretations on them; so that the same Actions may represent a Man as hypocritical and designing to one, which makes him appear a Saint or Hero to another. He therefore who looks upon the Soul through its outward Actions, often sees it through a deceitful Medium, which is apt to discolour and pervert the Object: So that on this Account also, *he* is the only proper Judge of our Perfections, who does not guess at the Sincerity of our Intentions from the Goodness of our Actions; but weighs the Goodness of our Actions by the Sincerity of our Intentions.

But further; it is impossible for outward Actions to represent the Perfections of the Soul, because they can never shew the Strength of those Principles from whence they proceed. They are not adequate Expressions of our Virtues, and can only shew us what Habits are in the Soul, without discovering the Degree and Perfection of such Habits. They are at best but weak Resemblances of our Intentions, faint and imperfect Copies that may acquaint us with the general Design, but can never express the Beauty and Life of the Original. But the great Judge of all the Earth knows every different State and Degree of humane Improvement, from those weak Stirrings and Tendencies of the Will which have not yet formed themselves into regular Purposes and Designs, to the last entire Finishing and Consummation of a good Habit. He beholds the first imperfect Rudiments of a Virtue in the Soul, and keeps a watchful Eye over it in all its Progress, 'till it has received every Grace it is capable of, and appears in its full Beauty and Perfection. Thus we see that none but the Supreme Being can esteem us according to our proper Merits, since all others must judge of us from our outward Actions, which can never give them a just Estimate of us, since there are many Perfections of a Man which are not capable of appearing in Actions; many which, allowing no natural Incapacity of shewing themselves, want an Opportunity of doing it; or should they all meet with an Opportunity of appearing by Actions, yet those Actions may be misinterpreted, and applied to wrong Principles; or though they plainly discovered the Principles from whence they proceeded, they could never shew the Degree, Strength, and Perfection of those Principles.

And as the Supreme Being is the only proper Judge of our Perfections, so is he the only fit Rewarder of them.   This is a Consideration that comes home to our Interest, as the other adapts it self to our Ambition.   And what could the most aspiring, or the most selfish Man desire more, were he to form the Notion of a Being to whom he could recommend himself, than such a Knowledge as can discover the least Appearance of Perfection in him, and such a Goodness as will proportion a Reward to it?

Let the ambitious Man therefore turn all his Desire of Fame this Way; and, that he may propose to himself a Fame worthy of his Ambition, let him consider that if he employs his Abilities to the best Advantage, the Time will come when the Supreme Governor of the World, the great Judge of Mankind, who sees every Degree of Perfection in others, and possesses all possible Perfection in himself, shall proclaim his Worth before Men and Angels, and pronounce to him in the Presence of the whole Creation that best and most significant of Applauses, *Well done thou good and faithful Servant, enter thou into Thy Master's Joy.*   C

No. 258.
[STEELE.]   Wednesday, December 26.

Divide & impera.

PLEASURE and Recreation of one Kind or other are absolutely necessary to relieve our Minds and Bodies from too constant Attention and Labour: Where therefore publick Diversions are tolerated, it behoves Persons of Distinction, with their Power and Example, to preside over them in such a Manner, as to check any Thing that tends to the Corruption of Manners, or which is too mean or trivial for the Entertainment of reasonable Creatures. As to the Diversions of this Kind in this Town, we owe them to the Arts of Poetry and Musick: My own private Opinion, with Relation to such Recreations, I have heretofore given with all the Frankness imaginable; what concerns those Arts at present the Reader shall have from my Correspondents. The first of the Letters with which I acquit my self for this Day, is written by one who proposes to improve our Entertainments of Dramatick Poetry, and the other comes from three Persons who as soon as named, will be thought capable of advancing the present State of Musick.

'*Mr.* SPECTATOR,

I am considerably obliged to you for your speedy Publication of my last in yours of the 18th Instant, and am in no small Hopes of being settled in the Post of *Comptroller of the Crys.* Of all the Objections I have hearkned after in publick Coffeehouses, there is but one that seems to carry any Weight with it, *viz.* That such a Post would come too near the Nature of a Monopoly. Now, Sir, because I would have all Sorts of People made easy, and being willing to have more Strings than one to my Bow; in Case that of *Comptroller* should fail me, I have since formed another Project, which, being grounded on the dividing a present Monopoly, I hope will give the Publick an Equivalent to their full Content. You know, Sir, it is allowed that the Business of the Stage is, as the Latin has it, *Jucunda & Idonea dicere Vitae.* Now there being but one Dramatick Theatre licensed for the Delight and Profit of this extensive Metropolis, I do humbly propose, for the Convenience of such of its Inhabitants as are too distant from *Covent-Garden,* that another *Theatre of Ease* may be erected in some spacious Part of the City; and that the Direction thereof may be made a Franchise in Fee to me, and my Heirs for ever. And that the Town may have no Jealousy of my ever coming to an Union with the Set of Actors now in Being, I do further propose to constitute for my Deputy my near Kinsman and Adventurer *Kitt Crotchet,* whose long Experience and Improvements in those Affairs need no Recommendation. 'Twas obvious to every Spectator what a quite different Foot the Stage was upon during his Government; and had he not been bolted out of his Trap-doors, his Garrison might have held out for ever, he having by long Pains and Perseverance arriv'd at the Art of making his Army fight without Pay or Provisions. I must confess it, with a melancholy Amazement, I see so wonderful a Genius laid aside, and the late Slaves of the Stage now become its Masters, Dunces that will be sure to suppress all theatrical Entertainments and Activities that they are not able themselves to shine in!

Every Man that goes to a Play is not obliged to have either Wit or Understanding; and I insist upon it, that all who go there should see something which may improve them in a Way of which they are capable. In short, Sir, I would have something *done* as well as *said* on the Stage. A Man may have an active Body, though he has not a quick Conception; for the Imitation therefore of such as are, as I may so speak, corporeal Wits or nimble Fellows, I would fain ask any of the present Mismanagers why should not Rope-dancers, Vaulters, Tumblers, Ladder - walkers, and Posture - makers appear again on our Stage? After such a Representation, a Five-bar Gate would be leaped with a better Grace next time any of the Audience went a Hunting. Sir, these Things cry loud for Reformation, and fall properly under the Province of SPECTATOR General; but how indeed should it be otherwise while Fellows (that for Twenty Years together were never paid but as their Master was in the Humour) now presume to pay others more than ever they had in their Lives; and, in Contempt of the Practice of Persons of Condition, have the Insolence to owe no Tradesman a Farthing at the End of the Week. Sir, all I propose is the publick Good; for no one can imagine I shall ever get a private Shilling by it; Therefore I hope you will recommend this Matter in one of your this Week's Papers, and desire when my house opens you will accept the Liberty of it for the Trouble you have received from,

Sir,

P. S. I have Assurances that   *Your humble Servant,*
the Trunk-maker will de-   Ralph Crotchet.'
clare for us.

'*Mr.* SPECTATOR,

We whose Names are subscribed think you the properest Person to signify what we have to offer the Town in Behalf of ourselves, and the Art which we profess, *Musick.* We conceive Hopes of your Favour from the Speculations on the Mistakes which the Town run into with Regard to their Pleasure of this Kind; and believing your Method of Judging is, that you consider Musick only valuable as it is agreeable to and heightens the Purpose of Poetry, we consent that That is not only the true Way of relishing that Pleasure, but also that without it a Composure of Musick is the same Thing as a Poem, where all the Rules of Poetical Numbers are observed, but the Words of no Sense or Meaning; to say it shorter, meer musical Sounds are in our Art no other than nonsense Verses are in Poetry. Musick therefore is to aggravate what is intended by Poetry; it must always have some Passion or Sentiment to express, or else Violins, Voices, or any other Organs of Sound, afford an Entertainment very little above the Rattles of Children. It was from this Opinion of the Matter, that when Mr. *Clayton* had finished his Studies in *Italy*, and brought over the Opera of *Arsinoe*, that Mr. *Haym* and Mr. *Dieupart*, who had the Honour to be well known and received among the Nobility and Gentry, were zealously enclined to assist, by their Sollicitations, in introducing so elegant an Entertainment as the *Italian* Musick grafted upon *English* Poetry. For this End Mr. *Dieupart* and Mr. *Haym*, according to their several Opportunities promoted the Introduction of *Arsinoe*, and did it to the best Advantage so great a Novelty would allow. It is not Proper to trouble you with Particulars of the just Complaints we all of us have to make; but so it is, that without Regard to our obliging Pains, we are all equally set aside in the present Opera. Our Application therefore to you is only to insert this Letter in your Papers that the Town may know we have all Three joined together to make Entertainments of Musick for the future at Mr. *Clayton's* House in *York-Buildings*. What we promise ourselves, is, to make a Subscription of Two Guineas for eight Times; and that the Entertainment, with the Names of the Authors of the Poetry, may be printed, to be sold in the House, with an Account of the several Authors of the vocal as well as instrumental Musick for each Night; the Money to be paid at the Receipt of the Tickets, at Mr. *Charles Lillie's*. It will, we hope, Sir, be easily allowed, that we are capable of Undertaking to exhibit by our joint Force and different Qualifications all that can be done in Musick; but lest you should think so dry a Thing as an Account of our Proposal should be a Matter unworthy your Paper, which generally contains something of publick Use; give us Leave to say, that favouring our Design is no less than reviving an Art, which runs to Ruin by the utmost Barbarism under an Affectation of Knowledge. We aim at establishing some settled Notion of what is Musick, at recovering from Neglect and Want very many Families who depend upon it, at making all Foreigners who pretend to succeed in *England* to learn the Language of it, as we ourselves have done, and not be so insolent as to expect a whole Nation, a refined and learned Nation, should submit to learn them. In a Word, Mr. SPECTATOR, with all Deference and Humility, we hope to behave ourselves in this Undertaking in such a Manner, that all *English* Men who have any Skill in Musick may be furthered in it for their Profit or Diversion by what new Things we shall produce; never pretending to surpass others, or asserting that any Thing which is a Science is not attainable by all Men of all Nations who have proper Genius for it: We say, Sir, what we hope for is not expected will arrive to us by contemning others, but through the utmost Diligence recommending ourselves.

We are,

Sir,

Your most humble Servants,

Thomas Clayton.

Nicolino Haym.

T   Charles Dieupart.'

No. 259.

[STEELE.]   Thursday, December 27.

Quod decet honestum est & quod honestum est decet.—Tull.

THERE are some Things which cannot come under certain Rules, but which one would think could not need them. Of this Kind are outward Civilities and Salutations. These one would imagine might be regulated by every Man's common Sense, without the Help of an Instructor, but that which we call common Sense suffers under that Word; for it sometimes implies no more than that Faculty which is common to all Men, but sometimes signifies right Reason, and what all Men should consent to. In this latter Acceptation of the Phrase, it is no great Wonder People err so much against it, since it is not every one who is possessed of it, and there are fewer who, against common Rules and Fashions, dare obey its Dictates. As to Salutations, which I was about to talk of, I observe, as I strole about Town, there are great Enormities committed with regard to this Particular. You shall sometimes see a Man begin the Offer of a Salutation, and observe a forbidding Air, or escaping Eye, in the Person he is going to salute, and stop short in the Pole of his Neck. This in the Person who believed he could do it with a good Grace, and was refused the Opportunity, is justly resented with a Coldness in the whole ensuing Season. Your great Beauties, People in much Favour, or by any Means, or for any Purpose overflattered, are apt to practise this which one may call the preventing Aspect, and throw their Attention another Way, lest they should confer a Bow or a

Curtsie upon a Person who might not appear to deserve that Dignity. Others you shall find so obsequious, and so very courteous, as there is no escaping their Favours of this Kind. Of this Sort may be a Man who is in the fifth or sixth Degree of Favour with a Minister; this good Creature is resolved to shew the World, that great Honours cannot at all Change his Manners, he is the same civil Person he ever was. He will venture his Neck to bow out of a Coach in full Speed, at once, to shew he is full of Business, and yet is not so taken up as to forget his old Friend. With a Man, who is not so well formed for Courtship and elegant Behaviour, such a Gentleman as this seldom finds his Account in the Return of his Complements, but he will still go on, for he is in his own Way, and must not omit; let the Neglect fall on your Side, or where it will, his Business is still to be well-bred to the End. I think I have read, in one of our *English* Comedies, a Description of a Fellow that affected knowing every Body, and for Want of Judgment in Time and Place, would bow and smile in the Face of a Judge sitting in the Court, would sit in an opposite Gallery, and smile in the Minister's Face as he came up into the Pulpit, and nod as if he alluded to some Familiarities between them in another Place. But now I happen to speak of Salutation at Church, I must take Notice that several of my Correspondents have importuned me to consider that Subject, and settle the Point of Decorum in that Particular.

I do not pretend to be the best Courtier in the World, but I have often on publick Occasions thought it a very great Absurdity in the Company (during the Royal Presence) to exchange Salutations from all Parts of the Room, when certainly common Sense should suggest that all Regards at that Time should be engaged, and cannot be diverted to any other Object, without Disrespect to the Sovereign. But as to the Complaint of my Correspondents, it is not to be imagined what Offence some of them take at the Custom of Saluting in Places of Worship. I have a very angry Letter from a Lady, who tells me one of her Acquaintance, out of meer Pride and a Pretence to be rude, takes upon her to return no Civilities done to her in Time of divine Service, and is the most religious Woman for no other Reason, but to appear a Woman of the best Quality in the Church. This absurd Custom had better be abolished than retained, if it were but to prevent Evils of no higher a Nature than this is, but I am informed of Objections much more considerable: A Dissenter of Rank and Distinction was lately prevailed upon by a Friend of his to come to one of the greatest Congregations of the Church of *England* about Town: After the Service was over, he declared he was very well satisfied with the little Ceremony which was used towards God Almighty; but at the same Time he feared he should not be able to go through those required towards one another: As to this Point he was in a State of Despair, and feared he was not well-bred enough to be a Convert. There have been many Scandals of this Kind given to our Protestant Dissenters, from the outward Pomp and Respect we take to ourselves in our religious Assemblies. A Quaker who came one Day into a Church, fixed his Eye upon an old Lady with a Carpet larger than that from the Pulpit before her, expecting when she would hold forth. An Anabaptist who designs to come over himself, and all his family, within a few Months, is sensible they want Breeding enough for our Congregations, and has sent his two elder Daughters to learn to dance, that they may not misbehave themselves at Church: It is worth considering whether, in regard to aukward People with scrupulous Consciences, a good Christian of the best Air in the World ought not rather to deny herself the Opportunity of shewing so many Graces, than keep a bashful Proselyte without the Pale of the Church.   T

No. 260.

[STEELE.]   Friday, December 28.

Singula de nobis anni praedantur euntes.—Hor.

'*Mr.* SPECTATOR,

I AM now in the sixty fifth Year of my Age, and having been the greater Part of my Days a Man of Pleasure, the Decay of my Faculties is a Stagnation of my Life. But how is it, Sir, that my Appetites are encreased upon me with the Loss of Power to gratify them? I write this, like a Criminal, to warn People to enter upon what Reformation they please to make in themselves in their Youth, and not expect they shall be capable of it from a fond Opinion some have often in their Mouths, that if we do not leave our Desires they will leave us. It is far otherwise: I am now as vain in my Dress, and as flippant if I see a pretty Woman, as when in my Youth I stood upon a Bench in the Pit to Survey the whole Circle of Beauties. The Folly is so extravagant with me, and I went on with so little Check of my Desires, or Resignation of them, that I can assure you I very often, meerly to entertain my own Thoughts, sit with my Spectacles on writing Love-Letters to the Beauties that have been long since in their Graves. This is to warm my

Heart with the feint Memory of Delights which were once agreeable to me; but how much happier would my Life have been now, if I could have looked back on any worthy Action done for my Country? If I had laid out that which I profused in Luxury and Wantonness, in Acts of Generosity or Charity? I have lived a Bachelour to this Day; and instead of a numerous Offspring, with which, in the regular Ways of Life, I might possibly have delighted my self, I have only to amuse my self with the Repetition of old Stories and Intrigues which no one will believe I ever was concerned in. I do not know whether you have ever treated of it or not; but you cannot fall on a better Subject, than that of the Art of growing old. In such a Lecture you must propose, that no one set his Heart upon what is transient; the Beauty grows wrinkled while we are yet gazing at her. The witty Man sinks into a Humorist imperceptibly, for want of reflecting that all Things around him are in a Flux, and continually changing: This he is in the Space of Ten or Fifteen Years surrounded by a new Set of People, whose Manners are as natural to them as his Delights, Method of Thinking, and Mode of Living, were formerly to him and his Friends. But the Mischief is, he looks upon the same Kind of Errors which he himself was guilty of with an Eye of Scorn, and with that Sort of ill-will which Men entertain against each other for different Opinions: Thus a crazy Constitution, and an uneasy Mind, is fretted with vexatious Passions for young Men's doing foolishly what it is Folly to do at all. Dear Sir, this is my present State of Mind; I hate those I should laugh at, and envy those I contemn. The Time of Youth and vigorous Manhood, passed the Way in which I have disposed of it, is attended with these Consequences; but to those who live and pass away Life as they ought, all Parts of it are equally pleasant; only the Memory of good and worthy Actions is a Feast which must give a quicker Relish to the Soul, than ever it could possibly taste in the highest Enjoyments or Jollities of Youth. As for me, if I sit down in my great Chair and begin to ponder, the Vagaries of a Child are not more ridiculous than the Circumstances which are heaped up in my Memory; fine Gowns, Country Dances, Ends of Tunes, interrupted Conversations, and mid-night Quarrels, are what must necessarily compose my Soliloquy. I beg of you to print this, that some Ladies of my Acquaintance, and my Years, may be perswaded to wear warm Night-caps this cold Season; and that my old Friend *Jack Tawdery* may buy him a Cane, and not creep with the Air of a Strut. I must add to all this, that if it were not for one Pleasure, which I thought a very mean one till of very late Years, I should have no one great Satisfaction left;

but if I live to the 10th of *March* 1714, and all my Securities
are good, I shall be worth fifty thousand Pound.

> *I am, Sir,*
>
> > *Your most humble Servant,*
> >
> > > Jack Afterday.'

'*Mr.* SPECTATOR,

You will infinitely oblige a distressed Lover, if you will
insert in your very next Paper the following Letter to my Mistress.   You must know I am not a Person apt to despair, but
she has got an odd Humour of stopping short unaccountably,
and, as she herself told a Confident of hers, she has cold Fits.
These Fits shall last her a Month or six Weeks together; and as
she falls into them without Provocation, so it is to be hoped
she will return from them without the Merit of new Services.
But Life and Love will not admit of such Intervals, therefore
pray let her be admonished as follows.

> "*Madam*,
>
> I love you, and I honour you; therefore pray do not tell me
> of waiting till Decencies, till Forms, till Humours are consulted
> and gratified. If you have that happy Constitution as to be
> indolent for ten Weeks together, you should consider that all
> that While I burn in Impatiences and Fevers; but still you say
> it will be Time enough, tho' I and you too grow older while
> we are yet talking.   Which do you think the more reasonable,
> that you should alter a State of Indifference for Happiness,
> and that to oblige me, or I live in Torment, and that to lay no
> Manner of Obligation upon you? While I indulge your In-
> sensibility I am doing nothing; if you favour my Passion, you
> are bestowing bright Desires, gay Hopes, generous Cares, noble
> Resolutions and transporting Raptures upon,
>
> > *Madam*,
> >
> > > *Your most devoted*
> > >
> > > > *humble Servant.*"'

'*Mr.* SPECTATOR,

Here's a Gentlewoman lodges in the same House with me,
that I never did any Injury to in my whole Life; and she is
always railing at me to those that she knows will tell me of it.
Don't you think she is in Love with me? or would you have me
break my Mind yet or not?

> *Your Servant,*
>
> > T. B.'

'*Mr.* SPECTATOR,

I am a Footman in a great Family, and am in Love with the

House-maid. We were all at Hot-cockles last Night in the Hall these Holidays; when I lay down and was blinded, she pull'd off her Shoe, and hit me with the Heel such a Rap, as almost broke my Head to Pieces. Pray, Sir, was this Love or Spite?'   T

No. 261.
[ADDISON.]   Saturday, December 29.

Γάμος γὰρ ἀνθρώποισιν εὐκταῖον κακόν.—Frag. vet. Po.

My Father, whom I mentioned in my first Speculation, and whom I must always Name with Honour and Gratitude, has very frequently talked to me upon the Subject of Marriage. I was in my younger Years engaged, partly by his Advice, and partly by my own Inclinations, in the Courtship of a Person who had a great Deal of Beauty, and did not at my first Approaches seem to have any Aversion to me; but as my natural Taciturnity hindered me from shewing my self to the best Advantage, she by Degrees began to look upon me as a very silly Fellow, and being resolved to regard Merit more than any Thing else in the Persons who made their Applications to her, she married a Captain of Dragoons who happened to be beating up for Recruits in those Parts.

This unlucky Accident has given me an Aversion to pretty Fellows ever since, and discouraged me from trying my Fortune with the fair Sex. The Observations which I made in this Conjuncture, and the repeated Advices which I received at that Time from the good old Man above-mentioned, have produced the following Essay upon Love and Marriage.

The pleasantest Part of a Man's Life is generally that which passes in Courtship, provided his Passion be sincere, and the Party beloved kind with Discretion. Love, Desire, Hope, all the pleasing Motions of the Soul rise in the Pursuit.

It is easier for an artful Man, who is not in Love, to persuade his Mistress he has a Passion for her, and to succeed in his Pursuits, than for one who loves with the greatest Violence. True Love has ten thousand Griefs, Impatiencies and Resentments, that render a Man unamiable in the Eyes of the Person whose Affection he sollicits; besides, that it sinks his Figure, gives him Fears, Apprehensions and Poorness of Spirit, and often makes him appear ridiculous where he has a Mind to recommend himself.

Those Marriages generally abound most with Love and Constancy, that are preceded by a long Courtship. The Passion should strike Root, and gather Strength before Marriage be grafted on it. A long Course of Hopes and Expectations fixes the Idea in our Minds, and habituates us to a Fondness of the Person beloved.

There is Nothing of so great Importance to us, as the good Qualities of one to whom we join our selves for Life; they do not only make our present State agreeable, but often determine our Happiness to all Eternity. Where the Choice is left to Friends, the chief Point under Consideration is an Estate: Where the Parties chuse for themselves, their Thoughts turn most upon the Person. They have both their Reasons. The first would procure many Conveniencies and Pleasures of Life to the Party whose Interests they espouse; and at the same Time may hope that the Wealth of their Friend will turn to their own Credit and Advantage. The others are preparing for themselves a perpetual Feast. A good Person does not only raise, but continue Love, and breeds a secret Pleasure and Complacency in the Beholder, when the first Heats of Desire are extinguished. It puts the Wife or Husband in Countenance both among Friends and Strangers, and generally fills the Family with a healthy and beautiful Race of Children.

I should prefer a Woman that is agreeable in my own Eye, and not deformed in that of the World, to a celebrated Beauty. If you marry one remarkably beautiful, you must have a violent Passion for her, or you have not the proper Taste of her charms; and if you have such a Passion for her, it is odds but it would be imbittered with Fears and Jealousies.

Good Nature, and Evenness of Temper, will give you an easie Companion for Life; Vertue and good Sense, an agreeable Friend; Love and Constancy, a good Wife or Husband. Where we meet one Person with all these Accomplishments, we find an Hundred without any one of them. The World notwithstanding, is more intent on Trains and Equipages, and all the showy Parts of Life; we love rather to dazzle the Multitude, than consult our proper Interests; and, as I have elsewhere observed, it is one of the most unaccountable Passions of humane Nature, that we are at greater Pains to appear easie and happy to others, than really to make our selves so. Of all Disparities, that in Humour makes the most unhappy Marriages, yet scarce enters into our Thoughts at the contracting of them. Several that are in this Respect unequally yoaked, and uneasie for Life, with a Person of a particular Character, might have been pleased and happy with a Person of a contrary one, notwithstanding they are both perhaps equally vertuous and laudable in their Kind.

Before Marriage we cannot be too inquisitive and discerning

in the Faults of the Person beloved, nor after it too dimsighted and superficial. However perfect and accomplish'd the Person appears to you at a Distance, you will find many Blemishes and Imperfections in her Humour, upon a more intimate Acquaintance, which you never discovered or perhaps suspected. Here therefore Discretion and good Nature are to shew their Strength; the first will hinder your Thoughts from dwelling on what is disagreeable, the other will raise in you all the Tenderness of Compassion and Humanity, and by Degrees soften those very Imperfections into Beauties.

Marriage enlarges the Scene of our Happiness and Miseries. A Marriage of Love is pleasant; a Marriage of Interest easie; and a Marriage, where both meet, happy. A happy Marriage has in it all the Pleasures of Friendship, all the Enjoyments of Sense and Reason, and, indeed, all the Sweets of Life. Nothing is a greater Mark of a degenerate and vitious Age, than the common Ridicule which passes on this State of Life. It is, indeed, only happy in those who can look down with Scorn or Neglect on the Impieties of the Times, and tread the Paths of Life together in a constant uniform Course of Virtue.

No. 262.

[ADDISON.]   Monday, December 31.

Nulla venenato littera mista joco est.—Ov.

I THINK my self highly obliged to the Publick for their kind Acceptance of a Paper which visits them every Morning, and has in it none of those *Seasonings* that recommend so many of the Writings which are in Vogue among us.

As, on the one Side, my Paper has not in it a single Word of News, a Reflection in Politicks, nor a Stroke of Party; so, on the other, there are no fashionable Touches of Infidelity, no obscene Ideas, no Satyrs upon Priesthood, Marriage, and the like popular Topicks of Ridicule; no private Scandal, nor any Thing that may tend to the Defamation of particular Persons, Families, or Societies.

There is not one of these abovementioned Subjects that would not sell a very indifferent Paper, could I think of gratifying the Publick by such mean and base Methods: But notwithstanding I have rejected every Thing that favours of Party, every Thing that is loose and immoral, and every Thing that might create Uneasiness in the Minds of particular Persons, I find that the Demand for my Papers has encreased every Month since their first Appearance in the World. This does not perhaps reflect so much Honour upon my self, as on my Readers, who give a much greater Attention to Discourses of Virtue and Morality, than ever I expected, or indeed could hope.

When I broke loose from that great Body of Writers who have employed their Wit and Parts in propagating Vice and Irreligion, I did not question but I should be treated as an odd Kind of Fellow that had a Mind to appear singular in my Way of Writing: But the general Reception I have found, convinces me that the World is not so corrupt as we are apt to imagine; and that if those Men of Parts who have been employed in vitiating the Age had endeavoured to rectify and amend it, they needed not have sacrificed their good Sense and Virtue to their Fame and Reputation. No Man is so sunk in Vice and Ignorance, but there are still some hidden Seeds of Goodness and Knowledge in him; which give him a Relish of such Reflections and Speculations as have an Aptness to improve the Mind and to make the Heart better.

I have shewn in a former Paper, with how much Care I have avoided all such Thoughts as are loose, obscene, or immoral; and I believe my Reader would still think the better of me, if he knew the Pains I am at in qualifying what I write after such a manner, that nothing may be interpreted as aimed at private Persons. For this Reason when I draw any faulty Character, I consider all those Persons to whom the Malice of the World may possibly apply it, and take care to dash it with such particular Circumstances as may prevent all such ill-natured Applications. If I write any Thing on a black Man, I run over in my Mind all the eminent Persons in the Nation who are of that Complection: When I place an imaginary Name at the Head of a Character, I examine every Syllable and Letter of it, that it may not bear any Resemblance to one that is real. I know very well the Value which every Man sets upon his Reputation, and how painful it is to be exposed to the Mirth and Derision of the Publick, and should therefore scorn to divert my Reader at the Expence of any private Man.

As I have been thus tender of every particular Person's Reputation, so I have taken more than ordinary Care not to give Offence to those who appear in the higher Figures of Life. I would not make my self merry even with a Piece of Pasteboard that is invested with a publick Character; for which Reason I have never glanced upon the late designed Procession of his Holiness and his Attendants, notwithstanding it might have afforded Matter to many ludicrous Speculations. Among those Advantages, which the Publick may reap from this Paper, it is not the least, that it draws Men's Minds off from the Bitterness of Party, and furnishes them with Subjects of Discourse that may be treated without Warmth or Passion. This is said to have been the first Design of those Gentlemen who set on Foot the Royal Society; and had then a very good Effect, as it turned many of the greatest Genius's of that Age to the Disquisitions of natural Knowledge, who, if they had engaged in Politicks with the same Parts and Application, might have set their Country in a Flame. The Air-Pump, the Barometer, the Quadrant, and the like Inventions, were thrown out to those busy Spirits, as Tubs and Barrels are to a Whale, that he may let the Ship sail on without Disturbance, while he diverts himself with those innocent Amusements.

I have been so very scrupulous in this Particular of not hurting any Man's Reputation, that I have forborn mentioning even such Authors as I could not name with Honour. This I must confess to have been a Piece of very great Self-denial: For as the Publick relishes nothing better than the Ridicule which turns upon a Writer of any Eminence, so there is nothing which a Man that has but a very ordinary Talent in Ridicule may execute with greater Ease. One might raise Laughter for a Quarter of a Year together upon the Works of a Person who has published but a very few Volumes. For which Reasons I am astonished, that those who have appeared against this Paper have made so very little of it. The Criticisms which I have hitherto published, have been made with an Intention rather to discover Beauties and Excellencies in the Writers of my own Time, than to publish any of their Faults and Imperfections. In the mean while I should take it for a very great Favour from some of my underhand Detractors, if they would break all Measures with me so far, as to give me a Pretence for examining their Performances with an impartial Eye: Nor shall I look upon it as any Breach of Charity to criticise the Author, so long as I keep clear of the Person.

In the mean While, till I am provoked to such Hostilities, I shall from Time to Time endeavour to do Justice to those who have distinguished themselves in the politer Parts of Learning, and to point out such Beauties in their Works as may have escaped the Observation of others.

As the first Place among our *English* Poets is due to *Milton*, and as I have drawn more Quotations out of him than from any other, I shall enter into a regular Criticism upon his *Paradise Lost*, which I shall publish every *Saurday* till I have given my Thoughts upon that Poem. I shall not however presume to impose upon others my own particular Judgment on this Author, but only deliver it as my private Opinion. Criticism is of a very large Extent, and every particular Master in this

Art has his favourite Passages in an Author, which do not equally strike the best Judges. It will be sufficient for me if I discover many Beauties or Imperfections which others have not attended to, and I should be very glad to see any of our eminent Writers publish their Discoveries on the same Subject. In short, I would always be understood to write my Papers of Criticism in the Spirit which *Horace* has expressed in those two famous Lines;

> . . . *Si quid novisti rectius istis,*
> *Candidus imperti; si non, his utere mecum.*

If you have made any better Remarks of your own, communicate them with Candour; if not, make Use of these I present you with.

No. 263.
[STEELE.]   Tuesday, January 1, 1712.

Gratulor . . . quod eum, quem necesse erat diligere, qualiscunque esset, talem habemus, ut libenter quoque diligamus.—Trebonius apud Tull.

'*Mr.* SPECTATOR,

I AM the happy Father of a very towardly Son, in whom I do not only see my Life, but also my Manner of Life, renewed. It would be extreamly beneficial to Society, if you would frequently resume Subjects which serve to bind these Sort of Relations faster, and endear the Tyes of Blood with those of Good-will, Protection, Observance, Indulgence and Veneration. I would, methinks, have this done after an uncommon Method, and do not think any one, who is not capable of writing a good Play, fit to undertake a Work wherein there will necessarily occur so many secret Instincts, and Biasses of humane Nature, which would pass unobserved by common Eyes. I thank Heaven I have no outragious Offence against my own excellent Parents to answer for, but when I am now and then alone, and look back upon my past Life, from my earliest Infancy to this Time, there are many Faults which I committed that did not appear to me, even till I my self became a Father. I had not till then a Notion of the Earnings of Heart, which a Man has when he sees his Child do a laudable Thing, or the sudden Damp which seizes him when he fears he will act something unworthy. It is not to be imagined, what a Remorse touched me for a long Train of childish Negligences of my Mother, when I saw my Wife the other Day look out of the Window, and turn as pale as Ashes upon seeing my younger Boy sliding upon the Ice. These slight

Intimations will give you to understand, that there are number-less little Crimes, which Children take no Notice of while they are doing, which, upon Reflection, when they shall themselves become Fathers, they will look upon with the utmost Sorrow and Contrition that they did not regard, before those whom they offended were to be no more seen. How many thousand Things do I remember, which would have highly pleased my Father, and I omitted for no other Reason, but that I thought what he proposed the Effect of Humour and old Age, which I am now convinced had Reason and good Sense in it. I cannot now go into the Parlour to him, and make his Heart glad with an Account of a Matter, which was of no Consequence, but that I told it, and acted in it. The good Man and Woman are long since in their Graves, who used to sit and plot the Welfare of us their Children, while, perhaps, we were sometimes laughing at the old Folks at another End of the House. The Truth of it is, were we merely to follow Nature in these great Duties of Life, tho' we have a strong Instinct towards the performing of them, we should be on both Sides very deficient. Age is so unwelcome to the Generality of Mankind, and Growth towards Manhood so desirable to all, that Resignation to Decay is too difficult a Task in the Father; and Deference, amidst the Impulse of gay Desires, appears unreasonable to the Son. There are so few who can grow old with a good Grace, and yet fewer who can come slow enough into the World, that a Father, were he to be actuated by his Desires, and a Son, were he to consult himself only, could neither of them behave himself as he ought to the other. But when Reason interposes against Instinct, where it would carry either out of the Interests of the other, there arises that happiest Intercourse of good Offices between those dearest Relations of humane Life. The Father, according to the Opportunities which are offered to him, is throwing down Blessings on the Son, and the Son endeavouring to appear the worthy Offspring of such a Father. It is after this Manner that *Camillus* and his first-born dwell together. *Camillus* enjoys a pleasing and indolent old Age, in which Passion is subdued, and Reason exalted. He waits the Day of his Dissolution with a Resignation mixed with Delight, and the Son fears the Accession of his Father's Fortune with Diffidence, least he should not enjoy or become it as well as his Predecessor. Add to this, that the Father knows he leaves a Friend to the Children of his Friends, an easie Land-lord to his Tenants, and an Agreeable Companion to his Acquaintance. He believes his Son's Behaviour will make him frequently remembred, but never wanted. This Commerce is so well cemented, that without the Pomp of saying, *Son, be a*

Friend to such a one when I am gone, Camillus knows, being in his Favour, is Direction enough to the grateful Youth who is to succeed him, without the Admonition of his mentioning it. These Gentlemen are honoured in all their Neighbourhood, and the same Effect which a Court has on the Manners of a Kingdom, their Characters have on all who live within the Influence of them.

My Son and I are out of Fortune to communicate our good Actions or Intentions to so many as these Gentlemen do; but I will be bold to say, my Son has, by the Applause and Approbation which his Behaviour towards me has gained him, occasioned that many an old Man, besides my self, has rejoiced. Other Men's Children follow the Example of mine, and I have the inexpressible Happiness of over-hearing our Neighbours, as we ride by, point to their Children, and say with a Voice of Joy, There they go.

You cannot, *Mr.* SPECTATOR, pass your Time better, than in insinuating the Delights which these Relations well regarded bestow upon each other. Ordinary Passages are no longer such, but mutual Love gives an Importance to the most indifferent Things, and a Merit to Actions the most insignificant. When we look round the World, and observe the many Misunderstandings which are created by the Malice and Insinuation of the meanest Servants between People thus related, how necessary will it appear that it were inculcated that Men would be upon their Guard to support a Constancy of Affection, and that grounded upon the Principles of Reason, not the Impulses of Instinct.

It is from the common Prejudices which Men receive from their Parents, that Hatreds are kept alive from one Generation to another; and when Men act by Instinct, Hatreds will descend when good Offices are forgotten. For the Degeneracy of humane Life is such, that our Anger is more easily transferred to our Children than our Love. Love always gives something to the Object it delights in, and Anger spoils the Person against whom it is moved of Something laudable in him : From this Degeneracy therefore, and a Sort of Self-Love, we are more prone to take up the Ill-will of our Parents, than to follow them in their Friendships.

One would think there should need no more to make Men keep up this Sort of Relation with the utmost Sanctity, than to examine their own Hearts. If every Father remembered his own Thoughts and Inclinations when he was a Son, and every Son remembered what he expected from his Father, when he himself was in a State of Dependance, this one Reflection would preserve Men from being dissolute or rigid in these several

Capacities. The Power and Subjection between them when broken, make them more emphatically Tyrants and Rebels against each other, with greater Cruelty of Heart than the Disruption of States and Empires can possibly produce. I shall end this Application to you with two Letters which passed between a Mother and Son very lately, and are as follows.

"*Dear* FRANK,

If the Pleasures, which I have the Grief to hear you pursue in Town, do not take up all your Time, do not deny your Mother so much of it, as to read seriously this Letter. You said before Mr. *Letacre*, that an old Woman might live very well in the Country upon half my Jointure, and that your Father was a fond Fool to give me a Rent-Charge of Eight hundred a Year to the Prejudice of his Son. What *Letacre* said to you upon that Occasion, you ought to have born with more Decency, as he was your Father's well-beloved Servant, than to have called him *Country-putt*. In the first Place, *Frank*, I must tell you I will have my Rent duly paid, for I will make up to your Sisters for the Partiality I was guilty of, in making your Father do so much as he has done for you. I may, it seems, live upon half my Jointure! I lived upon much less, *Frank*, when I carried you from Place to Place in these Arms, and could neither eat, dress, or mind any Thing for Feeding and Tending you a weakly Child, and shedding Tears when the Convulsions you were then troubled with returned upon you. By my Care you outgrew them, to throw away the Vigour of your Youth in the Arms of Harlots, and deny your Mother what is not yours to detain. Both your sisters are crying to see the Passion which I smother; but if you please to go on thus like a Gentleman of the Town, and forget all Regards to your self and Family, I shall immediately enter upon your Estate for the Arrear due to me, and without one Tear more contemn you for forgetting the Fondness of your Mother, as much as you have the Example of your Father. O *Frank*, do I live to omit writing my self,

Your Affectionate Mother,

A. T."

"*Madam*,

I will come down to Morrow and pay the Mony on my Knees. Pray write so no more. I will take care you never shall, for I will be for ever hereafter

Your most Dutiful Son,

F. T.

I will bring down new Heads for my Sisters. Pray let all be forgotten."'   T

No. 264.

[STEELE.]   Wednesday, January 2.

. . . Secretum iter & fallentis semita vitae.—Hor.

It has been from Age to Age an Affectation to love the Pleasure
of Solitude, among those who cannot possibly be supposed
qualified for passing Life in that Manner. This People have
taken up from reading the many agreeable Things which have
been writ on that Subject, for which we are beholden to excellent Persons who delighted in being retired and abstracted
from the Pleasures that enchant the Generality of the World.
This Way of Life is recommended indeed with great Beauty,
and in such a Manner as disposes the Reader for the Time to a
pleasing Forgetfulness, or Negligence of the particular Hurry
of Life in which he is engaged, together with a longing for that
State which he is charmed with in Description. But when we
consider the World it self, and how few there are capable of a
religious, learned, or philosophick Solitude, we shall be apt to
change a Regard to that Sort of Solitude, for being a little
singular in enjoying Time after the Way a Man himself likes
best in the World, without going so far as wholly to withdraw
from it. I have often observed, there is not a Man breathing
who does not differ from all other Men, as much in the Sentiments of his Mind, as the Features of his Face. The Felicity is,
when any one is so happy as to find out and follow what is the
Proper Bent of his Genius, and turn all his Endeavours to exert
himself according as that prompts him. Instead of this, which
is an innocent Method of enjoying a Man's self, and turning out
of the general Tracts wherein you have Crouds of Rivals, there
are those who pursue their own Way out of a Sourness and
Spirit of Contradiction: These Men do every Thing which they
are able to support, as if Guilt and Impunity could not go
together. They chuse a Thing only because another dislikes
it; and affect forsooth an inviolable Constancy in Matters of no
manner of Moment. Thus sometimes an old Fellow shall wear
this or that Sort of Cut in his Cloaths with great Integrity,
while all the rest of the World are degenerated into Buttons,
Pockets and Loops unknown to their Ancestors. As insignificant as even this is, if it were searched to the Bottom, you
perhaps would find it not sincere, but that he is in the Fashion
in his Heart, and holds out from mere Obstinacy. But I am
running from my intended Purpose, which was to celebrate a
certain particular Manner of passing away Life, and is a Contradiction to no Man, but a Resolution to contract none of the
exorbitant Desires by which others are enslaved. The best
Way of separating a Man's self from the World, is to give up

the Desire of being known to it. After a Man has preserved his Innocence, and performed all Duties incumbent upon him, his Time spent his own Way is what makes his Life differ from that of a Slave. If they who affect Show and Pomp knew how many of their Spectators derided their trivial Taste, they would be very much less elated, and have an Inclination to examine the Merit of all they have to do with: They would soon find out that there are many who make a Figure below what their Fortune or Merit entitles them to, out of mere Choice, and an elegant Desire of Ease and Disincumbrance. It would look like Romance to tell you in this Age of an old Man who is contented to pass for an Humourist, and one who does not understand the Figure he ought to make in the World, while he lives in a Lodging of ten Shillings a Week with only one Servant. While he dresses himself according to the Season in Cloath or in Stuff, and has no one necessary Attention to any Thing but the Bell which calls to Prayers twice a Day. I say it would look like a Fable to report that this Gentleman gives away all which is the Overplus of a great Fortune, by secret Methods, to other Men. If he has not the Pomp of a numerous Train, and of Professors of Service to him, he has every Day he lives the Conscience that the Widow, the Fatherless, the Mourner, and the Stranger bless his unseen Hand in their Prayers. This Humourist gives up all the Compliments which People of his own Condition could make to him, for the Pleasures of helping the afflicted, supplying the needy, and befriending the neglected. This Humourist keeps to himself much more than he wants, and gives a vast Refuse of his Superfluities to purchase Heaven, and by freeing others from the Temptations of worldly Want, to carry a Retinue with him thither.

Of all Men who affect living in a particular Way, next to this admirable Character, I am the most enamoured of *Irus*, whose Condition will not admit of such Largesses, and perhaps would not be capable of making them, if it were. *Irus*, tho' he is now turned of fifty, has not appeared in the World, in his real Character, since five and twenty, at which Age he ran out a small Patrimony, and spent some Time after with Rakes who had lived upon him: A Course of ten Years Time passed in all the little Alleys, By Paths, and sometimes open Taverns and Streets of this Town, gave *Irus* a perfect Skill in judging of the Inclinations of Mankind, and acting accordingly. He seriously considered he was poor, and the general Horrour which most Men have of all who are in that Condition. *Irus* judged very rightly, that while he could keep his Poverty a Secret, he should not feel the Weight of it; he improved this Thought into an

Affectation of Closeness and Covetousness. Upon this one Principle he resolved to govern his future Life; and in the thirty sixth Year of his Age he repaired to *Long-lane*, and looked upon several Dresses which hung there deserted by their first Masters, and exposed to the Purchase of the best Bidder. At this Place he exchanged his gay Shabbyness of Cloaths fit for a much younger Man, to warm ones that would be decent for a much older one. *Irus* came out thoroughly equipped from Head to Foot, with a little oaken Cane in the Form of a substantial Man that did not mind his Dress, turned of fifty. He had at this Time fifty Pounds in ready Money; and in this Habit, with this Fortune, he took his present Lodging in St. *John-street*, at the Mansion-House of a Taylor's Widow, who washes and can clear-starch his Bands. From that Time to this, he has kept the main Stock, without Alteration under or over, to the Value of five Pounds. He left off all his old Acquaintance to a Man, and all his Arts of Life, except the Play of Back-gammon, upon which he has more than bore his Charges. *Irus* has, ever since he came into this Neighbourhood, given all the Intimations, he skilfully could, of being a close Hunks worth Money: No body comes to visit him, he receives no Letters, and tells his Money Morning and Evening. He has from the publick Papers, a Knowledge of what generally passes, shuns all Discourses of Money, but shrugs his Shoulder when you talk of Securities; he denies his being rich with the Air, which all do who are vain of being so: He is the Oracle of a Neighbouring Justice of Peace who meets him at the Coffee-House; the Hopes that what he has must come to Somebody, and that he has no Heirs, have that Effect wherever he is known, that he every Day has three or four Invitations to dine at different Places, which he generally takes Care to chuse in such a manner, as not to seem inclined to the richer man. All the young Men respect him, and say he is just the same Man he was when they were Boys. He uses no Artifice in the World, but makes Use of Men's Designs upon him to get a Maintenance out of them. This he carries on by a certain Peevishness (which he acts very well), that no one would believe could possibly enter into the Head of a poor Fellow. His Meen, his Dress, his Carriage, and his Language are such, that you would be at a Loss to guess, whether in the active Part of his Life he had been a sensible Citizen, or Scholar that knew the World. These are the great Circumstances in the Life of *Irus*, and thus does he pass away his Days a Stranger to Mankind; and at his Death, the worst that will be said of him will be, that he got by every Man, who had Expectations from him, more than he had to leave him.

I have an Inclination to print the following Letters; for that I have heard the Author of them has some where or other seen me, and by an excellent Faculty in Mimickry my Correspondents tell me he can assume my Air, and give my Taciturnity a Slyness which diverts more than any Thing I could say if I were present. Thus I am glad my Silence is atoned for to the good Company in Town. He has carryed his Skill in Imitation so far, as to have forged a Letter from my Friend Sir ROGER in such a manner, that any one but I who am thoroughly acquainted with him, would have taken it for genuine.

   '*Mr.* SPECTATOR,

Having observ'd in *Lilly's* Grammar how sweetly *Bacchus* and *Apollo* run in a Verse: I have (to preserve the Amity between them) call'd in *Bacchus* to the Aid of my Profession of the *Theatre.* So that while some People of Quality are bespeaking Plays of me to be acted upon such a Day, and others, Hogsheads for their Houses, against such a Time; I am wholly employ'd in the agreeable Service of Wit and Wine: Sir, I have sent you Sir *Roger de Coverley's* Letter to me, which pray comply with in Favour of the *Bumper* Tavern. Be kind, for you know a Player's utmost Pride is the Approbation of the SPECTATOR.

        I am your Admirer, tho' unknown,
                    Richard Estcourt.'

  'To Mr. *Estcourt* at his House in *Covent-Garden.*
                    Coverly, December
                    the 18*th,* 1711.

   Old Comical One,

The Hogshead of Neat Port came safe, and have gotten the good Reputation in these Parts; and I am glad to hear, that a Fellow who has been laying out his Money, ever since he was born, for the meer Pleasure of Wine, has bethought himself of joining Profit and Pleasure together. Our Sexton (poor Man) having receiv'd Strength from thy Wine, since his fit of the Gout is hugely taken with it: He says it is given by Nature for the Use of Families, that no Steward's Table can be without it, that it strengthens Digestion, excludes Surfeits, Fevers, and Physick; which Green Wines of any kind can't do. Pray get a pure snug Room, and I hope next Term to help fill your Bumper with our People of the Club; but you must have no Bells stirring when the *Spectator* comes; I forebore ringing to Dinner while he was down with me in the Country. Thank you for the little Hams and *Portugal* Onions; pray keep some always by you. You know my Supper is only good *Cheshire* Cheese, best Mustard, a Golden Pippin, attended with a Pipe of *John Sly's* Best. Sir *Harry* has stoln all your Songs, and tells the Story of the 5th of *November* to Perfection.

Yours to serve you,

Roger de Coverley.

We 've lost old *John* since you were here.'   T

No. 265.

[ADDISON.]   Thursday, January 3.

*Dixerit e multis aliquis, quid virus in angues
Adjicis? & rabidae tradis ovile lupae?*—Ov. de Art. Am.

ONE of the Fathers, if I am rightly informed, has defined a Woman to be ζῷον φιλόκοσμον, *an Animal that delights in Finery.* I have already treated of the Sex in two or three Papers, conformably to this Definition, and have in particular observed, that in all Ages they have been more careful than the Men to adorn that Part of the Head, which we generally call the Outside.

This Observation is so very notorious, that when in ordinary Discourse we say a Man has a fine Head, a long Head, or a good Head, we express our selves metaphorically, and speak in relation to his Understanding; whereas when we say of a Woman, she has a fine, a long, or a good Head, we speak only in relation to her Commode.

It is observed among Birds, that Nature has lavished all her Ornaments upon the Male, who very often appears in a most beautiful Head-dress: Whether it be a Crest, a Comb, a Tuft of Feathers, or a natural little Plume, erected like a kind of Pinacle on the very Top of the Head. As Nature on the contrary has poured out her Charms in the greatest Abundance upon the female Part of our Species, so they are very assiduous in bestowing upon themselves the finest Garnitures of Art. The Peacock, in all his Pride, does not display half the Colours that appear in the Garments of a *British* Lady, when she is dressed either for a Ball or a Birth-day.

But to return to our Female Heads. The Ladies have been for some Time in a Kind of *moulting Season,* with regard to that Part of their Dress, having *cast* great Quantities of Ribbon, Lace, and Cambrick, and in some measure reduced that Part of the humane Figure to the beautiful globular Form, which is natural to it. We have for a great While expected what Kind of Ornament would be substituted in the Place of those antiquated Commodes. But our Female Projectors were all the last Summer so taken up with the Improvement of their Petticoats, that they had not Time to attend to any Thing else; but having at length sufficiently adorned their lower Parts, they now begin to turn their Thoughts upon the other Extremity, as well remembring the old Kitchin Proverb, that if you light your Fire at both Ends, the middle will shift for its self.

I am engaged in this Speculation by a Sight which I lately met with at the Opera. As I was standing in the hinder Part of the Box, I took notice of a little Cluster of Women sitting together in the prettiest coloured Hoods that I ever saw. One of them was blue, another yellow, and another philomot; the fourth was of a Pink Colour, and the fifth of a pale Green. I looked with as much Pleasure upon this little party-coloured Assembly, as upon a Bed of Tulips, and did not know at first whether it might not be an Embassie of *Indian* Queens; but upon my going about into the Pit, and taking them in Front, I was immediately undeceived, and saw so much Beauty in every Face, that I found them all to be *English*. Such Eyes and Lips, Cheeks and Foreheads, could be the Growth of no other Country. The Complection of their Faces hindered me from observing any further the Colour of their Hoods, though I could easily perceive by that unspeakable Satisfaction which appeared in their Looks, that their own Thoughts were wholly taken up on those pretty Ornaments they wore upon their Heads.

I am informed that this Fashion spreads daily, insomuch that the Whig and Tory Ladies begin already to hang out different Colours, and to shew their Principles in their Head-dress. Nay, if I may believe my Friend WILL HONEYCOMB, there is a certain old Coquet of his Acquaintance, who intends to appear very suddenly in a Rainbow Hood, like the *Iris* in *Dryden's Virgil*, not questioning but that among such Variety of Colours she shall have a Charm for every Heart.

My Friend WILL, who very much values himself upon his great Insights into Gallantry, tells me, that he can already guess at the Humour a Lady is in by her Hood, as the Courtiers of *Morocco* know the Disposition of their present Emperor by the Colour of the Dress which he puts on. When *Melesinda* wraps her Head in Flame Colour, her Heart is set upon Execution. When she covers it with Purple, I would not, says he, advise her Lover to approach her; but if she appears in White, it is Peace, and he may hand her out of her Box with Safety.

WILL informs me likewise, that these Hoods may be used as Signals. Why else, says he, does *Cornelia* always put on a Black Hood when her Husband is gone into the Country?

Such are my Friend HONEYCOMB's Dreams of Gallantry For my own Part, I impute this Diversity of Colours in the Hoods to the Diversity of Complection in the Faces of my pretty Country Women. *Ovid* in his Art of Love has given some Precepts as to this Particular, though I find they are different from those which prevail among the Moderns. He recommends a red striped Silk to the pale Complection; White to the Brown, and Dark to the Fair. On the contrary, my Friend WILL, who pretends to be a greater Master in this Art than *Ovid*, tells me, that the palest Features look the most agreeable in white Sarsenet; that a Face which is overflushed appears to advantage in the deepest Scarlet, and that the darkest Complection is not a little alleviated by a Black Hood. In short, he is for losing the Colour of the Face in that of the Hood, as a Fire burns dimly, and a Candle goes half out in the Light of the Sun. This, says he, your *Ovid* himself has hinted, where he treats of these Matters, when he tells us that the blue Water Nymphs are dressed in Sky-coloured Garments; and that *Aurora*, who always appears in the Light of the Rising Sun, is robed in Saffron.

Whether these his Observations are justly grounded I cannot tell: but I have often known him, as we have stood together behind the Ladies, praise or dispraise the Complection of a Face which he never saw, from observing the Colour of her Hood, and has been very seldom out in these his Guesses.

As I have Nothing more at Heart than the Honour and Improvement of the fair Sex, I cannot conclude this Paper without an Exhortation to the *British* Ladies, that they would excel the Women of all other Nations as much in Vertue and good Sense, as they do in Beauty; which they may certainly do, if they will be as industrious to cultivate their Minds, as they are to adorn their Bodies: In the mean while I shall recommend to their most serious Consideration the Saying of an old *Greek* Poet,

$$\Gamma\upsilon\nu\alpha\iota\kappa\grave{\iota}\ \kappa\acute{o}\sigma\mu\sigma\varsigma\ \acute{o}\ \tau\rho\acute{o}\pi\sigma\varsigma,\ \kappa'\ o\grave{\upsilon}\ \chi\rho\upsilon\sigma\acute{\iota}\alpha.$$

C

No. 266.
[STEELE.] Friday, January 4.

> *Id vero est, quod ego mihi puto palmarium,*
> *Me reperisse, quomodo adolescentulus*
> *Meretricum ingenia & mores posset noscere:*
> *Mature ut cum cognorit perpetuo oderit.*—Ter.

No Vice or Wickedness, which People fall into from Indulgence to Desires which are natural to all, ought to place them below

the Compassion of the virtuous Part of the World; which
indeed often makes me a little apt to suspect the Sincerity of
their Virtue who are too warmly provoked at other People's
personal Sins. The unlawful Commerce of the Sexes is of all
other the hardest to avoid; and yet there is no one which you
shall hear the rigider Part of Womankind speak of with so little
Mercy. It is very certain that a modest Woman cannot abhor
the Breach of Chastity too much; but pray let her hate it
for herself, and only pity it in others. WILL HONEYCOMB calls
these over-offended Ladies, the outragiously virtuous.

I do not design to fall upon Failures in general, with Relation
to the Gift of Chastity, but at present only enter upon that
large Field, and begin with the Consideration of poor and
publick Whores. The other Evening passing along near
Covent-Garden, I was jogged on the Elbow as I turned into the
Piazza, on the right Hand coming out of *James-street,* by a
slim young Girl of about Seventeen, who with a pert Air asked
me if I was for a Pint of Wine. I do not know but I should
have indulged my Curiosity in having some Chat with her, but
that I am informed the Man of the *Bumper* knows me; and it
would have made a Story for him not very agreeable to some
Part of my Writings, though I have in others so frequently said
that I am wholly unconcerned in any Scene I am in, but merely
as a Spectator. This Impediment being in my Way, we stood
under one of the Arches by Twilight; and there I could observe
as exact Features as I had ever seen, the most agreeable Shape,
the finest Neck and Bosom, in a Word, the whole Person
of a Woman exquisitely beautiful. She affected to allure me
with a forced Wantonness in her Look and Air; but I saw it
checked with Hunger and Cold: Her Eyes were wan and eager,
her Dress thin and tawdry, her Meen genteel and childish.
This strange Figure gave me much Anguish of Heart, and to
avoid being seen with her I went away, but could not forbear
giving her a Crown. The poor Thing sighed, curtsied, and with
a Blessing, expressed with the utmost Vehemence, turned
from me. This Creature is what they call *newly come upon the
Town,* but who, I suppose, falling into cruel Hands, was left
in the first Month from her Dishonour, and exposed to pass
through the Hands and Discipline of one of those Hags of Hell
whom we call Bawds. But lest I should grow too suddenly
grave on this Subject, and be my self outragiously good, I shall
turn to a Scene in one of *Fletcher*'s Plays, where this Character
is drawn, and the Oeconomy of Whoredom most admirably
described. The Passage I would point to is in the third Scene
of the second Act of the *Humorous Lieutenant.* *Leucippe,*
who is Agent for the King's Lust, and bawds at the same

Time for the whole Court, is very pleasantly introduced,
reading her Minutes as a Person of Business, with two Maids,
her Under-Secretaries, taking Instructions at a Table before
her. Her Women, both those under her present Tutelage, and
those which she is laying Wait for, are alphabetically set down
in her Book; and she is looking over the Letter *C*, in a muttering
Voice, as if between Soliloquy and speaking out, she says,

> *Her Maiden-head will yield me; let me see now;*
> *She is not Fifteen, they say: For her Complexion——*
> Cloe, Cloe, Cloe, *here I have her,*
> Cloe, *the Daughter of a Country Gentleman;*
> *Her Age upon Fifteen. Now her Complexion,*
> *A lovely brown; here 'tis; Eyes black and rowling,*
> *The Body neatly built; she strikes a Lute well,*
> *Sings most enticingly: These Helps consider'd,*
> *Her Maiden-head will amount to some three hundred,*
> *Or three hundred and fifty Crowns, 'twill bear it handsomly.*
> *Her Father's poor, some little Share deducted,*
> *To buy him a Hunting-Nag* . . .

These Creatures are very well instructed in the Circumstances
and Manners of all who are any Way related to the fair one
whom they have a Design upon. As *Cloe* is to be purchased
with 350 Crowns, and the Father taken off with a Pad; the
Merchant's Wife next to her, who abounds in Plenty, is not to
have downright Money, but the mercenary Part of her Mind is
engaged with a Present of Plate and a little Ambition: She is
made to understand that it is a Man of Quality who dies for her.
The Examination of a young Girl for Business, and the crying
down her Value for being a slight Thing, together with every
other Circumstance in the Scene, are inimitably excellent, and
have the true Spirit of Comedy; tho' it were to be wished the
Author had added a Circumstance which should make *Leucippe's* Baseness more odious.

It must not be Thought a Digression from my intended
Speculation, to talk of Bawds in a Discourse upon Wenches; for
a Woman of the Town is not thoroughly and properly such,
without having gone through the Education of one of these
Houses: But the compassionate Case of very many is, that they
are taken into such Hands without any the least Suspicion,
previous Temptation, or Admonition to what Place they are
going. The last Week I went to an Inn in the City, to enquire
for some Provisions which were sent by a Waggon out of the
Country; and as I waited in one of the Boxes till the Chamber-
lain had looked over his Parcels, I heard an old and a young
Voice repeating the Questions and Responses of the Church-
Catechism. I thought it no Breach of good Manners to peep

at a Crevise, and look in at People so well employed; but who should I see there but the most artful Procuress in the Town, examining a most beautiful Country-Girl, who had come up in the same Waggon with my Things, *Whether she was well educated, could forbear playing the Wanton with Servants and idle Fellows, of which this Town*, says she, *is too full:* At the same Time, *Whether she knew enough of Breeding; as that if a Squire or a Gentleman, or one that was her Betters, should give her a civil Salute, she could curtsie and be humble nevertheless.* Her innocent forsooths, yes's, and 't please you's, and she would do her *Endeavour*, moved the good old Lady to take her out of the Hands of a Country Bumkin her Brother, and hire her for her own Maid. I stay'd till I saw them all marched out to take Coach; the Brother loaded with a great Cheese, he prevailed upon her to take for her Civilities to Sister. This poor Creature's Fate is not far off that of her's whom I spoke of above; and it is not to be doubted, but after she has been long enough a Prey to Lust she will be delivered over to Famine; the Ironical Commendation of the Industry and Charity of these antiquated Ladies, these Directors of Sin, after they can no longer commit it, makes up the Beauty of the inimitable Dedication to the *Plain Dealer*, and is a Master-piece of Railery on this Vice: But to understand all the Purlues of this Game the better, and to illustrate this Subject in future Discourses, I must venture my self, with my Friend WILL, into the Haunts of Beauty and Gallantry; from pampered Vice in the Habitations of the Wealthy, to distressed indigent Wickedness expelled the Harbours of the Brothel.   T

No. 267.

[ADDISON.]   Saturday, January 5.

Cedite Romani scriptores, cedite Graii.—Propert.

THERE is Nothing in Nature so irksome as general Discourses, especially when they turn chiefly upon Words. For this Reason I shall wave the Discussion of that Point which was started some Years since, Whether *Milton*'s *Paradise Lost* may be called an Heroick Poem? Those who will not give it that Title, may call it (if they please) a *Divine Poem*. It will be sufficient to its Perfection, if it has in it all the Beauties of the highest Kind of Poetry; and as for those who alledge it is not an Heroick Poem, they advance no more to the Diminution of it, than if they should say *Adam* is not *Aeneas*, nor *Eve Helen*.

I shall therefore examine it by the Rules of Epic Poetry, and

see whether it falls short of the *Iliad* or *Aeneid*, in the Beauties
which are essential to that Kind of Writing. The first Thing
to be consider'd in an Epic Poem, is the Fable, which is perfect
or imperfect, according as the Action which it relates is more or
less so. This Action should have three Qualifications in it.
First, It should be but one Action. Secondly, It should be an
entire Action; and Thirdly, it should be a great Acton. To
consider the Action of the *Iliad*, *Aeneid*, and *Paradise Lost*, in
these three several Lights. *Homer* to preserve the Unity of his
Action hastens into the Midst of Things, as *Horace* has observed:
Had he gone up to *Leda*'s Egg, or begun much later, even at
the Rape of *Helen*, or the Investing of *Troy*, it is manifest that
the Story of the Poem would have been a Series of several
Actions. He therefore opens his Poem with the Discord of
his Princes, and with great Art interweaves in the several
succeeding Parts of it, an Account of every Thing material
which relates to them, and had passed before that fatal Dis-
sension. After the same Manner *Aeneas* makes his first
Appearance in the *Tyrrhene* Seas, and within Sight of *Italy*,
because the Action proposed to be celebrated was that of his
settling himself in *Latium*. But because it was necessary
for the Reader to know what had happened to him in the
taking of *Troy*, and in the preceding Parts of his Voyage, *Virgil*
makes his Heroe relate it by Way of Episode in the second and
third Books of the *Aeneid*. The Contents of both which Books
come before those of the first Book in the Thread of the Story,
tho' for preserving this Unity of Action, they follow them in
the Disposition of the Poem. *Milton*, in Imitation of these
two great Poets, opens his *Paradise Lost*, with an infernal
Council plotting the Fall of Man, which is the Action he proposed to celebrate; and as for those great Actions which pre
ceded, in Point of Time, the Battle of the Angels, and the
Creation of the World, (which would have entirely destroyed
the Unity of his principal Action, had he related them in the
same Order that they happened) he cast them into the fifth,
sixth, and seventh Books, by way of Episode to this noble
Poem.

Aristotle himself allows, that *Homer* has nothing to boast of
as to the Unity of his Fable, tho' at the same Time that great
Critick and Philosopher endeavours to palliate this Imperfection in the *Greek* Poet, by imputing it in some Measure to the
very Nature of an Epic Poem. Some have been of Opinion,
that the *Aeneid* labours also in this Particular, and has Episodes
which may be looked upon as Excrescencies rather than as
Parts of the Action. On the contrary, the Poem which we
have now under our Consideration, hath no other Episodes

than such as naturally arise from the Subject, and yet is filled with such a Multitude of astonishing Incidents, that it gives us at the same Time a Pleasure of the greatest Variety, and of the greatest Simplicity.

I must observe also, that as *Virgil* in the Poem which was designed to celebrate the Original of the *Roman* Empire, has described the Birth of its great Rival, the *Carthaginian* Commonwealth: *Milton* with the like Art in his Poem on the Fall of Man, has related the Fall of those Angels who are his professed Enemies. Besides the many other Beauties in such an Episode, it's running parallel with the great Action of the Poem, hinders it from breaking the Unity so much as another Episode would have done, that had not so great an Affinity with the principal Subject. In short, this is the same Kind of Beauty which the Criticks admire in the *Spanish Fryar*, or the *Double Discovery*, where the two different Plots look like Counterparts and Copies of one another.

The second Qualification required in the Action of an Epic Poem is, that it should be an *entire* Action: An Action is entire when it is compleat in all its Parts; or as *Aristotle* describes it, when it consists of a Beginning, a Middle, and an End. Nothing should go before it, be intermix'd with it, or follow after it, that is not related to it. As on the contrary, no single Step should be omitted in that just and regular Process which it must be supposed to take from its Original to its Consumma- tion. Thus we see the Anger of *Achilles* in its Birth, its Continuance and Effects; and *Aeneas*'s Settlement in *Italy*, carried on through all the Oppositions in his Way to it both by Sea and Land. The Action in *Milton* excels (I think) both the former in this Particular; we see it contrived in Hell, executed upon Earth, and punished by Heaven. The Parts of it are told in the most distinct Manner, and grow out of one another in the most natural Method.

The third Qualification of an Epic Poem is its *Greatness*. The Anger of *Achilles* was of such Consequence, that it em- broiled the Kings of *Greece*, destroy'd the Heroes of *Troy*, and engaged all the Gods in Factions. *Aeneas*'s Settlement in *Italy* produced the *Caesars*, and gave Birth to the *Roman* Empire. *Milton*'s Subject was still greater than either of the former; it does not determine the Fate of single Persons or Nations, but of a whole Species. The united Powers of Hell are joined together for the Destruction of Mankind, which they effected in Part, and would have completed, had not Omnipotence it self interposed. The principal Actors are Man in his greatest Perfection, and Woman in her highest Beauty. Their Enemies are the fallen Angels: The Messiah their Friend, and the

Almighty their Protector. In short, every Thing that is great in the whole Circle of Being, whether within the Verge of Nature, or out of it, has a proper Part assigned it in this noble Poem.

In Poetry, as in Architecture, not only the Whole, but the principal Members, and every Part of them. should be Great. I will not presume to say, that the Book of Games in the *Aeneid*, or that in the *Iliad*, are not of this Nature, nor to reprehend *Virgil*'s Simile of the Top, and many other of the same Nature in the *Iliad*, as liable to any Censure in this Particular; but I think we may say, without derogating from those wonderful Performances, that there is an unquestionable Magnificence in every Part of *Paradise Lost*, and indeed a much greater than could have been formed upon any Pagan System.

But *Aristotle*, by the Greatness of the Action, does not only mean that it should be great in its Nature, but also in its Duration, or in other Words, that it should have a due Length in it, as well as what we properly call Greatness. The just Measure of the Kind of Magnitude he explains by the following Similitude. An Animal, no bigger than a Mite, cannot appear perfect to the Eye, because the Sight takes it in at once, and has only a confused Idea of the Whole, and not a distinct Idea of all its Parts; If on the contrary you should suppose an Animal of ten thousand Furlongs in Length, the Eye would be so filled with a single Part of it, that it could not give the Mind an Idea of the Whole. What these Animals are to the Eye, a very short or a very long Action would be to the Memory. The first would be, as it were, lost and swallowed up by it, and the other difficult to be contained in it. *Homer* and *Virgil* have shewn their principal Art in this Particular; the Action of the *Iliad*, and that of the *Aeneid*, were in themselves exceeding short, but were so beautifully extended and diversified by the Invention of *Episodes*, and the Machinery of Gods, with the like poetical Ornaments, that they make up an agreeable Story sufficient to employ the Memory without overcharging it. *Milton*'s Action is enriched with such a Variety of Circumstances, that I have taken as much Pleasure in reading the Contents of his Books, as in the best invented Story I ever met with. It is possible, that the Traditions on which the *Iliad* and *Aeneid* were built, had more Circumstances in them than the History of *the Fall of Man*, as it is related in Scripture. Besides it was easier for *Homer* and *Virgil* to dash the Truth with Fiction, as they were in no danger of offending the Religion of their Country by it. But as for *Milton*, he had not only a very few Circumstances upon which to raise his Poem, but was also obliged to proceed with the greatest Caution in every Thing that he added out of his own Invention. And, indeed, notwithstanding all the Restraints he was under, he has filled his Story with so many surprising Incidents, which bear so close an Analogy with what is delivered in Holy Writ, that it is capable of pleasing the most delicate Reader, without giving Offence to the most scrupulous.

The modern Criticks have collected from several Hints in the *Iliad* and *Aeneid* the Space of Time, which is taken up by the Action of each of those Poems; but as a great Part of *Milton*'s Story was transacted in Regions that lie out of the Reach of the Sun and the Sphere of Day, it is impossible to gratifie the Reader with such a Calculation, which indeed would be more curious than instructive; None of the Criticks, either Antient or Modern, having laid down Rules to circumscribe the Action of an Epic Poem with any determined Number of Years, Days or Hours.

This Piece of Criticism on Milton's Paradise Lost *shall be carried on in the following* Saturdays *Papers.* L

No. 268.

[STEELE.] Monday, January 7.

. . . *Minus aptus acutis*
Naribus horum hominum . . . —Hor.

It is not that I think I have been more witty than I ought of late, that at present I wholly forbear any Attempt towards it: I am of Opinion that I ought some times to lay before the World the plain Letters of my Correspondents in the artless Dress in which they hastily send them, that the Reader may see I am not Accuser and Judge my self, but that the Indictment is properly and fairly laid, before I proceed against the Criminal.

'*Mr.* Spectator,

As you are *Spectator General*, I apply my self to you in the following Case; *viz.* I do not wear a Sword, but I often divert my self at the Theatre, where I frequently see a Set of Fellows pull plain People, by way of Humour or Frolick, by the Nose, upon frivolous or no Occasions. A Friend of mine the other Night applauding what a graceful exit Mr. *Wilks* made, one of these Nose-wringers over-hearing him, pinch'd him by the Nose. I was in the Pit the other Night, (when it was very much crouded) a Gentleman leaning upon me, and very heavily, I very civilly requested him to remove his Hand; for which he pulled me by the Nose. I would not resent it in so publick a

Place, because I was unwilling to create a Disturbance; but have since reflected upon it as a Thing that is unmanly and disingenuous, renders the Nose-puller odious, and makes the Person pulled by the Nose look little and contemptible. This Grievance I humbly request you would endeavour to redress.

I am your Admirer, &c.

James Easy.'

'*Mr*. SPECTATOR,

Your Discourse of the 29th of *December* on Love and Marriage is of so useful a Kind, that I cannot forbear adding my Thoughts to yours on that Subject. Methinks it is a Misfortune, that the Marriage State, which in its own Nature is adapted to give us the compleatest Happiness this Life is capable of, should be so uncomfortable a one to so many as it daily proves. But the Mischief generally proceeds from the unwise Choice People make for themselves, and an Expectation of Happiness from Things not capable of giving it. Nothing but the good Qualities of the Person beloved, can be a Foundation for a Love of Judgment and Discretion; and whoever expect Happiness from any Thing but Virtue, Wisdom, Good-humour, and a Similitude of Manners, will find themselves widely mistaken. But how few are there who seek after these Things, and do not rather make Riches their chief if not their only Aim? How rare it is for a Man, when he engages himself in the Thoughts of Marriage, to place his Hopes of having in such a Woman a constant, agreeable Companion? One who will divide his Cares and double his Joys? Who will manage that Share of his Estate he intrusts to her Conduct with Prudence and Frugality, govern his House with Oeconomy and Discretion, and be an Ornament to himself and Family? Where shall we find the Man who looks out for one who places her chief Happiness in the Practice of Virtue, and makes her Duty her continual Pleasure? No, Men rather seek for Mony as the Complement of all their Desires; and regardless of what Kind of Wives they take, they think Riches will be a Minister to all Kind of Pleasures, and enable them to keep Mistresses, Horses, Hounds, to drink, feast, and game with their Companions, pay their Debts contracted by former Extravagancies, or some such vile and unworthy End; and indulge themselves in Pleasures which are a Shame and Scandal to humane Nature. Now as for the Women; how few of them are there who place the Happiness of their Marriage in the having a wise and virtuous Friend? One who will be faithful and just to all, and constant and loving to them? Who with Care and Diligence will look after and improve the Estate, and without grudging allow whatever is prudent and convenient? Rather, How few are there who do not place their Happiness in out-shining others in Pomp and Show? And that do not think within themselves when they have married such a rich Person, that none of their Acquaintance shall appear so fine in their Equipage, so adorn'd in their Persons, or so magnificent in their Furniture as themselves? Thus their Heads are filled with vain Ideas; and I heartily wish I could say that Equipage and Show were not the chief Good of so many Women as I fear it is.

After this Manner do both Sexes deceive themselves, and bring Reflections and Disgrace upon the most happy and most honourable State of Life; whereas if they would but correct their depraved Taste, moderate their Ambition, and place their Happiness upon proper Objects, we should not find Felicity in the Marriage State such a Wonder in the World as it now is.

Sir, if you think these Thoughts worth inserting among your own, be pleas'd to give them a better Dress, and let them pass abroad; and you will oblige

Your Admirer,

A. B.'

'*Mr.* SPECTATOR,

As I was this Day walking in the Street, there happened to pass by on the other Side of the Way a Beauty, whose Charms were so attracting that it drew my Eyes wholly on that Side, insomuch that I neglected my own Way, and chanced to run my Nose directly against a Post; which the Lady no sooner perceived, but fell out into a Fit of Laughter, though at the same Time she was sensible that her self was the Cause of my Misfortune, which in my Opinion was the greater Aggravation of her Crime. I being busy wiping off the Blood which trickled down my Face, had not Time to acquaint her with her Barbarity, as also with my Resolution, *viz.* never to look out of my Way for one of her Sex more: Therefore, that your humble Servant may be revenged, he desires you to insert this in one of your next Papers, which he hopes will be a Warning to all the rest of the Women Gazers, as well as to poor

Anthony Gape.'

'*Mr.* SPECTATOR,

I desire to know in your next, if the merry Game of *the Parson has lost his Cloak*, is not mightily in Vogue amongst the fine Ladies this *Christmas*; because I see they wear Hoods of all Colours, which I suppose is for that Purpose: If it is, and you think it proper, I will carry some of those Hoods with me to our Ladies in *Yorkshire*; because they enjoyned me to bring them something from *London* that was very New.   If you can tell any Thing in which I can obey their Commands more agreeably, be pleas'd to inform me, and you will extremely oblige

Your humble Servant.'

'*Mr.* SPECTATOR,   *Oxford, Dec.* 29.

Since you appear inclined to be a Friend to the distressed, I beg you would assist me in an Affair under which I have suffered very much.   The reigning Toast of this Place is *Patetia*; I have pursued her with the utmost Diligence this Twelve-month, and find nothing stands in my Way but one who flatters her more than I can.   Pride is her Favourite Passion; therefore if you would be so far my Friend as to make a favourable Mention of her in one of your Papers, I believe I should not fail in my Addresses.   The Scholars stand in Rows, as they did to be sure in your Time, at her Pew-door; and she has all the Devotion paid to her by a Croud of Youths who are unacquainted with the Sex, and have Inexperience added to their Passion: However, if it succeeds according to my Vows, you will make me the happiest Man in the World, and the most obliged amongst all

Your humble Servants.'

'*Mr.* SPECTATOR,

I came to my Mistress's Toilet this Morning, for I am admitted when her Face is stark-naked: She frowned, and cryed pish when I said a Thing that I stole; and I will be judged by you whether it was not very pretty.   Madam, said I, you shall forbear that Part of your Dress, it may be well in others; but you cannot place a Patch where it does not hide a Beauty.'

                                                              T

No. 269.
[ADDISON.]   Tuesday, January 8.
         . . . *Aevo rarissima nostro,*
    Simplicitas . . .—Ov.

I WAS this Morning surprized with a great knocking at the Door, when my Landlady's Daughter came up to me and told me that there was a Man below desired to speak with me. Upon my asking her who it was, she told me it was a very grave elderly Person, but that she did not know his Name.   I immediately went down to him, and found him to be the Coachman of my worthy Friend Sir ROGER DE COVERLY.   He told me that his Master came to Town last Night, and would be glad to take a Turn with me in *Grays-Inn* Walks. As I was wondring in my self what had brought Sir ROGER to Town, not having lately received any Letter from him, he told me that his Master was come up to get a Sight of Prince *Eugene*, and that he desired I would immediately meet him.

I was not a little pleased with the Curiosity of the old Knight, though I did not much wonder at it, having heard him say more than once in private Discourse, that he looked upon Prince *Eugenio* (for so the Knight always calls him) to be a greater Man than *Scanderbeg*.

I was no sooner come into *Grays-Inn* Walks, but I heard my Friend upon the Terrace hemming twice or thrice to himself with great Vigour, for he loves to clear his Pipes in good Air (to make use of his own Phrase) and is not a little pleased with any one who takes Notice of the Strength which he still exerts in his Morning Hemms.

I was touched with a secret Joy at the Sight of the good old Man, who before he saw me was engaged in Conversation with a Beggar Man that had asked an Alms of him. I cou'd hear my Friend chide him for not finding out some Work; but at the same Time saw him put his Hand in his Pocket and give him Six-Pence.

Our Salutations were very hearty on both Sides, consisting of many kind Shakes of the Hand, and several affectionate Looks which we cast upon one another. After which the Knight told me my good Friend his Chaplain was very well, and much at my Service, and that the *Sunday* before, he had made a most incomparable Sermon out of Doctor *Barrow*. I have left, says he, all my Affairs in his Hands, and being willing to lay an Obligation upon him, have deposited with him thirty Marks, to be distributed among his poor Parishioners.

He then proceeded to acquaint me with the welfare of *Will Wimble*. Upon which he put his Hand into his Fob, and presented me in his Name with a Tobacco Stopper, telling me that *Will* had been busie all the Beginning of the Winter in turning great Quantities of them; and that he made a Present of one to every Gentleman in the Country who has good Principles, and smokes. He added, that poor *Will* was at present under great Tribulation, for that *Tom Touchy* had taken the Law of him for cutting some Hazle Sticks out of one of his Hedges.

Among other Pieces of News which the Knight brought from his Country Seat, he inform'd me that *Moll White* was dead, and that about a Month after her Death the Wind was so very high, that it blew down the End of one of his Barns. But for my own Part, says Sir ROGER, I do not think that the old Woman had any hand in it.

He afterwards fell into an Account of the Diversions which had passed in his House during the Holydays, for Sir ROGER, after the laudable Custom of his Ancestors, always keeps open House at *Christmas*. I learned from him, that he had killed eight fat Hogs for this Season, that he had dealt about his Chines very liberally amongst his Neighbours, and that in particular he had sent a string of Hogs-puddings with a pack of Cards to every poor Family in the Parish. I have often thought, says Sir ROGER, it happens very well that *Christmas* should fall out in the Middle of Winter. It is the most dead, uncomfortable Time of the Year, when the poor People would suffer very much from their Poverty and Cold, if they had not good Cheer, warm Fires, and *Christmas* Gambols to support them. I love to rejoyce their poor Hearts at this Season, and to see the whole Village merry in my great Hall. I allow a double Quantity of Malt to my small Beer, and set it a running for twelve Days to every one that calls for it. I have always a Piece of cold Beef and a Mince-Pye upon the Table, and am wonderfully pleased to see my Tenants pass away a whole Evening in playing their innocent Tricks, and smutting one another. Our Friend *Will Wimble* is as merry as any of them, and shews a thousand roguish Tricks upon these Occasions.

I was very much delighted with the Reflection of my old Friend, which carried so much Goodness in it. He then launched out into the Praise of the late Act of Parliament for securing the Church of *England*, and told me, with great Satisfaction, that he believed it already began to take Effect; for that a rigid Dissenter, who chanced to dine at his House on *Christmas* Day, had been observed to eat very plentifully of his Plumb-porridge.

After having dispatched all our Country Matters, Sir ROGER made several Enquiries concerning the Club, and particularly of his old Antagonist Sir ANDREW FREEPORT. He asked me with a Kind of a Smile, whether Sir ANDREW had not taken the Advantage of his Absence, to vent among them some of his Republican Doctrines; but soon after gathering up his Countenance into a more than ordinary Seriousness, Tell me truly, says he, don't you think Sir ANDREW had a Hand in the Pope's Procession——but without giving me time to answer him, Well, well, says he, I know you are a wary Man, and do not care to talk of publick Matters.

The Knight then asked me, if I had seen Prince *Eugenio*, and made me promise to get him a Stand in some convenient Place where he might have a full Sight of that extraordinary Man, whose Presence does so much Honour to the *British* Nation. He dwelt very long on the Praises of this great

General, and I found that since I was with him in the Country, he had drawn many Observations together out of his reading in *Baker's* Chronicle, and other Authors, who always lie in his Hall Window, which very much redound to the Honour of this Prince.

Having passed away the greatest Part of the Morning in hearing the Knight's Reflections, which were partly private, and partly political, he asked me if I would smoke a Pipe with him over a Dish of Coffee at *Squire's*. As I love the old Man, I take Delight in complying with every Thing that is agreeable to him, and accordingly waited on him to the Coffeehouse, where his venerable Figure drew upon us the Eyes of the whole Room. He had no sooner seated himself at the upper End of the high Table, but he called for a clean Pipe, a Paper of Tobacco, a Dish of Coffee, a Wax Candle, and the *Supplement*, with such an Air of Cheerfulness and Good-humour, that all the Boys in the Coffee-room (who seemed to take Pleasure in serving him) were at once employed on his several Errands, insomuch that no Body else could come at a Dish of Tea, till the Knight had got all his Conveniencies about him.   L

No. 270.

[STEELE.]   Wednesday, January 9.

*Discit enim citius meminitque libentius illud
Quod quis deridet, quam quod probat. . . .*

I do not know that I have been in greater Delight for these many Years, than in beholding the Boxes at the Play the last Time the *Scornful-Lady* was acted. So great an Assembly of Ladies placed in gradual Rows in all the Ornaments of Jewels, Silks, and Colours, gave so lively and gay an Impression to the Heart, that methought the Season of the Year was vanished; and I did not think it an ill Expression of a young Fellow who stood near me, that called the Boxes those Beds of Tulips. It was a pretty Variation of the Prospect, when any one of these fine Ladies rose up and did Honour to herself and Friend at a Distance, by curtisying; and gave Opportunity to that Friend to shew her Charms to the same Advantage in returning the Salutation. Here that Action is as proper and graceful, as it is at Church unbecoming and impertinent. By the Way, I must take the Liberty to observe, that I did not see any one who is usually so full of Civilities at Church, offer at any such Indecorum during any Part of the Action of the Play. Such beautiful Prospects gladden our Minds, and when considered in general, give innocent and pleasing Ideas. He that dwells upon

any one Object of Beauty, may fix his Imagination to his
Disquiet; but the Contemplation of a whole Assembly together,
is a Defence against the Encroachment of Desire: At least to
me, who have taken pains to look at Beauty abstracted from
the Consideration of its being the Object of Desire; at Power,
only as it sits upon another without any Hopes of partaking
any Share of it; at Wisdom and Capacity without any Pretensions to rival or envy its Acquisitions: I say to me who am
really free from forming any Hopes by beholding the Persons
of beautiful Women, or warming my self into Ambition from
the Successes of other Men, this World is not only a mere
Scene, but a very pleasant one.   Did Mankind but know the
Freedom which there is in keeping thus aloof from the World,
I should have more Imitators, than the powerfullest Man in the
Nation has Followers.   To be no Man's Rival in Love, or Competitor in Business, is a Character which if it does not recommend you as it ought to Benevolence among those whom you
live with, yet has it certainly this Effect, that you do not stand
so much in need of their Approbation, as you would if you
aimed at it more, in setting your Heart on the same Things
which the Generality doat on.   By this Means, and with this
easy Philosophy, I am never less at a Play than when I am at
the Theatre; but indeed I am seldom so well pleased with
Action as in that Place, for most Men follow Nature no longer
than while they are in their Night-Gowns, and all the busy
Part of the Day are in Characters which they neither become
or act in with Pleasure to themselves or their Beholders.   But
to return to my Ladies, I was very well pleased to see so great
a Croud of them assembled at a Play, wherein the Heroine, as
the Phrase is, is so just a Picture of the Vanity of the Sex in
tormenting their Admirers.   The Lady who pines for the Man
whom she treats with so much Impertinence and Inconstancy,
is drawn with much Art and Humour.   Her Resolutions to be
extremely civil, but her Vanity arising just at the Instant
that she resolved to express herself kindly, are described as
by one who had studied the Sex.   But when my Admiration
is fixed upon this excellent Character, and two or three others
in the Play, I must confess I was moved with the utmost
Indignation at the trivial, senseless, and unnatural Representation of the Chaplain.   It is possible there may be a Pedant
in Holy Orders, and we have seen one or two of them in the
World; but such a Driveler as Sir *Roger*, so bereft of all Manner
of Pride, which is the Characteristick of a Pedant, is what one
would not believe could come into the Head of the same Man
who drew the rest of the Play.   The Meeting between *Welford*
and him shews a Wretch without any Notion of the Dignity

of his Function; and it is out of all common Sense, that he should give an Account of himself *as one sent four or five Miles in a Morning on Foot for Eggs.* It is not to be denied, but his Part, and that of the Maid, whom he makes Love to, are excellently well performed; but a Thing which is blameable in it self, grows still more so by the Success in the Execution of it. It is so mean a Thing to gratify a loose Age with a scandalous Representation of what is reputable among Men, not to say what is sacred, that no Beauty, no Excellence in an Author ought to atone for it; nay, such Excellence is an Aggravation of his Guilt, and an Argument that he errs against the Conviction of his own Understanding and Conscience. Wit should be tried by this Rule, and an Audience should rise against such a Scene, as throws down the Reputation of any Thing which the Consideration of Religion or Decency should preserve from Contempt. But all this Evil arises from this one Corruption of Mind, that makes Men resent Offences against their Virtue, less than those against their Understanding. An Author shall write as if he thought there was not one Man of Honour or Woman of Chastity in the House, and come off with Applause: For an Insult upon all the Ten Commandments, with the little Criticks, is not so bad as the Breach of an Unity of Time or Place. Half wits do not apprehend the Miseries that must necessarily flow from Degeneracy of Manners; nor do they know that Order is the Support of Society. Sir *Roger* and his Mistress are Monsters of the Poets own forming; the Sentiments in both of them are such as do not arise in Fools of their Education. We all know that a silly Scholar, instead of being below every one he meets with, is apt to be exalted above the Rank of such as are really his Superiors: His Arrogance is always founded upon particular Notions of Distinction in his own Head, accompanied with a pedantick Scorn of all Fortune and Preheminence when compared with his Knowledge and Learning. This very one Character of Sir *Roger*, as silly as it really is, has done more towards the Disparagement of Holy Orders, and consequently of Virtue it self, than all the Wit that Author or any other could make up for in the Conduct of the longest Life after it. I do not pretend, in saying this, to give my self Airs of more Virtue than my Neighbours, but assert it from the Principles by which Mankind must always be governed. Sallies of Imagination are to be overlooked, when they are committed out of Warmth in the Recommendation of what is praise-worthy; but a deliberate advancing of Vice with all the Wit in the World, is as ill an Action as any that comes before the Magistrate, and ought to be received as such by the People.   T

No. 271.

[ADDISON.]   Thursday, January 10.

Mille trahens varios adverso sole colores.—Virg.

I RECEIVE a double Advantage from the Letters of my Correspondents; first, as they shew me which of my Papers are most acceptable to them; and in the next Place, as they furnish me with Materials for new Speculations.   Sometimes indeed I do not make Use of the Letter it self, but form the Hints of it into Plans of my own Invention; sometimes I take the Liberty to change the Language or Thought into my own Way of speaking and thinking, and always (if it can be done without Prejudice to the Sense) omit the many Compliments and Applauses which are usually bestowed upon me.

Besides the two Advantages above-mentioned, which I receive from the Letters that are sent me, they give me an Opportunity of lengthening out my Paper by the Skilful Management of the subscribing Part at the End of them, which perhaps does not a little conduce to the Ease, both of my self and Reader.

Some will have it, that I often write to my self, and am the only punctual Correspondent I have.   This Objection would indeed be material, were the Letters I communicate to the Publick stuffed with my own Commendations, and if, instead of endeavouring to divert or instruct my Readers, I admired in them the Beauty of my own Performances.   But I shall leave these wise Conjecturers to their own Imaginations, and produce the three following Letters for the Entertainment of the Day.

'*Sir,*

It was last *Thursday* in an Assembly of Ladies, where there were thirteen different coloured Hoods.   Your *Spectator* of that Day lying upon the Table, they ordered me to read it to them, which I did with a very clear Voice, 'till I came to the *Greek* Verse at the End of it.   I must confess I was a little startled at its popping upon me so unexpectedly: However, I covered my Confusion as well as I could, and after having muttered two or three hard Words to my self, laught heartily, and cryed *A very good Jest, Faith*.   The Ladies desired me to explain it to them, but I begg'd their Pardon for that, and told them that if it had been proper for them to hear, they may be sure the Author would not have wrapt it up in *Greek*.   I then let drop several Expressions, as if there were something in it that was not fit to be spoken before a Company of Ladies. Upon which the Matron of the Assembly, who was dressed in a Cherry-coloured Hood, commended the Discretion of the Writer, for having thrown his filthy Thoughts into *Greek*, which was likely to corrupt but few of his Readers. At the same Time she declared herself very well pleased, that he had not given a decisive Opinion upon the new-fashioned Hoods; for to tell you truly, says she, I was afraid he would have made us ashamed to show our Heads. Now, Sir, you must know, since this unlucky Accident happened to me in a Company of Ladies, among whom I passed for a most ingenious Man, I have consulted one who is well versed in the *Greek* Language, and assures me upon his Word, that your late Quotation means no more, than that *Manners and not Dress are the Ornaments of a Woman.* If this comes to the Knowledge of my Female Admirers, I shall be very hard put to it to bring my self off handsomely. In the mean While I give you this Account, that you may take Care hereafter not to betray any of your Well-wishers into the like Inconveniencies. It is in the Number of these that I beg Leave to subscribe my self

Tom Trippit.'

'*Mr.* SPECTATOR,

Your Readers are so well pleased with your Character of Sir ROGER DE COVERLY, that there appeared a sensible Joy in every Coffee-house, upon hearing the old Knight was come to Town. I am now with a Knot of his Admirers, who make it their joint Request to you, that you would give us publick Notice of the Window or Balcony where the Knight intends to make his Appearance. He has already given great satisfaction to several who have seen him at *Squire's* Coffee-house. If you think fit to place your short Face at Sir ROGER'S Left Elbow, we shall take the Hint, and gratefully acknowledge so great a Favour.

I am, Sir,

Your most Devoted

Humble Servant,

C. D.'

'*Sir,*

Knowing that you are very inquisitive after every Thing that is curious in Nature, I will wait on you if you please in the Dusk of the Evening, with my *Show* upon my Back, which I carry about with me in a Box, as only consisting of a Man a Woman, and an Horse. The two first are married, in which State the little Cavalier has so well acquitted himself, that his Lady is with Child. The big-bellied Woman, and her Husband, with their whimsical Palfry are so very light, that when they are put together into a Scale, an ordinary Man may weigh down the whole Family. The little Man is a Bully in his Nature, but when he grows cholerick, I confine him to his Box till his Wrath is over, by which Means I have hitherto prevented him from doing Mischief. His Horse is likewise very vicious, for which Reason I am forced to tie him close to his Manger with a Pack-thread. The Woman is a Coquet. She struts as much as it is possible for a Lady of two Foot high, and would ruin me in Silks, were not the Quantity that goes to a large Pin-cushion sufficient to make her a Gown and Petticoat. She told me the other Day, that she heard the Ladies wore coloured Hoods, and ordered me to get her one of the finest Blue. I am forced to comply with her Demands while she is in her present Condition, being very willing to have more of the same Breed. I do not know what she may produce me, but provided it be a *Show* I shall be very well satisfied. Such Novelties should not, I think, be concealed from the *British Spectator*; for which Reason I hope you will excuse this presumption in

> *Your most Dutiful,*
> *most Obedient,*
> *and most humble Servant,*

L   S. T.'

No. 272.
[STEELE.]   Friday, January 11.

> . . . *Longa est injuria, longae*
> *Ambages* . . .—Virg.

'*Mr.* SPECTATOR,

THE Occasion of this Letter is of so great Importance, and the Circumstances of it such, that I know you will but think it just to insert it, in Preference of all other Matters that can present themselves to your Consideration. I need not, after I have said this, tell you that I am in Love. The Circumstances of my Passion I shall let you understand as well as a disordered Mind will admit. That cursed Pickthank Mrs. *Jane*! Alass, I am railing at one to you by her Name as familiarly, as if you were acquainted with her as well as my self: But I will tell you all as fast as the alternate Interruptions of Love and Anger will give me Leave. There is a most agreeable young Woman in the World whom I am passionately in Love with, and from whom I have for some Space of Time received as great Marks of Favour as were fit for her to give, or me to desire. The successful Progress of the Affair of all others the most essential

towards a Man's Happiness, gave a new Life and Spirit not
only to my Behaviour and Discourse, but also a certain Grace
to all my Actions in the Commerce of Life, in all Things,
tho' never so remote from Love. You know the predominant
Passion spreads itself thro' all a Man's Transactions, and exalts
or depresses him according to the Nature of such Passion. But
alass, I have not yet begun my Story, and what is making
Sentences and Observations when a Man is pleading for his
Life? To begin then: This Lady has corresponded with me
under the Names of Love, she my *Belinda*, I her *Cleanthes*.
Tho' I am thus well got into the Account of my Affair, I cannot
keep in the Thread of it so much as to give you the Character
of Mrs. *Jane*, whom I will not hide under a borrowed Name;
but let you know that this Creature has been since I knew her
very handsome, (tho' I will not allow her even she *has been* for
the Future) and during the Time of her Bloom and Beauty was
so great a Tyrant to her Lovers, so overvalued her self and
under-rated all her Pretenders, that they have deserted her to
a Man; and she knows no Comfort but that common one to all
in her Condition, the Pleasure of interrupting the Amours of
others. It is impossible but you must have seen several of
these Volunteers in Malice, who pass their whole Time in the
most laborious Way of Life, in getting Intelligence, running
from Place to Place with new Whispers, without reaping any
other Benefit but the Hopes of making others as unhappy as
themselves. Mrs. *Jane* happened to be at a Place where I,
with many others well acquainted with my Passion for *Belinda*,
passed a *Christmas* Evening. There was among the rest a
young Lady so free in Mirth, so amiable in a just Reserve that
accompanied it, I wrong her to call it a Reserve, but there
appeared in her a Mirth or Chearfulness which was not a For-
bearance of more immoderate Joy, but the natural Appearance of all which could flow from a Mind possessed of an Habit
of Innocence and Purity. I must have utterly forgot *Belinda*
to have taken no Notice of one who was growing up to the same
womanly Virtues which shine to Perfection in her, had I not
distinguished one who seemed to promise to the World the
same Life and Conduct with my faithful and lovely *Belinda*.
When the Company broke up, the fine young Thing permitted
me to take Care of her Home; Mrs. *Jane* saw my particular
Regard to her, and was informed of my attending her to her
Father's House. She came early to *Belinda* the next Morning,
and asked her if Mrs. *Such-a-one* had been with her? No: If
Mr. *Such-a-one*'s Lady? No; Nor your Cousin *Such-a-one?*
No. Lord, says Mrs. *Jane*, what is the Friendship of Women
—— Nay they may well laugh at it. And did no one tell

you any Thing of the Behaviour of your Lover Mr. *What-d'ye call* last Night? But perhaps it is Nothing to you that he is to be married to young Mrs. —— on *Tuesday* next? *Belinda* was here ready to die with Rage and Jealousie. Then *Mrs. Jane* goes on: I have a young Kinsman who is Clerk to a great Conveyancer, who shall shew you the rough Draught of the Marriage-Settlement. The World says her Father gives him two thousand Pounds more than he could have with you. I went innocently to wait on *Belinda* as usual, but was not admitted; I writ to her, and my Letter was sent back unopened. Poor *Betty* her Maid, who was on my Side, has been here just now blubbering, and told me the whole Matter. She says she did not think I could be so base; and that she is now so odious to her Mistress for having so often spoke well of me, that she dare not mention me more. All our Hopes are placed in having these Circumstances fairly represented in the SPECTA-TOR, which *Betty* says she dare not but bring up as soon as it is brought in; and has promised when you have broke the Ice to own this was laid between us: And when I can come to an Hearing, the young Lady will support what we say by her Testimony, that I never saw her but that once in my whole Life. Dear Sir, do not omit this true Relation, nor think it too particular; for there are Crouds of forlorn Coquets who inter-mingle themselves with other Ladies, and contract Familiar-ities out of Malice, and with no other Design but to blast the Hopes of Lovers, the Expectation of Parents, and the Benevo-lence of Kindred. I doubt not but I shall be,

Sir,

Your most obliged
humble Servant,

CLEANTHES.'

'*Sir*,   *Will*'s Coffee-house, *Jan.* 10.

The other Day entering a Room adorned with the Fair-Sex, I offered, after the usual Manner, to each of them a Kiss; but one, more scornful than the rest, turned her Cheek. I did not think it proper to take any Notice of it till I had asked your Advice.

Your humble Servant,

E. S.'

The Correspondent is desired to say which Cheek the Offender turned to him.   T

No. 273.

[ADDISON.] Saturday, January 12.

. . . *Notandi sunt tibi mores.*—Hor.

HAVING examined the Action of *Paradise Lost*, let us in the next Place consider the Actors. This is *Aristotle*'s Method of considering; first the Fable, and secondly the Manners, or as we generally call them in *English*, the Fable and the Characters.

Homer has excelled all the heroic Poets that ever wrote, in the Multitude and Variety of his Characters. Every God that is admitted into his Poem, acts a Part which would have been suitable to no other Deity. His Princes are as much distinguished by their Manners as by their Dominions; and even those among them, whose Characters seem wholly made up of Courage, differ from one another as to the particular Kinds of Courage in which they excel. In short, there is scarce a Speech or Action in the *Iliad*, which the Reader may not ascribe to the Person that speaks or acts, without seeing his Name at the Head of it.

Homer does not only out-shine all other Poets in the Variety, but also in the Novelty of his Characters. He has introduced among his *Grecian* Princes a Person, who had lived thrice the Age of Man, and conversed with *Theseus, Hercules, Polyphemus,* and the first Race of Heroes. His principal Actor is the Son of a Goddess, not to mention the Off-spring of other Deities, who have likewise a Place in his Poem, and the venerable *Trojan* Prince who was the Father of so many Kings and Heroes. There is in these several Characters of *Homer*, a certain Dignity as well as Novelty, which adapts them in a more peculiar manner to the Nature of an heroic Poem. Tho', at the same Time, to give them the greater Variety, he has described a *Vulcan*, that is a Buffoon among his Gods, and a *Thersites* among his Mortals.

Virgil falls infinitely short of *Homer* in the Characters of his Poem, both as to their Variety and Novelty. *Aeneas* is indeed a perfect Character, but as for *Achates*, tho' he is stiled the Hero's Friend, he does nothing in the whole Poem which may deserve that Title. *Gyas, Mnesteus, Sergestus* and *Cloanthus*, are all of them Men of the same Stamp and Character,

Fortemque Gyan, fortemque Cloanthum : Virg.

There are indeed several natural Incidents in the Part of *Ascanius*; as that of *Dido* cannot be sufficiently admired. I do not see any Thing new or particular in *Turnus*. *Pallas* and *Evander* are remote Copies of *Hector* and *Priam*, as *Lausus* and *Mezentius* are almost Parallels to *Pallas* and *Evander*. The Characters of *Nisus* and *Eurialus* are beautiful, but common. We must not forget the Parts of *Sinon, Camilla,* and some few others, which are beautiful improvements on the Greek Poet. In short, there is neither that Variety nor Novelty in the Persons of the *Aeneid*, which we meet with in those of the *Iliad*.

If we look into the Characters of *Milton*, we shall find that he has introduced all the Variety his Poem was capable of receiving. The whole Species of Mankind was in two Persons at the Time to which the Subject of his Poem is confined. We have, however, four distinct Characters in these two Persons. We see Man and Woman in the highest Innocence and Perfection, and in the most abject State of Guilt and Infirmity. The two last Characters are, indeed, very common and obvious, but the two first are not only more magnificent, but more new than any Characters either in *Virgil* or *Homer*, or indeed in the whole Circle of Nature.

Milton was so sensible of this Defect in the Subject of his Poem, and of the few Characters it would afford him, that he has brought into it two Actors of a shadowy and fictitious Nature, in the Persons of Sin and Death, by which Means he has interwoven in the Body of his Fable a very beautiful and well invented Allegory. But notwithstanding the Fineness of this Allegory may atone for it in some Measure; I cannot think that Persons of such a chymerical Existence are proper Actors in an Epic Poem; because there is not that Measure of Probability annexed to them, which is requisite in Writings of this Kind, as I shall shew more at large hereafter.

Virgil has, indeed, admitted Fame as an Actress in the *Aeneid*, but the Part she acts is very short, and none of the most admired Circumstances in that Divine Work. We find in Mock-Heroic Poems, particularly in the *Dispensary* and the *Lutrin*, several allegorical Persons of this Nature, which are very beautiful in those Compositions, and may, perhaps, be used as an Argument, that the Authors of them were of Opinion, such Characters might have a Place in an Epic Work. For my own Part, I should be glad the Reader would think so, for the sake of the Poem I am now examining, and must further add, that if such empty unsubstantial Beings may be ever made Use of on this Occasion, there were never any more nicely imagined, and employed in more proper Actions, than those of which I am now speaking.

Another principal Actor in this Poem is the great Enemy of Mankind. The Part of *Ulysses* in Homer's *Odyssey* is very much admired by *Aristotle*, as perplexing that Fable with very agreeable Plots and Intricacies, not only by the many Adventures in his Voyage, and the Subtilty of his Behaviour, but by the various Concealments and Discoveries of his Person in several Parts of that Poem. But the crafty Being I have now mentioned, makes a much longer Voyage than *Ulysses*, puts in Practice many more Wiles and Stratagems, and hides himself under a greater Variety of Shapes and Appearances, all of which are severally detected, to the great Delight and Surprise of the Reader.

We may likewise observe with how much Art the Poet has varied several Characters of the Persons that speak in his infernal Assembly. On the contrary, how has he represented the whole Godhead exerting it self towards Man in its full Benevolence under the Three-fold Distinction of a Creator, a Redeemer and a Comforter!

Nor must we omit the Person of *Raphael*, who amidst his Tenderness and Friendship for Man, shews such a Dignity and Condescention in all his Speech and Behaviour, as are suitable to a Superior Nature. The Angels are indeed as much diversified in *Milton*, and distinguished by their proper Parts, as the Gods are in *Homer* or *Virgil*. The Reader will find nothing ascribed to *Uriel*, *Gabriel*, *Michael* or *Raphael*, which is not in a particular manner suitable to their respective Characters.

There is another Circumstance in the principal Actors of the *Iliad* and *Aeneid*, which gives a peculiar Beauty to those two Poems, and was therefore contrived with very great Judgment. I mean the Authors having chosen for their Heroes Persons who were so nearly related to the People for whom they wrote. *Achilles* was a *Greek*, and *Aeneas* the remote Founder of *Rome*. By this means their Countrymen (whom they principally proposed to themselves for their Readers) were particularly attentive to all the Parts of their Story, and sympathized with their Heroes in all their Adventures. A *Roman* could not but rejoice in the Escapes, Successes and Victories of *Aeneas*, and be grieved at any Defeats, Misfortunes or Disappointments that befel him; as a *Greek* must have had the same Regard for *Achilles*. And it is plain, that each of those Poems have lost this great Advantage, among those Readers to whom their Heroes are as Strangers, or indifferent Persons.

Milton's Poem is admirable in this respect, since it is impossible for any of its Readers, whatever Nation, Country or People he may belong to, not to be related to the Persons who are the principal Actors in it; but what is still infinitely more to its Advantage, the principal Actors in this Poem are not only our Progenitors, but our Representatives. We have an actual Interest in every Thing they do, and no less than our utmost Happiness is concerned, and lies at Stake in all their Behaviour.

I shall subjoyn as a Corollary to the foregoing Remark, an admirable Observation out of *Aristotle*, which hath been very much misrepresented in the Quotations of some modern Criticks. 'If a Man of perfect and consummate Virtue falls into a Misfortune, it raises our Pity, but not our Terror, because we do not fear that it may be our own Case, who do not resemble the Suffering Person.' But as that great Philosopher adds, 'If we see a Man of Virtues mixt with Infirmities, fall into Misfortune, it does not only raise our Pity but our Terror; because we are afraid that the like Misfortunes may happen to our selves, who resemble the Character of the Suffering Person.'

I shall take another Opportunity to observe, that a Person of an absolute and consummate Virtue should never be introduced in Tragedy, and shall only remark in this Place, that the foregoing Observation of *Aristotle*, tho' it may be true in other Occasions, does not hold in this; because in the present Case, though the Persons who fall into Misfortune are of the most perfect and consummate Virtue, it is not to be considered as what may possibly be, but what actually is our own Case; since we are embark'd with them on the same Bottom, and must be Partakers of their Happiness or Misery.

In this, and some other very few Instances, *Aristotle*'s Rules for Epic Poetry (which he had drawn from his Reflections upon *Homer*) cannot be supposed to quadrate exactly with the heroic Poems which have been made since his Time; as it is plain his Rules would have been still more perfect, could he have perused the *Aeneid* which was made some hundred Years after his Death.

In my next I shall go through other Parts of *Milton*'s Poem; and hope that what I shall there advance, as well as what I have already written, will not only serve as a Comment upon *Milton*, but upon *Aristotle*. L

No. 274.
[STEELE.]   Monday, January 14.

Audire est operae pretium procedere recte
Qui moechis non vultis. . . .—Hor.

I HAVE upon several Occasions (that have occurred since I first took into my Thoughts the present State of Fornication) weighed with my self, in Behalf of guilty Females, the Impulses of Flesh and Blood, together with the Arts and Gallantries of crafty Men; and reflect with some Scorn, that most Part of what we in our Youth think gay and polite, is nothing else but an Habit of indulging a Pruriency that Way. It will cost some Labour to bring People to so lively a Sense of this, as to recover the manly Modesty in the Behaviour of my Men Readers, and the bashful Grace in the Faces of my Women: But in all Cases which come into Debate, there are certain Things previously to be done before we can have a true Light into the subject Matter; therefore it will, in the first Place, be necessary to consider the impotent Wenchers and industrious Haggs who are supplied with, and are constantly supplying new Sacrifices to the Devil of Lust. You are to know then, if you are so happy as not to know it already, that the great Havock which is made in the Habitations of Beauty and Innocence, is committed by such as can only lay waste and not enjoy the Soil. When you observe the present State of Vice and Vertue, the Offenders are such as one would think should have no Impulse to what they are pursuing; as in Business, you see sometimes Fools pretend to be Knaves, so in Pleasure, you will find old Men set up for Wenchers. This latter Sort of Men are the great Basis and Fund of Iniquity in the Kind we are speaking of: You shall have an old rich Man often receive Scrawls from the several Quarters of the Town, with Descriptions of the new Wares in their Hands, if he will please to send Word when he will be waited on. This Interview is contrived, and the Innocent is brought to such Indecencies as from Time to Time banish Shame and raise Desire. With these Preparatives the Haggs break their Wards by little and little, till they are brought to lose all Apprehensions of what shall befal them in the Possession of younger Men. It is a common Postscript of an Hagg to a young Fellow whom she invites to a new Woman, *She has, I assure you, seen none but old Mr. Such-a-one.* It pleases the old Fellow that the Nymph is brought to him unadorned, and from his Bounty she is accommodated with enough to dress her for other Lovers. This is the most ordinary Method of bringing Beauty and Poverty into the Possession of the Town: But the particular Cases of kind Keepers, skilful Pimps, and all others who drive a separate Trade, and are not in the general Society or Commerce of Sin, will require distinct Consideration. At the same Time that we are thus severe on the Abandoned, we are to represent the Case of others with that Mitigation as the Circumstances demand. Calling Names does no Good; to speak worse of any Thing than it deserves, does only take off from the Credit of the Accuser, and has implicitly the Force of an Apology in the Behalf of the Person accused. We shall therefore, according as the Circumstances differ, vary our Appellations of these Criminals:

Those who offend only against themselves, and are not Scandals to Society, but out of Deference to the sober Part of the World, have so much Good left in them as to be ashamed, must not be huddled in the common Word due to the worst of Women; but Regard is to be had to their Circumstances when they fell, to the uneasy Perplexity under which they lived under senseless and severe Parents, to the Importunity of Poverty, to the Violence of a Passion in its Beginning well grounded, and all other Alleviations which make unhappy Women resign the Characteristick of their Sex, Modesty. To do otherwise than thus, would be to act like a pedantick Stoick, who thinks all Crimes alike, and not like an impartial SPECTATOR, who looks upon them with all the Circumstances that diminish or enhance the Guilt. I am in Hopes if this Subject be well pursued, Women will hereafter from their Infancy be treated with an Eye to their future State in the World; and not have their Tempers made too untractable from an improper Sourness or Pride, or too complying from Familiarity or Forwardness contracted at their own Houses. After these Hints on this Subject, I shall end this Paper with the following genuine Letter; and desire all who think they may be concerned in future Speculations on this Subject, to send in what they have to say for themselves for some Incidents in their Lives, in order to have proper Allowances made for their Conduct.

'*Mr.* SPECTATOR,   *January* 5, 1711.

The Subject of your Yesterday's Paper is of so great Importance, and the thorough handling of it may be so very useful to the Preservation of many an innocent young Creature, that I think every one is obliged to furnish you with what Lights he can to expose the pernicious Arts and Practices of those unnatural Women call'd Bawds. In order to this the enclosed is sent you, which is *verbatim* the Copy of a Letter written by a Bawd of Figure in this Town to a noble Lord. I have concealed the Names of both, my Intention being not to expose the Persons but the Thing.

    I am,

      Sir,

        Your humble Servant.'

'*My Lord.*

I having a great Esteem for your Honour, and a better Opinion of you than of any of the Quality, makes me acquaint you of an Affair that I hope will oblige you to know. I have a Niece that came to Town about a Fortnight ago. Her Parents being lately dead she came to me, expecting to a found me in

so good a Condition as to a set her up in a Milliner's Shop.
Her Father gave fourscore Pound with her for five Years:
Her Time is out, and she is not Sixteen; as pretty a black
Gentlewoman as ever you saw, a little Woman, which I know
your Lordship likes; well shaped, and as fine a Complection for
Red and White as ever I saw; I doubt not but your Lordship
will be of the same Opinion. She designs to go down about a
Month hence except I can provide for her, which I cannot at
present. Her Father was one with whom all he had died with
him, so there is four Children left destitute; so if your Lordship thinks fit to make an Appointment, where I shall wait on
you with my Niece, by a Line or two, I stay for your Answer;
for I have no Place fitted up since I left my House, fit to
entertain your Honour. I told her she should go with me to
see a Gentleman a very good Friend of mine; so I desire you
to take no Notice of my Letter, by Reason she is ignorant of
the Ways of the Town. My Lord, I desire if you meet us to
come alone; for upon my Word and Honour you are the first
that ever I mentioned her to. So I remain,

> *Your Lordship's*
>> *Most humble Servant to command.*

I beg of you to burn it when you 've read it.'
T

No. 275.
[ADDISON.]   Tuesday, January 15.

. . . *tribus Anticyris caput insanabile.* . . .—Hor.

I was Yesterday engaged in an Assembly of Virtuosos, where
one of them produced many curious Observations, which he
had lately made in the Anatomy of an humane Body. Another
of the Company communicated to us several wonderful Discoveries, which he had also made on the same Subject, by the
Help of very fine Glasses. This gave Birth to a great Variety of
uncommon Remarks, and furnished Discourse for the remaining Part of the Day.

The different Opinions which were started on this Occasion,
presented to my Imagination so many new Ideas, that by
mixing with those which were already there, they employed
my Fancy all the last Night, and composed a very wild
extravagant Dream.

I was invited, methought, to the Dissection of a *Beau's
Head*, and of a *Coquet's Heart*, which were both of them laid

on a Table before us. An imaginary Operator opened the first with a great deal of Nicety, which, upon a cursory and superficial View, appeared like the Head of another Man; but, upon applying our Glasses to it, we made a very odd Discovery, namely, that what we looked upon as Brains, were not such in Reality, but an Heap of strange Materials wound up in that Shape and Texture, and packed together with wonderful Art in the several Cavities of the Skull. For, as *Homer* tells us, that the Blood of the Gods is not real Blood, but only Something like it; so we found that the Brain of a Beau is not real Brain, but only Something like it.

The *Pineal Gland*, which many of our Modern Philosophers suppose to be the Seat of the Soul, smelt very strong of Essence and Orange-Flower Water, and was encompas'd with a Kind of horny Substance, cut into a thousand little Faces or Mirrours, which were imperceptible to the naked Eye; insomuch that the Soul, if there had been any here, must have been always taken up in contemplating her own Beauties.

We observed a large *Antrum* or Cavity in the *Sinciput,* that was filled with Ribbons, Lace and Embroidery, wrought together in a most curious Piece of Network, the Parts of which were likewise imperceptible to the naked Eye. Another of these *Antrums* or Cavities was stuffed with invisible Billet-doux, Love-Letters, pricked Dances, and other Trumpery of the same Nature. In another we found a Kind of Powder, which set the whole Company a Sneezing, and by the Scent discovered it self to be right *Spanish.* The several other Cells were stored with Commodities of the same Kind, of which it would be tedious to give the Reader an exact Inventory.

There was a large Cavity on each Side of the Head, which I must not omit. That on the right Side was filled with Fictions, Flatteries and Falsehoods, Vows, Promises and Protestations; that on the left with Oaths and Imprecations. There issued out a *Duct* from each of these Cells, which ran into the Root of the Tongue, where both joined together, and passed forward in one common *Duct* to the Tip of it. We discovered several little Roads or Canals running from the Ear into the Brain, and took particular Care to trace them out through their several Passages. One of them extended it self to a Bundle of Sonnets and little Musical Instruments. Others ended in several Bladders which were filled either with Wind or Froth. But the large Canal entered into a great Cavity of the Skull, from whence there went another Canal into the Tongue. This great Cavity was filled with a Kind of spongy Substance, which the *French* Anatomists call *Galimatias*, and the *English* Nonsense.

The Skins of the Forehead were extreamly tough and thick, and, what very much surpris'd us, had not in them any single Blood-Vessel that we were able to discover, either with or without our Glasses; from whence we concluded, that the Party when alive must have been entirely deprived of the Faculty of Blushing.

The *Os Cribriforme* was exceedingly stuffed, and in some Places damaged with Snuff. We could not but take Notice in particular of that small Muscle, which is not often discovered in Dissections, and draws the Nose upwards, when it expresses the Contempt which the Owner of it has, upon seeing any Thing he does not like, or fearing any Thing he does not understand. I need not tell my learned Reader, this is that Muscle which performs the Motion so often mentioned by the *Latin* Poets, when they talk of a Man's cocking his Nose, or playing the Rhinoceros.

We did not find any Thing very remarkable in the Eye, saving only, that the *Musculi Amatorii*, or as we may translate it into *English*, the *Ogling Muscles*, were very much worn and decayed with Use; whereas on the contrary, the *Elevator* or the Muscle which turns the Eye towards Heaven, did not appear to have been used at all.

I have only mentioned in this Dissection such new Discoveries as we were able to make, and have not taken any Notice of those Parts which are to be met with in common Heads. As for the Skull, the Face, and indeed the whole outward Shape and Figure of the Head, we could not discover any Difference from what we observe in the Heads of other Men. We were informed, that the Person to whom this Head belonged, had passed for *a Man* above five and thirty Years; during which Time he eat and drank like other People, dressed well, talked loud, laught frequently, and on particular Occasions had acquitted himself tolerably at a Ball or an Assembly, to which one of the Company added, that a certain Knot of Ladies took him for a Wit. He was cut off in the Flower of his Age, by the Blow of a Paring-Shovel, having been surprised by an eminent Citizen, as he was tendring some Civilities to his Wife.

When we had thoroughly examin'd this Head with all its Apartments, and its several Kinds of Furniture, we put up the Brain, such as it was, into its proper Place, and laid it aside under a broad Piece of Scarlet Cloth, in order to be *prepared*, and kept in a great Repository of Dissections, our Operator telling us that the Preparation would not be so difficult as that of another Brain, for that he had observed several of the little Pipes and Tubes which ran through the Brain were already filled with a Kind of mercurial Substance, which he looked upon to be true Quick Silver.

He applied himself in the next Place to the *Coquet's Heart*, which he likewise laid open with great Dexterity. There occurred to us many Particularities in this Dissection; but being unwilling to burden my Reader's Memory too much, I shall reserve this Subject for the Speculation of another Day.

L

No. 276.

[STEELE.] Wednesday, January 16.

Errori nomen virtus posuisset honestum.—Hor.

'*Mr.* SPECTATOR,

I HOPE you have Philosophy enough to be capable of bearing the Mention of your Faults. Your Papers which regard the fallen Part of the fair Sex, are, I think, written with an Indelicacy which makes them unworthy to be inserted in the Writings of a Moralist who knows the World. I cannot allow that you are at Liberty to observe upon the Actions of Mankind with the Freedom which you seem to resolve upon; at least if you do so, you should take along with you the Distinction of Manners of the World, according to the Quality and Way of Life of the Persons concerned. A Man of Breeding speaks of even Misfortune among Ladies, without giving it the most terrible Aspect it can bear; and this Tenderness towards them, is much more to be preserved when you speak of Vices. All Mankind are so far related, that Care is to be taken, in Things to which all are liable, you do not mention what concerns one in Terms which shall disgust another. Thus to tell a rich Man of the Indigence of a Kinsman of his, or abruptly inform a virtuous Woman of the Lapse of one who 'till then was in the same Degree of Esteem with her self, is in a Kind involving each of them in some Participation of those Disadvantages. It is therefore expected from every Writer, to treat his Argument in such a Manner, as is most proper to entertain the Sort of Readers to whom his Discourse is directed. It is not necessary, when you write to the Tea-Table, that you should draw Vices which carry all the Horrour of Shame and Contempt: If you paint an impertinent Self-love, an artful Glance, an assumed Complection, you say all which you ought to suppose they can possibly be guilty of. When you talk with this Limitation, you behave your self so that you may expect others in Conversation may second your Raillery; but when you do it in a Stile which every Body else forbears in Respect to their

Quality, they have an easy Remedy in forbearing to read you, and hearing no more of their Faults.   A Man that is now and then guilty of an Intemperance, is not to be called a Drunkard; but the Rule of polite Raillery, is to speak of a Man's Faults as if you loved him.   Of this Nature is what was said by *Caesar*: When one was railing with an uncourtly Vehemence, and broke out, What must we call him who was taken in an Intrigue with another Man's Wife? *Caesar* answered very gravely, *A Careless Fellow.*   This was at once a Reprimand for speaking of a Crime which in those Days had not the Abhorrence attending it as it ought, as well as an Intimation that all intemperate Behaviour before Superiours loses its Aim, by accusing in a Method unfit for the Audience.   A Word to the Wise.   All I mean here to say to you is, That the most free Person of Quality can go no further than being an unkind Woman; and you should never say of a Man of Figure worse, than that he knows the World.

I am,

Sir,

Your most humble Servant,

Francis Courtly.'

'*Mr.* SPECTATOR,

I am a Woman of an unspotted Reputation, and know Nothing I have ever done which should encourage such Insolence; but here was one the other Day, and he was dressed like a Gentleman too, who took Liberty to Name the Words lusty Fellow in my Presence.   I doubt not but you will resent it in Behalf of,

Sir,

Your humble Servant,

Celia.'

'*Mr.* SPECTATOR,

You lately put out a dreadful Paper, wherein you promise a full Account of the State of criminal Love; and call all the Fair who have transgressed in that Kind by one very rude Name which I do not care to repeat: But I Desire to know of you whether I am or I am not one of those?   My Case is as follows.   I am kept by an old Batchelour, who took me so young that I knew not how he came by me: He is a Bencher of one of the Inns of Court, a very gay healthy old Man; which is a very lucky Thing for him, who has been, he tells me, a Scowrer, a Scamperer, a Breaker of Windows, and Invader of Constables, in the Days of Yore, when all Dominion ended with the Day, and Males and Females met helter-skelter, and the Scowrers drove before them all who pretended to keep up

Order or Rule to the Interruption of Love and Honour. This is his Way of Talk, for he is very gay when he visits me; but as his former Knowledge of the Town has alarmed him into an invincible Jealousy, he keeps me in a Pair of Slippers, neat Boddice, warm Petticoats, and my own Hair woven in Ringletts, after a Manner, he says, he remembers. I am not Mistress of one Farthing of Money, but have all Necessaries provided for me, under the Guard of one who procured for him while he had any Desires to gratify. I know Nothing of a Wench's Life, but the Reputation of it: I have a natural Voice, and a pretty untaught Step in Dancing. His Manner is to bring an old Fellow who has been his Servant from his Youth, and is grey-headed: This Man makes on the Violin a certain Jiggish Noise, to which I dance, and when that is over I sing to him some loose Air that has more Wantonness than Musick in it. You must have seen a strange windowed House near *Hide-Park*, which is so built that no one can look out of any of the Apartments; my Rooms are after that Manner, and I never see Man, Woman or Child but in Company with the two Persons abovementioned. He sends me in all the Books, Pamphlets, Plays, Operas and Songs that come out; and his utmost Delight in me, as a Woman, is to talk over all his old Amours in my Presence, to play with my Neck, say *the Time was*, give me a Kiss, and bid me be sure to follow the Directions of my Guardian (the abovementioned Lady), and I shall never want. The Truth of my Case is, I suppose, that I was educated for a Purpose he did not know he should be unfit for when I came to Years. Now, Sir, what I ask of you, as a Casuist, is to tell me how far in these Circumstances I am innocent, though submissive; he guilty, though impotent?

> *I am,*
>> *Sir,*
>>> *Your constant Reader,*
>>>> PUCELLA.'

'*To the Man called the* SPECTATOR.

Friend,

Forasmuch as at the Birth of thy Labour, thou didst promise upon thy Word, that letting alone the Vanities that do abound, thou wouldest only endeavour to strengthen the crooked Morals of this our *Babylon*, I gave Credit to thy fair Speeches, and admitted one of thy Papers, every Day, save *Sunday*, into my House; for the Edification of my Daughter *Tabitha*, and to the End that *Susanna* the Wife of my Bosom might profit thereby. But alas! my Friend, I find that thou art a Liar, and that the

*L 165

Truth is not in thee; else why didst thou in a Paper which thou didst lately put forth, make Mention of those vain Coverings for the Heads of our Females, which thou lovest to liken unto Tulips, and which are lately sprung up among us? Nay, why didst thou make Mention of them in such a Seeming, as if thou didst approve the Invention, insomuch that my Daughter *Tabitha* beginneth to wax wanton, and to lust after these foolish Vanities? Surely thou dost see with the Eyes of the Flesh. Verily therefore, unless thou dost speedily amend and leave off following thine own Imaginations, I will leave off thee.

Thy Friend as hereafter thou dost demean thy self,

T   Hezekiah Broadbrim.'

No. 277.
[BUDGELL.]   Thursday, January 17.

　. . . *Fas est & ab hoste doceri.*—Ovid.

I PRESUME I need not inform the polite Part of my Readers, that before our Correspondence with *France* was unhappily interrupted by the War, our Ladies had all their Fashions from thence; which the Milliners took Care to furnish them with by Means of a jointed Baby, that came regularly over, once a Month, habited after the Manner of the most eminent Toasts in *Paris*.

I am credibly informed that even in the hottest Time of the War, the Sex made several Efforts, and raised large Contributions towards the Importation of this wooden *Mademoiselle*.

Whether the Vessel they set out was lost or taken, or whether its Cargo was seized on by the Officers of the Custom-house, as a Piece of Contraband Goods, I have not yet been able to learn; it is, however, certain, their first Attempts were without Success, to the no small Disappointment of our whole Female World; but as their Constancy and Application, in a Matter of so great Importance, can never be sufficiently commended, I am glad to find, that in Spight of all Opposition, they have at length carried their Point, of which I received Advice by the two following Letters.

　'*Mr.* SPECTATOR,

I am so great a Lover of whatever is *French*, that I lately discarded an humble Admirer, because he neither spoke that Tongue, nor drank Claret. I have long bewailed, in Secret, the Calamities of my Sex during the War, in all which Time we have laboured under the insupportable Inventions of *English* Tire-women, who, tho' they sometimes copy indifferently well, can never compose with that *Gout* they do in *France*.

I was almost in Despair of ever more seeing a Model from that dear Country, when last *Sunday* I overheard a Lady, in the next Pew to me, whisper another, that at the *Seven Stars* in *King-Street, Covent-garden*, there was a *Mademoiselle* compleatly dressed just come from *Paris*.

I was in the utmost Impatience during the remaining Part of the Service, and as soon as ever it was over, having learnt the Millener's *Addresse*, I went directly to her House in *King-street*, but was told that the *French* Lady was at a Person of Quality's in *Pall-Mall*, and would not be back again till very late that Night. I was therefore obliged to renew my Visit early this Morning, and had then a full View of the dear Moppet from Head to Foot.

You cannot imagine, worthy Sir, how ridiculously I find we have all been trussed up during the War, and how infinitely the *French* Dress excells ours.

The Mantua has no Leads in the Sleeves, and I hope we are not lighter than the *French* Ladies, so as to want that Kind of Ballast; the Petticoat has no Whalebone, but sits with an Air altogether gallant and *dégagée*; the *Coiffeure* is inexpressibly pretty, and in short, the whole dress has a thousand Beauties in it, which I would not have as yet made too publick.

I thought fit, however, to give you this Notice, that you may not be surprized at my appearing *à la mode de Paris* on the next Birth-Night.

> *I am,*
>> *Sir,*
>>> *Your humble Servant,*
>>>> Teraminta.'

Within an Hour after I had read this Letter, I received another from the Owner of the Puppet.

' *Sir,*

On *Saturday* last, being the 12th Instant, there arrived at my House in *King-street, Covent-garden*, a *French* Baby for the Year 1712. I have taken the utmost Care to have her dressed by the most celebrated Tyre-women and Mantua-makers in *Paris*, and do not find that I have any Reason to be sorry for the Expence I have been at in her Cloaths and Importation: However, as I know no Person who is so good a Judge of Dress, as your self, if you please to call at my House in your Way to the City, and take a View of her, I promise to amend whatever you shall disapprove in your next Paper, before I admit her as a Pattern to the Publick.

> *I am,*
>> *Sir,*
>>> *Your most humble Admirer,*
>>> *and most obedient Servant,*
>>>> Betty Cross-stitch.'

As I am willing to do any Thing in Reason for the Service of my Country-women, and had much rather prevent Faults than find them, I went last Night to the House of the above-mentioned Mrs. *Cross-stitch*. As soon as I enter'd, the Maid of the Shop, who, I suppose, was prepared for my coming, without asking me any Questions introduced me to the little Damsel, and ran away to call her Mistress.

The Puppet was dressed in a Cherry-coloured Gown and Petticoat, with a short working Apron over it, which discovered her Shape to the most Advantage. Her Hair was cut and divided very prettily, with several Ribbons stuck up and down in it. The Millener assured me, that her Complexion was such as was worn by all the Ladies of the best Fashion in *Paris*. Her Head was extreamly high, on which Subject having long since declared my Sentiments, I shall say Nothing more to it at present. I was also offended at a small Patch she wore on her Breast, which I cannot suppose is placed there with any good Design.

Her Necklace was of an immoderate Length, being tied before in such a Manner, that the two Ends hung down to her Girdle; but whether these supply the Place of Kissing-Strings in our Enemy's Country, and whether our *British* Ladies have any Occasion for them, I shall leave to their serious Consideration.

After having observed the Particulars of her Dress, as I was taking a View of it all together, the Shop-Maid, who is a pert Wench, told me that *Mademoiselle* had something very curious in the tying of her Garters; but as I pay a due Respect even to a Pair of Sticks when they are under Petticoats, I did not examine into that Particular.

Upon the whole I was well enough pleased with the Appearance of this gay Lady, and the more so, because she was not talkative, a Quality very rarely to be met with in the rest of her Country-women.

As I was taking my Leave, the Millener farther informed me, that with the Assistance of a Watch-maker, who was her Neighbour, and the ingenious Mr. *Powell*, she had also contrived another Puppet, which by the Help of several little Springs to be wound up within it, could move all its Limbs, and that she had sent it over to her Correspondent in *Paris*, to be taught the various Leanings and Bendings of the Head, the Risings of the Bosome, the Curtesy and Recovery, the genteel Trip, and the agreeable Jet, as they are now practised at the Court of *France*.

She added, that she hoped she might depend upon having my Encouragement as soon as it arrived; but as this was a Petition of too great Importance to be answered *extempore*, I left her without a Reply, and made the best of my Way to WILL HONEYCOMB's Lodgings, without whose Advice I never communicate any Thing to the Publick of this Nature.

X

No. 278.
[STEELE.]   Friday, January 18.

. . . *Sermones ego mallem*
Repentes per humum . . .—Hor.

'*Mr.* SPECTATOR,

Sir,

YOUR having done considerable Services in this great City by rectifying the Disorders of Families, and several Wives having preferr'd your Advice and Directions to those of their Husbands, emboldens me to apply to you at this Time. I am a Shop-keeper, and tho' but a young Man, I find by Experience that nothing but the utmost Diligence both of Husband and Wife (among trading People) can keep Affairs in any tolerable Order. My Wife at the Beginning of our Establishment shewed her self very assisting to me in my Business as much as could lie in her Way, and I have Reason to believe 'twas with her Inclination: But of late she has got acquainted with a School-man, who values himself for his great Knowledge in the Greek Tongue. He entertains her frequently in the Shop with Discourses of the Beauties and Excellencies of that Language, and repeats to her several Passages out of the Greek Poets, wherein he tells her there is unspeakable Harmony and agreeable Sounds that all other Languages are wholly unacquainted with. He has so infatuated her with his Jargon, that instead of using her former Diligence in the Shop, she now neglects the Affairs of the House, and is wholly taken up with her Tutor in Learning by Heart Scraps of Greek, which she vents upon all Occasions.

She told me some Days ago, that whereas I use some Latin Inscriptions in my Shop, she advised me with a great deal of Concern to have them changed into Greek; it being a Language less understood, would be more conformable to the Mistery of my Profession; that our good Friend would be assisting to us in this Work; and that a certain Faculty of Gentlemen would find themselves so much obliged to me, that they would infallibly make my Fortune: In short, her frequent Importunities upon this and other Impertinencies of the like Nature make me very uneasy; and if your Remonstrances have no more Effect upon her than mine, I am afraid I shall be obliged to ruin my self to procure her a Settlement at *Oxford* with her Tutor, for she's already too mad for *Bedlam.* Now, Sir, you see the Danger my Family is exposed to, and the Likelihood of my Wife's becoming both troublesome and useless, unless her reading her self, in your Paper, may make her reflect. She is so very learned, that I cannot pretend by Word of Mouth to argue with her: She laughed out at your ending a Paper in Greek, and said 'twas a Hint to Women of Literature, and very civil not to translate it to expose them to the Vulgar. You see how it is with,

Sir,

Your humble Servant.'

'*Mr.* Spectator,

If you have that Humanity and Compassion in your Nature that you take such Pains to make one think you have, you will not deny your Advice to a distressed Damsel, who intends to be determined by your Judgment in a Matter of great Importance to her. You must know then, There is an agreeable young Fellow, to whose Person, Wit, and Humour no Body makes any Objection, that pretends to have been long in Love with me. To this I must add, (whether it proceeds from the Vanity of my Nature, or the seeming Sincerity of my Lover, I won't pretend to say) that I verily believe he has a real Value for me; which, if true, you'll allow may justly augment his Merit with his Mistress. In short, I am so sensible of his good Qualities, and what I owe to his Passion, that I think I could sooner resolve to give up my Liberty to him than any Body else, were there not an Objection to be made to his Fortunes, in regard they don't answer the utmost mine may expect, and are not sufficient to secure me from undergoing the reproachful Phrase so commonly used, That she has play'd the Fool. Now, tho' I am one of those few who heartily despise Equipage, Diamonds, and a Coxcomb; yet since such opposite Notions from mine prevail in the World, even amongst the best, and such as are esteem'd the most prudent People, I can't find in my Heart to resolve upon incurring the Censure of those wise Folks, which I am conscious I shall do, if, when I enter into a married State, I discover a Thought beyond that of equalling, if not advancing my Fortunes. Under this Difficulty I now labour, not being in the least determin'd whether I shall be govern'd by the vain World, and the frequent Examples I meet with, or hearken to the Voice of my Lover, and the Motions I find in my Heart in favour of him. Sir, Your Opinion and Advice in this Affair, is the only Thing I know can turn the Ballance; and which I earnestly intreat I may receive soon; for, till I have your Thoughts upon it, I am engag'd not to give my Swain a final Discharge.

Besides the particular Obligation you will lay on me, by giving this Subject Room in one of your Papers, 'tis possible it may be of Use to some others of my Sex, who will be as grateful for the Favour as

Sir,

Your humble Servant,

Florinda.

P. S. *To tell you the Truth I am married to Him already, but pray something to justify me.'*

'Mr. SPECTATOR,

You will forgive Us Professors of Musick if We make a second Application to You, in Order to promote our Design of exhibiting Entertainments of Musick in *York-Buildings*. It is industriously insinuated, that Our Intention is to destroy Operas in General; but we beg of you to insert this plain Explanation of our selves in your Paper. Our Purpose is only to improve our Circumstances, by improving the Art which we profess. We see it utterly destroyed at present; and as we were the Persons who introduced Operas, we think it a groundless Imputation that we should set up against the Opera in it self. What we pretend to assert is, That the Songs of different Authors injudiciously put together, and a foreign Thing now performed amongst us, has put Musick it self to a stand; insomuch that the Ears of the People cannot now be entertained with any Thing but what has an impertinent Gayety, without any just Spirit; or a Languishment of Notes, without any Passion or common Sense. We hope those Persons of Sense and Quality who have done us the Honour to subscribe, will not be ashamed of their Patronage towards us, and not receive Impressions that patronising us is being for or against the Opera, but truly promoting their own Diversions in a more just and elegant Manner than has been hitherto performed.

We are,

Sir,

Your most humble Servants.

Thomas Clayton.
Nicolino Haym.
Charles Dieupart.

There will be no Performances in York-Buildings, *till after that of the Subscription.'* T

No. 279.

[ADDISON.]   Saturday, January 19.

Reddere personae scit convenientia cuique.—Hor.

WE have already taken a general Survey of the Fable and Characters in *Milton's Paradise Lost*: The Parts which remain to be considered, according to *Aristotle's* Method, are the *Sentiments* and the *Language*. Before I enter upon the first of these, I must advertise my Reader, that it is my Design as soon as I have finished my general Reflections on these four several Heads, to give particular Instances out of the Poem which is now before us of Beauties and Imperfections which may be observed under each of them, as also of such other Particulars as may not properly fall under any of them. This I thought fit to premise, that the Reader may not judge too hastily of this Piece of Criticism, or look upon it as Imperfect, before he has seen the whole Extent of it.

The Sentiments in all Epic Poems are the Thoughts and Behaviour which the Author ascribes to the Persons whom he introduces, and are *just* when they are conformable to the Characters of the several Persons. The Sentiments have likewise a Relation to *Things* as well as *Persons*, and are then perfect when they are such as are adapted to the Subject. If in either of these Cases the Poet argues, or explains, magnifies or diminishes, raises Love or Hatred, Pity or Terror, or any other Passion, we ought to consider whether the Sentiments he makes Use of are proper for their Ends. *Homer* is censured by the Criticks for his Defect as to this Particular in several Parts of the *Iliad* and *Odyssey*, tho' at the same Time those who have treated this great Poet with Candour, have attributed this Defect to the Times in which he lived. It was the Fault of the Age, and not of *Homer*, if there wants that Delicacy in some of his Sentiments, which appears in the Works of Men of a much inferior Genius. Besides, if there are Blemishes in any particular Thoughts, there is an infinite Beauty in the greatest Part of them. In short, if there are many Poets who would not have fallen into the Meanness of some of his Sentiments, there are none who could have risen up to the Greatness of others. *Virgil* has excelled all others in the Propriety of his Sentiments. *Milton* shines likewise very much in this Particular: Nor must we omit one Consideration which adds to his Honour and Reputation. *Homer* and *Virgil* introduced Persons whose Characters are commonly known among Men, and such as are to be met with either in History, or in ordinary Conversation. *Milton*'s Characters, most of them, lie out of Nature, and were to be formed purely by his own Invention. It shews a greater Genius in *Shakespear* to have drawn his *Calyban*, than his *Hotspur* or *Julius Caesar*: The one was to be supplied out of his own Imagination, whereas the other might have been formed upon Tradition, History and Observation. It was much easier therefore for *Homer* to find proper Sentiments for an Assembly of *Grecian* Generals, than for *Milton* to diversifie his infernal Council with proper Characters, and inspire them with a Variety of Sentiments. The Loves of *Dido* and *Aeneas* are only Copies of what has passed between other Persons. *Adam* and *Eve*, before the Fall, are a different Species from that of Mankind, who are descended from them; and none but a Poet of the most unbounded Invention, and the most exquisite Judgment, cou'd have filled their Conversation and Behaviour with such beautiful Circumstances during their State of Innocence.

Nor is it sufficient for an Epic Poem to be filled with such Thoughts as are *natural*, unless it abound also with such as are *sublime*. *Virgil* in this Particular falls short of *Homer*. He has not indeed so many Thoughts that are low and vulgar; but at the same Time has not so many Thoughts that are sublime and noble. The Truth of it is, *Virgil* seldom rises into very astonishing Sentiments, where he is not fired by the *Iliad*. He every where charms and pleases us by the Force of his own Genius; but seldom elevates and transports us where he does not fetch his Hints from *Homer*.

Milton's chief Talent, and indeed his distinguishing Excellence, lies in the Sublimity of his Thoughts. There are others of the Moderns who rival him in every other Part of Poetry; but in the Greatness of his Sentiments he triumphs over all the Poets both Modern and Ancient, *Homer* only excepted. It is impossible for the Imagination of Man, to distend it self with greater Ideas, than those which he has laid together in his first,

second, and tenth Books. The Seventh, which describes the
Creation of the World, is likewise wonderfully sublime, tho' not
so apt to stir up Emotion in the Mind of the Reader, nor consequently so perfect in the Epic Way of Writing, because it is
filled with less Action. Let the Reader compare what *Longinus*
has observed on several Passages in *Homer*, and he will find
Parallels for most of them in the *Paradise Lost*.

From what has been said we may infer, that as there are
two Kinds of Sentiments, the Natural and the Sublime, which
are always to be pursued in an heroick Poem, there are also two
Kinds of Thoughts which are carefully to be avoided. The first
are such as are affected and unnatural; the second such as are
mean and vulgar. As for the first Kind of Thoughts we meet
with little or Nothing that is like them in *Virgil*: He has none
of those little Points and Puerilities that are so often to be met
with in *Ovid*, none of the Epigrammatick Turns of *Lucan*,
none of those swelling Sentiments which are so frequently in
Statius and *Claudian*, none of those mixed Embellishments of
Tasso. Every Thing is just and natural. His Sentiments
shew that he had a perfect Insight into humane Nature, and
that he knew every Thing which was the most proper to affect it.

Mr. *Dryden* has in some Places, which I may hereafter take
Notice of, misrepresented *Virgil's* Way of Thinking as to this
Particular, in the Translation he has given us of the *Aeneid*.
I do not remember that *Homer* any where falls into the Faults
abovementioned, which were indeed the false Refinements of
later Ages. *Milton*, it must be confest, has sometimes erred
in this Respect, as I shall shew more at large in another Paper;
tho' considering all the Poets of the Age in which he writ, were
infected with this wrong Way of Thinking, he is rather to be
admired that he did not give more into it, than that he did
sometimes comply with the vicious Taste which prevails so
much among modern Writers.

But since several Thoughts may be natural which are low
and groveling, an Epic Poet should not only avoid such Sentiments as are unnatural or affected, but also such as are low and
vulgar. *Homer* has opened a great Field of Raillery to Men of
more Delicacy than Greatness of Genius, by the Homeliness
of some of his Sentiments. But, as I have before said, these are
rather to be imputed to the Simplicity of the Age in which he
lived, to which I may also add, of that which he described,
than to any Imperfection in that Divine Poet. *Zoilus*, among
the Ancients, and Monsieur *Perrault*, among the Moderns,
pushed their Ridicule very far upon him, on Account of some
such Sentiments. There is no Blemish to be observed in *Virgil*,
under this Head, and but very few in *Milton*.

I shall give but one Instance of this Impropriety of Sentiments in *Homer*, and at the same Time compare it with an Instance of the same Nature, both in *Virgil* and *Milton*. Sentiments which raise Laughter, can very seldom be admitted with any Decency into an heroick Poem, whose Business it is to excite Passions of a much nobler Nature.   *Homer*, however, in his Characters of *Vulcan* and *Thersites*, in his Story of *Mars* and *Venus*, in his Behaviour of *Irus*, and in other Passages, has been observed to have lapsed into the Burlesque Character, and to have departed from that serious Air which seems essential to the Magnificence of an Epic Poem.   I remember but one Laugh in the whole *Aeneid*, which rises in the fifth Book upon *Monoetes*, where he is represented as thrown overboard, and drying himself upon a Rock.   But this Piece of Mirth is so well timed, that the severest Critick can have Nothing to say against it, for it is in the Book of Games and Diversions, where the Reader's Mind may be supposed to be sufficiently relaxed for such an Entertainment.   The only Piece of Pleasantry in *Paradise Lost*, is where the evil Spirits are described as rallying the Angels upon the Success of their new invented Artillery.   This Passage I look upon to be the most exceptionable in the whole Poem, as being nothing else but a String of Puns, and those too very indifferent ones.

> . . . *Satan beheld their Plight,*
> *And to his Mates thus in Derision call'd.*
> *O Friends, why come not on these Victors proud!*
> *Ere while they fierce were coming, and when we,*
> *To entertain them fair with* open Front,
> *And Breast, (what could we more) propounded Terms*
> *Of Composition; straight they chang'd their Minds,*
> Flew off, *and into strange Vagaries fell,*
> *As they would dance: yet for a Dance they seem'd*
> *Somewhat extravagant and wild, perhaps*
> *For Joy of offer'd Peace; but I suppose*
> *If our Proposals once again were* heard,
> *We should compel them to a quick* Result.
> *To whom thus* Belial *in like gamesome Moode.*
> Leader, *the Terms we sent, were Terms of* Weight,
> *Of* hard Contents, *and full of Force urg'd home,*
> *Such as we might perceive amus'd them all,*
> *And* stumbled *many; who receives them right,*
> *Had need, from Head to Foot, well* understand;
> *Not* understood, *this Gift they have besides,*
> *They shew us when our Foes* walk not upright.
> *Thus they among themselves in pleasant vein*
> *Stood scoffing* . . .

L

No. 280.

[STEELE.]   Monday, January 21.

Principibus placuisse viris non ultima laus est.—Hor.

THE Desire of Pleasing makes a Man agreeable or unwelcome
to those with whom he converses, according to the Motive from
which that Inclination appears to flow. If your Concern for
pleasing others arises from innate Benevolence, it never fails
of Success; if from a Vanity to excel, its Disappointment is no
less certain. What we call an agreeable Man, is he who is
endowed with that natural Bent to do acceptable Things, from
a Delight he takes in them meerly as such; and the Affectation
of that Character is what constitutes a Fop. Under these
Leaders one may draw up all those who make any Manner of
Figure except in dumb Show. A rational and select Conversation is composed of Persons, who have the Talent of pleasing
with Delicacy of Sentiments flowing from habitual Chastity
of Thought; but mixed Company is frequently made up of
Pretenders to Mirth, and is usually pester'd with constrained,
obscene, and painful Witticisms. Now and then you meet
with a Man so exactly formed for Pleasing, that it is no Matter
what he is doing or saying, that is to say, that there need be no
Manner of Importance in it, to make him gain upon every
Body who hears or beholds him. This Felicity is not the Gift
of Nature only, but must be attended with happy Circumstances, which add a Dignity to the familiar Behaviour which
distinguishes him whom we call an agreeable Man. It is from
this that every *Body* loves and esteems *Polycarpus*. He is in
the Vigour of his Age and the Gayety of Life, but has passed
through very conspicuous Scenes in it; though no Soldier, he
has shared the Danger, and acted with great Gallantry and
Generosity on a Decisive Day of Battle. To have those
Qualities which only make other Men conspicuous in the World
as it were supernumerary to him, is a Circumstance which gives
Weight to his most indifferent Actions; for as a known Credit is
Ready-Cash to a Trader, so is acknowledged Merit immediate
Distinction, and serves in the Place of Equipage to a Gentle-
man. This renders *Polycarpus* graceful in Mirth, important in
Business, and regarded with Love in every ordinary Occurrence.
But not to dwell upon Characters which have such particular
Recommendations to our Hearts, let us turn our Thoughts
rather to the Methods of Pleasing, which must carry Men
through the World who cannot pretend to such Advantages.
Falling in with the particular Humour or Manner of one above
you, abstracted from the general Rules of good Behaviour, is
the Life of a Slave. A Parasite differs in nothing from the

meanest Servant, but that the Footman hires himself for bodily Labour, subjected to go and come at the Will of his Master, but the other gives up his very Soul: He is prostituted to speak, and professes to think after the Mode of him whom he courts. This Servitude to a Patron, in an honest Nature, would be more grievous than that of wearing his Livery; therefore we shall speak of those Methods only which are worthy and ingenuous.

The happy Talent of pleasing either those above you or below you, seems to be wholly owing to the Opinion they have of your Sincerity. This Quality is to attend the agreeable Man in all the Actions of his Life; and I think there need be no more said in Honour of it, than that it is what forces the Approbation even of your Opponents. The guilty Man has an Honour for the Judge who with Justice pronounces against him the Sentence of Death it self. The Author of the Sentence at the Head of this Paper was an excellent Judge of humane Life, and passed his own in Company the most agreeable that ever was in the World. *Augustus* lived amongst his Friends as if he had his Fortune to make in his own Court: Candour and Affability, accompanied with as much Power as ever Mortal was vested with, were what made him in the utmost Manner agreeable among a Set of admirable Men, who had Thoughts too high for Ambition, and Views too large to be gratified by what he could give them in the Disposal of an Empire, without the Pleasures of their mutual Conversation. A certain Unanimity of Taste and Judgment, which is natural to all of the same Order in the Species, was the Band of this Society; and the Emperour assumed no Figure in it but what he thought was his Due from his private Talents and Qualifications, as they contributed to advance the Pleasures and Sentiments of the Company.

Cunning People, Hypocrites, all who were but half virtuous or half wise, are incapable of tasting the refined Pleasure of such an equal Company as could wholly exclude the Regard of Fortune in their Conversations. *Horace*, in the Discourse from whence I take the Hint of the present Speculation, lays down excellent Rules for Conduct in Conversation with Men of Power; but he speaks it with an Air of one who had no Need of such an Application for any Thing which related to himself. It shows he understood what it was to be a skilful Courtier, by just Admonitions against Importunity, and shewing how forcible it was to speak modestly of your own Wants. There is indeed something so shameless in taking all Opportunities to speak of your own Affairs, that he who is guilty of it towards him upon whom he depends, fares like the Beggar who exposes his Sores, which instead of moving Compassion, makes the Man he begs of turn away from the Object.

I cannot tell what is become of him, but I remember about sixteen Years ago an honest Fellow, who so justly understood how disagreeable the Mention or Appearance of his Wants would make him, that I have often reflected upon him as a Counterpart of *Irus*, whom I have formerly mentioned. This Man, whom I have missed for some Years in my Walks, and have heard was some way employed about the Army, made it a Maxim, That good Wigs, delicate Linnen, and a chearful Air, were to a poor Dependant the same that working Tools are to a poor Artificer. It was no small Entertainment to me, who knew his Circumstances, to see him who had fasted two Days, attribute the Thinness they told him of to the Violence of some Gallantries he had lately been guilty of. The skilful Dissembler carried this on with the utmost Address; and if any suspected his Affairs were narrow, it was attributed to indulging himself in some fashionable Vice rather than an irreproachable Poverty, which saved his Credit with those on whom he depended.

The Main Art is to be as little troublesome as you can, and make all you hope for come rather as a Favour from your Patron than Claim from you. But I am here prating of what is the Method of Pleasing so as to succeed in the World, when there are Crouds who have, in City, Town, Court, and Country, arrived at considerable Acquisitions, and yet seem incapable of acting in any constant Tenour of Life, but have gone on from one successful Errour to another: Therefore I think I may shorten this Enquiry after the Method of Pleasing; and as the old Beau said to his Son, once for all, *Pray* Jack *be a fine Gentleman*, so may I to my Reader abridge my Instructions, and finish the Art of Pleasing in a Word, *Be rich.*   T

No. 281.

[ADDISON.]   Tuesday, January 22.

Pectoribus inhians spirantia consulit exta.—Virg.

HAVING already given an Account of the Dissection of a *Beau's Head*, with the several Discoveries made on that Occasion; I shall here, according to my Promise, enter upon the Dissection of a *Coquet's Heart*, and communicate to the Publick such Particularities as we observed in that curious Piece of Anatomy.

I should perhaps have waved this Undertaking, had not I

been put in Mind of my Promise by several of my unknown Correspondents, who are very importunate with me to make an Example of the Coquet, as I have already done of the Beau. It is therefore in Compliance with the Request of Friends, that I have looked over the Minutes of my former Dream, in order to give the Publick an exact Relation of it, which I shall enter upon without further Preface.

Our Operator, before he engaged in this visionary Dissection, told us, that there was Nothing in his Art more difficult, than to lay open the Heart of a Coquet, by reason of the many Labyrinths and Recesses which are to be found in it, and which do not appear in the Heart of any other Animal.

He desired us first of all to observe the *Pericardium*, or outward Case of the Heart, which we did very attentively; and by the Help of our Glasses discerned in it Millions of little Scars, which seem'd to have been occasioned by the Points of innumerable Darts and Arrows, that from Time to Time had glanced upon the outward Coat; though we could not discover the smallest Orifice, by which any of them had entered and pierced the inward Substance.

Every Smatterer in Anatomy knows, that this *Pericardium*, or Case of the Heart, contains in it a thin reddish Liquor, supposed to be bred from the Vapours which exhale out of the Heart, and being stopt here, are condensed into this watry Substance.   Upon examining this Liquor, we found that it had in it all the Qualities of that Spirit which is made Use of in the Thermometer, to shew the Change of Weather.

Nor must I here omit an Experiment one of the Company assured us he himself had made with this Liquor, which he found in great Quantity about the Heart of a Coquet whom he had formerly dissected.   He affirmed to us, that he had actually enclosed it in a small Tube made after the manner of a Weather-Glass; but that instead of acquainting him with the Variations of the Atmosphere, it showed him the Qualities of those Persons who entered the Room where it stood.   He affirmed also, that it rose at the Approach of a Plume of Feathers, an embroidered Coat, or a Pair of fringed Gloves; and that it fell as soon as an ill-shaped Perriwig, a clumsy pair of Shooes, or an unfashionable Coat came into his House: Nay, he proceeded so far as to assure us, that upon his Laughing aloud when he stood by it, the Liquor mounted very sensibly, and immediately sunk again upon his looking serious.   In short, he told us, that he knew very well by this Invention whenever he had a Man of Sense or a Coxcomb in his Room.

Having cleared away the *Pericardium*, or the Case and Liquor above-mentioned, we came to the Heart itself.   The

outward Surface of it was extremely slippery, and the *Mucro*,
or Point so very cold withal, that upon endeavouring to take
hold of it, it glided through the Fingers like a smooth Piece
of Ice.

The Fibres were turned and twisted in a more intricate and
perplexed Manner than they are usually found in other Hearts;
insomuch, that the whole Heart was wound up together like a
Gordian Knot, and must have had very irregular and unequal
Motions, whilst it was employed in its Vital Function.

One Thing we thought very observable, namely, that upon
examining all the Vessels which came into it or issued out of it,
we could not discover any Communication that it had with
the Tongue.

We could not but take Notice likewise, that several of those
little Nerves in the Heart which are affected by the Sentiments of Love, Hatred, and other Passions, did not descend to
this before us from the Brain, but from the Muscles which lie
about the Eye.

Upon weighing the Heart in my Hand, I found it to be
extreamly light, and consequently very hollow; which I did
not wonder at when upon looking into the Inside of it, I saw
Multitudes of Cells and Cavities running one within another,
as our Historians describe the Appartments of *Rosamond*'s
Bower. Several of these little Hollows were stuffed with innumerable Sorts of Trifles, which I shall forbear giving any
particular Account of, and shall therefore only take Notice of
what lay first and uppermost, which upon our unfolding it and
applying our Microscope to it appeared to be a Flame-coloured
Hood.

We were informed that the Lady of this Heart, when living,
received the Addresses of several who made Love to her, and
did not only give each of them Encouragement, but made
every one she conversed with believe that she regarded him
with an Eye of Kindness; for which Reason we expected to have
seen the Impression of Multitudes of Faces among the several
Plaites and Foldings of the Heart, but to our great Surprize
not a single Print of this Nature discovered it self till we came
into the very Core and Center of it. We there observed a
little Figure, which, upon applying our Glasses to it, appeared
dressed in a very Fantastick Manner. The more I looked upon
it, the more I thought I had seen the Face before, but could not
possibly recollect either the Place or Time; when at length one
of the Company, who had examined this Figure more nicely
than the rest, shew'd us plainly by the Make of its Face, and
the several Turns of its Features, that the little Idol that was
thus lodged in the very Middle of the Heart was the deceased

Beau, whose Head I gave some Account of in my last *Tuesday's* Paper.

As soon as we had finished our Dissection, we resolved to make an Experiment of the Heart, not being able to determine among our selves the Nature of its Substance, which differed in so many Particulars from that of the Heart in other Females. Accordingly we laid it into a Pan of burning Coals, when we observed in it a certain salamandrine Quality, that made it capable of living in the Midst of Fire and Flame, without being consum'd, or so much as singed.

As we were admiring this strange *Phaenomenon,* and standing round the Heart in a Circle, it gave a most prodigious Sigh, or rather Crack, and dispersed all at once in Smoke and Vapour. This imaginary Noise, which methought was louder than the Burst of a Cannon, produced such a violent Shake in my Brain, that it dissipated the Fumes of Sleep, and left me in an instant broad awake.   L

No. 282.

[STEELE.]   Wednesday, January 23.

. . . *Spes incerta futuri.*—Virg.

IT is a lamentable Thing that every Man is full of Complaints, and constantly uttering Sentences against the Fickleness of Fortune, when People generally bring upon themselves all the Calamities they fall into, and are constantly heaping up Matter for their own Sorrow and Disappointment. That which produces the greatest Part of the Pollutions of Mankind, is a false Hope which People indulge with so sanguine a Flattery to themselves, that their Hearts are bent upon fantastical Advantages which they had no Reason to believe should ever have arrived to them. By this unjust Measure of calculating their Happiness, they often mourn with real Affliction for imaginary Losses. When I am talking of this unhappy Way of accounting for our selves, I cannot but reflect upon a particular Set of People, who in their own Favour resolve every Thing that is possible into what is probable, and then reckon on that Probability as on what must certainly happen. WILL HONEYCOMB, upon my observing his looking on a Lady with some particular Attention, gave me an Account of the great Distresses which had laid waste that her very fine Face, and given an Air of Melancholy to a very agreeable Person. That Lady, and a Couple of Sisters of hers, were, said WILL, fourteen Years ago, the greatest Fortunes about Town; but without having any

Loss by bad Tenants, by bad Securities, or any Damage by
Sea or Land, are reduced to very narrow Circumstances. They
were at that Time the most inaccessible haughty Beauties in
Town; and their Pretensions to take upon them at that unmerciful Rate, was rais'd upon the following Scheme, according
to which all their Lovers were answered.

'Our Father is a youngish Man, but then our Mother is
somewhat older, and not likely to have any Children: His
Estate, being 800*l. per Annum*, at 20 Years Purchase, is worth
16,000*l.*   Our Uncle, who is above 50, has 400*l. per Annum*,
which, at the foresaid Rate, is 8000*l.*   There 's a Widow Aunt
who has 10,000*l.* at her own Disposal left by her Husband,
and an old Maiden-Aunt who has 6000*l.*   Then our Father's
Mother has 900*l. per Annum*, which is worth 18,000*l.* and 1000*l.*
each of us has of her own, which can't be taken from us.   These
summ'd up together stand thus;

		l.
Father's 800—16,000		
Uncle's 400— 8000		
Aunt's $\begin{cases} 10,000 \\ 6000 \end{cases}$ —16,000		
Grandmother 900—18,000		
Own 1000 each—— 3000		

Total 61,000

This equally divided between
us three, amounts to 20,000*l.*
each; and Allowance being
given for Enlargement upon
common Fame, we may
lawfully pass for 30,000*l.*
Fortunes.'

In Prospect of this, and the Knowledge of their own personal
Merit, every one was contemptible in their Eyes, and they
refus'd those Offers which had been frequently made 'em.
But *mark the End*: The Mother dies, the Father is married again
and has a Son; on him was entail'd the Father's, Uncle's, and
Grandmother's Estate.   This cut off 43,000*l.*   The Maiden-
Aunt married a tall Irishman, and with her went the 6000*l.*
The Widow died, and left but enough to pay her Debts and
bury her; so that there remain'd for these three Girls but their
own 1000*l.*   They had by this Time passed their Prime, and
got on the wrong Side of Thirty, and must pass the Remainder
of their Days, upbraiding Mankind that they mind nothing but
Money, and bewailing that Virtue, Sense, and Modesty are had
at present in no Manner of Estimation.

I mention this Case of Ladies before any other, because it is
the most irreparable: For tho' Youth is the Time less capable
of Reflection, it is in that Sex the only Season in which they
can advance their Fortunes.   But if we turn our Thoughts to
the Men, we see such Crouds of Unhappy from no other Reason
but an ill-grounded Hope, that it is hard to say which they

rather deserve, our Pity or Contempt. It is not unpleasant to see a Fellow after grown old in Attendance, and after having passed half a Life in Servitude, call himself the unhappiest of all Men, and pretend to be disappointed because a Courtier broke his Word. He that promises himself any Thing but what may naturally arise from his own Property or Labour, and goes beyond the Desire of possessing above two Parts in three even of that, lays up for himself an encreasing Heap of Afflictions and Disappointments. There are but two Means in the World of gaining by other Men, and these are by being either agreeable or considerable. The Generality of Mankind do all Things for their own Sakes; and when you hope any Thing from Persons above you, if you cannot say I can be thus agreeable, or thus serviceable, it is ridiculous to pretend to the Dignity of being unfortunate, when they leave you; you were injudicious in hoping for any other than to be neglected, for such as can come within these Descriptions of being capable to please, or serve your Patron, when his Humour or Interests calls for their Capacity either Way.

It would not methinks be an useless Comparison between the Condition of a Man who shuns all the Pleasures of Life, and of one who makes it his Business to pursue them. Hope in the Recluse makes his Austerities comfortable, while the luxurious Man gains Nothing but Uneasiness from his Enjoyments. What is the Difference in the Happiness of him who is macerated by Abstinence, and his who is surfeited with Excess? He who resigns the World, has no Temptation to Envy, Hatred, Malice, Anger, but is in constant Possession of a serene Mind; he who follows the Pleasures of it, which are in their very Nature disappointing, is in constant Search of Care, Solicitude, Remorse, and Confusion.

'*Mr.* SPECTATOR, *January* 14, 1712.

I am a young Woman, and have my Fortune to make; for which Reason I come constantly to Church to hear divine Service and make Conquests: But one great Hinderance in this my Design, is, that our Clerk, who was once a Gardener, has this *Christmas* so over deckt the Church with Greens, that he has quite spoilt my Prospect, insomuch that I have scarce seen the young Baronet I dress at these three Weeks, though we have both been very constant at our Devotions, and don't sit above three Pews off. The Church, as it is now equipt, looks more like a Green-house than a Place of Worship: The middle Isle is a very pretty shady Walk, and the Pews look like so many Arbours of each Side of it. The Pulpit it self has such Clusters of Ivy, Holly, and Rosemary about it, that a light

Fellow in our Pew took Occasion to say, that the Congregation heard the Word out of a Bush, like *Moses.* Sir *Anthony Love's* Pew in particular is so well hedged, that all my Batteries have no Effect. I am obliged to shoot at Random among the Boughs, without taking any Manner of Aim. *Mr.* SPECTATOR, unless you 'll give Orders for removing these Greens, I shall grow a very aukward Creature at Church, and soon have little else to do there but say my Prayers. I am in haste,

> *Dear Sir,*
>> *Your most Obedient Servant,*

T   Jenny Simper.'

No. 283.
[BUDGELL.]   Thursday, January 24.

Magister artis ingeni largitor
Venter . . .—Pers.

Lucian rallies the Philosophers in his Time, who could not agree whether they should admit *Riches* into the Number of *real Goods*; the Professors of the Severer Sects threw them quite out, while others as resolutely inserted them.

I am apt to believe, that as the World grew more polite, the rigid Doctrines of the first were wholly discarded; and I do not find any one so hardy at present, as to deny that there are very great Advantages in the Enjoyment of a plentiful Fortune. Indeed the best and wisest of Men, tho' they may possibly despise a good Part of those Things which the World calls Pleasures, can, I think, hardly be insensible of that Weight and Dignity which a moderate Share of Wealth adds to their Characters, Counsels and Actions.

We find it a general Complaint in Professions and Trades, that the richest Members of them are chiefly encouraged, and this is falsely imputed to the Ill-nature of Mankind, who are ever bestowing their Favours on such as least want them. Whereas, if we fairly consider their Proceedings in this Case, we shall find them founded on undoubted Reason: Since supposing both equal in their natural Integrity, I ought, in common Prudence, to fear foul Play from an indigent Person, rather than from one whose Circumstances seem to have placed him above the bare Temptation of Money.

This Reason also makes the Commonwealth regard her richest Subjects, as those who are most concerned for her Quiet and Interest, and consequently fittest to be entrusted with her highest Employments. On the contrary, *Cataline's* Saying to those Men of desperate Fortunes, who applyed themselves to him, and of whom he afterwards composed his Army, that *They had Nothing to hope for but a civil War*, was too true not to make the Impressions he desired.

I believe I need not fear but that what I have said in Praise of Money, will be more than sufficient with most of my Readers to excuse the Subject of my present Paper, which I intend, as an Essay on *The Ways to raise a Man's Fortune*; or *The Art of growing Rich*.

The first and most infallible Method towards the attaining of this End, is *Thrift*: All Men are not equally qualified for getting Money, but it is in the Power of every one alike to practise this Virtue, and I believe there are very few Persons, who, if they please to reflect on their past Lives, will not find that had they saved all those little Sums, which they have spent unnecessarily, they might at present have been Masters of a competent Fortune. *Diligence* justly claims the next Place to *Thrift*: I find both these excellently well recommended to common Use in the three following *Italian* Proverbs.

Never do that by Proxy which you can do yourself.
Never defer that till to Morrow which you can do to Day.
Never neglect small Matters and Expences.

A third Instrument of growing Rich, is *Method in Business*, which, as well as the two former, is also attainable by Persons of the meanest Capacities.

The famous *de Wit*, one of the greatest Statesmen of the Age in which he lived, being asked by a Friend, How he was able to dispatch that Multitude of Affairs in which he was engaged; replyed, That his whole Art consisted in doing *one Thing at once*. If, says he, I have any necessary Dispatches to make, I think of Nothing else 'till those are finished; If any Domestick Affairs require my Attention, I give my self up wholly to them till they are set in Order.

In short, we often see Men of dull and phlegmatick Tempers, arriving to great Estates, by making a regular and orderly Disposition of their Business, and that without it the greatest Parts and most lively Imaginations rather puzzle their Affairs, than bring them to an happy Issue.

From what has been said, I think I may lay it down as a Maxim, that every Man of good common Sense may, if he pleases, in his particular Station of Life, most certainly be rich. The Reason why we sometimes see the Men of the greatest Capacities are not so, is either because they despise Wealth in Comparison of Something else; or at least are not content to be getting an Estate, unless they may do it their own Way, and at the same Time enjoy all the Pleasures and Gratifications of Life.

But besides these ordinary Forms of growing rich, it must be allowed that there is Room for Genius, as well in this as in all other Circumstances of Life.

Tho' the Ways of getting Money were long since very numerous; and tho' so many new ones have been found out of late Years, there is certainly still remaining so large a Field for Invention, that a Man of an indifferent Head might easily sit down and draw up such a Plan for the Conduct and Support of his Life, as was never yet once thought of.

We daily see Methods put in Practice by hungry and ingenious Men, which demonstrate the Power of Invention in this Particular.

It is reported of *Scaramouche*, the first famous *Italian* Comedian, that being at *Paris*, and in great Want, he bethought himself of constantly plying near the Door of a noted Perfumer in that City, and when any one came out who had been buying Snuff, never failed to desire a Taste of them; when he had by this Means got together a Quantity made up of several different Sorts, he sold it again at a lower Rate to the same Perfumer, who finding out the Trick, called it *Tabac de mille fleures*, or *Snuff of a thousand Flowers*. The Story further tells us, that by this Means he got a very comfortable Subsistence, 'till making too much haste to grow rich, he one Day took such an unreasonable Pinch out of the Box of a *Swiss* Officer, as engaged him in a Quarrel, and obliged him to quit this ingenious Way of Life.

Nor can I in this Place omit doing Justice to a Youth of my own Country, who, tho' he is scarce yet twelve Years old, has with great Industry and Application attained to the Art of beating the Grenadiers March on his Chin. I am credibly informed, that by this Means he does not only maintain himself and his Mother, but that he is laying up Money every Day, with a Design, if the War continues, to purchase a Drum at least, if not a Colours.

I shall conclude these Instances with the Device of the famous *Rabelais*, when he was at a great Distance from *Paris*, and without Money to bear his Expences thither. This ingenious Author being thus sharp set, got together a convenient Quantity of Brick-Dust, and having disposed of it into several Papers, writ upon one *Poyson for Monsiuer*, upon a second *Poyson for the Dauphin*, and on a third, *Poyson for the King*. Having made this Provision for the Royal Family of *France*, he laid his Papers so that his Landlord, who was an inquisitive Man, and a good Subject, might get a Sight of them.

The Plot succeeded as he desired: The Host gave immediate Intelligence to the Secretary of State. The Secretary presently sent down a special Messenger, who brought up the Traitor to Court, and provided him at the King's Expence with proper Accommodations on the Road.   As soon as he appeared he was known to be the celebrated *Rabelais*, and his Powder upon Examination being found very innocent, the Jest was only laught at; for which a less eminent *Drole* would have been sent to the Gallies.

Trade and Commerce might doubtless be still varied a thousand Ways, out of which would arise such Branches as have not yet been touched.   The famous *Doily* is still fresh in every one's Memory, who raised a Fortune by finding out Materials for such Stuffs as might at once be cheap and genteel. I have heard it affirmed, that had not he discovered this frugal Method of gratifying our Pride, we should hardly have been able to carry on the last War.

I regard Trade not only as highly advantagious to the Common-wealth in general; but as the most natural and likely Method of making a Man's Fortune; having observed, since my being a Spectator in the World, greater Estates got above *Change*, than at *Whitehall* or St. *James's*.   I believe I may also add, that the first Acquisitions are generally attended with more Satisfaction, and as good a Conscience.

I must not however close this Essay, without observing, that what has been said is only intended for Persons in the common Ways of Thriving, and is not designed for those men who from low Beginnings push themselves up to the Top of States, and the most considerable Figures in Life.   My Maxim of *Saving* is not designed for such as these, since Nothing is more usual than for *Thrift* to disappoint the Ends of *Ambition*, it being almost impossible that the Mind should be intent upon Trifles, while it is at the same Time forming some great Design.

I may therefore compare these Men to a great Poet, who, as *Longinus* says, while he is full of the most magnificent Ideas, is not always at leisure to mind the little Beauties and Niceties of his Art.

I would however have all my Readers take great Care how they mistake themselves for uncommon *Genius's*, and Men above Rule, since it is very easie for them to be deceived in this Particular.   **X**

No. 284.
[STEELE.]   Friday, January 25.
        Posthabui tamen illorum mea seria ludo.—Virg.

AN unaffected Behaviour is without Question a very great

Charm; but under the Notion of being unconstrained and disengaged, People take upon them to be unconcerned in any Duty
of Life. A general Negligence is what they assume upon all
Occasions, and set up for an Aversion to all Manner of Business
and Attention. *I am the carelessest Creature in the World,
I have certainly the worst Memory of any Man living,* are
frequent Expressions in the Mouth of a Pretender of this Sort.
It is a professed Maxim with these People never to *think*;
there is Something so solemn in Reflexion, they, forsooth, can
never give themselves Time for such a Way of employing
themselves. It happens often that this Sort of Man is heavy
enough in his Nature to be a good Proficient in such Matters
as are attainable by Industry; but alas! He has such an ardent
Desire to be what he is not, to be too volatile, to have the Faults
of a Person of Spirit, that he professes himself the most unfit
Man living for any Manner of Application. When this Humour
enters into the Head of a Female, she generally professes
Sickness upon all Occasions, and acts all Things with an in-
disposed Air: She is offended, but her Mind is too lazy to raise
her to Anger; therefore she lives only as actuated by a violent
Spleen and gentle Scorn. She has hardly Curiosity to listen to
Scandal of her Acquaintance, and has never Attention enough
to hear them commended. This Affectation in both Sexes
makes them vain of being useless, and take a certain Pride in
their Insignificancy.

Opposite to this Folly is another no less unreasonable, and
that is the Impertinence of being always in a Hurry. There are
those who visit Ladies, and beg Pardon, afore they are well
seated in their Chairs, that they just called in, but are obliged
to attend Business of Importance elsewhere the very next
Moment: Thus they run from Place to Place, professing that
they are obliged to be still in another Company than that which
they are in. These Persons who are just a going some where
else should never be detained; let all the World allow that
Business is to be minded, and their Affairs will be at an End.
Their Vanity is to be importuned, and Compliance with their
Multiplicity of Affairs would effectually dispatch 'em. The
travelling Ladies who have half the Town to see in an Afternoon, may be pardoned for being in constant Hurry; but it is
inexcusable in Men to come where they have no Business, to
profess they absent themselves where they have. It has been
remarked by some nice Observers and Criticks, That there is
nothing discovers the true Temper of a Person so much as his
Letters. I have by me two Epistles, which are written by two
People of the different Humours above-mentioned. It is
wonderful that a Man cannot observe upon himself when he

sits down to write, but that he will gravely commit himself to Paper the same Man that he is in the Freedom of Conversation. I have hardly seen a Line from any of these Gentlemen, but spoke them as absent from what they were doing, as they profess they are when they come into Company: For the Folly is, that they have perswaded themselves they really are busy. Thus their whole Time is spent in Suspence of the present Moment to the next, and then from the next to the succeeding, which to the End of Life is to pass away with Pretence to many Things, and the Execution of Nothing.

'Sir,

The Post is just going out, and I have many other Letters of very great Importance to write this Evening, but I could not omit making my Compliments to you for your Civilities to me when I was last in Town. It is my Misfortune to be so full of Business, that I cannot tell you a thousand Things which I have to say to you. I must desire you to communicate the Contents of this to no one living; but believe me to be, with the greatest Fidelity,

Sir,
>Your most Obedient,
>Humble Servant,
>Stephen Courier.'

'Madam,

I hate Writing, of all Things in the World; however, tho' I have drunk the Waters, and am told I ought not to use my Eyes so much, I cannot forbear writing to you, to tell you I have been to the last Degree hipp'd since I saw you. How could you entertain such a Thought, as that I should hear of that silly Fellow with Patience? Take my Word for it, there is nothing in it; and you may believe it when so lazy a Creature as I am undergo the Pains to assure you of it by taking Pen, Ink, and Paper in my Hand. Forgive this, you know I shall not often offend in this Kind, I am very much

>Your Servant,
>Bridget Eitherdown.

The Fellow is of your Country, prithee send me Word, however, whether he has so great an Estate.'

'Mr. SPECTATOR,   *Jan. 24, 1712.*

I am Clerk of the Parish from whence Mrs. *Simper* sends her Complaint, in your Yesterday's *Spectator*. I must beg of you to publish this as a publick Admonition to the aforesaid Mrs. *Simper*, otherwise all my honest Care in the Disposition of the Greens in the Church will have no Effect: I shall therefore with your Leave lay before you the whole Matter. I was formerly, as she charges me, for several Years a Gardener in the County of *Kent*: But I must absolutely deny that 'tis out of any Affection I retain for my old Employment, that I have placed my Greens so liberally about the Church, but out of a particular Spleen I conceived against Mrs. *Simper* (and others of the same Sisterhood) some Time ago. As to herself, I had one Day set the hundredth *Psalm*, and was singing the first Line in order to put the Congregation into the Tune, she was all the while curtsying to Sir *Anthony* in so affected and indecent a Manner, that the Indignation I conceived at it made me forget my self so far, as from the Tune of that *Psalm* to wander into *Southwell* Tune, and from thence into *Windsor* Tune, still unable to recover my self till I had with the utmost Confusion set a new one. Nay, I have often seen her rise up and smile, and courtsy to one at the lower End of the Church, in the Midst of a *Gloria Patri*; and when I have spoke the Assent to a Prayer with a long *Amen* uttered with decent Gravity, she has been rowling her Eyes round about in such a Manner, as plainly shewed, however she was moved, it was not towards an heavenly Object. In fine, she extended her Conquests so far over the Males, and raised such Envy in the Females, that what between Love of those, and the Jealousy of these, I was almost the only Person that looked in a Prayer Book all Church Time. I had several Projects in my Head to put a Stop to this growing Mischief; but as I have long lived in *Kent*, and there often heard how the Kentish Men evaded the Conqueror, by carrying green Boughs over their Heads, it put me in Mind of practising this Device against Mrs. *Simper*. I find I have preserved many a young Man from her Eye-shot by this Means; therefore humbly pray the Boughs may be fixed, till she shall give Security for her peaceable Intentions.

Your Humble Servant,

T   Francis Sternhold.'

No. 285.

[ADDISON.]   Saturday, January 26.

Ne, quicunque Deus, quicunque adhibebitur heros,
Regali conspectus in auro nuper & ostro.
Migret in obscuras humili sermone tabernas:
Aut, dum vitat humum, nubes & inania captet.—Hor.

HAVING already treated of the Fable, the Characters, and Sentiments in the *Paradise Lost*, we are in the last Place to consider the *Language*; and as the learned World is very much divided upon *Milton*, as to this Point, I hope they will excuse me if I appear particular in any of my Opinions, and encline to those who judge the most advantagiously of the Author.

It is requisite that the Language of an heroick Poem should be both perspicuous and sublime. In proportion as either of these two Qualities are wanting, the Language is imperfect. Perspicuity is the first and most necessary Qualification; insomuch, that a good-natured Reader sometimes overlooks a little Slip even in the Grammar or Syntax, where it is impossible for him to mistake the Poet's Sense. Of this Kind is that Passage in *Milton*, wherein he speaks of *Satan*.

> . . . *God and his Son except,*
> *Created Thing Nought valued he nor shunn'd.*

And that in which he describes *Adam* and *Eve*.

> Adam *the goodliest Man of Men since born*
> *His Sons, the fairest of her Daughters* Eve.

It is plain, that in the former of these Passages, according to the natural Syntax, the Divine Persons mentioned in the first Line are represented as created Beings; and that in the other, *Adam* and *Eve* are confounded with their Sons and Daughters. Such little Blemishes as these, when the Thought is great and natural, we should, with *Horace*, impute to a pardonable Inadvertency, or to the Weakness of humane Nature, which cannot attend to each minute Particular, and give the last finishing to every Circumstance in so long a Work. The ancient Criticks therefore, who were acted by a Spirit of Candour, rather than that of Cavilling, invented certain Figures of Speech, on purpose to palliate little Errors of this Nature in the Writings of those Authors, who had so many greater Beauties to atone for them.

If Clearness and Perspicuity were only to be consulted, the Poet would have Nothing else to do but to cloath his Thoughts in the most plain and natural Expressions. But, since it often happens that the most obvious Phrases, and those which are used in ordinary Conversation, become too familiar to the Ear, and contract a Kind of Meanness by passing through the Mouths of the Vulgar, a Poet should take particular Care to guard himself against idiomatick Ways of Speaking. *Ovid* and *Lucan* have many Poornesses of Expression upon this Account, as taking up with the first Phrases that offered, without putting themselves to the Trouble of looking after such as would not only have been natural, but also elevated and sublime. *Milton* has but few Failings in this Kind, of which,

however, you may meet with some Instances, as in the following
Passages.

> *Embrio's and Idiots, Eremites and Fryars*
> White, Black, and Grey, *with all their* Trumpery.
> *Here Pilgrims roam . . .*
> *. . . A while Discourse they hold,*
> No fear lest Dinner cool; *when thus began*
> *Our Author . . .*
> *Who of all Ages to succeed, but feeling*
> *The Evil on him brought by me, will curse*
> *My Head, ill fare our Ancestor impure.*
> For this we may thank *Adam . . .*

The great Masters in Composition know very well that
many an elegant Phrase becomes improper for a Poet or an
Orator, when it has been debased by common Use. For this
Reason the Works of ancient Authors, which are written in
dead Languages, have a great Advantage over those which
are written in Languages that are now spoken. Were there
any mean Phrases or Idioms in *Virgil* and *Homer*, they would
not shock the Ear of the most delicate modern Reader, so
much as they would have done that of an old *Greek* or *Roman*,
because we never hear them pronounced in our Streets, or in
ordinary Conversation.

It is not therefore sufficient, that the Language of an
Epic Poem be perspicuous, unless it be also sublime. To this
End it ought to deviate from the common Forms and ordinary
Phrases of Speech. The Judgment of a Poet very much dis-
covers it self in shunning the common Roads of Expression,
without falling into such Ways of Speech as may seem stiff
and unnatural; he must not swell into a false Sublime, by
endeavouring to avoid the other Extream. Among the
Greeks, Eschylus, and sometimes *Sophocles,* were guilty of this
Fault; among the *Latins, Claudian* and *Statius*; and among our
own Countrymen, *Shakespear* and *Lee.* In these Authors the
Affectation of Greatness often hurts the Perspicuity of the
Stile, as in many others the Endeavour after Perspicuity
prejudices its Greatness.

Aristotle has observed, that the Idiomatick Stile may be
avoided, and the Sublime formed, by the following Methods.
First, by the Use of Metaphors, like those in *Milton.*

> Imparadised *in one another's Arms,*
> *. . . And in his Hand a Reed*
> *Stood waving* tipt *with Fire; . . .*
> *The grassie Clods now* calv'd. *. . . .*

In these and innumerable other Instances, the Metaphors

are very bold, but beautiful: I must however observe, that the Metaphors are not thick sown in *Milton*, which always savours too much of Wit; that they never clash with one another, which as *Aristotle* observes, turns a Sentence into a Kind of an Enigma or Riddle; and that he seldom makes Use of them where the proper and natural Words will do as well.

Another Way of raising the Language, and giving it a poetical Turn, is to make Use of the Idioms of other Tongues. *Virgil* is full of the *Greek* Forms of Speech, which the Criticks call *Hellenisms*, as *Horace* in his Odes abounds with them much more than *Virgil*. I need not mention the several Dialects which *Homer* has made Use of for this End. *Milton* in conformity with the Practice of the ancient Poets, and with *Aristotle*'s Rule, has infused a great many *Latinisms*, as well as *Graecisms*, and sometimes *Hebraisms*, into the Language of his Poem, as towards the Beginning of it.

> Nor *did they* not *perceive the evil Plight*
> *In which they were, or the fierce Pains* not *feel.*
> *Yet to their Gen'ral's Voice they soon obey'd.*
> . . . *Who shall tempt with wandring Feet*
> *The dark unbottom'd infinite Abyss,*
> *And through the* palpable Obscure *find out his Way,*
> *His uncouth Way, or spread his airy Flight*
> *Upborn with indefatigable Wings*
> *Over the* vast Abrupt! . . .
> . . . *So both ascend*
> *In the Visions of God.* . . .   B. 2.

Under this Head may be reckoned the placing the Adjective after the Substantive, the Transposition of Words, the turning the Adjective into a Substantive, with several other foreign Modes of Speech, which this Poet has naturalized to give his Verse the greater Sound, and throw it out of Prose.

The third Method mentioned by *Aristotle*, is what agrees with the Genius of the *Greek* Language more than with that of any other Tongue, and is therefore more used by *Homer* than by any other Poet. I mean the length'ning of a Phrase by the Addition of Words, which may either be inserted or omitted, as also by the extending or contracting of particular Words by the Insertion or Omission of certain Syllables. *Milton* has put in Practice this Method of raising his Language, as far as the Nature of our Tongue will permit, as in the Passage above-mentioned, *Eremite*, for what is Hermite in common Discourse. If you observe the Measure of his Verse, he has with great Judgment suppressed a Syllable in several Words, and shortned those of two Syllables into one, by which Method, besides the abovementioned Advantage, he has given a greater Variety

to his Numbers. But this Practice is more particularly remarkable in the Names of Persons and of Countries, as *Beelzebub*, *Hessebon*, and in many other Particulars, wherein he has
either changed the Name, or made Use of that which is not the
most commonly known, that he might the better deviate from
the Language of the Vulgar.

The same Reason recommended to him several old Words,
which also makes his Poem appear the more venerable, and
gives it a greater Air of Antiquity.

I must likewise take Notice, that there are in *Milton* several
Words of his own Coining, as *Cerberean, miscreated, Hell-
doom'd, Embryon* Atoms, and many Others. If the Reader is
offended at this Liberty in our *English* Poet, I would recommend him to a Discourse in *Plutarch*, which shews us how
frequently *Homer* has made Use of the same Liberty.

Milton, by the abovementioned Helps, and by the Choice of
the noblest Words and Phrases which our Tongue would afford
him, has carried our Language to a greater Height than any
of the *English* Poets have ever done before or after him, and
made the Sublimity of his Stile equal to that of his Sentiments.

I have been the more particular in these Observations of
Milton's Stile, because it is that Part of him in which he
appears the most singular. The Remarks I have here made
upon the Practice of other Poets, with my Observations out of
Aristotle, will perhaps alleviate the Prejudice which some have
taken to his Poem upon this Account; tho' after all, I must
confess, that I think his Stile, tho' admirable in general, is in
some Places too much stiffened and obscured by the frequent
Use of those Methods, which *Aristotle* has prescribed for the
raising of it.

This Redundancy of those several Ways of Speech which
Aristotle calls *foreign Language*, and with which *Milton* has so
very much enriched, and in some Places darkned the Language
of his Poem, was the more proper for his Use, because his
Poem is written in blank Verse; Rhyme, without any other
Assistance, throws the Language off from Prose, and very
often makes an indifferent Phrase pass unregarded; but where
the Verse is not built upon Rhymes, there Pomp of Sound, and
Energy of Expression, are indispensably necessary to support
the Stile, and keep it from falling into the Flatness of Prose.

Those who have not a Taste for this Elevation of Stile, and
are apt to ridicule a Poet when he departs from the common
Forms of Expression, would do well to see how *Aristotle* has
treated an ancient Author, called *Euclid*, for his insipid Mirth
upon this Occasion. Mr. *Dryden* used to call this Sort of Men
his Prose-Criticks.

I should, under this Head of the Language, consider *Milton*'s Numbers, in which he has made Use of several Elisions, that are not customary among other *English* Poets, as may be particularly observed in his cutting off the letter *Y*, when it precedes a Vowel. This, and some other Innovations in the Measure of his Verse, has varied his Numbers in such a Manner, as makes them incapable of satiating the Ear, and cloying the Reader, which the same uniform Measure would certainly have done, and which the perpetual Returns of Rhime never fail to do in long narrative Poems. I shall close these Reflections upon the Language of *Paradise Lost*, with observing that *Milton* has copied after *Homer,* rather than *Virgil*, in the Length of his Periods, the Copiousness of his Phrases, and the running of his Verses into one another.

L

No. 286.

[STEELE.]   Monday, January 28.

Nomina honesta praetenduntur vitiis.—Tacit.

'*Mr.* SPECTATOR,   *York, Jan.* 18, 1712.

I PRETEND not to inform a Gentleman of so just a Taste whenever he pleases to use it; but it may not be amiss to inform your Reader that there is a false Delicacy as well as a true one. True Delicacy, as I take it, consists in Exactness of Judgment and Dignity of Sentiment, or if you will, Purity of Affection, as this is opposed to Corruption and Grossness. There are Pedants in Breeding as well as in Learning. The Eye that cannot bear the Light is not delicate but sore. A good Constitution appears in the Soundness and Vigour of the Parts, not in the Squeamishness of the Stomach; And a false Delicacy is Affectation, not Politeness. What then can be the Standard of Delicacy but Truth and Virtue? Virtue, which, as the Satyrist long since observed, is real Honour; whereas the other Distinctions among Mankind are meerly titular. Judging by that Rule, in my Opinion, and in that of many of your virtuous female Readers, you are so far from deserving Mr. *Courtly*'s Accusation, that you seem too gentle, and to allow too many Excuses for an enormous Crime, which is the Reproach of the Age, and is in all its Branches and Degrees expresly forbidden by that Religion we pretend to profess; and whose Laws, in a Nation that calls it self Christian, one would think should take Place of those Rules, which Men of corrupt Minds, and those of weak Understandings follow. I know not any Thing more pernicious to good Manners, than the giving fair Names to foul Actions; for this confounds Vice and Virtue, and takes off that natural Horrour we have to Evil. An innocent Creature, who would start at the Name of Strumpet, may think it pretty to be called a Mistress, especially if her Seducer has taken Care to inform her, that a Union of Hearts is the principal Matter in the Sight of Heaven, and that the Business at Church is a mere idle Ceremony. Who knows not that the Difference between obscene and modest Words expressing the same Action, consists only in the accessary Idea, for there is Nothing immodest in Letters and Syllables. Fornication and Adultery are modest Words, because they express an evil Action as criminal, and so as to excite Horrour and Aversion: Whereas Words representing the Pleasure rather than the Sin, are for this Reason indecent and dishonest. Your Papers would be chargeable with Something worse than Indelicacy, they would be immoral, did you treat the detestable Sins of Uncleanness in the same Manner as you rally an impertinent Self-love and an artful Glance; As those Laws wou'd be very unjust, that shou'd chastise Murder and Petty Larceny with the same Punishment. Even Delicacy requires that the Pity shewn to distressed indigent Wickedness, first betrayed into, and then expelled the Harbours of the Brothel, shou'd be chang'd to Detestation,when we consider pamper'd Vice in the Habitations of the Wealthy. The most free Person of Quality, in Mr. *Courtly*'s Phrase, that is to speak properly, a Woman of Figure who has forgot her Birth and Breeding, dishonour'd her Relations and her self, abandon'd her Virtue and Reputation, together with the natural Modesty of her Sex, and risqued her very Soul, is so far from deserving to be treated with no worse Character than that of a Kind Woman (which is doubtless Mr. *Courtly*'s Meaning if he has any), that one can scarce be too severe on her, in as much as she Sins against greater Restraints, is less expos'd, and liable to fewer Temptations, than Beauty in Poverty and Distress. It is hop'd therefore, Sir, that you will not lay aside your generous Design of exposing that monstrous Wickedness of the Town, whereby a Multitude of Innocents are sacrificed in a more barbarous Manner than those who were offer'd to *Moloch*. The Unchaste are provoked to see their Vice expos'd, and the Chaste cannot rake into such Filth without Danger of Defilement; but a meer SPECTATOR, may look into the Bottom, and come off without partaking in the Guilt. The doing so will convince us you pursue publick Good, and not merely your own Advantage: But if your Zeal slackens, how can one help thinking that Mr. *Courtly*'s Letter is but a Feint to get off from a Subject, in which either your own, or the private and base Ends of others to whom you are partial, or of those of whom you are afraid, wou'd not endure a Reformation?

I am, Sir, your humble Servant and Admirer, so long as you tread in the Paths of Truth, Virtue and Honour.'

'Mr. SPECTATOR,

Trin. Col. Cantab. Jan. 12, 1711–12.

It is my Fortune to have a Chamber-Fellow, with whom, tho' I agree very well in many Sentiments, yet there is one in which we are as contrary as Light and Darkness. We are both in Love; his Mistress is a lovely Fair, and mine a lovely Brown. Now as the Praise of our Mistress's Beauty employs much of our Time, we have frequent Quarrels in entering upon that Subject, while each says all he can to defend his Choice. For my own Part, I have rack'd my Fancy to the utmost; and sometimes, with the greatest Warmth of Imagination, have told him, That Night was made before Day, and many more fine Things, tho' without any Effect: Nay, last Night I could not forbear saying, with more Heat than Judgment, that the Devil ought to be painted white. Now my Desire is, Sir, that you would be pleas'd to give us in Black and White your Opinion in the Matter of Dispute between us; which will either furnish me with fresh and prevailing Arguments to maintain my own Taste, or make me with less Repining allow that of my Chamber-Fellow. I know very well that I have *Jack Cleveland*, and *Bond*'s *Horace* on my Side; but then he has such a Band of Rhymers and Romance Writers, with which he opposes me, and is so continually chiming to the Tune of golden Tresses, yellow Locks, Milk, Marble, Ivory, Silver, Swans, Snow, Dazies, Doves, and the Lord knows what; which he is always Sounding with so much Vehemence in my Ears, that he often puts me into a brown Study how to answer him; and I find that I'm in a fair Way to be quite confounded, without your timely Assistance afforded to,

Sir,

Your humble Servant,

Philobrune.'

Z

No. 287.

[ADDISON.]   Tuesday, January 29.

'Ω φιλτάτη γῆ μῆτερ, ὡς σεμνὸν σφόδρ' εἶ
Τοῖς νοῦν ἔχουσι κτῆμα . . .—Menand.

I LOOK upon it as a peculiar Happiness, that were I to chuse of what Religion I would be, and under what Government I would live, I should most certainly give the Preference to that Form of Religion and Government which is established in my own Country. In this Point I think I am determined by Reason and Conviction; but if I shall be told that I am acted by Prejudice, I am sure it is an honest Prejudice, it is a Prejudice that arises from the Love of my Country, and therefore such an one as I will always indulge. I have in several Papers endeavoured to express my Duty and Esteem for the Church of *England*, and design this as an Essay upon the civil Part of our Constitution, having often entertained my self with Reflections on this Subject, which I have not met with in other Writers.

That Form of Government appears to me the most reasonable, which is most conformable to the Equality that we find in humane Nature, provided it be consistent with publick Peace and Tranquillity. This is what may properly be called Liberty, which exempts one Man from Subjection to another, so far as the Order and Oeconomy of Government will permit.

Liberty should reach every Individual of a People, as they all share one common Nature; if it only spreads among particular Branches, there had better be none at all since such a Liberty only aggravates the Misfortune of those who are deprived of it, by setting before them a disagreeable Subject of Comparison.

This Liberty is best preserved, where the Legislative Power is lodged in several Persons, especially if those Persons are of different Ranks and Interests; for where they are of the same Rank, and consequently have an Interest to manage peculiar to that Rank, it differs but little from a despotical Government in a single Person. But the greatest Security a People can have for their Liberty, is when the Legislative Power is in the Hands of Persons so happily distinguished, that by providing for the particular Interest of their several Ranks, they are providing for the whole Body of the People; or in other Words, when there is no Part of the People that has not a common Interest with at least one Part of the Legislators.

If there be but one Body of Legislators, it is no better than a Tyranny; if there are only two, there will want a casting Voice, and one of them must at Length be swallowed up by Disputes and Contentions that will necessarily arise between them. Four would have the same Inconvenience as two, and a greater Number would cause too much Confusion. I could never read a Passage in *Polybius*, and another in *Cicero*, to this Purpose, without a secret Pleasure in applying it to the *English* Constitution, which it suits much better than the *Roman*. Both these great Authors give the Pre-eminence to a mixt Government, consisting of three Branches, the Regal, the Noble, and the Popular. They had doubtless in their Thoughts the Constitution of the *Roman* Common-wealth, in which the Consul represented the King, the Senate the Nobles, and the Tribunes the People. This Division of the three Powers in the *Roman* Constitution, was by no means so distinct and natural, as it is in the *English* Form of Government. Among several Objections that might be made to it, I think the chief are those that affect the consular Power, which had only the Ornaments without the Force of the regal Authority. Their Number had not a casting Voice in it; for which Reason, if one did not chance to be employed Abroad, while the other sat at Home, the publick Business was sometimes at a Stand, while the Consuls pulled two different Ways in it. Besides, I do not find that the Consuls had ever a negative Voice in the passing of a Law, or Decree of Senate, so that indeed they were rather the chief Body of the Nobility, or the first Ministers of State, than a distinct Branch of the Soveraignty, in which none can be looked upon as a Part, who are not a Part of the Legislature. Had the Consuls been invested with the regal Authority to as great a Degree as our Monarchs, there would never have been any Occasions for a Dictatorship, which had in it the Power of all the three Orders, and ended in the subversion of the whole Constitution.

Such an History as that of *Suetonius*, which gives us a Succession of absolute Princes, is to me an unanswerable Argument against despotick Power. Where the Prince is a Man of Wisdom and Virtue, it is indeed happy for his People that he is absolute; but since in the common Run of Mankind, for one that is Wise and Good you find ten of a contrary Character, it is very dangerous for a Nation to stand to its Chance, or to have its publick Happiness or Misery depend on the Virtues or Vices of a single Person. Look into the Historian I have mentioned, or into any Series of absolute Princes, how many Tyrants must you read through, before you come to an Emperor that is supportable. But this is not all; an honest private Man often grows cruel and abandoned, when converted into an absolute Prince. Give a Man Power of doing what he pleases with Impunity, you extinguish his Fear, and consequently overturn in him one of the great Pillars of Morality. This too we find confirmed by Matter of Fact. How many hopeful Heirs apparent to great Empires, when in the Possession of them have become such Monsters of Lust and Cruelty as are a Reproach to Humane Hature?

Some tell us we ought to make our Governments on Earth like that in Heaven, which, say they, is altogether Monarchical and Unlimited. Was Man like his Creator in Goodness and

Justice, I should be for following this great Model; but where Goodness and Justice are not essential to the Ruler, I would by no Means put my self into his Hands to be disposed of according to his particular Will and Pleasure.

It is odd to consider the Connection between despotick Government and Barbarity, and how the making of one Person more than Man, makes the rest less. About nine Parts of the World in ten are in the lowest State of Slavery, and consequently sunk into the most gross and brutal Ignorance. *European* Slavery is indeed a State of Liberty, if compared with that which prevails in the other three Divisions of the World; and therefore it is no wonder that those who grovel under it, have many Tracks of Light among them, of which the others are wholly destitute.

Riches and Plenty are the natural Fruits of Liberty, and where these abound, Learning and all the liberal Arts will immediately lift up their Heads and flourish. As a Man must have no slavish Fears and Apprehensions hanging upon his Mind, who will indulge the Flights of Fancy or Speculation, and push his Researches into all the abstruse Corners of Truth, so it is necessary for him to have about him a Competency of all the Conveniencies of Life.

The first Thing every one looks after, is to provide himself with Necessaries. This Point will engross our Thoughts till it be satisfied: If this is taken Care of to our Hands, we look out for Pleasures and Amusements; and among a great Number of idle People, there will be many whose Pleasures will lie in Reading and Contemplation. These are the two great Sources of Knowledge, and as Men grow wise, they naturally Love to communicate their Discoveries; and others seeing the Happiness of such a learned Life, and improving by their Conversation, emulate, imitate and surpass one another, till a Nation is filled with Races of wise and understanding Persons. Ease and Plenty are therefore the great Cherishers of Knowledge; and as most of the despotick Governments of the World have neither of them, they are naturally over-run with Ignorance and Barbarity. In *Europe*, indeed, notwithstanding several of its Princes are absolute, there are Men famous for Knowledge and Learning, but the Reason is, because the Subjects are many of them rich and wealthy, the Prince not thinking fit to exert himself in his full Tyranny like the Princes of the eastern Nations, lest his Subjects should be invited to new-mould their Constitution, having so many Prospects of Liberty within their View. But in all despotick Governments, tho' a particular Prince may favour Arts and Letters, there is a natural Degeneracy of Mankind, as you may observe from

Augustus's Reign, how the *Romans* lost themselves by Degrees, till they fell to an Equality with the most barbarous Nations that surrounded them. Look upon *Greece* under its free States, and you would think its Inhabitants lived in different Climates, and under different Heavens, from those at present; so different are the Genius's which are formed under *Turkish* Slavery, and *Grecian* Liberty.

Besides Poverty and Want, there are other Reasons that debase the Minds of Men, who live under Slavery, though I look on this as the Principal. This natural Tendency of despotick Power to Ignorance and Barbarity, tho' not insisted upon by others, is, I think, an unanswerable Argument against that Form of Government, as it shows how repugnant it is to the Good of Mankind and the Perfection of humane Nature, which ought to be the great Ends of all civil Institutions.   L

No. 288.

[STEELE.]   Wednesday, January 30

. . . *Pavor est utrobique molestus.*—Hor.

'*Mr.* SPECTATOR,

WHEN you spoke of the Jilts and Coquets, you then promised to be very impartial, and not to spare even your own Sex, should any of their secret or open Faults come under your Cognizance; which has given me Encouragement to describe a certain Species of Mankind under the Denomination of *Male Jilts.* They are Gentlemen who do not design to marry, yet, that they may appear to have some Sense of Gallantry, think they must pay their *Devoirs* to one particular Fair; in order to which they single out from amongst the Herd of Females her to whom they design to make their fruitless Addresses. This done, they first take every Opportunity of being in her Company, and then never fail upon all Occasions to be particular to her, laying themselves at her Feet, protesting the Reality of their Passion with a thousand Oaths, solliciting a Return, and saying as many fine Things as their Stock of Wit will allow; and if they are not deficient that Way, generally speak so as to admit of a double Interpretation; which the credulous Fair is too apt to turn to her own Advantage, since it frequently happens to be a raw, innocent young Creature, who thinks all the World as sincere as her self; and so her unwary Heart becomes an easy Prey to those deceitful Monsters, who no sooner perceive it, but immediately they grow cool, and shun her whom they before seem'd so much to admire, and proceed to act the same common-place Villany towards another. A Coxcomb flushed with many of these infamous Victories shall say he is sorry for the poor Fools, protest and vow he never thought of Matrimony, and wonder talking civilly can be so strangely misinterpreted. Now, Mr. SPECTATOR, you that are a professed Friend to Love, will, I hope, observe upon those who abuse that noble Passion, and raise it in innocent Minds by a deceitful Affectation of it, after which they desert the Enamoured. Pray bestow a little of your Counsel to those fond believing Females who already have or are in Danger of broken Hearts; in which you will oblige a great Part of this Town, but in a particular Manner,

> *Sir,*
>
> *Your (yet Heart-whole) Admirer,*
> *and devoted humble Servant,*
>
> Melainia.'

Melainia's Complaint is occasioned by so general a Folly, that it is wonderful one could so long overlook it. But this false Gallantry proceeds from an Impotence of Mind, which makes those who are guilty of it incapable of pursuing what they themselves approve. Many a Man wishes a Woman his Wife, whom he dare not take for such. Tho' no one has Power over his Inclinations or Fortunes, he is a Slave to common Fame. For this Reason I think *Melainia* gives them too soft a Name in that of Male-Coquets. I know not why Irresolution of Mind should not be more contemptible than Impotence of Body; and these frivolous Admirers would be but tenderly used, in being only included in the same Term with the Insufficient another Way. They whom my Correspondent calls Male-Coquets, shall hereafter be called *Fribblers*. A Fribbler is one who professes Rapture and Admiration for the Woman to whom he addresses, and dreads Nothing so much as her Consent. His Heart can flutter by the Force of Imagination, but cannot fix from the Force of Judgment. It is not uncommon for the Parents of young Women of moderate Fortune to wink at the Addresses of Fribblers, and expose their Children to the ambiguous Behaviour which *Melainia* complains of, till by the Fondness to one they are to lose, they become incapable of Love towards others, and by Consequence in their future Marriage lead a joyless or a miserable Life. As therefore I shall in the Speculations which regard Love be as severe as I ought on Jilts and libertine Women, so will I be as little merciful to insignificant and mischievous Men. In order to this all Visitants who frequent Families wherein there are young Females, are forthwith required to declare them·

selves, or absent from Places where their Presence banishes such as would pass their Time more to the Advantage of those whom they visit. It is a Matter of too great Moment to be dallied with; and I shall expect from all my young People a satisfactory Account of Appearances. *Strephon* has from the Publication hereof seven Days to explain the Riddle he presented to *Eudamia*; and *Chloris* an Hour after this comes to her Hand, to declare whether she will have *Philotas*, whom a Woman of no less Merit than her self, and of superior Fortune, languishes to call her own.

'*To the* SPECTATOR.

Sir,

Since so many Dealers turn Authors, and write quaint Advertisements in Praise of their Wares, one, who from an Author turned Dealer, may be allowed for the Advancement of Trade to turn Author again. I will not however set up, like some of 'em, for Selling cheaper than the most able honest Tradesmen can; nor do I send this to be better known for Choice and Cheapness of China and Japan-Wares, Teas, Fans, Muslins, Pictures, Arrack, and other *Indian* Goods. Placed as I am in *Leaden-hall-street*, near the *India-Company*, and the Centre of that Trade, Thanks to my fair Customers, my Warehouse is graced as well as the Benefit Days of my Plays and Operas; and the foreign Goods I sell seem no less acceptable than the foreign Books I translated, *Rabelais* and Don *Quixote*: This the Criticks allow me, and while they like my Wares they may dispraise my Writing. But as 'tis not so well known yet that I frequently cross the Seas of late, and speaking *Dutch* and *French*, besides other Languages, I have the Conveniency of buying and importing rich Brocades, *Dutch* Atlasses, with Gold and Silver or without, and other foreign Silks of the newest Modes and best Fabricks, fine *Flanders* Lace, Linnens, and Pictures at the best Hand; this my new Way of Trade I have fallen into, I cannot better publish than by an Application to you. My Wares are fit only for such as your Readers; and I would beg of you to print this Address in your Paper, that those whose Minds you adorn may take the Ornaments for their Persons and Houses from me. This, Sir, if I may presume to beg it, will be the greater Favour, as I have lately received rich Silks and fine Lace to a considerable Value, which will be sold cheap for a quick Return, and as I have also a large Stock of other Goods. *Indian* Silks were formerly a great Branch of our Trade; and since we must not sell 'em, we must seek Amends by dealing in others. This I hope will plead for one who would lessen the Number of Teazers of the Muses, and who, suiting his Spirit to his Circumstances, humbles the Poet to exalt the Citizen. Like a true Tradesman, I hardly ever look into any Books but those of Accompts. To say the Truth, I cannot, I think, give you a better Idea of my being a downright Man of Traffick, than by acknowledging I oftner read the Advertisements, than the Matter of even your Paper. I am under a great Temptation to take this Opportunity of admonishing other Writers to follow my Example, and trouble the Town no more; but as it is my present Business to encrease the Number of Buyers rather than Sellers, I hasten to tell you that I am,

> *Sir,*
>
> *Your most humble,*
> *and most obedient Servant,*

T   Peter Motteux.'

No. 289.

[ADDISON.]   Thursday, January 31.

Vitae summa brevis spem nos vetat incohare longam.—Hor.

UPON taking my Seat in a Coffee-house, I often draw the Eyes of the whole Room upon me, when in the hottest Seasons of News, and at a Time that perhaps the *Dutch* Mail is just come in, they hear me ask the Coffee-man for his last Week's Bill of Mortality: I find that I have been sometimes taken on this Occasion for a Parish Sexton, sometimes for an Undertaker, and sometimes for a Doctor of Physick. In this, however, I am guided by the Spirit of a Philosopher, as I take Occasion from hence to reflect upon the regular Encrease and Diminution of Mankind, and consider the several various Ways through which we pass from Life to Eternity. I am very well pleased with these weekly Admonitions, that bring into my Mind such Thoughts as ought to be the daily Entertainment of every reasonable Creature; and can consider with Pleasure to my self, by which of those Deliverances, or, as we commonly call them, Distempers, I may possibly make my Escape out of this World of Sorrows, into that Condition of Existence, wherein I hope to be happier than it is possible for me at present to conceive.

But this is not all the Use I make of the above-mentioned weekly Paper. A Bill of Mortality is in my Opinion an un-answerable Argument for a Providence; how can we, without supposing our selves under the constant Care of a Supreme Being, give any possible Account for that nice Proportion which we find in every great City, between the Deaths and

Births of its Inhabitants, and between the Number of Males, and that of Females, who are brought into the World? What else could adjust in so exact a Manner the Recruits of every Nation to its Losses, and divide these new Supplies of People into such equal Bodies of both Sexes? Chance could never hold the Balance with so steady a Hand.   Were we not counted out by an intelligent Supervisor, we should be sometimes overcharged with Multitudes, and at others waste away into a Desart: We should be sometimes a *populus virorum*, as *Florus* elegantly expresses it, *a Generation of Males*, and at others a Species of Women.   We may extend this Consideration to every Species of living Creatures, and consider the whole animal World as an huge Army made up of innumerable Corps, if I may use that Term, whose Quotas have *been* kept entire near five thousand Years, in so wonderful a Manner, that there is not probably a single Species lost during this long Tract of Time.   Could we have general Bills of Mortality of every Kind of Animal, or Particular ones of every Species in each Continent and Island, I could almost say in every Wood, Marsh or Mountain, what astonishing Instances would they be of that Providence which watches over all its Works?

I have heard of a great Man in the *Romish* Church, who upon reading those Words in the fifth Chapter of *Genesis*, *And all the Days that* Adam *lived were nine hundred and thirty Years, and he died; and all the days of* Seth *were nine hundred and twelv Years, and he died; and all the Days of* Methusalah *were nine hundred and sixty nine Years, and he died*, immediately shut himself up in a Convent, and retired from the World, as not thinking any Thing in this Life worth Pursuing, which had not regard to another.

The Truth of it is, there is Nothing in History which is so improving to the Reader, as those Accounts which we meet with of the Deaths of eminent Persons, and of their Behaviour in that dreadful Season.   I may also add, that there are no Parts in History which affect and please the Reader in so sensible a Manner.   The Reason I take to be this, because there is no other single Circumstance in the Story of any Person which can possibly be the Case of every one who reads it.   A Battel or a Triumph are Conjunctures in which not one Man in a Million is likely to be engaged; but when we see a Person at the Point of Death, we cannot forbear being attentive to every Thing he says or does, because we are sure, that some Time or other we shall our selves be in the same melancholy Circumstances. The General, the Statesman, or the Philosopher, are perhaps Characters which we may never act in; but the dying Man is one whom, sooner or later, we shall certainly resemble.

It is, perhaps, for the same Kind of Reason, that few Books written in *English* have been so much perused as Doctor *Sherlock*'s Discourse upon Death; though at the same Time I must own, that he who has not perused this excellent Piece, has not perhaps read one of the strongest Persuasives to a religious Life that ever was written in any Language.

The Consideration, with which I shall close this Essay upon Death, is one of the most ancient and most beaten Morals that has been recommended to Mankind. But its being so very common, and so universally received, though it takes away from it the Grace of Novelty, adds very much to the Weight of it, as it shews that it falls in with the general Sense of Mankind. In short, I would have every one consider, that he is in this Life Nothing more than a Passenger, and that he is not to set up his Rest here, but to keep an attentive Eye upon that State of Being to which he approaches every Moment, and which will be for ever fixed and permanent. This single Consideration would be sufficient to extinguish the Bitterness of Hatred, the Thirst of Avarice, and the Cruelty of Ambition.

I am very much pleased with the Passage of *Antiphanes*, a very ancient Poet, who lived near an hundred Years before *Socrates*, which represents the Life of Man under this View, as I have here translated it Word for Word. *Be not grieved, says he, above Measure, for thy deceased Friends. They are not dead, but have only finished that Journey which it is necessary for every one of us to take. We our selves must go to that great Place of Reception in which they are all of them assembled, and, in this general Rendezvous of Mankind, live together in another State of Being.*

I think I have, in a former Paper, taken Notice of those beautiful Metaphors in Scripture, where Life is termed a Pilgrimage, and those who pass through it are called Strangers, and Sojourners upon Earth. I shall conclude this with a Story, which I have somewhere read in the Travels of Sir *John Chardin*; that Gentleman, after having told us, that the Inns which receive the Caravans in *Persia*, and the Eastern Countries, are called by the Name of *Caravansaries*, gives us a Relation to the following Purpose.

A *Dervise*, travelling through *Tartary*, being arrived at the Town of *Balk*, went into the King's Palace by a Mistake, as thinking it to be a publick Inn or Caravansary. Having looked about him for some Time, he entered into a long Gallery, where he laid down his Wallet, and spread his Carpet, in order to repose himself upon it, after the Manner of the Eastern Nations. He had not been long in this Posture before he was discovered by some of the Guards, who asked him what was his Business in that Place? The *Dervise* told them, he intended to take up his Night's Lodging in that Caravansary. The Guards let him know, in a very angry Manner, that the House he was in, was not a Caravansary, but the King's Palace. It happened that the King himself passed through the Gallery during this Debate, and smiling at the Mistake of the *Dervise*, asked him how he could possibly be so dull as not to distinguish a Palace from a Caravansary? Sir, says the *Dervise*, give me Leave to ask your Majesty a Question or two. Who were the Persons that lodged in this House when it was first built? The King replied, *His Ancestors*. And who, says the *Dervise*, was the last Person that lodged here? The King replied, *His Father*. And who is it, says the *Dervise*, that lodges here at present? The King told him *that it was he himself*. And who, says the *Dervise*, will be here after you? The King answer'd, *the young Prince his Son.* 'Ah Sir,' said the *Dervise*, 'a House that changes its Inhabitants so often, and receives such a perpetual Succession of Guests, is not a Palace, but a *Caravansary*.'   L

No. 290.

[STEELE.]   Friday, February 1.

Projicit ampullas & sesquipedalia verba.—Hor.

THE Players, who know I am very much their Friend, take all Opportunities to express a Gratitude to me for being so. They could not have a better Occasion of obliging me, than one which they lately took Hold of. They desired my Friend WILL HONEYCOMB to bring me to the Reading of a new Tragedy, it is called *The distressed Mother.* I must confess, tho' some Days are passed since I enjoyed that Entertainment, the Passions of the several Characters dwell strongly upon my Imagination; and I congratulate to the Age, that they are at last to see Truth and humane Life represented in the Incidents which concern Heroes and Heroines. The Stile of the Play is such as becomes those of the first Education, and the Sentiments worthy those of the highest Figure. It was a most exquisite Pleasure to me, to observe real Tears drop from the Eyes of those who had long made it their Profession to dissemble Affliction; and the Player who read, frequently throw down the Book, till he had given Vent to the Humanity which rose in him at some irresistible Touches of the imagined Sorrow. We have seldom had any Female Distress on the Stage, which did not, upon cool Imagination, appear to flow from the Weakness rather than the

Misfortune of the Person represented: But in this Tragedy you
are not entertained with the ungoverned Passions of such as
are enamoured of each other meerly as they are Men and
Women, but their Regards are founded upon high Conceptions
of each other's Virtue and Merit; and the Character which gives
Name to the Play, is one who has behaved her self with heroick
Virtue in the most important Circumstances of a female Life,
those of a Wife, a Widow, and a Mother. If there be those
whose Minds have been too attentive upon the Affairs of Life,
to have any Notion of the Passion of Love in such Extremes as
are known only to particular Tempers, yet, in the above-
mentioned Considerations, the Sorrow of the Heroine will
move even the Generality of Mankind. Domestick Virtues
concern all the World, and there is no one living who is not
interested that *Andromache* should be an imitable Character.
The generous Affection to the Memory of her deceased Husband, that tender Care for her Son, which is ever heightned
with the Consideration of his Father, and these Regards preserved in spite of being tempted with the Possession of the
highest Greatness, are what cannot but be venerable even to
such an Audience as at present frequents the *English* Theatre.
My Friend WILL HONEYCOMB commended several tender
Things that were said, and told me they were very
genteel; but whispered me, that he feared the Piece was not
busy enough for the present Taste. To supply this, he recommended to the Players to be very careful in their Scenes, and
above all Things, that every Part should be perfectly new
dress'd. I was very glad to find that they did not neglect my
Friend's Admonition, because there are a great many in his
Class of Criticism who may be gained by it; but indeed the
Truth is, that as to the Work it self, it is every where Nature.
The Persons are of the highest Quality in Life, even that of
Princes; but their Quality is not represented by the Poet with
Direction that Guards and Waiters should follow them in every
Scene, but their Grandeur appears in greatness of Sentiments,
flowing from Minds worthy their Condition. To make a
Character truly Great, this Author understands that it should
have its Foundation in superior Thoughts and Maxims of Conduct. It is very certain, that many an honest Woman would
make no Difficulty, tho' she had been the Wife of *Hector*, for
the Sake of a Kingdom, to marry the Enemy of her Husband's
Family and Country; and indeed who can deny but she
might be still an honest Woman, but no Heroine? That may
be defensible, nay laudable in one Character, which would be
in the highest degree exceptionable in another. When *Cato
Uticensis* killed himself, *Cottius*, a *Roman* of ordinary Quality

and Character, did the same Thing; upon which one said, smiling, '*Cottius* might have lived tho' *Caesar* has seized the *Roman* Liberty.' *Cottius*'s Condition might have been the same, let Things at the Upper-End of the World pass as they would. What is further very extraordinary in this Work, is, that the Persons are all of them laudable, and their Misfortunes arise rather from unguarded Virtue than Propensity to Vice. The Town has an Opportunity of doing it self Justice in supporting the Representations of Passion, Sorrow, Indignation, even Despair it self, within the Rules of Decency, Honour, and good Breeding; and since there is no one can flatter himself his Life will be always fortunate, they may here see Sorrow as they would wish to bear it whenever it arrives.

'*Mr.* SPECTATOR,

I am appointed to act a Part in the new Tragedy, called *The Distressed Mother*: It is the celebrated Grief of *Orestes* which I am to personate; but I shall not act as I ought, for I shall feel it too intimately to be able to utter it. I was last Night repeating a Paragraph to my self, which I took to be an Expression of Rage, and in the Middle of the Sentence there was a Stroke of Self-pity, which quite unmanned me. Be pleased, Sir, to print this Letter, that when I am oppressed in this Manner at such an Interval, a certain Part of the Audience may not think I am out; and I hope with this Allowance to do it to Satisfaction.

> *I am,*
>> *Sir,*
>>> *Your most humble Servant,*
>>>> George Powell.'

'*Mr.* SPECTATOR,

As I was walking t' other Day in the *Park*, I saw a Gentleman with a very short Face; I desire to know whether it was you. Pray inform me as soon as you can, lest I become the most heroick *Hecatissa*'s Rival.

> *Your humble Servant to Command,*
>> Sophia.'

'*Dear Madam,*

It is not me you are in love with, for I was very ill, and kept my Chamber all that Day.

> *Your most humble Servant,*

T
>> *The* SPECTATOR.'

No. 291.

[ADDISON.]   Saturday, February 2.

> . . . *Ubi plura nitent in carmine, non ego paucis*
> *Offendar maculis, quas aut incuria fudit,*
> *Aut humana parum cavit natura.* . . .—Hor.

I HAVE now consider'd *Milton*'s *Paradise Lost* under those
four great Heads of the Fable, the Characters, the Sentiments,
and the Language; and have shewn that he excels, in general,
under each of these Heads.   I hope that I have made several
Discoveries which may appear new, even to those who are
versed in Critical Learning.   Were I indeed to chuse my
Readers, by whose Judgment I would stand or fall, they should
not be such as are acquainted only with the *French* and *Italian*
Criticks, but also with the Antient and Moderns who have
written in either of the learned Languages.   Above all, I
would have them well versed in the *Greek* and *Latin* Poets,
without which a Man very often fancies that he understands
a Critick, when in reality he does not comprehend his
Meaning.

It is in Criticism, as in all other Sciences and Speculations;
one who brings with him any implicit Notions and Observations
which he has made in his reading of the Poets, will find his
own Reflections methodized and explained, and perhaps several
little Hints that had passed in his Mind, perfected and improved
in the Works of a good Critick; whereas one who has not these
previous Lights, is very often an utter Stranger to what he
reads, and apt to put a wrong Interpretation upon it.

Nor is it sufficient, that a Man who sets up for a Judge in
Criticism, should have perused the Authors above-mentioned,
unless he has also a clear and logical Head.   Without this
Talent he is perpetually puzzled and perplexed amidst his own
Blunders, mistakes the Sense of those he would confute, or if
he chances to think right, does not know how to convey his
Thoughts to another with Clearness and Perspicuity.   *Aristotle*,
who was the best Critick, was also one of the best Logicians
that ever appeared in the World.

Mr. *Lock*'s Essay on Human Understanding would be
thought a very odd Book for a Man to make himself Master of,
who would get a Reputation by Critical Writings; though at the
same Time it is very certain, that an Author who has not learned
the Art of distinguishing between Words and Things, and of
ranging his Thoughts, and setting them in proper Lights, whatever Notions he may have, will lose himself in Confusion and
Obscurity.   I might further observe, that there is not a *Greek*
or *Latin* Critick who has not shewn, even in the Stile of his

Criticisms, that he was a Master of all the Elegance and Delicacy of his Native Tongue.

The Truth of it is, there is nothing more absurd, than for a Man to set up for a Critick, without a good Insight into all the Parts of Learning; whereas many of those who have endeavoured to signalize themselves by Works of this Nature among our *English* Writers, are not only defective in the abovementioned Particulars, but plainly discover by the Phrases which they make use of, and by their confused way of thinking, that they are not acquainted with the most common and ordinary Systems of Arts and Sciences. A few general Rules extracted out of the *French* Authors, with a certain Cant of Words, has sometimes set up an illiterate heavy Writer for a most judicious and formidable Critick.

One great Mark, by which you may discover a Critick who has neither Taste nor Learning, is this, that he seldom ventures to praise any Passage in an Author which has not been before received and applauded by the Publick, and that his Criticism turns wholly upon little Faults and Errors. This Part of a Critick is so very easy to succeed in, that we find every ordinary Reader, upon the publishing of a new Poem, has Wit and Illnature enough to turn several Passages of it into Ridicule, and very often in the right Place. This Mr. *Dryden* has very agreeably remarked in those two celebrated Lines,

> *Errors, like Straws, upon the Surface flow;*
> *He who would search for Pearls must dive below.*

A true Critick ought to dwell rather upon Excellencies than Imperfections, to discover the concealed Beauties of a Writer, and communicate to the World such Things as are worth their Observation. The most exquisite Words and finest Strokes of an Author are those which very often appear the most doubtful and exceptionable, to a Man who wants a Relish for polite Learning; and they are these, which a soure undistinguishing Critick generally attacks with the greatest Violence. *Tully* observes, that it is very easy to brand or fix a Mark upon what he calls *Verbum ardens*, or, as it may be rendered into *English, a glowing bold Expression,* and to turn it into Ridicule by a cold ill-natured Criticism. A little Wit is equally capable of exposing a Beauty, and of aggravating a Fault; and though such a Treatment of an Author naturally produces Indignation in the Mind of an understanding Reader, it has however its Effect among the Generality of those whose Hands it falls into, the Rabble of Mankind being very apt to think that every Thing which is laughed at with any Mixture of Wit, is ridiculous in it self.

Such a Mirth as this, is always unseasonable in a Critick, as it rather prejudices the Reader than convinces him, and is capable of making a Beauty, as well as a Blemish, the Subject of Derision. A Man, who cannot write with Wit on a proper Subject, is dull and stupid, but one who shews it in an improper Place, is as impertinent and absurd. Besides, a Man who has the Gift of Ridicule is apt to find Fault with any Thing that gives him an Opportunity of exerting his beloved Talent, and very often censures a Passage, not because there is any Fault in it, but because he can be merry upon it. Such Kinds of Pleasantry are very unfair and disingenuous in Works of Criticism, in which the greatest Masters, both antient and modern, have always appeared with a serious and instructive Air.

As I intend in my next Paper to shew the Defects in *Milton's Paradise Lost*, I thought fit to premise these few Particulars, to the End that the Reader may know I enter upon it, as on a very ungrateful Work, and that I shall just point at the Imperfections, without endeavouring to enflame them with Ridicule. I must also observe with *Longinus*, that the Productions of a great Genius, with many Lapses and Inadvertencies, are infinitely preferable to the Works of an inferior Kind of Author, which are scrupulously exact and conformable to all the Rules of correct Writing.

I shall conclude my Paper with a Story out of *Boccalini*, which sufficiently shews us the Opinion that judicious Author entertained of the Sort of Criticks I have been here mentioning. A famous Critick, says he, having gathered together all the Faults of an eminent Poet, made a present of them to *Apollo*, who received them very graciously, and resolved to make the Author a suitable Return for the Trouble he had been at in collecting them. In order to this, he set before him a Sack of Wheat, as it had been just threshed out of the Sheaf. He then bid him pick out the Chaff from among the Corn, and lay it aside by it self. The Critick applied himself to the Task with great Industry and Pleasure, and after having made the due Separation, was presented by *Apollo* with the Chaff for his Pains.   L

No. 292.

Monday, February 4.

Illam, quicquid agit, quoquo vestigia flectit,
  Componit furtim, subsequiturque decor.—Tib. L. 4.

As no one can be said to enjoy Health, who is only not sick, without he feel within himself a lightsome and invigorating Principle, which will not suffer him to remain idle, but still spurs him on to Action; so in the Practice of every Virtue, there is some additional Grace required, to give a Claim of excelling in this or that particular Action. A Diamond may want polishing, though the Value be still intrinsically the same; and the same Good may be done with different Degrees of Lustre. No Man should be contented with himself that he barely does well, but he should perform every thing in the best and most becoming Manner that he is able.

Tully tells us, he wrote his Book of *Offices*, because there was no Time of Life in which some correspondent Duty might not be practis'd; nor is there a Duty without a certain Decency accompanying it, by which every Virtue 'tis joined to, will seem to be doubled. Another may do the same Thing, and yet the Action want that Air and Beauty which distinguish it from others; like that inimitable Sun-shine *Titian* is said to have diffus'd over his Landschapes; which denotes them his, and has been always unequall'd by any other Person.

There is one Action in which this Quality I am speaking of will be more sensibly perceived, than in granting a Request, or doing an Office of Kindness. *Mummius*, by his Way of consenting to a Benefaction, shall make it lose its Name; while *Carus* doubles the Kindness and the Obligation: From the first the desir'd Request drops indeed at last, but from so doubtful a Brow, that the obliged has almost as much Reason to resent the Manner of bestowing it, as to be thankful for the Favour it self. *Carus* invites with a pleasing Air, to give him an Opportunity of doing an Act of Humanity, meets the Petition half Way, and consents to a Request with a Countenance which proclaims the Satisfaction of his Mind in assisting the Distressed.

The Decency then that is to be observed in Liberality, seems to consist in its being performed with such Cheerfulness, as may express the godlike Pleasure is to be met with in obliging one's Fellow-Creatures; that may shew good Nature and Benevolence overflow'd, and do not, as in some Men, run upon the Tilt, and taste of the Sediments of a grutching uncommunicative Disposition.

Since I have intimated that the greatest Decorum is to be preserved in the bestowing our good Offices, I will illustrate it a little by an Example drawn from private Life, which carries with it such a Profusion of Liberality, that it can be exceeded by nothing but the Humanity and good Nature which accompanies it. It is a Letter of *Pliny*'s, which I shall here translate, because the Action will best appear in its first Dress of Thought, without any foreign or ambitious Ornaments.

'PLINY *to* QUINTILIAN.

Tho' I am fully acquainted with the Contentment and just Moderation of your Mind, and the Conformity the Education you have given your Daughter bears to your own Character; yet since she is suddenly to be married to a Person of Distinction, whose Figure in the World makes it necessary for her to be at a more than ordinary Expence in Cloaths and Equipage suitable to her Husband's Quality; by which, tho' her intrinsick Worth be not augmented, yet will it receive both Ornament and Lustre: And knowing your Estate to be as moderate as the Riches of your Mind are abundant, I must challenge to my self some Part of the Burthen; and as a Parent of your Child, I present her with Twelve hundred and fifty Crowns towards these Expences; which Sum had been much larger, had I not feared the Smallness of it would be the greatest Inducement with you to accept of it.   Farewell.'

Thus should a Benefaction be done with a good Grace, and shine in the strongest Point of Light; it should not only answer all the Hopes and Exigencies of the Receiver, but even out-run his Wishes: 'Tis this happy Manner of Behaviour which adds new Charms to it, and softens those Gifts of Art and Nature, which otherwise would be rather distasteful than agreeable. Without it Valour would degenerate into Brutality, Learning into Pedantry, and the genteelest Demeanour into Affectation. Even Religion it self, unless Decency be the Handmaid which waits upon her, is apt to make People appear guilty of Sourness and ill Humour: But this shews Virtue in her first original Form, adds a Comeliness to Religion, and gives its Professors the justest Title to the Beauty of Holiness.   A Man fully instructed in this Art, may assume a thousand Shapes. and please in all: He may do a thousand Actions shall become none other but himself; not that the Things themselves are different, but the Manner of doing them.

If you examine each Feature by its self, *Aglaura* and *Calliclea* are equally handsome; but take them in the Whole, and you cannot suffer the Comparison: The one is full of numberless nameless Graces, the other of as many nameless Faults.

The Comeliness of Person and Decency of Behaviour, add infinite Weight to what is pronounc'd by any one.   'Tis the Want of this that often makes the Rebukes and Advice of old rigid Persons of no Effect, and leave a Displeasure in the Minds of those they are directed to: But Youth and Beauty, if accompanied with a graceful and becoming Severity, is of mighty Force to raise, even in the most Profligate, a Sense of Shame.

In *Milton* the Devil is never describ'd asham'd but once, and
that at the Rebuke of a beauteous Angel.

> *So spake the Cherub, and his grave Rebuke*
> *Severe in youthful Beauty, added Grace*
> *Invincible : Abash'd the Devil stood,*
> *And felt how awful Goodness is, and saw*
> *Virtue in her own Shape how lovely! saw, and pin'd*
> *His Loss.*

The Care of doing nothing unbecoming has accompanied the
greatest Minds to their last Moments: They avoided even an
indecent Posture in the very Article of Death. Thus *Caesar*
gather'd his Robe about him, that he might not fall in a Manner
unbecoming of himself; and the greatest Concern that appeared
in the Behaviour of *Lucretia*, when she stabb'd her self, was,
that her Body should lie in an Attitude worthy the mind which
had inhabited it.

> *. . . Ne non procumbat honeste*
> *Extrema haec etiam cura, cadentis erat.*
> *'Twas her last Thought, How decently to fall.*

'*Mr.* Spectator,

I am a young Woman without a Fortune; but of a very high
Mind: That is, Good Sir, I am to the last Degree proud and vain.
I am ever railing at the Rich, for doing Things which, upon
Search into my Heart, I find I am only angry because I cannot
do the same my self. I wear the Hoop'd Petticoat, and am all
in Callicoes what the finest are in Silks. It is a dreadful Thing
to be poor and proud; therefore, if you please, a Lecture on
that Subject for the Satisfaction of

> *Your Uneasy*
> *Humble Servant,*
> Jezebell.'

No. 293.
[ADDISON.]   Tuesday, February 5.

Πᾶσιν γάρ εὖ φρονοῦσι συμμαχεῖ τύχη.—Frag. Vet. Po.

THE Famous *Gratian*, in his little Book wherein he lays down
Maxims for a Man's advancing himself at Court, advises his
Reader to associate himself with the Fortunate, and to shun
the Company of the Unfortunate; which, notwithstanding the
Baseness of the Precept to an honest Mind, may have some-
thing useful in it for those who push their Interest in the
World. It is certain a great Part of what we call good or ill
Fortune, rises out of right or wrong Measures, and Schemes of

Life. When I hear a Man complain of his being unfortunate in all his Undertakings, I shrewdly suspect him for a very weak Man in his Affairs. In conformity with this Way of thinking, Cardinal *Richelieu* used to say, that *unfortunate* and *imprudent* were but two Words for the same thing. As the Cardinal himself had a great Share both of Prudence and Good-Fortune, his famous Antagonist, the Count *d'Olivarez*, was disgraced at the Court of *Madrid*, because it was alledged against him that he had never any Success in his Undertakings. This, says an eminent Author, was *indirectly* accusing him of Imprudence.

Cicero recommended *Pompey* to the *Romans* for their General, upon three Accounts, as he was a Man of Courage, Conduct and Good-Fortune. It was, perhaps, for the Reason abovementioned, namely, that a Series of Good-Fortune supposes a prudent Management in the Person whom it befalls, that not only *Sylla* the Dictator, but several of the *Roman* Emperors, as is still to be seen upon their Medals, among their other Titles, gave themselves that of *Felix*, or Fortunate. The Heathens, indeed, seemed to have valued a Man more for his Good-Fortune than for any other Quality, which I think is very natural for those who have not a strong Belief of another World. For how can I conceive a Man crowned with many distinguishing Blessings, that has not some extraordinary Fund of Merit and Perfection in him, which lies open to the Supreme Eye, tho' perhaps it is not discovered by my Observation? What is the Reason *Homer*'s and *Virgil*'s Heroes do not form a Resolution, or strike a Blow, without the Conduct and Direction of some Deity? Doubtless, because the Poets esteemed it the greatest Honour to be favoured by the Gods, and thought the best Way of praising a Man was to recount those Favours which naturally implied an extraordinary Merit in the Person on whom they descended.

Those who believe a future State of Rewards and Punishments act very absurdly, if they form their Opinions of a Man's Merit from his Successes. But certainly, if I thought the whole Circle of our Being was concluded between our Births and Deaths, I should think of a Man's Good-Fortune the Measure and Standard of his real Merit, since Providence would have no Opportunity of rewarding his Virtues and Perfections, but in the present Life. A virtuous Unbeliever, who lies under the Pressure of Misfortunes, has Reason to cry out, as they say *Brutus* did a little before his Death. *O Virtue, I have worshipped thee as a substantial Good, but I find thou art an Empty Name.*

But to return to our first Point. Tho' Prudence does undoubtedly in a great measure produce our good or ill Fortune in the World, it is certain there are many unforeseen Accidents and Occurrences, which very often pervert the finest Schemes that can be laid by humane Wisdom. The Race is not always to the Swift, nor the Battel to the Strong. Nothing less than infinite Wisdom can have an absolute Command over Fortune; the highest Degree of it which Man can possess, is by no means equal to fortuitous Events, and to such Contingencies as may rise in the Prosecution of our Affairs. Nay, it very often happens, that Prudence, which has always in it a great Mixture of Caution, hinders a Man from being so fortunate as he might possibly have been without it. A Person who only aims at what is likely to succeed, and follows closely the Dictates of humane Prudence, never meets with those great and unforeseen Successes, which are often the Effect of a Sanguine Temper, or a more happy Rashness; and this perhaps may be the Reason, that according to the common Observation, Fortune, like other Females, delights rather in favouring the young than the old.

Upon the whole, since Man is so short-sighted a Creature, and the Accidents which may happen to him so various, I cannot but be of Dr. *Tillotson*'s Opinion in another Case, that were there any Doubt of a Providence, yet it certainly would be very desirable there should be such a Being of infinite Wisdom and Goodness, on whose Direction we might rely in the Conduct of Human Life.

It is a great Presumption to ascribe our Successes to our own Management, and not to esteem our selves upon any Blessing, rather as it is the Bounty of Heaven, than the Acquisition of our own Prudence. I am very well pleased with a Medal which was struck by Queen *Elizabeth* a little after the Defeat of the Invincible Armada, to perpetuate the Memory of that extraordinary Event. It is well known how the King of *Spain*, and others who were the Enemies of that great Princess, to derogate from her Glory, ascrib'd the Ruin of their Fleet rather to the Violence of Storms and Tempests, than to the Bravery of the *English*. Queen *Elizabeth*, instead of looking upon this as a Diminution of her Honour, valued her self upon such a signal Favour of Providence; and accordingly in the Reverse of the Medal above mentioned, has represented a Fleet beaten by a Tempest, and falling foul upon one another, with that Religious Inscription, *Afflavit Deus & dissipantur.* *He blew with his Wind, and they were scattered.*

It is remarked of a famous *Graecian* General, whose Name I cannot at present recollect, and who had been a particular Favourite of Fortune, that upon recounting his Victories among his Friends, he added at the End of several great Actions, *And in this Fortune had no Share.* After which it is observed in History, that he never prospered in any Thing he undertook.

As Arrogance, and a Conceitedness of our own Abilities, are very shocking and offensive to Men of Sense and Virtue, we may be sure they are highly displeasing to that Being who delights in an humble Mind, and by several of his Dispensations seems purposely to shew us, that our own Schemes or Prudence have no Share in our Advancement.

Since on this Subject I have already admitted several Quotations which have occurred to my Memory upon writing this Paper, I will conclude it with a little *Persian* Fable. A Drop of Water fell out of a Cloud into the Sea, and finding it self lost in such an Immensity of fluid Matter, broke out into the following Reflection: 'Alass! What an insignificant Creature am I on this prodigious Ocean of Waters; my Existence is of no Concern to the Universe, I am reduced to a Kind of Nothing, and am less than the least of the Works of God.' It so happened, that an Oyster, which lay in the Neighbourhood of this Drop, chanced to gape and swallow it up in the Midst of this his humble Soliloquy. The Drop, says the Fable, lay a great while hardning in the Shell, 'till by Degrees it was ripen'd into a Pearl, which falling into the Hands of a Diver, after a long Series of Adventures, is at present that famous Pearl which is fixed on the Top of the *Persian* Diadem.   L

No. 294.

[STEELE.]   Wednesday, February 6.

Difficile est plurimum virtutem revereri qui semper secunda fortuna sit usus.—Tull. *ad Herennium.*

INSOLENCE is the Crime of all others which every Man is most apt to rail at; and yet is there one Respect in which almost all Men living are guilty of it, and that is in the Case of laying a greater Value upon the Gifts of Fortune than we ought. It is here in *England* come into our very Language, as a Propriety of Distinction, to say, when we would speak of Persons to their Advantage, they are People of Condition. There is no Doubt but the proper Use of Riches implies that a Man should exert all the good Qualities imaginable; and if we mean by a Man of Condition or Quality one, who, according to the Wealth he is Master of, shews himself just, beneficent, and charitable, that Term ought very deservedly to be had in the highest Veneration; but when Wealth is used only as it is the Support of Pomp and Luxury, to be rich is very far from being a Recommendation to Honour and Respect. It is indeed the greatest Insolence imaginable, in a Creature who would feel the Extremes of Thirst and Hunger if he did not prevent his Appetites before they call upon him, to be so forgetful of the common Necessity of humane Nature as never to cast an Eye upon the Poor and Needy. The Fellow who escaped from a Ship which struck upon a Rock in the West, and joined with the Country-People to destroy his Brother-Sailors and make her a Wreck, was Thought a most execrable Creature; but does not every Man who enjoys the Possession of what he naturally wants, and is unmindful of the unsupplied Distress of other Men, betray the same Temper of Mind? When a Man looks about him, and with Regard to Riches and Poverty beholds some drawn in Pomp and Equipage, and they and their very Servants with an Air of Scorn and Triumph overlooking the Multitude that pass by them: And in the same Street a Creature of the same Make crying out in the Name of all that is good and sacred to behold his Misery, and give him some Supply against Hunger and Nakedness; who would believe these two Beings were of the same Species? But so it is, that the Consideration of Fortune has taken up all our Minds, and, as I have often complained, Poverty and Riches stand in our Imaginations in the Places of Guilt and Innocence. But in all Seasons there will be some Instances of Persons who have Souls too large to be taken with popular Prejudices, and while the rest of Mankind are contending for Superiority in Power and Wealth, have their Thoughts bent upon the Necessities of those below them. The Charity-Schools which have been erected of late Years, are the greatest Instances of publick Spirit the Age has produced: But indeed when we consider how long this Sort of Beneficence has been on Foot, it is rather from the good Management of those Institutions, than from the Number or Value of the Benefactions to them, that they make so great a Figure. One would think it impossible, that in the Space of fourteen Years there should not have been five thousand Pounds bestowed in Gifts this Way, nor sixteen hundred Children, including Males and Females, put out into Methods of Industry. It is not allowed me to speak of Luxury and Folly with the severe Spirit they deserve; I shall only therefore say, I shall very readily compound with any Lady in a Hoop-Petticoat, if she gives the Price of one half Yard of the Silk towards cloathing, feeding and instructing an innocent helpless Creature of her own Sex in one of these Schools. The Consciousness of such an Action will give her Features a nobler Life on this illustrious Day, than all the Jewels that can hang in her Hair, or can be clustred in her Bosom. It would be uncourtly to speak in harsher

Words to the Fair, but to Men one may take a little more Freedom. It is monstrous how a Man can live with so little Reflection, as to fancy he is not in a Condition very unjust, and disproportioned to the Rest of Mankind, while he enjoys Wealth, and exerts no Benevolence or Bounty to others. As for this particular Occasion of these Schools, there cannot any offer more worthy a generous Mind. Would you do an handsome Thing without Return? do it for an Infant that is not sensible of the Obligation: Would you do it for public Good? do it for one who would be an honest Artificer: Would you do it for the Sake of Heaven? give it to one who shall be instructed in the Worship of him for whose Sake you gave it. It is methinks a most laudable Institution, this, if it were of no other Expectation than that of producing a Race of good and useful Servants, who will have more than a liberal, a religious Education. What would not a Man do, in common Prudence, to lay out in Purchase of one about him, who would add to all his Orders he gave the Weight of the Commandments to inforce an Obedience to them? for one who would consider his Master as his Father, his Friend, and Benefactor upon the easy Terms, and in Expectation of no other Return but moderate Wages and gentle Usage? It is the common Vice of Children to run too much among the Servants; from such as are educated in these Places they would see Nothing but Lowliness in the Servant, which would not be disingenuous in the Child. All the ill Offices and defamatory Whispers, which take their Birth from Domesticks, would be prevented if this Charity could be made universal; and a good Man might have a Knowledge of the whole Life of the Persons he designs to take into his House for his own Service, or that of his Family or Children, long before they were admitted. This would create endearing Dependencies; and the Obligation would have a paternal Air in the Master, who would be relieved from much Care and Anxiety from the Gratitude and Diligence of an humble Friend attending him as his Servant. I fall into this Discourse from a Letter sent to me, to give me Notice that Fifty Boys would be clothed and take their Seats (at the Charge of some generous Benefactors) in St. *Bride's* Chuch on *Sunday* next. I wish I could promise to my self any Thing which my Correspondent seems to expect from a Publication of it in this Paper; for there can be Nothing added to what so many excellent and learned Men have said on this Occasion: But that there may be something here which would move a generous Mind, like that of him who writ to me, I shall transcribe an handsome Paragraph of Dr. *Snape's* Sermon on these Charities, which my Correspondent enclosed with this Letter.

The wise Providence has amply compensated the Disadvantages of the Poor and Indigent, in wanting many of the Conveniencies of this Life, by a more abundant Provision for their Happiness in the next. Had they been higher born, or more richly endowed, they would have wanted this Manner of Education, of which those only enjoy the Benefit, who are low enough to submit to it; where they have such Advantages without Money, and without Price, as the Rich cannot purchase with it. The Learning which is giv'n, is generally more edifying to them, than that which is sold to others: Thus do they become more exalted in Goodness, by being depressed in Fortune, and their Poverty is, in reality, their Preferment.   T

No. 295.

[ADDISON.]   Thursday, February 7.

Prodiga non sentit pereuntem femina censum:
Ac velut exhausta redivivus pullulet arca
Nummus, & e pleno tollatur semper acervo,
Non unquam reputant, quanti sibi gaudia constent.—Juv.

'Mr. SPECTATOR,

I AM turned of my great Climacterick, and am naturally a Man of a meek Temper. About a dozen Years ago I was married, for my Sins, to a young Woman of a good Family, and of an high Spirit; but could not bring her to close with me, before I had entered into a Treaty with her longer than that of the Grand Alliance. Among other Articles it was therein stipulated, that she should have 400*l.* a Year for *Pin-money*, which I obliged my self to pay quarterly into the Hands of one who acted as her Plenipotentiary in that Affair. I have ever since religiously observed my Part in this solemn Agreement. Now, Sir, so it is, that the Lady has had several Children since I married her; to which, if I should credit our malicious Neighbours, her *Pin-money* has not a little contributed. The Education of these my Children, who, contrary to my Expectation, are born to me every Year, streightens me so much, that I have begged their Mother to free me from the Obligation of the above-mentioned *Pin-money*, that it may go towards making a Provision for her Family. This Proposal makes her noble Blood swell in her Veins, insomuch that finding me a little tardy in her last Quarter's Payment, she threatens me every Day to arrest me; and proceeds so far as to tell me, that if I do not do her Justice, I shall dye in a Jayl, To this she adds, when her Passion will let her argue calmly, that she has several Play-Debts on her Hand, which must be discharged very suddenly, and that she cannot lose her Money as becomes a Woman of her Fashion, if she makes me any Abatements in this Article. I hope, Sir, you will take an Occasion from hence to give your Opinion upon a Subject which you have not yet touched, and inform us if there are any Precedents for this Usage among our Ancestors; or whether you find any Mention of *Pin-money* in *Grotius, Puffendorf,* or any other of the Civilians.

I am ever

the humblest of your Admirers,

Josiah Fribble, *Esq.*'

As there is no Man living, who is a more professed Advocate for the Fair-Sex than my self, so there is none that would be more unwilling to invade any of their Ancient Rights and Privileges; but as the Doctrine of *Pin-money* is of a very late Date, unknown to our Great Grand-mothers, and not yet received by many of our modern Ladies, I think it is for the Interest of both Sexes to keep it from spreading.

Mr. *Fribble* may not, perhaps, be much mistaken, where he intimates, that the supplying a Man's Wife with *Pin-money,* is furnishing her with Arms against himself, and in a Manner becoming accessary to his own Dishonour. We may, indeed, generally observe, that in Proportion as a Woman is more or less beautiful, and her Husband advanced in Years, she stands in need of a greater or less Number of *Pins,* and upon a Treaty of Marriage, rises or falls in her Demands accordingly. It must likewise be owned, that high Quality in a Mistress does very much inflame this Article in the Marriage-reckoning.

But where the Age and Circumstances of both Parties are pretty much upon a Level, I cannot but think the insisting upon *Pin-money* is very extraordinary; and yet we find several Matches broken off upon this very Head. What would a Foreigner, or one who is a Stranger to this Practice, think of a Lover that forsakes his Mistress, because he is not willing to keep her in *Pins*; but what would he think of the Mistress, shou'd he be inform'd that she asks five or six hundred Pounds a Year for this Use? Should a Man unacquainted with our Customs be told the Sums which are allowed in *Great-Britain,* under the Title of *Pin-money,* what a prodigious Consumption of *Pins* would he think there was in this Island? *A Pin a Day,* says our frugal Proverb, *is a Groat a Year*; so that according to this Calculation, my Friend *Fribble's* Wife must every Year make Use of Eight Millions six hundred and forty thousand *new Pins.*

I am not ignorant that our *British* Ladies alledge they comprehend under this general Term several other Conveniencies of Life; I cou'd therefore wish, for the Honour of my Country-women, that they had rather call'd it *Needle-Money*, which might have implied something of Good-housewifry, and not have given the malicious World occasion to think, that Dress and Trifles have always the uppermost Place in a Woman's Thoughts.

I know several of my fair Reasoners urge, in Defence of this Practice, that it is but a necessary Provision they make for themselves, in Case their Husband proves a Churle or a Miser; so that they consider this Allowance as a kind of Alimony, which they may lay their Claim to, without actually separating from their Husbands. But with Submission, I think a Woman who will give up her self to a Man in Marriage, where there is the least Room for such an Apprehension, and trust her Person to one whom she will not rely on for the common Necessaries of Life, may very properly be accused (in the Phrase of an homely Proverb) of being *Penny wise and Pound foolish*.

It is observed of over-cautious Generals, that they never engage in a Battel without securing a Retreat, in Case the Event should not answer their Expectations; on the other Hand, your greatest Conquerors have burnt their Ships, or broke down the Bridges behind them, as being determined either to succeed or die in the Engagement. In the same Manner I should very much suspect a Woman who takes such Precautions for her Retreat, and contrives Methods how she may live happily, without the Affection of one to whom she joins herself for Life. Separate Purses, between Man and Wife, are, in my Opinion, as unnatural as separate Beds. A Marriage cannot be happy, where the Pleasures, Inclinations and Interests of both Parties are not the same. There is no greater Incitement to Love in the Mind of Man, than the Sense of a Person's depending upon him for her Ease and Happiness; as a Woman uses all her Endeavours to please the Person whom she looks upon as her Honour, her Comfort, and her Support.

For this Reason I am not very much surprized at the Behaviour of a rough Country 'Squire, who, being not a little shocked at the Proceeding of a young Widow that would not recede from her Demands of *Pin-money*, was so enraged at her mercenary Temper, that he told her in great wrath, 'as much as she Thought him her Slave, he would shew all the World he did not care a Pin for her.' Upon which he flew out of the Room, and never saw her more.

Socrates, in *Plato*'s *Alcibiades*, says, he was informed by one, who had travelled through *Persia*, that as he passed over a great Tract of Lands, and enquired what the Name of the Place was, they told him it was the *Queen's Girdle*; to which he adds, that another wide Field, which lay by it, was called the *Queen's Veil*, and that in the same Manner there was a large Portion of Ground set aside for every Part of her Majesty's Dress. These Lands might not be improperly called the Queen of *Persia's Pin-money*.

I remember my Friend, Sir ROGER, who I dare say never read this Passage in *Plato*, told me some Time since, that upon his courting the perverse Widow (of whom I have given an Account in former Papers) he had disposed of an hundred Acres in a Diamond-Ring, which he would have presented her with, had she Thought fit to accept it; and that upon her Wedding-Day she should have carried on her Head fifty of the tallest Oaks upon his Estate. He further informed me, that he would have given her a Colepit to keep her in clean Linnen, that he would have allowed her the Profits of a Windmill for her Fans, and have presented her, once in three Years, with the Sheering of his Sheep for her Under-Petticoats. To which the Knight always adds, that though he did not Care for fine Cloaths himself, there should not have been a Woman in the Country better dressed than my Lady *Coverly*. Sir ROGER, perhaps, may in this, as well as in many other of his Devices, appear something odd and singular; but if the Humour of *Pin-money* prevails, I think it would be very proper for every Gentleman of an Estate, to marke out so many Acres of it under the Title of *The Pins*.   L

No. 296.
[STEELE.]   Friday, February **8**.
    . . . *Nugis addere pondus.*—Hor.

    '*Dear* SPEC.

HAVING lately conversed much with the fair Sex on the Subject of your Speculations (which, since their Appearance in Publick, have been the chief Exercise of the female loquacious Faculty) I found the fair Ones possess'd with a Dissatisfaction at your prefixing Greek Mottos to the Frontispiece of your late Papers; and, as a Man of Gallantry, I thought it a Duty incumbent on me to impart it to you, in Hopes of a Reformation, which is only to be affected by a Restoration of the Latin to the usual Dignity in your Papers, which of late the Greek, to the great Displeasure of your female Readers, has usurp'd; for tho' the Latin has the Recommendation of being as unintelligible to them as the Greek, yet being written of the same Character with their Mother Tongue, by the Assistance of a Spelling-Book it 's legible; which Quality the Greek wants: And since the Introduction of Opera's into this Nation, the Ladies are so charmed with Sounds abstracted from their Ideas, that they adore and honour the Sound of Latin as it is old Italian. I am a Sollicitor for the fair Sex, and therefore think my self in that Character more likely to be prevalent in this Request, than if I should subscribe my self by my proper Name.

J. M.

I desire you may insert this in one of your Speculations, to shew my Zeal for removing the Dissatisfaction of the fair Sex, and restoring you to their Favour.'

'Sir,

I was some Time since in Company with a young Officer, who entertained us with the Conquest he had made over a Female Neighbour of his; when a Gentleman who stood by, as, I suppose, envying the Captain's good Fortune, asked him what Reason he had to believe the Lady admired him? Why, says he, my Lodgings are opposite to hers, and she is continually at her Window either at Work, Reading, taking Snuff, or putting her self in some toying Posture on purpose to draw my Eyes that Way. The Confession of this vain Soldier made me reflect on some of my own Actions; for you must know, Sir, I am often at a Window which fronts the Apartments of several Gentlemen, who I doubt not have the same Opinion of me. I must own I love to look at them all, one for being well dressed, a second for his fine Eye, and one particular one because he is the least Man I ever saw; but there is something so easy and pleasant in the Manner of my little Man, that I observe he is a Favourite of all his Acquaintance. I could go on to tell you of many others that I believe think I have encouraged them from my Window: But pray let me have your Opinion of the Use of the Window in a Beautiful Lady; and how often she may look out at the same Man, without being supposed to have a Mind to jump out to him.

Yours,

Aurelia Careless.'

Twice.

'Mr. Spectator,

I have for some Time made Love to a Lady, who receiv'd it with all the kind Returns I ought to expect. But without any Provocation that I know of, she has of late shunned me with the utmost Abhorrence, insomuch that she went out of Church last *Sunday* in the Midst of Divine Service, upon my coming into the same Pew.   Pray, Sir, what must I do in this Business?

Your Servant,

Euphues.'

Let Her alone Ten Days.

'*Mr.* SPECTATOR,   *York, January* the 20th, 1711–12.

We have in this Town a Sort of People who pretend to Wit and write Lampoons: I have lately been the Subject of one of them.   The Scribbler had not Genius enough in Verse to turn my Age, as indeed I am an old Maid, into Raillery, for affecting a youthier Turn than is consistent with my Time of Day; and therefore he makes the Title to his Madrigal, the Character of Mrs. *Judith Lovebane,* born in the Year 1680.   What I desire of you is, That you disallow that a Coxcomb who pretends to write Verse, should put the most malicious Thing he can say in Prose.   This I humbly conceive will disable our Country Wits, who indeed take a great deal of Pains to say any thing in Rhime, tho' they say it very ill.

I am, Sir,

Your Humble Servant,

Susanna Lovebane.'

'*Mr.* SPECTATOR,

We are several of us, Gentlemen and Ladies, who board in the same House, and after Dinner one of our Company (an agreeable Man enough otherwise) stands up and reads your Paper to us all.   We are the civillest People in the World to one another, and therefore I am forced to this Way of desiring our Reader, when he is doing this Office, not to stand afore the Fire.   This will be a general Good to our Family this cold Weather.   He will, I know, take it to be our common Request when he comes to these Words, *Pray Sir sit down*; which I desire you to insert, and you will particularly oblige

Your Daily Reader,

Charity Frost.'

'*Sir,*

I am a great Lover of Dancing, but cannot perform so well as some others: However, by my Out-of-the-Way Capers, and some original Grimaces, I don't fail to divert the Company, particularly the Ladies, who laugh immoderately all the Time. Some, who pretend to be my Friends, tell me they do it in Derision, and would advise me to leave it off, withal that I make my self ridiculous.   I don't know what to do in this

Affair, but am resolved not to give over upon any Account till I have the Opinion of the SPECTATOR.

Your humble Servant,

John Trott.'

If Mr. *Trott* is not aukward out of Time, he has a Right to dance let who will laugh: But if he has no Ear he will interrupt others; and I am of Opinion he should sit still.   Given under my Hand this Fifth of *February,* 1711–12.

The SPECTATOR.

T

No. 297.

[ADDISON.]   Saturday, February 9.

. . . *Velut si*
Egregio inspersos reprendas corpore naevos.—Hor.

AFTER what I have said in my last *Saturday*'s Paper, I shall enter on the Subject of this without farther Preface, and remark the several Defects which appear in the Fable, the Characters, the Sentiments, and the Language of *Milton*'s *Paradise Lost;* not doubting but the Reader will pardon me, if I alledge at the same Time whatever may be said for the Extenuation of such Defects.   The first Imperfection which I shall observe in the Fable is, that the Event of it is unhappy.

The Fable of every Poem is according to *Aristotle*'s Division either *Simple* or *Implex.*   It is called Simple when there is no Change of Fortune in it, Implex when the Fortune of the chief Actor changes from Bad to Good, or from Good to Bad.   The Implex Fable is thought the most perfect; I suppose, because it is more proper to stir up the Passions of the Reader, and to surprize him with a greater Variety of Accidents.

The Implex Fable is therefore of two Kinds: In the first the chief Actor makes his Way through a long Series of Dangers and Difficulties, 'till he arrives at Honour and Prosperity, as we see in the Story of *Ulysses.*   In the second, the chief Actor in the Poem falls from some eminent Pitch of Honour and Prosperity, into Misery and Disgrace.   Thus we see *Adam* and *Eve* sinking from a State of Innocence and Happiness, into the most abject Condition of Sin and Sorrow.

The most taking Tragedies among the Antients were built on this last Sort of Implex Fable, particularly the Tragedy of *Oedipus,* which proceeds upon a Story, if we may believe *Aristotle,* the most proper for Tragedy that could be invented by the Wit of Man.   I have taken some pains in a former Paper to shew, that this Kind of Implex Fable, wherein the Event is unhappy, is more apt to affect an Audience than that of the first Kind; notwithstanding many excellent Pieces among the Antients, as well as most of those which have been written of late Years in our own Country, are raised upon contrary Plans. I must however own, that I think this Kind of Fable, which is the most perfect in Tragedy, is not so proper for an Heroick Poem.

Milton seems to have been sensible of this Imperfection in his Fable, and has therefore endeavoured to cure it by several Expedients; particularly by the Mortification which the great adversary of Mankind meets with upon his Return to the Assembly of Infernal Spirits, as it is described in a beautiful Passage of the tenth Book; and likewise by the Vision, wherein *Adam* at the Close of the Poem sees his Off-spring triumphing over his great Enemy, and himself restored to a happier *Paradise* than that from which he fell.

There is another Objection against *Milton's* Fable, which is indeed almost the same with the former, tho' placed in a different Light, namely, That the Hero in the *Paradise Lost* is unsuccessful, and by no means a Match for his Enemies. This gave Occasion to Mr. *Dryden's* Reflection, that the Devil was in reality *Milton's* Hero. I think I have obviated this Objection in my first Paper. The *Paradise Lost* is an Epic, or a Narrative Poem; he that looks for an Hero in it, searches for that which *Milton* never intended; but if he needs fix the Name of an Hero upon any Person in it, 'tis certainly the *Messiah* who is the Hero, both in the Principal Action, and in the chief Episodes. Paganism could not furnish out a real Action for a Fable greater than that of the *Iliad* or *Aeneid*, and therefore an Heathen could not form a higher Notion of a Poem than one of that Kind, which they call an Heroick. Whether *Milton's* is not of a sublimer Nature I will not presume to determine: It is sufficient that I shew there is in the *Paradise Lost* all the Greatness of Plan, Regularity of Design, and masterly Beauties which we discover in *Homer* and *Virgil*.

I must in the next Place observe, that *Milton* has interwoven in the Texture of his Fable some particulars which do not seem to have Probability enough for an Epic Poem, particularly in the Actions which he ascribes to *Sin* and *Death*, and the Picture which he draws of the *Lymbo of Vanity*, with other Passages in the second Book. Such Allegories rather savour of the Spirit of *Spencer* and *Ariosto*, than of *Homer* and *Virgil*.

In the Structure of his Poem he has likewise admitted too many Digressions. It is finely observed by *Aristotle*, that the Author of an Heroick Poem should seldom speak himself, but throw as much of his Work as he can into the Mouths of those who are his principal Actors. *Aristotle* has given no Reason for this Precept; but I presume it is because the Mind of the Reader is more awed and elevated when he hears *Aeneas* or *Achilles* speak, than when *Virgil* or *Homer* talk in their own Persons. Besides that assuming the Character of an eminent Man is apt to fire the Imagination, and raise the Ideas of the Author. *Tully* tells us, mentioning his Dialogue of Old Age, in which *Cato* is the chief Speaker, that upon a Review of it he was agreeably imposed upon, and fancied that it was *Cato*, and not he himself, who uttered his Thoughts on that Subject.

If the Reader would be at the pains to see how the Story of the *Iliad* and the *Aeneid* is delivered by those Persons who act in it, he will be surprized to find how little in either of these Poems proceeds from the Authors. *Milton* has, in the general Disposition of his Fable, very finely observed this great Rule; insomuch, that there is scarce a third Part of it which comes from the Poet; the rest is spoken either by *Adam* and *Eve*, or by some Good or Evil Spirit who is engaged either in their Destruction or Defence.

From what has been here observed it appears, that Digressions are by no means to be allowed of in an Epic Poem. If the Poet, even in the ordinary Course of his Narration, should speak as little as possible, he should certainly never let his Narration sleep for the sake of any Reflections of his own. I have often observed, with a secret Admiration, that the longest Reflection in the *Aeneid* is in that Passage of the Tenth Book, where *Turnus* is represented as dressing himself in the Spoils of *Pallas*, whom he had slain. *Virgil* here lets his Fable stand still for the sake of the following Remark. *How is the Mind of Man ignorant of Futurity, and unable to bear prosperous Fortune with Moderation? The Time will come when* Turnus *shall wish that he had left the Body of* Pallas *untouched, and curse the Day on which he dressed himself in these Spoils*. As the great Event of the *Aeneid*, and the Death of *Turnus*, whom *Aeneas* slew because he saw him adorned with the Spoils of *Pallas*, turns upon this Incident, *Virgil* went out of his way to make this Reflection upon it, without which so small a Circumstance might possibly have slipped out of his Reader's Memory. *Lucan*, who was an Injudicious Poet, lets drop his Story very frequently for the sake of his unnecessary Digressions, or his *Diverticula*, as *Scaliger* calls them. If he gives us an Account of the Prodigies which preceded the Civil War, he declaims upon the Occasion, and shews how much happier it would be for Man, if he did not feel his Evil Fortune before it comes to pass, and suffer not only by its real Weight, but by the Apprehension of it. *Milton*'s Complaint for his Blindness, his Panegyrick on Marriage, his Reflections on *Adam* and *Eve*'s going

naked, of the Angels eating, and several other Passages in his
Poem, are liable to the same Exception, tho' I must confess
there is so great a Beauty in these very Digressions, that I
would not wish them out of his Poem.

I have, in a former Paper, spoken of the *Characters* of
Milton's *Paradise Lost*, and declared my Opinion, as to the
Allegorical Persons who are introduced in it.

If we look into the *Sentiments*, I think they are sometimes
defective under the following Heads; First, as there are several
of them too much pointed, and some that degenerate even into
Punns. Of this last Kind I am afraid is that in the First
Book, where, speaking of the Pigmies, he calls them.

> . . . *The small* Infantry
> *Warr'd on by Cranes* . . .

Another Blemish that appears in some of his Thoughts, is
his frequent Allusion to Heathen Fables, which are not certainly of a Piece with the Divine Subject, of which he treats.
I do not find fault with these Allusions, where the Poet himself
represents them as fabulous, as he does in some Places, but
where he mentions them as Truths and Matters of Fact. The
Limits of my Paper will not give me leave to be particular in
Instances of this Kind: The Reader will easily remark them in
his Perusal of the Poem.

A third Fault in his Sentiments, is an unnecessary Ostentation of Learning, which likewise occurs very frequently. It
is certain that both *Homer* and *Virgil* were Masters of all
the Learning of their Times, but it shews it self in their
Works after an indirect and concealed Manner. *Milton* seems
ambitious of letting us know, by his Excursions on Free-Will
and Predestination, and his many Glances upon History,
Astronomy, Geography and the like, as well as by the Terms
and Phrases he sometimes makes use of, that he was acquainted
with the whole Circle of Arts and Sciences.

If, in the last Place, we consider the *Language* of this great
Poet, we must allow what I have hinted in a former Paper,
that it is often too much laboured, and sometimes obscured
by old Words, Transpositions, and Foreign Idioms. *Seneca*'s
Objection to the Stile of a great Author, *Riget ejus oratio, nihil
in ea placidum, nihil lene*, is what many Criticks make to *Milton;*
As I cannot wholly refute it, so I have already apologized for it
in another Paper; to which I may further add, that *Milton*'s
Sentiments and Ideas were so wonderfully sublime, that it
would have been impossible for him to have represented them in
their full Strength and Beauty, without having Recourse to
these Foreign Assistances. Our Language sunk under him,

and was unequal to the Greatness of Soul, which furnished him with such glorious Conceptions.

A second Fault in his Language is, that he often affects a Kind of Jingle in his Words, as in the following Passages, and many others:

> *And brought into the* World *a* World *of woe.*
> *. . . Begirt th' Almighty throne*
> Beseeching *or* besieging . . .
> *This* tempted *our* Attempt . . .
> *At one slight* Bound *high overleapt all* Bound.

I know there are Figures for this Kind of Speech, that some of the greatest Antients have been guilty of it, and that *Aristotle* himself has given it a Place in his Rhetorick among the Beauties of that Art.   But as it is in itself poor and trifling, it is I think at present universally exploded by all the Masters of polite Writing.

The last Fault which I shall take notice of in *Milton*'s Stile, is the frequent Use of what the Learned call *Technical Words,* or Terms of Art.   It is one of the greatest Beauties of Poetry, to make hard Things intelligible, and to deliver what is abstruse of it self in such easy Language as may be understood by ordinary Readers: Besides that the Knowledge of a Poet should rather seem born with him, or inspired, than drawn from Books and Systems.   I have often wondered how Mr. *Dryden* could translate a Passage out of *Virgil* after the following manner.

> *Tack to the Larboard, and stand off to Sea.*
> *Veer Star-board Sea and Land. . . .*

Milton makes use of *Larboard* in the same manner.   When he is upon Building he mentions *Doric Pillars, Pilasters, Cornice, Freeze, Architrave.*   When he talks of Heavenly Bodies, you meet with *Ecliptic* and *Eccentric, the Trepidation, Stars dropping from the Zenith, Rays culminating from the Equator.*   To which might be added many Instances of the like Kind in several other Arts and Sciences.

I shall in my next Papers give an Account of the many particular Beauties in *Milton,* which would have been too long to insert under those general Heads I have already treated of, and with which I intend to conclude this Piece of Criticism.   L

No. 298.
[STEELE.]   Monday, February 11.
> *Nusquam tuta fides . . .*—Virg.

'*Mr.* SPECTATOR,   *London,* Feb. 9, 1711–12.

I AM a Virgin, and in no Case despicable; but yet such as I

am I must remain, or else become, 'tis to be feared, less happy: For I find not the least good Effect from the just Correction you some Time since gave that too free, that looser Part of our Sex which spoils the Men; the same Connivance at the Vices, the same easy Admittance of Addresses, the same vitiated Relish of the Conversation of the greatest of Rakes (or in a more fashionable Way of expressing one's self, of such as have seen the World most) still abounds, increases, multiplies.

The humble Petition therefore of many of the most strictly virtuous, and of my self, is, That you 'l once more exert your Authority, and that, according to your late Promise, your full, your impartial Authority, on this sillier Branch of our Kind: For why should they be the uncontroulable Mistresses of our Fate? Why should they with Impunity indulge the Males in Licenciousness whilst single, and we have the dismal Hazard and Plague of Reforming them when married? Strike home, Sir, then, and spare not, or all our maiden Hopes, our gilded Hopes of nuptial Felicity are frustrated, are vanished, and you your self, as well as Mr. *Courtly*, will, by smoothing over immodest Practices with the Gloss of soft and harmless Names, for ever forfeit our Esteem. Nor think that I 'm herein more severe than need be: If I have not Reason more than enough, do you and the World judge from this ensuing Account, which, I think, will prove the Evil to be universal.

You must know then, that since your Reprehension of this Female Degeneracy came out, I 've had a Tender of Respects from no less than five Persons, of tollerable Figure too as Times go: But the Misfortune is, that four of the five are professed Followers of the Mode. They would face me down, that all Women of good Sense ever were, and ever will be, Latitudinarians in Wedlock; and always did, and will, give and take what they profanely term conjugal Liberty of Conscience.

The two first of them, a Captain and a Merchant, to strengthen their Argument, pretend to repeat after a Couple, a Brace of Ladies of Quality and Wit, That *Venus* was always kind to *Mars*; and what Soul that has the least Spark of Generosity, can deny a Man of Bravery any Thing? And how pitiful a Trader that, whom no Woman but his own Wife will have Correspondence and Dealings with? Thus these; whilst the third, the Country Squire, confess'd, That indeed he was surpriz'd into good Breeding, and enter'd into the Knowledge of the World unawares. That dining the other Day at a Gentleman's House, the Person who entertained, was obliged to leave him with his Wife and Nieces; where they spoke with so much Contempt of an absent Gentleman for being slow at a Hint, that he had resolved never to be drowsy, unmannerly, or

stupid for the future at a Friend's House; and on a hunting
Morning, not to pursue the Game either with the Husband
abroad, or with the Wife at home.

The next that came was a Tradesman, nor less full of the
Age than the former; for he had the Gallantry to tell me, that
at a late Junket which he was invited to, the Motion being
made, and the Question being put, 'twas by Maid, Wife and
Widow resolv'd, *nemine contradicente*, That a young sprightly
Journeyman is absolutely necessary in their Way of Business:
To which they had the Assent and Concurrence of the Husbands
present. I dropp'd him a Curtsy, and gave him to understand that was his Audience of Leave.

I am reckoned pretty, and have had very many Advances
besides these; but have been very averse to hear any of them,
from my Observation on these above-mentioned, 'till I hoped
some Good from the Character of my present Admirer, a
Clergy-man. But I find even amongst them there are indirect Practices in Relation to Love, and our Treaty is at
present a little in Suspence, till some Circumstances are cleared.
There is a Charge against him among the Women, and the Case
is this: It is alledged, That a certain endowed Female would
have appropriated herself to, and consolidated herself with a
Church, which my Divine now enjoys; (or, which is the same
Thing, did prostitute herself to her Friend's doing this for her):
That my Ecclesiastick, to obtain the one, did engage himself to
take off the other that lay on Hand; but that on his Success
in the Spiritual, he again renounced the Carnal.

I put this closely to him, and tax'd him with Disingenuity.
He to clear himself made the subsequent Defence, and that
in the most solemn Manner possible: That he was applied
to, and instigated to accept of a Benefice: That a con-
ditional Offer thereof was indeed made him at first, but with
Disdain by him rejected: That when Nothing (as they easily
perceived) of this Nature could bring him to their Purpose,
Assurance of his being entirely unengaged before-hand, and safe
from all their After-Expectations (the only Stratagem left
to draw him in) was given him: That pursuant to this, the
Donation it self was without Delay, before several reputable
Witnesses, tender'd to him *gratis*, with the open Profession of
not the least Reserve, or most minute Condition; but that yet
immediately after Induction, his insidious Introducer (or her
crafty Procurer, which you will) industriously spread the Report; which had reach'd my Ears not only in the Neighbourhood of that said Church, but in *London*, in the University, in
mine and his own Country, and where-ever else it might probably obviate his Application to any other Woman, and so confine

him to this alone: And in a Word, That as he never did make
any previous Offer of his Service, or the least Step to her
Affection; so on his Discovery of these Designs thus laid to
trick him, he could not but afterwards, in Justice to himself,
vindicate both his Innocence and Freedom, by keeping his
proper Distance.

This is his Apology, and I think I shall be satisfied with it.
But I cannot conclude my tedious Epistle, without recommending to you not only to resume your former Chastisement,
but to add to your Criminals the simoniacal Ladies, who seduce
the sacred Order into the Difficulty of either breaking a mercenary Troth made to them whom they ought not to deceive,
or by breaking or keeping it offending against him whom they
cannot deceive. Your Assistance and Labours of this Sort
would be of great Benefit, and your speedy Thoughts on this
Subject would be very seasonable to,

> *Sir,*
> *Your most obedient Servant,*
> Chastity Loveworth.'

T

No. 299.
[ADDISON.]   Tuesday, February 12.

> *Malo Venusinam, quam te, Cornelia, mater*
> *Gracchorum, si cum magnis virtutibus affers*
> *Grande supercilium, & numeras in dote triumphos.*
> *Tolle tuum, precor, Annibalem victumque Syphacem*
> *In castris, & cum tota Carthagine migra.*—Juv.

It is observed, that a Man improves more by reading the
Story of a Person eminent for Prudence and Virtue, than by
the finest Rules and Precepts of Morality. In the same
Manner a Representation of those Calamities and Misfortunes
which a weak Man suffers from wrong Measures, and ill-con-
certed Schemes of Life, is apt to make a deeper Impression
upon our Minds, than the wisest Maxims and Instructions that
can be given us, for avoiding the like Follies and Indiscretions
in our own private Conduct. It is for this Reason that I lay
before my Reader the following Letter, and leave it with him
to make his own Use of it, without adding any Reflections of
my own upon the Subject-Matter.

'*Mr.* Spectator,

Having carefully perused a Letter sent you by *Josiah
Fribble*, Esq; with your subsequent Discourse upon *Pin-money*,
I do presume to trouble you with an Account of my own Case,

which I look upon to be no less deplorable than that of Squire *Fribble.* I am a Person of no Extraction, having begun the World with a small Parcel of rusty Iron, and was for some Years commonly known by the Name of *Jack Anvil.* I have naturally a very happy Genius for getting Money, insomuch that by the Age of five and twenty I had scraped together four thousand two hundred Pounds, five Shillings and a few odd Pence. I then launched out into considerable Business, and became a bold Trader both by Sea and Land, which in a few Years raised me a very considerable Fortune. For these my good Services I was knighted in the thirty fifth Year of my Age, and lived with great Dignity among my City-Neighbours by the Name of Sir *John Anvil.* Being in my Temper very ambitious, I was now bent upon making a Family, and accordingly resolved that my Descendants should have a Dash of good Blood in their Veins. In Order to this I made Love to the Lady *Mary Oddly,* an indigent young Woman of Quality. To cut short the Marriage Treaty, I threw her a *Charte Blanche,* as our News Papers call it, desiring her to write upon it her own Terms. She was very concise in her Demands, insisting only that the Disposal of my Fortune, and the Regulation of my Family, should be entirely in her Hands. Her Father and Brothers appeared exceedingly averse to this Match, and would not see me for some Time; but at present are so well reconciled, that they dine with me almost every Day, and have borrowed considerable Sums of me, which my Lady *Mary* very often twits me with, when she would shew me how kind her Relations are to me. She had no Portion, as I told you before, but what she wanted in Fortune, she makes up in Spirit. She at first changed my Name to Sir *John Envil,* and at present writes herself *Mary Enville.* I have had some Children by her, whom she has Christned with the Sirnames of her Family, in order, as she tells me, to wear out the Homeliness of their Parentage by the Father's Side. Our eldest Son is the Honourable *Oddly Enville,* Esq; and our eldest Daughter *Harriot Enville.* Upon her first coming into my Family, she turned off a Parcel of very careful Servants, who had been long with me, and introduced in their stead a couple of Black-a-moors, and three or four very genteel Fellows in laced Liveries, besides her *French*-woman, who is perpetually making a Noise in the House in a Language which no body understands except my Lady *Mary.* She next set herself to reform every Room of my House, having glazed all my Chimney pieces with Looking-glass, and planted every Corner with such Heaps of *China,* that I am obliged to move about my own House with the greatest Caution and Circumspection, for fear of hurting some of our brittle Furniture.

She makes an Illumination once a Week with Wax-Candles in one of the largest Rooms, in Order, as she phrases it, to see Company. At which Time she always desires me to be Abroad, or to confine my self to the Cock-loft, that I may not disgrace her among her Visitants of Quality. Her Footmen, as I told you before, are such Beaus that I do not much care for asking them Questions; when I do, they answer me with a sawcy Frown, and say that every Thing, which I find Fault with, was done by my Lady *Mary*'s Order. She tells me that she intends they shall wear Swords with their next Liveries, having lately observed the Footmen of two or three Persons of Quality hanging behind the Coach with Swords by their Sides. As soon as the first Honey-moon was over, I represented to her the Unreasonableness of those daily Innovations which she made in my Family; but she told me I was no longer to consider my self as Sir *John Anvil*, but as her Husband; and added, with a Frown, that I did not seem to know who she was. I was surprised to be treated thus, after such Familiarities as had passed between us. But she has since given me to know, that whatever Freedoms she may sometimes indulge me in, she expects in general to be treated with the Respect that is due to her Birth and Quality. Our Children have been trained up from their Infancy with so many Accounts of their Mother's Family, that they know the Stories of all the great Men and Women it has produced. Their Mother tells them, that such an one commanded in such a Sea Engagement; that their great Grandfather had a Horse shot under him at *Edge-hill*; that their Uncle was at the Siege of *Buda*; and that her Mother danced at a Ball at Court, with the Duke of *Monmouth*; with Abundance of Fiddle-faddle of the same Nature. I was, the other Day, a little out of Countenance at a Question of my little Daughter *Harriot*, who asked me, with a great deal of Innocence, why I never told them of the Generals and Admirals that had been in *my* Family. As for my eldest Son *Oddly*, he has been so spirited up by his Mother, that if he does not mend his Manners I shall go near to disinherit him. He drew his Sword upon me before he was nine Years old, and told me, that he expected to be used like a Gentleman. Upon my Offering to correct him for his Insolence, my Lady *Mary* stept in between us, and told me, that I ought to consider there was some Difference between his Mother and mine. She is perpetually finding out the Features of her own Relations in every one of my Children, tho' by the Way, I have a little Chub-faced Boy as like me as he can stare, if I durst say so; but what most angers me, when she sees me playing with any of them upon my Knee, she has begged me more than once to converse with the Children as little as possibly, that they may not learn any of my aukward Tricks.

You must farther know, since I am opening my Heart to you, that she thinks herself my superior in Sense, as much as she is in Quality, and therefore treats me like a plain well-meaning Man, who does not know the World. She dictates to me in my own Business, sets me right in Point of Trade, and if I disagree with her about any of my Ships at Sea, wonders that I will dispute with her, when I know very well that her great Grandfather was a Flag-Officer.

To compleat my Sufferings, she has teised me for this Quarter of a Year last past, to remove into one of the Squares at the other End of the Town, promising for my Encouragement, that I shall have as good a Cock-loft as any Gentleman in the Square; to which the honourable *Oddly Enville*, Esq., always adds, like a Jack-a-napes as he is, that he hopes 'twill be as near the Court as possible.

In short, Mr. SPECTATOR, I am so much out of my natural Element, that to recover my old Way of Life, I would be content to begin the World again, and be plain *Jack Anvil*; but alas! I am in for Life, and am bound to Subscribe my self, with great sorrow of Heart,

Your humble Servant,

L   John Enville, *Knt.*'

No. 300.

[STEELE.]   Wednesday, February 13.

. . . *Diversum vitio vitium prope majus.*—Hor.

'*Mr.* SPECTATOR,

WHEN you talk of the Subject of Love, and the Relations arising from it, methinks you should take Care to leave no Fault unobserved which concerns the State of Marriage. The great Vexation that I have observed in it, is, that the wedded Couple seem to want Opportunities of being often enough alone together, and are forced to quarrel and be fond before Company. Mr. *Hotspur* and his Lady, in a Room full of their Friends, are ever saying something so smart to each other, and that but just within Rules, that the whole Company stand in the utmost Anxiety and Suspence for Fear of their falling into Extremities which they could not be present at. On the other side, *Tom. Faddle* and his pretty Spouse, wherever they come are billing at such a Rate, as they think must do our Hearts good to behold 'em. Cannot you possibly propose a Mean between being Wasps and Doves in Publick? I should think if you advised to hate or love sincerely it would be better: For if they would be so discreet as to hate from the very Bottom of their Hearts, their Aversion would be too strong for their Gibes every Moment; and if they loved with that calm and noble Value which dwells in the Heart, with a Warmth like that of Life-Blood, they would not be so impatient of their Passion as to fall into observable Fondness. This Method, in each Case, would have Appearances; but as those who offend on the fond Side are by much the fewer, I would have you begin with them, and go on to take Notice of a most impertinent Licence married Women take, not only to be very loving to their Spouses in Publick, but also make nauseous Allusions to private Familiarities and the like. *Lucina* is a Lady of the greatest Discretion you must know in the World; and withal very much a Physician: Upon the Strength of these two Qualities there is nothing she will not speak of before us Virgins; and she every Day talks with a very grave Air in such a Manner, as is very improper so much as to be hinted at, but to obviate the greatest Extremity. Those whom they call good Bodies, notable People, hearty Neighbours, and the purest goodest Company in the World, are the great Offenders in this Kind. Here I think I have laid before you an open Field for Pleasantry; and hope you will shew these People that at least they are not witty: In which you will save from many a Blush a daily Sufferer, who is very much

> *Your most humble Servant,*
>
> Susanna Decent.'

'*Mr.* Spectator,

In yours of *Wednesday* the 30th past, you and your Correspondent are very severe on a Sort of Men, whom you call Male Coquets; but without any other Reason, in my Apprehension, than that of paying a shallow Compliment to the fair Sex, by accusing some Men of imaginary Faults, that the Women may not seem to be the more faulty Sex; though at the same Time you suppose there are some so weak as to be imposed upon by fine Things and false Addresses. I can't perswade my self that your Design is to debar the Sexes the Benefit of each other's Conversation within the Rules of Honour; nor will you, I dare say, recommend to 'em, or encourage the common Tea-Table Talk, much less that of Politicks and Matter of State: And if these are forbidden Subjects of Discourse, then, as long as there are any Women in the World who take a Pleasure in hearing themselves praised, and can bear the Sight of a Man prostrate at their Feet, so long I shall make no Wonder that there are those of the other Sex who will pay them those Impertinent Humiliations. We should have few People such Fools as to practise Flattery, if all were so wise as to despise it. I don't deny but you would do a meritorious Act, if you could prevent all Impositions on the Simplicity of young Women; but I must confess I don't apprehend you have laid the Fault on the proper Person, and if I trouble you with my Thoughts upon it I promise my self your Pardon. Such of the Sex as are raw and innocent, and most exposed to these Attacks, have, or their Parents are much to blame if they have not, one to advise and guard 'em, and are obliged themselves to take Care of 'em; but if these, who ought to hinder Men from all Opportunities of this Sort of Conversation, instead of that encourage and promote it, the Suspicion is very just that there are some private Reasons for it; and I 'll leave it to you to determine on which Side a Part is then acted. Some Women there are who are arrived at Years of Discretion, I mean are got out of the Hands of their Parents and Governours, and are set up for themselves, who yet are liable to these Attempts; but if these are prevail'd upon, you must excuse me if I lay the Fault upon them that their Wisdom is not grown with their Years. My Client, Mr. *Strephon*, whom you summoned to declare himself, gives you Thanks however for your Warning; and begs the Favour only to inlarge his Time for a Week, or to the last Day of the Term, and then he 'll appear *gratis* and pray no Day over.

Yours,

Philanthropos.'

' *Mr.* Spectator,

I was last Night to visit a Lady whom I much esteem, and always took for my Friend; but met with so very different a Reception from what I expected, that I cannot help applying my self to you on this Occasion. In the Room of that Civility and Familiarity I used to be treated with by her, an affected Strangeness in her Looks and Coldness in her Behaviour, plainly told me I was not the welcome Guest which the Regard and Tenderness she has often expressed for me gave me Reason to flatter my self to think I was. Sir, this is certainly a great Fault, and I assure you a very common one; therefore I hope you will think it a fit Subject for some Part of a *Spectator*. Be pleased to acquaint us how we must behave our selves towards this valetudinary Friendship, subject to so many Heats and Colds; and you will oblige,

Sir,

Your humble Servant,

Miranda.'

'*Sir,*

I cannot forbear acknowledging the Delight your late *Spectators* on *Saturdays* have given me; for it is writ in the honest Spirit of Criticism, and called to my Mind the following four Lines I had read long since in a Prologue to a Play called *Julius Caesar,* which has deserved a better Fate. The Verses are addressed to the little Criticks.

> *Shew your small Talent, and let that suffice ye;*
> *But grow not vain upon it, I advise ye.*
> *For every Fop can find out Faults in Plays;*
> *You'll ne'er arrive at Knowing when to praise.*

Yours,

T   *D. G.'*

No. 301
[BUDGELL.]   Thursday, February 14.

> *Possent ut juvenes visere fervidi*
> *Multo non sine risu*
> *Dilapsam in cineres facem.*—Hor.

WE are generally so much pleased with any little Accomplishments, either of Body or Mind, which have once made us remarkable in the World, that we endeavour to perswade our selves it is not in the Power of Time to rob us of them. We are eternally pursuing the same Methods which first procured us the Applauses of Mankind. It is from this Notion that an Author writes on, tho' he is come to Dotage; without ever considering that his Memory is impair'd, and that he hath lost that Life, and those Spirits, which formerly raised his Fancy, and fired his Imagination. The same Folly hinders a Man from submitting his Behaviour to his Age, and makes *Clodius,* who was a celebrated Dancer at five and twenty, still love to hobble in a Minuet, tho' he is past Threescore. It is this, in a Word, which fills the Town with elderly Fops, and superannuated Coquets.

Canidia, a Lady of this latter Species, passed by me yesterday in her Coach. *Canidia* was an haughty Beauty of the last Age, and was followed by Crouds of Adorers, whose Passions only pleased her, as they gave her Opportunities of playing the Tyrant. She then contracted that awful Cast of the Eye and forbidding Frown, which she has not yet laid aside, and has still all the Insolence of Beauty without its Charms. If she now attracts the Eyes of any Beholders, it is only by being remarkably ridiculous; even her own Sex laugh at her Affectation; and the Men, who always enjoy an ill-natured Pleasure in seeing an imperious Beauty humbled and neglected, regard her with the same Satisfaction that a free Nation sees a Tyrant in Disgrace.

WILL HONEYCOMB, who is a great Admirer of the Gallantries in King *Charles* the Second's Reign, lately communicated to me a Letter written by a Wit of that Age to his Mistress, who, it seems, was a Lady of *Canidia*'s Humour; and tho' I do not always approve of my Friend WILL's Taste, I liked this Letter so well, that I took a Copy of it, with which I shall here present my Reader.

'*To* CLOE.

Madam,

Since my waking Thoughts have never been able to influence you in my Favour, I am resolved to try whether my Dreams can make any Impression on you. To this End I shall give you an Account of a very odd one which my Fancy presented to me last Night, within a few Hours after I left you.

Methought I was unaccountably conveyed into the most delicious Place my Eyes ever beheld, it was a large Valley divided by a River of the purest Water I had ever seen. The Ground on each Side of it rose by an easy Ascent, and was cover'd with Flowers of an infinite Variety, which as they were reflected in the Water doubled the Beauties of the Place, or rather formed an imaginary Scene more beautiful than the real. On each Side of the River was a Range of lofty Trees, whose Boughs were loaden with almost as many Birds as Leaves. Every Tree was full of Harmony.

I had not gone far in this pleasant Valley, when I perceived that it was terminated by a most magnificent Temple. The Structure was ancient, and regular. On the Top of it was figured the God *Saturn*, in the same Shape and Dress that the Poets usually represent *Time*.

As I was advancing to satisfy my Curiosity by a nearer View, I was stopped by an Object far more beautiful than any I had before discovered in the whole Place. I fancy, Madam, you will easily guess that this could hardly be any Thing but your self; in reality it was so; you lay extended on the Flowers by the Side of the River, so that your Hands which were thrown in a negligent Posture, almost touched the Water. Your Eyes were closed; but if your Sleep deprived me of the Satisfaction of seeing them, it left me at leisure to contemplate several other Charms, which disappear when your Eyes are open. I could not but admire the Tranquillity you slept in, especially when I considered the Uneasiness you produce in so many others.

While I was wholly taken up in these Reflections, the Doors

of the Temple flew open, with a very great Noise; and lifting up my Eyes, I saw two Figures, in humane Shape, coming into the Valley. Upon a nearer Survey, I found them to be YOUTH and LOVE. The first was encircled with a kind of Purple Light, that spread a Glory over all the Place; the other held a flaming Torch in his Hand. I could observe, that all the Way as they came towards us, the Colours of the Flowers appeared more lively, the Trees shot out in Blossoms, the Birds threw themselves into Pairs, and serenaded them as they passed. The whole Face of Nature glowed with new Beauties. They were no sooner arrived at the Place where you lay, when they seated themselves on each Side of you. On their Approach, methought I saw a new Bloom arise in your Face, and new Charms diffuse themselves over your whole Person. You appeared more than Mortal; but, to my great Surprise, continued fast asleep, tho' the two Deities made several gentle Efforts to awaken you.

After a short Time, YOUTH (displaying a Pair of Wings, which I had not before taken Notice of) flew off. LOVE still remained, and holding the Torch which he had in his Hand before your Face, you still appeared as beautiful as ever. The glaring of the Light in your Eyes at length awaken'd you, when, to my great Surprise, instead of acknowledging the Favour of the Deity, you frowned upon him, and struck the Torch out of his Hand into the River. The God after having regarded you with a Look that spoke at once his Pity and Displeasure, flew away. Immediately a Kind of Gloom overspread the whole Place. At the same Time I saw an hideous Spectre enter at one End of the Valley. His Eyes were sunk into his Head, his Face was pale and withered, and his Skin puckered up in Wrinkles. As he walked on the Sides of the Bank the River froze, the Flowers faded, the Trees shed their Blossoms, the Birds dropp'd from off the Boughs, and fell dead at his Feet. By these Marks I knew him to be OLD-AGE: You were seized with the utmost Horror and Amazement at his Approach. You endeavoured to have fled, but the Phantome caught you in his Arms. You may easily guess at the Change you suffered in this Embrace. For my own Part, tho' I am still too full of the dreadful Idea, I will not shock you with a Description of it: I was so startled at the Sight that my Sleep immediately left me, and I found my self awake, at leisure to consider of a Dream which seems too extraordinary to be without a Meaning. I am, Madam, with the greatest Passion,

Your most obedient,
Most humble Servant, &c.'

X

No. 302.

[STEELE.] Friday, February 15.

> . . . *Lacrimaeque decorae,*
> *Gratior & pulchro veniens in corpore virtus.*—V. *Ae.* 5.

I READ what I give for the Entertainment of this Day with a great deal of Pleasure, and publish it just as it came to my Hands. I shall be very glad to find there are many guessed at for *Emilia.*

'*Mr.* SPECTATOR,

If this Paper has the good Fortune to be honoured with a Place in your Writings, I shall be the more pleased, because the Character of *Emilia* is not an imaginary but a real one. I have industriously obscured the whole by the Addition of one or two Circumstances of no Consequence, that the Person it is drawn from might still be concealed; and that the Writer of it might not be in the least suspected, and for some other Reasons, I chuse not to give it the Form of a Letter: But if, besides the Faults of the Composition, there be any Thing in it more proper for a Correspondent than the SPECTATOR himself to write, I submit it to your better Judgment, to receive any other Model you think fit.

> *I am,*
> *Sir,*
> *Your very humble Servant.*'

There is Nothing which gives one so pleasing a prospect of humane Nature, as the Contemplation of Wisdom and Beauty: The latter is the peculiar Portion of that Sex which is therefore called Fair; but the happy Concurrence of both these Excellencies in the same Person, is a Character too celestial to be frequently met with. Beauty is an over-weaning self-sufficient Thing, careless of providing it self any more substantial Ornaments; nay so little does it consult its own Interests, that it too often defeats it self, by betraying that Innocence which renders it lovely and desirable. As therefore Virtue makes a beautiful Woman appear more beautiful, so Beauty makes a virtuous Woman really more virtuous. Whilst I am considering these two Perfections gloriously united in one Person, I cannot help representing to my Mind the Image of *Emilia.*

Who ever beheld the charming *Emilia,* without feeling in his Breast at once the Glow of Love and the Tenderness of virtuous Friendship? The unstudied Graces of her Behaviour, and the pleasing Accents of her Tongue, insensibly draw you on to wish for a nearer Enjoyment of them; but even her Smiles carry

in them a silent Reproof to the Impulses of licentious Love.
Thus, tho' the Attractives of her Beauty play almost irresist-
ibly upon you and create Desire, you immediately stand corrected not by the Severity but the Decency of her Virtue.
That Sweetness and Good-humour which is so visible in her
Face, naturally diffuses it self into every Word and Action:
A Man must be a Savage, who, at the Sight of *Emilia*, is not
more inclined to do her Good than gratify himself: Her Person
as it is thus studiously embellished by Nature, thus adorned
with unpremeditated Graces, is a fit Lodging for a Mind so
fair and lovely; there dwell rational Piety, modest Hope, and
chearful Resignation.

Many of the prevailing Passions of Mankind do undeservedly
pass under the Name of Religion; which is thus made to express
it self in Action, according to the Nature of the Constitution
in which it resides: So that were we to make a Judgment from
Appearances, one would imagine Religion in some is little better
than Sullenness and Reserve, in many Fear, in others the De-
spondings of a melancholy Complexion, in others the Formality
of insignificant unaffecting Observances, in others Severity,
in others Ostentation. In *Emilia* it is a Principle founded in
Reason and enlivened with Hope; it does not break forth into
irregular Fits and Sallies of Devotion, but is an uniform and
consistent Tenour of Action: It is strict without Severity,
compassionate without Weakness; it is the Perfection of that
good Humour which proceeds from the Understanding, not
the Effect of an easy Constitution.

By a generous Sympathy in Nature, we feel our selves disposed to mourn when any of our Fellow Creatures are afflicted;
but injured Innocence and Beauty in Distress, is an Object
that carries in it something inexpressibly moving: It softens
the most manly Heart with the tenderest Sensations of Love
and Compassion, till at length it confesses its Humanity, and
flows out into Tears.

Were I to relate that Part of *Emilia*'s Life which has given
her an Opportunity of exerting the Heroism of Christianity,
it would make too sad, too tender a Story: But when I consider her alone in the Midst of her Distresses, looking beyond
this gloomy Vale of Affliction and Sorrow in the Joys of Heaven
and Immortality, and when I see her in Conversation thoughtless and easy as if she were the most happy Creature in the
World, I am transported with Admiration. Surely never did
such a philosophical Soul inhabit such a beauteous Form!
For Beauty is often made a Privilege against Thought and
Reflection; it laughs at Wisdom, and will not abide the Gravity
of its Instructions.

Were I able to represent *Emilia*'s Virtues in their Proper Colours and their due Proportions, Love or Flattery might perhaps be thought to have drawn the Picture larger than Life; but as this is but an imperfect Draught of so excellent a Character, and as I cannot, will not hope to have any Interest in her Person, all that I can say of her is but impartial Praise extorted from me by the prevailing Brightness of her Virtues. So rare a Pattern of Female Excellence ought not to be concealed, but should be set out to the View and Imitation of the World; for how amiable does Virtue appear thus as it were made visible to us in so fair an Example!

Honoria's Disposition is of a very different Turn: Her Thoughts are wholly bent upon Conquest and arbitrary Power. That she has some Wit and Beauty no Body denies, and therefore has the Esteem of all her Acquaintance as a Woman of an agreeable Person and Conversation; but (whatever her Husband may think of it) that is not sufficient for *Honoria*: She waves that Title to Respect as a mean Acquisition, and demands Veneration in the Right of an Idol; for this Reason her natural Desire of Life is continually checked with an inconsistent Fear of Wrinkles and old Age.

Emilia cannot be supposed ignorant of her personal Charms, tho' she seems to be so; but she will not hold her Happiness upon so precarious a Tenure, whilst her Mind is adorned with Beauties of a more exalted and lasting Nature. When in the full Bloom of Youth and Beauty we saw her surrounded with a Croud of Adorers, she took no Pleasure in Slaughter and Destruction, gave no false deluding Hopes which might encrease the Torments of her disappointed Lovers; but having for some Time given to the Decency of a Virgin Coyness, examined the Merit of their several Pretensions, she at length gratified her own, by resigning herself to the ardent Passion of *Bromius*. *Bromius* was then Master of many good Qualities and a moderate Fortune, which was soon after unexpectedly encreased to a plentiful Estate. This for a good while prov'd his Misfortune, as it furnish'd his unexperienc'd Age with the Opportunities of evil Company and a sensual Life. He might have longer wander'd in the Labyrinths of Vice and Folly, had not *Emilia*'s prudent Conduct won him over to the Government of his Reason. Her Ingenuity has been constantly employed in humanizing his Passions and refining his Pleasures. She has shew'd him by her own Example, that Virtue is consistent with decent Freedoms and good Humour, or rather, that it cannot subsist without 'em. Her good Sense readily instructed her, that a silent Example and an easy unrepining Behaviour, will always be more perswasive than the Severity of Lectures and Admonitions; and that there is so much Pride interwoven into the Make of humane Nature, that an obstinate Man must only take the Hint from another, and then be left to advise and correct himself. Thus by an artful Train of Management and unseen Perswasions, having at first brought him not to dislike, and at length to be pleased with that which otherwise he would not have bore to hear of, she then knew how to press and secure this Advantage, by approving it as his Thought, and seconding it as his Proposal. By this Means she has gain'd an Interest in some of his leading Passions, and made them accessary to his Reformation.

There is another Particular of *Emilia*'s Conduct which I can't forbear mentioning: To some perhaps it may at first Sight appear but a trifling inconsiderable Circumstance; but for my Part, I think it highly worthy of Observation, and to be recommended to the Consideration of the fair Sex. I have often thought wrapping Gowns and dirty Linnen, with all that huddled Oeconomy of Dress which passes under the general Name of a Mob, the Bane of conjugal Love, and one of the readiest Means imaginable to alienate the Affection of an Husband, especially a fond one. I have heard some Ladies who have been surprized by Company in such a Deshabille, apologize for it after this Manner; *Truly I am ashamed to be caught in this Pickle; but my Husband and I were sitting all alone by ourselves, and I did not expect to see such good Company.* . . . This by the Way is a fine Compliment to the good Man, which 'tis ten to one but he returns in dogged Answers and a churlish Behaviour, without knowing what it is that puts him out of Humour.

Emilia's Observation teaches her, that as little Inadvertencies and Neglects cast a Blemish upon a great Character; so the Neglect of Apparel, even among the most intimate Friends, does insensibly lessen their Regards to each other, by creating a Familiarity too low and contemptible. She understands the Importance of those Things which the Generality account Trifles; and considers every Thing as a Matter of Consequence, that has the least Tendency towards keeping up or abating the Affection of her Husband; him she esteems as a fit Object to employ her Ingenuity in pleasing, because he is to be pleased for Life.

By the Help of these, and a thousand other nameless Arts, which 'tis easier for her to practise than for another to express, by the Obstinacy of her Goodness and unprovoked Submission, in spight of all her Afflictions and ill Usage, *Bromius* is become a Man of Sense and a kind Husband, and *Emilia* a happy Wife.

Ye guardian Angels to whose Care Heaven has entrusted its

dear *Emilia*, guide her still forward in the Paths of Virtue, defend her from the Insolence and Wrongs of this undiscerning World; at length when we must no more converse with such Purity on Earth, lead her gently hence innocent and unreprovable to a better Place, where by an easy Transition from what she now is, she may shine forth an Angel of Light.

T

No. 303.
[ADDISON.]   Saturday, February 16.

. . . Volet haec sub luce videri,
Judicis argutum quae non formidat acumen.—Hor.

I HAVE seen in the Works of a Modern Philosopher, a Map of the Spots in the Sun. My last Paper of the Faults and Blemishes in *Milton's Paradise Lost*, may be considered as a Piece of the same Nature. To pursue the Allusion: As it is observed, that among the bright Parts of the luminous Body above-mentioned, there are some which glow more intensely, and dart a stronger Light than others; so, notwithstanding I have already shewn *Milton*'s Poem to be very beautiful in general, I shall now proceed to take notice of such Beauties as appear to me more exquisite than the rest. *Milton* has proposed the Subject of his Poem in the following Verses.

Of Man's first Disobedience, and the fruit
Of that forbidden tree, whose mortal taste
Brought Death into the World and all our woe,
With loss of Eden, *'till one greater Man*
Restore us, and regain the blissful Seat,
Sing Heav'nly Muse . . .

These Lines are perhaps as plain, simple and unadorned as any of the whole Poem, in which Particular the Author has conform'd himself to the Example of *Homer*, and the Precept of *Horace*.

His Invocation to a Work which turns in a great Measure upon the Creation of the World, is very properly made to the Muse who inspired *Moses* in those Books from whence our Author drew his Subject, and to the Holy Spirit who is therein represented as operating after a particular Manner in the first Production of Nature. This whole Exordium rises very happily into noble Language and Sentiment, as I think the Transition to the Fable is exquisitely beautiful and natural.

The Nine-days Astonishment, in which the Angels lay entranced after their dreadful Overthrow and Fall from Heaven, before they could recover either the Use of Thought or Speech, is a noble *Circumstance*, and very finely imagined. The Division of Hell into Seas of Fire and into firm Ground impregnate with the same furious Element, with that particular Circumstance of the Exclusion of *Hope* from those Infernal Regions, are Instances of the same great and fruitful Invention.

The Thoughts in the first Speech and Description of *Satan*, who is one of the principal Actors, in this Poem, are wonderfully proper to give us a full Idea of him. His Pride, Envy and Revenge, Obstinacy, Despair and Impenitence, are all of them very artfully interwoven. In short, his first Speech is a Complication of all those Passions which discover themselves separately in several other of his Speeches in the Poem. The whole Part of this great Enemy of Mankind is filled with such Incidents as are very apt to raise and terrify the Reader's Imagination. Of this Nature, in the Book now before us, is his being the first that awakens out of the general Trance, with his Posture on the burning Lake, his rising from it, and the Description of his Shield and Spear.

> *Thus* Satan *talking to his nearest mate,*
> *With head up-lift above the wave, and eyes*
> *That sparkling blazed, his other parts beside*
> *Prone on the Flood, extended long and large,*
> *Lay floating many a rood. . . .*
> *Forthwith upright he rears from off the pool*
> *His mighty Stature; on each hand the flames*
> *Driv'n backward slope their pointing Spires, and rowl'd*
> *In Billows, leave i' th' midst a horrid vale.*
> *Then with expanded wings he steers his flight*
> *Aloft, incumbent on the dusky Air*
> *That felt unusual weight . . .*
> *. . . His pondrous Shield*
> *Ethereal temper, massie, large and round,*
> *Behind him cast; the broad circumference*
> *Hung on his Shoulders like the Moon, whose orb*
> *Thro' Optick Glass the* Tuscan *Artist views*
> *At Ev'ning from the top of* Fesole,
> *Or in* Valdarno *to descry new Lands,*
> *Rivers or Mountains on her spotted Globe.*
> *His Spear to equal which the tallest pine*
> *Hewn on* Norwegian *Hills to be the Mast*
> *Of some great Ammiral, were but a wand*
> *He walk'd with to support uneasy Steps*
> *Over the burning Marl. . . .*

To which we may add his Call to the fallen Angels that lay plunged and stupified in the Sea of Fire.

> *He call'd so loud, that all the hollow deep*
> *Of Hell resounded. . . .*

But there is no single Passage in the whole Poem worked up to a greater Sublimity, than that wherein his Person is described in those celebrated Lines:

> . . . *He, above the rest*
> *In shape and gesture proudly eminent*
> *Stood like a Tower,* &c.

His Sentiments are every way answerable to his Character, and suitable to a created Being of the most exalted and most depraved Nature. Such is that in which he takes possession of his Place of Torments.

> . . . *Hail Horrors, hail*
> *Infernal World, and thou profoundest Hell*
> *Receive thy new Possessor, one who brings*
> *A mind not to be changed by place or time.*

And afterwards,

> . . . *Here at least*
> *We shall be free; th' Almighty hath not built*
> *Here for his envy, will not drive us hence:*
> *Here we may reign secure; and in my choice*
> *To reign is worth ambition, tho' in Hell:*
> *Better to reign in Hell than serve in Heaven.*

Amidst those Impieties which this Enraged Spirit utters in other Places of the Poem, the Author has taken care to introduce none that is not big with Absurdity, and incapable of shocking a Religious Reader; his Words, as the Poet himself describes them, bearing only a *Semblance of Worth, not Substance.* He is likewise with great Art described as owning his Adversary to be Almighty. Whatever perverse Interpretation he puts on the Justice, Mercy, and other Attributes of the Supreme Being, he frequently confesses his Omnipotence, that being the Perfection he was forced to allow him, and the only Consideration which could support his Pride under the Shame of his Defeat.

Nor must I here omit that beautiful Cirumstance of his bursting out in Tears, upon his Survey of those innumerable Spirits whom he had involved in the same Guilt and Ruin with himself.

> . . . *He now prepared*
> *To speak; whereat their doubled ranks they bend*
> *From wing to wing, and half enclose him round*
> *With all his Peers: Attention held them mute.*
> *Thrice he assay'd, and thrice in spite of Scorn*
> *Tears such as Angels weep, burst forth.* . . .

The Catalogue of Evil Spirits has Abundance of Learning in it, and a very agreeable Turn of Poetry, which rises in a great measure from its describing the Places where they were worshipped, by those beautiful Marks of Rivers so frequent among the Antient Poets. The Author has doubtless in this place *Homer*'s Catalogue of Ships, and *Virgil*'s List of Warriors in his View. The Characters of *Moloch* and *Belial* prepare the Reader's Mind for their respective Speeches and Behaviour in the second and sixth Book. The Account of *Thammuz* is finely Romantick, and suitable to what we read among the Antients of the Worship which was paid to that Idol.

The Passage in the Catalogue, explaining the manner how Spirits transform themselves by Contraction, or Enlargement of their Dimensions, is introduced with great Judgment, to make way for several surprising Accidents in the Sequel of the Poem. There follows one, at the very End of the First Book, which is what the *French* Criticks call *Marvellous*, but at the same Time *probable* by reason of the Passage last mentioned. As soon as the Infernal Palace is finished, we are told the Multitude and Rabble of Spirits immediately shrunk themselves into a small Compass, that there might be Room for such a numberless Assembly in this capacious Hall. But it is the Poet's Refinement upon this Thought, which I most admire, and which is indeed very noble in its self. For he tells us, that notwithstanding the vulgar, among the fallen Spirits, contracted their Forms, those of the first Rank and Dignity still preserved their natural Dimensions.

> *Thus incorporeal Spirits to smallest Forms*
> *Reduc'd their Shapes immense, and were at large*
> *Though without Number still amidst the Hall*
> *Of that infernal Court.   But far within,*
> *And in their own Dimensions like themselves,*
> *The Great Seraphick Lords and Cherubim,*
> *In close recess and Secret conclave sate,*
> *A thousand Demy Gods on Golden Seats,*
> *Frequent and full. . . .*

The Character of *Mammon*, and the Description of the *Pandaemonium*, are full of Beauties.

There are several other Strokes in the First Book wonderfully poetical, and Instances of that Sublime Genius so peculiar to the Author. Such is the Description of *Azazel*'s Stature, and the Infernal Standard, which he unfurls; as also of that ghastly Light, by which the Fiends appear to one another in their Place of Torments.

> *The Seat of Desolation, void of Light,*
> *Save what the glimm'ring of those livid Flames*
> *Casts pale and dreadful . . .*

The Shout of the whole Host of fallen Angels when drawn up in Battel Aray;

> *. . . The Universal Host up sent*
> *A Shout that tore Hell's Concave, and beyond*
> *Frighted the Reign of* Chaos *and old Night.*

The Review, which the Leader makes of his Infernal Army;

> *. . . He thro' the armed files*
> *Darts his experienc'd eye, and soon traverse*
> *The whole Battalion views, their order due,*
> *Their Vizages and Stature as of Gods,*
> *Their number last he sums. And now his Heart*
> *Distends with pride, and hard'ning in his strength*
> *Glories . . .*

The Flash of Light, which appeared upon the drawing of their Swords;

> *He spake: and to confirm his Words out flew*
> *Millions of flaming Swords, drawn from the Thighs*
> *Of mighty* Cherubim; *the sudden Blaze*
> *Far round illumin'd Hell. . . .*

The sudden Production of the *Pandaemonium;*

> *Anon out of the Earth a Fabrick huge*
> *Rose like an Exhalation, with the Sound*
> *Of Dulcet Symphonies and Voices sweet.*

The artificial Illuminations made in it;

> *. . . From the arched Roof*
> *Pendent by subtle Magick, many a Row*
> *Of Starry Lamps and blazing Crescets, fed*
> *With* Naphtha *and* Asphaltus, *yielded Light*
> *As from a Sky . . .*

There are also several noble Similes and Allusions in the first Book of *Paradise Lost.* And here I must observe, that when *Milton* alludes either to Things or Persons, he never quits his Simile till it rises to some very great Idea, which is often foreign to the Occasion that gave Birth to it. The Resemblance does not, perhaps, last above a Line or two, but the Poet runs on with the Hint, till he has raised out of it some glorious Image or Sentiment, proper to inflame the Mind of the Reader, and to give it that sublime Kind of Entertainment, which is suitable to the Nature of an Heroick Poem. Those, who are acquainted with *Homer's* and *Virgil's* Way of Writing, cannot but be pleased with this kind of Structure in *Milton's* Similitudes. I am the more particular on this Head, because ignorant Readers, who have formed their Taste upon the quaint Similes, and little Turns of Wit, which are so much in

Vogue among modern Poets, cannot relish these Beauties which
are of a much higher Nature, and are therefore apt to censure
Milton's Comparisons, in which they do not see any surprising
Points of Likeness. Monsieur *Perrault* was a Man of this
vitiated Relish, and for that very Reason has endeavoured to
turn into Ridicule several of *Homer*'s Similitudes, which he
calls *Comparaisons à longue queue, Long-tail'd Comparisons.*
I shall conclude this Paper on the First Book of *Milton* with the
Answer which Monsieur *Boileau* makes to *Perrault* on this
Occasion; 'Comparisons,' says he, 'in Odes and Epic Poems are
not introduced only to illustrate and embellish the Discourse,
but to amuse and relax the Mind of the Reader, by frequently
disengaging him from too painful an Attention to the principal
Subject, and by leading him into other agreeable Images.
Homer,' says he, 'excelled in this Particular, whose Comparisons abound with such Images of Nature as are proper to
relieve and diversifie his Subjects. He continually instructs
the Reader, and makes him take notice, even in Objects which
are every Day before our Eyes, of such Circumstances as we
should not otherwise have observed.' *To this he adds, as a
Maxim universally acknowledged,* 'That it is not necessary in
Poetry for the Points of the Comparison to correspond with one
another exactly, but that a general Resemblance is sufficient,
and that too much Nicety in this Particular savours of the
Rhetorician and Epigrammatist.'

In short, if we look into the Conduct of *Homer*, *Virgil* and
Milton, as the great Fable is the Soul of each Poem, so to give
their Works an agreeable Variety, their Episodes are so many
short Fables, and their Similes so many short Episodes; to
which you may add, if you please, that their Metaphors are so
many short Similes. If the Reader considers the Comparisons
in the first Book of *Milton*, of the Sun in an Eclipse, of the
sleeping *Leviathan*, of the Bees swarming about their Hive,
of the fairy Dance, in the View wherein I have here placed them,
he will easily discover the great Beauties that are in each of
those Passages.   L

No. 304.
[STEELE.]   Monday, February 18.
Vulnus alit venis & caeco carpitur igni.—Virg.

THE Circumstances of my Correspondent, whose Letter I now
insert, are so frequent, that I cannot want Compassion so much

as to forbear laying it before the Town. There is something so mean and inhumane in a direct *Smithfield* Bargain for Children, that if this Lover carries his Point, and observes the Rules he pretends to follow, I do not only wish him Success, but also that it may animate others to follow his Example. I know not one Motive relating to this Life which would produce so many honourable and worthy Actions, as the Hopes of obtaining a Woman of Merit; there would ten thousand Ways of Industry and honest Ambition be pursued by young Men, who believed that the Persons admired had Value enough for their Passion to attend the Event of their good Fortune in all their Applications, in order to make their Circumstances fall in with the Duties they owe to themselves, their Families, and their Country: All these Relations a Man should think of, who intends to go into the State of Marriage, and expects to make it a State of Pleasure and Satisfaction.

' *Mr.* SPECTATOR,

I have for some Years indulged a Passion for a young Lady of Age and Quality suitable to my own, but very much superior in Fortune. It is the Fashion with Parents (how justly I leave you to judge) to make all Regards give Way to the Article of Wealth. From this one Consideration is that I have concealed the ardent Love I have for her; but I am beholden to the Force of my Love for many Advantages which I reaped from it towards the better Conduct of my Life. A certain Complacency to all the World, a strong Desire to oblige where-ever it lay in my Power, and a circumspect Behaviour in all my Words and Actions, have rendered me more particularly acceptable to all my Friends and Acquaintance. Love has had the same good Effect upon my Fortune; and I have encreased in Riches, in Proportion to my Advancement in those Arts, which make a Man agreeable and amiable. There is a certain Sympathy which will tell my Mistress from these Circumstances, that it is I who write this for her Reading, if you will please to insert it. There is not a downright Enmity, but a great Coldness between our Parents; so that if either of us declared any kind Sentiments for each other, her Friends would be very backward to lay an Obligation upon our Family, and mine to receive it from hers. Under these delicate Circumstances it is no easy Matter to act with Safety. I have no Reason to fancy my Mistress has any Regard for me, but from a very disinterested Value which I have for her. If from any Hint in any future Paper of yours she gives me the least Encouragement, I doubt not but I shall surmount all other Difficulties; and inspired by so noble a Motive for the Care of my Fortune, as the Belief she is to be concerned in it, I will not despair of receiving her one Day from her Father's own Hand.

> *I am,*
> > *Sir,*
> > > *Your most obedient humble Servant,*
> > > > Clytander.'

To his Worship the SPECTATOR.

The humble PETITION of *Anthony Title-Page*, Stationer, in the Centre of *Lincoln's-Inn-Fields*.

Sheweth,

That your Petitioner and his Fore-fathers have been Sellers of Books for Time immemorial: That your Petitioner's Ancestor, *Crouchback Title-Page*, was the first of that Vocation in *Britain*; who keeping his Station (in fair Weather) at the Corner of *Lothbury*, was by way of Eminency call'd *the Stationer*, a Name which from him all succeeding Booksellers have affected to bear: That the Station of your Petitioner and his Father has been in the Place of his present Settlement ever since that Square has been built: That your Petitioner has formerly had the Honour of your Worship's Custom, and hopes you never had Reason to complain of your Pennyworths, that particularly he sold you your first *Lilly*'s Grammar, and at the same time a *Wit's Common-wealth* almost as good as new: Moreover, that your first rudimental Essays in Spectatorship were made in your Petitioner's Shop, where you often practis'd for Hours together sometimes on his Books upon the Rails, sometimes on the little Hieroglyphicks either gilt, silver'd, or plain, which the *Egyptian* Woman on the other Side of the Shop had wrought in Gingerbread, and sometimes on the *English* Youth, who in sundry Places there were exercising themselves in the traditional Sports of the Field.

From these Considerations it is, that your Petitioner is encouraged to apply himself to you, and to proceed humbly to acquaint your Worship, That he has certain Intelligence that you receive great Numbers of defamatory Letters design'd by their Authors to be publish'd, which you throw aside, and totally Neglect: Your Petitioner therefore prays, that you will please to bestow on him those refuse Letters, and he hopes by printing them to get a more plentiful Provision for his Family; or at the worst, he may be allowed to sell them by the Pound Weight to his good Customers the Pastry-Cooks of *London* and *Westminster*.

And your Petitioner shall ever pray, &c.

To the SPECTATOR.

The humble PETITION of *Bartholomew Ladylove,* of *Round-Court,* in the Parish of St. *Martin's in the Fields,* in Behalf of himself and Neighbours.

Sheweth,

That your Petitioners have with great Industry and Application arrived at the most exact Art of Invitation or Entreaty: That by a beseeching Air and perswasive Address, they have for many Years last past peaceably drawn in every tenth Passenger, whether they intended or not to call at their Shops, to come in and buy; and from that Softness of Behaviour, have arrived among Tradesmen at the gentle Appellation of the *Fawners.*

That there have of late set up amongst us certain Persons of *Monmouth-street* and *Long-lane,* who by the Strength of their Arms, and Loudness of their Throats, draw off the Regard of all Passengers from your said Petitioners; from which Violence they are distinguished by the Name of *the Worriers.*

That while your Petitioners stand ready to receive Passengers with a submissive Bow, and repeat with a gentle Voice, *Ladies what do you want? pray look in here,* the Worriers reach out their Hands at Pistol-shot, and seize the Customers at Arms-Length.

That while the Fawners strain and relax the Muscles of their Faces, in making Distinction between a Spinster in a coloured Scarf, and an Hand-maid in a Straw-hat, the Worriers use the same Roughness to both, and prevail upon the Easiness of the Passengers to the Impoverishment of your Petitioners.

Your Petitioners therefore most humbly pray, that the Worriers may not be permitted to inhabit the politer Parts of the Town; and that *Round-Court* may remain a Receptacle for Buyers of a more soft Education.

And your Petitioners, &c.

The Petition of the New-Exchange *concerning the Arts of Buying and Selling, and particularly valuing Goods by the Complexion of the Seller, will be considered on another Occasion.* T

No. 305.
[ADDISON.]   Tuesday, February 19.

Non tali auxilio, nec defensoribus istis
Tempus eget . . .—Virg.

OUR late News-Papers being full of the Project now on Foot in the Court of *France,* for establishing a Political Academy, and I myself having received Letters from several Virtuosos among my foreign Correspondents, which give some Light into that Affair, I intend to make it the Subject of this Day's Speculation. A general Account of this Project may be met with in the *Daily Courant* of last *Friday* in the following Words, translated from the Gazette of *Amsterdam*.

Paris, February 12. ''Tis confirmed that the King has resolv'd to establish a new Academy for Politicks, of which the Marquess de *Torcy*, Minister and Secretary of State, is to be Protector. Six Academicians are to be chosen, endow'd with proper Talents, for beginning to form this Academy, into which no Person is to be admitted under twenty five Years of Age: They must likewise have each an Estate of two thousand Livres a Year, either in Possession, or to come to 'em by Inheritance. The King will allow to each a Pension of a thousand Livres. They are likewise to have able Masters to teach 'em the necessary Sciences, and to instruct them in all the Treaties of Peace, Alliance, and others which have been made in several Ages past. These Members are to meet twice a Week at the *Louvre.* From this Seminary are to be chosen Secretaries to Ambassies, who by Degrees may advance to higher Employments.'

Cardinal *Richelieu*'s Politicks made *France* the Terror of *Europe.* The Statesmen who have appeared in that Nation of late Years, have on the contrary rendered it either the Pity or Contempt of its Neighbours. The Cardinal erected that famous Academy which has carried all the Parts of polite Learning to the greatest Height. His chief Design in that Institution was to divert the Men of Genius from meddling with Politicks, a Province in which he did not care to have any one else interfere with him. On the contrary, the Marquess de *Torcy* seems resolved to make several young Men in *France* as wise as himself, and is therefore taken up at present in establishing a Nursery of Statesmen.

Some private Letters add, that there will also be erected a Seminary of Petticoat Politicians, who are to be brought up at the Feet of Madam de *Maintenon*, and to be dispatched into Foreign Courts upon any Emergencies of State; but as the News of this last Project has not been yet confirmed, I shall take no farther Notice of it.

Several of my Readers may doubtless remember, that upon the Conclusion of the last War, which had been carried on so successfully by the Enemy, their Generals were many of them transformed into Ambassadors; but the Conduct of those who have commanded in the present War, has, it seems, brought so little Honour and Advantage to their great Monarch, that he is resolved to trust his Affairs no longer in the Hands of those military Gentlemen.

The Regulations of this new Academy very much deserve our Attention. The Students are to have in Possession, or Reversion, an Estate of two thousand *French* Livres *per Annum*, which, as the present Exchange runs, will amount to at least one hundred and twenty six Pounds English. This, with the royal Allowance of a Thousand Livres, will enable them to find themselves in Coffee and Snuff; not to mention News Papers, Pen and Ink, Wax and Wafers, with the like Necessaries for Politicians.

A Man must be at least five and twenty before he can be initiated into the Misteries of this Academy, tho' there is no Question but many grave Persons of a much more advanced Age, who have been constant Readers of the *Paris* Gazette, will be glad to begin the World a-new, and enter themselves upon this List of Politicians.

The Society of these hopeful young Gentlemen is to be under the Direction of six Professors, who, it seems, are to be speculative Statesmen, and drawn out of the Body of the Royal Academy. These six wise Masters, according to my private Letters, are to have the following Parts alloted them.

The first is to instruct the Students in *State Legerdemain*, as how to take off the Impression of a Seal, to split a Wafer, to open a Letter, to fold it up again, with other the like ingenious Feats of Dexterity and Art. When the Students have accomplished themselves in this Part of their Profession, they are to be delivered into the Hands of their second Instructor, who is a kind of *Posture-master*.

This Artist is to teach them how to nod judiciously, to shrug up their Shoulders in a dubious Case, to connive with either Eye, and in a Word, the whole Practice of *Political Grimace*.

The third is a Sort of *Language Master*, who is to instruct them in the Stile proper for a Foreign Minister in his ordinary Discourse. And to the End that this College of Statesmen may be thoroughly practised in the political Stile, they are to make use of it in their common Conversations, before they are employed either in Foreign or Domestick Affairs. If one of them asks another, what a Clock it is, the other is to answer him indirectly, and, if possible, to turn off the Question. If he is desired to change a *Louis d'or*, he must beg Time to consider of it. If it be enquired of him, whether the King is at *Versailles* or *Marly*, he must answer in a Whisper. If he be ask'd the News of the late *Gazette*, or the Subject of a Proclamation, he is to reply, that he has not yet read it: Or if he does not care for explaining himself so far, he needs only draw his Brow up in Wrinkles, or elevate the left Shoulder.

The fourth Professor is to teach the whole Art of political

Characters and Hieroglyphicks; and to the End that they may be perfect also in this Practice, they are not to send a Note to one another (tho' it be but to borrow a *Tacitus* or a *Machiavel*) which is not written in Cypher.

Their fifth Professor, it is thought, will be chosen out of the Society of Jesuits, and is to be well read in the Controversies of probable Doctrines, mental Reservations, and the Rights of Princes. This Learned Man is to instruct them in the Grammar, Syntax, and construing Part of *Treaty-latin;* how to distinguish between the Spirit and the Letter, and likewise demonstrate how the same Form of Words may lay an Obligation upon any Prince in Europe, different from that which it lays upon his most Christian Majesty. He is likewise to teach them the Art of finding Flaws, Loop-holes, and Evasions, in the most solemn Compacts, and particularly a great *Rabbinical Secret*, revived of late Years by the Fraternity of Jesuits, namely, that contradictory Interpretations of the same Article, may both of them be true and valid.

When our Statesmen are sufficiently improved by these several Instructors, they are to receive their last Polishing from one who is to act among them as *Master of the Ceremonies*. This Gentleman is to give them Lectures upon those important Points of the *Elbow-Chair*, and the *Stair-Head;* to instruct them in the different Situations of the Right-Hand, and to furnish them with Bows and Inclinations of all Sizes, Measures and Proportions. In short, this Professor is to give the Society their *stiffening*, and infuse into their Manners that beautiful political Starch, which may qualifie them for Levees, Conferences, Visits, and make them shine in what Vulgar Minds are apt to look upon as Trifles.

I have not yet heard any further Particulars, which are to be observed in this Society of unfledged Statesmen; but I must confess, had I a Son of five and twenty, that shou'd take it into his Head at that Age to set up for a Politician, I think I shou'd go near to disinherit him for a Block-head. Besides, I should be apprehensive lest the same Arts which are to enable him to negotiate between Potentates, might a little infect his ordinary Behaviour between Man and Man. There is no Question but these young *Machiavels* will, in a little Time, turn their College upside-down with Plots and Stratagems, and lay as many Schemes to circumvent one another in a Frog or a Sallad, as they may hereafter put in Practice to over-reach a neighbouring Prince or State.

We are told that the *Spartans*, tho' they punish'd Theft in their young Men, when it was discovered, looked upon it as honourable if it succeeded. Provided the Conveyance was clean and unsuspected, a Youth might afterwards boast of it. This, say the Historians, was to keep them sharp, and to hinder them from being imposed upon, either in their publick or private Negociations. Whether any such Relaxations of Morality, such little *Jeux d'esprit*, ought not to be allowed in this intended Seminary of Politicians, I shall leave to the Wisdom of their Founder.

In the mean Time we have fair Warning given us by this doubty Body of Statesmen; and as *Sylla* saw many *Marius's* in *Caesar*, so I think we may discover many *Torcis* in this College of *Academicians*. Whatever we think of our selves, I am afraid neither our *Smyrna* or St. *James's* will be a Match for it. Our Coffee-houses are, indeed, very good Institutions, but whether or no these our *British* Schools of Politicks may furnish out as able Envoys and Secretaries as an Academy that is set a-part for that Purpose, will deserve our serious Consideration; especially if we remember that our Country is more famous for producing Men of Integrity than Statesmen; and that, on the contrary, *French* Truth, and *British* Policy make a Conspicuous Figure in NOTHING, as the Earl of *Rochester* has very well observed in his admirable Poem upon that barren Subject. L

No. 306.
[STEELE.]   Wednesday, February 20.

> . . . *Quae forma, ut se tibi semper*
> *Imputet?* . . .—Juv.

'*Mr.* SPECTATOR,

I WRITE this to communicate to you a Misfortune which frequently happens, and therefore deserves a consolatory Discourse on the Subject. I was within this Half-Year in the Possession of as much Beauty and as many Lovers as any young Lady in *England*. But my Admirers have left me, and I cannot complain of their Behaviour. I have within that Time had the Small-Pox; and this Face, which (according to many amorous Epistles which I have by me) was the Seat of all that is beautiful in Woman, is now disfigured with Scars. It goes to the very Soul of me to speak what I really think of my Face; and tho' I think I did not over-rate my Beauty while I had it, it has extremely advanced in its Value with me now it is lost. There is one Circumstance which makes my Case very Particular; the ugliest Fellow that ever pretended to me, was, and is most in my Favour, and he treats me at Present the most unreasonably. If you could make him return an Obligation

which he owes me, in liking a Person that is not amiable;——
But there is, I fear, no Possibility of making Passion move by
the Rules of Reason and Gratitude. But say what you can to
one who has survived herself, and knows not how to act in
a new Being. My Lovers are at the Feet of my Rivals, my
Rivals are every Day bewailing me, and I cannot enjoy what
I am, by Reason of the distracting Reflection upon what I was.
Consider the Woman I was did not dye of old Age, but I was
taken off in the Prime of my Youth, and according to the
Course of Nature may have forty Years After-Life to come.
I have Nothing of my self left which I like, but that

> I am,
> Sir,
>> Your most humble Servant,
>>> Parthenissa.'

When *Lewis* of *France* had lost the Battle of *Ramelies*, the
Addresses to him at that Time were full of his Fortitude, and
they turned his Misfortune to his Glory; in that, during his
Prosperity, he could never have manifested his heroick Constancy under Distresses, and so the World had lost the most
eminent Part of his Character. *Parthenissa*'s Condition gives
her the same Opportunity: and to resign Conquests is a Task
as difficult in a Beauty as an Hero. In the very Entrance
upon this Work she must burn all her Love-Letters; or since
she is so candid as not to call her Lovers, who follow her no
longer, unfaithful, it would be a very good Beginning of a new
Life from that of a Beauty, to send them back to those who
writ them, with this honest Inscription, *Articles of a Marriage
Treaty broken off by the Small-Pox.* I have known but one
Instance where a Matter of this Kind went on after a like
Misfortune; where the Lady, who was a Woman of Spirit, writ
this Billet to her Lover.

> ' *Sir,*
>
> If you flattered me before I had this terrible Malady, pray
> come and see me now: But if you sincerely liked me, stay away;
> for I am not the same
>> *Corinna.*'

The Lover thought there was something so sprightly in her
Behaviour, that he answered,

> ' *Madam,*
>
> I am not obliged since you are not the same Woman, to let
> you know whether I flatter'd you or not; but I assure you, I
> do not, when I tell you I now like you above all your Sex, and

hope you will bear what may befall me when we are both one, as well as you do what happens to your self now you are single; therefore I am ready to take such a Spirit for my Companion as soon as you please.

Amilcar.'

If *Parthenissa* can now possess her own Mind, and think as little of her Beauty as she ought to have done when she had it, there will be no great Diminution of her Charms; and if she was formerly affected too much with them, an easy Behaviour will more than make up for the Loss of them. Take the whole Sex together, and you find those who have the strongest Possession of Men's Hearts are not eminent for their Beauty: You see it often happen that those who engage Men to the greatest Violence, are such as those who are Strangers to them would take to be remarkably defective for that End. The fondest Lover I know, said to me one Day in a Croud of Women at an Entertainment of Musick, You have often heard me talk of my Beloved; That Woman there, continued he, smiling when he had fixed my Eye, is her very Picture. The Lady he showed me was by much the least remarkable for Beauty of any in the whole Assembly; but having my Curiosity extremely raised, I could not keep my Eyes off of her. Her Eyes at last met mine, and with a sudden Surprize she looked round her to see who near her was remarkably handsome that I was gazing at. This little Act explain'd the Secret: She did not understand herself for the Object of Love, and therefore she was so. The Lover is a very honest plain Man; and what charmed him was a Person that goes along with him in the Cares and Joys of Life, not taken up with herself, but sincerely attentive with a ready and chearful Mind to accompany him in either.

I can tell *Parthenissa* for her Comfort, That the Beauties, generally speaking, are the most impertinent and disagreeable of Women. An apparent Desire of Admiration, a Reflection upon their own Merit, and a precious Behaviour in their general Conduct, are almost inseparable Accidents in Beauties. All you obtain of them is granted to Importunity and Sollicitation for what did not deserve so much of your Time, and you recover from the Possession of it, as out of a Dream.

You are asham'd of the Vagaries of Fancy which so strangely misled you, and your Admiration of a Beauty, merely as such, is inconsistent with a tolerable Reflection upon your self: The chearful good humoured Creatures, into whose Heads it never entered that they could make any Man unhappy, are the Persons formed for making Men happy. There 's Miss *Liddy* can dance a Jigg, raise Paste, write a good Hand, keep an Accompt, give a reasonable Answer, and do as she is bid, while her elder Sister Madam *Martha* is out of Humour, has the Spleen, learns by Reports of People of higher Quality new Ways of being uneasy and displeas'd. And this happens for no Reason in the World, but that poor *Liddy* knows she has no such Thing as a certain Negligence *that is so becoming*, that there is not I know not what in *her Air*: And that if she talks like a Fool, there is no one will say, Well! I know not what it is, but *every Thing pleases when she speaks it*.

Ask any of the Husbands of your great Beauties, and they 'll tell you that they hate their Wives nine Hours of every Day they pass together. There is such a Particularity for ever affected by them, that they are incumbered with their Charms in all they say or do. They pray at publick Devotions as they are Beauties; they converse on ordinary Occasions as they are Beauties. Ask *Bellinda* what it is a Clock, and she is at a Stand whether so great a Beauty should answer you. In a Word, I think instead of Offering to administer Consolation to *Parthenissa*, I should congratulate her Metamorphosis; and however she thinks she was not in the least insolent in the Prosperity of her Charms, she was enough so to find she may make herself a much more agreeable Creature in her present Adversity. The Endeavour to please is highly promoted by a Consciousness that the Approbation of the Person you would be agreeable to, is a Favour you do not deserve; for in this Case Assurance of Success is the most certain Way to Disappointment. Good Nature will always supply the Absence of Beauty, but Beauty cannot long supply the Absence of Good Nature.

P. S.

   '*Madam*,   *February* 18.

I have yours of this Day, wherein you twice bid me not disoblige you, but you must explain your self further before I know what to do.

               Your most obedient Servant,

T   The SPECTATOR.'

No. 307.

[BUDGELL.]   Thursday, February 21.

   . . . *Versate diu quid ferre recusent*
   Quid valeant umeri . . .—Hor.

I AM so well pleased with the following Letter, that I am in Hopes it will not be a disagreeable Present to the Publick.

'*Sir*,

Though I believe none of your Readers more admire your agreeable Manner of Working up Trifles than my self, yet as your Speculations are now swelling into Volumes, and will in all probability pass down to future Ages, methinks I would have no single Subject in them, wherein the general Good of Mankind is concern'd, left unfinished.

I have a long Time expected with great Impatience, that you would enlarge upon the ordinary Mistakes which are committed in the Education of our Children. I the more easily flatter'd my self that you would one Time or other resume this Consideration, because you tell us that your 168th Paper was only composed of a few broken Hints; but finding my self hitherto disappointed, I have ventured to send you my own Thoughts on this Subject.

I remember *Pericles*, in his famous Oration at the Funeral of those *Athenian* young Men who perished in the *Samian* Expedition, has a Thought very much celebrated by several ancient Criticks, namely, That the Loss which the Commonwealth suffered by the Destruction of its Youth, was like the Loss which the Year would suffer by the Destruction of the Spring. The Prejudice which the Publick sustains from a wrong Education of Children, is an Evil of the same Nature, as it in a Manner starves Posterity, and defrauds our Country of those Persons, who, with due Care, might make an eminent Figure in their respective Posts of Life.

I have seen a Book written by *Juan Huartes*, a *Spanish* Physician, Entitled, *Examen de Ingenios*, wherein he lays it down as one of his first Positions, that Nothing but Nature can qualifie a Man for Learning; and that without a proper Temperament for the particular Art or Science which he studies, his utmost Pains and Application, assisted by the ablest Masters, will be to no Purpose.

He illustrates this by the Example of *Tully*'s Son *Marcus*.

Cicero, in Order to accomplish his Son in that Sort of Learning which he designed him for, sent him to *Athens*, the most celebrated Academy at that Time in the World, and where a vast Concourse, out of the most polite Nations, could not but furnish the young Gentleman with a Multitude of great Examples, and Accidents that might insensibly have instructed him in his designed Studies: He placed him under the Care of *Cratippus*, who was one of the greatest Philosophers of the Age, and, as if all the Books which were at that Time written, had not been sufficient for his Use, he composed others on purpose for him: Notwithstanding all this, History informs us, that *Marcus* proved a meer Blockhead, and that Nature (who it seems was even with the Son for her Prodigality to the Father) rendered him incapable of improving by all the Rules of Eloquence, the Precepts of Philosophy, his own Endeavours, and the most refined Conversation in *Athens*.

This Author therefore proposes, that there should be certain Tryers or Examiners appointed by the State to inspect the Genius of every particular Boy, and to allot him the Part that is most suitable to his natural Talents.

Plato in one of his Dialogues tells us, that *Socrates*, who was the Son of a Midwife, used to say, that as his Mother, tho' she was very skilful in her Profession, could not deliver a Woman, unless she was first with Child; so neither could he himself raise Knowledge out of a Mind, where Nature had not planted it.

Accordingly the Method this Philosopher took, of instructing his Scholars by several Interrogatories or Questions, was only helping the Birth, and bringing their own Thoughts to Light.

The *Spanish* Doctor abovementioned, as his Speculations grow more refined, asserts that every Kind of Wit has a particular Science corresponding to it, and in which alone it can be truly excellent. As to those Genius's, which may seem to have an equal Aptitude for several Things, he regards them as so many unfinished Pieces of Nature wrought off in haste.

There are, indeed, but very few to whom Nature has been so unkind, that they are not capable of shining in some Science or other. There is a certain Byass towards Knowledge in every Mind, which may be strengthened and improved by proper Applications.

The Story of *Clavius* is very well known; he was entered in a College of Jesuits, and after having been tryed at several Parts of Learning, was upon the Point of being dismissed as an hopeless Blockhead, till one of the Fathers took it into his Head to make an Assay of his Parts in Geometry, which it seems hit his Genius so luckily, that he afterwards became one of the greatest Mathematicians of the Age. It is commonly thought that the Sagacity of these Fathers, in discovering the Talent of a young Student, has not a little contributed to the Figure which their Order has made in the World.

How different from this Manner of Education is that which prevails in our own Country? Where nothing is more usual than to see forty or fifty Boys of several Ages, Tempers and Inclinations, ranged together in the same Class, employed upon the same Authors, and enjoyned the same Tasks? Whatever their natural Genius may be, they are all to be made Poets, Historians, and Orators alike. They are all obliged to have the same Capacity, to bring in the same Tale of Verse, and to furnish out the same Portion of Prose. Every Boy is bound to have as good a Memory as the Captain of the Form. To be brief, instead of adapting Studies to the particular Genius of a Youth, we expect from the young Man, that he should adapt his Genius to his Studies. This, I must confess, is not so much to be imputed to the Instructor, as to the Parent, who will never be brought to believe, that his Son is not capable of performing as much as his Neighbours, and that he may not make him whatever he has a Mind to.

If the present Age is more laudable than those which have gone before it in any single Particular, it is in that generous Care which several well-disposed Persons have taken in the education of poor Children; and as in these Charity-Schools there is no Place left for the over-weening Fondness of a Parent, the Directors of them would make them beneficial to the Publick, if they consider'd the Precept which I have been thus long inculcating. They might easily, by well examining the Parts of those under their Inspection, make a just Distribution of them into proper Classes and Divisions, and allot to them this or that particular Study, as their Genius qualifies them for Professions, Trades, Handicrafts, or Service by Sea or Land.

How is this Kind of Regulation wanting in the three great Professions!

Dr. *South* complaining of Persons who took upon them Holy Orders, tho' altogether unqualified for the sacred Function, says somewhere, that many a Man runs his Head against a Pulpit, who might have done his Country excellent Service at a Plough-tail.

In like Manner many a Lawyer, who makes but an indifferent Figure at the Bar, might have made a very elegant Waterman, and have shined at the *Temple* Stairs, tho' he can get no Business in the House.

I have known a Corn-cutter, who with a right Education would have been an excellent Physician.

To descend lower, are not our Streets filled with sagacious Draymen and Politicians in Liveries? We have several Taylors of six Foot high, and meet with many a broad Pair of Shoulders that are thrown away upon a Barber, when perhaps at the same Time we see a pigmy Porter reeling under a Burthen, who might have managed a Needle with much Dexterity, or have snapped his Fingers with great Ease to himself, and Advantage to the Publick.

The *Spartans*, tho' they acted with the Spirit which I am here speaking of, carried it much farther than what I propose: Among them it was not lawful for the Father himself to bring up his Children after his own Fancy. As soon as they were seven Years old they were all listed in several Companies, and disciplined by the Publick. The old Men were Spectators of their Performances, who often raised Quarrels among them, and set them at Strife with one another, that by those early Discoveries they might see how their several Talents lay, and without any Regard to their Quality, dispose of them accordingly for the Service of the Common-wealth. By this Means *Sparta* soon became the Mistress of *Greece*, and famous through the whole World for her civil and military Discipline.

If you think this Letter deserves a Place among your Speculations, I may perhaps trouble you with some other Thoughts on the same Subject.

X   *I am,* &c.

No. 308.
[STEELE.]   Friday, February 22.

. . . *Jam proterva*
Fronte petet Lalage maritum.—Hor.

'*Mr.* SPECTATOR,

I GIVE you this Trouble in order to propose my self to you as an Assistant in the weighty Cares which you have thought fit to undergo for the publick Good. I am a very great Lover of Women, that is to say honestly; and as it is natural to study what one likes, I have industriously applied my self to understand them. The present Circumstance relating to them, is, that I think there wants under you, as SPECTATOR, a Person to be distinguished and vested in the Power and Quality of a Censor on Marriages. I lodge at the *Temple*, and know, by seeing Women come hither, and afterwards observing them conducted by their Council to Judges Chambers, that there is a Custom in Case of making Conveyance of a Wife's Estate, that she is carried to a Judge's Apartment and left alone with him, to be examined in private whether she has not been frightened or sweetned by her Spouse into the Act she is going to do, or whether it is of her own free Will. Now if this be a Method founded upon Reason and Equity, why should there not be also a proper Officer for examining such as are entering into the State of Matrimony, whether they are forced by Parents on one Side, or moved by Interest only on the other, to come together, and bring forth such aukward Heirs as are the Product of half Love and constrained Compliances? There is no Body, though I say it my self, would be fitter for this Office than I am; for I am an ugly Fellow of great Wit and Sagacity. My Father was an hail Country-'Squire, my Mother a witty

Beauty of no Fortune: The Match was made by Consent of my Mother's Parents against her own; and I am the Child of the Rape on the Wedding-Night; so that I am as healthy and homely as my Father, but as sprightly and agreeable as my Mother.   It would be of great Ease to you if you would use me under you, that Matches might be better regulated for the future, and we might have no more Children of Squabbles. I shall not reveal all my Pretensions till I receive your Answer; and am,

Sir,

Your most humble Servant,

Mules Palfrey.'

'*Mr.* SPECTATOR,

I am one of those unfortunate Men within the City-Walls who am married to a Woman of Quality, but her Temper is something different from that of Lady *Anvill*.   My Lady's whole Time and Thoughts are spent in keeping up to the Mode both in Apparel and Furniture.   All the Goods in my House have been changed three times in seven Years.   I have had seven Children by her; and by our Marriage-Articles she was to have her Apartment new furnish'd as often as she lay in. Nothing in our House is useful but that which is fashionable; my Pewter holds out generally half a Year, my Plate a full Twelve-month; Chairs are not fit to sit in that were made two Years since, nor Beds fit for any thing but to sleep in, that have stood up above that Time.   My Dear is of Opinion that an old-fashion Grate consumes Coals, but gives no Heat: If she drinks out of Glasses of last Year, she cannot distinguish Wine from Small-Beer.   Oh dear Sir you may guess all the rest.

Yours.

P. S. I could bear even all this, if I were not obliged also to eat *fashionably*.   I have a plain Stomach, and have a constant Loathing of whatever comes to my own Table; for which Reason I dine at the *Chop-House* three Days a Week: Where the good Company wonders they never see you of late.   I am sure by your unprejudiced Discourses you love Broth better than Soup.'

'*Mr.* SPECTATOR,   *Will*'s, *Feb.* 19.

You may believe you are a Person as much talked of as any Man in Town.   I am one of your best Friends in this House, and have laid a Wager you are so candid a Man and so honest a Fellow, that you will print this Letter, tho' it is in Recommendation of a new Paper called *The Historian*.   I have read it carefully, and find it written with Skill, good Sense, Modesty, and Fire. You must allow the Town is kinder to you than you deserve; and I doubt not but you have so much Sense of the World, Change of Humour, and Instability of all humane Things, as to understand, that the only Way to preserve Favour, is to communicate it to others with Good-Nature and Judgment. You are so generally read, that what you speak of will be read. This with Men of Sense and Taste is all that is wanting to recommend *The Historian.*

> *I am,*
>> *Sir,*
>>> *Your daily Advocate,*
>>>> Reader Gentle.'

I was very much surprized this Morning, that any one should find out my Lodging, and know it so well, as to come directly to my Closet-Door, and knock at it, to give me the following Letter. When I came out I opened it, and saw by a very strong Pair of Shooes and a warm Coat the Bearer had on, that he walked all the Way to bring it me, tho' dated from *York.* My Misfortune is that I cannot talk, and I found the Messenger had so much of me, that he could think better than speak. He had, I observed, a polite Discerning hid under a shrewd Rusticity: He delivered the Paper with a Yorkshire Tone and a Town Leer.

'*Mr.* SPECTATOR,

The Privilege you have indulg'd *John Trot* has prov'd of very bad Consequence to our illustrious Assembly, which, besides the many excellent Maxims it is founded upon, is remarkable for the extraordinary Decorum always observed in It. One Instance of which is, that the *Carders,* (who are always of the first Quality) never begin to play 'till the French-Dances are finish'd and the Country-Dances begin: But *John Trot* having now got your Commission in his Pocket, (which every one here has a profound Respect for) has the Assurance to set up for a Minuit-Dancer. Not only so, but he has brought down upon us the whole Body of the *Trots,* which are very numerous, with their Auxiliaries the Hobblers and the Skippers; by which Means the Time is so much wasted, that unless we break all Rules of Goverment, it must redound to the utter Subversion of the *Brag-table,* the discreet Members of which value Time as *Fribble*'s Wife does her Pin-Money. We are pretty well assur'd that your Indulgence to *Trot* was only in Relation to Country-Dances; however we have deferred the issuing an Order of Council upon the Premisses, hoping to get you to joyn with us, that *Trot,* nor any of his Clan, presume for the future to dance any but Country-Dances, unless a Horn Pipe upon a Festival Day. If you will do this you will oblige a great many Ladies, and particularly

Your most humble Servant,

York, Feb. 16.   Eliz. Sweepstakes.'

I never meant any other than that Mr. *Trot* should confine himself to Country-Dances: And I further direct, that he shall take out none but his own Relations according to their Nearness of Blood; but any Gentlewoman may take out him.

London, Feb. 21.   *The* SPECTATOR.

T

No. 309.

[ADDISON.]   Saturday, February 23.

Di, quibus imperium est animarum, umbraeque silentes,
Et Chaos, & Phlegethon, loca nocte tacentia late;
Sit mihi fas audita loqui: sit numine vestro
Pandere res alta terra & caligine mersas.—Virg.

I HAVE before observed in general, that the Persons whom *Milton* introduces into his Poem always discover such Sentiments and Behaviour, as are in a peculiar Manner conformable to their respective Characters. Every Circumstance in their Speeches and Actions, is with great Justness and Delicacy adapted to the Persons who speak and act. As the Poet very much excels in this Consistency of his Characters, I shall beg Leave to consider several Passages of the Second Book in this Light. That superior Greatness, and Mock-Majesty, which is ascribed to the Prince of the fallen Angels, is admirably preserved in the Beginning of this Book. His opening and closing the Debate; his taking on himself that great Enterprize at the Thought of which the whole internal Assembly trembled; his encountring the hideous Phantom who guarded the Gates of Hell, and appeared to him in all his Terrors, are Instances of that proud and daring Mind which could not brook Submission even to Omnipotence.

> *Satan was now at Hand, and from his Seat*
> *The Monster moving onward came as fast*
> *With horrid Strides, Hell trembled as he strode,*
> *Th' undaunted Fiend what this might be admir'd,*
> *Admir'd, not fear'd . . .*

The same Boldness and Intrepidity of Behaviour discovers it self in the several Adventures which he meets with during his Passage through the Regions of unformed Matter, and particularly in his Address to those tremendous Powers who are described as presiding over it.

The Part of *Moloch* is likewise in all its Circumstances full of that Fire and Fury which distinguish this Spirit from the rest of the fallen Angels. He is described in the first Book as be-smeared with the Blood of humane Sacrifices, and delighted with the Tears of Parents and the Cries of Children. In the second Book he is marked out as the fiercest Spirit that fought in Heaven; and if we consider the Figure which he makes in the sixth Book, where the Battel of the Angels is described, we find it every Way answerable to the same furious enraged Character.

> . . . *Where the might of* Gabriel *fought,*
> *And with fierce Ensigns pierc'd the deep array*
> *Of* Moloc, *furious King, who him defy'd,*
> *And at his Chariot wheels to drag him bound*
> *Threaten'd, nor from the holy one of Heav'n*
> *Refrain'd his Tongue blasphemous; but anon*
> *Down cloven to the waste, with shatter'd arms*
> *And uncouth pain fled bellowing.* . . .

It may be worth while to observe, that *Milton* has repre-sented this violent impetuous Spirit, who is hurried on by such precipitate Passions, as the *first* that rises in the Assembly, to give his Opinion upon their present Posture of Affairs. Accordingly he declares himself abruptly for War, and appears incensed at his Companions, for losing so much Time as even to deliberate upon it. All his Sentiments are rash, audacious, and desperate. Such is that of arming themselves with their Tortures, and turning their Punishments upon him who inflicted them.

> . . . *No, let us rather chuse,*
> *Arm'd with Hell-flames and fury, all at once*
> *O'er Heavens high tow'rs to force resistless Way,*
> *Turning our Tortures into horrid Arms*
> *Against the Tort'rer; when to meet the Noise*
> *Of his almighty Engine he shall hear*
> *Infernal Thunder, and for Lightning see*
> *Black fire and horror shot with equal rage*
> *Among his Angels; and his Throne it self*
> *Mixt with* Tartarean *Sulphur, and strange Fire,*
> *His own invented Torments.* . . .

His preferring Annihilation to Shame or Misery, is also highly suitable to his Character; as the Comfort he draws from their disturbing the Peace of Heaven, that if it be not Victory is Revenge, is a Sentiment truly diabolical, and becoming the Bitterness of this implacable Spirit.

Belial is described, in the first Book, as the Idol of the lewd and luxurious. He is in the second Book, pursuant to that Description, characterised as timorous and slothful; and if we look in the sixth Book we find him celebrated in the Battel of Angels for Nothing but that Scoffing Speech which he makes to *Satan*, on their supposed Advantage over the Enemy. As his Appearance is uniform, and of a Piece, in these three several Views, we find his Sentiments in the infernal Assembly every Way conformable to his Character. Such are his Apprehensions of a second Battel, his Horrors of Annihilation, his preferring to be miserable rather than *not to be.* I need not observe, that the Contrast of Thought in this Speech, and that which precedes it, gives an agreeable Variety to the Debate.

Mammon's Character is so fully drawn in the first Book, that the Poet adds Nothing to it in the Second. We were before told, that he was the first who taught Mankind to ransack the Earth for Gold and Silver, and that he was the Architect of *Pandaemonium,* or the infernal Palace, where the evil Spirits were to meet in Council. His Speech in this Book is every where suitable to so depraved a Character. How proper is that Reflection, of their being unable to taste the Happiness of Heaven were they actually there, in the Mouth of one, who while he was in Heaven, is said to have had his Mind dazled with the outward Pomps and Glories of the Place, and to have been more intent on the Riches of the Pavement, than on the beatifick Vision. I shall also leave the Reader to judge how agreeable the following Sentiments are to the same Character.

> . . . *This deep World*
> *Of Darkness do we dread? How oft amidst*
> *Thick Cloud and dark doth Heav'ns all-ruling Sire*
> *Chuse to reside, his Glory unobscured,*
> *And with the Majesty of Darkness round*
> *Covers his Throne; from whence deep Thunders roar*
> *Mustring their Rage, and Heav'n resembles Hell?*
> *As he our Darkness, cannot we his Light*
> *Imitate when we please? This desart Soil,*
> *Wants not her hidden Lustre, Gems and Gold;*
> *Nor want we Skill or Art, from whence to raise*
> *Magnificence, and what can Heav'n shew more?*

Beelzebub, who is reckon'd the second in Dignity that fell, and is, in the first Book, the second that awakens out of the Trance, and confers with *Satan* upon the Situation of their Affairs, maintains his Rank in the Book now before us. There is a wonderful Majesty described in his rising up to speak. He acts as a Kind of Moderator between the two opposite Parties, and proposes a third Undertaking, which the whole

Assembly gives into. The Motion he makes of detaching one of their Body in Search of a new World is grounded upon a Project devised by *Satan,* and cursorily proposed by him in the following Lines of the first Book.

> *Space may produce new Worlds, whereof so rife*
> *There went a Fame in Heav'n, that he e'er long*
> *Intended to create, and therein plant*
> *A Generation, whom his choice regard*
> *Should favour equal to the Sons of Heav'n:*
> *Thither, if but to pry, shall be perhaps*
> *Our first Eruption, thither or elsewhere:*
> *For this infernal Pit shall never hold*
> *Celestial Spirits in bondage, nor th' Abyss*
> *Long under Darkness cover. But these Thoughts*
> *Full Counsel must mature: . . .*

It is on this Project that *Beelzebub* grounds his Proposal.

> *. . . What if we find*
> *Some easier Enterprize? There is a Place*
> *(If ancient and prophetic Fame in Heav'n*
> *Err not) another World, the happy Seat*
> *Of some new Race call'd* Man, *about this Time*
> *To be created like to us, though less*
> *In Power and Excellence, but favour'd more*
> *Of him who rules above; so was his Will*
> *Pronounc'd among the Gods, and by an Oath,*
> *That shook Heav'n's whole Circumference, confirm'd.*

The Reader may observe how just it was, not to omit in the first Book the Project upon which the whole Poem turns: As also that the Prince of the fall'n Angels was the only proper Person to give it Birth, and that the next to him in Dignity was the fittest to second and support it.

There is besides, I think, something wonderfully beautiful, and very apt to affect the Reader's Imagination, in this antient Prophecy or Report in Heaven, concerning the Creation of Man. Nothing could shew more the Dignity of the Species, than this Tradition which ran of them before their Existence. They are represented to have been the Talk of Heaven, before they were created. *Virgil* in compliment to the *Roman* Common-wealth, makes the Heroes of it appear in their State of Pre-existence; but *Milton* does a far greater Honour to Mankind in general, as he gives us a Glimpse of them even before they are in Being.

The rising of this great Assembly is described in a very sublime and poetical Manner.

> *Their rising all at once was as the sound*
> *Of Thunder heard remote . . .*

The Diversions of the fallen Angels, with the particular Account of their Place of Habitation, are described with great Pregnancy of Thought, and Copiousness of Invention. The Diversions are every way suitable to Beings who had Nothing left them but Strength and Knowledge misapplied. Such are their Contentions at the Race, and in Feats of Arms, with their Entertainment in the following Lines.

> *Others with vast* Typhaean *Rage more fell*
> *Rend up both Rocks and Hills and ride the Air*
> *In Whirlwind; Hell scarce holds the wild uproar.*

Their Musick is employed in celebrating their own criminal Exploits, and their Discourse in sounding the unfathomable Depths of Fate, Free-will, and Fore-Knowledge.

The several Circumstances in the Description of Hell are very finely imagined; as the four Rivers which disgorge themselves into the Sea of Fire, the Extreams of Cold and Heat, and the River of Oblivion. The monstrous Animals produced in that infernal World are represented by a single Line, which gives us a more horrid Idea of them, than a much longer Description would have done.

> *. . . Nature breeds,*
> *Perverse, all monstrous, all prodigious Things,*
> *Abominable, inutterable, and worse*
> Than Fables yet have feign'd, or fear conceiv'd,
> *Gorgons and Hydras, and Chimeras dire.*

This Episode of the fallen Spirits, and their Place of Habitation, comes in very happily to unbend the Mind of the Reader from its Attention to the Debate. An ordinary Poet would indeed have spun out so many Circumstances to a great Length, and by that Means have weakned, instead of illustrated, the principal Fable.

The Flight of *Satan* to the Gates of Hell is finely imaged.

I have already declared my Opinion of the Allegory concerning *Sin* and *Death*, which is however a very finished Piece in its Kind, when it is not considered as Part of an Epic Poem. The Genealogy of the several Persons is contrived with great Delicacy. *Sin* is the Daughter of *Satan*, and *Death* the Offspring of *Sin*. The incestuous Mixture between *Sin* and *Death* produces these Monsters and Hell-hounds which from Time to Time enter into their Mother, and tear the Bowels of her who gave them Birth. These are the Terrors of an evil Conscience, and the proper Fruits of *Sin*, which naturally rise from the Apprehensions of *Death*. This last beautiful Moral is, I think, clearly intimated in the Speech of *Sin*, where complaining of this her dreadful Issue, she adds,

> Before mine Eyes in Opposition sits
> Grim Death thy Son and Foe, who sets them on.
> *And me his Parent would full soon devour*
> *For want of other Prey, but that he knows*
> *His End with mine involv'd . . .*

I need not mention to the Reader the beautiful Circumstance in the last Part of this Quotation. He will likewise observe how naturally the three Persons concerned in this Allegory are tempted by one common Interest to enter into a Confederacy together, and how properly Sin is made the Portress of Hell, and the only Being that can open the Gates to that World of Tortures.

The descriptive Part of this Allegory is likewise very strong, and full of sublime Ideas. The Figure of Death, the Regal Crown upon his Head, his Menace to Satan, his advancing to the Combat, the Outcry at his Birth, are Circumstances too noble to be past over in Silence, and extreamly suitable to this *King of Terrors*. I need not Mention the Justness of Thought which is observed in the Generation of these several Symbolical Persons, that Sin was produced upon the first Revolt of Satan, that Death appeared soon after he was cast into Hell, and that the Terrors of Conscience were conceived at the Gate of this Place of Torments. The Description of the Gates is very poetical, as the opening of them is full of *Milton*'s Spirit.

> *. . . On a sudden open fly*
> *With impetuous recoil and jarring sound*
> *Th' infernal Doors, and on their Hinges grate*
> *Harsh Thunder, that the lowest bottom shook*
> *Of* Erebus. *She open'd, but to shut*
> *Excell'd her Pow'r; the Gates wide open stood,*
> *That with extended Wings a banner'd host*
> *Under spread Ensigns marching might pass through*
> *With Horse and Chariots rank'd in loose array;*
> *So wide they stood, and like a Furnace Mouth*
> *Cast forth redounding Smoak and ruddy Flame.*

In Satan's Voyage through the Chaos there are several imaginary Persons described, as residing in that immense Waste of Matter. This may perhaps be conformable to the Taste of those Criticks who are pleased with Nothing in a Poet which has not Life and Manners ascribed to it; but for my own Part, I am pleased most with those Passages in this Description which carry in them a greater Measure of Probability, and are such as might possibly have happened. Of this Kind is his first Mounting in the Smoak, that rises from the infernal Pit, his falling into a Cloud of Nitre, and the like combustible Materials, that by their Explosion still hurried him forward in his Voyage; his springing upward like a Pyramid of Fire, with his laborious Passage through that Confusion of Elements, which the Poet calls

The Womb of Nature, and perhaps her Grave.

The Glimmering Light which shot into the *Chaos* from the utmost Verge of the Creation, with the distant Discovery of the Earth that hung close by the Moon, are wonderfully Beautiful and Poetical. L

No. 310.
[STEELE.] Monday, February 25.

Connubio jungam stabili . . .—Virg.

'*Mr.* SPECTATOR,

I AM a certain young Woman, that love a certain young Man very heartily; and my Father and Mother were for it a great While, but now they say I can do better, but I think I cannot. They bid me love him, and I cannot unlove him. What must I do? Speak quickly.

Biddy Doughbake.'

'*Dear* SPEC. *Feb.* 19, 1712.

I have lov'd a Lady entirely for this Year and Half, tho' for a great Part of the Time (which has contributed not a little to my Pain) I have been debarred the Liberty of conversing with her. The Grounds of our Difference was this; That when we had enquired into each other's Circumstances, we found that at our first setting out into the World we should owe five hundred Pounds more than her Fortune would pay off. My Estate is seven hundred Pounds a Year, besides the Benefit of Tin-Mines. Now, dear SPEC. upon this State of the Case, and the Lady's positive Declaration that there is still no other Objection, I beg you'll not fail to insert this, with your Opinion, as soon as possibly, whether this ought to be esteemed a just Cause or Impediment why we should not be join'd; and you will for ever oblige

Yours sincerely,

Dick Lovesick.

P. S. Sir, if I marry this Lady by the Assistance of your Opinion, you may expect a Favour for it.'

'*Mr.* SPECTATOR,

I have the Misfortune to be one of those unhappy Men who

are distinguished by the Name of discarded Lovers; but I am the less mortified at my Disgrace, because the young Lady is one of those Creatures who set up for Negligence of Men, are forsooth the most rigidly virtuous in the World, and yet their Nicety will permit them, at the Command of Parents, to go to Bed to the most utter Stranger that can be proposed to them. As to me my self, I was introduced by the Father of my Mistress; but find I owe my being at first received to a Comparison of my Estate with that of a former Lover, and that I am now in a like Manner turned off, to give Way to an humble Servant still richer than I am. What makes this Treatment the more extravagant, is, that the young Lady is in the Management of this Way of Fraud, and obeys her Father's Orders on these Occasions without any Manner of Reluctance, but does it with the same Air that one of your Men of the World would signify the Necessity of Affairs for turning another out of Office. When I came home last Night I found this Letter from my Mistress.

"*Sir,*

I hope you will not think it is any Manner of Disrespect to your Person or Merit that the intended Nuptials between us are interrupted. My Father says he has a much better Offer for me than you can make, and has ordered me to break off the Treaty between us. If it had proceeded, I should have behaved my self with all suitable Regard to you; but as it is, I beg we may be Strangers for the Future. Adieu.

Lydia."

This great Indifference on this Subject, and the mercenary Motives for making Alliances, is what I think lies naturally before you, and I beg of you to give me your Thoughts upon it. My Answer to *Lydia* was as follows, which I hope you will approve; for you are to know the Woman's Family affect a wonderful Ease on these Occasions, tho' they expect it should be painfully received on the Man's Side.

"*Madam,*

I have received yours, and knew the Prudence of your House so well, that I always took Care to be ready to obey your Commands, tho' they should be to see you no more. Pray give my Service to all the good Family. *Adieu.*

The Opera Subscription is full.

Clitophon."'

Memorandum. *The Censor of Marriage to consider this Letter, and report the common Usages on such Treaties, with how many Pounds or Acres are generally esteemed sufficient*

Reason for preferring a new to an old Pretender; with his Opinion what is proper to be determined in such Cases for the future.

'Mr. SPECTATOR,

There is an elderly Person, lately left off Business and settled in our Town, in order, as he thinks, to retire from the World; but he has brought with him such an Inclination to Talebearing, that he disturbs both himself and all our Neighbourhood.   Notwithstanding this Frailty, the honest Gentleman is so happy as to have no Enemy: At the same time he has not one Friend who will venture to acquaint him with his Weakness.   It is not to be doubted but if this Failing were set in a proper Light, he would quickly perceive the Indecency and evil Consequences of it.   Now, Sir, this being an Infirmity which I hope may be corrected, and knowing that he pays much Deference to you, I beg that, when you are at Leisure to give us a Speculation on Gossiping, you would think of my Neighbour: You will hereby oblige several who will be glad to find a Reformation in their gray-hair'd Friend: And how becoming will it be for him, instead of pouring forth Words at all Adventures, to set a Watch before the Door of his Mouth, to refrain his *Tongue*, to check its Impetuosity, and guard against the Sallies of that *little, pert, forward, busy Person;* which, under a sober Conduct, might prove a useful Member of a Society, In Compliance with whose Intimations, I have taken the Liberty to make this Address to you.

> I am,
> > Sir,
> > > *Your most obscure Servant,*
> > > > Philanthropos.'

'Mr. SPECTATOR,   *Feb.* 16, 1712.

This is to petition you, in Behalf of my self and many more of your gentle Readers, that at any Time when you may have private Reasons against letting us know what you think your self, you would be pleased to pardon us such Letters of your Correspondents as seem to be of no Use but to the Printer.

It is further our humble Request, that you would substitute Advertisements in the Place of such Epistles; and that in Order hereunto Mr. *Buckley* may be authorized to take up of your zealous Friend Mr. *Charles Lillie*, any Quantity of Words he shall from time to time have Occasion for.

The many useful Parts of Knowledge which may be communicated to the Publick this Way, will, we hope, be a Consideration in Favour of your Petitioners.

> *And your Petitioners, &c.*'

Note. That particular Regard be had to this Petition; and the Papers marked Letter R may be carefully examined for the future.   T

No. 311.

[ADDISON.]   Tuesday, February 26.

Nec pharetris Veneris macer est aut lampade fervet:
Inde faces ardent, veniunt a dote sagittae.—Juv.

'*Mr.* Spectator,

I am amazed that among all the Variety of Characters, with which you have enriched your Speculations, you have never given us a Picture of those audacious young Fellows among us, who commonly go by the Name of *Fortune-Stealers.* You must know, Sir, I am one who live in a continual Apprehension of this Sort of People, that lie in wait, Day and Night, for our Children, and may be considered as a Kind of Kidnappers within the Law. I am the Father of a Young Heiress, whom I begin to look upon as marriageable, and who has looked upon her self as such for above these Six Years. She is now in the eighteenth Year of her Age. The Fortune-hunters have already cast their Eyes upon her, and take care to plant themselves in her View whenever she appears in any publick Assembly. I have my self caught a young Jackanapes, with a Pair of Silver fringed Gloves, in the very Fact. You must know, Sir, I have kept her as a Prisoner of State ever since she was in her Teens. Her Chamber Windows are cross-barred, she is not permitted to go out of the House but with her Keeper, who is a stayed Relation of my own; I have likewise forbid her the Use of Pen and Ink for this Twelve-Month last past, and do not suffer a Ban-box to be carried into her Room before it has been searched. Notwithstanding these Precautions, I am at my Wits End for fear of any sudden Surprize. There were, two or three Nights ago, some Fiddles heard in the Street, which I am afraid portend me no Good; not to mention a tall *Irish*-Man, that has been seen walking before my House more than once this Winter. My Kinswoman likewise informs me, that the Girl has talked to her twice or thrice of a Gentleman in a fair Wig, and that she loves to go to Church more than ever she did in her Life. She gave me the Slip about a Week ago, upon which my whole House was in Alarm. I immediately dispatched a Hue-and-Cry after her to the Change, to her Mantua-maker, and to the young Ladies that visit her; but after above an Hour's Search she returned of herself, having been taking a Walk, as she told me, by *Rosamond's* Pond. I have hereupon turned off her Woman, doubled her Guards, and given new Instructions to my Relation, who, to give her her due, keeps a watchful Eye over all her Motions. This, Sir, keeps me in a perpetual Anxiety, and makes me very often watch when my Daughter sleeps, as I am afraid she is even with me in her Turn. Now, Sir, what I would desire of you, is, to represent to this fluttering Tribe of young Fellows, who are for making their Fortunes by these indirect Means, that stealing a Man's Daughter for the Sake of her Portion, is but a Kind of tolerated Robbery; and that they make but a poor Amends to the Father, whom they plunder after this Manner, by going to Bed with his Child. Dear Sir, be speedy in your Thoughts on this Subject, that, if possible they may appear before the Disbanding of the Army.

> *I am,*
> > *Sir,*
> > > *Your most obedient humble Servant,*
> > > > Tim. Watchwell.'

Themistocles, the great *Athenian* General, being asked whether he would chuse to marry his Daughter to an indigent Man of Merit, or to a worthless Man of an Estate, replied, That he should prefer a Man without an Estate, to an Estate without a Man. The worst of it is, our modern Fortune-Hunters are those who turn their Heads that Way, because they are good for Nothing else. If a young Fellow finds he can make Nothing of *Cook and Littleton,* he provides himself with a Ladder of Ropes, and by that Means very often enters upon the Premises.

The same Art of Scaling has likewise been practised with good Success by many Military Ingineers. Stratagems of this Nature make Parts and Industry superfluous, and cut short the Way to Riches.

Nor is Vanity a less Motive than Idleness to this Kind of mercenary Pursuit. A Fop who admires his Person in a Glass, soon enters into a Resolution of making his Fortune by it, not questioning but every Woman that falls in his Way will do him as much Justice as he does himself. When an Heiress sees a Man, throwing particular Graces into his Ogle, or talking loud within her Hearing, she ought to look to herself; but if withall she observes a Pair of Red-Heels, a Patch, or any other Particularity in his Dress, she cannot take too much Care of her Person. These are Baits not to be trifled with, Charms that have done a World of Execution, and made their Way into Hearts which have been Thought impregnable. The

Force of a Man with these Qualifications is so well known, that I am credibly inform'd there are several Female Undertakers about the Change, who upon the Arrival of a likely Man out of a neighbouring Kingdom, will furnish him with proper Dress from Head to Foot, to be paid for at a double Price on the Day of Marriage.

We must however distinguish between Fortune-Hunters and Fortune-Stealers. The first are those assiduous Gentlemen who employ their whole Lives in the Chace, without ever coming at the Quarry. *Suffenus* has combed and powdered at the Ladies for thirty Years together, and taken his Stand in a Side-Box, 'till he is grown wrinkled under their Eyes. He is now laying the same Snares for the present Generation of Beauties, which he practised on their Mothers. *Cottilus*, after having made his Applications to more than you meet with in Mr. *Cowley*'s Ballad of Mistresses, was at last smitten with a City Lady of 20000*l*. Sterling; but died of old Age before he could bring Matters to bear. Nor must I here omit my worthy Friend Mr. HONEYCOMB, who has often told us in the Club, that for twenty years successively, upon the Death of a childless rich Man, he immediately drew on his Boots, called for his Horse, and made up to the Widow, When he is rallied upon his ill Success, WILL with his usual Gayety tells us, that he always found her Prae-engaged.

Widows are indeed the great Game of your Fortune-Hunters. There is scarce a young Fellow in the Town of six Foot high, that has not passed in Review before one or other of these wealthy Relicts. *Hudibras*'s *Cupid*, who

> . . . *took his Stand*
> *Upon a Widow's Jointure-Land,*

is daily employed in throwing Darts, and kindling Flames. But as for Widows, they are such a subtle Generation of People, that they may be left to their own Conduct; or, if they make a false Step in it, they are answerable for it to no Body but themselves. The young innocent Creatures who have no Knowledge and Experience of the World, are those whose Safety I would principally consult in this Speculation. The Stealing of such an one should, in my Opinion, be as punishable as a Rape. Where there is no Judgment, there is no Choice; and why the inveigling a Woman before she is come to Years of Discretion, should not be as criminal as the seducing of her before she is ten Years old, I am at a Loss to comprehend.

L

No. 312.

[STEELE.]   Wednesday, February 27.

Quod huic officium, quae laus, quod decus erit tanti, quod adipisci cum
    dolore corporis velit, qui dolorem summum malum sibi esse
    persuaserit? Quam porro quis ignominiam, quam turpitudinem
    non pertulerit, ut effugiat dolorem, si id summum malum esse
    decreverit?—Tull. *De Dolore tolerando.*

It is a very melancholy Reflection, that Men are usually so
weak, that it is absolutely necessary for them to know Sorrow
and Pain to be in their right Senses. Prosperous People (for
happy there are none) are hurried away with a fond Sense of
their present Condition, and thoughtless of the Mutability of
Fortune.   Fortune is a Term which we must use in such Discourses as these, for what is wrought by the unseen Hand of
the Disposer of all Things.   But methinks the Disposition of a
Mind which is truly great, is that which makes Misfortunes and
Sorrows little when they befall our selves, great and lamentable
when they befall other Men.   The most unpardonable Male-
factor in the World, going to his Death, and bearing it with
Composure, would win the Pity of those who should behold him;
and this not because his Calamity is deplorable, but because he
seems himself not to deplore it. We suffer for him who is less
sensible of his own Misery, and are inclined to despise him who
sinks under the Weight of his Distresses.   On the other Hand,
without any Touch of Envy, a temperate and well-governed
Mind looks down on such as are exalted with Success, with a
certain Shame for the Imbecillity of human Nature, that can
so far forget how liable it is to Calamity, as to grow giddy with
only the Suspence of Sorrow, which is the Portion of all Men.
He therefore who turns his Face from the unhappy Man, who
will not look again when his Eye is cast upon modest Sorrow,
who shuns Affliction like a Contagion, does but pamper himself
up for a Sacrifice, and contract in himself a greater Aptitude
to Misery by attempting to escape it.   A Gentleman where I
happened to be last night, fell into a Discourse which I thought
shewed a good Discerning in him: He took Notice, that whenever Men have looked into their Heart for the Idea of true
Excellency in Humane Nature, they have found it to consist
in Suffering after a right Manner and with a good Grace.
Heroes are always drawn bearing Sorrows, struggling with
Adversities, undergoing all Kinds of Hardships, and having in
the Service of Mankind a Kind of Appetite to Difficulties and
Dangers.   The Gentleman went on to observe, that it is from
this secret Sense of the high Merit which there is in Patience
under Calamities, that the Writers of Romances, when they

attempt to furnish out Characters of the highest Excellence, ransack Nature for Things terrible; they raise a new Creation of Monsters, Dragons, and Giants; Where the Danger ends, the Heroe ceases; when he won an Empire, or gained his Mistress, the rest of his Story is not worth relating. My Friend carried his Discourse so far as to say, that it was for higher Beings than Men to join Happiness and Greatness in the same Idea; but that in our Condition we have no Conception of superlative Excellence, or Heroism, but as it is surrounded with a Shade of Distress.

It is certainly the proper Education we should give our selves, to be prepared for the ill Events and Accidents we are to meet with in a Life sentenced to be a Scene of Sorrow: But instead of this Expectation, we soften our selves with Prospects of constant Delight, and destroy in our Minds the Seeds of Fortitude and Virtue, which should support us in Hours of Anguish. The constant Pursuit of Pleasure has in it something insolent and improper for our Being. There is a pretty sober Liveliness in the Ode of *Horace* to *Delius*, where he tells him, loud Mirth, or immoderate Sorrow, Inequality of Behaviour either in Prosperity or Adversity, are alike ungraceful in Man that is born to die. Moderation in both Circumstances is peculiar to generous Minds: Men of that Sort ever taste the Gratifications of Health, and all other Advantages of Life, as if they were liable to part with them; and when bereft of them, resign them with a Greatness of Mind which shews they knew their Value and Duration. The Contempt of Pleasure is a certain Preparatory for the Contempt of Pain: Without this, the Mind is as it were taken suddenly by an unforeseen Event; but he that has always, during Health and Prosperity, been abstinent in his Satisfactions, enjoys, in the worst of Difficulties, the Reflection, that his Anguish is not aggravated with the Comparison of past Pleasures which upbraid his present Condition. *Tully* tells us a Story after *Pompey*, which gives us a good Taste of the pleasant Manner the Men of Wit and Philosophy had in old Times, of alleviating the Distresses of Life by the Force of Reason and Philosophy. *Pompey*, when he came to *Rhodes*, had a Curiosity to visit the famous Philosopher *Possidonius*; but finding him in his sick Bed, he bewailed the Misfortune that he should not hear a Discourse from him: But you may, answered *Possidonius*; and immediately entered into the Point of Stoical Philosophy, which says Pain is not an Evil. During the Discourse, upon every Puncture he felt from his Distemper, he smiled and cried out, Pain, Pain, be as impertinent and troublesome as you please, I shall never own that thou art an Evil.

'Mr. SPECTATOR,

Having seen in several of your Papers, a Concern for the Honour of the Clergy, and their doing every Thing as becomes their Character, and particularly performing the publick Service with a due Zeal and Devotion; I am the more encouraged to lay before them, by your Means, several Expressions used by some of them in their Prayers before Sermon, which I am not well satisfied in: As their giving some Titles and Epithets to great Men, which are indeed due to them in their several Ranks and Stations, but not properly used, I think, in our Prayers. Is it not Contradiction to say, Illustrious, Right Reverend, and Right Honourable poor Sinners? These Distinctions are suited only to our State here, and have no Place in Heaven: We see they are omitted in the Liturgy, which I think the Clergy should take for their Pattern in their own Forms of Devotion. There is another Expression which I would not mention, but that I have heard it several Times before a learned Congregation, to bring in the last Petition of the Prayer in these Words, *O let not the Lord be angry, and I will speak but this once;* as if there was no Difference between *Abraham*'s interceding for *Sodom*, for which he had no Warrant as we can find, and our asking those Things which we are required to pray for; they would therefore have much more Reason to fear his Anger if they did not make such Petitions to him. There is another pretty Fancy: When a young Man has a Mind to let us know who gave him his Scarf, he speaks a Parenthesis to the Almighty, Bless, *as I am in Duty bound to pray*, the right honourable the Countess; is not that as much as to say, Bless her, for thou knowest I am her Chaplain?

Your humble Servant,

T
J. O.'

No. 313.
[BUDGELL.]
Thursday, February 28.

Exigite ut mores teneros ceu pollice ducat,
Ut si quis cera vultum facit . . . —Juv.

I SHALL give the following Letter no other Recommendation, than by telling my Readers that it comes from the same Hand with that of last *Thursday*.

'Sir,

I send you, according to my Promise, some farther Thoughts on the Education of Youth, in which I intend to discuss that famous Question, *Whether the Education at a Publick School, or under a private Tutor is to be preferr'd?*

As some of the greatest Men in most Ages have been of very different Opinions in this Matter, I shall give a short Account of what I think may be best urged on both Sides, and afterwards leave every Person to determine for himself.

It is certain from *Suetonius*, that the *Romans* thought the Education of their Children a Business properly belonging to the Parents themselves; and *Plutarch*, in the Life of *Marcus Cato* tells us, that as soon as his Son was capable of Learning, *Cato* would suffer no Body to teach him but himself, tho' he had a Servant named *Chilo*, who was an excellent Grammarian, and who taught a great many other Youths.

On the contrary, the *Greeks* seemed more enclined to publick Schools and Seminaries.

A private Education promises in the first place Virtue and good Breeding, a publick School manly Assurance, and an early Knowledge in the Ways of the World.

Mr. *Locke*, in his celebrated Treatise *of Education*, confesses that there are Inconveniences to be feared on both Sides; *if*, says he, *I keep my Son at Home, he is in Danger of becoming my young Master; if I send him Abroad, it is scarce possible to keep him from the reigning Contagion of Rudeness and Vice. He will perhaps be more innocent at Home, but more ignorant of the World, and more sheepish when he comes Abroad:* However, as this learned Author asserts, That Virtue is much more difficult to be attained than Knowledge of the World; and that Vice is a more stubborn, as well as a more dangerous Fault than Sheepishness, he is altogether for a private Education; and the more so, because he does not see why a Youth, with right Management, might not attain the same Assurance in his Father's House, as at a publick School.   To this End he advises Parents to accustom their Sons to whatever strange Faces come to the House, to take them with them when they visit their Neighbours, and to engage them in Conversation with Men of Parts and Breeding.

It may be objected to this Method, that Conversation is not the only Thing necessary, but that unless it be a Conversation with such as are in some Measure their Equals in Parts and Years, there can be no Room for Emulation, Contention, and several of the most lively Passions of the Mind; which, without being sometimes moved by these Means, may possibly contract a Dullness and Insensibility.

One of the greatest Writers our Nation ever produced observes, That a Boy who forms Parties, and makes himself popular in a School or a College, would act the same Part with equal Ease in a Senate or a Privy-Council; and Mr. *Osburn* speaking like a Man versed in the Ways of the World, affirms, that the well-laying and carrying on of a Design to rob an Orchard, trains up a Youth insensibly to Caution, Secrecy and Circumspection, and fits him for Matters of greater Importance.

In short, a private Education seems the most natural Method for the forming of a virtuous Man; a publick Education for making a Man of Business.   The first would furnish out a good Subject for *Plato*'s Republick, the latter a Member for a Community over-run with Artifice and Corruption.

It must however be confessed, that a Person at the Head of a publick School, has sometimes so many Boys under his Direction, that it is impossible he should extend a due Proportion of his Care to each of them.   This is, however, in reality the Fault of the Age, in which we often see twenty Parents, who, tho' each expects his Son should be made a Scholar, are not contented all together to make it worth while, for any Man of a liberal Education to take upon him the Care of their Instruction.

In our great Schools indeed this Fault has been of late Years rectified, so that we have at present not only ingenious Men for the chief Masters, but such as have proper Ushers and Assistants under them. I must nevertheless own, that for Want of the same Encouragement in the Country, we have many a promising Genius spoiled and abused in those little Seminaries.

I am the more inclined to this Opinion, having my self experienced the Usage of two rural Masters, each of them very unfit for the Trust they took upon them to discharge.   The first imposed much more upon me than my Parts, tho' none of the weakest, could endure; and used me barbarously for not performing Impossibilities.   The latter was of quite another Temper; and a Boy, who would run upon his Errands, wash his Coffee Pot, or ring the Bell, might have as little Conversation with any of the Classicks as he thought fit.   I have known a Lad at this Place excused his Exercise for assisting the Cook-maid; and remember a Neighbouring Gentleman's Son was among us five Years, most of which Time he employ'd in airing and watering our Master's grey Pad.   I scorned to compound for my Faults, by doing any of these elegant Offices, and was accordingly the best Scholar, and the worst used of any Boy in the School.

I shall conclude this Discourse with an Advantage mentioned by *Quintilian*, as accompanying a publick way of Education, which I have not yet taken notice of; namely, That we very often contract such Friendships at School, as are a Service to us all the following Parts of our Lives.

I shall give you, under this Head, a Story very well known to several Persons, and which you may depend upon as real Truth.

Every one, who is acquainted with *Westminster*-School,

knows that there is a Curtain which used to be drawn a-cross the Room, to separate the upper School from the lower. A Youth happened, by some Mischance, to tear the above-mentioned Curtain. The Severity of the Master was too well known for the Criminal to expect any Pardon for such a Fault; so that the Boy, who was of a meek Temper, was terrified to Death at the Thoughts of his Appearance, when his Friend, who sat next to him, bade him be of good Cheer, for that he would take the Fault on himself. He kept his Word accordingly. As soon as they were grown up to be Men, the civil War broke out, in which our two Friends took the opposite Sides, one of them followed the Parliament, the other the Royal Party.

As their Tempers were different, the Youth, who had torn the Curtain, endeavoured to raise himself on the civil List, and the other, who had born the Blame of it, on the Military: The first succeeded so well, that he was in a short Time made a Judge under the Protector. The other was engaged in the unhappy Enterprize of *Penruddock* and *Grove* in the West. I suppose, Sir, I need not acquaint you with the Event of that Undertaking. Every one knows that the Royal Party was routed, and all the Heads of them, among whom was the Curtain Champion, imprisoned at *Exeter*. It happened to be his Friend's Lot at that Time to go the Western Circuit: The Tryal of the Rebels, as they were then called, was very short, and Nothing now remained but to pass Sentence on them; when the Judge hearing the Name of his old Friend, and ob-serving his Face more attentively, which he had not seen for many Years, asked him, if he was not formerly a *Westminster*-Scholar? By the Answer, he was soon convinced that it was his former generous Friend; and, without saying any Thing more at that Time, made the best of his Way to *London*, where employing all his Power and Interest with the Protector, he saved his Friend from the Fate of his unhappy Associates.

The Gentleman, whose Life was thus preserved by the Gratitude of his School-Fellow, was afterwards the Father of a Son, whom he lived to see promoted in the Church, and who still deservedly fills one of the highest Stations in it.' **X**

No. 314.
[STEELE.]   Friday, February 29.

> *Tandem desine matrem*
> *Tempestiva sequi viro.*—Hor. Od. 23.

'*Mr.* SPECTATOR,   *Feb.* 7, 1711–12.

I AM a Young Man about eighteen Years of Age, and have been

in Love with a young Woman of the same Age about this half
Year. I go to see her six Days in the Week, but never could
have the Happiness of being with her alone. If any of her
Friends are at home, she will see me in their Company; but if
they be not in the Way, she flies to her Chamber. I can discover no Signs of her Aversion; but, either a Fear of falling into
the Toils of Matrimony, or a childish Timidity, deprives us of an
Interview a-part, and drives us upon the Difficulty of languishing out our Lives in fruitless Expectation. Now, Mr. SPECTA-
TOR, if you think us ripe for Oeconomy, perswade the dear
Creature, that to pine away into Barrenness and Deformity
under a Mother's Shade, is not so honourable, nor does she
appear so amiable, as she would in full Bloom.

[*There is a great deal left out before he concludes.*]

Mr. SPECTATOR,

Your humble Servant,

Bob Harmless.'

If this Gentleman be really no more than Eighteen, I must do
him the Justice to say he is the most knowing Infant I have
yet met with. He does not, I fear, yet understand, that all he
thinks of is another Woman; therefore, till he has given a
further Account of himself, the young Lady is hereby directed
to keep close to her Mother.

The SPECTATOR.

I cannot comply with the Request in Mr. *Trott*'s Letter; but
let it go just as it came to my Hands, for being so familiar with
the old Gentleman, as rough as he is to him. Since Mr. *Trott*
has an Ambition to make him his Father-in-Law, he ought to
treat him with more Respect; besides, his Stile to me might
have been more distant than he has thought fit to afford me:
Moreover, his Mistress shall continue in her Confinement, till
he has found out which Word in his Letter is not writely spelt.

'*Mr.* SPECTATOR,

I shall ever own myself your obliged humble Servant for the
Advice you gave me concerning my Dancing; which unluckily
came too late: For, as I said, I would not leave off Capering till
I had your Opinion of the Matter; was at our famous Assembly
the Day before I received your Papers, and there was observed
by an old Gentleman, who was informed I had a Respect for
his Daughter, told me I was an insignificant little Fellow, and
said that for the future he would take Care of his Child, so that
he did not doubt but to crosse my amerous Inclinations. The
Lady is confined to her Chamber, and for my Part, I am ready
to hang my self with the Thoughts that I have danced my self

out of Favour with her Father. I hope you will pardon the Trouble I give; but shall take it for a mighty Favour, if you will give me a little more of your Advice to put me in a write Way to cheat the old Dragon and obtain my Mistress. I am once more,

Sir,

York, Feb. 23,   *Your obliged humble Servant,*
   1711–12.   John Trott.

Let me desire you to make what Alterations you please, and insert this as soon as possible. Pardon Mistake by Haste.'

I never do pardon Mistakes by Haste.

The SPECTATOR.

'*Sir,*   *Feb. 27, 1711–12.*

Pray be so kind as to let me know what you esteem to be the chief Qualification of a good Poet, especially of one who writes Plays; and you will very much oblige,

Sir, Your very humble Servant,

N. B.'

To be a very well-bred Man.

The SPECTATOR.

'*Mr.* SPECTATOR,

You are to know that I am naturally brave, and love Fighting as well as any Man in *England*. This gallant Temper of mine makes me extremely delighted with Battles on the Stage. I give you this Trouble to complain to you, that *Nicolini* refused to gratifie me in that Part of the Opera for which I have most Taste. I observe it 's become a Custom, that whenever any Gentlemen are particularly pleased with a Song, at their crying out *Encore* or *Altro Volto*, the Performer is so obliging as to sing it over again. I was at the Opera the last time *Hydaspes* was performed. At that Part of it where the Heroe engages with the Lion, the graceful Manner with which he put that terrible Monster to Death gave me so great a Pleasure, and at the same time so just a Sense of that Gentleman's Intrepidity and Conduct, that I could not forbear desiring a Repetition of it, by crying out *Altro Volto* in a very audible Voice; and my Friends flatter me that I pronounced those Words with a tolerable good Accent, considering that was but the third Opera I had ever seen in my Life. Yet, notwithstanding all this, there was so little Regard had to me, that the Lion was carried off, and went to Bed, without being killed any more that Night. Now, Sir, pray consider that I did not understand a Word of what Mr. *Nicolini* said to this cruel Creature; besides, I have no Ear for Musick; so that during the long Dispute between 'em, the whole Entertainment I had was from my Eye: Why then have not I as much Right to have a graceful Action repeated as another has a pleasing Sound, since he only hears, as I only see, and we neither of us know that there is any reasonable thing a doing? Pray, Sir, settle the Business of this Claim in the Audience, and let us know when we may cry *Altro Volto, Anglice, again, again,* for the future. I am an *English*-Man, and expect some Reason or other to be given me, and perhaps an ordinary one may serve; but I expect your Answer.

> I am,
> > Sir,
> > > *Your most humble Servant,*
> > > > Toby Rentfree.'

'*Mr.* SPECTATOR,　　　　　　　　　　　*Nov.* 29.

You must give me Leave, amongst the rest of your Female Correspondents, to address you about an Affair which has already given you many a Speculation; and which, I know I need not tell you, have had a very happy influence over the adult Part of our Sex: But as many of us are either too old to learn, or too obstinate in the Pursuit of the Vanities which have been bred up with us from our Infancy, and all of us quitting the Stage whilst you are prompting us to act our Part well; you ought, methinks, rather to turn your Instructions for the Benefit of that Part of our Sex who are yet in their native Innocence, and ignorant of the Vices, and that Variety of Unhappiness that reign amongst us.

I must tell you, Mr. SPECTATOR, that it is as much a Part of your Office to oversee the Education of the Female Part of the Nation, as well as of the Male; and to convince the World you are not partial, pray proceed to detect the Male-Administration of Governesses as successfully as you have expos'd that of Pedagogues; and rescue our Sex from the Prejudice and Tyranny of Education as well as that of your own, who without your seasonable Interposition are like to improve upon the Vices that are now in Vogue.

I who know the Dignity of your Post, as SPECTATOR, and the Authority a skilful Eye ought to bear in the Female World, could not forbear consulting you, and beg your Advice in so critical a Point, as is that of the Education of young Gentle-women: Having already provided my self with a very convenient House in a good Air, I 'm not without Hope but that you will promote this generous design. I must farther tell you, Sir, that all who shall be committed to my Conduct, beside the usual Accomplishments of the Needle, Dancing, and the *French* Tongue, shall not fail to be your constant Readers.

It is therefore my humble Petition, that you will entertain the Town on this important Subject, and so far oblige a Stranger, as to raise a Curiosity and Enquiry in my Behalf, by publishing the following Advertisement.

I am, Sir,

Your constant Admirer,

M. W.'

ADVERTISEMENT.

The Boarding-School for young Gentlewomen, which was formerly kept on Mile-End-Green, being laid down, there is now one set up almost opposite to it at the two Golden-Balls, and much more convenient in every Respect; where, beside the common Instructions given to young Gentlewomen, they will be taught the whole Art of Pastrey and Preserving, with whatever may render them accomplished. Those who please to make trial of the Vigilance and Ability of the Persons concerned, may enquire at the two Golden-Balls on Mile-End-Green, near Stepney, where they will receive further Satisfaction.

This is to give Notice, that the SPECTATOR *has taken upon him to be Visitant of all Boarding-Schools where young Women are educated; and designs to proceed in the said Office after the same Manner that the Visitants of Colleges do in the two famous Universities of this Land.*

All Lovers who write to the SPECTATOR, *are desired to forbear one Expression which is in most of the Letters to him, either out of Laziness or Want of Invention, and is true of not above two thousand Women in the whole World; viz.* She has in her all that is valuable in Woman.   T

No. 315.
[ADDISON.]   Saturday, March 1.

*Nec deus intersit, nisi dignus vindice nodus
Inciderit . . .—Hor.*

Horace advises a Poet to consider thoroughly the Nature and Force of his Genius. *Milton* seems to have known, perfectly well, wherein his Strength lay, and has therefore chosen a Subject entirely conformable to those Talents, of which he was Master. As his Genius was wonderfully turned to the Sublime, his Subject is the noblest that could have entered into the Thoughts of Man. Every Thing that is truly great and astonishing, has a Place in it. The whole Systeme of the intellectual World; the *Chaos*, and the Creation; Heaven, Earth and Hell; enter into the Constitution of his Poem.

Having in the First and Second Book represented the Infernal World with all its Horrours, the Thread of his Fable naturally leads him into the opposite Regions of Bliss and Glory.

If *Milton*'s Majesty forsakes him any where, it is in those Parts of his Poem, where the Divine Persons are introduced as Speakers. One may, I think, observe that the Author proceeds with a Kind of Fear and Trembling, whilst he describes the Sentiments of the Almighty. He dares not give his Imagination its full Play, but chuses to confine himself to such Thoughts as are drawn from the Books of the most Orthodox Divines, and to such Expressions as may be met with in Scripture. The Beauties, therefore, which we are to look for in these Speeches, are not of a poetical Nature, or so proper to fill the Mind with Sentiments of Grandeur, as with Thoughts of Devotion. The Passions, which they are designed to raise, are a Divine Love and Religious Fear. The particular Beauty of the Speeches in the Third Book, consists in that Shortness and Perspicuity of Stile, in which the Poet has couched the greatest Mysteries of Christianity, and drawn together, in a regular Scheme, the whole Dispensation of Providence, with respect to Man. He has represented all the abstruse Doctrines of Predestination, Free-Will and Grace, as also the great Points of Incarnation and Redemption (which naturally grow up in a Poem that treats of the Fall of Man), with great Energy of Expression, and in a clearer and stronger Light than I ever met with in any other Writer. As these Points are dry in themselves to the Generality of Readers, the concise and clear Manner in which he has treated them, is very much to be admired, as is likewise that particular Art which he has made Use of, in the interspersing of all those Graces of Poetry, which the Subject was capable of receiving.

The Survey of the whole Creation, and of every Thing that is transacted in it, is a Prospect worthy of Omniscience; and as much above that, in which *Virgil* has drawn his *Jupiter*, as the Christian Idea of the Supream Being is more Rational and Sublime than that of the Heathens. The particular Objects on which he is described to have cast his Eye, are represented in the most beautiful and lively Manner:

> *Now had th' Almighty Father from above,*
> *From the pure Empyrean where he sits*
> *High thron'd above all height, bent down his Eye,*
> *His own Works and their Works at once to View.*
> *About him all the Sanctities of Heav'n*
> *Stood thick as Stars, and from his Sight receiv'd*
> *Beatitude past utterance: On his Right*
> *The radiant Image of his Glory sat,*

His only Son; On earth he first beheld
Our two first Parents, yet the only two
Of Mankind, in the happy Garden plac'd,
Reaping immortal fruits of Joy and Love,
Uninterrupted joy, unrival'd Love,
In blisful Solitude; he then survey'd
Hell and the Gulf between, and Satan *there*
Coasting the Wall of Heav'n on this Side Night
In the dun air sublime, and ready now
To stoop with wearied Wings and willing Feet
On the bare outside of this World, that seem'd
Firm Land imbosom'd without firmament,
Uncertain which, in Ocean or in Air.
Him God beholding from his prospect high,
Wherein past, present, future he beholds,
Thus to his only Son foreseeing spake.

Satan's Approach to the Confines of the Creation, is finely imaged in the Beginning of the Speech, which immediately follows. The Effects of this Speech in the blessed Spirits, and in the divine Person to whom it was addressed, cannot but fill the Mind of the Reader with a secret Complacency.

Thus while God spake, ambrosial Fragrance fill'd
All Heav'n, and in the blessed Spirits elect
Sense of new Joy ineffable diffus'd:
Beyond compare the Son of God was seen
Most glorious; in him all his Father shone
Substantially express'd; and in his Face
Divine Compassion visibly appear'd,
Love without End, and without Measure Grace.

I need not Point out the Beauty of that Circumstance, wherein the whole Host of Angels are represented as standing mute; nor shew how proper the Occasion was to produce such a Silence in Heaven. The Close of this Divine Colloquy, with the Hymn of Angels that follows upon it, are so wonderfully beautiful and poetical, that I should not forbear inserting the whole Passage, if the Bounds of my Paper would give me leave.

No sooner had th' Almighty ceas'd, but all
The multitudes of Angels with a shout,
Loud as from Numbers without Number, sweet
As from blest Voices, utt'ring Joy, Heav'n rung
With Jubilee, and loud Hosannas fill'd
Th' eternal Regions; &c., &c. . . .

Satan's Walk upon the Outside of the Universe, which, at a Distance, appeared to him of a globular Form, but, upon his nearer Approach, looked like an unbounded Plain, is natural and noble. As his Roaming upon the Frontiers of the Creation,

between that Mass of Matter, which was wrought into a
World, and that shapeless unformed Heap of Materials, which
still lay in *Chaos* and Confusion, strikes the Imagination with
something astonishingly great and wild. I have before spoken
of the Limbo of Vanity, which the Poet places upon this outer-
most Surface of the Universe, and shall here explain my self
more at large on that, and other Parts of the Poem, which
are of the same shadowy Nature.

Aristotle observes, that the Fable of an Epic Poem should
abound in Circumstances that are both credible and astonish-
ing; or, as the *French* Criticks chuse to phrase it, the Fable
should be filled with the Probable and the Marvellous. This
Rule is as fine and just as any in *Aristotle*'s whole Art of Poetry.
If the Fable is only probable, it differs Nothing from a true
History; if it is only marvellous, it is no better than a Romance.
The great Secret therefore of Heroick Poetry, is to relate such
Circumstances, as may produce in the Reader at the same
Time both Belief and Astonishment. This is brought to pass
in a *well chosen* Fable, by the Account of such Things as have
really happened, or at least of such Things as have happened
according to the received Opinions of Mankind. *Milton*'s
Fable is a Master-piece of this Nature; as the War in Heaven,
the Condition of the fallen Angels, the State of Innocence, the
Temptation of the Serpent, and the Fall of Man, though they
are very astonishing in themselves, are not only credible, but
Actual Points of Faith.

The next Method of reconciling Miracles with Credibility, is
by a happy Invention of the Poet; as in particular, when he
introduces Agents of a superior Nature, who are capable of
effecting what is wonderful, and what is not to be met with in
the ordinary Course of Things. *Ulysses*'s Ship being turned
into a Rock, and *Aeneas*'s Fleet into a Shoal of Water Nymphs,
though they are very surprising Accidents, are nevertheless
probable, when we are told that they were the Gods who thus
transformed them. It is this Kind of Machinery which fills
the Poems both of *Homer* and *Virgil* with such Circumstances
as are wonderful, but not impossible, and so frequently produce
in the Reader the most pleasing Passion that can rise in the
Mind of Man, which is Admiration. If there be any Instance
in the *Aeneid* liable to Exception upon this Account, it is in the
Beginning of the Third Book, where *Aeneas* is represented as
tearing up the Myrtle that dropped Blood. To qualifie this
wonderful Circumstance, *Polydorus* tells a Story from the Root
of the Myrtle, that the barbarous Inhabitants of the Country
having pierced him with Spears and Arrows, the Wood which
was left in his Body took Root in his Wounds, and gave Birth

to that bleeding Tree. This Circumstance seems to have the Marvellous without the Probable, because it is represented as proceeding from natural Causes, without the Interposition of any God, or other supernatural Power capable of producing it. The Spears and Arrows grow of themselves, without so much as the modern Help of an Enchantment. If we look into the Fiction of *Milton*'s Fable, though we find it full of surprising Incidents, they are generally suited to our Notions of the Things and Persons described, and tempered with a due Measure of Probability. I must only make an Exception to the Limbo of Vanity, with his Episode of Sin and Death, and some of the imaginary Persons in his *Chaos*. These Passages are astonishing, but not credible; the Reader cannot so far impose upon himself as to see a Possibility in them; they are the Description of Dreams and Shadows, not of Things or Persons. I know that many Criticks look upon the Stories of *Circe, Polypheme,* the *Sirens,* nay the whole *Odissey* and *Illiad* to be Allegories; but allowing this to be true, they are Fables, which considering the Opinions of Mankind that prevailed in the Age of the Poet, might possibly have been according to the Letter. The Persons are such as might have acted what is ascribed to them, as the Circumstances, in which they are represented, might possibly have been Truths and Realities. This Appearance of Probability is so absolutely requisite in the greater Kinds of Poetry, that *Aristotle* observes the ancient tragick Writers made Use of the Names of such great Men as had actually lived in the World, tho' the Tragedy proceeded upon Adventures they were never engaged in, on Purpose to make the Subject more credible. In a Word, besides the hidden Meaning of an Epic Allegory, the plain literal Sense ought to appear probable. The Story should be such as an ordinary Reader may acquiesce in, whatever natural, moral, or political Truth may be discovered in it by Men of greater Penetration.

Satan after having long wandred upon the Surface, or outmost Wall of the Universe, discovers at last a wide Gap in it, which led into the Creation, and is described as the Opening through which the Angels pass to and fro into the lower World, upon their Errands to Mankind. His Sitting upon the Brink of this Passage, and taking a Survey of the whole Face of Nature, that appeared to him new and fresh in all its Beauties, with the Simile illustrating this Circumstance, fills the Mind of the Reader with as surprising and glorious an Idea as any that arises in the whole Poem. He looks down into that vast Hollow of the Universe with the Eye, or (as *Milton* calls it in his first Book) with the Kenn of an Angel. He surveys all the

Wonders in this immense Amphitheatre that lye between both the Poles of Heaven, and takes in at one View the whole Round of the Creation.

His Flight between the several Worlds that shined on every Side of him, with the particular Description of the Sun, are set forth in all the Wantonness of a luxuriant Imagination. His Shape, Speech and Behaviour upon his transforming himself into an Angel of Light, are touched with exquisite Beauty. The Poet's Thought of directing *Satan* to the Sun, which in the Vulgar Opinion of Mankind is the most conspicuous Part of the Creation, and the placing in it an Angel, is a Circumstance very finely contrived, and the more adjusted to a poetical Probability, as it was a received Doctrine among the most famous Philosophers, that every Orb had its *Intelligence*; and as an Apostle in sacred Writ is said to have seen such an Angel in the Sun. In the Answer which this Angel returns to the disguised Evil Spirit, there is such a becoming Majesty as is altogether suitable to a superior Being. The Part of it in which he represents himself as present at the Creation, is very noble in it self, and not only proper where it is introduced, but requisite to prepare the Reader for what follows in the Seventh Book.

> *I saw when at his Word the formless Mass,*
> *This World's Material Mould came to a Heap:*
> *Confusion heard his Voice, and wild uproar*
> *Stood rul'd, stood vast infinitude confin'd;*
> *Till at his second bidding Darkness fled.*
> *Light shon,* &c.

In the following Part of the Speech he points out the Earth with such Circumstances, that the Reader can scarce forbear fancying himself employed on the same distant View of it.

> *Look downward on that Globe whose hither Side*
> *With light from hence, tho' but reflected, shines;*
> *That Place is Earth, the Seat of Man, that light*
> *His day,* &c.

I must not conclude my Reflections upon this third Book of *Paradise Lost*, without taking Notice of that celebrated Complaint of *Milton* with which it opens, and which certainly deserves all the Praises that have been given it; tho' as I have before hinted, it may rather be looked upon as an Excrescence, than as an essential Part of the Poem. The same Observation might be applied to that beautiful Digression upon Hypocrisie, in the same Book. **L**

No. 316.

[HUGHES.]   Monday, March 3.

Libertas; quae sera tamen respexit inertem.—Virg. Ecl. 1.

'*Mr.* SPECTATOR,

IF you ever read a Letter, which is sent, with the more Pleasure for the Reality of its Complaints, this may have Reason to hope for a favourable Acceptance; and if Time be the most irretrievable Loss, the Regrets which follow will be thought, I hope, the most justifiable. The regaining of my Liberty from a long State of Indolence and Inactivity, and the Desire of resisting the farther Encroachments of Idleness, make me apply to you; and the Uneasiness with which I recollect the past Years, and the Apprehensions with which I expect the Future, soon determined me to it.

Idleness is so general a Distemper, that I cannot but imagine a Speculation on this Subject will be of universal Use. There is hardly any one Person without some Allay of it; and thousands besides my self spend more Time in an idle Uncertainty which to begin first of two Affairs, than would have been sufficient to have ended them both. The Occasion of this seems to be the Want of some necessary Employment, to put the Spirits in Motion, and awaken them out of their Lethargy. If I had less Leisure, I should have more; for I should then find my Time distinguished into Portions, some for Business, and others for the indulging of Pleasures: But now one Face of Indolence over-spreads the Whole, and I have no Landmark to direct my self by. Were one's Time a little straitned by Business, like Water inclosed in its Banks, it would have some determined Course; but unless it be put into some Channel it has no Current, but becomes a Deluge without either Use or Motion.

When *Scanderbeg* Prince of *Epirus* was dead, the *Turks*, who had but too often felt the Force of his Arm in the Battles he had won from them, imagined that by wearing a Piece of his Bones near their Heart, they should be animated with a Vigour and Force like to that which inspired him when living. As I am like to be but of little Use whilst I live, I am resolved to do what Good I can after my Decease; and have accordingly ordered my Bones to be disposed of in this Manner for the Good of my Countrymen, who are troubled with too exorbitant a Degree of Fire. All Fox-hunters upon wearing me, would in a short Time be brought to endure their Beds in a Morning, and perhaps even quit them with Regret at Ten: Instead of hurrying away to teaze a poor Animal, and run away from their own Thoughts, a Chair or a Chariot would be thought the most desirable Means of performing a Remove from one Place to another. I should be a Cure for the unnatural Desire of *John Trott* for Dancing, and a Specifick to lessen the Inclination Mrs. *Fidget* has to Motion, and cause her always to give her Approbation to the present Place she is in. In fine, no *Egyptian* Mummy was ever half so useful in Physick, as I should be to these feaverish Constitutions, to repress the violent Sallies of Youth, and give each Action its proper Weight and Repose.

I can stifle any violent Inclination, and oppose a Torrent of Anger, or the Sollicitations of Revenge, with Success. But Indolence is a Stream which flows slowly on, but yet undermines the Foundation of every Virtue. A Vice of a more lively Nature were a more desirable Tyrant than this Rust of the Mind, which gives a Tincture of its Nature to every Action of one's Life. It were as little Hazard to be lost in a Storm, as to lye thus perpetually becalmed: And it is to no Purpose to have within one the Seeds of a thousand good Qualities, if we want the Vigour and Resolution necessary for the exerting them. Death brings all Persons back to an Equality; and this Image of it, this Slumber of the Mind, leaves no Difference between the greatest Genius and the meanest Understanding: A Faculty of doing Things remarkably praise-worthy thus concealed, is of no more Use to the Owner, than a Heap of Gold to the Man who dares not use it.

To-morrow is still the fatal Time when all is to be rectified: To morrow comes, it goes, and still I please my self with the Shadow, whilst I lose the Reality; unmindful that the present Time alone is ours, the future is yet unborn, and the past is dead, and can only live (as Parents in their Children) in the Actions it has produced.

The Time we live ought not to be computed by the Number of Years, but by the Use has been made of it; thus 'tis not the Extent of Ground, but the yearly Rent which gives the Value to the Estate. Wretched and thoughtless Creatures, in the only Place where Covetousness were a Virtue we turn Prodigals! Nothing lies upon our Hands with such Uneasiness, nor has there been so many Devices for any one Thing, as to make it slide away imperceptibly and to no Purpose. A Shilling shall be hoarded up with Care, whilst that which is above the Price of an Estate, is flung away with Disregard and Contempt. There is Nothing now-a-days so much avoided, as a sollicitous Improvement of every Part of Time; 'tis a Report must be shunned as one tenders the Name of a Wit and a fine Genius, and as one fears the dreadful Character of a laborious Plodder:

But notwithstanding this, the greatest Wits any Age has produced thought far otherwise; for who can think either *Socrates* or *Demosthenes* lost any Reputation, by their continual Pains both in overcoming the Defects and improving the Gifts of Nature.   All are acquainted with the Labour and Assiduity with which *Tully* acquired his Eloquence.   *Seneca* in his Letters to *Lucilius* assures him, there was not a Day in which he did not either write Something, or read and epitomize some good Author; and I remember *Pliny* in one of his Letters, where he gives an Account of the various Methods he used to fill up every Vacancy of Time, after several Imployments, which he enumerates; Sometimes, says he, I hunt; but even then I carry with me a Pocket-Book, that whilst my Servants are busied in disposing of the Nets and other Matters, I may be employed in something that may be useful to me in my Studies; and that if I miss of my Game, I may at least bring home some of mine own Thoughts with me, and not have the Mortification of having caught Nothing all Day.

Thus, Sir, you see how many Examples I recal to Mind, and what Arguments I use with my self to regain my Liberty: But as I am afraid 'tis no Ordinary Perswasion that will be of Service, I shall expect your Thoughts on this Subject with the greatest Impatience, especially since the Good will not be confined to me alone, but will be of universal Use.   For there is no Hopes of Amendment where Men are pleased with their Ruin, and whilst they think Laziness is a desirable Character: Whether it be that they like the State it self, or that they think it gives them a new Lustre when they do exert themselves, seemingly to be able to do that without Labour and Application, which others attain to but with the greatest Diligence.

> *I am, Sir,*
>> *Your most obliged humble Servant,*
>>> Samuel Slack.'

'CLYTANDER *to* CLEONE.

Madam,

Permission to love you is all that I desire, to conquer all the Difficulties those about you place in my Way to surmount, and acquire all those Qualifications you expect in him who pretends to the Honour of being,

> *Madam,*
>> *Your most humble Servant,*
>>> Clytander.'

Z

No. 317.
[ADDISON.]   Tuesday, March 4.

. . . *Fruges consumere nati.*—Hor.

Augustus, a few Moments before his Death, asked his Friends
who stood about him, if they thought he had acted his Part
well; and upon receiving such an Answer as was due to his
extraordinary Merit, *Let me then*, says he, *go off the Stage
with your Applause*, using the Expression with which the
Roman Actors made their *Exit* at the Conclusion of a dramatick
Piece. I could wish that Men, while they are in Health, would
consider well the Nature of the Part they are engaged in, and
what Figure it will make in the Minds of those they leave
behind them: Whether it was worth coming into the World
for, whether it be suitable to a reasonable Being; in short,
whether it appears graceful in this Life, or will turn to an
Advantage in the next. Let the Sycophant, or Buffoon, the
Satyrist, or the good Companion, consider with himself, when
his Body shall be laid in the Grave, and his Soul pass into another State of Existence, how much it will redound to his
Praise to have it said of him, that no Man in *England* eat better,
that he had an admirable Talent at turning his Friends into
Ridicule, that no Body out-did him at an ill-natured Jest, or
that he never went to Bed before he had dispatched his third
Bottle. These are, however, very common funeral Orations,
and Elogiums on deceased Persons who have acted among
Mankind with some Figure and Reputation.

But if we look into the Bulk of our Species, they are such as
are not likely to be remember'd a Moment after their Dis-
appearance. They leave behind them no Traces of their
Existence, but are forgotten as tho' they had never been.
They are neither wanted by the Poor, regretted by the Rich,
nor celebrated by the Learned. They are neither missed in
the Common-wealth, nor lamented by private Persons. Their
Actions are of no Significancy to Mankind, and might have been
performed by Creatures of much less Dignity, than those who
are distinguished by the Faculty of Reason. An eminent
French Author speaks somewhere to the following Purpose:
I have often seen from my Chamber-window two noble Creatures, both of them of an erect Countenance, and endowed
with Reason. These two intellectual Beings are employed
from Morning to Night, in rubbing two smooth Stones one upon
another; that is, as the vulgar phrase it, in polishing Marble.

My Friend, Sir ANDREW FREEPORT, as we were sitting in the
Club last Night, gave us an Account of a sober Citizen, who
died a few Days since. This honest Man being of greater

Consequence in his own Thoughts, than in the Eye of the World, had for some Years past kept a Journal of his Life. Sir ANDREW shewed us one Week of it. Since the Occurrences set down in it mark out such a Road of Action as that I have been speaking of, I shall present my Reader with a faithful Copy of it; after having first informed him, that the deceased Person had in his Youth been bred to Trade, but finding himself not so well turned for Business, he had for several Years last past lived altogether upon a moderate Annuity.

MONDAY, *Eight a Clock.* I put on my Cloaths and walked into the Parlour.

Nine a Clock ditto. Tied my Knee-strings, and washed my Hands.

Hours Ten, Eleven and Twelve. Smoaked three Pipes of *Virginia.* Read the *Supplement* and *Daily Courant.* Things go ill in the North. Mr. *Nisby*'s Opinion thereupon.

One a Clock in the Afternoon. Chid *Ralph* for mislaying my Tobacco-Box.

Two a Clock. Sat down to Dinner. *Mem.* Too many Plumbs, and no Sewet.

From Three to Four. Took my Afternoon's Nap.

From Four to Six. Walked into the Fields. Wind, S.S.E.

From Six to Ten. At the Club. Mr. *Nisby*'s Opinion about the Peace.

Ten a Clock. Went to Bed, slept sound.

TUESDAY, BEING HOLIDAY, *Eight a Clock.* Rose as usual.

Nine a Clock. Washed Hands and Face, shaved, put on my double Soaled shoes.

Ten, Eleven, Twelve. Took a walk to *Islington.*

One. Took a Pot of Mother *Cob*'s Mild.

Between two and three. Returned, dined on a Knuckle of Veal and Bacon. *Mem.* Sprouts wanting.

Three. Nap as usual.

From Four to Six. Coffee-house. Read the News. A Dish of Twist. Grand Vizier strangled.

From Six to Ten. At the Club. Mr. *Nisby*'s Account of the great Turk.

Ten. Dream of the Grand Vizier. Broken Sleep.

WEDNESDAY, *Eight a Clock.* Tongue of my Shoe-Buckle broke. Hands, but not Face.

Nine. Paid off the Butcher's Bill. *Mem.* To be allowed for the last Leg of Mutton.

Ten, Eleven. At the Coffee-House. More Work in the North. Stranger in a black Wigg asked me how Stocks went.

From Twelve to One. Walked in the Fields. Wind to the South.

From One to Two. Smoaked a Pipe and a half.

Two. Dined as usual. Stomach good.

Three. Nap broke by the falling of a Pewter-Dish. *Mem.* Cook-maid in Love, and grown careless.

From Four to Six. At the Coffee-house. Advice from *Smyrna*, that the Grand Vizier was first of all strangled, and afterwards beheaded.

Six a Clock in the Evening. Was half an Hour in the Club before any Body else came. Mr. *Nisby* of Opinion, that the Grand Vizier was not strangled the sixth Instant.

Ten at Night. Went to Bed. Slept without waking till Nine next Morning.

THURSDAY, *Nine a Clock.* Staid within till two a Clock for Sir *Timothy.* Who did not bring me my Annuity according to his Promise.

Two in the Afternoon. Sate down to Dinner. Loss of Appetite. Small beer soure. Beef overcorned.

Three. Could not take my Nap.

Four and Five. Give *Ralph* a Box on the Ear. Turned off my Cookmaid. Sent a Message to Sir *Timothy.* *Mem.* I did not go to the Club to Night. Went to Bed at Nine a Clock.

FRIDAY. Passed the Morning in Meditation upon Sir *Timothy*, who was with me a Quarter before Twelve.

Twelve a Clock. Bought a new Head to my Cane, and a Tongue to my Buckle. Drank a Glass of Purl to recover Appetite.

Two and Three. Dined, and slept well.

From Four to Six. Went to the Coffee-house. Met Mr. *Nisby* there. Smoaked several Pipes. Mr. *Nisby* of Opinion that laced Coffee is bad for the Head.

Six a Clock. At the Club as Steward. Sat late.

Twelve a Clock. Went to Bed, dreamt that I drank Small-beer with the Grand Vizier.

SATURDAY. Waked at Eleven, walked in the Fields, Wind N.E.

Twelve. Caught in a Shower.

One in the Afternoon. Returned home, and dryed my self.

Two. Mr. *Nisby* dined with me. First Course Marrow-bones, Second Ox-Cheek, with a Bottle of *Brook*'s and *Hellier.*

Three a Clock. Over slept my self.

Six. Went to the Club. Like to have faln into a Gutter. Grand Vizier certainly Dead, &c.

I Question not, but the Reader will be surprized to find the above-mentioned Journalist taking so much Care of a Life that was filled with such inconsiderable Actions and received so very small Improvements; and yet, if we look into the

Behaviour of many whom we daily converse with, we shall find that most of their Hours are taken up in those three Important Articles of Eating, Drinking and Sleeping. I do not suppose that a Man loses his Time, who is not engaged in publick Affairs, or in an illustrious Course of Action. On the contrary, I believe our Hours may very often be more profitably laid out in such Transactions as make no Figure in the World, than in such as are apt to draw upon them the Attention of Mankind. One may become wiser and better by several Methods of Employing one's self in Secrecy and Silence, and do what is laudable without Noise or Ostentation. I would, however, recommend to every one of my Readers, the keeping a Journal of their Lives for one Week, and setting down punctually their whole Series of Employments during that Space of Time. This Kind of Self-Examination would give them a true State of themselves, and incline them to consider seriously what they are about. One Day would rectifie the Omissions of another, and make a Man weigh all those indifferent Actions, which, though they are easily forgotten, must certainly be accounted for.   L

No. 318.

[STEELE.]   Wednesday, March 5.

. . . *Non omnia possumus omnes.*—Virg.

'*Mr.* SPECTATOR,

A CERTAIN Vice which you have lately attacked, has not yet been considered by you as growing so deep in the Heart of Man, that the Affectation outlives the Practice of it. You must have observed, that Men who had been bred in Arms, preserve to the most extreme and feeble old Age a certain Daring in their Aspect: In like Manner, they who have past their time in Gallantry and Adventure, keep up, as well as they can, the Appearance of it, and carry a petulant Inclination to their last Moments. Let this serve for a Preface to a Relation I am going to give you of an old Beau in Town, that has not only been amorous, and a Follower of Women in general, but also, in spite of the Admonition of grey Hairs, been, from his sixty third Year to his present seventieth, in an actual Pursuit of a young Lady, the Wife of his Friend, and a Man of Merit. The gay old *Escalus* has Wit, good Health, and is perfectly well-bred; but from the Fashion and Manners of the Court when he was in his Bloom, has such a natural Tendency to amorous Adventure, that he thought it would be an endless Reproach to him to make no Use of a Familiarity he was allowed at a Gentleman's House, whose good Humour and Confidence exposed his Wife to the Addresses of any who should take in their Head to do him the good Office. It is not impossible that *Escalus* might also resent that the Husband was particularly negligent of him; and tho' he gave many Intimations of a Passion towards the Wife, the Husband either did not see them, or put him to the Contempt of overlooking them. In the mean Time *Isabella*, for so we shall call our Heroine, saw his Passion, and rejoyced in it as a Foundation for much Diversion, and an Opportunity of indulging her self in the dear Delight of being admired, addressed to, and flatter'd with no ill Consequence to her Reputation. This Lady is of a free and disengaged Behaviour, ever in good Humour, such as is the Image of Innocence with those who are innocent, and an Encouragement to Vice with those who are abandoned. From this Kind of Carriage, and an apparent Approbation of his Gallantry, *Escalus* had frequent Opportunities of laying amorous Epistles in her Way, of fixing his Eyes attentively upon her Action, of performing a thousand little Offices which are neglected by the Unconcerned, but are so many Approaches towards Happiness with the Enamoured. It was now, as is above hinted, almost the End of the seventh Year of his Passion, when *Escalus* from general Terms, and the ambiguous Respect which criminal Lovers retain in their Addresses, began to bewail that his Passion grew too violent for him to answer any longer for his Behaviour towards her; and that he hoped she would have Consideration for his long and patient Respect, to excuse the Motions of a Heart now no longer under the Direction of the unhappy Owner of it. Such for some Months had been the Language of *Escalus* both in his Talk and his Letters to *Isabella*; who returned all the Profusion of kind Things which had been the Collection of Fifty Years, with *I must not hear you; you will make me forget that you are a Gentleman; I would not willingly lose you as a Friend;* and the like Expressions, which the Skilful interpret to their own Advantage, as well knowing that a feeble Denial is a modest Assent. I should have told you, that *Isabella*, during the whole Progress of this Amour, communicated it to her Husband; and that an Account of *Escalus*'s Love was their usual Entertainment after Half a Day's Absence: *Isabella* therefore, upon her Lover's late more open Assaults, with a Smile told her Husband she could hold out no longer, but that his Fate was now come to a Crisis. After she had explained herself a little farther, with her Husband's Approbation she proceeded in the following Manner. The next Time that *Escalus* was alone with her, and repeated his

Importunity, the crafty *Isabella* looked on her Fan with an Air of great Attention, as considering of what Importance such a Secret was to her; and upon the Repetition of a warm Expression, she looked at him with an Eye of Fondness, and told him he was past that Time of Life which could make her fear he would boast of a Lady's Favour; then turned away her Head with a very well acted Confusion, which favoured the Escape of the Aged *Escalus*. This Adventure was Matter of great Pleasantry to *Isabella* and her Spouse; and they had enjoyed it two days before *Escalus* could recollect himself enough to form the following Letter.

"*Madam*,

What happened the other Day, gives me a lively Image of the Inconsistency of humane Passions and Inclinations. We pursue what we are denied, and place our Affections on what is absent, tho' we neglected it when present. As long as you refused my Love, your Refusal did so strongly excite my Passion, that I had not once the Leisure to think of recalling my Reason to aid me against the Design upon your Virtue. But when that Virtue began to comply in my Favour, my Reason made an Effort over my Love, and let me see the Baseness of my Behaviour in attempting a Woman of Honour. I own to you, it was not without the most violent Struggle that I gained this Victory over my self; nay I will confess my Shame, and acknowledge I could not have prevailed but by Flight. However, Madam, I beg that you will believe a Moment's Weakness has not destroyed the Esteem I had for you, which was confirmed by so many Years of obstinate Virtue. You have Reason to rejoyce that this did not happen within the Observation of one of the young Fellows, who would have exposed your Weakness, and gloried in his own brutish Inclinations.

> *I am, Madam,*
> *Your most devoted humble Servant.*"

Isabella, with the Help of her Husband, returned the following Answer.

"*Sir*,

I cannot but account my self a very happy Woman, in having a Man for a Lover that can write so well, and give so good a Turn to a Disappointment. Another Excellence you have above all other Pretenders I ever heard of, on Occasions where the most reasonable Men lose all their Reason, you have yours most powerful. We are each of us to thank our Genius, that the Passion of one abated in Proportion as that of the other grew violent. Does it not yet come into your Head, to imagine that I knew my Compliance was the greatest Cruelty I could be guilty of towards you? In Return for your long and faithful Passion, I must let you know that you are old enough to become a little more Gravity; but if you will leave me and coquet it any where else, may your Mistress yield.

T   *Isabella.*' '

No. 319.

[BUDGELL.]   Thursday, March 6.

Quo teneam vultus mutantem Protea nodo?—Hor.

I HAVE endeavoured, in the Course of my Papers, to do Justice to the Age, and have taken Care as much as possible to keep my self a Neuter between both Sexes. I have neither spared the Ladies out of Complaisance, nor the Men out of Partiality; but notwithstanding the great Integrity with which I have acted in this Particular, I find my self taxed with an Inclination to favour my own Half of the Species. Whether it be that the Women afford a more fruitful Field for Speculation, or whether they run more in my Head than the Men, I cannot tell, but I shall set down the Charge as it is laid against me in the following Letter.

'*Mr.* SPECTATOR,

I always make one among a Company of young Females, who peruse your Speculations every Morning. I am at present commissioned, by our whole Assembly, to let you know, that we fear you are a little enclined to be partial towards your own Sex. We must however acknowledge, with all due Gratitude, that in some Cases you have given us our Revenge on the Men, and done us Justice. We could not easily have forgiven you several Strokes in the Dissection of the *Coquet's Heart*, if you had not, much about the same Time, made a Sacrifice to us of a *Beau's Scull*.

You may, however, Sir, please to remember, that not long since you attacked our Hoods and Commodes in such Manner, as, to use your own Expression, made very many of us ashamed to shew our Heads. We must, therefore, beg Leave to represent to you, that we are in Hopes, if you would please to make a due Enquiry, the Men in all Ages would be found to have been little less whimsical in adorning that Part, than our selves. The different Forms of their Wiggs, together with the various Cocks of their Hats, all flatter us in this Opinion.

I had an humble Servant last Summer, who the first Time

he declared himself, was in a Full-Bottom Wigg; but the Day after, to my no small Surprize, he accosted me in a thin Natural one. I received him, at this our second Interview, as a perfect Stranger, but was extreamly confounded, when his Speech discovered who he was. I resolved, therefore, to fix his Face in my Memory for the future; but as I was walking in the Park the same Evening, he appeared to me in one of those Wiggs that I think you call a *Night-cap*, which had altered him more effectually than before. He afterwards played a Couple of Black Riding Wiggs upon me, with the same Success; and, in short, assumed a new Face almost every Day in the first Month of his Courtship.

I observed afterwards, that the Variety of Cocks into which he moulded his Hat, had not a little contributed to his Impositions upon me.

Yet, as if all these Ways were not sufficient to distinguish their Heads, you must, doubtless, Sir, have observed, that great Numbers of young Fellows have, for several Months last past, taken upon them to wear Feathers.

We hope, therefore, that these may, with as much Justice, be called *Indian Princes*, as you have stiled a Woman in a coloured Hood an *Indian* Queen; and that you will, in due Time, take these airy Gentlemen into Consideration.

We the more earnestly beg that you would put a Stop to this Practice, since it has already lost us one of the most agreeable Members of our Society, who after having refused several good Estates, and two Titles, was lured from us last Week by a *mixed Feather*.

I am ordered to present you the Respects of our whole Company, and am,

Sir,

Your very humble Servant,

DORINDA.

Note. *The Person wearing the Feather, tho' our Friend took him for an Officer in the Guards, has proved to be an arrant Linnen-Draper.*'

I am not now at Leisure to give my Opinion upon the Hat and Feather; however, to wipe off the present Imputation, and gratifie my Female Correspondent, I shall here print a Letter which I lately received from a Man of Mode, who seems to have a very extraordinary genius in his way.

'*Sir,*

I presume I need not inform you, that among Men of Dress it is a common Phrase to say, *Mr.* Such-an-one *has struck a bold Stroke*; by which we understand, that he is the first Man who has had Courage enough to lead up a Fashion. Accordingly, when our Taylors take Measure of us, they always demand *whether we will have a plain Suit, or strike a bold Stroke?* I think I may without Vanity say, that I have struck some of the boldest and most successful Strokes of any Man in *Great Britain.* I was the first that struck the long Pocket about two Years since: I was likewise the Author of the frosted Button, which when I saw the Town came readily into, being resolved to strike while the Iron was hot, I produced much about the same Time the Scollop Flap, the knotted Cravat, and made a fair push for the Silver-clocked Stocking.

A few Months after I brought up *the modish Jacket*, or the Coat with close Sleeves. I struck this at first in a plain *Doily*; but that failing, I struck it a second Time in blue Camlet; and repeated the Stroke in several Kinds of Cloth, till at last it took Effect. There are two or three young Fellows at the other End of the Town, who have always their Eye upon me, and answer me Stroke for Stroke. I was once so unwary as to mention my Fancy in Relation to a new-fashioned *Surtout* before one of these Gentlemen, who was disingenuous enough to steal my Thought, and by that Means prevented my intended Stroke.

I have a Design this Spring to make very considerable Innovations in the Wastcoat, and have already begun with a *Coup d'essai* upon the Sleeves which has succeeded very well.

I must further inform you, if you will promise to encourage, or at least to connive at me, that it is my Design to strike such a Stroke the Beginning of the next Month, as shall surprise the whole Town.

I do not think it prudent to acquaint you with all the Particulars of my intended Dress; but will only tell you as a Sample of it, that I shall very speedily appear at *White's* in a *Cherry-coloured Hat.* I took this Hint from the Ladies' Hoods, which I look upon as the boldest Stroke that Sex has struck for these hundred Years last past.

> *I am, Sir,*
>> *Your most Obedient, most humble Servant,*
>>> Will Sprightly.'

I have not Time at present to make any Reflections on this Letter, but must not however omit, that having shewn it to WILL HONEYCOMB, he desires to be acquainted with the Gentleman who writ it. **X**

No. 320.

[STEELE.]   Friday, March 7.

. . . *Non pronuba Juno,*
Non Hymenaeus adest, non illi Gratia lecto. . . .
Eumenides stravere torum . . .—Ov.

'Mr. SPECTATOR,

You have given many Hints in your Papers, to the Disadvantage of Persons of your own Sex, who lay Plots upon Women. Among other hard Words you have published the Term Male-Coquets, and been very severe upon such as give themselves the Liberty of a little Dalliance of Heart, and playing fast and loose, between Love and Indifference, till perhaps an easie young Girl is reduced to Sighs, Dreams and Tears; and languishes away her Life for a careless Coxcomb, who looks astonished, and wonders at such an Effect from what in him was all but common Civility. Thus you have treated the Men who are irresolute in Marriage; but if you design to be impartial, pray be so honest as to print the Information I now give you, of a certain Sett of Women who never coquet for the Matter, but with an high Hand marry whom they please to whom they please. As for my Part, I should not have concerned my self with them, but that I understand I am pitched upon by them, to be married, against my Will, to one I never saw in my Life. It has been my Misfortune, Sir, very innocently to rejoice in a plentiful Fortune, of which I am Master, to bespeak a fine Chariot, to give Direction for two or three handsome Snuff-Boxes, and as many Suits of fine Cloaths; but before any of these were ready, I heard Reports of my being to be married to two or three different young Women. Upon my taking Notice of it to a young Gentleman who is often in my Company, he told me smiling, I was in the Inquisition. You may believe I was not a little startled at what he meant, and more so when he asked me if I had bespoke any Thing of late that was fine. I told him several; upon which he produced a Description of my Person from the Tradesmen whom I had employed, and told me that they had certainly informed against me. Mr. SPECTATOR, Whatever the World may think of me, I am more Coxcomb than Fool, and I grew very inquisitive upon this Head, not a little pleased with the Novelty. My Friend told me, there were a certain Sett of Women of Fashion, whereof the Number of Six made a Committee, who sat thrice a Week, under the Title of the Inquisition on Maids and Batchelours. It seems, whenever there comes such an unthinking gay Thing as my self to Town, he must want all Manner of Necessaries, or be put into the Inquisition by the first Tradesmen he employs. They have constant Intelligence with Cane-shops, Perfumers, Toymen, Coach-makers, and China-Houses. From these several Places these Undertakers for Marriages have as constant and regular Correspondence, as the funeral Men have with Vintners and Apothecaries. All Batchelors are under their immediate Inspection, and my Friend produced to me a Report given in to their Board, wherein an old Unkle of mine, who came to Town with me, and my self, were inserted, and we stood thus; the Unkle smoaky, rotten, poor; the Nephew raw, but no Fool, sound at present, very rich. My Information did not end here, but my Friend's Advices are so good, that he could shew me a Copy of the Letter sent to the young Lady who is to have me; which I enclose to you.

> *"Madam,*
>
> This is to let you know, that you are to be married to a Beau that comes out on *Thursday* six in the Evening. Be at the *Park*: You cannot but know a Virgin-Fop; they have a Mind to look saucy, but are out of Countenance. The Board has denied him to several good Families. I wish you Joy.
>
> *Corinna."'*

What makes my Correspondent's Case the more deplorable, is, that as I find by the Report from my Censor of Marriages, the Friend he speaks of is employed by the Inquisition to take him in, as the Phrase is. After all that is told him, he has Information only of one Woman that is laid for him, and that the wrong one; for the Lady-Commissioners have devoted him to another than the Person against whom they have employed their Agent his Friend to alarm him. The Plot is laid so well about this young Gentleman, that he has no Friend to retire to, no Place to appear in, or Part of the Kingdom to fly into, but he must fall into the Notice, and be subject to the Power of the Inquisition. They have their Emissaries and Substitutes in all Parts of this united Kingdom. The first Step they usually take, is to find from a Correspondence, by their Messengers and Whisperers with some Domestick of the Batchelor (who is to be hunted into the Toils they have laid for him) what are his Manners, his Familiarities, his good Qualities, or Vices; not as the Good in him is a Recommendation, or the Ill a Diminution, but as they affect or contribute to the main Enquiry, What Estate he has in him? When this Point is well reported to the Board, they can take in a wild roaring Fox-hunter, as easily as a soft gentle young Fop of the Town. The Way is to make all Places uneasie to him, but the Scenes in which they have allotted him to act. His Brother Huntsmen, Bottle

Companions, his Fraternity of Fops, shall be brought into the Conspiracy against him. Then this Matter is not laid in so barefaced a Manner before him, as to have it intimated Mrs. Such-a-one would make him a very proper Wife; but by the Force of their Correspondence they shall make it (as Mr. *Waller* said of the Marriage of the Dwarfs) as impracticable to have any Woman besides her they design him, as it would have been in *Adam* to have refused *Eve*. The Man named by the Commission for Mrs. Such-a-one, shall neither be in Fashion, nor dare ever to appear in Company, should he attempt to evade their Determination.

The female Sex wholly govern domestick Life; and by this Means, when they think fit they can sow Dissentions between the dearest Friends, nay make Father and Son irreconcilable Enemies, in spite of all the Ties of Gratitude on one Part, and the Duty of Protection to be paid on the other. The Ladies of the Inquisition understand this perfectly well; and where Love is not a Motive to a Man's chusing one whom they allot, they can, with very much Art, insinuate Stories to the Disadvantage of his Honesty or Courage, till the Creature is too much dispirited to bear up against a general ill Reception which he every where meets with, and in due Time falls into their appointed Wedlock for Shelter. I have a long Letter bearing Date the fourth Instant, which gives me a large Account of the Policies of this Court; and find there is now before them a very refractory Person who has escaped all their Machinations for two Years last past: But they have prevented two successive Matches which were of his own Inclination, the one, by a Report that his Mistress was to be married, and the very Day appointed, Wedding-Clothes bought, and all Things ready for her being given to another; the second Time, by insinuating to all his Mistress's Friends and Acquaintance, that he had been false to several other Women, and the like. The poor Man is now reduced to profess he designs to lead a single Life; but the Inquisition give out to all his Acquaintance, that nothing is intended but the Gentleman's own Welfare and Happiness. When this is urged, he talks still more humbly, and protests he aims only at a Life without Pain or Reproach: Pleasure, Honour or Riches are Things for which he has no Taste. But notwithstanding all this and what else he may defend himself with, as that the Lady is too old or too young, of a suitable Humour, or the quite contrary, and that it is impossible they can ever do other than wrangle from *June* to *January*, every Body tells him all this is Spleen, and he must have a Wife; while all the Members of the Inquisition are unanimous in a certain Woman for him, and they think they all together are better able to judge, than he or any other private person whatsoever.

'*Sir,*   *Temple, March* 3, 1711.

Your Speculation this Day on the Subject of Idleness has employed me, ever since I read it, in sorrowful Reflections on my having loitered away the Term (or rather the Vacation) of ten Years in this Place, and unhappily suffered a good Chamber and Study to lye idle as long. My Books (except those I have taken to sleep upon) have been totally neglected, and my Lord *Coke* and other venerable Authors were never so slighted in their Lives. I spend most of the Day at a neighbouring Coffee-House, where we have what I may call a lazy Club. We generally come in Night-Gowns, with our Stockings about our Heels, and sometimes but one on. Our Salutation at Entrance is a Yawn and a Stretch, and then without more Ceremony we take our Place at the Lolling-Table; where our Discourse is, what I fear you would not read out, therefore shall not insert. But I assure you, Sir, I heartily lament this Loss of Time, and am now resolved (if possible, with double Diligence) to retrieve it, being effectually awakened by the Arguments of Mr. *Slack* out of the senseless Stupidity that has so long possessed me. And to demonstrate, that Penitence accompanies my Confession, and Constancy my Resolutions, I have locked my Door for a Year, and desire you would let my Companions know I am not within. I am with great Respect,

> *Sir,*
> *Your most obedient Servant,*

T   N. B.'

No. 321.
[ADDISON.]   Saturday, March 8.

Non satis est pulchra esse poemata, dulcia sunto.—Hor.

THOSE, who know how many Volumes have been written on the Poems of *Homer* and *Virgil*, will easily pardon the Length of my Discourse upon *Milton.* The *Paradise Lost* is looked upon, by the best Judges, as the greatest Production, or at least the noblest Work of Genius, in our Language, and therefore deserves to be set before an *English* Reader in its full Beauty. For this Reason, tho' I have endeavoured to give a general Idea of its Graces and Imperfections in my six first Papers, I thought my self obliged to bestow one upon every Book in particular. The Three first Books I have already dispatched, and am now entring upon the Fourth. I need not acquaint my Reader, that there are Multitudes of Beauties in this great Author, especially in the descriptive Parts of this Poem, which I have not touched upon; it being my Intention to point out those only, which appear to me the most exquisite, or those which are not so obvious to ordinary Readers. Every one that has read the Criticks, who have written upon the *Odissy*, the *Illiad* and the *Aeneid*, knows very well, that though they agree in their Opinions of the great Beauties in those Poems, they have nevertheless each of them discovered several Master-Strokes, which have escaped the Observation of the rest. In the same Manner, I question not, but any Writer, who shall treat of this Subject after me, may find several Beauties in *Milton*, which I have not taken notice of. I must likewise observe, that as the greatest Masters of critical Learning differ among one another, as to some particular Points in an Epic Poem, I have not bound my self scrupulously to the Rules which any one of them has laid down upon that Art, but have taken the Liberty sometimes to join with one, and sometimes with another, and sometimes to differ from all of them, when I have thought that the Reason of the Thing was on my side.

We may consider the Beauties of the Fourth Book under three Heads. In the first are those Pictures of Still-Life, which we meet with in the Description of *Eden, Paradise, Adam*'s Bower, &c. In the next are the Machines, which comprehend the Speeches and Behaviour of the good and bad Angels. In the last is the Conduct of *Adam* and *Eve*, who are the principa Actors in the Poem.

In the Description of *Paradise*, the Poet has observed *Aristotle*'s Rule of lavishing all the Ornaments of Diction on the weak unactive Parts of the Fable, which are not supported by the Beauty of Sentiments and Characters. Accordingly the Reader may observe, that the Expressions are more florid and elaborate in these Descriptions, than in most other Parts of the Poem. I must further add, that tho' the *Drawings* of Gardens, Rivers, Rainbows, and the like dead Pieces of Nature, are justly censured in an heroic Poem, when they run out into an unnecessary Length; the Description of *Paradise* would have been faulty, had not the Poet been very particular in it, not only as it is the Scene of the principal Action, but as it is requisite to give us an Idea of that Happiness from which our first Parents fell. The Plan of it is wonderfully beautiful, and formed upon the short Sketch which we have of it, in Holy Writ. *Milton*'s Exuberance of Imagination, has poured forth such a Redundancy of Ornaments on this Seat of Happiness and Innocence, that it would be endless to point out each Particular.

I must not quit this Head, without further observing, that there is scarce a Speech of *Adam* or *Eve* in the whole Poem, wherein the Sentiments and Allusions are not taken from this their delightful Habitation. The Reader, during their whole Course of Action, always finds himself in the Walks of *Paradise*. In short, as the Cricks have remarked, that in those Poems, wherein Shepherds are Actors, the Thoughts ought always to take a Tincture from the Woods, Fields and Rivers; so we may observe, that our first Parents seldom lose Sight of their happy Station in any Thing they speak or do; and, if the Reader will give me Leave to use the Expression, that their Thoughts are always *paradisiacal*.

We are in the next Place to consider the Machines of the Fourth Book. *Satan* being now within Prospect of *Eden*, and looking round upon the Glories of the Creation, is filled with Sentiments different from those which he discovered whilst he was in Hell. The Place inspires him with Thoughts more adapted to it: He reflects upon the happy Condition from whence he fell, and breaks forth into a Speech that is softned with several transient Touches of Remorse and Self-Accusation: But at length, he confirms himself in Impenitence, and in his Design of drawing Man into his own State of Guilt and Misery. This Conflict of Passions is raised with a great deal of Art, as the Opening of his Speech to the Sun is very bold and noble.

> *O thou that with surpassing Glory crown'd*
> *Look'st from thy sole Dominion like the God*
> *Of this new World, at whose Sight all the Stars*
> *Hide their diminish'd Heads, to thee I call*
> *But with no friendly Voice, and add thy Name*
> *O Sun, to tell thee how I hate thy Beams*
> *That bring to my Remembrance from what State*
> *I fell, how glorious once above thy Sphere.*

This Speech is, I think, the finest that is ascribed to *Satan* in the whole Poem. The Evil Spirit afterwards proceeds to make his Discoveries concerning our first Parents, and to learn after what Manner they may be best attacked. His bounding over the Walls of *Paradise*; his sitting in the Shape of a Cormorant upon the Tree of Life, which stood in the Center of it, and over-topped all the other Trees of the Garden; his alighting among the Herd of Animals, which are so beautifully represented as playing about *Adam* and *Eve*, together with his transforming himself into different Shapes, in order to hear their Conversation, are Circumstances that give an agreeable

Surprise to the Reader, and are devised with great Art, to connect that Series of Adventures in which the Poet has engaged
this Artificer of Fraud.

The Thought of *Satan's* Transformation into a Cormorant,
and placing himself on the Tree of Life, seems raised upon that
Passage in the *Iliad*, where two Deities are described, as perch-
ing on the Top of an Oak in the Shape of Vulturs.

His planting himself at the Ear of *Eve* under the Form of a
Toad, in order to produce vain Dreams and Imaginations, is a
Circumstance of the same Nature; as his starting up in his own
Form is wonderfully fine, both in the Literal Description, and
in the Moral which is concealed under it. His Answer upon
his being discovered, and demanded to give an Account of
himself, is conformable to the Pride and intrepidity of his
Character.

> *Know ye not then, said* Satan, *fill'd with Scorn,*
> *Know ye not me? ye knew me once no Mate*
> *For you, there sitting where you durst not soare;*
> *Not to know me argues your-selves unknown,*
> *The lowest of your throng; . . .*

Zephon's Rebuke, with the Influence it had on *Satan*, is
exquisitely graceful and moral. *Satan* is afterwards led away
to *Gabriel*, the chief of the guardian Angels, who kept Watch in
Paradise. His disdainful Behaviour on this Occasion is so
remarkable a Beauty, that the most ordinary Reader cannot
but take Notice of it. *Gabriel's* discovering his Approach at a
Distance, is drawn with great Strength and Liveliness of
Imagination.

> *O Friends, I hear the tread of nimble Feet*
> *Hast'ning this Way, and now by glimps discern*
> Ithuriel *and* Zephon *through the shade;*
> *And with them comes a third of regal Port*
> *But faded splendor wan; who by his gait*
> *And fierce demeanor seems the Prince of Hell,*
> *Not likely to part hence without contest;*
> *Stand firm, for in his look defiance lours.*

The Conference between *Gabriel* and *Satan* abounds with
Sentiments proper for the Occasion, and suitable to the Persons
of the two Speakers. *Satan's* cloathing himself with Terror,
when he prepares for the Combat, is truly sublime, and at least
equal to *Homer's* Description of Discord celebrated by *Longinus*, or to that of Fame in *Virgil*, who are both represented with
their Feet standing upon the Earth, and their Heads reaching
above the Clouds.

> *While thus he spake, th' Angelic Squadron bright*
> *Turn'd fiery red, sharpning in mooned Horns*
> *Their Phalanx, and began to hem him round*
> *With ported Spears, &c.*
> *. . . On th' other Side, Satan, alarm'd,*
> *Collecting all his might dilated stood*
> *Like* Teneriff *or* Atlas *unremov'd.*
> *His Stature reach'd the Sky, and on his Crest*
> *Sat horrour plum'd ; . . .*

I must here take notice, that *Milton* is every where full of Hints, and sometimes literal Translations, taken from the greatest of the *Greek* and *Latin* Poets.   But this I may reserve for a Discourse by it self, because I would not break the Thread of these Speculations, that are designed for *English* Readers, with such Reflections as would be of no Use but to the Learned.

I must however observe in this Place, that the breaking off the Combat between *Gabriel* and *Satan*, by the hanging out of the golden Scales in Heaven, is a Refinement upon *Homer's* Thought, who tells us, that before the Battle between *Hector* and *Achilles*, *Jupiter* weighed the Event of it in a Pair of Scales. The Reader may see the whole Passage in the 22d *Iliad*.

Virgil, before the last decisive Combat, describes *Jupiter* in the same Manner, as weighing the Fates of *Turnus* and *Aeneas*. *Milton*, though he fetched this beautiful Circumstance from the *Iliad* and *Aeneid*, does not only insert it as a poetical Embellishment, like the Authors above-mentioned; but makes an artful Use of it for the proper carrying on of his Fable, and for the breaking off the Combat between the two Warriors, who were upon the point of engaging.   To this we may further add, that *Milton* is the more justified in this Passage, as we find the same noble Allegory in Holy Writ, where a wicked Prince is said to have been *weigh'd in the Scales, and to have been found wanting*.

I must here take Notice under the Head of the Machines, that *Uriel's* gliding down to the Earth upon a Sunbeam, with the Poet's Device to make him *descend*, as well in his Return to the Sun, as in his coming from it, is a Prettiness that might have been admired in a little fanciful Poet, but seems below the Genius of *Milton*.   The Description of the Host of armed Angels walking their nightly Round in *Paradise*, is of another Spirit;

> *So saying, on he led his radiant files,*
> *Dazling the Moon;*

as that Account of the Hymns which our first Parents used to hear them sing in these their Midnight-Walks, is altogether Divine, and inexpressibly amusing to the Imagination.

We are, in the last place, to consider the Parts which *Adam*

and *Eve* act in the fourth Book. The Description of them as
they first appeared to *Satan*, is exquisitely drawn, and sufficient
to make the fallen Angel gaze upon them with all that Astonishment, and those Emotions of Envy, in which he is represented.

> *Two of far nobler Shape erect and tall,*
> *God-like erect, with native honour clad*
> *In naked Majesty seem'd lords of all,*
> *And worthy seem'd, for in their looks Divine*
> *The Image of their glorious Maker shon.*
> *Truth, Wisdom, Sanctitude severe and pure;*
> *Severe, but in true filial Freedom plac'd:*
> *For Contemplation he and valour form'd,*
> *For softness she and sweet attractive Grace;*
> *He for God only, she for God in him:*
> *His fair large Front, and Eye sublime declar'd*
> *Absolute Rule; and* Hyacinthin *Locks*
> *Round from his parted forelock manly hung*
> *Clustring, but not beneath his Shoulders broad;*
> *She as a Vail down to her slender Waste*
> *Her unadorned golden Tresses wore*
> *Dis-shevel'd, but in wanton Ringlets wav'd.*
> *So pass'd they naked on, nor shun'd the Sight*
> *Of God or Angel, for they Thought no ill:*
> *So Hand in Hand they pass'd, the loveliest Pair*
> *That ever since in love's Embraces met.*

There is a fine Spirit of Poetry in the Lines which follow,
wherein they are described as sitting on a Bed of Flowers by
the Side of a Fountain, amidst a mixed Assembly of Animals.

The Speeches of these two first Lovers flow equally from
Passion and Sincerity. The Professions they make to one
another are full of Warmth; but at the same Time founded on
Truth. In a Word, they are the Gallantries of *Paradise.*

> *. . . When* Adam *first of Men . . .*
> *Sole Partner and sole Part of all these Joys*
> *Dearer thy self than all; . . .*
> *But let us ever praise him, and extol*
> *His bounty, following our delightful task,*
> *To prune those growing plants, and tend these flowers,*
> *Which were it toilsome, yet with thee were sweet.*
> *To whom thus* Eve *repli'd. O thou for whom*
> *And from whom I was form'd, Flesh of thy Flesh,*
> *And without whom am to no end, my Guide*
> *And Head, what thou hast said is just and right.*
> *For we to him indeed all Praises owe,*
> *And daily Thanks, I chiefly who enjoy*
> *So far the happier Lot, enjoying thee*
> *Prae-eminent by so much odds, while thou*
> *Like Consort to thy self canst no where find, &c.*

The remaining Part of *Eve*'s Speech, in which she gives an Account of her self upon her first Creation, and the Manner in which she was brought to *Adam*, is I think as beautiful a Passage as any in *Milton*, or perhaps in any other Poet whatsoever. These Passages are all worked off with so much Art, that they are capable of pleasing the most delicate Reader, without offending the most severe.

> *That Day I oft remember, when from Sleep*, &c.

A Poet of less Judgment and Invention than this great Author, would have found it very difficult to have filled these tender Parts of the Poem with Sentiments proper for a State of Innocence; to have described the Warmth of Love, and the Professions of it, without Artifice or Hyperbole; to have made the Man speak the most endearing Things, without descending from his natural Dignity, and the Woman receiving them without Departing from the Modesty of her Character; in a Word, to adjust the Prerogatives of Wisdom and Beauty, and make each appear to the other in its proper Force and Loveliness. This mutual Subordination of the two Sexes is wonderfully kept up in the whole Poem, as particularly in the Speech of *Eve* I have beforementioned, and upon the Conclusion of it in the following Lines;

> *So spake our general Mother, and with Eyes*
> *Of conjugal Attraction unreprov'd,*
> *And meek surrender, half embracing lean'd*
> *On our first Father, half her swelling breast*
> *Naked met his under the flowing Gold*
> *Of her loose Tresses hid; he in Delight*
> *Both of her Beauty and submissive Charms*
> *Smil'd with superior Love. . . .*

The Poet adds, that the Devil turned away with Envy at the Sight of so much Happiness.

We have another View of our first Parents in their evening Discourses, which is full of pleasing Images, and Sentiments suitable to their Condition and Characters. The Speech of *Eve*, in particular, is dressed up in such a soft and natural Turn of Words and Sentiments, as cannot be sufficiently admired.

I shall close my Reflections upon this Book, with observing the Masterly Transition which the Poet makes to their Evening Worship, in the following Lines.

> *Thus at their shadie lodge arriv'd, both stood,*
> *Both turn'd, and under open Sky ador'd*
> *The God that made both Sky, Air, Earth, and Heav'n*

Which they beheld, the Moons resplendent Globe
And Starry Pole: Thou also mad' st the Night
Maker Omnipotent, and thou the Day, &c.

Most of the modern heroick Poets have imitated the Ancients, in beginning a Speech without premising, that the Person said thus or thus; but as it is easie to imitate the Ancients in the Omission of two or three Words, it requires Judgment to do it in such a Manner as they shall not be missed, and that the Speech may begin naturally without them. There is a fine Instance of this Kind out of *Homer*, in the Twenty Third Chapter of *Longinus*.

L

The End of the Fourth Volume.

NOTES

$A.$ = Original Daily Issue.
$B. I.$ = Biographical Index.

Dedication. PAGE I. Henry Boyle, brother of the Earl of Burlington, and nephew of the more famous Robert Boyle, was created Baron Carleton in October 1714 (see $B. I.$). Pope speaks of his 'calm sense' in the *Epilogue to the Satires* (ii. 80), and Gay introduces him in *Mr. Pope's Welcome from Greece* (xv).

Any particular Person. See i. 514–15. Jeremy Collier pleads for the same general interpretation in the Preface to his *Essays* (second edition, 1697).

A List of Subscribers follows the Dedication. It contains over four hundred names, chiefly those of noblemen or of well-to-do merchants, such as Thomas Brooke and John Hellier (of the *Spectator* advertisements). Among the subscribers are Sir Richard Blackmore, Eustace Budgell, William Clayton, Dr. Garth, Sir Godfrey Kneller, Sir Isaac Newton, Mr. Pearce, Dr. Shadwell, John Vanbrugh, Robert Walpole, and Christopher Wren.

170. PAGE 3. *Motto*. Terence, *Eunuchus*, I. i.

Advice to a Daughter, by George Savile, Marquess of Halifax, printed on pages 1–84 of the 1700 edition of his *Miscellanies*. It is one of the books in Leonora's library, *ante*, i. 112 and note.

PAGE 4. *Phaedria's Request*. Terence, *Eunuchus*, I. ii. 112–16.

PAGE 5. *Be not jealous*, etc. Ecclesiasticus, ix. 1.

171. PAGE 7. *Motto*. Ovid, *Metamorphoses*, vii. 826.

Ode to Lydia. Horace, *Odes*, I. xiii. 1–8. In A is added: 'part of which I find Translated to my Hand.'

PAGE 8. *Ardeat*, etc. Juvenal, *Satires*, vi. 209.

PAGE 9. *Herod and Mariamne*. Josephus's *Antiquities of the Jews*, xv. iii and vii.

This paper and the preceding are referred to in No. 547.

172. PAGE II. *Motto*. Cicero, *De Officiis*, I. xix.

Omnamante. See i. 436.

173. PAGE 14. *Motto*. Ovid, *Metamorphoses*, v. 216–17.

In a late Paper. See i. 487.

PAGE 15. *Dutch Painter*. Cf. i. 259.

Milton's Death. *Paradise Lost*, ii. 846. Correctly, 'horrible.'

174. PAGE 16. *Motto*. Virgil, *Eclogues*, vii. 69.

PAGE 16. *The old Roman Fable*, as in Livy (II. xxxii), Plutarch, and Annaeus Florus (I. xxiii), but more familiar by Shakespeare's rendering in *Coriolanus* (I. i).

PAGE 17. *Carthaginian Faith.* The *Punica fides* of the Roman historians.

Landed and trading Interest. See No. 69. Sir Andrew Freeport's defence of his class is that of Mr. Sealand in *The Conscious Lovers* (IV. i).

175. PAGE 20. *Motto.* Ovid, *Remedia Amoris*, 625.

PAGE 22. *In a late Speculation.* No. 119.

PAGE 23. *Button-makers.* This is a reference to a statute of 1709, in the interests of 'the many thousands of men, women, and children,' who depended 'upon the making of silk, mohair, gimp, and thread buttons and button-holes with the needle.' As early as 1609 they had petitioned against 'the making and binding button-holes with cloth, serge, etc.'

176. *Motto.* Lucretius, *De Rerum Natura*, iv. 1155.

PAGE 25. Harington's *Oceana*, which appeared in 1656, was edited in 1700, with Harington's other works, by John Toland (referred to in i. 566).

177. PAGE 26. *Motto.* Juvenal, *Satires*, xv. 140–2.

One of my last Week's Papers. See No. 169.

Milkiness of Blood.

> Would I could share thy balmy, even temper,
> And milkiness of blood.
>
>   Dryden's *Cleomenes*, I. i. 119–20.

PAGE 28. See Sir Thomas Browne's *Religio Medici*, Part II, § xiii.

PAGE 29. *What I spent*, etc. Percy refers to an epitaph which was to be found in St. George's church, Doncaster, thus:

> How now, who is heare?
> I, Robin of Doncastere,
> And Margaret my feare.
> That I spent, that I had:
> That I gave, that I have:
> That I left, that I lost.

See also Camden's *Remaines* (1674), page 519.

178. PAGE 30. *Motto.* Horace, *Epistles*, II. ii. 133.

179. PAGE 32. *Motto.* Horace, *Ars Poetica*, 341–4.

This reference to the variety of subjects discussed in the *Spectator* recalls, by way of contrast, Boswell's plaint about the slow success of the *Rambler*, because of the 'uniformity in its texture' (*Life of Johnson*, edited by Birkbeck Hill, i. 208).

PAGE 33. *Passage in Waller.* From his verses *Upon the Earl of Roscommon's Translation of Horace*, lines 41–2, correctly thus:

> Poets lose half the praise they should have got,
> Could it be known what they discreetly blot.

PAGE 34. *Pickled-Herring.* See i. 539.
Children in the Wood. See i. 550.

180. PAGE 35. *Motto.* Horace, *Epistles*, I. ii. 14.

Philarithmus, the writer of the letter, was said to be Henry Martyn, who, among others, is thanked by Steele, in No. 555, for contributions to the *Spectator*. See also *Cottilus*, i. 563. Further ingenuity has discovered in him the model, or one of the models, of Sir Andrew Freeport.

Louis XIV, the 'hardened Sinner,' is the subject of an earlier attack in the *Spectator*. See No. 139 (i. 419).

PAGE 38. The anecdotes will be found in Plutarch's *Life of Pyrrhus*.

181. *Motto.* Virgil, *Aeneid*, ii. 145.

PAGE 39. *Illustrated this kind*, etc. See Nos. 120, 121.

PAGE 40. *Freher.* Addison got his material from Bayle's *Dictionary*, article 'Eginhart.' The story of Eginhart is there transcribed from the *Chronicon Laurishamensis Coenobii*, as printed by the Heidelberg lawyer, Marquard Freher, in the first volume of his *Rerum Germanicarum Scriptores* (1600). Bayle introduces the story with the reflection that it deserves the attention of authors, and especially of such a story-teller as La Fontaine.

Among the advertisements at the end of this number (*A*) is the following, which illustrates No. 191: 'At Sam's Coffee-house in Ludgate-street, during the Time of drawing the Million and Half Lottery, will be kept a most correct Numerical Table (tho' not examin'd by a celebrated Mathematician, as is lately set forth by some ignorant Upstarts, to give Credit to their Undertaking) where all Persons may know whether their Tickets are Benefits or Blanks, every half hour, paying for every Benefit 2s. 6d. and, if a Blank, nothing.' In subsequent numbers there are rival advertisements by the Cross Keys and Bible in Cornhill (under the charge of Andrew Bell, Printer to the Hon. Commissioners of the Lottery), Jack's in Birchin Lane, the Turk's Head in Ironmonger Lane, the Guildhall, the Rainbow, the British, and others.

182. PAGE 41. *Motto.* Juvenal, *Satires*, vi. 181.

183. PAGE 44. *Motto.* Hesiod, *Theogonia*, 27–8.

Jothram's [Jotham's] Fable. Judges, ix. 8 et sqq.
Nathan's Fable. 2 Samuel xii. 1 et sqq.
Fable of the Belly. See No. 174, note.
Boileau. 'This is somewhat curious, considering that Boileau did not include the fable in his *Art poétique* (ii) and

considering too that there are so few fables in his works. Perhaps Addison was thinking of the fable at the end of the second *Epistle*, which, however, is mediocre and not to be compared with the *chef d'œuvre* of La Fontaine on the same subject.'— D. Nichol Smith.

PAGE 45. *As for the Odissey.* Cf. Le Bossu, I. xii: 'Ce que l'Iliade et l'Odyssée ont de commun, c'est que l'une et l'autre est une instruction morale, déguisée sous les allégories d'une Action. C'est ce qu'Horace y reconnoît; et par conséquent l'une et l'autre, au sentiment de ce Critique, est une Fable, telle que nous l'avons proposée.' Cf. also Book IV, *Des Mœurs*.

Invented by Prodicus, etc. Xenophon's *Memorabilia*, ii. The Dutch issue of the *Journal des Sçavans* of November 1712 contained a paper by Lord Shaftesbury on the Judgment of Hercules, afterwards published in English in the posthumous edition of his works.

Plato's *Account* will be found in the *Phaedo*, § 10.

184. PAGE 47. *Motto.* Horace, *Ars Poetica*, 360. Cf. No. 124 ('Rests and Nodding-places'): also Quintilian, x. i.

PAGE 48. The subject of the advertisement was one Nicholas Hart (see *B. I.*) and 'his Historiographer' was William Hill senior, of Lincoln's Inn (see *B. I.*).

PAGE 49. Lines 8, 9. Probably a reference to the session of Parliament at this time.

Juvenal. Satires, i. 55 et sqq.

185. PAGE 50. *Motto.* Virgil, *Aeneid*, i. 11.

Video, etc. Ovid, *Metamorphoses*, vii. 20–1.

186. PAGE 52. *Motto.* Horace, *Odes*, I. iii. 38.

PAGE 55. *Pythagoras's first Rule* is the motto of No. 112.

A Cock to Aesculapius, from the *Phaedo*, lxvi.

Xenophon tells us. *Cyropaedia*, viii. 7.

187. *Motto.* Horace, *Odes*, I. v. 12–13.

PAGE 56. *Scrutore*, or scrutoire, the older (seventeenth-century) aphetic form of escritoire.

PAGE 58. *Mr. Sly.* See *B. I.*

188. *Motto.* Adapted from Cicero, *Epistolae ad Familiares*, xv. vi. 1: 'Laetus sum laudari me, inquit Hector, opinor apud Naevium, abs te, pater, a laudato viro.' See also v. xii. 7.

PAGE 59. *The Satyrist.* Persius, *Satires*, iv. 51–2.

Tollat sua munera cerdo:
Tecum habita.

The Lacedemonians. See Plutarch's *Life of Lycurgus*.

PAGE 60. *Equally the objects of ridicule.* Cf. the *Guardian*, No. 4 (16th March 1713), in which Pope comments severely on 'this prostitution of praise.'

PAGE 60. *Bulfinch*, in Brome's *Northern Lasse* (1632), again referred to in No. 468.

> *Phocion.* See Plutarch's life. Cf. Bacon, *Apophthegms*, 291: 'Has any foolish thing dropped from me unawares?'

189. PAGE 61. *Motto.* Virgil, *Aeneid*, ix. 294; x. 824.

PAGE 62. *Sir Sampson Legend*, the heavy father in Congreve's comedy *Love for Love*.

> *Crudelis*, etc. Virgil, *Eclogues*, viii. 48–50.
> *Subject of my Paper.* No. 181.

PAGE 63. *Father le Conte.* See Part II, letter i, of *The Present State of China*, an English translation of his work which was published in London in 1697.

> *A Passage.* Herodotus, I. cxxxvii.

190. PAGE 64. *Motto.* Horace, *Odes*, II. viii. 18.

> On the subject of this paper cf. the *Guardian*, No. 105, by Addison.

PAGE 66. *The greatest Politicians of the Age.* A supposed reference to Secretary St. John, afterwards Lord Bolingbroke.

191. PAGE 67. *Motto.* Homer, *Iliad*, ii. 6.

> *Mahomet's Burying Place.* Addison again makes use of Bayle. See article 'Mahomet.'
> *A Tacker . . . Number* 134. In 1704 a Bill was introduced into the House of Commons against occasional conformity, and, that it might the more surely pass the Lords, was tacked to a Money Bill. A large majority, however, opposed this procedure, and the Bill was thrown out. The minority numbered 134.

PAGE 68. *Acted*=actuated. Cf. No. 287, first paragraph.

> *Lottery.* See note to No. 181.

PAGE 69. *Disburse*, reimburse.

192. *Motto.* Terence, *Andria*, I. i. 69–71.

PAGE 71. *The Cornelii.* Identified by some with Francis Eyles, director of the East India Company, and afterwards created a baronet; his son, Sir John, Lord Mayor of London in 1727, and his other son, Sir Joseph, Sheriff of London in 1725.

193. PAGE 73. *Motto.* Virgil, *Georgics*, ii. 461–2.

PAGE 74. *Difference in the Military and Civil List.* The Duke of Marlborough had the reputation of receiving *en déshabillé*. Steele may also hint at the Tory ministers Oxford and Ormond, the former the 'close' minister, the latter an 'open-breasted' officer.

> Line 25. *A* and the 1712–13 edition read 'Beauteous,' which is probably a misprint.

PAGE 75. *The Satyrist says.* Juvenal, *Satires*, viii. 73:

> Rarus enim ferme sensus communis in illa
> Fortuna.

194. PAGE 76. *Motto.* Horace, *Odes*, I. xiii. 4. See also page 7 of this volume. Previous editors have found in the first letter a direct reference by Steele to his relations with his wife, 'Dear Prue.'

195. PAGE 78. *Motto.* Hesiod, *Works and Days*, lines 40–1.
    Arabian Nights. See the 'History of the Greek King and Douban, the Physician,' in the tale of the *Fisherman*.

    PAGE 79. *Diogenes.* Diogenes Laertius, *Vitae Philosophorum*, VI. ii. 6.

    PAGE 80. *Sir William Temple's* axiom is his own. '. . . All excess is to be avoided, especially in the common use of wine: whereof the first Glass may pass for Health, the second for good Humour, the third for our Friends: but the fourth is for our Enemies' (*Essays*, 'Of Health and Long Life,' ii. 428, 1754 edition).
    Ancient Authors. Diogenes Laertius, *Life of Socrates*; Aelian, *Variae Historiae*, xiii. 27.

    PAGE 81. Luigi Cornaro's *Trattato de la vita sobria* appeared at Padua in 1558, and was the first of the *Discorsi della vita sobria* (Milan, 1627). *Cornaro's Treatise of Temperance and Sobrietie, translated by Master George Herbert* (the poet), had appeared in 1634. The English version incorrectly referred to by Addison is *Sure and certain Methods of attaining a long and healthful Life . . . made English by W. Jones*, second edition, London, 1704. It is advertised in No. 196 (*A*). Many reissues followed from the London and provincial presses: the fifty-fifth appeared at Leeds in 1832.

196. *Motto.* Horace, *Epistles*, I. xi. 30.
    PAGE 82. The 'Young Woman' at Hackney refers to the petition of Benjamin Easie in No. 134.

197. PAGE 84. *Motto.* Horace, *Epistles*, I. xviii. 15–20.
    PAGE 85. *Hudibras*, I. i. 69–70 ('change *hands*').

198. PAGE 88. *Motto.* Horace, *Odes*, IV. iv. 50–3. The original reads *Cervi*, which Addison alters for his present purpose.
    Visitant to her Bed-side. See note, i. 538.
    Queen Emma. Mother of Edward Confessor. Addison probably refreshed his memory by the perusal of Bayle's *Dictionary*, in which the tale is given. See article 'Emma.'
    PAGE 89. *Chamont.* A young soldier of fortune in Otway's tragedy of *The Orphan*. The lines are in Act II.

199. PAGE 91. *Motto.* Ovid, *Heroides*, iv. 10.
    Oroondates. From Mlle de Scudéry's romance of *Artamène ou le Grand Cyrus* (1649–53).

200. PAGE 93. *Motto.* Virgil, *Aeneid*, vi. 823 ('Vincet amor patriae').

PAGE 94. 'Philarithmus' himself, i.e. Henry Martyn (*ante*, page 35), may have been the author of this further politico-economic study.

PAGE 96. *The Schoolmen's Ass*. See page 67.

PAGE 97. πλέον, etc. See the motto of No. 195, *ante*, page 78.
　　Sir William Petty (1623–87). His *Essays in Political Arithmetic* had been published in 1699: and a new edition had just appeared (in 1711).

201. *Motto*. Aulus Gellius, *Noctes Atticae*, IV. ix. 'Nigidius Figulus, homo, ut ego arbitror, juxta M. Varronem doctissimus, in undecimo commentariorum grammaticorum versum ex antiquo carmine refert, memoria hercle dignum: religentem esse oportet; religiosum nefas. Cujus autem id carmen sit, non scribit.'

202. PAGE 100. *Motto*. Horace, *Epistles*, I. xviii. 25.
　　PAGE 101. *Make-Bates*. See i. 562.

203. PAGE 103. *Motto*. Ovid, *Metamorphoses*, ii. 36–8.
　　PAGE 104. Virgil, *Georgics*, ii. 80–2.
　　Addison takes the *Fragment of Apollodorus* from his Winterton (*Poetae Minores Graeci*, page 485). See i. 547.

204. PAGE 106. *Motto*. Horace, *Odes*, I. xix. 7–8.
　　PAGE 107. *Sothades*. This is Belinda's Portuguese for the dictionary *Saudades*. *Saudade* signifies a 'tender regard' or appreciation for something absent, combined with an earnest longing for its attainment.
　　PAGE 108. *The Lover in the Way of the World*. See Congreve's *Way of the World*, I. ii, where Mirabell says of Millamant's failings: 'I studied 'em, and got 'em by rote. . . . They are now grown as familiar to me as my own frailties; and in all probability, in a little time longer, I shall like 'em as well.'
　　R——s. Interpreted by the early editors as Rivers.

205. PAGE 109. *Motto*. Horace, *Ars Poetica*, 25.
　　PAGE 111. *Foolish Roderigos*. A reference to the character in Shakespeare's *Othello*.
　　PAGE 112. *Nicolini*. See i. 17 and *B. I*.
　　Hopkins and Sternhold, the metrical translators of the Psalms.
　　Sir William Temple. See page 80.
　　Errata. Perhaps an intentional error, at the expense of Robin Good-fellow.
　　This and subsequent numbers contain a long advertisement of 'Proposals for Graving and Printing the Gallery of Raphael at Hampton-court.' Her Majesty having been graciously pleased to grant her Licence to Signor Nicola Dorigny (lately arrived from Rome) to copy and engrave these 'the most valuable set of portable Pictures in the World,' the said Signor proposed to issue 8 plates (7 cartoons and a frontispiece),

*Q 165

19 × 30 and 19 × 25, at four guineas per set, 'a modest price,' as the Undertaker 'aims at Reputation rather than profit.' The nobility and gentry are reminded of Signor Dorigny's work 'after Raphael' during the past twenty years. Steele makes this proposal the topic of No. 226 (page 168), q.v.

206. PAGE 113. *Motto.* Horace, *Odes*, III. xvi. 21–2.

207. PAGE 115. *Motto.* Juvenal, *Satires*, x. 1–4.
  PAGE 117. *Verses out of Homer.* *Iliad*, viii. 548–9.
      As Homer tells us. *Iliad*, v. 127.
  PAGE 119. Other editions add the signature 'L' to this paper.

208. *Motto.* Ovid, *Ars Amatoria*, i. 99. The motto in *A* is '*Spectaret populum ludis attentius ipsis.—Hor.*'
      Mackbeth the other Night. Played on Saturday, 20th October.
  PAGE 120. *The Prude.* See note, i. 554.

209. PAGE 122. *Motto.* Simonides (Amorginus), *Iambics*, iii (Περὶ γυναικῶν). Addison derives his motto and his remarks about Simonides from Winterton's *Poetae Minores Graeci*, page 442. The text from which he made his English version will be found on pages 443–7.
  PAGE 123. *Bienséance.* See i. 565.
  PAGE 125. *Boileau . . . his last Satyr.* This is the tenth *Satire* (written in 1693), the last in the edition of 1694.
      The Satyr upon Man is the eighth *Satire* (1667).
      In *A* is printed the following advertisement, which is here quoted in further illustration of the note on page 534 of volume i: 'Hungary Water, right and fine, large half Pint (Flint) Bottles for 15d. at Strahan's, Bookseller, against the Royal Exchange. . . . Note, it is the same sort by which Isabella, Queen of Hungary, so long preserved her Life and Health. She always poured a small quantity in the Water she washed her Hands and Face withal.' She 'used it with great success in old Pains and the Rheumatism' and commended it especially for pains in the head and the vapours. It is to be taken in a morning draught of ale to aid digestion; to be used by barbers, on their customers' heads and faces after shaving, and by bagnio keepers, 'who should pour some of these Bottles over the Gentlemen and Ladies when they came out of the Bath.'

210. *Motto.* Cicero, *Tusculan Disputations*, I. xv.
  PAGE 126. *Traveller upon the Alps.* The metaphor may have been suggested by the well-known lines in Pope's *Essay on Criticism* (ii. 225–32), which, again, may be an echo of a passage in Drummond of Hawthornden's *Hymn of the Fairest Fair* in his *Flowers of Zion*.
  PAGE 127. *Lord Cardinal*, etc. *2 Henry VI*, IV. iii. 27–9.
      The signature in *A* and in the editions after the octavo of

1712–13 is Z, which here and elsewhere may stand for John Hughes. The signature 'T' may mean that Steele, as editor, transcribed it. These considerations, however, recall Addison's paragraphs in No. 221.

211. PAGE 128. *Motto*. Phaedrus, *Fables*, i, Prologue, 7.
   Horace has a thought. Odes, I. xvi.
   PAGE 129. *Dryden*, *Of the Pythagorean Philosophy, from the Fifteenth Book of Ovid's Metamorphoses*, lines 239–46, 254–9. Scott and Saintsbury's text reads *Man or Beast* in line 242.
   Congreve in a Prologue to one of his Comedies. The passage is in the Epilogue to *Love for Love* (lines 21–4).

212. PAGE 131. *Motto*. Horace, *Satires*, II. vii. 91–2.
   PAGE 132. The passage from Tully will be found in the *Paradoxa*, v. ii.
   On this day Swift writes in his *Journal to Stella*: 'The Spectators are likewise printing in a larger and smaller volume, so I believe they are going to leave them off, and indeed people grow weary of them, though they are often prettily written.' See note to No. 226.

213. PAGE 133. *Motto*. Virgil, *Aeneid*, i. 604.
   PAGE 134. *Acosta's Answer to Limborch.* Addison alludes to the *Amica Collatio de Veritate Religionis Christianae cum Erudito Judaeo*, by Philippe de Limborch, professor of theology at Amsterdam, published in 1667. His opponent was the physician Isaac Orobio; not Uriel Acosta, the convert to Judaism, who died at Amsterdam as early as 1640. See Bayle.
   Saint-Evremond's *Works*, iii (*Sur la Religion*).
   PAGE 136. *Erasmus*. Apophthegms, iii.

214. *Motto*. Juvenal, *Satires*, iii. 124–5. In *A* the motto is
   Dulcis inexpertis cultura potentis amici ;
   Expertus metuit.—Hor.
   PAGE 139. *Plato's Guardian Angels.* See the *Phaedo*.

215. *Motto*. Ovid, *Ex Ponto*, II. ix. 47–8.

216. PAGE 142. *Motto*. Terence, *Eunuchus*, I. i. 5–10.
   Mr. Freeman. Cf. page 133.

217. PAGE 144. *Motto*. Juvenal, *Satires*, vi. 327–8.
   PAGE 145. *Demolish a Prude.* See note, page 484.
   PAGE 146. *All over in a Sweat.* The *Vicar of Wakefield* (1766) had a like complaint against the 'Two Ladies of Great Distinction' at the ball. 'One of them, I thought, expressed her sentiments upon this occasion in a very coarse manner, when she observed that, "by the living jingo, she was all of a muck of sweat"' (Chapter IX).

PAGE 147. The clergyman's wife refers to No. 209 (page 124).

218. *Motto.* Horace, *Epistles*, I. xviii. 68. The 1712 edition prints 'Caveto.'
Great Benefit Ticket. Cf. note, page 479; also No. 242.

219. PAGE 149. *Motto.* Ovid, *Metamorphoses*, xiii. 141.
PAGE 151. *Epictetus. Enchiridion*, xxiii.
PAGE 152. *Then shall*, etc. Wisdom of Solomon, v. 1–5 and 8–14.

220. *Motto.* Virgil, *Aeneid*, xii. 228. The motto in *A* is

> . . . *Aliena negotia centum*
> *Per caput, et circa saliunt latus.*—Hor.

PAGE 153. The second letter in this paper is said to be by John Hughes.
Stood upon one Leg. Horace, *Satires*, I. iv. 9–10.
Accipe si vis. Ib. 14–16.
German Wits. Another of the *Spectator's* hits at German dullness. Cf. i. 184 and 260.
Ingenious Projector. This is a reference to John Peter, physician, who wrote a pamphlet, entitled *Artificial Versifying, a new way to make Latin Verses*, London, 1678. 'I believe,' says Percy, 'it is a plan of his scheme which is given in Nat. Bailey's Dictionary, folio, under the word Hexameter.'

PAGE 154. *Last Great Storm.* 26th November 1703.
The project of the Duke of Buckingham (joint author of *The Rehearsal*) may have suggested to Swift the image of the engine for making sentences (*Gulliver's Travels*, III. v).

221. PAGE 155. *Motto.* Horace, *Satires*, I. iii. 6–7.
PAGE 156. *Quae Genus* and *As in praesenti* are the initial words in certain rules in Lily's *Grammar*, which was still in use. Cf. No. 230 (page 184).
PAGE 157. *I cover it on purpose*, etc. Cf. the Dedication of *The Drummer*, where Steele says that Tickell, the editor of Addison's works, 'will not let me or any body else obey Mr. Addison's commands, in hiding any thing he desires should be concealed.' On the general interpretation of the initials see the elaborate notes in Chalmers's edition. Addison's warning to the curious, analogous to the warning against the identification of the characters of the *Spectator*, has been treated with some disrespect by the editors. The safe inference that Addison's papers were signed 'C' 'L' 'I' or 'O' did not satisfy Dr. Calder, who held the absurd opinion that 'C' meant 'written at Chelsea,' 'L' at London, 'I' in Ireland, and 'O' at the Office. See also iv. 480.

222. PAGE 158. *Motto.* Horace, *Epistles*, II. ii. 183–4.
PAGE 159. *Tigellius.* Horace, *Satires*, I. ii.
Character of Zimri. From Dryden's *Absalom and Achitophel*, Part I. See *ante*, i. 490 and note.

PAGE 160. *Whetters.* See i. 547.

223. *Motto.* Phaedrus, *Fables*, III. i. 5.

PAGE 161. *Apparent*, etc. Virgil, *Aeneid*, i. 118.

PAGE 162. *A Friend, whose admirable Pastorals*, etc. Ambrose
Philips (see *B. I.*). *The Winter-Piece* had appeared in the
Tatler, No. 12, where Philips is introduced as 'the author of
several choice Poems in Mr. Tonson's new Miscellany.' The
other ode translated 'by the same hand' will be found in
No. 229. Pope in his *Macer, a Character*, written after his
quarrel with 'Namby Pamby,' says:

> 'Twas all th' ambition his high soul could feel,
> To wear red stockings, and to dine with Steele.

PAGE 163. *Greek Critick.* Dionysius Halicarnassensis, *De Struc-
tura Orationis*, London, 1702, page 202.

Advertisement in *A*: 'Just Publish'd. The Spectator In-
spected, or a Letter to the Spectator from an Officer of the
Army in Flanders, touching the use of French Terms, in Relations from the Army: Occasioned by the Spectator of the
8th of September 1711. Written by the Author of the Spy
upon the Spectator.' See i. 566.

224. PAGE 164. *Motto.* Horace, *Satires*, I. vi. 23-4.

PAGE 165. *Mr. Waller's Opinion.* *To Zelinda*, lines 19-22.

225. PAGE 168. *Motto.* Juvenal, *Satires*, x. 365.

A Bewrayer. Ecclesiasticus, vi. 9, xxvii. 17.

PAGE 170. *Wisdom is glorious*, etc. Wisdom of Solomon, vi. 12-16.

226. *Motto.* The motto in *A* is 'Pictura poesis erit.' See note
to No. 58 (i. 543).

Swift writes on 18th November, in his *Journal to Stella*: 'Do
you read the Spectators? I never do; they never come in my
way; I go to no Coffee-houses. They say abundance of them
are very pretty; they are going to be printed in small volumes;
I 'll bring them over with me.' Cf. note to No. 212.

PAGE 171. *The Cartons.* See the advertisement in No. 205.
Steele, it may be noted, resided at Hampton. See also No. 244.

PAGE 172. *That noble Artist.* Nicholas Dorigny (1658-1746).
See *B. I.*

227. PAGE 173. *Motto.* Theocritus, *Idyllia*, iii. 24-7.

PAGE 176. The following advertisement, referring to the 1712-13
edition, appears in *A* in this and subsequent numbers: 'There is
now Printing by Subscription two Volumes of the SPECTATORS
on a large Character in Octavo; the price of the two Vols. well
bound and Gilt two Guineas. Those who are inclined to Subscribe, are desired to make their first Payments to Jacob
Tonson, Bookseller in the Strand; the Books being so near
finished, that they will be ready for the Subscribers at, or before
Christmas next.'

'The Third and Fourth Volumes of the LUCUBRATIONS of Isaac Bickerstaff, Esq; are ready to be delivered at the same Place.

'*N.B.* The Author desires that such Gentlemen who have not received their Books for which they have Subscribed, would be pleased to signify the same to Mr. Tonson.'

228. *Motto.* Horace, *Epistles*, I. xviii. 69.

PAGE 177. *I am all face.* Cf. Montaigne's *Essays*, translated by Florio, I. xxxv: 'A certaine man demanded of one of our loytring rogues, whom in the deep of frosty winter, he saw wandring up and downe with nothing but his shirt about him, and yet as blithe and lusty as an other that keepes himselfe muffled and wrapt in warme furres up to the eares; how he could have patience to go so. "And have not you, good Sir" (replied he), "your face all bare? Imagine I am all face."'

PAGE 178. *Plutarch. Lives of the Gracchi.*

PAGE 179. *Buckley.* See *B. I.* and i. 523.

229. PAGE 180. *Motto.* Horace, *Odes*, IV. ix. 10–12.

The translations are: (1) by Catullus, li; (2) by Boileau, translation of Longinus, viii; (3) by Ambrose Philips, reprinted in the collected edition of 1748, page 146 (cf. *ante*, page 487). Welsted's *Remarks on Longinus, in a Letter to a Friend*, printed at the end of Welsted's translation, London 1712, rather unblushingly reproduces the sentiments and references in this paper. Curiously enough, he refers to, among other things, his correspondent's admiration of the ballad of *Chevy Chace* ('your beloved Chevy Chace'); but the correspondent cannot well be Addison, and Welsted's letter cannot claim priority, for it refers to a criticism on Milton in the *Spectator*, which appeared in No. 333.

PAGE 182. *Plutarch. Life of Demetrius.*

230. *Motto.* Cicero?

PAGE 183. *Pliny. Epistles*, II. ii.
As if he had asked it. 'Thus far by Mr. John Hughes,' say the previous editors.

PAGE 184. *Lilly.* Cf. page 486.

231. PAGE 185. *Motto.* Martial, *Epigrams*, VIII. lxxviii. 4. The letter is by John Hughes.

PAGE 186. *Almahide*, an opera composed by Buononcini, founded on the romance by Scudéry, which had been translated in 1677 by John Phillips, Milton's nephew. Dryden's *Almanzor and Almahide or The Conquest of Granada* (two parts), which is only in a general way inspired by Scudéry's work, may have served as a model for the opera. It was produced in 1710 with Nicolini (i. 17) and Marguerite de l'Épine in the cast.
A young Singer. Mrs. Barbier.

PAGE 186. *Lingua melior*, etc. Virgil, *Aeneid*, xi. 338–9.
  Homer. Iliad, i. 225.

PAGE 187. *Seneca. Epistles*, I. xi.

PAGE 188. *Imitate Caesar.* Suetonius, *De Vita Caesarum*, i. 45.

232. *Motto.* Sallust, *Bellum Catilinarium*, lvii. Probably by Henry Martyn (cf. No. 200). In *A* the signature is X.

  PAGE 190. *Sir William Petty. Ante*, page 97 and note. See his *Discourse on Taxes*.

233. PAGE 192. *Motto.* Virgil, *Eclogues*, x. 60–1.
  Greek Manuscript. Cf. page 176.

  PAGE 194. '350.' More correctly 250. '120,' printed '150' in *A*.

234. PAGE 195. *Motto.* Horace, *Satires*, I. iii. 41. The motto in *A* is 'Splendide mendax.—Hor.'

  PAGE 196. *Free-thinker.* See i. 566.

235. PAGE 198. *Motto.* Horace, *Ars Poetica*, 81–2.

  PAGE 199. *Nicolini.* See *B. I.* and note to page 186.
  Dogget (Thomas). See *B. I.*
  Virgil's Ruler of the Winds. Aeneid, I. 80.

236. PAGE 200. *Motto.* Horace, *Ars Poetica*, 398.

  PAGE 201. *Ridiculed : To avoid.* In *A*, 'Ridiculed: For this Reason should they appear the least like what they were so much used to laugh at, they would become the Jest of themselves, and the object of that Raillery they formerly bestowed on others. To avoid . . .'

237. PAGE 203. *Motto.* Seneca, *Oedipus*, line 295 (Actus II).
  This paper, which is unsigned, is printed in the fourth edition of Addison's works, 1720, and referred to as by Hughes in the preface to the poems of the latter, 1735.

  PAGE 204. *Milton. Paradise Lost*, ii. 557–61.
  Seneca. De Constantia Sapientis.

  PAGE 205. *Jewish Tradition.* Henry More's *Divine Dialogues* (H. Morley's *Spectator*).

238. PAGE 206. *Motto.* Persius, *Satires*, iv. 50–1.
  So softens, etc. Waller, *Of my Lady Isabella, playing on the Lute*, lines 11–12.
  A and '1712' read 'recompence the Artifices made Use of.'

  PAGE 207. *Manly in the Play.* Wycherley's *Plain Dealer*.
  Tacitus. Annals, II. xiii.

  PAGE 208. *Precious Ointment.* Ecclesiastes, vii. 1.
  A Collection of Letters. As, e.g., in Tom Brown's *Works*. Henry Morley refers to Boyer's *Letters on Wit, Politicks, and Morality*, 1701. In 1715 appeared *Letters of Love an Gallantry*,

written in Greek by Aristenaetus, with a Dedication to Eustace Budgell, who is there referred to as the 'X' of the *Spectator.*

239. PAGE 209. *Motto.* Virgil, *Aeneid,* vi. 86.

　　PAGE 210. *Logic Lane* (still so named) runs off the High Street by University College.

　　　Smiglesians, the followers of Martin Smiglecius (died 1618), a Polish Jesuit. His *Logic,* praised by Rapin and Bayle, was reprinted at Oxford in 1658.

　　　Erasmus. Probably in his *Letters.*

　　PAGE 211. *Grand Monarch.* Louis XIV (*le grand monarque*).

　　　With one of the Roman Emperors. Hadrian. Bacon's *Apophthegms,* iii.

　　　Hudibras, II. i. 297. Cf. *ante,* i. 43 and note.

　　　Author quoted by M. Bayle. And. Ammonius. The saying is of Henry VIII's reign.

240. PAGE 213. *Motto.* Martial, *Epigrams,* I. xvi. 2.

　　PAGE 214. *Philaster* by Beaumont and Fletcher is advertised in *A* (No. 236) to be played on Friday, 30th November.

　　　Trunk-maker. See page 198.

　　　Side-boxes. See i. 549.

　　　The Hunting-Match is in the fourth act of *Philaster; the Rebellion* in the fifth.

　　　Made it criminal. The playbills now read: 'By Her Majesty's Command no Person is to be admitted behind the Scenes.'

241. *Motto.* Virgil, *Aeneid,* iv. 466–8.

　　PAGE 215. *Otway's Monimia.* In *The Orphan,* Act II.

　　PAGE 216. *Strada. Prolusions,* II. vi. See the *Guardian,* Nos. 115, 119, 122.

242. PAGE 217. *Motto.* Horace, *Epistles,* II. i. 168–9.

　　　A former paper. No. 132.

　　PAGE 218. *Duelling.* See i. 521.

　　　Ticket in the present Lottery. Cf. page 479.

243. PAGE 220. *Motto.* Cicero, *De Officiis,* I. v.

　　PAGE 221. *Hierocles.* Needham's edition, page 56.

244. PAGE 223. *Motto.* Horace, *Satires,* II. vii. 101.

　　　The Cartons. See pages 171–2.

　　PAGE 224. *Simonides.* See pages 122–3.

　　　Chalmers is at some pains to correct the syntax and vocabulary of the 'deserving' *Constantia.*

　　PAGE 225. *Comprehend all others.* 'Ingratum si disceris, omnia dixeris.'

245. *Motto.* Horace, *Ars Poetica,* 338.

　　PAGE 226. *Cordeliers.* The Minorites (Franciscan), so called from the knotted cord worn at the waist.

PAGE 226. *As Shakespear expresses.* 'So common-hackneyed in the *eyes* of men.'—*1 Henry IV*, III. i. 40.

    Hot-Cockles (French, *la main chaude*), a game in which the player shuts his eyes, puts his hand on his back, and is required to guess who strikes it. Cf. Eugène Sue, *Mysteries of Paris*, III. vii.

    Questions and Commands. See iv. 471.

    Whisk. See i. 547.

    Lanterloo. A card game in which the knave of clubs is the highest card. Cf. *Tatler*, No. 245.

PAGE 228. *Joshua Barnes* (died 1714), Professor of Greek at Cambridge.

    Graecum est, etc. A saying of Franciscus Accursius, when he encountered a Greek quotation in his Justinian. See Bayle.

246. *Motto.* Homer, *Iliad*, xvi. 33–5.

    Equipage of the Tea-Table. See i. 522.

247. PAGE 231. *Motto.* Hesiod, *Theogonia*, lines 39–40.

PAGE 232. *British Fishery.* Alias 'Billingsgate,' as in No. 451, and in the *Tatler*, No. 79.

PAGE 233. *Hudibras*, III. ii. 443.

PAGE 234. *Wanton Wife of Bath.* The ballad is given *in extenso* in Percy's *Reliques*, edited by Wheatley, iii. 336.

    Ovid. Metamorphoses, vi. 556–60.

    The Story of the Pippin Woman. Gay in his *Trivia* (ii) refers to the loquacious dame who, when the Thames was frozen over, had her head cut off by the ice.

> The cracking Crystal yields, she sinks, she dyes;
> Her Head chopt off, from her lost Shoulders flies:
> Pippins she cry'd, but Death her Voice confounds,
> And Pip-Pip-Pip along the Ice resounds.

248. *Motto.* Cicero, *De Officiis*, I. xv.

PAGE 236. *A City Romance.* The 'eminent trader' was a Mr. John Moreton, referred to again in No. 546; and the 'generous merchant' Sir William Scawen, the 'W. S.' of the letter. Cf. No. 346. The initials at the end of the letter are 'W. P.,' though a correction to 'W. S.' had been made in No. 252 of *A*.

    It has been heretofore urged. See No. 218.

    A Tradition, etc. See Goldsmith's *Life of Richard Nash*: 'An instance of his humanity is told us in the Spectator, though his name is not mentioned. When he was to give in his accounts to the Masters of the Temple, among other articles, he charged "For making one man happy, 10 *l.*,"' etc.

249. PAGE 237. *Motto.* Taken from Winterton's *Poetae Minores Graeci*, page 507.

PAGE 239. *Burlesque . . . of two kinds.* Addison here borrows from Boileau. See the Preface to the *Lutrin*.

PAGE 239. *The Dispensary.* By Samuel Garth.
  Waller. The Countess of Carlisle in Mourning, line **13**.
  Horace. Odes, I. xxxiii, II. viii, etc.
  Milton. L'Allegro, 11, etc.

250. PAGE 240. *Motto.* Horace, *Epistles* I. xvii. 3–5.

  PAGE 241. *Pious Man.* Cf. the image in Young's *Night Thoughts.*

  PAGE 242. *Ardentis,* etc. Virgil, *Aeneid,* xii. 101–2.
  'T. B.' is said to be Mr. Golding.
  Starers. See i. 61 et sqq.
  Perspective-glasses. Cf. Tatler, No. 77.

251. PAGE 243. *Motto.* Virgil, *Aeneid,* vi. 625–6 (*Si linguae centum
  sint,* etc.).

  PAGE 244. *Card-matches.* See i. 533.

  PAGE 245. *Colly-Molly-Puff.* 'This little man was but just able to
  support the basket of pastry which he carried on his head, and
  sung in a very peculiar tone the cant words which passed into
  his name Colly-Molly-Puff. There is a half sheet print of him
  in the Set of London Cries, M. Lauron *del.* P. Tempest, *exc.*'—
  Grainger's *Biographical History,* quoted by Chalmers.

252. PAGE 249. *Motto.* Virgil, *Aeneid,* ii. 570.

  PAGE 250. The last letter is by John Hughes.

  PAGE 251. *She keeps a Squirrel.* Cf. Steele's *Funeral or Grief à-la-
  Mode,* v. iii. See also volume i of this edition, page 534 (note
  to page 112).

253. *Motto.* Horace, *Epistles,* II. i. 76–7.

  PAGE 252. Line 6. *Sole Wonder.* 'Single Product' in *A.*
  The Art of Criticism. The *Essay on Criticism* had been
  advertised in the 65th *Spectator* (i. 355). Pope was grateful for this favourable critique, and, imagining Steele to have
  been the author, wrote to him ten days later: I have passed
  part of this Christmas with some honest country gentlemen, who
  have wit enough to be good-natured, but no manner of relish for
  criticism or polite writing, as you may easily conclude when I tell
  you they never read the *Spectator.* This was the reason I did
  not see that of the 20th till yesterday at my return home,
  wherein, though it be the highest satisfaction to find oneself
  commended by a person whom all the world commends, yet I
  am not more obliged to you for that, than for your candour and
  frankness in acquainting me with the error I have been guilty
  of in speaking too freely of my brother moderns. It is indeed
  the common method of all counterfeits in wit, as well as in
  physic, to begin with warning us of other's cheats, in order to
  make the more way for their own. But if ever this Essay be
  thought worth a second edition, I shall be very glad to strike
  out all such strokes which you shall be so kind as to point out
  to me. I shall really be proud of being corrected. . . . Some

of the faults of that book I have myself found, and more, I am confident, others have,—enough at least to have made me very humble, had you not given this public approbation of it, which I can look upon only as the effect of that benevolence you have ever been so ready to show to any who but make it their endeavour to do well. . . . Moderate praise encourages a young writer, but a great deal may injure him; and you have been so lavish in this point, that I almost hope—not to call in question your judgment in the piece—that it was some particular partial inclination to the author which carried you so far' (*Letters*, edited by Elwin, i. 388). Warton in his *Essay on the Genius of Pope* hints that the young author did not see 'a small mixture of ill-nature' in the words, 'the observations . . . are some of them uncommon.' But the young author was too delighted with this counterblast to the cavillings of Dennis to consider such a subtlety, and might well rest pleased with the *Spectator's* appreciation of the opinion that

> True wit is nature to advantage dressed,
> What oft was thought, but ne'er so well expressed.

Pope probably did not think so well of the *Spectator's* 'benevolence' in its puffs of the volumes of Ambrose Philips. The advertisement of the *Essay* reappears opportunely in No. 263.

PAGE 253. *Boileau.* 'Un bon mot n'est bon mot qu'en ce qu'il dit une chose que chacun pensait, et qu'il la dit d'une manière vive, fine, et nouvelle' (Preface to the edition of 1701).

These equal syllables, etc. *Essay on Criticism*, lines 344–7. *A needless Alexandrine*, etc., lines 356–7. *'Tis not enough*, etc. lines 364–73.

PAGE 254. καὶ μὴν Σίσυφον, etc. *Odyssey*, xi. 593–8.

Essay on Translated Verse, by the Earl of Roscommon, 1681. *Essay on Poetry*, by the Duke of Buckingham (Earl of Mulgrave), 1682.

254. *Motto.* Phocylides, line 62. Winterton's *Poetae Minores Graeci*, page 411.

PAGE 255. *Madam in her Grogram Gown*, an echo from Swift's *Baucis and Philemon* (1706):

> Her petticoat, transformed apace,
> Became black satin flounc'd with lace,
> 'Plain Goody' would no longer down;
> 'Twas 'Madam,' in her grogram gown.

Will Honeycomb confesses, in the 530th *Spectator*, that his humble-born wife 'did more execution upon me in Grogram, than the greatest Beauty in Town or Court had ever done in Brocade.'

The Ring. See i. 539.

255. PAGE 257. *Motto.* Horace, *Epistles*, I. i. 36–7.

Sallust. 'Quo minus gloriam petebat, eo magis illum adsequebatur' (*Bellum Catilinarium*, lvii).

256. PAGE 260. *Motto.* Hesiod, *Works and Days*, ii. 379–80.

   PAGE 263. *Cicero.* *Oratio pro M. Marcello*, viii.

   PAGE 264. *A* adds, at the end: ' I shall conclude this Subject in my next Paper.'

257. *Motto.* Stobaeus, *Florilegium*, I. iii. 9.

258. PAGE 267. *Motto.* ?

   PAGE 268. *As the Latin has it.* Horace, *Ars Poetica*, 334.

    Kitt Crotchet. Christopher Rich. See i. 518.

   PAGE 269. *Rope-dancers*, etc. 'But he [Rich] having no Understanding in this polite Way, brought in upon us, to get in his Money, Ladder-dancers, Rope-dancers, Jugglers, and Montebanks, to strut in the Place of *Shakespear's* Heroes, and *Johnson's* Humourists' (*Tatler*, No. 12).

    The Trunk-maker. See page 198.

   PAGE 270. *Mr. Clayton.* See i. 526, and *B. I.* For *Nicolino Haym* and *Charles Dieupart*, see *B. I.* Clayton and his friends started the Concert-room at York-buildings, Strand, after Handel had ousted them from the theatres. Steele was interested in their venture, and wrote to Pope ' to know whether you are at leisure to help Mr. Clayton, that is me, to some words for music against winter' (26th July 1711). Pope, writing on 2nd August to Caryll, refers to Steele's request in behalf of Clayton 'whose interest he (Steele) espouses with great zeal. His expression is Pray oblige Mr. Clayton, that is me, so far as, etc. The desire I have to gratify Mr. Steele has made me consent to his request, though it is a task that otherwise I am not very fond of.' Steele had also persuaded John Hughes to adapt Dryden's *Alexander's Feast* for a musical setting by Clayton.

    Charles Lillie's. See i. 539.

259. PAGE 271. *Motto.* Cicero, *De Officiis*, I. xxvii.

    Salutations. See the reference to the Spectator's 'odd humour' in No. 454.

260. PAGE 273. *Motto.* Horace, *Epistles*, II. ii. 55.

   PAGE 276. *Hot-cockles.* See page 491. Austin Dobson adds from Gay's *Shepherd's Week*, 1714, page 9:

> As at *Hot-Cockles* once I laid me down,
> And felt the weighty Hand of many a Clown;
> *Buxoma* gave a gentle Tap, and I
> Quick rose, and read soft Mischief in her Eye.

261. *Motto.* Menander, *Monost.* 102 (Winterton, page 505).

262. PAGE 278. *Motto.* Ovid, *Tristia*, ii. 566.

   PAGE 279. *A black Man.* Cf. No. 1. Steele 'was, in fact, what in those days was called a "black man"' (Dobson's *Selections from Steele*, xliii). Surly John Dennis made pointed reference to his dark complexion and his black periwig. Pepys always calls a brunette a 'black woman.'

PAGE 279. *The Procession of his Holiness* had taken place annually in 17th November, in commemoration of the accession of Queen Elizabeth. Dryden frequently refers to it in his plays, notably in the Epilogue to *Oedipus*. A print of the ceremony in 1679 is reproduced in Scott and Saintsbury's edition of his *Works* (vi. 240). These processions were the occasion of much party tumult, especially after the trial of the bishops, and of Dr. Sacheverell. The celebration of 1711 was planned on an elaborate scale. The Tory Government however intervened, and seized the images. Swift describes the episode in his *Journal to Stella*, 17th November and 26th November 1711. See also *The Relation of the Facts and Circumstances of the Intended Riot*, written at Swift's request; and *The March of the Chevalier de St. George, or an Account of the Mock Procession . . . intended . . . on 17th Nov.* 1711 (advertised in No. 271 of the *Spectator*).

PAGE 280. *Tubs*. Probably suggested by Swift's recent book, the *Tale of a Tub* (1704).

Criticism upon his Paradise Lost. See note in volume i, page 523; to which we may add that, in the 6th *Tatler*, Steele's Sappho discourses enthusiastically on Milton.

PAGE 281. *Horace. Epistles*, I. vi. 67–8.

263. *Motto.* From a letter by Trebonius to Cicero, in the *Epistolae ad Familiares*, xii. 16.

PAGE 284. *Heads.* Cf. page 289 (line 23); also i. 555.

264. *Motto.* Horace, *Epistles*, I. xviii. 103.

PAGE 287. *Long-lane.* A mart for cast-off clothes in West Smith-field. 'Hung with tatters, like a Long-lane penthouse.'— Congreve, *Way of the World*, III. i.

St. John Street. St. John Street, Clerkenwell.

PAGE 288. *The Bumper Tavern.* Richard Estcourt, of the Beef-steak Club (see i. 521), had advertised in Nos. 260, 261, and 263 of the *Spectator* that he would on 1st January open the *Bumper Tavern* in James Street, Covent Garden, where the best wines, from Brook and Hellier, would be delivered by 'trusty Anthony' in 'the same natural purity that he receives it from the said merchants.'

PAGE 289. *John Sly's Best.* Sly was a tobacconist, as well as a haberdasher of hats. See No. 526.

265. *Motto.* Ovid, *De Arte Amatoria*, iii. 7.

A good Head. Cf. page 284 and note.

PAGE 290. *Improvement of their Petticoats.* See i. 560.

Philomot (filemot), a corruption of 'feuillemorte,' the colour of a dead or faded leaf.

PAGE 291. Γυναικὶ, etc. Menander, *Monost.* 92. (Winterton, page 507). Meineke reads οὐ τὰ χρυσία. Cf. *Spectator*, No. 271.

266. *Motto.* Terence, *Eunuchus*, v. iv. 8–11.

  PAGE 292. *The Man of the Bumper.* 'Trusty Anthony'; probably
  Anthony Aston, as Genest suggests. See page 288 and note.
  Fletcher's Humorous Lieutenant. Steele quotes II. iii. 15–26.

  PAGE 293. *An Inn in the City.* We are reminded of the first plate
  of Hogarth's *Harlot's Progress* (1731), which may have been
  inspired by this paper.

  PAGE 294. *Dedication to the Plain Dealer.* Wycherley's play was
  dedicated 'To My Lady B[ennet],' in the form of a *billet-doux*.
  Cf. Pepys's *Diary*, 30th May 1668 (Globe edition, page 656,
  note).

267. *Motto.* Propertius, *Elegies*, III. xxvi (34), line 65.

  Addison's papers on Milton's *Paradise Lost*, of which this
  is the first, were reprinted in 1719, under the title of *Notes on the
  Twelve Books of Paradise Lost, Collected from the Spectator.* For
  the bibliography of later issues, see Arber's reprint, page 8.

  Gildon, in his *Laws of Poetry* (1721), endeavoured to con-
  trovert Addison's application of 'the rules of epopoeia.' Gott-
  sched having in his *Critische Dichtkunst* (1730) expressed the
  dislike of the French school of critics to Milton's epic, Bodmer
  was prompted to reply, in 1732, with a prose translation of
  Paradise Lost, in the preface of which he gives Addison the
  honour of having aroused the eighteenth-century writers to an
  interest in Milton. In 1740 Bodmer published his *Critische
  Abhandlung | von dem | Wunderbaren | in der Poesie | und
  dessen Verbindung mit dem | Wahrscheinlichen | In einer Ver-
  theidigung des Gedichtes | Joh. Miltons von dem verlohrnen
  Paradiese ; | Der beygefüget ist | Joseph Addisons | Abhandlung |
  von den Schönheiten in demselben | Gedichte.* His friend Breitin-
  ger, also of the opposing Zürich school, supported the same
  views in his *Critische Dichtkunst* (1740).

  I shall therefore examine it by the Rules of Epic Poetry.
  Though the *Spectator* pokes fun at the English critics who earn
  their reputation by the unacknowledged help of the French,
  its editors can hardly escape the charge of having borrowed
  from the same quarter without acknowledgment. Addison is
  indebted in No. 70, to Le Bossu's *Traité du Poème épique*, 1675
  (see i. 546), and he must be suspected of another borrowing here
  in his 'Rules of Epic Poetry.' Addison's Aristotle, too, is at
  second hand, from the translation and notes of André Dacier.
  Aristotle had said that 'Epic poetry . . . is an imitation . . .
  of characters of a higher type' (c. v); that 'the Epic action has
  no limits of time' (c. v); and that 'it should have for its subject
  a single action, whole and complete, with a beginning, a middle,
  and an end' (c. xxiii). Le Bossu formulated this, as follows:
  'L'action épique a quatre conditions. La première est son
  Unité; la seconde, son *Intégrité*; la troisième, son *Importance*;
  et la quatrième, sa *Durée*' (II. vii). Addison's 'one action,'
  'entire action,' and 'great action' correspond, and in the same
  order, with Le Bossu's 'unité,' 'intégrité,' and 'importance':

and though 'duration' is not mentioned here, it is discussed, at considerable length, at the end of the paper.

Likewise, when Addison remarks that '*Aristotle* himself allows, that *Homer* has nothing to boast of as to the Unity of his Fable, tho' at the same Time that great Critick and Philosopher endeavours to palliate this Imperfection in the *Greek* Poet, by imputing it in some Measure to the very Nature of an Epic Poem,' he is probably indebted to the sixth chapter of the second book of Le Bossu; and the remark, at the end of the paper, that 'modern Criticks have collected from several Hints in the *Iliad* and *Aeneid* the Space of Time, which is taken up by the Action of each of those Poems,' may be a direct reference to the eighteenth chapter of the same book.

PAGE 295. *As Horace has observed. Ars Poetica*, 147. Cf. Vida, *Ars Poetica*, ii. 74–108; Scaliger, *Libri Poetices Septem*, Idea, xcvi; Spenser's *Faerie Queene*, 'Letter of the Author's.'

PAGE 296. *The Spanish Fryar or The Double Discovery*, by Dryden (1681). It is also praised by Johnson 'for the happy coincidence and coalition of the two plots' (*Life of Dryden*).

PAGE 297. *Simile of the Top. Aeneid*, vii. 378–84.
The following Similitude. Poetics, vii. 4.

268. PAGE 298. *Motto.* Horace, *Satires*, I. iii. 29–30.
Mr. Wilks. His histrionic 'skill' is praised in the 19th *Tatler*; and in the 182nd Mr. Bickerstaff contrasts 'his singular Talent in representing the Graces of Nature,' with that of Cibber in showing 'the Deformity in the affectation of them.' See *B. I.*

PAGE 299. *James Easy.* See i. 540.

269. PAGE 301. *Motto.* Ovid, *De Arte Amatoria*, i. 241–2.

PAGE 302. *Gray's-Inn Walks.* Gray's Inn Gardens are frequently mentioned in plays of this time as a fashionable resort or place of assignation. See the note in W. Henry Wills's *Roger de Coverley*, page 211.

Prince Eugene had come to England (on 5th January 1712) to endeavour to arrange for the active alliance of Austria and England against France, and also to reinstate the Duke of Marlborough, His visit caused intense excitement, especially among the Whigs, who welcomed him with enthusiasm. (See the advertisements in *A*, Nos. 279, 286, and 291.) He was received by the queen; but failed in his mission. References to the visit will be found in Swift's *Journal to Stella* (13th January and 10th February). The character of Prince Eugene is the subject of the 340th *Spectator*. No. 471 of the *Spectator* contains an advertisement of a Whig pamphlet, *Prince Eugene not the Man you took him for ; or a Merry Tale of a Modern Hero.* A doubtful tradition says that the prince stood sponsor to Steele's third son, Eugene. (See Austin Dobson's *Selections from Steele*, page 498.)
Thirty Marks. £20.

PAGE 302. *Will had been busie.* Cf. i. 329–30.
    Moll White. See i. 357.

PAGE 303. *Late Act of Parliament.* A Bill against Occasional Conformity was passed without opposition in December 1711.
    Pope's Procession. See page 279 and note.

PAGE 304. *Baker's Chronicle.* See i. 534.
    Squire's. See i. 540. It was noted for its coffee, and was frequented chiefly by the benchers and students of Gray's Inn.

270. *Motto.* Horace, *Epistles*, II. i. 262–3.
    The Scornful Lady, by Beaumont and Fletcher.

271. PAGE 307. *Motto.* Virgil, *Aeneid*, iv. 701.
    The Greek Verse. See No. 265.

272. PAGE 309. *Motto.* Virgil, *Aeneid*, i. 341–2.

273. PAGE 312. *Motto.* Horace, *Ars Poetica*, 156.

PAGE 313. *More new.* Dennis's praise of *Paradise Lost* was founded on its originality. 'His Thoughts, his Images, and, by consequence too, his Spirit are actually new, and different from those of Homer and Virgil' (*Grounds of Criticism in Poetry*, 1704).
    The Dispensary, by Sir Samuel Garth (see page 239); *Le Lutrin*, by Boileau.
    Admired by Aristotle. *Poetics*, xvii and xxiv.

PAGE 314. *The Angels . . . respective Characters.* Not in *A*.

PAGE 315. *Observation out of Aristotle.* *Poetics*, xiii. Cf. Le Bossu, *Du Poème épique*, II. xvii.

274. *Motto.* Horace, *Satires*, I. ii. 37–8.

275. PAGE 318. *Motto.* Horace, *Ars Poetica*, 300.

276. PAGE 321. *Motto.* Horace, *Satires*, I. iii. 42.
    The Tea-Table. See i. 517.

PAGE 322. *Scowrer*, etc. See i. 532, 556.

PAGE 324. *Liken unto Tulips. Ante*, No. 265.

277. *Motto.* Ovid, *Metamorphoses*, iv. 428.
    All their Fashions from thence. Cf. i. 566.

PAGE 326. *Mr. Powell.* See i. 524; also *B. I.*

278. PAGE 327. *Motto.* Horace, *Epistles*, II. i. 250–1.

PAGE 328. *Ending a Paper in Greek.* See No. 265.

PAGE 329. *Second Application.* See No. 258.
    'A neat Pocket Edition of the Spectator, in 2 vol. 12' is advertised in *A*.

279. PAGE 330. *Motto.* Horace, *Ars Poetica*, 316.
    The Criticks . . . the times in which he lived. Cf. Le Bossu, *Du Poème épique*, VI. iii.

PAGE 332. *Longimus.* *On the Sublime*, ix.

Affect it. Addison continues thus in *A*: 'I remember but one Line in him which has been objected against, by the Criticks, as a point of Wit. It is in the ninth Book, where Juno, speaking of the Trojans, how they survived the Ruins of their City, expresses her self in the following Words;

Num capti potuere capi, num incensa cremarunt Pergama?

Were the Trojans *taken even after they were Captives, or did* Troy *burn even when it was in Flames?* '

Zoilus, 'Homeromastix,' frequently referred to by Dryden, Swift, and Pope. Parnell's *Life of Zoilus* (1715) was to have been included in the first volume of Pope's *Iliad*.

Perrault. Charles Perrault's criticisms on Homer began in his poem *Le Siècle de Louis le Grand* (27th January 1687), and were elaborated in the *Parallèles des anciens et des modernes* (1688–97).

280. PAGE 334. *Motto.* Horace, *Epistles*, i. xvii. **35.**

281. PAGE 336. *Motto.* Virgil, *Aeneid*, iv. 64.

PAGE 337. *Plume of Feathers.* Cf. page 464.
Fringed gloves. Cf. i. 525.

282. PAGE 339. *Motto.* Virgil, *Aeneid*, viii. 580.

283. PAGE 342. *Motto.* Persius, *Satires*, Prologue, 10.
Lucian. 'In his *Auction of Philosophers*.'—H. Morley.

PAGE 344. The familiar, but imaginary, tale concerning Rabelais is discussed in Louis Moland's *Rabelais*, page xxvi.

284. PAGE 345. *Motto.* Virgil, *Eclogues*, vii. 17. In *A* the motto is that of No. 54 of this edition.

285. PAGE 348. *Motto.* Horace, *Ars Poetica*, 227–30.

PAGE 349. *Both perspicuous and sublime.* Aristotle, *Poetics*, xxii. 1.
With Horace. *Ars Poetica*, 351–3.

PAGE 350. *By the following Methods.* Aristotle, *Poetics*, xxii.

PAGE 352. *Discourse in Plutarch.* 'On the Life and Poetry of Homer, wrongly ascribed to Plutarch, Book I, § 16.'—H. Morley.
Euclid. Aristotle, *Poetics*, xxii. 5.

286. PAGE 353. *Motto.* Adapted from Tacitus, *Annals*, xiv. 21.

PAGE 355. J. Cleveland in his *Senses' Festival*, included in his *Poems* published in 1653, upholds the brunette. John Bond wrote commentaries on Horace and Persius.

287. *Motto.* Menander, *Nauclerus*, ii (Meineke, *Fragmenta*, iv. 175). It is quoted by Athenaeus, iv. 166.

PAGE 356. *Acted.* Cf. page 67 and note.

288. PAGE 359. *Motto.* Horace, *Epistles*, I. vi. 10.

    PAGE 362. *Peter Motteux* (see. i. 526), the translator of Rabelais, *Don Quixote*, and Bayle's *Dictionary*.

289. *Motto.* Horace, *Odes*, I. iv. 15.

    PAGE 364. *Dr. Sherlock's Discourse.* See i. 533.
        Passage of Antiphanes. No. vi in Winterton's *Poetae Minores Graeci* (page 482).
        Sir John Chardin. The first (and only) volume of the translation, *The Travels of Sir John Chardin into Persia and the East Indies*, appeared in 1686.

290. PAGE 365. *Motto.* Horace, *Ars Poetica*, 97.
        The Distrest Mother, a version of Racine's *Andromaque* by Ambrose Philips, first acted on 17th March 1712, and printed in 1713. Sir Roger de Coverley's interest in the piece is the theme of No. 335. It could hardly escape the kind attentions of the *Spectator*, for Steele wrote the Prologue, and Addison and Budgell the Epilogue.

    PAGE 367. *George Powell*, the actor. See i. 524 and *B. I.*

291. PAGE 368. *Motto.* Horace, *Ars Poetica*, 351–3; referred to in No. 285.

    PAGE 369. *French Authors.* Dryden has the credit of an early appreciation of French criticism. The 'illiterate writers' followed and compiled their critical essays from Rapin, Le Bossu, Bouhours, Boileau, Perrault, Fontenelle, and the Daciers. Much of this borrowed critical wisdom was unacknowledged by Grub Street—and by the more respectable *Spectator*.
        Errors, like Straws. Dryden's *All for Love*, Prologue, 25–6.
        Verbum ardens. Cicero, *Ad Marcum Brutum Orator*, viii. 27. 'Facile est enim verbum aliquod ardens (ut ita dicam) notare.'

    PAGE 370. *Longinus. On the Sublime*, xxvi.
        Boccalini. His *Ragguagli di Parnasso* was Englished in 1656 under the title of *Advertisements from Parnassus*. It was reprinted in 1669, 1674, and 1704. An edition, called *Advices from Parnassus*, by T. B., was revised by Hughes in 1706.

292. *Motto.* Tibullus, IV. ii. 7–8.

    PAGE 371. *Letter of Pliny's.* Book VI, letter xxxii.

    PAGE 373. *So spake the Cherub. Paradise Lost*, iv. 844–9.
    Ne non procumbat. Ovid, *Fasti*, ii. 833–4.

293. *Motto.* See Winterton's *Poetae Minores Graeci*, page 527.
        The 'little Book' is *The Courtier's Oracle or The Art of Prudence*, 1694 (also 1702 and 1705), a translation of Balthazar Gracian's *El Oraculo Manual*. See Nos. 379 and 409.

    PAGE 376. The *Persian Fable* is derived from Chardin's *Travels* (see page 364). The original version will be found in the *Bustan* of Hafiz.

294. *Motto.* Cicero, *Ad Herennium.*

PAGE 377. *This illustrious Day.* Queen Anne's birthday.

PAGE 378. *St. Bride's Church,* etc. Cf. the sexton's letter in No. 380.
   Dr. Snape's sermons were published, posthumously, in 1745. He opposed Hoadly, in the Bangorian controvrsey.

295. PAGE 379. *Motto.* Juvenal, *Satires,* vi. 362-5.

296. PAGE 382. *Motto.* Horace, *Epistles,* i. xix. 42.

297. PAGE 385. *Motto.* Horace, *Satires,* i. vi. 66-7.
   Simple or Implex. Aristotle's *Poetics,* x. Addison borrows the term 'implex' from the French critics, and especially from André Dacier's translation of Aristotle. Cf. F. Brunetière, *Etudes critiques,* iv. 181. Johnson uses the term 'implex' in his *Life of Cowley* (1790 edition, i. 87).
   Most proper for Tragedy. Poetics, xi.

PAGE 386. *Mr. Dryden's Reflection.* Dedication of the *Aeneis.* (*Works,* edited by Scott and Saintsbury, xiv. 144).
   Mouths of . . . his principal Actors. Poetics, xxiv.

PAGE 387. *Scaliger,* as in the *Poetice;* but the word occurs in the favourite Tully.

PAGE 389. *A Place in his Rhetorick.* iii. xi.
   Tack to the Larboard. Dryden's *Aeneis,* iii. 526-7. Milton, *Paradise Lost,* ii. 1019.

298. *Motto.* Virgil, *Aeneid,* iv. 373.

299. PAGE 392. *Motto.* Juvenal, *Satires,* vi. 167-71.
   Addison may, as the editors tell us, have had in mind a successful ironmonger, Crowley, afterwards Sir Ambrose Crawley; but the satire will stand without this individual interest.

PAGE 393. *Charte Blanche, as our News Papers call it.* A hit at the foreign phrases in the continental news-letters (cf. i. 499). Addison was almost the first to use the term: he probably (against his intention) popularized it.

300. PAGE 395. *Motto.* Horace, *Epistles,* i. xviii. 5.

PAGE 398. *The following four Lines.* The editor has failed to trace these.

301. *Motto.* Horace, *Odes,* iv. xiii. 26-8.

302. PAGE 401. *Motto.* Virgil, *Aeneid,* v. 343-4.
   Guessed at for Emilia. Steele pokes fun at the commentators cf. i. 515, etc.). The more popular 'guesses' are 'the mother of Mr. Ascham of Conington, in Cambridgeshire, and grandmother of Lady Hatton,' and 'Anne, Countess of Coventry.'

The authorship of the sketch has been claimed for Hughes (*Letters*, iii. 8), and also for Dr. Brome, the clergyman of the parish in which the aforesaid Mrs. Ascham lived. The *Bromius* of this paper rather suggests the latter. If that be so, there may be some 'basis of fact' in Mrs. Ockley's ascription to Mrs. Ascham.

303. PAGE 405. *Motto.* Horace, *Ars Poetica*, 363–4.

    PAGE 408. *Paid to that Idol.* Addison subsequently interpolated here lines 446–57 of book i of *Paradise Lost*, with a note on the same by 'the late ingenious Mr. Maundrell,' taken from his *Journey from Aleppo to Jerusalem.* It will be found in the text of the *Notes upon the Twelve Books of Paradise Lost*, published separately in 1719.

    What the French Critics call Marvellous. See Boileau, *Réflexions sur Longin*, v.

    PAGE 410. *Perrault* and *Boileau.* Addison's reference to Perrault's phrase and his quotation from Boileau are taken from the *Réflexions sur Longin*, iv. The English translation of *The Whole Works of Mons. Boileau* is advertised in No. 272 (*A*) as 'just published.'

304. *Motto.* Virgil, *Aeneid*, iv. 2.

    PAGE 412. *Wit's Commonwealth.* A popular school-book, by J. Bodenham.

    The desire of 'Anthony Title-Page' was realized in Charles Lillie's two volumes, referred to *ante*, i. 539.

    PAGE 413. *New-Exchange.* See i. 555.

305. *Motto.* Virgil, *Aeneid*, ii. 521–2.

    PAGE 417. *Our Smyrna or St. James's.* See i. 514.

    Earl of Rochester. See i. 516.

306. *Motto.* Juvenal, *Satires*, vi. 178–9.

    Small-Pox. It is difficult for us to understand how terrible were the ravages of this disease in English society at this time. Swift's *Journal to Stella* is full of references to its havoc. Inoculation was introduced by Lady Mary Wortley Montagu, after her return from Turkey in 1718. See Pope's letter to Broome, 16th July 1721 (Elwin and Courthope, viii. 47).

    PAGE 420. *Good Nature will always*, etc. 'Perhaps Goldsmith was thinking of this paper when he wrote the little tale in verse called *The Double Transformation*, 1765, the heroine of which is reformed by an attack of small-pox:

> "No more presuming on her sway,
> She learns good nature every day:
> Serenely gay, and strict in duty,
> Jack finds his wife—a perfect beauty."'

(Austin Dobson's *Selections from Steele*, page 476.)

307.   *Motto.*   Horace, *Ars Poetica*, 39–40.

PAGE 421. The *Examen de Ingenios* of Huarte is described in Bayle. Budgell probably obtained his information there.

PAGE 422. *Clavius.* Christopher Clavius, who czrried out the reform of the calendar by order of Gregory XIII. See Bayle.

308. PAGE 424. *Motto.* Horace, *Odes*, II. v. 15–16.

PAGE 425. *The Historian.* One of the numerous imitators of the *Tatler* and *Spectator.*

PAGE 426. *Brag-table.* Brag was a game of cards, similar to the modern poker.

309. PAGE 427. *Motto.* Virgil, *Aeneid*, vi. 264–7.
Addison's papers on Milton are from this point of greater length. The type in *A* is closer, and there are, of necessity, very few advertisements. A larger sheet is sometimes used.

310. PAGE 433. *Motto.* Virgil, *Aeneid*, i. 73.

311. PAGE 436. *Motto.* Juvenal, *Satires*, vi. 138–9.
Silver fringed Gloves. See page 337 and note.
Irish-Man. Cf. i. 141.

PAGE 437. *Rosamond's Pond.* Cf. Defoe's *Advice from the Scandalous Club*, No. 45.

PAGE 438. *Side-Box.* See i. 549.
Hudibras. I. iii. 311–12.

312. PAGE 439. *Motto.* Cicero, *Tusculan Disputations*, II. vi.

PAGE 440. *Story after Pompey.* *Tusculan Disputations*, II. xxiv

PAGE 441. *Devotion.* A long passage in *A* is here omitted.

313. *Motto.* Juvenal, *Satires*, vii. 237–8.

PAGE 442. *Suetonius . . . Mr. Locke.* *Of Education*, §§ 69, 70.
Mr. Osburn. See i. 564.

PAGE 443. *A Story very well known.* The *Master* is the famous Dr. Busby. The 'Gentleman whose life was preserv'd' has been identified as Colonel Wake, father of William Wake, then Bishop of Lincoln; but in a communication to the editor the Rev. Rashleigh Duke, Rector of Birlingham, Pershore, gave his opinion that the hero of the rent curtain was Colonel Robert Duke of Wiltshire. 'Col. Duke was engaged with Penruddocke and Grove and others in the rising in 1655, and was taken prisoner and tried with them at Exeter, and with them was sentenced to death. The original MS. of that sentence exists now, and it bears the name of Robert Duke following on those of Penruddocke and Grove, and the warrant is signed by Cromwell; but the name of R. Duke, which occurs twice in the body of the warrant, is cancelled. His life was saved, and he was banished to the E. Indies, where he died.'

314. PAGE 444. *Motto*. Horace, *Odes*, I. xxiii. 11–12.

　　PAGE 446. *Nicolini*. See I. 518.
　　　　Hydaspes. See i. 523. It was played on 26th December and 12th January (see advertisements in the issues of *A* of these dates).

315. PAGE 448. *Motto*. Horace, *Ars Poetica*, 191–2.
　　　　Horace advises. *Ars Poetica*, 38–40; the motto of No. 307.

　　PAGE 451. *Aristotle observes*. *Poetics*, xxiv. 8.

316. PAGE 454. *Motto*. Virgil, *Eclogues*, i. 28.

　　PAGE 456. *Pliny*. *Letters*, i. 6.

317. PAGE 457. *Motto*. Horace, *Epistles*, I. ii. 27.

　　PAGE 459. *Purl*. See i. 552.
　　　　Laced Coffee. Coffee dashed with spirits.
　　　　Brook and Hellier, the famed wine-merchants, advertised regularly in the *Spectator*. See note on the Bumper Tavern, page 495. They intimate that 'At the Bumper every Bottle of Port Wine sent out is sealed upon the Cork with the Bumper by Anthony.' Cf. D'Urfey's *Pills to purge Melancholy*, 'A new Ballad Sung at Messieurs Brook & Hellier's Club, at the Temple Tavern in Fleet Street' (vi. 340):

> Each Vintner of late, has got an Estate,
> 　　By brewing and Sophistication:
> With Syder and Sloes, they 've made a damn'd Dose,
> 　　Has Poisoned one half of the Nation.
> But Hellier & Brook, a Method have took,
> 　　To prove them all Scoundrels and Noddys;
> And shew'd us a way which (if we don't stray)
> 　　Will save both our Pockets and Bodies.

318. PAGE 460. *Motto*. Virgil, *Eclogues*, viii. 63.

319. PAGE 463. *Motto*. Horace, *Epistles*, I. i. 90.
　　　　Various Cocks. Cf. i. 560. The paper recalls Hogarth's plate of the 'Five Orders of Periwigs.'

　　PAGE 464. *Wear Feathers*. See page 337.
　　　　An arrant Linnen-Draper. 'Only an Ensign in the Train Bands' in *A*. Budgell may have been thinking of an advertisement in No. 259 (*A*), which describes a deserter from the 1st Foot Guards, 'a Linnen-draper by Trade.'

　　PAGE 465. *White's*. See i. 552.

320. PAGE 466. *Motto*. Ovid, *Metamorphoses*, vi. 428–9, 431.

PAGE 468. *Mr. Waller. Of the Marriage of the Dwarfs*, lines 1–6:

> Design, or chance, makes others wive;
> But Nature did this match contrive;
> Eve might as well have Adam fled,
> As she denied her little bed
> To him, for whom Heaven seemed to frame,
> And measure out, this only dame.

PAGE 469. *Lazy Club.* Cf. i. 520.

321. *Motto.* Horace, *Ars Poetica*, 99.

PAGE 470. *Aristotle's Rule. Poetics*, xxiv. 11.